55 *Victorian Prose Writers Before 1867*, edited by William B. Thesing (1987)

56 *German Fiction Writers, 1914-1945*, edited by James Hardin (1987)

57 *Victorian Prose Writers After 1867*, edited by William B. Thesing (1987)

58 *Jacobean and Caroline Dramatists*, edited by Fredson Bowers (1987)

59 *American Literary Critics and Scholars, 1800-1850*, edited by John W. Rathbun and Monica M. Grecu (1987)

60 *Canadian Writers Since 1960*, Second Series, edited by W. H. New (1987)

61 *American Writers for Children Since 1960: Poets, Illustrators, and Nonfiction Authors*, edited by Glenn E. Estes (1987)

62 *Elizabethan Dramatists*, edited by Fredson Bowers (1987)

63 *Modern American Critics, 1920-1955*, edited by Gregory S. Jay (1988)

64 *American Literary Critics and Scholars, 1850-1880*, edited by John W. Rathbun and Monica M. Grecu (1988)

65 *French Novelists, 1900-1930*, edited by Catharine Savage Brosman (1988)

66 *German Fiction Writers, 1885-1913*, 2 parts, edited by James Hardin (1988)

67 *Modern American Critics Since 1955*, edited by Gregory S. Jay (1988)

68 *Canadian Writers, 1920-1959*, First Series, edited by W. H. New (1988)

69 *Contemporary German Fiction Writers*, First Series, edited by Wolfgang D. Elfe and James Hardin (1988)

70 *British Mystery Writers, 1860-1919*, edited by Bernard Benstock and Thomas F. Staley (1988)

71 *American Literary Critics and Scholars, 1880-1900*, edited by John W. Rathbun and Monica M. Grecu (1988)

72 *French Novelists, 1930-1960*, edited by Catharine Savage Brosman (1988)

73 *American Magazine Journalists, 1741-1850*, edited by Sam G. Riley (1988)

74 *American Short-Story Writers Before 1880*, edited by Bobby Ellen Kimbel, with the assistance of William E. Grant (1988)

75 *Contemporary German Fiction Writers*, Second Series, edited by Wolfgang D. Elfe and James Hardin (1988)

76 *Afro-American Writers, 1940-1955*, edited by Trudier Harris (1988)

77 *British Mystery Writers, 1920-1939*, edited by Bernard Benstock and Thomas F. Staley (1988)

78 *American Short-Story Writers, 1880-1910*, edited by Bobby Ellen Kimbel, with the assistance of William E. Grant (1988)

79 *American Magazine Journalists, 1850-1900*, edited by Sam G. Riley (1988)

80 *Restoration and Eighteenth-Century Dramatists*, First Series, edited by Paula R. Backscheider (1989)

81 *Austrian Fiction Writers, 1875-1913*, edited by James Hardin and Donald G. Daviau (1989)

82 *Chicano Writers*, First Series, edited by Francisco A. Lomelí and Carl R. Shirley (1989)

83 *French Novelists Since 1960*, edited by Catharine Savage Brosman (1989)

84 *Restoration and Eighteenth-Century Dramatists*, Second Series, edited by Paula R. Backscheider (1989)

85 *Austrian Fiction Writers After 1914*, edited by James Hardin and Donald G. Daviau (1989)

86 *American Short-Story Writers, 1910-1945*, First Series, edited by Bobby Ellen Kimbel (1989)

87 *British Mystery and Thriller Writers Since 1940*, First Series, edited by Bernard Benstock and Thomas F. Staley (1989)

88 *Canadian Writers, 1920-1959*, Second Series, edited by W. H. New (1989)

89 *Restoration and Eighteenth-Century Dramatists*, Third Series, edited by Paula R. Backscheider (1989)

90 *German Writers in the Age of Goethe, 1789-1832*, edited by James Hardin and Christoph E. Schweitzer (1989)

91 *American Magazine Journalists, 1900-1960*, First Series, edited by Sam G. Riley (1990)

92 *Canadian Writers, 1890-1920*, edited by W. H. New (1990)

93 *British Romantic Poets, 1789-1832*, First Series, edited by John R. Greenfield (1990)

94 *German Writers in the Age of Goethe: Sturm und Drang to Classicism*, edited by James Hardin and Christoph E. Schweitzer (1990)

95 *Eighteenth-Century British Poets*, First Series, edited by John Sitter (1990)

96 *British Romantic Poets, 1789-1832*, Second Series, edited by John R. Greenfield (1990)

97 *German Writers from the Enlightenment to Sturm und Drang, 1720-1764*, edited by James Hardin and Christoph E. Schweitzer (1990)

98 *Modern British Essayists*, First Series, edited by Robert Beum (1990)

99 *Canadian Writers Before 1890*, edited by W. H. New (1990)

100 *Modern British Essayists*, Second Series, edited by Robert Beum (1990)

101 *British Prose Writers, 1660-1800*, First Series, edited by Donald T. Siebert (1991)

102 *American Short-Story Writers, 1910-1945*, Second Series, edited by Bobby Ellen Kimbel (1991

103 *American Literary Biographers*, First Series, edited by Steven Serafin (1991)

104 *British Prose Writers, 1660-1800*, Second Series, edited by Donald T. Siebert (1991)

105 *American Poets Since World War II*, Second Series, edited by R. S. Gwynn (1991)

106 *British Literary Publishing Houses, 1820-1880*, edited by Patricia J. Anderson and Jonathan Rose (1991)

107 *British Romantic Prose Writers, 1789-1832*, First Series, edited by John R. Greenfield (1991)

108 *Twentieth-Century Spanish Poets*, First Series, edited by Michael L. Perna (1991)

109 *Eighteenth-Century British Poets*, Second Series, edited by John Sitter (1991)

110 *British Romantic Prose Writers, 1789-1832*, Second Series, edited by John R. Greenfield (1991)

111 *American Literary Biographers*, Second Series, edited by Steven Serafin (1991)

112 *British Literary Publishing Houses, 1881-1965*, edited by Jonathan Rose and Patricia J. Anderson (1991)

113 *Modern Latin-American Fiction Writers*, First Series, edited by William Luis (1992)

114 *Twentieth-Century Italian Poets*, First Series, edited by Giovanna Wedel De Stasio, Glauco Cambon, and Antonio Illiano (1992)

115 *Medieval Philosophers*, edited by Jeremiah Hackett (1992)

(Continued on back endsheets)

Dictionary of Literary Biography® • Volume One Hundred Thirty-Seven

American Magazine Journalists, 1900–1960

Second Series

Dictionary of Literary Biography® • Volume One Hundred Thirty-Seven

American Magazine Journalists, 1900–1960

Second Series

Edited by
Sam G. Riley
Virginia Polytechnic Institute
and State University

A Bruccoli Clark Layman Book
Gale Research Inc.
Detroit, Washington, D.C., London

Printed in the United States of America

Published simultaneously in the United Kingdom
by Gale Research International Limited
(An affiliated company of Gale Research Inc.)

The paper used in this publication meets the minimum requirements of American National Standard for Information Sciences–Permanence Paper for Printed Library Materials, ANSI Z39.48-1984. ∞™

Permission to quote from the works of H. L. Mencken was granted by the Enoch Pratt Free Library in accordance with the terms of Mr. Mencken's will.

Library of Congress Catalog Card Number 93-081176
ISBN 0-8103-5396-2

The trademark **ITP** is used under license.

10 9 8 7 6 5 4 3 2 1

Contents

Plan of the Series

... Almost the most prodigious asset of a country, and perhaps its most precious possession, is its native literary product – when that product is fine and noble and enduring.

Mark Twain*

The advisory board, the editors, and the publisher of the *Dictionary of Literary Biography* are joined in endorsing Mark Twain's declaration. The literature of a nation provides an inexhaustible resource of permanent worth. We intend to make literature and its creators better understood and more accessible to students and the reading public, while satisfying the standards of teachers and scholars.

To meet these requirements, *literary biography* has been construed in terms of the author's achievement. The most important thing about a writer is his writing. Accordingly, the entries in *DLB* are career biographies, tracing the development of the author's canon and the evolution of his reputation.

The purpose of *DLB* is not only to provide reliable information in a convenient format but also to place the figures in the larger perspective of literary history and to offer appraisals of their accomplishments by qualified scholars.

The publication plan for *DLB* resulted from two years of preparation. The project was proposed to Bruccoli Clark by Frederick C. Ruffner, president of the Gale Research Company, in November 1975. After specimen entries were prepared and typeset, an advisory board was formed to refine the entry format and develop the series rationale. In meetings held during 1976, the publisher, series editors, and advisory board approved the scheme for a comprehensive biographical dictionary of persons who contributed to North American literature. Editorial work on the first volume began in January 1977, and it was published in 1978. In order to make *DLB* more than a reference tool and to compile volumes that individually have claim to status as literary history, it was decided to organize volumes by topic, period, or genre. Each of these freestanding volumes provides a biographical-bibliographical guide and overview for a particular area of literature. We are convinced that this organization – as opposed to a single alphabet method – constitutes a valuable innovation in the presentation of reference material. The volume plan necessarily requires many decisions for the placement and treatment of authors who might properly be included in two or three volumes. In some instances a major figure will be included in separate volumes, but with different entries emphasizing the aspect of his career appropriate to each volume. Ernest Hemingway, for example, is represented in *American Writers in Paris, 1920–1939* by an entry focusing on his expatriate apprenticeship; he is also in *American Novelists, 1910–1945* with an entry surveying his entire career. Each volume includes a cumulative index of the subject authors and articles. Comprehensive indexes to the entire series are planned.

With volume ten in 1982 it was decided to enlarge the scope of *DLB*. By the end of 1986 twenty-one volumes treating British literature had been published, and volumes for Commonwealth and Modern European literature were in progress. The series has been further augmented by the *DLB Yearbooks* (since 1981) which update published entries and add new entries to keep the *DLB* current with contemporary activity. There have also been *DLB Documentary Series* volumes which provide biographical and critical source materials for figures whose work is judged to have particular interest for students. One of these companion volumes is entirely devoted to Tennessee Williams.

We define literature as the *intellectual commerce of a nation:* not merely as belles lettres but as that ample and complex process by which ideas are generated, shaped, and transmitted. *DLB* entries are not limited to "creative writers" but extend to other figures who in their time and in their way influenced the mind of a people. Thus the series encompasses historians, journalists, publishers, and screenwriters. By this means readers of *DLB* may be aided to perceive literature not as cult scripture in the keeping of intellectual high priests but firmly po-

**From an unpublished section of Mark Twain's autobiography, copyright by the Mark Twain Company* sitioned at the center of a nation's life.

DLB includes the major writers appropriate to each volume and those standing in the ranks immediately behind them. Scholarly and critical counsel has been sought in deciding which minor figures to include and how full their entries should be. Wherever possible, useful references are made to figures who do not warrant separate entries.

Each *DLB* volume has a volume editor responsible for planning the volume, selecting the figures for inclusion, and assigning the entries. Volume editors are also responsible for preparing, where appropriate, appendices surveying the major periodicals and literary and intellectual movements for their volumes, as well as lists of further readings. Work on the series as a whole is coordinated at the Bruccoli Clark Layman editorial center in Columbia, South Carolina, where the editorial staff is responsible for accuracy of the published volumes.

One feature that distinguishes *DLB* is the illustration policy – its concern with the iconography of literature. Just as an author is influenced by his surroundings, so is the reader's understanding of the author enhanced by a knowledge of his environment. Therefore *DLB* volumes include not only drawings, paintings, and photographs of authors, often depicting them at various stages in their careers, but also illustrations of their families and places where they lived. Title pages are regularly reproduced in facsimile along with dust jackets for modern authors. The dust jackets are a special feature of *DLB* because they often document better than anything else the way in which an author's work was perceived in its own time. Specimens of the writers' manuscripts are included when feasible.

Samuel Johnson rightly decreed that "The chief glory of every people arises from its authors." The purpose of the *Dictionary of Literary Biography* is to compile literary history in the surest way available to us – by accurate and comprehensive treatment of the lives and work of those who contributed to it.

The *DLB* Advisory Board

Introduction

This volume of the *Dictionary of Literary Biography* is the second of two devoted to publishers and editors of American magazines in the period 1900 to 1960, years marked by the emergence of the magazine as a truly mass medium and the subsequent decline of this status after the success of television. A fuller general account of American magazine publishing in this period appears in the foreword to *DLB 91: American Magazine Journalists, 1900–1960,* First Series. The scope of the magazine industry in this period was such that an additional volume was required to do justice to its leading editorial figures.

The considerable growth in the importance of the magazine during the early years of the twentieth century was a result of an economics of plenty, with large-scale retailers selling an abundance of standardized, brand goods that required a more efficient national advertising medium than had existed previously. The magazine, specifically the kind of magazine that was affordably priced and that appealed to a large audience by offering varied, easy-to-understand editorial content, was the answer to this need. Thanks to favorable postal regulations and improved transportation, such magazines as the *Ladies' Home Journal, Munsey's,* and *McClure's* were able to pioneer in achieving mass circulations. Ads were more aggressively solicited than they had been in the 1800s, and ad/editorial ratios began to change from roughly 50/50 to 65/35 by the midcentury mark. By this time magazine publishers had come to see their subscribers less as readers and more as consumers. Concurrently, magazines evolved from being basically an elitist medium into a far more popular one – a medium that more nearly reflected than led popular taste. As this change was occurring, editorial content also became more closely geared to ad content.

As the century progressed, magazine publishers paid close attention to their own marketing needs. Newsstand sales lost ground to subscriptions, first solicited mainly door-to-door, then by direct-mail offers. By the 1930s drugstores, soon to be joined by high-traffic grocery chains, were beginning to replace bookstores and newsstands as the most important outlets for single-copy sales. From the emergence of the national magazine until antitrust decisions in the 1950s, distribution of magazines to retailers was dominated by the American News Company, which had been founded in 1864. (In the early 1900s, however, a few large-scale publishers, such as Curtis and McCall, had begun severing ties with American News and formed independent distribution firms of their own.) These factors, along with a higher education level, broadened affluence, and expanded leisure time, led to dramatic growth in overall magazine circulation and in the total number of magazines from which the public could choose. By the conclusion of World War II more than two-thirds of adult Americans were magazine readers.

Also by this time "positioning" had become vital to many magazines. Given the considerable competition for readers and subscribers among these many magazines, each title needed to establish a niche that distinguished it from the other titles in its general category. This niche might be large – for instance, consider the ways in which *Look* sought to differentiate itself from *Life* and the *Saturday Evening Post:* more features oriented than news-intensive *Life,* more picture oriented than the *Post* – or it might involve the more precise positioning of a smaller-circulation specialized magazine that aimed its product at a particular reader age, occupation, or subject interest rather than at a mass audience. In addition to this developing trend toward specialization, which would become far more important in the 1960s and 1970s, the first sixty years of the century saw magazine article length become briefer, a growing dominance of photography over other forms of illustration, and an ever-increasing interest in people (as opposed to places, things, and ideas).

Editors and publishers profiled in this volume include those who carried on magazines that had been founded in the nineteenth century. Orison Marden, one of America's apostles of self-help, founded *Success* in 1897, continued the magazine until 1912, and then resurrected it for another run from 1918 to 1924. Edward Weeks became in 1938 the ninth editor of the *Atlantic Monthly* (founded 1857) and made it a magazine not of literature for its own sake but for exploring important social issues. Herbert Mayes began in 1939 to rescue *Good Housekeeping* (founded 1885) from stodginess; he was joined in 1945 by Margaret Cousins, and in 1958 this team brought their editorial skills to a similarly afflicted *McCall's* (founded 1886). In 1942 Ben Hibbs took over the editorship of the *Saturday Evening Post* (founded 1821), giving the then-troubled magazine the God-fearing, patriotic family appeal that made it so popular in the pretelevision years. In 1948 Gerard Piel purchased the old, slumping *Scientific American* (founded 1845) and made it the leader in its field by aiming it largely at corporate and academic readers and concentrating on examining the impact of scientific advances on modern society. Beginning in 1951 editor Carey McWilliams made the venerable weekly the *Nation* (founded 1865) into America's leading exponent of liberal opinion in the cold-war era.

Also appearing in this volume are editors of magazines that originated in the period being covered. The beginning of this period includes the *Smart Set,* a monthly magazine of literary interest founded in 1900 by former Civil War colonel William D'Alton Mann. The publication was shaped by a series of editors, including Mann, before attaining its most influential editors in 1914: the iconoclastic social critic H. L. Mencken and his coeditor, theater critic George Jean Nathan. The two men went on to found in 1924 a magazine of their own, the *American Mercury,* though the periodical was edited by Mencken alone after 1925. Other early-twentieth-century magazines of note were *Mid-Week Pictorial* and *Current History,* both founded in 1914 and both edited starting in 1915 by George Washington Ochs-Oakes, younger brother of the celebrated Adolph Ochs, publisher of the *New York Times.*

The magazine genre known collectively as the "pulps" dates from 1896, when Frank Munsey converted *Argosy* to an all-fiction content and printed it on inexpensive pulpwood stock, but the genre did not fully develop until the 1920s. The pulps were priced from ten to twenty-five cents a copy and reached millions of readers in the 1920s, 1930s, and 1940s – before television and paperback books became popular conveyors of inexpensive entertainment to mass audiences. Although the early pulps each contained a varied diet of fiction, the genre eventually began to specialize in subject matter. Important categories were mystery/detective, Western, romance, science fiction, and sports.

Black Mask, the most renowned of the pulp mystery magazines, was founded in 1920 by Mencken and Nathan. Edited from 1926 to 1936 by Joseph Thompson Shaw, it showcased the work of the "hard-boiled" school of detective fiction, most notably Dashiell Hammett and Raymond Chandler. Another important pulp was *Amazing Stories,* founded in 1926 by Hugo Gernsback, the Luxembourg-born writer and inventor who became known as America's foremost early editor and publisher of scientific fiction. Gernsback created several other pulps, including *Wonder Stories* and *Scientific Detective Monthly* (both founded 1929), specializing in fiction which offered readers technologically plausible extrapolations from existing scientific knowledge. After World War II, the popularity of paperback books cut into the pulp market, the television Western eventually drew off the market of the Western pulps, and soap operas took away some of the market for the romance end of the pulp business. The most resilient of all the pulps were the science-fiction titles, which outlasted the others perhaps due to society's ever-increasing scientific and technological complexity.

The worldwide publishing empire of the *Reader's Digest* had its beginning in 1922, when husband-wife team DeWitt and Lila Wallace founded their pocket-sized magazine of optimism, patriotism, and the American way. The Wallaces' idea was not merely to clip or appropriate existing articles as many of America's earliest magazines had done, but to pay for them and edit them to give busy readers a quick read and a bargain as well. The success of the publication led to other digests: *Catholic Digest* (1936), *Book Digest* (1938), *Everybody's Digest* (1938), *Cartoon Digest* (1939), *Negro Digest* (1942), *Editorial Digest* (1947), and others. The small page size of the *Reader's Digest,* which made the magazine handy for carrying about and for reading in crowded places, also appealed to other publishers and was emulated in 1935 by Robb Sagendorph, founder of the early regional magazine *Yankee;* in 1936 by David Smart's *Coronet,* initially an art magazine; and in 1944 by *Pageant,* published by Alex Hillman. Most successful of the more recent "digest-sized" periodicals has been *TV Guide,* founded in 1948 and taken over in 1953 by Walter Annenberg.

The witty, sophisticated *New Yorker* appeared in 1925. It employed James Thurber, E. B. White, K. A. White, and Wolcott Gibbs; and it published such writers as Dorothy Parker, John O'Hara, S. J. Perelman, and Alexander Woollcott. Both its founding editor, Harold Ross, and his successor, William Shawn, are included in this volume.

A general trend away from the use of fiction in most of the larger-circulation U.S. magazines was responsible for the 1931 founding by husband-wife team Martha Foley and Whit Burnett of *Story,* a magazine devoted to short stories and novellas. Before it perished in 1965, *Story* had carried the work of Erskine Caldwell, John Cheever, Truman Capote, William Faulkner, William Saroyan, and Norman Mailer.

Reaching a larger audience was the men's magazine *Esquire,* founded in 1933 by David Smart, who hired Arnold Gingrich as editor. Originally a fashion magazine, *Esquire* became known for the quality of its writing, contributed by such writers as Ernest Hemingway, D. H. Lawrence, and F. Scott Fitzgerald. Yet another launch in this decade was *Look,* a monthly specializing in photo features that grew out of the rotogravure section and photo syndicate of the *Des Moines Register,* an earlier property of the Cowles family. In 1941 appeared *Ellery Queen's Mystery Magazine,* edited for three decades by cousins Frederic Dannay and Manfred Lee and published by Lawrence Spivak, who later was the publisher and sometimes editor of the more political post-Mencken *American Mercury.*

The travel magazine *Holiday,* edited by Ted Patrick, appeared in 1946, and in 1948 Edwin Self and his wife Gloria brought out what many have called the first modern city magazine (independent of chamber-of-commerce control), *San Diego,* which became known for its emphasis on preservation and conservation. Also in the 1940s Ken Purdy edited both the picture magazine *Parade,* boosting its circulation to more than five million, and *True,* a men's magazine of nonfiction.

What public taste would have rendered an improbable success prior to the early 1950s was the appearance of a new genre of "skin magazines," pioneered in 1953 by Hugh Hefner and his *Playboy,* which quickly bred innumerable competitors with such titles as *Dude, Gent,* and *Monsieur.* Along different lines, the most recent of the magazines whose editors and publishers are addressed in this volume is the *National Review,* an opinion journal founded by William F. Buckley, Jr., in 1955 and which is now a leading voice of the American Right.

By 1960 the competition of television was causing magazine publishers to rethink the role of the mass-market periodical. The *American Magazine* had folded in 1956; *Collier's,* in 1957. *Coronet* was to follow in 1961, the *Saturday Evening Post* in 1969, *Look* in 1971, and *Life* in 1972. Although the *Post* and *Life* were later resurrected, the end of this period brought with it the demise of most of the nationally distributed magazines whose editors had tried to include content that would appeal to nearly everyone.

– *Sam G. Riley*

ACKNOWLEDGMENTS

This book was produced by Bruccoli Clark Layman, Inc. Karen L. Rood is senior editor for the *Dictionary of Literary Biography* series. Sam Bruce was the in-house editor.

Photography editors are Edward Scott and Timothy C. Lundy. Layout and graphics supervisor is Penney L. Haughton. Copyediting supervisor is Bill Adams. Typesetting supervisor is Kathleen M. Flanagan. Darren Harris-Fain and Julie E. Frick are editorial associates. Systems manager is George F. Dodge. The production staff includes Phyllis Avant, Joseph Matthew Bruccoli, Ann M. Cheschi, Patricia Coate, Denise Edwards, Sarah A. Estes, Joyce Fowler, Laurel Gladden, Jolyon M. Helterman, Rebecca Mayo, Kathy Lawler Merlette, Sean Moriarty, Pamela D. Norton, Thomas J. Pickett, Patricia F. Salisbury, Maxine K. Smalls, William L. Thomas, Jr., and Wilma Weant.

Walter W. Ross and Deborah M. Chasteen did library research. They were assisted by the following librarians at the Thomas Cooper Library of the University of South Carolina: Linda Holderfield and the interlibrary-loan staff; reference librarians Gwen Baxter, Daniel Boice, Faye Chadwell, Cathy Eckman, Gary Geer, Qun "Gerry" Jiao, Jean Rhyne, Carol Tobin, Carolyn Tyler, Virginia Weathers, Elizabeth Whiznant, and Connie Widney; circulation-department head Thomas Marcil; and acquisitions-searching supervisor David Haggard.

Dictionary of Literary Biography® • Volume One Hundred Thirty-Seven

American Magazine Journalists, 1900–1960

Second Series

Dictionary of Literary Biography

Frederick Lewis Allen

(5 July 1890 - 13 February 1954)

Sam G. Riley
Virginia Polytechnic Institute & State University

MAJOR POSITIONS HELD: Assistant editor, *Atlantic Monthly* (1914); managing editor, *Century Magazine* (1916-1917); editorial assistant (1923-1925), assistant editor (1925-1930), associate editor (1931-1941), editor (1941-1953), consulting editor, *Harper's Magazine* (1954).

BOOKS: *Frederick Baylies Allen; A Memoir* (Cambridge, Mass.: Riverside, 1929);

Only Yesterday: An Informal History of the Nineteen-Twenties (New York & London: Harper & Brothers, 1931);

The Lords of Creation (New York & London: Harper & Brothers, 1935);

In a Time of Apprehension, A Commencement Address Delivered at the Bennington College in Bennington, Vermont (North Bennington, Vt.: Catamount, 1938);

Since Yesterday: The Nineteen-Thirties in America (New York: Harper & Brothers, 1940);

American Magazines, 1741-1941, by Allen, William L. Chenery, and Fulton Oursler (New York: New York Public Library, 1941);

Paul Revere Reynolds, A Biographical Sketch (New York: Privately printed, 1944);

The Great Pierpont Morgan (New York: Harper, 1949);

Harper's Magazine, 1850-1950; A Centenary Address (New York: Newcomen Society in North America, 1950);

The Big Change: America Transforms Itself, 1900-1950 (New York: Harper, 1952).

OTHER: Mason Locke Weems, *Anecdote from the Life of George Washington, from the History of that Very Extraordinary Man,* preface by Allen (Madison, N.J.: Golden Hind, 1932);

Frederick Lewis Allen

The American Procession, American Life since 1860 in Photographs, commentary by Allen, photographs compiled by Agnes Rogers (New York & London: Harper & Brothers, 1933);

Metropolis; An American City in Photographs, commentary by Allen, photographs compiled by Rogers (New York & London: Harper & Brothers, 1934);

I Remember Distinctly: A Family Album of the American People, 1918–1941, commentary by Allen, photographs compiled by Rogers (New York: Harper, 1947).

SELECTED PERIODICAL PUBLICATIONS – UNCOLLECTED: "The Creative Gift," *Punch,* 145 (9 July 1913): 42;

"Who Shall Ascend into the Hill of the Lord," *Atlantic Monthly,* 112 (October 1913): 516–519;

"Terpsichore: The Present Rage for Rhythmic Dancing and Blurred Art," *Vanity Fair,* 4 (March 1915): 47–48;

"Small Talk," *Century,* 93 (February 1917): 636–639;

"An Opportunity for Critics," *New Republic,* 10 (31 March 1917): 264–265;

"The American Tradition and the War," *Nation,* 104 (April 1917): 484–485;

"President Wilson: A Political and Personal Interpretation," *Outlook,* 121 (23 April 1919): 693–696;

"The Goon and His Style," *Harper's,* 144 (December 1921): 121–123;

"Newspapers and the Truth," *Atlantic Monthly,* 129 (January 1922): 44–54;

"University and College Publicity," *School and Society,* 15 (6 May 1922): 485–489;

"Mountain Mania," *Atlantic Monthly,* 129 (June 1922): 852–854;

"Intensive Flivving," *Atlantic Monthly,* 132 (August 1923): 278–280;

"A Little Lecture on the Atom," *Harper's,* 148 (March 1924): 545–547;

"Public Opinion," *Forum,* 74 (December 1925): 894–896;

"The Fetish of the Ph.D.," *Independent,* 116 (10 April 1926): 411–412, 430–431;

"The House Terrible," *Harper's,* 153 (October 1926): 647–650;

"These Disillusioned Highbrows," *Independent,* 118 (9 April 1927): 378–379;

"Liquidation Day Parade," *New Yorker,* 5 (7 December 1929): 61–62;

"What Are You Doing for Prosperity?," *New Yorker,* 5 (28 December 1929): 19–20;

"Westchester Squeeze," *New Yorker,* 5 (4 January 1930): 73–76;

"The End of an Era," *Outlook and Independent,* 154 (5 February 1930): 239–240;

"Those Fifth Avenue Girls," *New Yorker,* 5 (8 February 1930): 19–20;

"Paul Revere's Ride," *New Yorker,* 6 (19 April 1930): 19–21;

"Give Me the Facts," *New Yorker,* 6 (12 July 1930): 49–55;

"Best-Sellers: 1900–1935," *Saturday Review of Literature,* 13 (7 December 1935): 3–4, 20, 24, 26;

"Breaking World Records," *Harper's,* 173 (August 1936): 302–310;

"Who's Getting the Money?," *Harper's,* 189 (June 1944): 1–10;

The Function of a Magazine in America, special issue of *The University of Missouri Bulletin,* 46, no. 23 (1945);

"This Time and Last Time," *Harper's,* 194 (March 1947): 193–203;

"The American Magazine Grows Up," *Atlantic Monthly,* 180 (November 1947): 77–82;

"The Big Change: The Coming – and Disciplining – of Industrialism, 1850–1950," *Harper's,* 201 (October 1950): 145–160;

"What Have We Got Here?," *Life,* 34 (5 January 1953): 47;

"An Editor's Creed," *Atlantic Monthly,* 192 (December 1953): 46–47;

"The Big Change in Suburbia," *Harper's,* 208 (June 1954): 21–28;

"Crisis in the Suburbs," *Harper's,* 209 (July 1954): 47–53.

Frederick Lewis Allen is remembered mainly as a longtime editor of *Harper's* magazine and as a popular social historian. His tenure with *Harper's* began in 1923 with the position of editorial assistant and continued through 1953, when he resigned his position as editor in chief. Allen might be described as a New England, Ivy League gentleman editor. His biographer, Darwin Payne, regards Allen's career as a bridge between the proprieties and elitism of America's Victorian age and the leveling mass culture that began to spread rapidly in the 1950s. Both as editor and author, Allen was much concerned with traditional values in this changing culture.

Allen was born into a line of prosperous merchants and churchmen who traced their ancestry to not one but seven Plymouth Colony Pilgrims. His father, Frederick Baylies Allen, was a minister, first a Congregationalist and later an Episcopalian, whose first wife, Louisa Ripley Vose, died in 1871 soon after the birth of the couple's third child. More

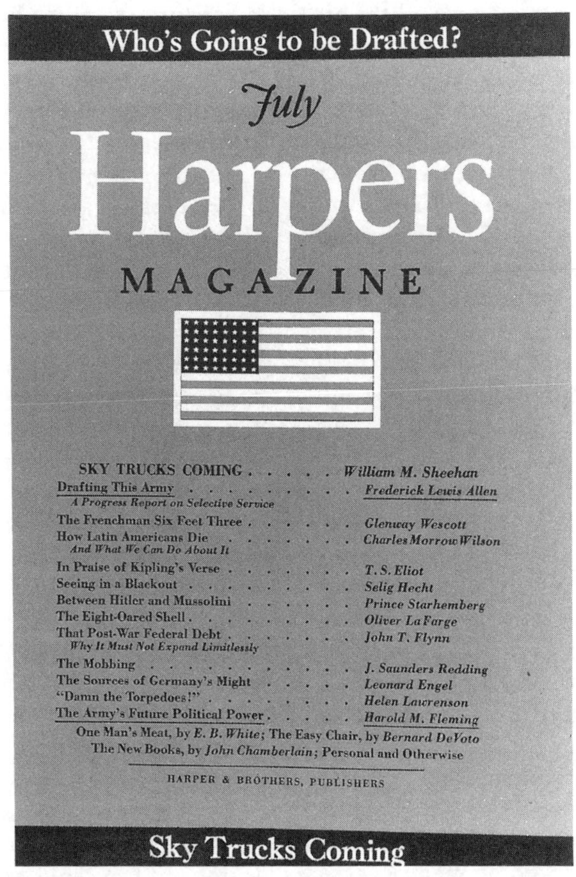

Who's Going to be Drafted?

July

Harpers

MAGAZINE

SKY TRUCKS COMING . . . . . *William M. Sheehan*
Drafting This Army . . . . . *Frederick Lewis Allen*
A Progress Report on Selective Service
The Frenchman Six Feet Three . . . . . *Glenway Wescott*
How Latin Americans Die . . . . . *Charles Morrow Wilson*
And What We Can Do About It
In Praise of Kipling's Verse . . . . . *T. S. Eliot*
Seeing in a Blackout . . . . . *Selig Hecht*
Between Hitler and Mussolini . . . . . *Prince Starhemberg*
The Eight-Oared Shell . . . . . *Oliver La Farge*
That Post-War Federal Debt . . . . . *John T. Flynn*
Why It Must Not Expand Limitlessly
The Mobbing . . . . . *J. Saunders Redding*
The Sources of Germany's Might . . . . . *Leonard Engel*
"Damn the Torpedoes!" . . . . . *Helen Lawrenson*
The Army's Future Political Power . . . . . *Harold M. Fleming*
One Man's Meat, by *E. B. White*; The Easy Chair, by *Bernard DeVoto*
The New Books, by *John Chamberlain*; Personal and Otherwise

HARPER & BROTHERS, PUBLISHERS

Sky Trucks Coming

Cover for a 1942 issue reflecting the patriotic mood of the nation after the Japanese bombed Pearl Harbor on 7 December 1941

than a decade later, in 1883, the Reverend Allen married Alberta Hildegarde Lewis, and on 5 July 1890 Frederick Lewis Allen was born. While not truly wealthy, the Allens were far more affluent and well connected than most ministers and their families. The Reverend Mr. Allen, educated at Harvard, Amherst, and the Andover Theological Seminary, had family money, was a skilled artist and an avid golfer, and owned a large house, complete with servants, in a good section of Boston plus a summer place in New Hampshire. He was active in social and charitable works in Boston, turning an Episcopal mission there into a welfare agency; serving as president of the Robert Gould Shaw House, a charity that benefited blacks; and founding the New England Watch and Ward Society, which became known under Allen's successor, J. Frank Chase, for its ambitious efforts at censorship.

At age twelve, Allen, known in his youth as Fritz, was sent to America's most prestigious boarding school, Groton, where he compiled a fine academic record and wrote for the *Weekly Groton,* but he disliked the hazing and snobbishness of the other students. He became the sports editor of the *Weekly Groton* and also wrote poetry for that paper. At his graduation in 1908 he took several honors in English and left the school well prepared for Harvard University, which he entered in 1909.

Under its new president, Abbott Lawrence Lowell, Harvard was at that time attempting to give up certain elements of its entrenched New England elitism in order to become more of a force nationally. Here Allen met fellow students Walter Lippmann and Robert Benchley, one of his cohorts on the *Lampoon,* the campus humor magazine. In addition to his *Lampoon* work, Allen, now called Freddie, was an editor of Harvard's monthly literary magazine, the *Advocate,* in which he published short stories, poetry, reviews, and essays. One of his poems, "Tripoli," won Harvard's Lloyd McKim Garrison Prize in 1912. Later in the year Allen completed his A.B. degree and was inducted into the Institute of 1770 and the Hasty Pudding Club, the latter a distinction he shared with classmate Joseph P. Kennedy. While working on his A.M. degree, which he received in 1913, Allen taught English composition at Harvard.

Allen's work for the *Lampoon* attracted the attention of Frank Crowinshield, then an editor for *Century*. Crowinshield encouraged Allen to prepare himself for a magazine career by writing sophisticated humor copy. Allen took this advice, first publishing in 1913 three pieces in London's venerable humor periodical *Punch*. One of these, "The Creative Gift," is a brief reflection with an anticlimactic ending on the notion that characters in a play, once created by their author, take on lives of their own that determine their subsequent actions. This early work, while rather stiff, at least showed promise. The young English teacher also sold a more serious story, "Who Shall Ascend into the Hill of the Lord," to *Atlantic Monthly*.

When Allen's teaching obligations were completed, he immediately entered magazine work. Turning down Crowninshield's offer to become assistant editor of the new Conde-Nast magazine *Vanity Fair,* Allen opted instead for an assistant editor spot with the long-established, high-prestige *Atlantic Monthly* under owner and editor Ellery Sedgwick, a fellow Groton graduate. At this time Sedgwick was changing the magazine's focus from art and literature to a wider examination of public issues, a move that saved the *Atlantic* from extinction and again gave it a competitive circulation. From August 1914 until December 1915 Allen worked on manuscripts, did layout and proofing, and corresponded with writers during the day while doing his own writing by night, occasionally publishing in *Vanity Fair*.

In December 1915 Allen accepted a new job as managing editor of *Century* and left Boston for New York. Working under the editorship of former newspaperman and dramatist Douglas Doty, Allen had considerable input as this magazine, like the *Atlantic,* shifted emphasis from the literary to broader coverage of public issues. His life in a new city was made more congenial through the Harvard Club and by the Coffee House, a club for artists, musicians, and writers.

Allen wrote as well as edited for *Century;* one of his better efforts was the 1917 short story "Small Talk," a wry first-person account of a chance meeting with an important businessman, described as "a whole corporation on two legs," and the "perfunctory rallies of talk" as the two men try to find common ground for conversation. This sketch constitutes a nice job of upper-crust humor in a style similar to that of Allen's old *Lampoon* mate Benchley. Allen was not to give up his interest in humor writing for some years yet, but already he was giving more attention to penning serious articles, such as a *New Republic* piece complaining that the magazine as a medium was not being taken seriously enough and an essay for *Nation* in April 1917 examining the American tradition of individualism and how it might react to the need for greater discipline should the United States join the war in Europe.

Soon thereafter Allen received and accepted an invitation to leave his magazine post and serve as director of the press bureau of Boston's Writers' Committee for Patriotic Service. In this new job he was to serve as publicist for the war effort, yet he resigned after only two months and the Writers' Committee was disbanded. Allen moved quickly to a similar position in Washington, D.C., with the Council of National Defense as head of this group's Section on Cooperation with States. As such, he served as a liaison, conveying information between the national council and the National Committee on Public Information and the individual state-defense councils then being created.

His public-relations experience during this period might be regarded as a mixture of good works and propaganda. Admirers would regard his efforts as helpful in gaining public support for involvement in the "War To End All Wars"; detractors might see Allen more as a protected young man shouting "Let's you men go and fight" to the sons of parents lacking the powerful connections of the Allens. As legions of U.S. soldiers were training and fighting, Allen was enjoying a courtship with Vassar graduate Dorothy Penrose Cobb, who was working in Washington in the War Department. The couple became engaged in September 1918. To the thirty-year-old Allen's credit, he determined to enlist in the Army's Chemical Warfare Service, but he was finally persuaded to give up this plan in favor of a better position on the council and on 29 November married Dorothy, with Benchley as his best man. Demobilization began, and the newlyweds settled into a comfortable life with a maid and a cook, and Allen contributed serious articles, unsigned, to *Outlook,* offering an appraisal of the war effort and President Woodrow Wilson's role in it.

Inquiries about a new magazine or even a newspaper position failed to produce anything to Allen's liking, but in the war years and postwar period the job field of public relations was enjoying enormous growth. One of the first universities to aggressively market its image was Harvard, which initially hired an outside agency, then decided to handle publicity in-house. Allen's name was suggested by his staunch supporter Sedgwick. In September 1919 Allen assumed the job of the school's publicity director, though his official title was secretary to the corporation. Many of his duties con-

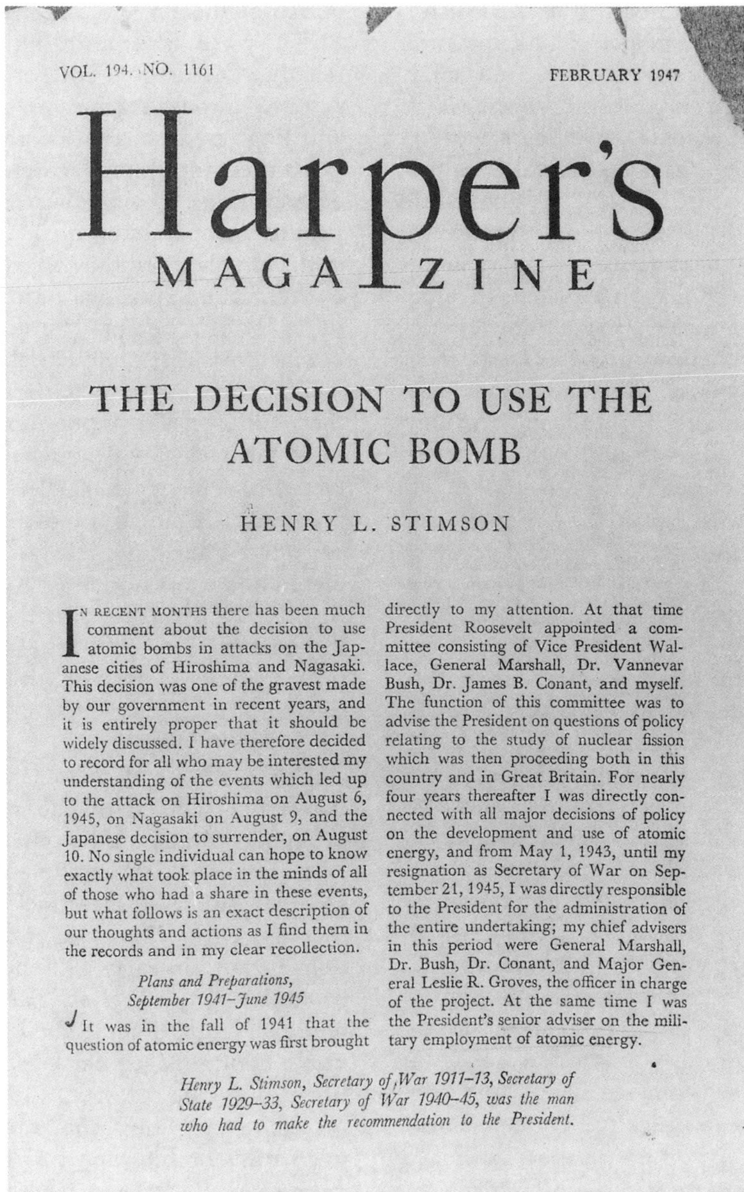

VOL. 194. NO. 1161 FEBRUARY 1947

Harper's MAGAZINE

THE DECISION TO USE THE ATOMIC BOMB

HENRY L. STIMSON

In recent months there has been much comment about the decision to use atomic bombs in attacks on the Japanese cities of Hiroshima and Nagasaki. This decision was one of the gravest made by our government in recent years, and it is entirely proper that it should be widely discussed. I have therefore decided to record for all who may be interested my understanding of the events which led up to the attack on Hiroshima on August 6, 1945, on Nagasaki on August 9, and the Japanese decision to surrender, on August 10. No single individual can hope to know exactly what took place in the minds of all of those who had a share in these events, but what follows is an exact description of our thoughts and actions as I find them in the records and in my clear recollection.

Plans and Preparations, September 1941–June 1945

It was in the fall of 1941 that the question of atomic energy was first brought directly to my attention. At that time President Roosevelt appointed a committee consisting of Vice President Wallace, General Marshall, Dr. Vannevar Bush, Dr. James B. Conant, and myself. The function of this committee was to advise the President on questions of policy relating to the study of nuclear fission which was then proceeding both in this country and in Great Britain. For nearly four years thereafter I was directly connected with all major decisions of policy on the development and use of atomic energy, and from May 1, 1943, until my resignation as Secretary of War on September 21, 1945, I was directly responsible to the President for the administration of the entire undertaking; my chief advisers in this period were General Marshall, Dr. Bush, Dr. Conant, and Major General Leslie R. Groves, the officer in charge of the project. At the same time I was the President's senior adviser on the military employment of atomic energy.

Henry L. Stimson, Secretary of War 1911–13, Secretary of State 1929–33, Secretary of War 1940–45, was the man who had to make the recommendation to the President.

First page of one of the most acclaimed nonfiction articles published by Harper's *in the postwar period, former secretary of war Henry L. Stimson's account of the 1945 decision to employ atomic weapons against Japan*

sisted of "putting out fires" to control bad press, yet Allen provided a measure of national leadership in the new field of university public relations with a 1922 *School and Society* article discussing what such work entailed.

During these years in Cambridge – 1919–1923 – Dorothy Allen gave birth to two children, Elizabeth Penrose and Oliver Ellsworth. In addition, Allen freelanced frequently for the humor section of *Harper's Magazine,* "The Lion's Mouth." One of these sketches, "The Goon and His Style," divided people into two types: "goons" and "jiggers," goons being those with a heavy touch, jiggers being people marked by wit and playfulness. Germans, he wrote, tended to be goons; Frenchmen, jiggers. Allen's point was to lambaste the pompous and ponderous – he specifically named George Washington and James Fenimore Cooper as goons – and young writers who try to appear wise and dignified beyond their years.

The frustrations the young public-relations man experienced are evident in a more serious 1922 article Allen published in *Atlantic,* "Newspapers and the Truth." Though he approvingly cites Lippmann's little book *Liberty and the News* (1920) for its exposition of the importance of a free press to freedom in general, Allen's sympathies are clearly more in line with Upton Sinclair's *Brass Check* (1919), a book that presents, in Allen's words, "case after case in which the press has falsified the news." Allen discusses the difficulty of achieving true accuracy in news stories; the indifference to accuracy displayed by many reporters and editors; the limited educations of many newsmen; the tendency to embellish to make a more entertaining story; "pack journalism," in which, "like a gang of small boys after a stray dog," reporters fall into the pack to hunt down "wounded" public figures; and the tendency of newspapers to side with moneyed interests.

Allen's frustrations with his often thankless public-relations tasks led to a 1923 career move that would result in a long and happy association with one of the nation's leading magazine and book publishers, Harper and Brothers in New York City. Allen's first duties as editorial assistant were in the firm's literary and tradebook division, then headed by William H. Briggs. Working mainly with book manuscripts, Allen began to ease into editing articles for *Harper's Magazine* under editor Thomas B. Wells, who in 1925 revamped the slumping monthly in much the same way Sedgwick had changed the *Atlantic* while Allen had been with that magazine. Again, fiction and poetry were de-emphasized to make room for more nonfiction that addressed the issues of the day. The change was successful, and in 1925 Allen was named the magazine's assistant editor. He and Dorothy built a new house in Scarsdale, New York, which motivated Allen to redouble his freelancing in order to help cover this large expense.

Allen sold picture ideas to the humor magazine *Life* and continued writing short humor for *Harper's,* including "A Little Lecture on the Atom," a 1924 spoof of science using the device of personification. Allen likened the atom's tiny size to that of congressmen's brains and noted that once the public grasps that even structural steel is composed of atoms, each of which is hollow, upper floors in New York's skyscrapers would likely become harder to rent. Another such sketch, "The House Terrible," appeared in the October 1926 issue and drew on Allen's own building experience. His last fling at humor writing consisted of six sketches for the *New Yorker* in 1929 and 1930, beginning with "Liquidation Day Parade" and ending with "Give Me the Facts."

In a more earnest vein, Allen placed in *The Independent,* a weekly Boston opinion journal, "The Fetish of the Ph.D.," an overstated attack on the Ph.D. system in American higher education. Allen felt that "professors with the Ph.D. virus in their systems" should teach more and spend less time on "piffling research" that narrows their interests and turns them into "small, careful, timid men ignorant of everything which educated citizens of the world should know outside their own acre of specialization." He regarded the concept of knowledge for its own sake as a spurious rationalization used to justify a lot of academic "bunk." Another *Independent* article of Allen's, "These Disillusioned Highbrows," attacked H. L. Mencken and Sinclair Lewis and their followers as supercilious snobs who underrated the everyday American.

In 1926 and 1927 Allen took on a longer writing project, a biography of a Scarsdale friend, literary agent Paul Revere Reynolds. Though he completed the manuscript in April 1927, *Paul Revere Reynolds, a Biographical Sketch* was not published until Reynolds's death in 1944. Meanwhile, Allen undertook a similar project about his own father; the resulting book, *Frederick Baylies Allen; A Memoir,* was published in 1929.

The Allens' daughter Elizabeth died of spinal meningitis on 11 November 1928, and this event probably stimulated the reflective side of Frederick Allen's nature. Later, as he pondered the stock-market crash of 1929, he concluded that much more than money was involved in this dramatic economic debacle, and in early 1930 he published "The End of an Era" in *Outlook and Independent.* By spring he had decided to expand the idea behind this article into a book. In October Dorothy died of complications following surgery, and Allen used the book project to help him through his grief. By the following spring he had begun a courtship with fellow *Harper's* employee Agnes Rogers Hyde, and in May he was promoted to the magazine's assistant editorship under new editor in chief Lee Foster Hartman.

In autumn 1931 Allen's expansion of "The End of an Era," titled *Only Yesterday: An Informal History of the Nineteen-Twenties,* was published and immediately became a Book-of-the-Month Club selection. *Only Yesterday* was a best-seller and to date has sold more than one million copies. Allen, not a professional historian, called the method he used in writing the book "retrospective journalism." It can be viewed from today's perspective as a cross between history and popular culture, and it has had a decided impact on how educated Americans remember the decade of the 1920s. Kenneth Lynn, writing in 1980 in *American Scholar,* said that the book actually reveals more about its author than about the

Cover for the October 1950 issue, celebrating one hundred years of publication

1920s, a conclusion seconded by John D. Stevens in his 1991 book *Sensationalism and the New York Press,* in which he points out that for the majority of Americans, "the twenties no more roared than the nineties had been gay." It is probably fair to say that this, the best-known of Allen's books, did an accurate job of depicting life as he and other members of the loftier social orders knew and lived it.

Allen married Agnes on 29 September 1932 and, while continuing his normal editorial duties at *Harper's,* began preparing for a book that would examine American style capitalism and how its practice had led to the 1929 Wall Street collapse that ushered in the Great Depression. He worked on this book, *The Lords of Creation,* from October 1933 until June 1935. His own position was the essentially liberal stance of the New Deal Democrat who felt that raw, undiluted capitalism would have to give way to new measures that would improve the lot of the common man.

Around this same time Allen and his new wife came up with a new idea involving photography: pictorial history books. Their first, *The American Procession,* which addressed American life between 1860 and 1917, appeared in 1933. A second, *Metropolis,* published in 1934, was a photographic look at New York City; and more than a decade later, in 1947, appeared a pictorial view of the years 1918–1941 titled *I Remember Distinctly.* Agnes collected and arranged the photos, while Frederick wrote the accompanying captions. The books sold well and the first two helped the Allens to ride out the Depression in fine style. Agnes went on to write and edit other books of her own and eventually left *Harper's* for a job with the *Literary Digest.* In 1936 the couple moved to Manhattan where they bought an elegant brownstone.

At *Harper's,* Allen campaigned for a new writer to take over the long-running "Editor's Easy Chair" section of the magazine, then being conducted by Edward Martin, age eighty. Martin's successor, in November 1935, was frequent contributor Bernard DeVoto. The magazine's circulation had declined somewhat due to the Depression, yet quality remained high, with fiction by the likes of William Faulkner, John Steinbeck, and G. K. Chesterton and nonfiction by such writers as Elmer Davis, Stuart Chase, Harold Laski, and John Gunther. Allen edited some of Gunther's work and recommended that writer's *Inside Europe* to the *Harper's* book division, a canny move. He also edited Marquis Childs and worked on an unflattering, highly controversial article on Boston's storied mayor James Curley.

In 1937 Allen risked pushing for several rather large changes in the magazine. By this time he considered the venerable "Easy Chair" department to be so outdated that it should be put to rest, and he thought book reviewer Harry Hansen should be replaced by someone more critical. He also favored a wider range of topics, greater flexibility as to the length of articles – then standardized at roughly five thousand words – and verse, the inclusion of first-person narratives, payment in excess of the usual $250 per article for favored contributors, a new cover design, and more writing time for himself and assistant editor George Leighton. Editor in chief Hartman began making changes in 1938, beginning with a new cover; replacing "The Lion's Mouth" department with "One Man's Meat," to be written by E. B. White; the addition of longer verse contributions, the first of which was by Edna St. Vincent Millay; and a new book reviewer, John Chamberlain. The "Easy Chair" remained, however.

While serving as *Harper's* associate editor, Allen managed to keep up his freelance productivity on a wide variety of contemporary topics that touched upon American life. In the *Saturday Review of Literature* he published "Best-Sellers: 1900–1935," which concluded that the U.S. reading public had become more intellectually sophisticated, due in large part, he wrote, to the effect of the mass media. Also, Allen had been putting aside material for a sequel to *Only Yesterday*. In 1939 he requested and received a four-month leave from the magazine to work on *Since Yesterday: The Nineteen-Thirties in America,* which appeared in February 1940 and became another best-seller.

Harper's editor Hartman died in September 1941, and in early October company officials chose Allen to succeed him despite some apprehension that Allen's own book projects might divert his attention from the magazine. The appointment brought Allen an outpouring of attention from other magazines, newspapers, and radio. Due to the success of his books, he was by this time as much a "public editor" as Hartman had been a private, company man. The new editor wrote in the December issue that *Harper's* would continue on its existing course, taking a long view of news events and offering interpretation. The times were uncertain, of course, because of the success the Nazis were having in Europe. Allen and most editors of American opinion journals had initially opposed intervention in the conflict but with only a few exceptions had, after the fall of France, grown more willing to commit American troops. Aside from war concerns, the very survival of serious magazines seemed in doubt. By the early 1940s the most financially successful magazines were such titles as *Time,* the new *Life,* and *Reader's Digest,* the contents of which were far less literary and less directed at an elite audience than were *Harper's* and competing periodicals of serious commentary. The larger circulations of the new "consumer magazines" allowed them to pay contributors much higher rates than could *Harper's* and to attract more advertising as well. How best to position *Harper's* in this milieu was Allen's immediate problem.

The Japanese attack at Pearl Harbor in December 1941 rendered obsolete most of the war-connected articles scheduled for the February *Harper's*. Given the new sense of urgency, travel and fiction content was de-emphasized, making room for new coverage of the war effort. Allen worked closely with DeVoto's commentary in "The Easy Chair," at times softening that writer's attacks on such isolationist holdouts as Charles Lindbergh. Allen kept *Harper's* attuned to a broad, strategic coverage of the war, both abroad and on the home front, rather than trying to compete in coverage of spot news. He anguished over the military censorship that hampered military writer Fletcher Pratt's series on major naval battles, working as best he could with the federal Office of Censorship under former Associated Press news director Byron Price and the Office of War Information under frequent *Harper's* contributor Elmer Davis. John Dos Passos wrote "The People at War," a series on home-front war issues, and, due to Allen's own experiences in World War I, the editor began soliciting stories on postwar-planning topics well before the war ended. In 1943 Allen took advantage of a British Ministry of Information–sponsored trip to London for a first-hand look at German air raids.

Paper shortages and requirements to submit multiple sets of proofs for advance censorship of each issue were Allen's greatest trials as editor during the war. The intelligent reading public's desire to make sense of what was happening abroad and at home actually strengthened *Harper's* wartime circulation, though advertisers scaled back until 1943, when ad revenues surged as companies tried to keep their name recognition high. Allen made George Leighton his associate editor in 1942, but the two men differed often, resulting in Leighton's resignation two years later and his replacement by John Kouwenhoven. Russell Lynes and book reviewer Katherine Gauss were named assistant editors, and DeVoto was given a raise as recognition of his good work.

As for content, war-related articles continued to dominate *Harper's*. Fiction was limited: usually only one short story appeared per issue, although much high-quality fiction appeared during the war – by such authors as Eudora Welty, Pearl S. Buck, H. G. Wells, and Faulkner. During these years Allen also resolved to use more verse and to cease using it as filler. He was known as a fiction editor who could make corrections and changes without irritating even the most celebrated writers, and his rejection letters were couched in the most gentle, polite wording.

In nonfiction, Allen strove for modest but steady coverage of developments in science, education, business, and economics. The magazine took a liberal stance on racial issues, which the war had brought to the fore, and spoke out against war profiteering. Allen personally covered the April 1945 conference in San Francisco at which the charter for the United Nations was drafted. A few years later he became embroiled in attempts to counter Whittaker Chambers's alarmist stories of Communist infiltration into U.S. institutions and Sen. Joseph McCarthy's anticommunist witch-hunts. Realizing that the international spread of communism was a real enough menace, Allen nevertheless recognized that its threat was far less serious domestically. As editor, he favored calmly written articles that opposed repressive measures, and he rejected submissions that would use *Harper's* to pander for political gain, including a manuscript by Richard Nixon. Allen became a director of the prestigious Foreign Policy Association and a member of the liberal National Committee for an Effective Congress.

The postwar years brought a boom for the magazine industry in general. Most of the new titles were aimed more at entertainment than at offering serious information of the sort *Harper's* provided. Allen's views as to the role of his own magazine were laid out in "The Functions of a Magazine in America," a speech he was to have delivered to the nation's oldest journalism school at the University of Missouri, but he contracted pneumonia and was unable to appear on stage. *Harper's* should, Allen wrote, serve as a forum for important public issues and for a variety of independent voices that were neither academic nor compromisingly populist. The editor of a serious magazine, he continued, had to resist pressures: from advertisers, from overzealous government censorship, and from some readers' desires for more entertainment-oriented content. This last kind of pressure received expanded treatment in a speech Allen delivered to the National Publishers Association in 1947.

During the postwar period *Harper's* was, according to Allen's biographer, Payne, receiving articles and stories from five hundred to six hundred writers each week. These manuscripts were parceled out among the six in-house editors for an initial decision. Those that were initially approved were read by some of the other editors; Allen usually had the final say as to acceptance or rejection. Nonfiction continued to dominate content, but a typical issue also carried two pieces of quality fiction by such writers as Faulkner, Truman Capote, J. D. Salinger, Arthur Miller, and John Cheever.

Of all the nonfiction carried by *Harper's* in the postwar years, the most acclaimed was the former secretary of war Henry L. Stimson's "The Decision to Use the Atomic Bomb," which appeared in February 1947. Another article that excited unusual comment was Eric Larrabee's "The Day the Earth Stood Still," in the January 1950 issue. This article summarized the work of Immanuel Velikovsky, author of *Worlds in Collision* (1950), which proposed that catastrophic cosmic events had affected the earth's surface and life-forms. The October *Harper's* celebrated the magazine's hundredth anniversary.

Though never a big seller for its parent company, *Harper's* under Allen's leadership did better financially than its chief rival, the *Atlantic Monthly*, then edited by Allen's friend Edward Weeks. The possibility of the two distinguished magazines merging was discussed, though this did not occur. In 1952, however, the two combined their advertising operations as Harper-Atlantic Sales in order to achieve cost savings. With a circulation of roughly 160,000, *Harper's* hovered around the break-even point. One revenue enhancer during Allen's years as editor was a contract with *Reader's Digest* that allowed the digest-sized monthly to condense and reuse any article that had first appeared in *Harper's*.

The war's end gave Allen a bit more time to devote to his own writing. He briefly considered doing a biography of President Franklin D. Roosevelt but deferred to John Gunther on this project. During 1946 and 1947 Allen and Agnes collaborated on a third photo book, *I Remember Distinctly*, which covers a wide swath of American life in the 1920s and 1930s and which became a best-seller. The editor's next book was a generally sympathetic biography of financier J. P. Morgan, *The Great Pierpont Morgan*, which appeared in

1949. His final book, *The Big Change: America Transforms Itself, 1900–1950,* appeared in 1952. This ambitious, thoroughly optimistic account of how the nation's capitalism had become more democratic became a Book-of-the-Month selection and sold extremely well.

Another activity to which Allen devoted considerable time and effort was serving two terms as a overseer of Harvard, first from 1942 to 1948, then from 1950 until his death in 1954. During these years he headed committees dealing with a number of different aspects of university life. Following his resignation as editor of *Harper's,* effective 30 September 1953, Allen also became a trustee of the Ford Foundation. In 1952 he and Agnes were asked to write a script for a two-hour television special to be sponsored by Ford Motor Company. The program was to show how life had changed during the first half of the twentieth century. Carried by both CBS and NBC, the show won the Allens a Christopher Award.

The Allens enjoyed a secure, pleasant retirement, with tennis, travel, entertaining, and Allen continuing his hobby of watercolor painting. His last magazine articles, published posthumously in *Harper's,* were about overdevelopment of America's suburbs. On 13 February 1954 Allen died from the effects of a cerebral hemorrhage he had suffered two weeks earlier. He was buried at Boston's Forest Hills Cemetery. Obituaries and other tributes remembered him as an admired and well-liked editor and as an accomplished popular historian.

Biography:

Darwin Payne, *The Man of Only Yesterday: Frederick Lewis Allen, Former Editor of Harper's Magazine, Author, and Interpreter of His Times* (New York: Harper & Row, 1975).

References:

Norman Kolin, "Frederick Lewis Allen and Harper's Magazine." Master's thesis, University of Missouri, 1950;

Kenneth Lynn, "Only Yesterday," *American Scholar,* 49 (Autumn 1980): 513–518;

Theodore Peterson, *Magazines in the Twentieth Century* (Urbana: University of Illinois Press, 1964), pp. 408–414;

John D. Stevens, *Sensationalism and the New York Press* (New York: Columbia University Press, 1991), p. 103;

John Tebbel and Mary Ellen Zuckerman, *The Magazine in America, 1741–1990* (New York: Oxford University Press, 1991), pp. 199–201, 318–322.

Papers:

Frederick Lewis Allen's papers are housed in two collections in the Manuscript Division of the Library of Congress: the Frederick Lewis Allen papers and the *Harper's Magazine* Editorial Correspondence files.

John Shaw Billings

(11 May 1898 - 25 August 1975)

Daniel Morris
Harvard University

MAJOR POSITIONS HELD: Washington correspondent, *Brooklyn Daily Eagle* (1921–1929); Washington correspondent (1928–1929), national affairs editor (1929–1933), managing editor, *Time* (1933–1936); managing editor, *Life* (1936–1944); director of all Time, Inc., publications (1944–1955).

SELECTED PERIODICAL PUBLICATION – UNCOLLECTED: "Death of Coolidge," anonymous, *Time,* 21 (16 January 1933): 9–10.

John Shaw Billings (John Shaw Billings Papers, South Caroliniana Library, University of South Carolina)

John Shaw Billings was a master of the groundbreaking narrative prose style of *Time* magazine in the 1920s and a pioneer in photojournalism, playing a key role in developing the "photo essay," or story that was told through a filmic sequence of photographs and only spare, but suggestive, textual captions. As a managing editor for *Time* from 1933 to 1936 and then for *Life* from 1936 to 1944, Billings was a gifted enabler of the talents of staff members whose areas of expertise differed from his own. He also excelled in his ability to mediate disputes between politically diverse factions at *Time* and *Life,* to gain the respect of his staff due to his combination of geniality and strong will, and, perhaps more important, to maintain the favor of the editor in chief of Time, Henry R. Luce. This relationship of trust, built over three decades, allowed Billings to become one of the most powerful and well-paid journalists in the United States: even during the economic decline of the 1930s, he earned twenty-seven thousand dollars a year plus stock profits as a managing editor for *Time.* He was also second in command at Time, Inc., between 1944 and 1955, a period when its publications were believed to hold sway over public opinion about international events and in the choosing of American presidents. A fellow editor at Time, Hedley Donovan has written in his memoirs that if Luce had died during those years, Billings might well have succeeded him. It is not an exaggeration to say that without his ability to mediate between the egos and political ambitions of the stars at Time, *Life* may never have gotten off the ground or, having done so, probably would never have achieved its place in the history of American periodicals as the nation's first mass-circulation picture weekly and as one of America's greatest publication success stories.

The son of John S. and Katherine Hammond Billings, John Shaw was born on 11 May 1898 in Beech Island, South Carolina. As a graduate of Saint Paul's School about to enter Harvard University in 1916, Billings wandered around New England, slept in barns, and talked to farmers with a copy of Vachel Lindsay's poems in his pocket. During World War I he was an ambulance driver in France and an aviation cadet.

Unlike most of the other journalists who made their reputations at *Time,* Billings actually toiled as a newspaperman before entering magazine journalism. After graduating from Harvard in 1920, Billings began his career as a reporter for the *Bridgeport* (Connecticut) *Telegram.* In 1921 he began as a reporter for the *Brooklyn Daily Eagle,* and in September of that year he became its Washington correspondent. He would remain with the paper for eight years, alternately content and dissatisfied with his position there.

In April 1924 Billings married Frederica Washburn Wade, the daughter of the chief judge of the Georgia Court of Appeals. Married life agreed with Billings, who approached his job at the *Eagle* with renewed vigor. His happiness was marred, however, by the death of his mother on 5 July 1925. Billings's relations with his father had always been strained, but when the latter announced his intention to remarry only a few months after his wife's death, an alienation between father and son ensued. Billings's father died on 27 April 1927 after a painful illness, which, Billings noted in his diary, "moved me to great pity and blotted out most of my bitterness toward him."

In May 1928 Billings began as a stringer correspondent for *Time* magazine, and in January 1929 he left the *Eagle* to take over as national affairs editor at *Time.* Yet Billings was never one to inflate his own importance, looking on journalism as "an honorable trade . . . but certainly not a profession." In spite of this modesty Billings's contribution to the innovative writing style of *Time* in the late 1920s and early 1930s would have been a significant contribution to American journalism had he never become an editor of *Life.* Although he was trained in the 1920s on daily newspapers that adhered to the "inverted pyramid" style of reporting – the most important facts in the lead paragraph with additional materials appearing in descending order of significance to facilitate easier editing – Billings quickly mastered a new style of reporting events with a novelist's sense of drama and narrative shape.

Instead of the traditional "who, what, where" style of reporting news, Luce's first partner, Britton Hadden, felt that in a weekly newsmagazine that based its reports primarily on earlier wire service reports, each story, even if only four hundred words long, should follow literary conventions of narrative by having a beginning, a middle, and an end. Whether or not the reporter had actually witnessed the event firsthand, the task was to re-create the event in the reader's mind through vivid imagery. Billings excelled at this style of reporting, setting the standard for the magazine's other writers. An outstanding example of Billings's narrative style of reporting is his story "Death of Coolidge" (16 January 1933). Working with a set of clippings that told in detail the events of the president's last day and funeral, Billings tried to capture the mood of the day as news of the president's death had spread. He invented his own images to convey the somber tone of the "cheerless afternoon." The tires of the procession of twenty motorcars "droned a dirge on the rutty mud." Near the end came a one-sentence paragraph reminiscent of the conclusion of James Joyce's short story "The Dead" (1914): "That night snow fell blotting out all trace of the new grave." This piece was widely reprinted in contemporary anthologies as a model of journalistic narrative.

According to W. A. Swanberg, Luce was famous for "roosevelting," a term that referred to the president's penchant for shuffling men around into similar positions within his cabinet, but Luce's shuffling of his staff was more often known at Time as "Chinese checkers." The only key player who was seldom, if ever, thrust into a Chinese checkers game was Billings. Billings's uncanny ability to gain favor with Luce while others around him faded into inferior positions first became evident after Hadden, Luce's partner first at the *Yale Daily News* and then at *Time,* died in 1929.

At the time of Hadden's death the managing editor of *Time* was Hadden's cousin, John Martin. By all accounts Martin was a brilliant editor, but his short fuse and erratic temperament led to clashes between him and Luce. Martin was a drinker, used tough words, was combative, and held little favor with Luce. After Hadden's death Luce began to call on Billings with increasing frequency to fill in as managing editor whenever Martin was absent or on vacation. In 1933 Luce decided to name Martin as the head of an experimental department that would study the creation of new publications, thus making room for Billings as managing editor of *Time.* Billings was in South Carolina, halfway through a long-delayed, long-promised eight-week vacation with his family, when he received the job offer, and his response was indicative of his dedication to the company: he cut short his holiday to take on the new challenge in New York. Thus, only four years after Hadden's death and only five since joining the staff full-time, Billings was managing editor of *Time.*

Where Martin had been a brilliant editor, Billings was steady and predictable, sometimes to a

John Shaw Billings and Henry Luce selecting photographs for an early issue of Life *(John Shaw Billings Papers, South Caroliniana Library, University of South Carolina)*

fault. In spite of the new managing editor's hard work, Luce felt the first issues of *Time* under Billings lacked dramatic flair, yet the writers at the magazine quickly grew to like and respect him. Elizabeth Armstrong, the music writer, thought he gave the organization a sense of balance and inspired the staff to do their best. Robert Cantwell, one of the book reviewers, discovered that Billings had a literary background, though the editor never called attention to it. Cantwell admired the way Billings would pose as the average reader of *Time,* saying that if Cantwell could interest him in a particular book, the chances were he could interest other readers as well. Billings did not change the magazine's narrative style of reporting, but he curbed some of the more exuberant writers.

Perhaps because he did not inherit a uniformly strong staff, Billings's recollection in his diary of his early months as managing editor reveals more challenges than triumphs. "Nobody but a managing editor will ever know the agony of bad writing by staff," he wrote. During this initial period Luce was constantly critical of his efforts, and, to a degree, Billings welcomed the attention. Billings looked to Luce as a "critical gadfly to keep me and staff from getting soft and flabby." Billings also felt *Time* needed Luce's running comments to keep the weekly "jacked up and taut."

While Billings may at times have appreciated Luce's interventions into his day-to-day practice, Billings's diaries also reveal how challenging it was for him to work under the eye of Luce, whose lack of consistent interest in the daily operations of the magazine often upset the flow of the editorial process and who did not suffer fools gladly. Luce would typically come into the office on a Sunday af-

115

.... F. & I lay down. She got a nap but I was too nervous and excited to go to sleep. She & I later both wrote Uncle Henry letters, telling him that my days with TIME are now over and my career now moves off in a new direction.

Oct. 28– Wed Because I am far behind on what LIFE is doing (and because LIFE itself is also far behind), I went to the office at 10 a.m.— and straight in to spend an hour with Luce. He made a speech to me on LIFE's principles and purposes, explained the departments, etc. My job is to pick up his ideas as quickly as possible—& carry them out, without too much criticism. (I think Luce is damned smart—& I have little or no criticism of his ideas).... Longwell is ill with grippe—a sad circumstance because he is to initiate me into the LIFE personnel and machine. Back to my old office (I hate to swap it for Martin's smaller one), looking over layouts and captions, to get acquainted with material in the works. Luce & I went to lunch at the Ritz where he continued to explain and expound (he talked in such a low voice I had to strain to hear him.) This last for an hour & a half. Back to Chrysler Bldg. I was assigned a gas mask

Pages from Billings's diary (John Shaw Billings Papers, South Caroliniana Library, University of South Carolina)

116

story for the first issue and went to work on it in Longwell's empty office. There was nobody around to do a thing—and I had a horrible sense of disorganization. In two weeks we start to press & everything is near chaos: no office space, no worthwhile help, no system. Left at 5:30—& home to find F in the dumps because I had spent a TIME-off day at the office. An idle evening. After 10 I went down to see Bertie and tell him of the change in M-E's. He seemed truly distressed at my going. Then he brought up the matter of his salary—& why it wasn't raised last year and would it be this year. Luckily I could honestly say that it was none of business—that I always felt that his salary was something private between him & Luce.

Oct. 29 – To the office and officially moving into
Thurs Martin's 51st floor office—with Miss Bradley just outside. I collected the gas mask material—and got Ravesen to start laying it out for me. Tons of stuff were dumped on me. Martin came in, friendly & nice. Later we ate a sandwich lunch together in my

ternoon, read some copy, and then point out to Billings what Luce called "sour spots." Luce would also undermine Billings's authority over his staff by pointing out "who was good and who was bad" among the writers. If Luce did not think a staff member had an "interesting mind," Billings would be strongly advised to discharge that staffer. In spite of the intrusions that left the staff "nearly ragged," Billings welcomed Luce's Sunday visits, the assumption being that no attention from Luce meant real trouble.

The most obvious positive influence of Billings's tenure as managing editor at *Time* was his ability to bring discipline, a professional attitude, and a sense of calm to a young magazine that was in transition from being the collaborative effort of Luce and Hadden to being the sole property of the erratic Luce. Billings's tastes in literary and journalistic style, however, also marked him as willing to risk being innovative. His ability to change his mind about how to approach the reporting of news (evident in his own piece about Coolidge) would serve him well as he was thrust into the editorship of the nation's first mass-marketed picture weekly in 1936, only weeks before its first number was to go to press.

In February 1936, in a private room at New York's Cloud Club with Billings, Ralph Ingersoll, and Roy Larsen, Luce broached the idea of starting a picture magazine. The senior editors had different opinions about whether this new project was a good idea. Larsen's solution to meeting public demand for photography was simply to make *Time* more pictorial. Billings agreed that the idea of founding a new periodical was risky but countered with the observation that adding more pictures to *Time* would not be as likely to prevent competitors from starting their own picture weeklies as would a new, separate publication. Luce, who according to Billings had the idea "in his blood," favored Billings's more radical position. Billings's instincts in this meeting about Luce's desires reveal why he, from the start, won the games of Chinese checkers that occurred when Luce was in the mood to shift the positions of key staff members.

The meeting at the Cloud Club also illustrates how Billings mediated conflicts among key members at *Time* and *Life*. As managing editor at *Time* in the politically turbulent 1930s, Billings's relatively nonideological approach to editing allowed him to find a common ground between Whittaker Chambers and Laird Goldsborough, two of the magazine's crusading anticommunist foreign editors, and key reporters such as John Osborne and John Hersey, who held more-liberal views. In the case of Chambers, whose position as foreign editor especially upset Osborne, Billings was able to calm the waters at *Time* by assuring his reporters that a new department – international – would take over from Chambers many of the stories that had given them cause for complaint. Osborne returned from Europe to head the new international department, and while Chambers remained as the permanent foreign news editor, staff members agreed that the new department undercut and neutralized Chambers's power to control editorial content from abroad.

Although Billings would become an indispensable member of *Life,* Luce originally chose Martin, Billings's predecessor as managing editor of *Time,* to manage the new picture magazine. As had been the case three years earlier, Martin's drinking and hot temper made Luce reconsider his original choice, and he once again turned to the "organization man" he could most trust, Billings, to pull the magazine together during a time of crisis. Six months before *Life* went to press, however, Luce had offered Billings no indication that he was considering replacing Martin. "I want you to be the one person who doesn't bother his head about it," Luce told Billings. "Just keep *Time* going."

But less than three weeks from the publication date the editorial management of *Life* underwent a shakeup. Martin's personality had begun to have a corrosive effect on everyone. He handled innovative picture editor Daniel Longwell roughly, criticizing him before an embarrassed staff. He arbitrarily rejected pictures and layouts and was at odds with Luce. At one luncheon he shouted down all of Luce's suggestions as "buckeye." On 23 October Billings recorded in his diary the visit with Luce that would thrust the managing editor, a print man all his life, into the editorship of an entirely new type of magazine. Billings wrote that at five o'clock Luce had called him into his office, shut the door, and told him that Martin's behavior had led to a "great crisis" at *Life*. According to Luce, the magazine was disorganized and not nearly ready to go to press. Luce's idea was to return Martin to *Time* and to have Billings take over for Martin at *Life*. Billings, who knew little at that point about the new magazine's philosophy and who was devoted to *Time,* was, in his words, "surprised and startled" at the offer. In spite of his contentment at *Time,* Billings accepted the appointment as a "fresh excitement." The idea pleased Billings because it offered him "much harder work" and because Luce thought the change was "best for the organization."

Cover for the first issue of the magazine that revolutionized photojournalism

Billings took over just seventeen days before the first issue of *Life* was scheduled to go to press. He later recalled that the staff was inexperienced; that the picture editor, Longwell, was out with the flu; and that Luce gave each editorial decision a "final yes or no." When he was not squinting critically at layouts or editing captions, Luce was filling his new managing editor full of the principles and purposes of *Life*. The magazine would inform, but it would also entertain. There was to be a lot of show business about it. According to Luce, *Life* must attain a paradoxical quality of unity in flow, pace and change of pace, charm, and shock.

Billings turned out to be a surprisingly appropriate choice for *Life*. In spite of being a print man, he displayed an intuitive feel for the new developments in the "mini cam" and "documentary realism" revolutions in photojournalism. Billings's editorial instincts quickly became apparent in his choice of the cover for the first issue of *Life*. Although Luce and Billings were Republicans who supported Wendell Willkie and John Dewey in their pages and who by no means unequivocally supported Roosevelt's New Deal, Billings chose Margaret Bourke-White's picture of the massive Fort Peck Dam then being built by the Works Progress Administration in New Deal, Montana. This photograph, part of her photo-essay on the workers who were constructing the dam, managed to make the structure seem exotic. Its turrets were mistaken by some viewers for those of a castle. The first issue also highlighted aerial shots of the king of England's country residence and of the San Francisco Bay Bridge, and it revealed Billings's flair for the metaphorical and the comical: the frontispiece, captioned "Life Begins," showed an obstetrician holding a newborn baby by its heels.

Billings's contribution to *Life* becomes most evident when one learns of the complexities of the publication schedule he had to meet each week. With the exception of one advance form, *Time* had a single deadline. *Life,* on the other hand, had to be

Billings cutting the cake at the celebration of the first anniversary of Life, *1937. At far right is Joseph J. Thorndike, who would become managing editor in 1946 (John Shaw Billings Papers, South Caroliniana Library, University of South Carolina).*

put to press in sections, which meant that the editors had to meet a succession of deadlines. Assembling the layout was also complex because of geographical concerns. Editors in New York would lay out their pages and choose preliminary photographs and then would have to ship these materials to Chicago for publication. Wirephotos would be inserted and corrections teletyped, in case of last-minute changes. In the case of the first issue, pictures for the lead story did not arrive in Chicago until one day before the publication date. In the early days Billings and his colleagues were so overburdened that writers from other Luce publications, such as Archibald MacLeish of *Fortune,* were called to help write captions. Needless to say, the situation was stressful.

Given that Billings had so little experience working with the photo-essay format prior to his appointment and given his lack of time to prepare for his new position, it is astonishing that the first issue of *Life* became an unprecedented success in magazine publishing and that its pages nicely showcased Luce's notion of a magazine that would both entertain and inform the reader. Almost immediately vendors sold out of all 200,000 copies of the initial run. Including subscription sales *Life* had a first-issue circulation of 435,000, and, after four weeks, that figure rose to over 500,000. Only the lack of availability of a special coated paper that allowed for a better reproduction quality of the photographs kept *Life* in its initial weeks from selling even more copies. No magazine in American history had passed the half-million mark so soon after its launch.

In spite of Billings's herculean effort to put together a first issue on time with only seventeen days notice and in spite of his ability to deal with the labyrinth of deadlines and revisions, Luce, typically, was not satisfied with the final product. In his diary Billings recalled that when Luce saw the first proofs from Chicago, he thought the whole issue had "gone sour on the press," but Luce may only have had himself to blame if the first issues of *Life* appeared, to him, disorganized. Luce's role in the editorial process was often a disruptive, rather than constructive, influence on Billings's already daunting task. "He tosses everything up in the air like a juggler," Billings wrote, leaving the staff with the task of catching "the pieces as they come down." Billings felt Luce did not understand that *Life* did not have a format like the *New York Times,* where "all the news" could be crammed onto one page or even into one issue.

In his diary Billings revealed how Luce wounded him in front of his staff during meetings that were supposed to be forums to discuss how to improve the magazine. At these three-hour meetings, when Billings started to speak, Luce would cut him short with "I don't want to hear from you" and then proceed to listen to ideas from junior members of Billings's staff. The conflict over editorial control left Billings with sore feelings toward Luce in the 1940s and 1950s, ironically, a period when Billings's authority at Time increased. To a degree the managing editor sublimated his feelings by writing them down as private grumblings. "I'm so worn down by his talk that I don't even bother to answer him back," Billings confided to his diary. Billings believed that success had changed Luce, that he had become insensitive to the personal and professional needs of staff, and that he was no longer the "shy, simple fellow I first knew."

Even as he continued to shoulder the brunt of Luce's antics in front of the editorial staff, Billings remained dedicated to his task of improving *Life*. Billings endured Luce's tirades by focusing on the aesthetic development of the magazine. Adopting the attitude of a romantic artist, Billings viewed the week-to-week development of *Life* as an organic process. He accepted the fact that it would take four or five years of trial and error for *Life* to evolve from its cluttered look of the 1930s into a distinctive style, which it eventually attained in the 1940s with its prominently featured photo-essays, taken almost exclusively by *Life* staffers, with generous amounts of white space surrounding each picture.

In the 1940s Billings played a fundamental role in sharpening the editorial definition of *Life*. He allowed his photographers to decide what to shoot, and he paid tribute to a new generation of photographers by identifying them as colleagues and creative journalists, as essayists who used pictures rather than words to educate and to move readers. *Life* staff photographers had their names on the masthead, right along with those of Luce and Billings. Billings's decision to hire a staff of photographers rather than to rely on wire services remains one of his most important legacies at *Life,* ensuring the magazine's trademark sequences of pictures that told a coherent story. To the original quartet of staff photographers – Alfred Eisenstaedt, Thomas McAvoy, Peter Stackpole, and Bourke-White – were added other gifted professionals: William Vandivert, Carl Mydans, Hansel Mieth, and John Phillips among them.

Because the emphasis in *Life* was from the start on its "show-book" qualities, Billings also soon realized that the dramatic, imagistic writing style he had used in *Time* to describe the death of Coolidge in 1933 would serve no purpose except redundancy when placed next to the documentary photographs of *Life*. Billings had to fight against the penchant of former *Time* editors and writers to bring their favorite words and sentence rhythms to a magazine that privileged dramatic pictures over literary style. Just as Billings had been able to adapt to the unique writing format at *Time* and to make this new style his own, he understood that *Life,* the showcase for pictures, called for a return to the stricter, more spare prose style that he had practiced for the *Brooklyn Daily Eagle*.

In addition to its narrative photographic sequences *Life* was also known for promoting itself through displays of sensationalism and sex. One of the magazine's most controversial articles in its early period was a domestic striptease entitled "How to Undress in Front of Your Husband" (15 February 1937). Although accounts of Billings's management style stress his social conservatism and his desire to uphold high professional standards as editor, his begrudging acceptance of these displays suggests that he possessed a touch of the huckster. He wrote in his diary, "crude and vulgar as it was this act did a promotional job. It got the magazine talked about, and by March we had attracted enough attention to be denounced, burlesqued and reviled."

By 1944 Luce's attention to extramarital love affairs had damaged his ability to watch over his company, affording Billings a unique opportunity to run *Life* without interference. But Billings was also left with a growing disenchantment with Luce, as a journalist and as a moral person. While the postwar years might have been the crowning moments of Billings's career at Time, his personal animosities toward Luce made his last decade there less rewarding than had been his tenure as managing editor.

These animosities can be gleaned from Billings's diary commentary during a period of crisis in Luce's personal life. In 1944, in the midst of his struggles with his wife, Clare, and his infatuation with Jean Dalrymple, Luce also conducted a brief affair with a member of his and Clare's circle. The woman was threatening to expose the affair if Luce did not pay her one hundred thousand dollars. Billings, who had heard that his boss was suffering from "chronic exhaustion," showed little sympathy for this man who had displayed such bad manners and inconsiderate behavior. While Billings felt that Luce's troubles with his romantic entanglements

Billings at his desk, circa 1940

were well deserved, he also wrote in his diary that he did not want the dirt to "splatter on the company and therefore on me."

Luce's attention to Willkie's unsuccessful campaign for the Republican nomination of 1944 represents another aspect of the publisher's conflicting loyalties, divided between a dedication to the successful operations of his magazines and other interests, in this case his growing concern with American and international politics. Disenchanted with his role as unofficial propagandist for American interests abroad and as one who had influence with the powerful but who was himself never an elected official, Luce began to angle for a secretary of state nomination and planned to run for the Senate, as well as devoting attention to his wife's career as a congresswoman and, later, as an ambassador to Italy.

Considering Luce's distractions, it was, perhaps, no surprise that in 1944, sensing he could no longer juggle his interest in his own political ambitions and the smooth running of his magazines, Luce turned over the operations of all his magazines to Billings. When the change was announced, Billings recorded the extraordinary news in his diary with little enthusiasm: "I must spend much time listening to his roaming rambling ideas." Billings did not relish the task of trying to make sense out of these "rambling ideas" to the rest of Time. Perhaps it is fitting that Billings, a newsman since the 1920s, never felt comfortable in his executive role. Once removed from the daily struggles of putting together *Life,* Billings allowed his contribution to the company to wane. He became more embroiled in debates over Luce's personal affairs and political opinions and less involved in the job he was trained to do.

As editorial director of Time, Billings never equaled his earlier accomplishments at *Life.* Exhausted and disappointed with Luce's liberal stance on civil rights, Billings left New York City to retire in the South in 1955. In 1960 Luce began looking for a replacement editor in chief at Time, and Billings was a clear favorite for the job even though he had been in retirement for five years. But, according to Ralph G. Martin, Billings had moved back to

South Carolina because a black couple had moved into his New York apartment house. He refused to return to New York in order to be considered for the position. The incident reveals Billings's racial prejudices, but by all accounts he was always able to separate his personal beliefs from his judgment as an editor.

If Billings was an organization man, he was an unusually individualistic one. His diaries reveal his ambivalent relationship with Luce, as well as his struggle to suppress his political and personal views so as to fulfill his role as a professional journalist committed to inventing new ways to tell stories in words and pictures. While Luce has been the object of far greater attention than Billings, the decision made by the managing editors at Time affected both the quality of the magazine and the whole production process. Billings proved to be a perfect choice as managing editor of *Life*. He had an instinctive liking and feel for pictures and made up his mind quickly. He saw most pictures and approved all layouts. To his staff he was a formidable figure. According to Robert T. Elson's history of Time only Luce, Roy Larsen, and a few of the older hands addressed Billings by his first name. To others, writes Elson, "he was always 'Mr. Billings,' and his summons on the inter-office communicator brought them running." Because his authority was respected by staffers, deadlines were met promptly. Under his editorship morale was high, and the staff enjoyed a sense of freedom and adventure. In his memoir *More Than Meets the Eye* (1959), Carl Mydans recalls his experience as a staff photographer for *Life*. Mydans describes an atmosphere during Billings's tenure in which no idea for a story was too absurd to be tried, producing in the magazine's staff "an insatiable drive to search out every facet of American life." Billings devoted his energy and talent to the development of the technical and stylistic innovations introduced by Luce's magazines, and the result was a model of how news would be handled in magazines, newspapers, and television for the rest of the century.

References:

James L. Baughman, *Henry R. Luce and the Rise of the American News Media* (Boston: Twayne, 1987);

Hedley Donovan, *Right Places, Right Times: Forty Years in Journalism Not Counting My Paper Route* (New York: Holt, 1989);

Robert T. Elson, *Time Inc.: The Intimate History of a Publishing Enterprise 1923–1941* (New York: Atheneum, 1968);

Elson, *Time Inc.: The Intimate History of a Publishing Enterprise 1941–1960,* edited by Duncan Norton-Taylor (New York: Atheneum, 1973);

Ralph G. Martin, *Henry and Clare: An Intimate Portrait of the Luces* (New York: Putnam, 1991);

Carl Mydans, *More Than Meets the Eye* (New York: Harper, 1959);

Patricia Neils, *China Images in the Life and Times of Henry Luce* (Savage, Md.: Rowman & Littlefield, 1990);

W. A. Swanberg, *Luce and His Empire* (New York: Scribners, 1972);

William H. Whyte, Jr., *The Organization Man* (New York: Simon & Schuster, 1956).

Papers:

The principal collection of John Shaw Billings's papers is at the Caroliniana Library of the University of South Carolina in Columbia.

Bruce Bliven

(27 July 1889 - 27 May 1977)

Peyton Brien
University of Toronto

MAJOR POSITIONS HELD: Director, Department of Journalism, University of Southern California (1914–1916); editorial staff member, *Printer's Ink* (1917–1919); editorial board member, *New York Globe* (1919–1923); managing editor (1923–1930), editor, *New Republic* (1930–1955); New York correspondent, *Manchester Guardian* (1927–1947); lecturer in communication and journalism, Stanford University (1956–1977).

BOOKS: *The Jewish Refugee Problem* (New York: League for Industrial Democracy, 1939);
The Men Who Make the Future (New York: Duell, Sloan & Pearce, 1942);
Preview For Tomorrow: The Unfinished Business of Science (New York: Knopf, 1953);
The World Changers (New York: John Day, 1965);
Five Million Words Later: An Autobiography (New York: John Day, 1970);
A Mirror For Greatness: Six Americans (New York: McGraw-Hill, 1975).

OTHER: "Slaves of the Roof," in *Modern Essays*, edited by Christopher D. Morley (New York: Harcourt, Brace, 1924), pp. 264-275.
What the Informed Citizen Needs To Know, edited by Bliven and Avrahm G. Mezerik (New York: Duell, Sloan & Pierce, 1945);
Twentieth Century Unlimited, from the Vantage Point of the First Fifty Years, edited by Bliven (Philadelphia: Lippincott, 1950).

SELECTED PERIODICAL PUBLICATIONS – UNCOLLECTED: "Journalism and Public Affairs," *New York University Bulletin*, 35, no. 16 (1935);
"The Genes and the Hope of Mankind," *New Republic*, 104 (14 April 1941): 493–497;
"A Prairie Boyhood," *Palimpsest*, 49, no. 8 (1968).

Bruce Bliven

In a *New York Times* interview, Bruce Bliven described what he called the "essence of liberalism": "to have an open mind, a desire to have an open society, a desire to know the fundamental truth, a desire that as many people as possible should have a better life . . . I don't know of any better ambition for society." Throughout his career as a journalist Bliven worked to achieve these social aims through statements of belief and ideals, both in print and from the speaker's podium, and through constant research and consistent intellectual striving to develop clear formulas for liberal political and economic agendas. Although his résumé is more extensive, Bliven is best known for his editorial capacities at the *New Republic,* a weekly periodical, and secondarily perhaps as New York correspondent for the *Manchester Guardian.* His activities both professional and personal extended far beyond this. In a review of his autobiography, *Five Million Words Later* (1970), Helen Fuller depicts Bliven as "a compulsive worker," pointing out that he typically held three jobs at a time and worked seven days a week, reading, editing, and writing "reams of . . . copy" for the *New Republic* during his tenure there, even as he was producing freelance work for other publications.

Fuller describes Bliven's lasting position in journalism as being "the back-up man supreme – ready and able to jump into any weak spot in an emergency, remarkably free from pride of place in organizations of which he was a part." This description is partly accurate but does not tell the entire story. Bliven was criticized on occasion by certain of his editors for autocratic behavior; however, he did not maintain his position as chief editor at a powerful magazine for a quarter of a century without meeting and overcoming substantial opposition.

Bliven's personal life remains a relative enigma – even in his autobiography he manages rarely to discuss himself. Fuller attributes this to, essentially, a journalistic instinct to focus not on oneself but on "the center of the stage"; Bliven's attention is directed at the remarkable world on which he reported, often with an insider's view, rather than on himself. Yet in doing this, Bliven sometimes forgets himself to a degree that might lead to omission of valuable information.

Bliven's father, Charles Franklin Bliven, was a farmer who had little formal education but who was, according to his son, an "incessant reader." Bliven also characterizes his father as "a wonderful person, loved by all who knew him, and he could do almost anything, but among the exceptions were making and saving money."

In 1876 Charles married Lillah Cordelia Ormsby; both were natives of Emmetsburg, Iowa. Bliven later believed that the citizens of the town perceived his mother, whose family included landowners and businessmen, as having married beneath her station. Bruce was born on 27 July 1889. In his autobiography Bliven describes the world into which he was born and in which he grew up, an image of Middle America at the turn of the century: "we . . . lived in an orderly, disciplined, and authoritarian world. God was an old gentleman with a long beard, up in the sky, who watched every detail of the life of every one of us." Ideas inspired by figures such as Freud were "unheard of," and social life included "lawn suppers in summer with Japanese lanterns tied in the trees, and card tables set out on the grass for the diners. In winter there were bobsled rides in a wagon equipped with runners. . . ."

Even with assistance from Lillah's family, life was often economically challenging in the Bliven household. Lillah's brothers gave them 160 acres of good farmland where the family grew wheat, corn, and oats, and carried a dairy herd plus a few breeding bulls. The Blivens found it difficult to achieve all of their needs through farming, beset as it could often be with both climatic and economic problems, so Lillah's brothers eventually offered Charles a position in their new mortgage and loan company. He was well paid, and life became more comfortable for the Blivens.

Then, in the economic panic of 1893, the mortgage and loan company failed and much of the farmland had to be sold off. Lillah was able to supplement their income through selling toilet and cosmetic supplies and, less successfully, as a subscription agent for forthcoming books. The maternal brothers had all moved elsewhere or were dead, so their assistance was no longer available. Although they were poor now, life in the Midwest was probably not as tough on the Bliven family as it would have been in a more urban setting. They still had some livestock, a rather large vegetable garden, and apple trees and some vineyards in the surrounding fields as well as their ties in a small town. In the end, as the family did not need an especially large income, they were able to subsist in reasonable comfort through all of Bruce's formative years.

Bliven showed an interest in literature and writing from an early age. Before he left Emmetsburg he had read almost all that was available in his home and various town libraries, including some encyclopedias. At the age of ten he won two essay contests for children, held by the *Woman's Home Companion* and *Success Magazine.* In high school he began and organized a student paper in which he handled almost every aspect of writing and publication, including soliciting advertisers and setting type. Some of Bliven's short stories were printed in one of the town newspapers (at the prompting, he believed, of his mother). At age sixteen he starred in an operetta, which Lillah directed, and later won a countywide oratorical contest for a speech he composed and memorized, praising "the sturdy inhabitants of the Mississippi Valley."

Bliven remained constantly active throughout his formative years. He held several different sum-

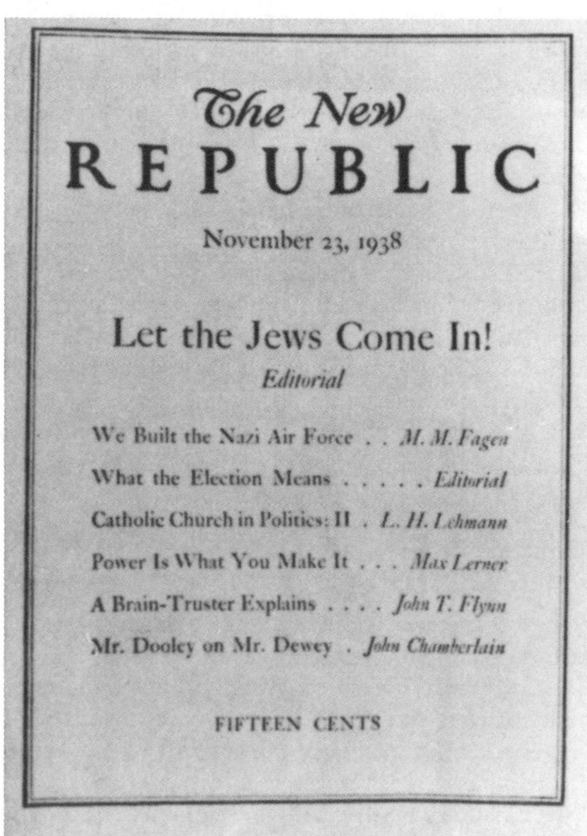
The New
REPUBLIC

November 23, 1938

Let the Jews Come In!
Editorial

We Built the Nazi Air Force . . *M. M. Fagen*

What the Election Means . . . . . *Editorial*

Catholic Church in Politics: II . *L. H. Lehmann*

Power Is What You Make It . . . *Max Lerner*

A Brain-Truster Explains . . . . *John T. Flynn*

Mr. Dooley on Mr. Dewey . *John Chamberlain*

FIFTEEN CENTS

Cover for a pre–World War II issue, including articles revealing the liberal stance that the magazine maintained throughout the war

mer jobs, including work in a steam laundry, selling subscriptions to the *Saturday Evening Post,* and as a crewman on a tourist sailboat. Thus he was also able to provide some support for his family. But despite his achievements and strong work ethic, there were serious economic concerns in the Bliven household as Bruce neared the end of his high-school career as to whether his future education, at least at a reputable school, would be a viable possibility. Those concerns were largely resolved when a cousin agreed to give Bliven forty dollars a month to assist him in covering his personal expenses. Bliven applied to and was accepted by several universities; he decided to attend Stanford.

In his later life, although he was glad also to identify the merits of his college life, Bliven was critical of some aspects of the Stanford academic program. At that time, still in the early stages of its accredited existence, Stanford operated primarily through an elective system with few required courses. It was all too possible because of this, he said, to obtain a degree "having acquired a shockingly small amount of really useful knowledge."

Bliven concluded that the best experiences of his college life came, as they do for many people, outside the classroom. The most important of those extracurricular activities for Bliven's future career was the position he attained as a college correspondent for the *San Francisco Bulletin.* Although some references record that between 1909 and 1912 Bliven was a "member of the editorial staff" at the *Bulletin,* Bliven himself characterized it somewhat less becomingly – he mentions in his autobiography that during these years he was first a "college correspondent" doing strings for fifteen cents an hour and after a couple of years of this was able to spend his summers as a "cub reporter" earning fifteen dollars a week.

Bliven was proud and excited, though, about his association with the editor of the *Bulletin,* Fremont Older, who was to have considerable influence in developing Bliven as a journalist. Older was a dynamic editor who wanted to shake up the world. He was intent on exposing the rampant corruption in San Francisco, including its drugs, graft, prostitution, and bribery. Another powerful influence in Bliven's intellectual and political development was N. L. Griest, the owner of a secondhand bookstore in nearby San Jose and a socialist "who refrained from proselyting." The back room of Griest's store was a headquarters of sorts for the larger portion of San Jose's intellectual community, and Bliven was a regular visitor.

Toward the end of his junior year at Stanford, Bliven met Rose Frances Emery at a college dance. She registered for her first year of courses at Stanford as Bliven began his senior year. In 1912 he decided to stay on for a fifth year but soon came to feel this had been a mistake. He found the direction of the graduate courses "too remote from reality." After a few weeks he signed out of Stanford and moved to Los Angeles, leaving his fiancée behind temporarily. After this move, Bliven was able to live in the apartment of his older sister, Maude, while he searched for employment.

It seems whimsically symbolic that Bliven gained his first job there, in the advertising business, through more than a touch of deception. Having never been involved previously in the business of advertising, he designed an ad and convinced the vice-president of the department store Harris and Frank that he knew the advertising business quite well. His delivery was convincing enough that he was offered a position with them on the spot. He then spent the entire weekend in the local public library reading everything available about advertising techniques in a dire effort to prepare himself for the job he would begin the following Monday.

Bliven forthwith joined Los Angeles's Advertising Club; within a year he had become vice-president. He began reviewing books for a weekly magazine, the *Outlook,* in return for the books he reviewed. He acquired a low-paying spare-time job at the YMCA teaching English, and he was contracted by Southern Pacific Railroad to write their official booklet about Riverside County. Amid all of this activity he also managed to marry Rose in May 1913.

By the end of the year Bliven had become bored with advertising. In 1914 he convinced President Bovard of the University of Southern California that the school needed a department of journalism and that Bliven was the man to organize and direct it. He then procured several capable friends for teachers and began sessions that autumn with perhaps one hundred students. Within a year, upon learning that his president hated making public appearances, Bliven took on a role which he describes as "official spokesman" for the university.

During this same period Bliven acquired another pastime to keep himself active, as music critic for a Los Angeles morning newspaper, the *Tribune.* Also, he and Rose, through an acquaintance which blossomed into friendship with Dr. Josephine Jackson, became "enthusiastic Freudians," perhaps compensating for a way of perceiving the social world which Bliven had noted was absent in his earlier years in Emmetsburg, and apparently at Stanford as well, and which would no doubt have its influence on his journalistic style.

On 31 January 1916 Bruce Bliven, Jr., was born to Bruce and Rose. Bliven's typical reticence regarding personal and family matters is apparent once again in his treatment of this episode in *Five Million Words Later,* in which the proud father does not get around to mentioning the name of his only child until six pages after the birth is noted.

Still in 1916 Bliven began writing as an unpaid theater critic for the *Los Angeles Daily News.* Early in the following year, after attending an advertising convention in New York City, he dropped in at the offices of the advertising trade journal *Printers' Ink.* Not long after he returned home he received a letter from that periodical inviting him to move to New York and join them on their editorial staff. He accepted their offer, and on 1 March 1917 the Bliven family moved to New York.

Bliven soon accepted an invitation to teach evening classes in writing at the Washington Square campus of New York University. Every Sunday, weather permitting, Bruce and Rose would travel to chosen spots outside of the city and spend the afternoon hiking, covering distances of five to ten miles. Almost every Saturday evening between September and June they attended a theater matinee, where they were able to see almost every important current Broadway production. Rose, who Bliven credits as being more ambitious scholastically than he, eventually obtained her M.A. in educational psychology and completed most of her Ph.D. work.

Early in 1919 Bliven interviewed Jason Rogers, publisher of the *Globe.* After this experience Bliven was invited to move to the *Globe* as its chief editorial writer. He accepted and began his work at his new post on 1 March of that year. Among his more important writings for the paper was an article in which Bliven proposed an urban development and taxation method, which he believed could, through subsidies, encourage development of new housing projects and a decrease in the cost to the builder without any actual loss of city or state revenues. The article led to a meeting with Gov. Alfred E. Smith, who proposed and passed legislation putting the newspaperman's scheme into effect, altering in the process much of the demographic structure of New York, both city and state. This legislation also encouraged a great deal of needed construction, which likely would not otherwise have occurred at the time.

The following year Bliven reluctantly accepted the position of managing editor of the *Globe,* although he would have preferred to continue as a writer. Slightly earlier he had received and subsequently turned down a job offer from William Randolph Hearst, whose journalistic philosophies Bliven unabashedly loathed. (In the *New Republic* some years later he would publish a lengthy open letter to Hearst urging him to retire.)

As managing editor, Bliven evidently managed to accomplish some writing at the *Globe,* including articles which discussed in favorable terms Darwinian ideas of evolution; and a series (against the express wishes of Secretary of War Newton D. Baker) detailing the subversion by one of their own officers of American soldiers' rights in Europe. Opposed by some of his staff, Bliven established a policy wherein reporting of union strikes would feature both sides of the dispute rather than the blatant support of the owners' position, which was the general policy adopted by most newspapers of the time. He also developed a marked improvement in the paper's cultural reporting of literature, theater, music, and film.

During this period Bliven began with some diligence to cultivate professional and friendly relations with several well-placed individuals who were to prove valuable resources during much of his later career. Among the earliest were Bernard Baruch and Averill Harriman. Bliven's encouragement was significant to DeWitt Wallace, founder of the *Reader's Digest* (in which Bliven would later publish freelance articles), and Briton Haden, cofounder of *Time*. As ever, Bliven continued his incessant activities in projects outside of his primary employment.

The most important of these outside activities were the articles he submitted to the *New Republic*. He had been contributing to the liberal political magazine since shortly before the turn of the decade; the seventeen articles that he sent them were all accepted. By early 1922 Bliven had begun finding irksome the "mess of endless routine and petty personnel problems" which he had to administrate at the *Globe*. When the newspaper went out of business following the death in 1923 of its publisher, Edward Searles, Bliven was able to move into the position of managing editor at the *New Republic*.

On 1 March 1923 Bliven began his new position at the magazine where he would spend his next thirty years, and the 4 April 1923 edition of the *New Republic* announced that Bliven had joined its editorial board. For the next three decades the greater portion of what can be said about Bruce Bliven must be said in conjunction with what was happening at the *New Republic*. To speak of the editorial positions of the magazine, although there was room in its policies for differing opinions, is in large degree to speak of what Bliven believed. The numerous contributors and the editorial staff at the *New Republic* were made up of people in whom Bliven believed and whose views he wished to see expressed on a national platform. This situation is especially apparent after 1930.

Bliven's first credited article, appearing in the 4 April issue, was a movie review titled "The Thespian Whale." The article discussed a film produced by the citizens of New Bedford, Massachusetts, "Down to the Sea in Ships," and made recommendations about the directions which cinema marketing must take if it was to survive as a viable industry. In his second article, "A Main Street Realist," Bliven delivered a favorable review of Thyra Samler Winslow's first book, a collection of short stories titled *Picture Frames* (1923), while expressing his dislike for the writing of T. S. Eliot and James Joyce. In the next issue of the *New Republic*, Bliven graduated to the General Articles department with a short piece called "The Great Sugar Mystery," which looked at the economics of sugar production and contended that recent increases in sugar prices were totally unnecessary.

In his history of the *New Republic*, David Seideman asserts that Bliven did not fit the pattern of editors for the *New Republic*. He lacked the philosophical training, for instance, of Walter Lippmann or Herbert Croly, and he did not have the technical knowledge of George Soule, with whom he would later collaborate in operating the magazine. However, no other editor in the magazine's history began with as much actual journalistic experience as Bliven. He quickly instituted a change in the direction and thrust of the periodical, increasing the proportion of actual reporting in relation to opinion pieces espousing liberal economic and political agendas.

This change was doubtless the source of some conflict; the staff of the *New Republic* was a disparate group when Bliven joined. Shortly after arriving at the magazine, Bliven compared his job to "conducting an orchestra with members who do not want to play, perform special compositions of their own, or make discordant noises that are the equivalent of Bronx cheers." There may have been, for instance, some differences between Bliven and Croly. Bliven comments in his autobiography that Croly was "naive in dealing with would-be contributors." Croly, for his part, considered Bliven a "trustworthy and able" editor but told Dorothy Elmhirst that Bliven's editorial work lacked "intellectual distinction and drive." Whatever the challenges Bliven had breaking into his new position and managing a talented pool of strong-willed editors and writers, it was also an exciting position for him, thrusting him into the midst of almost every economic and political event in the United States and often the world for the next thirty years.

During his editorship of the *New Republic*, Bliven added Stark Young, Robert Morss Lovett, and Malcolm Cowley, among others, to the magazine's staff. He also lined up many illustrious contributors including Felix Frankfurter (later a Supreme Court justice); Heywood Broun; Charles A. Beard; Harold Laski; Mike Gold; Julian Huxley; Lewis Mumford; Max Lerner; Wendell L. Willkie; Charles Wright Mills; S. I. Hayakawa; Carl Menninger, the secretary of labor under President Franklin D. Roosevelt; Frances Perkins; anthropologist Melville J. Herskovits; and I. F. Stone. Although much of the periodical's emphasis was on economic and political concerns, the *New Republic* under Bliven also presented a great number of figures more recognized for their literary contributions. Some of them were in the earlier stages of their careers, but many were already well established. A partial list of these includes Mark Van

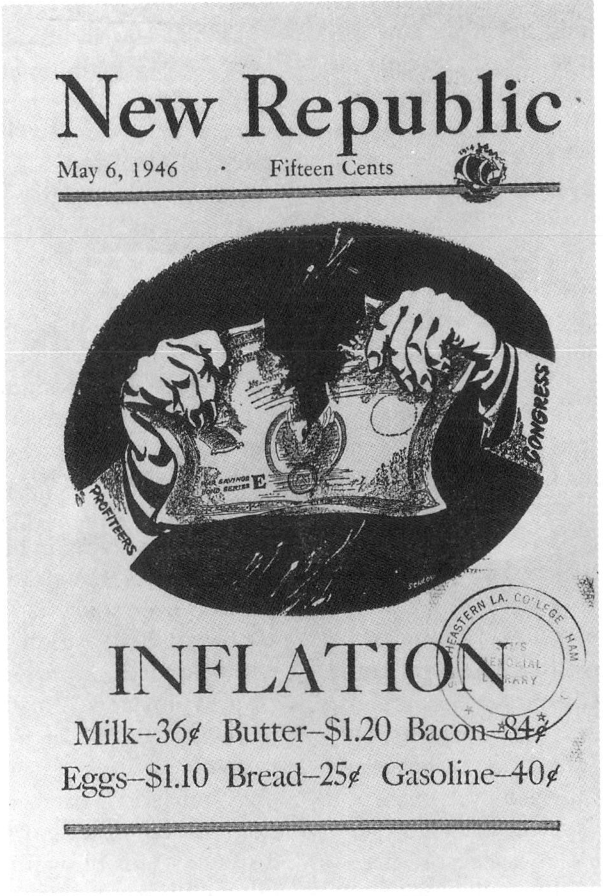

Cover for an issue focusing on post–World War II economic conditions in the United States

Doren, R. P. Blackmur, Conrad Aiken, William Saroyan, Muriel Rukeyser, Hart Crane (his last work was among those the magazine published), Marianne Moore, Stephen Spender, W. H. Auden, Theodore Roethke, Henry Miller, and Delmore Schwartz.

Although the *New Republic* had been an early supporter of President Woodrow Wilson, it had broken with him in disillusionment over the Treaty of Versailles and the U.S. entry into the League of Nations. The magazine subsequently became a caustic critic of the Warren G. Harding, Calvin Coolidge, and Herbert E. Hoover presidential administrations. Bliven again took the opportunity to stir up the political situation. He wrote the first really comprehensive account of the "Ohio Gang," one that would play an important part in exposing the Teapot Dome scandals in the 1920s.

Bliven had also been closely involved with the case of Nicola Sacco and Bartolomeo Vanzetti, two Italian anarchists charged with murder, for three years before coming to the *New Republic.* He continued doing all he could through his reporting to aid them. He proclaimed himself deeply disturbed by the "shocking irregularities" of the prosecution of their case, calling both defendants "intelligent men . . . highly read." Forty years later, when writing his autobiography, Bliven would still assert the likelihood of Sacco and Vanzetti's innocence but would add that the most important issue regarding their case was the fact that "the majestic Commonwealth of Massachusetts put them to death without a fair trial because they were foreigners and radicals." Bliven was able to pay the two men a visit in their cell shortly before they were executed in 1927, able only to offer his belief in them and his condolences.

In 1930, following Croly's death from a stroke incurred some eighteen months earlier, Bliven took control of the *New Republic* along with Soule. Although there were some later disagreements between them, Bliven has commented that the two of them agreed on most political and economic issues.

His schedule changed from a six-day to a seven-day workweek. Feeling some trepidation at his new duties, Bliven at first considered attempting to operate the magazine by forming an editorial advisory committee to make its decisions. He reports that he was eventually talked out of this by Frankfurter, who convinced him that such a government-by-committee "would either be a nuisance . . . or deadwood."

Even after the onset of the Great Depression in 1929 and then Roosevelt's election to the presidency in 1933, the *New Republic* could rarely be accused of taking a blindly liberal stand. In some cases Bliven sided with the New Deal, but at least as often he stood against it. He assailed from its beginning, for instance, the National Recovery Agency but spoke quite favorably of the Civilian Works Administration. Later asserting the creatively progressive positions of his magazine, Bliven remarked that "Almost all the ideas of the New Deal had been threshed out in our pages – and in very few other places – years before Roosevelt became President."

One important element Bliven brought into his journalism that had some influence on the *New Republic* was his layman's interest in the sciences. He was well aware of the changes in the world being wrought by accelerated scientific achievement, and he understood that in many instances a fuller understanding even of the economic and political direction of the world could not be fully realized without an eye also to scientific progress of the day. Probably his most noted single example here is "The Genes and the Hope of Mankind." First published in the 1941 *Smithsonian Institute Annual Report,* it also appeared that year in the 14 April *New Republic* and was published the following year as one of the articles in Bliven's book *The Men Who Make The Future.* The essay was, for its time, a searching effort to explicate some basic issues in genetic research for the public, including the possible influences of genes on human social behavior.

The circulation of the *New Republic* was never great – thirty-five thousand copies a week is the figure regularly quoted as its norm for the Depression and war years. But this number does not reflect the magazine's impact upon the country. Its well-thought-out and intensively researched editorials and Bliven's public lectures, both aimed at encouraging moderate to left-wing political factions, are credited with having influenced the national thinking on hundreds of political and social issues of the day. This impact was due to the fact that the magazine's primary readership consisted of those in positions of power and/or influence, including newspaper editors and reporters, educators, clergymen, social workers, and such politicians as the president and all of his cabinet members.

Bliven maintained his title at the *New Republic* until 1955. In 1953, however, he suffered a heart attack and was ordered by his doctors to slow his pace. Bliven and his wife returned to Stanford, where he lectured part-time in journalism and communications. Bliven occasionally missed the excitement of New York but was generally happy at Stanford. Comfortable in the self-contained entity of the college community, he had access to excellent library facilities and regular association with many knowledgeable and intriguing personalities, including Alekandr Kerensky, who had been premier of Russia at the time of the Bolshevik takeover and with whom Bliven became good friends.

During the larger part of the period when Bliven was serving in his various editorial capacities at the *New Republic,* he was also reporting for the *Manchester Guardian* as its New York correspondent. He began this position on 1 March 1927 and continued into 1947, a period which included the Great Depression and World War II. Bliven's work for the *Guardian* was far from a casual undertaking, for it involved filing a story of from three hundred to one thousand words, six days a week, with a 3:00 P.M. (Eastern Standard Time) deadline for every dispatch. This obligation consistently made scheduling his life a far more hectic affair. Even when on scheduled vacations from the *New Republic,* Bliven's duties for the *Guardian* continued (while he was in the United States, at least). The farther west he traveled, as time zones changed, the earlier he had to have his report prepared and sent to England via Western Union. It was not a highly paid position by any means. Bliven reported his salary as approximately twenty-five hundred dollars a year and that this did not change during his entire twenty years with the *Guardian.*

Bliven was forthcoming about his motivations for adding this complexity to his life. "The chief reason I took the job was simple egoism. *The Guardian* was . . . the best written newspaper in the English language, and one of the three or four most prestigious in the world." Bliven's connection with *The Guardian* was also quite useful for him as an editor of the *New Republic.* Articles for one publication often appeared in a somewhat changed format in the other. Bliven made valuable personal contacts due to his connection with the *Guardian,* and some of them served Bliven well also as editor of the *New Republic.*

One such contact, which Bliven reports as one of the greatest experiences of his life, came when visiting London and Cambridge as a consequence of his position with the English newspaper. He was able to spend several hours alone with Mahatma Gandhi, who had been temporarily released from prison in India to attend the Imperial Conference in London. Although Gandhi knew he would be returning to a jail in his homeland as soon as the conference was over, Bliven would recall in his autobiography that he had perceived no sign of bitterness in the man: "He seemed to me a man of transcendent sweetness; I instantly felt at ease with him as I have with few others in my life . . . when I said good-bye, I felt that I was leaving the greatest man I had ever encountered, and a friend."

Bliven also met John Maynard Keynes, Winston Churchill, Malcolm Muggeridge, and numerous other important figures through his association with the *Guardian.* He was aided by the auspices of that periodical in visits to several capitals of Western Europe (although much of the writing he did while there may have been for the *New Republic*). Bliven parted company amicably with the *Guardian* in 1947. His responsibilities with the *New Republic* had become more demanding, as had his part-time freelance efforts for several high-circulation U.S. magazines, including the *Saturday Evening Post, Ladies Home Journal, Reader's Digest, Harper's Magazine, Redbook, Collier's Magazine, Atlantic Monthly, Current History,* and *Century.* He was succeeded as New York correspondent for the *Guardian* by Alistair Cooke.

In retirement Bliven maintained a creative and active life, even after a second and more serious heart attack suffered toward the end of the 1950s. Besides teaching, he accepted an occasional public speaking engagement. He also continued to write – several books and more than thirty magazine articles.

On 27 May 1977, following complications from a broken hip suffered in a fall, Bliven died at the Stanford Medical Center in Palo Alto, California. Besides his wife, he left behind his son, Bruce, Jr., who had become an author in his own right, and a grandson, Frederic Bruce Bliven.

Essentially, Bliven could be characterized as an example of a success story of a type highly popular in the American mainstream. Emanating from humble origins in the heart of Middle America, he was a proponent of liberal democracy who was able through consistent, sober, diligent effort and humanitarian goodwill combined with a hard-headed realism to climb to a professional peak, where at times he succeeded in influencing the opinions and perceptions of those who generated national policies and legislated the social order of his country. Thus he exercised a positive influence as well on a great proportion of the American public.

Yet Bliven would not be one to overrate his achievements. He perhaps made the best summation of these during a 1969 interview with Steven V. Roberts. While speaking generally of the objectives of journalism, Bliven said, "You make people conscious of themselves, of where they stand in relation to the world, where they stand in relation to history, what is possible to be done, and then they do it, with heartbreaking slowness. But the world does move, eventually, it moves."

Interview:

Stephen V. Roberts, "At 80, Bruce Bliven Still Finds Liberalism in the Way," *New York Times,* 27 July 1969, p. 33.

References:

Helen Fuller, "An Editor Reminisces," *New Republic,* 165 (9 January 1971): 32–36;

David Seideman, *The New Republic: A Voice of Modern Liberalism* (New York: Praeger, 1986).

William F. Buckley, Jr.

(24 November 1925 –)

James W. Hipp

See also the Buckley entry in *DLB Yearbook: 1980.*

MAJOR POSITIONS HELD: Publisher (1955–1957), editor in chief (1955–1990), editor at large, *National Review* (1990–).

SELECTED BOOKS: *God and Man at Yale: The Superstitions of "Academic Freedom"* (Chicago: Regnery, 1951);

McCarthy and His Enemies: The Record and Its Meaning, by Buckley and L. Brent Bozell (New York: McDowell Oblensky, 1954);

Up From Liberalism (New York: McDowell Oblensky, 1959);

Rumbles Left and Right: A Book About Troublesome People and Ideas (New York: Putnam, 1962);

The Committee and Its Critics: A Calm Review of the House Committee on Un-American Activities (New York: Putnam, 1962);

The Unmaking of a Mayor (New York: Viking, 1966);

The Governor Listeth: A Book of Inspired Political Observations (New York: Putnam, 1970);

Quotations from Chairman Bill: The Best of William F. Buckley, Jr., compiled by David Franke (New Rochelle, N.Y.: Arlington House, 1970);

Cruising Speed: A Documentary (New York: Putnam, 1971);

The Jeweler's Eye (New York: Putnam, 1971);

Inveighing We Will Go (New York: Putnam, 1972);

Four Reforms: A Guide for the Seventies (New York: Putnam, 1973);

United Nations Journal: A Delegate's Odyssey (New York: Putnam, 1974);

Execution Eve and Other Contemporary Ballads (New York: Putnam, 1975);

Airborne: A Sentimental Journey (New York: Macmillan, 1976);

Saving the Queen (Garden City, N.Y.: Doubleday, 1976);

A Hymnal: The Controversial Arts (New York: Putnam, 1978);

Stained Glass (Garden City, N.Y.: Doubleday, 1978);

William F. Buckley, Jr. (photograph by Gert Berliner)

Who's On First (Garden City, N.Y.: Doubleday, 1980);

Atlantic High: A Celebration (Boston: Little, Brown, 1982);

Marco Polo If You Can (Garden City, N.Y.: Doubleday, 1982);
Overdrive: A Personal Documentary (Garden City, N.Y.: Doubleday, 1983);
The Story of Henri Tod (Garden City, N.Y.: Doubleday, 1984);
See You Later Alligator (Garden City, N.Y.: Doubleday, 1985);
Right Reason: A Collection (Garden City, N.Y.: Doubleday, 1985);
The Temptation of Wilfred Malachey (New York: Workman, 1985);
High Jinx (Garden City, N.Y.: Doubleday, 1986);
Mongoose, R.I.P. (New York: Random House, 1987);
Racing Through Paradise: A Pacific Passage (New York: Random House, 1987);
On the Firing Line: The Public Life of Public Figures (New York: Random House, 1989);
Gratitude: Reflections on What We Owe to Our Country (New York: Random House, 1990);
Tucker's Last Stand (New York: Random House, 1990);
Windfall: The End of the Affair (New York: Random House, 1992);
In Search of Anti-Semitism (New York: Continuum, 1992);
Happy Days Were Here Again: Reflections of a Libertarian Journalist (New York: Random House, 1993);
A Very Private Plot (New York: Morrow, 1993).

OTHER: *The Committee and Its Critics: A Calm Review of the House Committee on Un-American Activities,* edited by Buckley (Chicago: Regnery, 1963);
Did You Ever See a Dream Walking?: American Conservative Thought in the Twentieth Century, edited by Buckley (Indianapolis: Bobbs-Merrill, 1970);
Odyssey of a Friend: Whittaker Chambers' Letters to William F. Buckley, Jr., 1954–1961, edited by Buckley (New York: Putnam, 1970);
Keeping the Tablets: Modern American Conservative Thought, edited by Buckley and Charles R. Kesler (New York: Harper & Row, 1988).

When William F. Buckley, Jr., stepped down as editor in chief of the *National Review* in November 1990, he ended day-to-day involvement with the magazine he founded in 1955 to present a "responsible dissent from Liberal orthodoxy." During Buckley's thirty-five-year editorship, the magazine became one of the most influential journals of political opinion in the United States. He himself became one of the most recognizable figures in American journalism in addition to becoming both an inspiration and an icon to several generations of political conservatives. Although dismissed by some critics as a mere gadfly, Buckley's success as an editor, novelist, syndicated newspaper columnist, television host, and sometime politician mark him as more than that. Buckley's sometimes-lonely and sometimes-strident advocacy of conservative policies was instrumental in laying the foundation for the conservative revival of the 1960s and its triumph in the 1980s.

William Francis Buckley, Jr., was born on 24 November 1925 in New York City. At the age of five he changed his middle name to Frank in order that he might have his father's name. The symbolism in this action is significant, as William Frank Buckley, Sr., was the primary influence on his son's development. A devout Catholic and self-described counterrevolutionary, the elder Buckley infused his children not only with the staunchly traditional values he held but also with an insurgent's eye toward promoting them.

Buckley, Sr., known as Will, and his wife, Aloise Steiner Buckley, had ten children and raised them as a close-knit family, despite the somewhat peripatetic lifestyle of a Texas lawyer with foreign oil interests. The Buckleys spent 1926 in Venezuela and lived from 1929 to 1933 in Europe. The Buckley fortune had arisen from Mexican oil interests, and Mexico was a country where the elder Buckley had great influence until the revolution of the late 1910s. Will joined in counterrevolutionary activities to support the government against the insurgents, and when the government was overthrown, his activities led the new regime to confiscate all of his Mexican holdings in 1922. This experience reinforced his hatred of revolution, a hatred he worked to instill in all of his ten children.

After the Mexican revolution, Will spent more time with his growing family and overseeing his Venezuelan oil interests. The Buckley family was intensely competitive, and the lessons imparted by Will and Aloise infused the intellects of all the children with a fierce family pride, a strong Catholic faith, and a hatred of revolution and communism.

William F. Buckley was privately tutored and went to school in England and France, an experience which helped to moderate the isolationism so much favored by his father. But in England he attended Saint John's Beaumont, an exclusive Catholic public school, and his father's isolationism was still a tremendous influence. The day in 1938 that Buckley enrolled at the school, Neville Chamberlain's agreement with Adolf Hitler at Munich was announced. Buckley hung an American flag over his bed. As John Judis recounts in *William*

Cover for the issue dealing with the 1978 debate between Buckley and presidential candidate Ronald Reagan

F. Buckley, Jr.: Patron Saint of the Conservatives (1988), Buckley once "lowered the British flag that flew over the school and replaced it by a small American flag." Despite the fact that the Buckley children were pulled out of their English schools in 1939 and taken on a tour of Fascist Italy, Buckley's time at Saint John's Beaumont was quite influential on his intellectual development. The coming war and his mother's fragile health – she was again pregnant – turned him even more toward religion, and he was quite receptive to the instruction by the Jesuits, which cemented his Catholic faith at the same time he began to pursue more-secular intellectual interests. His time at Saint John's Beaumont, which included a protest of the conditions at the school, was probably a model for the public school attended for a short time by Blackford Oakes, the hero of Buckley's spy novels.

In 1943 Buckley graduated from Millbrook, a small, private, Protestant preparatory school in New York, not far from his family's home in Sharon, Connecticut. During his time at Millbrook from 1940 to 1943, Buckley was fully under the influence of his father's isolationist views and vociferously opposed the United States entering World War II on behalf of Great Britain. He also came under the influence of the brilliant, anarchic essayist Albert Jay Nock, whose antiegalitarianism and suspicion of democracy and authority were appealing to the young Buckley. Nock was also a favorite of the elder Buckley, who often invited the writer, then unable to find commercial magazine outlets for his writing, to the Buckley home. While Nock would be influential on Buckley's later thought and writing, Buckley would struggle to refine, though not eliminate, his suspicion of democracy. He never embraced Nock's anti-Semitism; in fact, he contributed an issue-length article in the *National Review* in 1992 ("In Search of Anti-Semitism"), later published in book form, which, among other purposes, sought to define and delegitimatize anti-Semitism in contemporary conservative thought and politics.

Buckley was inducted into the army in June 1944 and barely passed his Officer Candidate School program. He left the army as a second lieutenant. He entered Yale in fall 1946, part of the great influx of older, former servicemen entering college for the first time. It was at Yale that Buckley's influences first began to gel and his provocative activities began to bear fruit or at least notoriety. He carried on battles with students, the administration, and the faculty through letters in the *Yale Daily News* and debates in class. He also came under the influence of Yale professor Wilmoore Kendall. His association with Kendall, a former Trotskyite who had become a fervent anticommunist, was the first example of Buckley's tendency to gravitate toward people who had disaffected from the Left toward the Right. Kendall's political intensity and cultural conservatism attracted Buckley, and he learned much from them.

During his junior year at Yale, Buckley became increasingly involved in the running of the *Yale Daily News,* becoming the editor through an election he believed he had no chance of winning. Buckley was controversial in this position; he used the editorial columns of the paper to attack the demands on professors to publish at the expense of their teaching and to begin his attack on the idea of academic freedom. Although he was opposed politically by most of the Yale administration, he was named student speaker at Alumni Day in 1950. He planned to deliver a scathing speech on the shortcomings of the Yale faculty, but the speech he wrote was opposed by the administration, and he withdrew from the honor. The rejection stung Buckley, and he soon made plans to write a book attacking the anticapitalist and irreligious thought of much of the Yale faculty.

On 6 July 1950 Buckley married Patricia Austin Taylor, with whom he had a son, Christopher Taylor Buckley, in 1952. In April 1951, as he was finishing work on his book, Buckley was accepted into service in the Central Intelligence Agency. After a training period, he and his wife were stationed in Mexico City in September 1951. Buckley's book on his academic travails, *God and Man at Yale: The Superstitions of "Academic Freedom,"* was published by Regnery in October 1951, the 250th anniversary of Yale's founding, and vaulted Buckley into controversy and the national limelight. The book expands the idea he first expounded in the undelivered Alumni Day speech that Yale faculty members – many of them attacked by name in the text – were atheists and socialists and therefore unfit to teach at a university that still claimed a Christian heritage in a capitalist nation. He derided academic freedom as a delusional, irresponsible dictum in which teachers take no note of what students and alumni, whom Buckley thought should be the real power in a university setting, believed and thought was right and true.

As reasoned argument, *God and Man at Yale* was not without fault; as polemic, the book was a brilliant success. McGeorge Bundy contributed a blisteringly negative review to *Atlantic Monthly,* calling Buckley a twisted and ignorant young man. There were negative notices in the *New Republic* by Robert Hatch and in the *New York Times Book Review* by Peter Viereck. In an issue of *Life* covering Yale's 250th anniversary, Henry Luce criticized *God and Man at Yale* in his editorial. But the book also had its champions, receiving positive reviews in the *Saturday Review*, the *Chicago Tribune*, the *Freeman*, and the *American Mercury.* The coverage of the book and the controversy over it helped to make it an unlikely best-seller. Regnery sold more than eleven thousand copies of the book in November 1951, vaulting the book to number sixteen on the *New York Times* best-seller list.

In March 1952 Buckley went to work for the *American Mercury* as an associate editor. The magazine, along with the *Freeman,* the magazine voice of conservatives, was destitute. Its circulation was still ninety thousand, but its finances were suspect, and much of its cachet was left over from its association with H. L. Mencken in the 1920s. After less than a year Buckley resigned over an editorial disagreement – the magazine refused to print one of his articles. The experience left him more sure of the need for a new conservative magazine.

The taste of controversy and public success with *God and Man at Yale* and the frustration with his experience at the *American Mercury* had much to do with Buckley's interest in starting the *National Review.* The conservative movement lacked a mainstream magazine venue in which conservative ideas could effect national debate over political and social issues. Many in the conservative camp shared this idea, but no one had a firm idea about how to proceed. Buckley came to the forefront of the push for a magazine after another controversial book publication. In early 1954 Regnery published *McCarthy and His Enemies: The Record and Its Meaning,* which Buckley wrote with his brother-in-law, Brent Bozell. The book, because of its controversial subject and its even more controversial point of view of supporting McCarthyism, was greeted with silence. It had only one major review outside the conservative press, a negative notice in the *New York Times.* When his book was ignored by the mainstream press, Buckley became more involved in starting a magazine, in the vein of the *New Republic* and the *Nation,* and in which conservative books would be neither ignored nor vilified.

In summer 1954 Willi Schlamm, an Austrian former Communist who was part of Henry Luce's staff on *Time* and a staunch anticommunist, pushed Buckley in the direction of starting a new magazine from scratch instead of buying *American Mercury* or the *Freeman,* as Buckley had been contemplating. Schlamm was a conservative, but he was Jewish and an internationalist, which made him the opposite of the Old Right isolationists and anti-Semites who were a major factor in the traditional right wing in America. Indeed, part of the motivation behind the new magazine was to remake the public image of the Right.

Schlamm and Buckley began the arduous task of raising money and attracting editors. By September 1955 the two had raised $290,000, slightly more than half of what Buckley needed to launch the magazine, now christened the *National Review.* Among the donors were Buckley, Sr., who gave $100,000, and South Carolina textile magnate and arch–trade protectionist Roger Milliken. Buckley recruited Wall Street lawyer William Casey, who later became the director of the Central Intelligence Agency under President Ronald Reagan, to draw up legal papers for the founding of the *National Review.* Schlamm and Buckley had great trouble convincing wealthy donors to back such a risky venture. Most potential investors were little concerned about the financial risk but instead were doubtful that the magazine would have any real effect on political debate in the country.

Many of the editors Buckley wanted to hire were compelled to refuse his offer because of the

Cover for the thirty-fifth-anniversary issue of the National Review, *in which the announcement of Buckley's retirement as editor in chief was published*

personal financial risk they would incur. Thus David Lawrence of *U.S. News & World Report* and Ralph de Toledano of *Newsweek* each turned down an offer to become managing editor of *National Review.* But there were many other problems in recruiting editors for the magazine. Russell Kirk, author of the widely praised *The Conservative Mind: From Burke to Santayana* (1953), turned down an editorial position because he lived in Minnesota and did not want to relocate to New York. Buckley also wanted to hire Whittaker Chambers, the accuser of Alger Hiss and author of *Witness* (1952), as an editor, but political differences of a significant but rarefied kind led to his refusal of an editorial position at the time. Chambers was a supporter of Eisenhower and Nixon and was much attuned to the need for moderation in political tactics if not in ideological beliefs. Buckley and Schlamm were of a more apocalyptic frame of mind, which Chambers believed would reduce the magazine's appeal to the masses and therefore its effectiveness as a conservative voice.

One immediate recruiting success was James Burnham, a former Troskyite academic, editor, author, and CIA consultant. Though for much of the 1940s and early 1950s he had been regarded as a staunchly liberal anticommunist, his refusal to denounce unequivocally McCarthy had made him a pariah among the liberal intelligentsia. He gratefully accepted a senior editorial position on the magazine. He became one of the magazine's strongest and most effective voices during its early years. Other editors included Kendall, in charge of the book section; Suzanne La Follette, a former editor on the staff of the *Freeman,* as managing editor; and Bozell as a contributor of a Washington column. Buckley was editor in chief as well as publisher, serving in the latter position until 1957, when William Rusher joined the magazine.

The first weekly issue of the *National Review* appeared on 14 November 1955. Even in the first issue Buckley attempted to enliven conservatism with wit and sarcasm instead of relying entirely on the deadly serious moralism so common in other right-wing journals. His own attitude toward conservatism made it easier to adopt such an editorial rationale. Unlike many conservatives and moderates, Buckley saw his political persuasion in full opposition to the status quo. His magazine was one of dissent and radical opposition. He made this clear in the Publisher's Statement included in the first issue:

> Let's face it: Unlike Vienna, it seems altogether possible that did *National Review* not exist, no one would have invented it. The launching of a conservative weekly in a country widely assumed to be a bastion of conservatism at first glance looks like a work of supererogation, rather like publishing a royalist weekly within the walls of Buckingham Palace. It is not that, of course: if *National Review* is superfluous, it is so for very different reasons: It stands athwart history, yelling Stop, at a time when no one is inclined to do so, or to have much patience with those who do.

The development of Buckley's thought and the editorial outlook of the *National Review* over the course of the next four decades had a profound effect on conservative politics in the United States. From a voice "yelling Stop," the *National Review* and much of mainstream conservatism evolved into a voice that was much more reconciled to the political status quo – at least a minimal welfare state and a government big enough to fund the anticommunist crusade – and which counseled if not stop, then at least slow down a little.

But during the early years, especially during the 1950s, the *National Review* made few concessions to the reality, and seeming permanence, of the welfare state instituted during the New Deal. Indeed, the magazine seemed to follow the line that it would support most anyone on the Right, regardless of the position expounded. This stance led to editorial opinions that were morally questionable, if not overtly racist. The 18 August 1957 issue featured an editorial that argued that the white race in southern states had a right "to take such measures as are necessary to prevail, politically and culturally, in areas in which it does not predominate numerically. . . . It is so entitled because, for the time being it is the advanced race."

But Buckley's political outlook was growing as the magazine began to increase its circulation. The average circulation of an issue of the *National Review* during its first year of publication was 18,000 copies. In 1959 it reached 25,385. As the *National Review* became more widely read and more influential, its editors became more assured of its character and what they felt should be the defining traits of American conservatism. In late December 1957, even before circulation had begun to grow, Chambers, who had agreed to contribute articles and joined the editorial staff for a short time in the late 1950s, attempted to define the philosopher Ayn Rand and her philosophy of objectivism from the perspective of mainstream conservative thought. In a review of her novel *Atlas Shrugged* (1957), Chambers attacked Rand's atheistic materialism as being philosophically little different than Marxism, drawing little distinction between the determinism of Hitler from that of Joseph Stalin. This review, which outraged the nonreligious libertarian wing of conservatives, did much to emphasize the importance of Judeo-Christianity in Buckley's vision of conservatism.

As a corollary to this episode, Buckley explicitly placed anti-Semitism outside the pale of responsible conservative thought, which meant outside the *National Review*. On 1 April 1959 Buckley circulated a memo to *National Review* writers which stated that no names would appear on the magazine's masthead that appeared on the masthead of the *American Mercury,* which under new management had, in Buckley's opinion, become anti-Semitic. Actions such as these were particularly powerful in defining conservatism and also in building the power and reputation of the *National Review* as the leading voice of conservative politics in America.

The end of the 1950s brought little sign of the political upheaval of the following decade. Yet the election in 1960 of John F. Kennedy as president coincided with a revival in political thought and activity on both the Right and the Left. By 1961 circulation had grown to 54,000. The world situation – the Cuban revolution, the Berlin Wall crisis, the Cuban Missile Crisis – all contributed to a heightened sense of the possibilities and necessity of political action. Buckley used his reputation and influence, and the pages of the *National Review,* to aid the formation of such conservative organizations as the Young Americans for Freedom in 1960 and the Conservative Party of New York State in 1961.

These activities outside the narrow realm of the *National Review* began to be more common for Buckley in the early 1960s. In 1962 Buckley began writing a syndicated newspaper column on current events which limited somewhat his hands-on time at the magazine. But under the editorial leadership of Burnham and Buckley's sister Priscilla, the *National Review* required much less of its founder's attention. Its finances, while always experiencing deficits, were not so bad that outside donations and the Buckley fortune could not balance them. His newspaper column attracted much press coverage, including a guest spot on "The Jack Paar Show" in 1962 that was the beginning of the very public feud between Buckley and novelist Gore Vidal.

His growing public persona and his increased knowledge of public opinions through his travels led to a modification of his politics. He became convinced that much of the public was aware of the basic rightness of the civil-rights movement; he ceased to support archsegregationists and began to argue over the methods rather than the basic goals of the movement. He also led the *National Review* through an extended intraconservative argument which led in 1965 to the excommunication of the staunchly anticommunist John Birch Society from the mainstream conservative movement.

In the aftermath of the 1964 Lyndon Johnson landslide victory over Barry Goldwater, the first truly conservative postwar presidential candidate, Buckley decided to try politics for himself. It was a decision that cemented his place in the public's, or at least the media's, eye. In 1965 he declared himself a Conservative party candidate for mayor of New York. His wit and love of controversy found fertile ground in the race against Democrat Abraham Beame and liberal Republican John Lindsay, the eventual winner. Surprising everyone, including himself, Buckley received 13.4 percent of the vote. While not coming close to winning – or even helping Beame defeat the liberal Lindsay, which had been the more realistic goal – Buckley had made real strides in giving respectability to conservative

Buckley in 1971 (Gale International Portrait Gallery)

policies. Unlike Goldwater, Buckley was able to debate effectively that the liberal policies of his opponents were not in the interest of most voters. Many commentators, Kevin Phillips in *The Coming Republican Majority* (1969) among them, argued that Buckley had created the makings of a viable conservative election strategy. Buckley recounted his New York election experience in *The Unmaking of a Mayor* (1966).

His media success in the New York mayoral race led to the beginning of a debate and interview show, "Firing Line," which was first broadcast on New York station WOR on 30 April 1966. Buckley's appeal eventually began to supersede that of the *National Review,* a trend that along with a more powerful conservative critique of political issues had the cumulative effect of creating additional conservative media outlets. By the late 1960s and early 1970s many liberal anticommunists were becoming disenchanted with the avowedly anti-American New Left and the perceived continued failure of liberal domestic policies. While ideologically unable to accept the conservatism of Buckley and the *National Review,* writers and thinkers such as Irving Kristol, Norman Podhoretz, and Nathan Glazer began a critique of American politics that later became known as neoconservatism. They carried on this critique in such journals as *Public Interest* and *Commentary,* effectively opening up much more of the mainstream to conservative thought.

Buckley's accomplishments during the 1970s and 1980s became less and less solely associated with the *National Review.* His nonfiction books, his Blackford Oakes spy novels, "Firing Line," and his syndicated column all gave him media outlets outside the magazine he had founded, which was still known as Buckley's *National Review.* The magazine, however, remained influential. The long-running disputation between the *National Review* and President Richard Nixon over relations with the Soviet Union and the People's Republic of China weakened Nixon's hard-core conservative support. In the 1972 campaign the magazine's staff even flirted with supporting editorially the more conservative John Ashbrook of California in the Republican primaries. But the emergence of the New Left candidate George McGovern convinced Buckley and the *National Review* editors that practical politics was more important than ideological purity.

Yet the Watergate affair brought the Nixon presidency, and the conservative movement, to a crisis. Throughout 1973 Buckley, who along with Burnham viewed the scandal as a damning indictment of Nixon's character, entertained editorially the ramifications of a possible Nixon resignation. But it was not until June 1974 that Buckley publicly called for Nixon's resignation. His reluctance to do so stemmed from his realization of what the disaster of Nixon would do to the Republican party and therefore, in his view, the nation. But although the consequences of Nixon's downfall would be just as dreadful as Buckley predicted, they would have the effect of revitalizing conservative prospects during the late 1970s.

Buckley and the *National Review* had supported Reagan in his bid to unseat Gerald Ford as the Republican presidential nominee in 1976, a bid that fell short and helped, along with the president's poor campaign, to elect Jimmy Carter. As the 1980 election approached, conservatives once again supported Reagan. But during the debate over the Panama Canal treaties, which Carter had negotiated, Buckley supported Carter and opposed Reagan. Buckley and Reagan went as far as to debate each other in 1978, an event which brought Reagan a national audience. Buckley's stance brought condemnation from many conservatives, but as Buckley noted in his book *Overdrive* (1983), his public support of the treaties and his opposition to Reagan may have ensured the latter's election in 1980: "I think, ironically, that Reagan would not have been nominated if he had favored the Panama Canal Treaty, and that he wouldn't have been elected if it hadn't passed. He'd have lost the conservatives if he had backed the treaty, and lost the election if we'd subsequently faced, in Panama, insurrection, as in my opinion we would have."

But while he angered many conservatives, he did not endanger his friendship with Reagan, with whose election the *National Review* reached the pinnacle of its influence on official Washington. Reagan publicly declared that the *National Review* was his favorite magazine and acknowledged its influence in advancing conservative political fortunes. Circulation increased, though financial deficits continued. But change was in the air at the magazine. In 1978 Burnham had suffered a severe stroke and was forced to cease work on the magazine, thus removing Buckley's closest aide. As the Reagan years passed into the George Bush years, and euphoria passed into frustration and disappointment, Buckley began to concern himself with how to keep the *National Review* alive after he was unable to guide its fate. In late 1989 Rusher resigned as publisher of the magazine and was replaced by Wick Allison, who instituted an aggressive marketing program, including television advertising, in order to increase circulation. Actors Charlton Heston and Tom Selleck appeared in commercials extolling the virtues of the *National Review,* helping to produce a surge in circulation that reached nearly 300,000 by 1993. In 1990, on the thirty-fifth anniversary of the first issue of the *National Review,* Buckley announced that he was stepping down as editor in chief to become editor at large. As successor he named John O'Sullivan, a former aide to British prime minister Margaret Thatcher.

Buckley's career as a magazine editor succeeded far beyond his wildest imaginings or those of his critics. The character of American conservatism, and therefore of contemporary American politics, would be quite different without the influence and the writing of Buckley. While the *National Review* has continued successfully without Buckley's daily involvement, it has struggled to define a post-Buckley conservatism.

Biography:

John B. Judis, *William F. Buckley, Jr.: Patron Saint of the Conservatives* (New York: Simon & Schuster, 1988).

References:

McGeorge Bundy, "The Attack on Yale," *Atlantic Monthly,* 188 (November 1951): 51;

David Burner and Thomas R. West, eds., *Column Right: Conservative Journalists in the Service of Nationalism* (New York: New York University Press, 1988);

Seymour Martin Lipset and Earl Raab, *The Politics of Unreason,* second edition (Chicago: University of Chicago Press, 1978);

Henry Luce, "God, Socialism, and Yale," *Life,* 15 (29 October 1951);

John Lukacs, *Outgrowing Democracy: A History of the United States in the Twentieth Century* (Garden City, N.Y.: Doubleday, 1984);

George H. Nash, *The Conservative Intellectual Movement in America Since 1945* (New York: Basic Books, 1976);

Terry Teachout, ed., *Ghosts on the Roof: Selected Journalism of Whittaker Chambers, 1931–1959* (Washington, D.C.: Regnery Gateway, 1989).

Papers:

The Buckley Papers at the Beinecke Library at Yale University contain Buckley's correspondence since 1951 and material concerning the *National Review.*

Whit Burnett

(14 August 1899 - 22 April 1973)

and

Martha Foley

(1897 - 5 September 1977)

Edd Applegate
Middle Tennessee State University

MAJOR POSITIONS HELD (by Burnett): Coeditor (1931–1942), editor, *Story* (1942–1951, 1960–1964); editor, Story Press (1935–1952); editor, Hawthorn Books (1958–1961).

MAJOR POSITIONS HELD (by Foley): Coeditor, *Story* (1931–1941).

BOOKS (by Burnett): *The Maker of Signs: A Variety* (New York: Smith & Haas, 1934);
The Literary Life and the Hell with It (New York: Harper, 1939).

BOOK (by Foley): *The Story of STORY Magazine: A Memoir,* edited by Jay Neugeboren (New York: Norton, 1980).

OTHER: *A Story Anthology, 1931–1933: Thirty-three Selections from the European Years of "Story," the Magazine Devoted Solely to the Short Story,* edited by Burnett and Foley (New York: Vanguard, 1933);
Story in America, 1933–1934: Thirty-four Selections from the American Issues of "Story," the Magazine Devoted Solely to the Short Story, edited by Burnett and Foley (New York: Vanguard, 1934);
The Flying Yorkshireman: A Book of Novellas, edited by Burnett and Foley (New York: Harper, 1937);
The Best American Short Stories, edited by Foley (New York: Houghton Mifflin, 1942–1957);
This Is My Best, edited by Burnett (New York: Dial, 1942);
Two Bottles of Relish: A Book of Strange and Unusual Stories, edited by Burnett (New York: Dial, 1943);
18 Great Stories of Today, edited by Burnett (New York: Avon, 1944);

Martha Foley and Whit Burnett

The Seas of God: Great Stories of the Human Spirit, edited by Burnett (Philadelphia: Lippincott, 1944);
The Story Pocket Book, edited by Burnett (New York: Pocket Books, 1945);
Time to Be Young, edited by Burnett (Philadelphia: Lippincott, 1945);
American Authors Today, edited by Burnett and Charles Slatkin (New York: Ginn, 1947);

Story: The Fiction of the Forties, edited by Whit and Hallie Burnett (New York: Dutton, 1949);

U.S. Stories: Regional Stories from the Forty-Eight States, edited, with a foreword, by Foley and Abraham Rothberg (New York: Hendricks House Farrar Straus, 1949);

The World's Best, edited by Burnett (New York: Dial, 1950);

Sextet: Six Story Discoveries in the Novella Form, edited by Whit and Hallie Burnett (New York: McKay, 1951);

The Best of the Best American Short Stories, 1915–1950, edited by Foley (New York: Houghton Mifflin, 1952);

The Tough Ones: A Collection of Realistic Short Stories, edited by Whit and Hallie Burnett (New York: Popular Library, 1954);

This Is My Best Humor, edited by Whit Burnett (New York: Dial, 1955); abridged as *This Is My Funniest* (New York: Perma, 1957);

The Spirit of Adventure: The Challenge and the Fascination of the Strange, the Impossible, and the Dangerous, as told by 38 Famous Writer-Adventurers, edited by Whit Burnett (New York: Holt, 1956);

19 Tales of Terror, edited by Whit and Hallie Burnett (New York: Bantam, 1957);

Animal Spirits: A Carnival of Prose, Poetry, and Cartoons, edited by Whit Burnett (Philadelphia: Lippincott, 1957);

This Is My Philosophy: Twenty of the World's Outstanding Thinkers Reveal the Deepest Meanings They Have Found in Life, edited by Whit Burnett (New York: Harper, 1957; London: Allen & Unwin, 1958);

The Scarlet Treasury of Great Confessions by World-Famous Diarists, Letter-Writers and Lovers, edited by Whit Burnett (New York: Pyramid, 1958);

The Spirit of Man: Great Stories and Experiences of Spiritual Crisis, Inspiration, and the Joy of Life, by Forty Famous Contemporaries, edited by Whit Burnett (New York: Hawthorn, 1958); republished as *The Human Spirit: A Quest Among Its Mysteries by Forty World-famous Men and Women* (London: Allen & Unwin, 1958);

The Best American Short Stories, edited by Foley and David Burnett (New York: Houghton Mifflin, 1958–1976);

Fiction of a Generation, edited by Whit and Hallie Burnett (London: Macgibbon & Kee, 1959);

Things with Claws, edited by Whit and Hallie Burnett (New York: Ballantine, 1961);

Best College Writing, 1961, edited by Whit and Hallie Burnett (New York: Random House, 1961);

Firsts of the Famous, edited by Whit Burnett (New York: Ballantine, 1962);

Yearbook of the American Short Story, edited by Foley and David Burnett (New York: Ballantine, 1963);

The Modern Short Story in the Making, edited by Whit and Hallie Burnett (New York: Hawthorn, 1964);

The Stone Soldier, edited by Whit and Hallie Burnett (New York: Fleet, 1964);

Story Jubilee: Thirty-three Years of Story, edited by Whit and Hallie Burnett (New York: Doubleday, 1965);

Fifty Best American Short Stories: 1915–1965, edited by Foley (New York: Houghton Mifflin, 1965);

Thomas Hardy: The Return of the Native, edited by Whit Burnett (New York: Barnes & Noble, 1966);

Discovery, edited by Whit Burnett (New York: Four Winds, 1967);

Henry Fielding: Joseph Andrews, edited by Whit Burnett (New York: Barnes & Noble, 1968);

Story: The Yearbook of Discovery, edited by Whit and Hallie Burnett, 4 volumes (New York: Four Winds, 1968–1971);

That's What Happened to Me, edited by Whit Burnett (New York: Four Winds, 1969);

America's 85 Greatest Living Authors Present This Is My Best: In the Third Quarter of the Century, edited by Whit Burnett (New York: Doubleday, 1970);

Black Hands on a White Face: A Timepiece of Experiences in a Black and White America, edited by Whit Burnett (New York: Dodd, Mead, 1971);

The Best American Short Stories: The Yearbook of the American Short Story, edited by Foley (New York: Ballantine, 1973);

Two Hundred Years of Great American Short Stories, edited by Foley (New York: Houghton Mifflin, 1975).

Whit Burnett and Martha Foley founded *Story,* a magazine devoted solely to the short story, in Vienna in 1931. Almost from the beginning *Story* was recognized by Edward J. O'Brien, an editor of short-story anthologies, as a magazine of distinction. In the introduction to his *Best Short Stories of 1932,* he wrote that *Story* "is now the most distinguished short story magazine in the world." O'Brien published four stories from the magazine in that 1932 anthology.

Martha Foley, the daughter of Walter and Margaret Millicent McCarthy Foley, was born in Boston in 1897. She attended the Boston Girls' Latin School from 1909 to 1915. Although her fa-

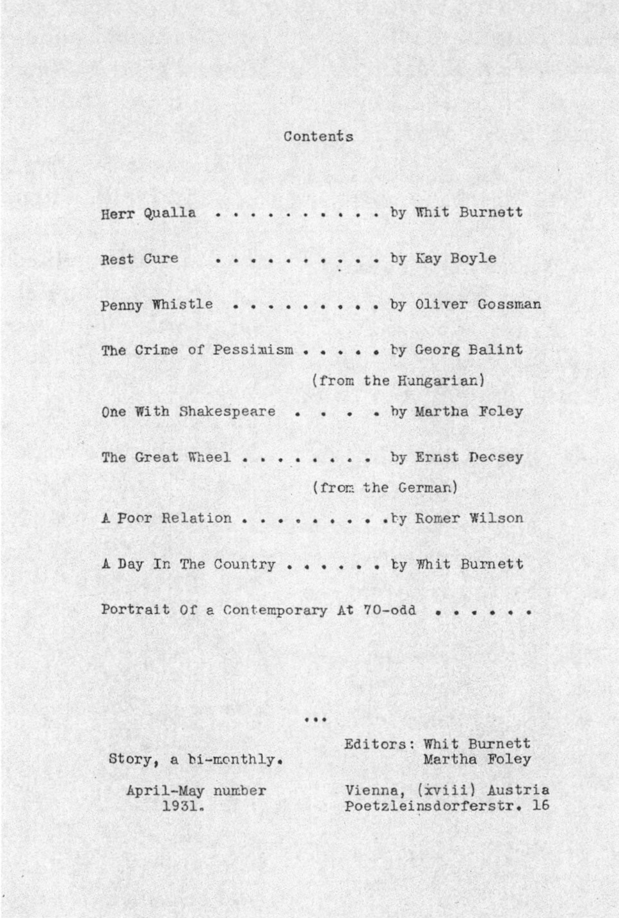
Contents

...

Story, a bi-monthly.

April-May number
1931.

Editors: Whit Burnett
Martha Foley

Vienna, (xviii) Austria
Poetzleinsdorferstr. 16

Contents for the first issue of the little magazine that Burnett and Foley founded to enlarge the market for short fiction

ther, a doctor, had wanted her to be a teacher like her mother, she longed to be a writer. Her first short story was published in the school magazine, the *Jabberwock,* when she was eleven. She attended Boston University for two years, then moved to New York, where she obtained a position as a copy editor at the *New York Ledger.* As she wrote in *The Story of STORY Magazine* (1980), "Getting a job on the *Ledger* was a simple business. All one had to do was walk in and ask. I could probably have been managing editor if I'd thought of it." Foley soon quit her job and moved to California. After writing for the *Glendale Evening News* and then the *San Francisco Journal* – where she met Whit Burnett, who was working for the Associated Press – Foley moved to Los Angeles in 1923 and worked as a feature writer and later a feature editor for the *Los Angeles Illustrated Daily News.* Douglas Turney, the managing editor who had hired her, contributed fiction to the *Smart Set* and constantly complained that markets for fiction were decreasing. Foley exclaimed to him in 1925 that they should publish "a serious fiction magazine." Turney seriously considered the idea; however, he rejected it, primarily because he had a regular column to produce for the *Daily News.*

Whitney Ewing Burnett, the son of Benjamin James and Anna Marian Christensen Burnett, was born on 14 August 1899 in Salt Lake City. Educated in public schools, he worked as a reporter before moving to California to attend the University of Southern California and to be a reporter for the *Evening Express.* Within a year he was working as an editor for the Associated Press in Los Angeles. In 1920 he returned to his native state and enrolled in the University of Utah, where he remained until 1921. He enjoyed furthering his education, but he also enjoyed earning money, so he returned to California, where he was hired as an editor in the Associated Press office in San Francisco. Burnett liked his work and for several years remained content. He enrolled in the University of California, Berkeley, in 1922. As mentioned, he and Foley had met when she worked in San Francisco. Their paths did not cross again, however, until 1925, when he came to Los Angeles, out of money, and she loaned him a hundred dollars to buy a ticket for a freighter bound for New York. Burnett soon got a job as a copyreader with the *New York Times.*

On her way to Boston, Foley stopped in New York to change trains, and Burnett was at the station waiting for her. "I think I'm falling in love with you," he said. Foley did not go on to Boston or back to Los Angeles; she stayed with Burnett and got a job as a caption writer for the *New York Daily News,* then for the *New York Mirror.* She wanted to be a reporter, but she was stuck in this position until she visited Paris. Burnett, who had been given his two weeks' notice by the *Times* in 1927, had, at Foley's suggestion, gone there to write fiction. In Paris, Foley got a temporary position with the *Paris Herald.* When this job ended, she and Burnett returned to New York. He got a job as an assistant city editor with the Associated Press, but she yearned for Paris and soon returned. She was hired as a reporter for the Paris edition of the *New York Herald.* As she recalled, "The *Herald* had a record-breaking year. We doubled the number of men, and two women were added to the city room staff." She cabled Burnett, informing him about a job. He resigned from his position in New York and immediately went to Paris to join the *Herald* staff. First he was a copyreader, then a city editor, and then a feature writer. The European manager of the Consolidated Press, William Bird, had read Burnett's work and offered him a job in Vienna at twice the salary; meanwhile Foley wrote to William Hillman, head of the Universal Service in Europe, about a job in Vienna. Hillman made her a correspondent, and at the end of 1929, Foley and Burnett moved to Vienna. The couple worked as correspondents during a time when many thought the world as they knew it was about to end – the 1929 stock market crash had occurred. Burnett and Foley were young, in love, and somewhat naive. As reporters, they missed the major stories. Years later she wrote, "We looked beyond newspaper work to more important writing. We did not plan to spend our lives at ephemeral day-to-day reporting. We wanted to produce literature." Indeed it was this desire that eventually caused her to force Burnett into coediting a magazine for writers.

Before the founding of *Story,* Foley quit the Universal Service over an article that she had not written but that had been published with her byline. She joined Burnett and the Consolidated Press. However, like him, she wrote for other publications, including the prestigious *American Mercury,* which was edited by H. L. Mencken, and *transition,* which was edited by Eugene Jolas. In 1930 Edward J. O'Brien asked Burnett's permission to reprint his "Two Men Free" in *The Best American Short Stories of 1930.* This request caused Foley to think, as she reported in *The Story of STORY Magazine,* "Now Whit will only have to send his story to an editor to have it accepted. . . . " Reality forced her to realize, however, that most magazines, even the *American Mercury* and *transition,* were no longer publishing short stories. Mencken and Jolas were interested in articles. She then approached Burnett about publishing a magazine devoted solely to short stories. Although he agreed that there was a need for a literary magazine; he refused to help her publish one. She made preparations, nonetheless, and she intuitively knew that he eventually would give in. She made out a list of names for it and wrote to friends all over the world, informing them that she was planning to publish a short-story magazine. When manuscripts began arriving in the mail, Burnett changed his mind.

Story began as a mimeographed publication. The opening announcement in the first issue (April–May 1931) set out the purpose of the publication: "to present . . . Short Stories of exceptional merit. . . . Only Short Stories are considered, and if and when any articles are used, they will be as rare as Short Stories of Creative importance are today in the article-ridden magazines of America."

As Foley recalled, "*Story* was not conceived as a money-making enterprise but as a crusade"; indeed the publication appeared during the Depression. The first issue had stories by Burnett, Foley, Romer Wilson, Kay Boyle, Oliver Gossman, George Balint, and Ernst Decsey, and 167 copies were printed. Foley mailed at least one copy each to the *Sunday London Times Literary Supplement;* the *New York Times;* the *New York Herald Tribune;* O'Brien; and Blanche Colton Williams, editor of the annual *O. Henry Memorial Award Collection.* The magazine received considerable recognition, particularly from the *Sunday London Times Literary Supplement* and the *New York Herald Tribune.* O'Brien asked permission to reprint four stories – "the most ever chosen from a magazine in a whole year, let alone a single issue," as Foley noted.

The second issue presented stories by Robert Musil and G. M. Noxon, among others. *Story* received unusual encouragement from the Viennese who had been impressed that "the great Musil" had contributed a story. To them, Musil was one of the

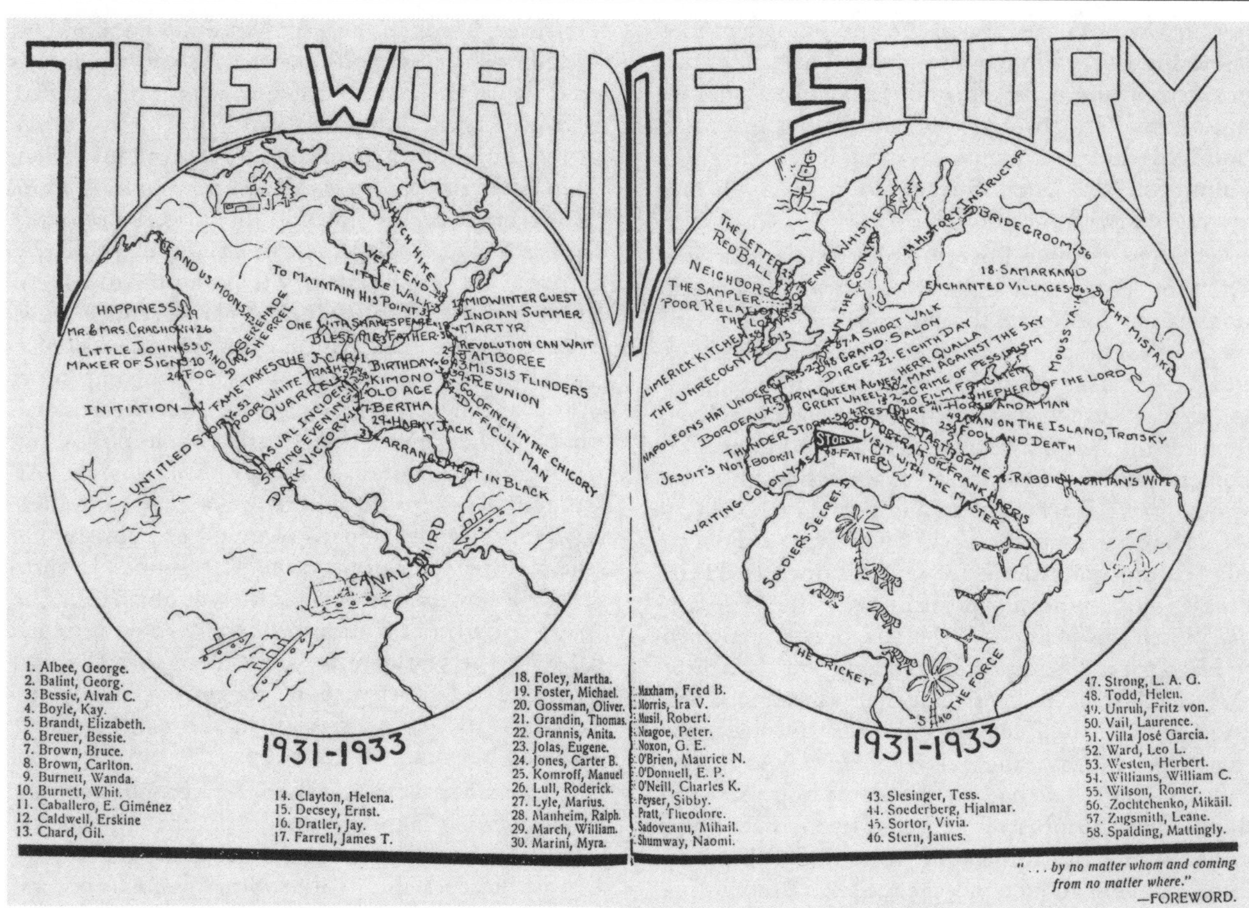

Illustration from the December 1932 issue of Story, *showing the international scope of its contents. Settings for stories are indicated on the maps, with numbers keying them to their authors.*

great writers of the century. Ironically the two young editors had never heard of him.

Burnett and Foley had been living together for several years. In 1931, when they realized they would like to have children, they married in a Vienna *Rathaus,* or town hall, which contained a small but charming chapel.

The third issue of *Story* introduced James T. Farrell, who later wrote the "Studs Lonigan" trilogy. Farrell was one of the most important proletarian writers of the 1930s. As the reputation of *Story* spread, other writers of distinction became contributors, including Jolas, José García Villa, Ralph Manheim, William Carlos Williams, George Albee, Conrad Aiken, E. P. O'Donnell, Pietro Solari, Manuel Komroff, Tess Slesinger, John Cowles, Peter Neagoe, L. A. G. Strong, H. E. Bates, Alvah Bessie, John Fante, L. A. Pavey, Charles Kendall, E. Gimeney Caballero, and Noah Fabricant. Other writers and editors visited Burnett and Foley.

As the circulation of *Story* grew, the editors realized that in addition to needing a circulation manager they needed a rejection slip. Foley composed a kind, considerate one in 1932:

> Dear Contributor:
>
> This, alas, is a rejection slip. And, heaven knows, the editors, who have had their own full share of them, have no affection for them.
>
> It has been found, however, that it is physically impossible to enter into correspondence with everyone who has been kind enough to send in a manuscript. And the editors have had to resort to this.
>
> It is, fortunately, thus far our only recourse to formality. And you may rest assured that this manuscript, like every other that comes to *Story,* has been sympathetically read and carefully considered before it is now, finally, for one or perhaps more reasons, put back in circulation.
>
> Thank you for letting us see the story.
>
> Cordially,
> THE EDITORS

Whenever they received more stories of merit than they could use, they would add a postscript to let the author know that they liked it. This nicety was an unusual practice at the time. Most magazine editors would not inform authors of their reaction to manuscripts. Of course, most magazines paid for what was used; the editors of *Story* could not afford to pay contributors. Yet writers continued to supply Burnett and Foley with top-quality short stories.

Their son, David, was born on 5 November 1931. Although the couple continued to work for the Consolidated Press, raise David, and write, their devotion to *Story* became systematic, in the sense that Foley read and selected most of the manuscripts while Burnett worked on layouts and other areas of production. By this time they had found a printer, Herr Hollinek, to produce the magazine professionally.

Early in 1932, when David was about four months old, the couple planned to take him to Romania on a trip for the press. However, on the way they stopped in Majorca and decided to stay. Within days the Vienna post office and the Vienna printer forwarded their mail and proofs for the final Vienna issue of *Story*. Manuscripts from writers living in Sweden, Spain, Russia, Austria, Germany, Hungary, France, Italy, England, and the United States continued to come in. A printer who had extremely old equipment was hired in Majorca: the magazine usually contained eighty pages, yet only four pages could be produced at one time. Of course, time was the major problem in preparing the first Majorca issue; then, as Foley recalled, "The installment reading of the proofs . . . became a pleasant routine."

Subscriptions and bookstore sales grew, and the fact that O'Brien selected eight stories from the issues printed in 1932 drew widespread attention. Nonetheless Burnett and Foley needed money. They wrote letters to publishers in New York to determine whether one was interested in financing the magazine. Manuel Komroff, who had contributed several stories, responded, saying that Harry Schuman, president of the Book-of-the-Month Club, and Bennett Cerf and Donald Klopfer, owners of Random House, wanted to discuss the matter. Komroff added, "Come to New York at once."

The couple and their son, using Foley's recent inheritance, set sail for New York, where she and Burnett met with Klopfer, Cerf, and Schuman. As Foley later wrote, "The magazine would be brought to America, and . . . would [eventually] become a monthly. Its office would be at Random House. All five of us would have an equal share in a corporation to be formed, and Whit and I, as editors, would draw weekly salaries. . . . Contributors would be paid . . . twenty-five dollars a story. The first American issue was to be ready for distribution in early March and would . . . be dated ahead – April 1933."

The magazine received enthusiastic support. For example, Mencken provided a flattering full-page advertisement that read, "*The American Mercury* welcomes *Story* to America." He even invited the editors to lunch. The *New Republic* held a luncheon, and a literary club, the Meeting Place, held a cocktail party. The editors of *Story,* as before, got to know many of the contributors: Erskine Caldwell became a friend, as did Nelson Algren, Tennessee Williams, Cornell Woolrich, and Malcolm Lowry.

The first American issue featured a brief sketch of the remarkable two-year history of *Story,* and fiction by such writers as Caldwell, Elizabeth Wagner, John Cowles, Kay Boyle, Mikhail Zoshchenke, and Conrad Aiken. Before 1933 ended, readers had been introduced to Lowry, Algren, Alan Marshall, Frederick Scribner, Bernadine Kielty, John S. McNamara, and Linda Henly. Other writers included William Faulkner, A. E. Coppard, Zora Neale Hurston, and Ted Pratt.

Story grew in popularity – so much so that the editors, in October 1933, informed the readers that the cost of the publication would be cut in half: from fifty cents to twenty-five cents. In addition they formally announced the decision made earlier: the magazine would be published every month, as opposed to every other month. To assure readers that these changes would not weaken the content, the editors wrote,

> *Story* will continue to be the medium, and, at present, the sole medium, for the presentation to intelligent readers of the new, significant writing in the short story form as it is being practised (if not printed) by the significant writers in America and abroad . . . Reducing the price will entail no attempt to lessen the quality or vulgarize the appeal. *Story* was brought to America as an experiment in the presentation of writing which generally was being ignored by the commercial magazines of this country although hailed critically when this same writing appeared in books. . . . With this issue's radical change in both price and frequency of appearance, the editors hope to bring *Story* to an even larger reading public – and still a public which makes no compromise with its taste. . . .

In the next issue the editors began to publish the first regular editorial column in *Story*. Titled "Notes," it featured appraisals of new works of fiction and introduced Kielty as the new associate editor and George Cronyn as the new business manager.

Before 1933 ended, Burnett and Foley had discovered William Saroyan, and they published his short story "The Daring Young Man on the Flying Trapeze." Saroyan, who was living in San Francisco, upon learning that his story had been accepted, wrote a short story every day for a month and mailed them to Foley. She accepted a few and tried to sell the rest to other editors. In 1933 the editors also announced their first annual "College Short Story Contest." This contest lasted fourteen years and introduced such writers as James Laughlin, Budd Schulberg, Norman Mailer, and Elizabeth Janeway.

In March 1934 *Story* marked its first anniversary in America. More short stories had been published in *Story* than in any other American magazine. In addition Burnett and Foley's first compilation, *A Story Anthology, 1931–1933,* had been published the year before. Like the magazine the book received favorable reviews. Another anthology followed in 1934.

In 1935 the editors included another column in the magazine. "End Pages," which was signed by Burnett, appeared after the last story and was nothing more than an informally written, inside look at the editors' lives. The column grew in length, however, and eventually incorporated comments about books, publishers, and writers. The editors decided to move the column to the second or third page. If the column was longer, it continued after the last story. These columns were eventually collected and published under the title *The Literary Life and the Hell with It* (1939). The year 1935 saw the circulation of *Story* grow to more than twenty-one thousand. This growth, coupled with the editors' need for more office space to handle other enterprises, forced them to move.

In the March 1935 issue the editors reiterated the purpose of *Story* and explained that the magazine was for all writers, particularly the unknown:

> *Story* has no feeling that it has been on the wrong track in giving more prominence to the work of "unknown" writers than it has to the known. But here, too, it has no feeling of rigidity; it has printed the short stories of the best short story writers now practicing, and usually in such a balanced number as to place the unknown writer in as close proximity as possible to the known, for contrast, occasionally; for comparison, as often. . . .

In the November 1935 issue the editors informed their readers that changes would be made to the magazine to make "it the most definitive magazine of its kind on the short story and contemporary writing in English. . . ." Contributions or "notes" from other writers, letters to the editors, and attention to books, "with a regularly departmentalized monthly survey of the reviews for and against the most significant. . . ," would be printed in every issue. Consequently the editors introduced the following columns: "*Story* Recommends," "(+) BOOKS (–)" (including a "Survey of Reviews"), and "Most in Demand." These columns allowed such writers as Sherwood Anderson, Bernard Shaw, Thomas Mann, Dorothy Thompson, Hendrik William Van Loon, James Laughlin, and others to write about various subjects – from fascism to motivations for creating literature.

In 1936 Burnett and Foley established the *Story* Service Bureau, which provided six services: the *Story* "Press-to-Reader" Service discounted books to readers; the *Story* Bureau Information Service helped readers learn of new books or publishers; the *Story* Bureau Study Service helped students learn about the short story; the *Story* Bureau School Service provided names of colleges that had courses in creative writing; the *Story* Bureau Reading Service recommended books to readers; and the *Story* Bureau "Best Seller" Service printed in *Story* the titles of best-sellers based on bookstore sales. As the editors wrote in the August 1936 issue, "*Story* was founded to present good stories. *Story* now takes the next logical step forward in assisting the reading public to find and to buy the best in modern writing."

In the July 1936 issue the editors announced that the Story Press, "in association with Harper & Brothers," would publish "a limited number of books of high distinction." The editors pointed out that they were interested in fiction and nonfiction by unknown as well as established writers. They emphasized that the unknown writer's work would "be given a warm welcome, a fair and sympathetic reading, and – when published – the greatest possible chance for recognition." Their first book, *Bread and Wine,* by Ignazio Silone, was published a year later and sold one hundred thousand copies. Eric Knight's *Song on Your Bugles* (1937) was the second book published. The third book, also published in 1937, was a collection of four stories, *Uncle Tom's Children,* by Richard Wright.

In the fall of 1936 the editors informed their readers that Horace Gregory, who had written essays and reviews for the *Atlantic Monthly,* the *Nation, Poetry, Life and Letters Today,* and the *New Republic,* would write a column concerning new writers and their first books. The column, although enlightening, appeared in only a few issues.

In its first five years of publication, the circulation of *Story* grew to more than twenty-three

Cover for the issue with which Story *resumed publication as a quarterly*

thousand. The editors had published hundreds of stories by such writers as Nelson Algren, H. E. Bates, Alvah C. Bessie, Hal Borland, Erskine Caldwell, Dorothy Canfield, Richard Carroll, Madelene Cole, Cronyn, William Faulkner, Richard Greenleaf, Sara Haardt, Doris Kirkpatrick, Edwin Lanham, Malcolm Lowry, Alan Marshall, Dorothy McCleary, McNamara, Peter Neagoe, Charles Kendall O'Neill, Doris Peel, Mary Brinker Post, Richard B. Sale, Saroyan, Richard Sherman, L. A. G. Strong, Jerome Weidman, Romer Wilson, John Cheever, Charles Cooke, Chester Crowell, Peter De Vries, Martha Dodd, Nancy Evans, Vardis Fisher, Roy Flannagan, Oliver Gossman, Emily Hahn, William Haslan Hale, Elizabeth Hart, Frank K. Kelly, Eric Knight, Ruth Lambert, Meyer Levin, Virginia Moore, Frank O'Connor, Sean O'Faolain, Alice Beal Parsons, L. A. Pavey, Luigi Pirandello, William Polk, Tess Slesinger, Jesse Stuart, Leane Zugsmith, Villa Stiles, Robert Traver, Edward North Robinson, Graham Greene, Carson Smith (McCullers), and Elizabeth Janeway.

In February 1937 the editors mentioned a new form of fiction that had appeared in a few previous issues, the "novelette." However, as the editors strongly emphasized, they did not care to use this term, which they referred to as "cheap and banal." Instead they used "the ancient and traditional Italian word novella. . . . " About forty novellas appeared in *Story*. Five were collected and published under the title *The Flying Yorkshireman* in 1938.

Lewis Gannett began to contribute a column titled "Behind the Books" in the October 1937 issue, and he continued to do so through the March–April 1939 issue. Gannett's column was in a sense similar to Gregory's in that Gannett discussed writers and their books.

In the July–August 1938 issue the following announcement belatedly appeared on the second page:

> *Story* announces a return to its original policy of bimonthly publication. Established in Vienna ... as a magazine to appear every two months, and continued on that schedule in Palma de Mallorca and later for the first year or so in New York City, its publishers revert to the original rhythm with the feeling that it is a tempo naturally suited to a magazine which has never aimed at mere short-lived topicality but at relative literary permanence in the selection and presentation of its material....

This was the only explanation given to the readers. However, it was during this period that the editors introduced photo essays, play adaptations, and poetry, thus indicating that interest in the publication was on the decline. These innovations failed to attract new readers and were consequently discontinued, as was the *Story* Service Bureau. The circulation fell to seventeen thousand in 1938 and 1939 and to eight thousand in 1940 and 1941. Although the magazine and the Story Press continued, the latter moved from Harper to Lippincott, perhaps another indication that something was wrong.

In the July–August 1940 issue the editors announced that "weekly dramatizations of distinguished *Story* stories have been and will be aired on the radio. This is the first attempt to bring to radio listeners the same quality of vital literature that has made *Story* the outstanding literary magazine of the day.... " Writers such as John Gunther, Sherwood Anderson, Rex Stout, John W. Vandercook, Erika Mann, Helen Hull, Wright, Cronyn, Irwin Shaw, Saroyan, and Eric Knight either read, discussed, or authored the programs.

To commemorate ten years of publication, the editors, in their May–June 1941 issue, not only discussed the purpose of the magazine but what it had achieved: "In ten years nearly a thousand short stories were published.... The editors have chosen these stories not only for their literary quality but because in addition to being good stories they seem, in one way or another, to illuminate the years in which they were published...." Later in the announcement the editors, in effect, seemed to confront what was to occur within a relatively short time when they either acknowledged or thanked the authors for the short stories, the distinguished critics who had supported the magazine, the anthologists who had provided numerous stories a more permanent place, the thousands of readers, and Kurt Semon, the publisher who had been with the magazine since 1936.

In the November–December 1941 issue readers were informed that Foley was no longer with the magazine. A one-page announcement, signed by Semon and Burnett, read:

> With this issue, the name of Martha Foley disappears from the editorial title page of *Story*. Miss Foley is on a leave of absence in order that she may edit the Edward J. O'Brien Memorial Anthology, *The Best Short Stories*....
>
> Miss Foley, a co-founder of *Story* in Vienna, has been for ten years one of its editors. Her experience during that period of reading and editing innumerable thousands of short-story manuscripts well equips her for her new task.
>
> While Miss Foley will no longer be an editor of the magazine, she will continue as an editor of The Story Press, book publishers, in association with the J. B. Lippincott Company.
>
> After ten years of daily association, it would be impossible in a few brief words here to express our gratitude for and appreciation of Miss Foley's work on *Story*. We greatly regret her loss to the magazine and its readers, but we join with them in wishing her the very best in her new undertaking.

Foley and Burnett separated and then divorced in 1941. She edited or coedited the annual anthology *The Best American Short Stories* from 1942 to 1976. The couple's son, David, coedited the volumes from 1958 to 1971, the year he died. However, Foley listed him as coeditor on the other volumes, too. She died of heart disease on 5 September 1977.

Burnett married Hallie Southgate Abbett in 1942. Hallie, a writer, helped him edit *Story* until its demise. Edith Kean joined *Story* as an assistant editor with the January–February 1944 issue. She left before publication of the July–August 1944 issue, however, and Eleanor Gilchrist took her place.

The magazine struggled from 1948 to 1951 and appeared only twice a year, in book form. It did not appear again until the spring of 1960, when it was sponsored by the University of Missouri. As the editors – who now included William Peden, Richard Wathen, H. E. Bates, Allan Seager, and Kenneth T. Hurst – announced:

> With this issue, the magazine *Story* ... resumes publication as a quarterly.
>
> The magazine ... is being revived with a new group editorship and the official sponsorship of a large midwestern university, the University of Missouri....
>
> The policy of the new *Story* will be the publication of good short stories coming from no matter whom and from no matter where. Emphasis will be on the fictional sources of America, but its readers will find no iron-clad rigidity about this since even in [this] the first issue there are stories from England's Mr. Bates, a novella by the

> Parisian satirist Marcel Azme, and, among others, work by a young Korean writer now studying at Harvard....
>
> The editors believe that there is even more demand now for a magazine of distinguished and readable short stories than there was when *Story* first began nearly thirty years ago....

Later in the announcement the editors paid tribute to early associates of *Story,* including Foley, Kielty, Schuman, Cerf, Klopfer, Semon, Gilchrist, Donald Friede, Leonard Amster, Victor Keller, James Light, and Ronald Kirkbride.

The popularity of *Story* fluctuated for two years; in 1962 the editors informed readers that the magazine would increase the number of pages yet decrease the price, as a result of "two great national institutions and the support of a few old friends of the magazine."

> *Story* from now on will have the sponsorship of the University of Cincinnati, and the support of the Reader's Digest through the Reader's Digest Foundation, a non-profit organization which will hereafter sponsor *Story's* Annual College Prize Short Story Contests among the universities and colleges of America....
>
> The only change in *Story* will be the opening up of certain pages of *Story* to advertising of a highly selective nature designed to appeal to the selective audience among which *Story* circulates.

This support could not keep *Story* going, however. In 1964 the magazine, like similar literary publications, suspended publication. In the few issues published between 1960 and 1964 works by such writers as Borden Deal, Shirley Ann Grau, Maksim Gorky, A. B. Guthrie, Jr., George Hitchcock, Evan Hunter, Robert Lowry, Tom McAfee, Thomas Mann, Don Robertson, and Jeb Stuart appeared.

Burnett edited many short-story anthologies and several books of humor. He worked as an editor for Hawthorn, a book publisher, before he died on 22 April 1973.

Hallie Burnett mentioned that Scholastic Magazines made an effort to bring *Story* back in 1968: "The one issue was a highly contemporary looking magazine, slick pages, psychedelic art, with some good material, and it cost $60,000 – enough to bring out a year's issues in other days!" The effort was futile; the magazine flopped. Apparently readers were no longer interested in the short story. But *Story* had introduced readers to hundreds of writers who otherwise might never have seen their work in print.

References:

Hallie Burnett, "Personal Recollections of a *Story* Editor," *Connecticut Review,* 6 (April 1973): 5–12;

Jay Neugeboren, "Story," *American Scholar* (Summer 1983): 396–406.

Margaret Cousins

(26 January 1905 -)

Shirley M. Mundt
Louisiana State University

MAJOR POSITIONS HELD: Editor, *Southern Pharmaceutical Journal* (1932–1937); associate editor, *Pictorial Review* (1937–1938); managing editor, *Good Housekeeping* (1945–1958); managing editor, *McCall's* (1958–1961); senior editor, Doubleday (1961–1970); special editor, Holt, Rinehart & Winston (1970); fiction and book editor, *Ladies' Home Journal* (1971–1973).

BOOKS: *Big Spring,* by Cousins and Shine Philips (New York: Prentice-Hall, 1942);

The Strange Christmas Dinner (Sioux City, Iowa: Wetmore Declamation Bureau, 1945);

Uncle Edgar and the Reluctant Saint (New York: Farrar, Straus, 1948);

Ben Franklin of Old Philadelphia (New York: Random House, 1952);

Christmas Gift (Garden City, N.Y.: Doubleday, 1952);

Souvenir, Margaret Truman's Own Story, by Cousins and Truman (New York: McGraw-Hill, 1956);

We Were There at the Battle of the Alamo (New York: Grosset & Dunlap, 1958); republished as *The Boy in the Alamo* (San Antonio, Tex.: Corona, 1983);

Traffic with Evil, as Avery Johns (Garden City, N.Y.: Doubleday, 1962);

The Story of Thomas Alva Edison (New York: Random House, 1965).

OTHER: "The Popular Short Story," in *Writer's Roundtable,* edited by Helen Hull and Michael Drury (New York: Harper, 1959), pp. 10–16;

Stories of Love and Marriage, edited by Cousins (Garden City, N.Y.: Doubleday, 1961);

The Salty Thumb: Your Garden by the Sea, edited by Cousins (Montauk, N.Y.: Montauk Village Association, 1967);

Claudia Alta Taylor (Lady Bird) Johnson, *A White House Diary,* edited by Cousins (New York: Holt, Rinehart & Winston, 1970);

Margaret Cousins (Gale International Portrait Gallery)

Lyndon Baines Johnson, *The Vantage Point: Perspectives of the Presidency 1963–1969,* edited by Cousins (New York: Holt, Rinehart & Winston, 1971);

"One More Adventure," in *The Courage to Grow Old,* edited by Phillip Berman (New York: Ballantine, 1989), pp. 208–211.

SELECTED PERIODICAL PUBLICATIONS – UNCOLLECTED:

POETRY

"Indian Summer," *Good Housekeeping,* 91 (November 1930): 40;

"Salute to a Tenement Window," *Pictorial Review,* 37 (February 1936): 51;

"Spring Again," *Good Housekeeping,* 110 (April 1940): 92;

"Bashful Armadillo," as Mary Parrish, *Good Housekeeping,* 120 (January 1945): 11;

"Visitor," *Good Housekeeping,* 143 (December 1956): 8;

"Christmas Day, 4:00 P.M.," as Parrish, *McCall's,* 88 (December 1960): 146-147;

"Peace on Earth," *McCall's,* 91 (December 1964): 173.

FICTION

"Age of Reason," *Pictorial Review,* 37 (April 1936): 18-19;

"The Boy from Home," *Mademoiselle,* 2 (February 1937): 42+

"Emancipation," *Pictorial Review,* 39 (February 1938): 18-19;

"Baghdad on the Subway," *Pictorial Review,* 40 (January 1939): 4+; (February 1939): 56+; (March 1939): 51;

"Career Woman," *Good Housekeeping,* 108 (January 1939): 16-17+;

"Words without Music," *Good Housekeeping,* 110 (January 1940): 32-33+;

"Mrs. Butch," *Good Housekeeping,* 110 (March 1940): 40-41+;

"First Formal," *Good Housekeeping,* 111 (September 1940): 26-27+;

"Whisper of Spring," *Good Housekeeping,* 111 (December 1940): 42-43+;

"Romantic Encounter," *Good Housekeeping,* 112 (May 1941): 32-33+;

"Little Brother," *Good Housekeeping,* 113 (October 1941): 32-33+;

"Dangerous Corner," *Good Housekeeping,* 114 (January 1942): 16-17+;

"Kiss," *Good Housekeeping,* 115 (August 1942): 22-23+;

"Dance Remembered," *Good Housekeeping,* 115 (September 1942): 22-23+;

"At a Sacrifice," *Good Housekeeping,* 115 (November 1942): 28-29+;

"Beautiful Friendship," *Good Housekeeping,* 116 (April 1943): 34-35+;

"Mr. Custer and His Lasting Love," *Good Housekeeping,* 117 (September 1943): 42-43+;

"How Long Can a Girl Go on Dreaming?," *Good Housekeeping,* 118 (January 1944): 44-45+;

"She Didn't Like People," *Good Housekeeping,* 118 (February 1944): 24-25+;

"The Natural History of Stacey Spender," *Good Housekeeping,* 118 (May 1944): 18-19+; (June 1944): 42-43+;

"The Girl Who Did Everything," *Good Housekeeping,* 119 (July 1944): 34-35+;

"Awakening," *Good Housekeeping,* 119 (November 1944): 20-21+;

"Sandra Stone Will Be a Belle," *Good Housekeeping,* 120 (April 1945): 18-19+; (May 1945): 40-41+;

"The Worshipper," *Good Housekeeping,* 121 (September 1945): 30-31+;

"The Outsider," *Good Housekeeping,* 122 (March 1946): 24-25+;

"The Schoolteacher and the Cad," *Good Housekeeping,* 122 (April 1946): 38-39+;

"The Man Who Married Money," *Good Housekeeping,* 122 (June 1946): 28-29+; (July 1946): 40-41+;

"All That Matters," *Good Housekeeping,* 124 (June 1947): 22-23+;

"Marvin Hobbs," *Good Housekeeping,* 125 (September 1947): 22-23+;

"Eighth-Avenue Look," *Good Housekeeping,* 125 (October 1947): 48-49+;

"Letter to Mr. Priest," *Good Housekeeping,* 125 (November 1947): 38-39+;

"An Apple for Miss Myrtle," *Woman's Day,* 11 (May 1948): 28+;

"Simple Faith," *Good Housekeeping,* 127 (September 1948): 44-45+;

"One Thing in Common," *Good Housekeeping,* 128 (January 1949): 34-35+;

"A Minority Report," *Good Housekeeping,* 131 (November 1950): 52-53+;

"Complicated Road," *Good Housekeeping,* 132 (January 1951): 60-61+;

"Dover," *Good Housekeeping,* 133 (August 1951): 58-59+;

"Ex-Hermit," *Good Housekeeping,* 134 (March 1952): 54-55+;

"Trouble with Love," *Good Housekeeping,* 135 (August 1952): 54-55+;

"The Man Who Won the Waldorf," *Good Housekeeping,* 135 (September 1952): 50-51+;

"Queen's Husband," *Good Housekeeping,* 135 (December 1952): 52-53+;

"Long, Low Whistle," *Good Housekeeping,* 136 (February 1953): 60-61+;

"The Life of Lucy Gallant," *Good Housekeeping,* 136 (May 1953): 54-57+;

"The Believer," *Good Housekeeping,* 137 (December 1953): 50-51+;

"Quarrel," *Good Housekeeping,* 138 (February 1954): 54-55+;

"Kismet," *Good Housekeeping,* 139 (November 1954): 52-53+;

"Love Is a Complicated Thing," *Good Housekeeping,* 140 (March 1955): 52–53+;
"The Girl Who Made Herself Over," *Good Housekeeping,* 141 (July 1955): 50–51+;
"Affair at the Plaza," *Good Housekeeping,* 143 (August 1956): 64–65+;
"What Miracles Are Made Of," *Good Housekeeping,* 143 (December 1956): 84–85+;
"Desert Flower," *Good Housekeeping,* 145 (September 1957): 76–77+;
"Not Required Reading," *Good Housekeeping,* 145 (December 1957): 78–79+;
"The Legend of Adele Mercer," *Good Housekeeping,* 146 (May 1958): 102–103+;
"The Shy One," *Good Housekeeping,* 146 (June 1958): 58–59+;
"The President's Daughter," *Good Housekeeping,* 147 (September 1958): 76–77+;
"Paris Opening," *Cosmopolitan,* 145 (October 1958): 91–95;
"The House," *McCall's,* 86 (July 1959): 38–39+;
"Lover's Leap," *McCall's,* 87 (January 1960): 40–41+;
"Civilized Couple," *Good Housekeeping,* 150 (March 1960): 70–71+;
"Excerpt from the Autobiography of Carol Lorillard," *McCall's,* 87 (March 1960): 96–97+;
"Romantic Names, Exotic Places," *McCall's,* 87 (April 1960): 78–79+;
"The Rockefeller Center Romance," *McCall's,* 88 (December 1960): 86–87+;
"Love in a Crowd," *McCall's,* 88 (June 1961): 72–73+;
"Anything Can Happen," *McCall's,* 89 (November 1961): 92–93+;
"The Day of the Wedding," *McCall's,* 89 (June 1962): 70–71+;
"Oliver and the Rich Rich Girl," *McCall's,* 89 (August 1962): 74–75+;
"Talisman," *McCall's,* 90 (December 1962): 116–117+;
"Friend of a Friend," *McCall's,* 90 (March 1963); 98–99+;
"Charmed Life," *McCall's,* 90 (July 1963): 66–67+;
"New Girl," *Good Housekeeping,* 157 (August 1963): 74–85;
"Suburban Matron's Story," *McCall's,* 91 (November 1963): 104–105+;
"The Enchanted Cottage," *Good Housekeeping,* 157 (December 1963): 104–109;
"Feminine Mystique," *McCall's,* 91 (June 1964): 72–73+;
"Christmas in Town," *McCall's,* 92 (December 1964): 130–131+;
"The Incident at Versailles," *McCall's,* 92 (May 1965): 114–115;
"Still Waters," *Good Housekeeping,* 162 (April 1966): 90–91+;
"O. J. Hazeltine," *Ladies' Home Journal,* 83 (May 1966): 90–91+;
"Band of Angels," *McCall's,* 94 (December 1966): 78–79+;
"Gifted Child," *Ladies' Home Journal,* 86 (December 1969): 32+;
"Remembrance of Things Future," *Ladies' Home Journal,* 88 (October 1971): 110–111+;
"Once Upon a Time," *Good Housekeeping,* 178 (April 1974): 90–91+;
"Promises to Keep," *Ladies' Home Journal,* 92 (January 1975): 64–65+;
"Visit to Aunt Adeline," *McCall's,* 105 (December 1977): 118–119+;

NONFICTION

"I Remember . . the Story of a Girl Who Knew a Drug Store as Her Home," *American Druggist,* 81 (March 1930): 48–49+;
" 'Hello World' Henderson," *American Druggist,* 81 (April 1930): 28+;
"Pharmacy's Gift to Literature – O. Henry," *American Druggist,* 81 (June 1930): 28–29+;
"Wednesday Was Different," *American Druggist,* 82 (August 1930): 22–23+;
"They Call Him Major – Bernard Ruppe," *American Druggist,* 82 (November 1930): 40–41+;
"Like a Self-service Grocery," *American Druggist,* 83 (March 1931): 40–41+;
"Out of an Oil Field . . . A Drug Chain," *American Druggist,* 84 (December 1931): 34–35+;
"Gone to the Dogs," *American Druggist,* 85 (January 1932): 30–31+;
"In the Shadow of the Lone Star Capitol," *American Druggist,* 85 (June 1932): 51+;
"Four Good Texas Drug Stores," *American Druggist,* 86 (July 1932): 33+;
"Figure It Out for Yourself," *American Druggist,* 86 (October 1932): 66–67+;
"This Little Druggist Beats This Big Store," *American Druggist,* 87 (February 1933): 52–53+;
"Something Unusual Has Happened in the State of Oklahoma," 87 (June 1933): 74+;
"The Book Says So," *American Druggist,* 88 (July 1933): 44–45+;
"A Drug Store Takes Up with a New Fad," *American Druggist,* 88 (August 1933): 46–47+;
"A Drug Store That Remembers an Old War," *American Druggist,* 90 (July 1934): 44–45+;

I Remember..

The Story of a Girl who Knew a Drug Store as Her HOME

Pages from an early autobiographical article in which Cousins describes growing up in her father's drugstore

"He Sells Sodas to Indians," *American Druggist,* 91 (April 1935): 42-43+;

"Ranchers Won't Write," *American Druggist,* 91 (June 1935): 36-37+;

"Ring the Bell: Texas Convention Circus," *American Druggist,* 94 (September 1936): 62+;

"T. G. Cressner – Miracle Man of Weslaco," *American Druggist,* 96 (July 1937): 44-45+;

"Home Is the Place," *Good Housekeeping,* 113 (October 1941): 115;

"Let's Never Give Up Christmas in America," *Good Housekeeping,* 113 (December 1941): 48;

"What Does the Heart Remember?," *Good Housekeeping,* 114 (February 1942): 107;

"The Shape of Security," *Good Housekeeping,* 116 (June 1943): 81;

"The Fine Art of Being an Aunt," *Good Housekeeping,* 117 (October 1943): 38+;

"Opportunities for the Free Lance Writer in the Post-War World," *Writer,* 58 (October 1945): 305-307;

"What the Editors Want," *Writer,* 62 (October 1949): 335;

"Books and the Modern Magazine," *Wilson Library Bulletin,* 25 (October 1950): 161-163;

"Combing the Haystack," *Saturday Review of Literature,* 34 (17 February 1951): 12-13;

"What's Ahead for Fiction?," *Writer,* 67 (July 1954): 224;

"Give a Child a Toy Collection," *Good Housekeeping,* 141 (December 1955): 82-83;

"All the Love in the World," as Mary Parrish, *McCall's,* 99 (June 1961): 64-71;

"Is Fiction Here to Stay?," *Writer,* 77 (January 1964): 9-15; 81 (December 1968): 16-21+;

"San Antonio, I Love You!," *McCall's,* 93 (November 1965): 72+;

"Christmas Is (Not) for Children," *Ladies' Home Journal,* 84 (December 1967): 59;

"Fire on the Eighth Floor," *House Beautiful,* 110 (May 1968): 146-147+;

"Garland of Wishes for the Seven Ages of Christmas," *McCall's,* 96 (December 1968): 73-77;

"Love Story; Runaway Hit: Why?," *Vogue,* 157 (1 March 1971): 130-132+;

"Vogue Books," *Vogue,* 159 (1 April 1972): 64+;

"Words to Warm the Heart," *Reader's Digest,* 100 (April 1972): 217+;

"The Place for Christmas Is Within Our Hearts," *Ladies' Home Journal,* 91 (December 1974): 98–99;

"Valentine for Bess Truman," *McCall's,* 102 (February 1975); 91+.

In a career spanning more than seventy-five years, Margaret Cousins has written many short stories, nonfiction articles, biographies, children's books, novels, poems, and inspirational essays, and she has edited thousands of manuscripts in these same genres. As a writer for mass-circulation magazines, she regarded editors for whom she worked as kind, considerate, helpful, patient, and hardworking; as an editor at *Good Housekeeping, McCall's, Ladies' Home Journal,* and Doubleday, she tried to meet all those standards. Her essays in the *Writer,* the *Saturday Review of Literature,* and the *Wilson Library Bulletin* offered encouragement and clear, practical advice to those who hoped to publish fiction in the popular-magazine market. Nearly two hundred of her own stories and articles were published in United States and foreign magazines. At age eighty-five, looking back over her career in the magazine industry, Cousins recalled: "I wrote what it was my job to buy, and I knew what the magazine press needed and wanted. I was never ashamed of my stories, nor did I offer anything not good enough to print, but I never really confused them with Literature."

Born on the prairie of Knox County, near Munday, Texas, on 26 January 1905, Sue Margaret Cousins was brought up in a close-knit family where morality, courtesy, integrity, discipline, and self-reliance were stressed but were accompanied by love and affection; all are themes that appear repeatedly in the short stories she later wrote. Her father, Walter Henry Cousins, of French-Irish descent, worked on a ranch as a young man but became a registered pharmacist in 1902. He wrote humorous stories, essays, and cowboy verse, and he contributed to several magazines. He communicated his love for literature to his two children, Margaret (who learned to read at age four) and Walter, Jr., by reading to them from the works of Charles Dickens, Edgar Allan Poe, O. Henry, and others. Sue Margaret Reeves Cousins, Margaret's mother, was a descendant of Scottish and Welsh families who moved to Texas after the Civil War. For her and her young daughter, home-service magazines were a "cultural lifeline," and Margaret Cousins believes that being introduced to this medium at an early age led her into a career of writing and editing for women's magazines.

Despite their prairie-life surroundings, the Cousins family was not deprived of cultural experiences: they saw Giuseppe Verdi's opera *Il trovatore* (1853) when it came to Wichita Falls, Texas; heard Enrico Caruso in Fort Worth; saw Anna Pavlova in *The Dying Swan* in Dallas; and visited museums on the Eastern Seaboard. Cousins planned at one time to write an autobiography describing these pleasant experiences: "I really wanted to write a book called *A Happy Childhood,* because so many artists and writers whine and cry about their childhoods. My parents *lived* with my brother and me. They loved us and didn't think anything was more important. . . ." She did not write the autobiography because, she said, "I had a long list of people depending on me and I just never could catch up."

When she was ten, her family moved to Dallas, shortly after her father bought the *Southern Pharmaceutical Journal.* She was already writing stories and verse. At age twelve she sold a poem about Rudolph Valentino to *Motion Picture Magazine.* In high school she was active in school publications and was class poet. Cousins gives credit to her teachers at Bryan Street High School in Dallas for her background in literature, American history, and journalism.

After Cousins's graduation in 1922, her mother wanted her to enter Wellesley, Randolph-Macon, or Mills College, but her father wanted her to get an education that would equip her to join him in the magazine business. She entered the University of Texas at Austin. After studying journalism for four years, she took a bachelor of arts degree because funds for the school of journalism were suddenly cut before her graduation. At the university she joined Theta Sigma Phi, a society for female journalists, worked on the staffs of the *Texas Ranger* and *Longhorn Magazine,* and became issue editor (one night each week) for the *Daily Texan* – the first woman to be given this responsibility. She continued to write verse and was honored with the D. A. Frank Poetry Prize.

Upon graduation in 1926 she went to work for her father on the *Southern Pharmaceutical Journal,* which circulated in Arkansas, Louisiana, New Mexico, Oklahoma, and Texas, carrying news items of interest to druggists and price lists of pharmaceutical products. Cousins helped with the secretarial work, learned to set Linotype, solicited stories, compiled data, and wrote editorials and feature articles. In 1990 she recalled, "In my journalism classes at the University of Texas, I had learned a lot of notions about what would brighten up all this information. My father was not impressed with these notions and regularly declined my suggestions. I began to send my rejected manuscripts to places like *Drug Topics* and *The American Druggist.* To my own amazement and my father's chagrin, these New York editors began to take an interest in this stuff."

For more than ten years she worked for her father, moving up from apprentice to associate editor and finally to editor, but she contributed to other publications; she sent verse to *Holland's, Matrix,* and *Pictorial Review;* she wrote articles for the *American Druggist;* she edited the *Drug Traveler,* a quarterly published by the Drug Travelers Association; and she submitted fiction to *Pictorial Review* and *Woman's Home Companion.* In 1936 editor Herbert R. Mayes offered Cousins a job on the staff of *American Druggist.* She declined because she felt the magazine was possibly a competitor to her father's magazine, and she told Mayes that her real ambition was to work on a women's service magazine. He promised to call her later and did. She accepted from him a position as associate editor of *Pictorial Review* in 1937, leaving the responsibility of the *Southern Pharmaceutical Journal* to her brother, who edited that publication until 1952.

Years later Mayes paid tribute to Cousins in his autobiography, *The Magazine Maze* (1980): "At my invitation Miss Cousins came from her home in Texas to join me in magazine work. Then, wherever I went, she went. Of all the associates I ever had, she was my closest. For twenty-five years I had in her at my side the staunchest ally, adjutant, colleague, teammate and comforter. . . . There was no understudy for her. There couldn't be. She was irreplaceable."

At *Pictorial Review* Cousins went into training for the kind of work she would do for the remainder of her career: reading and editing manuscripts, writing promotional reviews, writing fiction, and writing verse. Mayes, she later wrote, was "a great teacher . . . a difficult boss, but a leader I would have followed into a fiery furnace." When Mayes took over *Pictorial Review,* it was already in financial trouble. He was able to bring up sales at the newsstands, but regular subscribers reacted negatively to some of the fiction he chose to publish. Soon after Cousins joined the editorial staff, Mayes began negotiating with Richard E. Berlin, president of the Hearst Corporation, for the position of editor of *Good Housekeeping. Pictorial Review* struggled on until March 1939; Cousins's column "Baghdad on the Subway" appeared in the last three issues. Before the collapse of *Pictorial Review* Mayes had made his move to *Good Housekeeping,* although he did not become editor until August 1939. Cousins moved to the general promotion department of Hearst Magazines, and for the next four years she wrote copy, most of it appearing in *House Beautiful* – seasonal features and essays on topics such as writing letters, gift-giving, and decorating. A few of her articles were accepted by *Good Housekeeping,* where her fiction was appearing regularly.

As publication of her stories increased, she spent less time writing poetry and, over the years, published only a few more poems, all competently written, mostly about nature or Christmas. About this time, however, she took on another kind of writing which she would continue sporadically – ghostwriting. In 1942 Shine Philips published his "casual biography of a prairie town," *Big Spring,* ghostwritten by Cousins. When Cousins later donated portions of the original manuscript to the Harry Ransom Humanities Research Center, University of Texas at Austin, she described Philips's book as "the first trade book ever to be published by Prentice-Hall and [it] became a best-seller during World War II."

In 1942 Mayes made her associate editor at *Good Housekeeping.* Many of her stories were published in the magazine, including "The Natural History of Stacey Spender," in which she sketches the lifetime of a poor, then rich, then poor-again oilman, who is never truly happy until he is penniless, ready to start over with his daughter at his side. The story is long enough to have been published separately but was not, although two of her shorter stories were: *The Strange Christmas Dinner* (1945) and *Uncle Edgar and the Reluctant Saint* (1948). These two stories move quickly to an unexpected outcome, whereas "Stacey Spender" is slow moving and predictable all the way. The characters in the shorter stories are also more appealing: Edgar, a heretofore irresponsible young uncle, comes to the defense of his six-year-old niece when she is harassed by the local sheriff, who thinks it is clever to tease youngsters. Edgar gives him a fat nose and later presses him into duty as Saint Nicholas when the train on which they are all traveling is snowbound. *The Strange Christmas Dinner* is the story of a Scrooge-like restaurant owner in New York City; he plans to serve pigs' knuckles for Christmas dinner, but his employees plan otherwise. They are able to carry out their plan when an unusual guest enters the restaurant and orders a Christmas feast with all the trimmings.

In September 1945 Cousins's name appeared for the first time on the masthead of *Good Housekeep-*

Cover for a 1945 issue featuring a story by Cousins

ing as managing editor, a new position no doubt created for her because she had become so valuable to Mayes and so popular with the 2.5 million subscribers to the magazine. Cousins was welcomed to her post in "Town Hall," the editors' column, as "one editor who has the affection and respect not only of her immediate associates but of all her contemporaries in the business as well. Never has a magazine known an abler executive, authors a more understanding counselor, literary agents a fairer negotiator, editors a more generous associate." It was an effusive note of praise, but the same kind of compliments came from the staffs at *McCall's* and *Ladies' Home Journal* in later years.

Appearing also in the September 1945 issue of *Good Housekeeping* was Cousins's story "The Worshipper." The story has a thin, romantic plot, which is hardly worthy of note, but the two main characters in the story resemble Cousins at different stages of her life: there is the curious, practical-minded, dependable, industrious, thirteen-year-old messenger girl who is awestruck by the affluent, powerful, busy female executive, impatient with interruptions and inefficiency but compassionate beneath the career-comes-first facade.

As managing editor, Cousins continued under Mayes's tutelage. Mayes, she wrote, was "completely in charge. When he chose art work or photographs, he often had me come and stand beside him and, if necessary, he would explain his choices. He taught me how to have ideas, and what to do with ideas after I had them. He ran a tight ship, and we all knew it."

Mayes and Cousins agreed that *Good Housekeeping* should buy the best fiction available and that they should pay authors well. It was common for stories by well-known writers to be featured in *Good Housekeeping* – including W. Somerset Maugham, Sinclair Lewis, Ellery Queen, Shirley Jackson, Edna St. Vincent Millay, A. A. Milne, James Thurber, Irving Stone, and Philip Wylie – but *Good Housekeeping* competed with other magazines for new writers as well. On 17 February 1951, in an essay for *Saturday Review of Literature,* "Combing the Haystack," Cousins described the duties of magazine editors, who take scouting for new talent seriously: reading manuscripts (at that time 150,000 a year were submitted to *Good Housekeeping* and *Cosmopolitan* combined), interviewing, attending writers' conferences, lecturing, listening, criticizing, and at times finding that writers they advised and assisted turned elsewhere when they were ready to publish. In a talk delivered to the Women's National Book Association on 24 May 1949, Cousins explained what *Good Housekeeping* looked for in fiction: wit, charm, suspense, philosophy, and humor – stories "free of profanity and abnormalities, salaciousness and violence, or other things which might corrupt the young" (*Wilson Library Bulletin,* October 1950). Cousins's own fiction met these criteria; she published thirty-three stories in *Good Housekeeping* during the thirteen years she served as managing editor, and she continued to send material to *American Magazine, Woman's Home Companion, Cosmopolitan,* and other magazines.

Cousins made her first contribution to juvenile literature in 1952. Bennett Cerf had begun the Landmark Series for children at Random House and asked Cousins to write a biography of Benjamin Franklin. She recalled, "I said I did not know how to write for children, and Bennett said 'Who do you think you write for now?' I was so mad I almost hung up, but he offered me a large advance." She wrote *Ben Franklin of Old Philadelphia* (1952), which has been published in Chinese, Spanish, Greek, and Oriya (a dialect of India). In twelve succinct chapters she outlines Franklin's life, adding just enough colorful detail to keep young readers interested. The book was last published in 1987.

Also in 1952 Doubleday published eight of Cousins's Christmas stories in a little volume called *Christmas Gift.* All revolve around someone who experiences a Christmas surprise: a small-time crook, required by the court to play Santa at a department store, is surprised by his own generosity – and honesty; a small-town music teacher discovers amid the chaos of the Christmas pageant that her secret admiration for the widowed pastor is reciprocated; and other realistic characters get involved in action that could take place but usually does not – the combination that goes over well in mass-circulation media. The stories had appeared in various magazines between 1941 and 1951. Cousins later wrote, "I specialized in Christmas stories (some of my friends called me 'the Kris Kringle Kid' as I might have a Christmas story in my own magazine and two others in December issues under assumed names)." She published under three pseudonyms: Mary Parrish, Avery Johns, and William Masters.

Cousins's work did not go unnoticed by the television and film industries. Her agent, Harold Matson, sold several of her short stories to television, among them "An Apple for Miss Myrtle" (May 1948). Adapted for television by Kathleen and Robert Howard Lindsay, the story appeared in 1955 on NBC's weekday series "Matinee Theatre" and starred Geraldine Page. Paramount bought her novelette, "The Life of Lucy Gallant" (May 1953) and filmed *Lucy Gallant,* with a screenplay by John Lee Mahin and Winston Miller. The movie starred Jane Wyman as a career-oriented department store owner, who eventually agrees to marry the local farmer-oilman millionaire, played by Charlton Heston. Released in 1955 to mixed reviews, the film is still aired occasionally on television.

Cousins was called on in 1956 to ghostwrite another book, the autobiography of Margaret Truman. Mayes had made a deal with Truman's agent for rights to a book to be serialized in *Good Housekeeping;* the president's daughter was in great demand socially, however, and had difficulty finding time to write. According to Cousins, "Mr. Mayes got very restive and decided I should persuade Margaret to write this book, though I was very busy being managing editor of the magazine. Needless to say, I did what Mr. Mayes wanted me to do. I did most of the research and I followed her around, day and night, and between us we got the manuscript together." Using playbills, programs, train schedules, photographs, Margaret Truman's diary, and Cousins's notes, the two were able to write a warm, frank, lively account of Truman's life with her parents in Independence, Missouri, in the Blair House, and in the White House. The result was *Souvenir, Margaret Truman's Own Story,* and reviewers were highly complimentary.

Cousins's second juvenile book, *We Were There at the Battle of the Alamo,* was published in 1958. It too was successful, selling more than one hundred thousand copies over the years. Corona republished it under a new title, *The Boy in the Alamo,* in 1983.

By October 1958 *Good Housekeeping* under Mayes had surpassed all records in circulation and advertising and was continuing to soar, but friction between Mayes and Richard E. Deems, executive vice-president of Hearst, resulted in Mayes's dismissal as editor of *Good Housekeeping.* Fortunately for Mayes, *McCall's* editor Otis Wiese had just resigned, and Mayes was offered the position. He took it on the condition that he would have "absolutely absolute" editorial autonomy. Cousins went with him, as did several of Mayes's other associates from *Good Housekeeping.*

Cousins was made managing editor of *McCall's,* where she charmed her associates, as is obvious in the "Living with People" column of February 1961: "Mention Margaret Cousins' name anywhere – among top authors, designers, literary agents, theater people, or just nice folks – and you always get a glowing reaction, because this girl has a heart as big as Texas . . . ; her infectious enthusiasm is mass therapy for all of us." Cousins entertained often in her apartment in New York City: she displayed artworks; her collections of silver boxes, antique eggs, and egg cups; and hundreds of books autographed by the authors. (Later fire damaged the apartment extensively, a traumatic event Cousins described in "Fire on the Eighth Floor" in *House Beautiful,* May 1968.) She also entertained at her two-hundred-year-old Montauk, Long Island, cottage.

Cousins was "a solid anchor" at *McCall's,* according to Mayes. She assisted wherever she was needed, even helping iron dresses for models at a fashion show. If Mayes saw a painting he liked and wanted a story to accompany it, he called on Cousins. She could write a story between dinner and four in the morning and often did. Nine of her stories were published in *McCall's* during the three years she was managing editor, and she continued to send stories elsewhere. Occasionally she was called on to edit celebrity columns such as those of Clare Boothe Luce and Eleanor Roosevelt.

In 1961 Cousins edited *Stories of Love and Marriage,* a collection of twenty-two short stories written mostly by authors who published in mass-circulation magazines during the 1940s and 1950s. In her

SOUVENIR

When I read in the paper not long ago that the USS *Missouri* was to be decommissioned, I experienced a pang above and beyond the call of duty. It seemed to me that the passing of the Big Mo set on an era in my life a seal of finality much more definite than the change of family address from 1600 Pennsylvania Avenue, Washington, D.C., to 219 North Delaware Street, Independence, Missouri. For the *Missouri* and I, in a manner of speaking, had started out together, and all her triumphs and vicissitudes were entwined with the strings of my heart. In many ways she had been deeply involved in my affairs, and whether she was serving as a setting for the signing of treaties or wallowing in a mudbank off the coast of Florida, I always felt as if I were her mother. When I went on to read that the *Missouri* was headed for scrap, I really saddened, but I decided at once that the identification ended there! That's my platform, and I'm sticking to it.

Still, the nostalgia brought on by my associations with that good gray battleship encouraged me to haul out the moth-eaten old suitcase trunk in which I had hastily stowed the scrapbooks, diaries, autographs, photographs, clippings, letters, telegrams, dance programs, place cards, ribbons, pressed flowers, and a few shreds of confetti when I left the White House. (My father and I are incapable of throwing anything away!) When I had got it out in the middle of the living-room floor and located the key, I sat staring at it—Pandora's box, full of so much that was glamorous, happy, exciting, and rewarding, and so much that was not—undecided whether it was time to let it all roll over me again or to wait for a more distant perspective.

But I wanted to remember the *Missouri* on the crest of the wave, so I fitted the key to the lock and my life literally sprang out at me. The suitcase had always been a little too small to hold it. (*Please turn the page*)

53

This is my story—of the people I love the best, and the good fortune I've had and the privileges enjoyed, of the great and near-great I have met and the rumors I've survived, of the White House I remember and the Missouri home I'll never forget

by Margaret Truman

Pages from the first installment of Margaret Truman's autobiography, ghostwritten by Cousins, in the March 1956 issue of Good Housekeeping

introduction to the book, Cousins capsulizes the philosophy that governs characterization in her own fiction: "The character in a short story must seize upon the reader's imagination, like a face in the window of a passing train, and make its indelible impression." One of her stories, "The Marabou Crisis," is included in the book but under her pseudonym Mary Parrish. The central character is a fun-loving, usually prudent housewife who splurges on a Christmas gift for herself, then agonizes throughout the holidays, fearing her husband's reaction when she opens the present on Christmas morning. The story has an O. Henry twist to the conclusion, but it is Cousins's success in creating the character that impresses the reader.

Mayes was made president and chief executive officer of the McCall's Corporation in 1961. According to Cousins, Mayes wanted to take her into "the business side of publishing" at that time. She did not want to become involved in the stressful politics of magazine management; she wanted to write and edit. In the fall of 1961 she resigned from *McCall's* and went to Doubleday as senior editor. John Mack Carter took the editorship of *McCall's*.

At Doubleday, under editor in chief Kenneth McCormick, Cousins worked on many of Doubleday's series, such as Mainstream of American History, Mainstream of Religious History, Mainstream of World History, and Crossroads of History; she corresponded with countless editors, authors, and illustrators; she made speeches on behalf of Doubleday; and she worked on promotion and publicity committees. In 1962 Doubleday published her *Traffic with Evil,* using her pseudonym Avery Johns. It is a Crime Club novel set in New York City and Montauk Point. The main character, the daughter of a judge, allows romance to lead her into trouble with the authorities. Before writing this novel, Cousins once said she did not believe she was profound enough to write serious novels. *Traffic with Evil* is her only published full-length novel.

In 1965 Random House published her third book for juveniles, *The Story of Thomas Alva Edison,* another biography in the Landmark Series. No other biographers in the United States had yet written Edison's story. Cousins had to write to London for much of her information. She portrays Edison realistically but understandably gives sketchy treatment to scientific detail. The book is intended for grades five to seven. It was last reprinted in 1981.

On Cousins's sixty-fifth birthday Doubleday retired her because of the automatic retirement clause in their pension plan. Furious, disappointed, and unwilling to retire, she went looking for another job.

She found a position as special editor with Holt, Rinehart and Winston, editing, among other works, the autobiographies of President and Mrs. Lyndon Baines Johnson. Lady Bird Johnson had begun dictating extensive tape recordings of her activities in the White House immediately after her husband took office. By the time they left the White House, she had several suitcases full of tapes. These had to be reviewed, and parts had to be cut for her book, *A White House Diary* (1970). Cousins assisted with the cutting and later said, "I did not 'help her' with her book. She is a *born* writer and should be writing books today, as she has much to say." Cousins also edited portions of the president's book, *The Vantage Point* (1971). When the Lyndon Baines Johnson Library was dedicated in May 1971 at the University of Texas at Austin, Cousins attended as Mrs. Johnson's guest.

In 1971 John Mack Carter, who had taken the editorship of *Ladies' Home Journal* after a short stint at *McCall's,* invited Cousins to take the position of book editor at *Ladies' Home Journal.* In the August 1971 issue, Carter boasted that Cousins had been instrumental in getting Daphne du Maurier and Katherine Anne Porter to submit stories to *Ladies' Home Journal.* Carter was pleased to have a "top editor" and an "accomplished writer" whose name was "familiar, friendly, golden" to join his staff.

Cousins worked at her new job for two years, but one day she fell down in the midst of noon traffic at Madison Avenue and 55th Street in New York City. When her doctor diagnosed the cause of her fall as rheumatoid arthritis, she decided to retire. She moved to San Antonio, where her father had taken her when she was a small child. In "San Antonio, I Love You!," a promotion piece she wrote for *McCall's* in November 1965, she said, "San Antonio always seemed to be peculiarly mine. My father, who loved it, made me a present of it."

In her last published essay, one of a group of essays written by prominent men and women in *The Courage to Grow Old* (1989), Cousins describes her retirement in San Antonio as "one of the most exciting periods of my whole life." She has spent her time "exploring churchwork, docentship, public service, fund-raising for worthy causes, educational projects, literacy campaigns, animal rights, preservation and conservation, local politics, storytelling, and even babysitting."

Since her retirement Cousins has received several awards and honors, including the Distinguished Alumna Award from the University of Texas (1973); an honorary literary doctorate from William Woods College (1980); the Arts and Letters Award from Friends of San Antonio Public Library (1982); and the Women in Communications Lifetime Achievement Award (1986). But for Margaret ("Maggie") Cousins, who has never lost her Texas twang and has always explained her versatile accomplishments and interests by simply saying she comes from Texas, the greatest honor of them all must have been her induction into the Texas Hall of Fame in 1986. As a final analysis of her career, Mayes wrote: "Editorially, there was nothing Miss Cousins couldn't and didn't do."

References:

Florence Elberta Barns, *Texas Writers of Today* (Dallas: Tardy, 1935), pp. 124, 125;

Herbert R. Mayes, *The Magazine Maze* (Garden City, N.Y.: Doubleday, 1980);

Frank Luther Mott, *A History of American Magazines,* volume 5 (Cambridge, Mass.: Harvard University Press, 1968), p. 141.

Papers:

The principal collection of Margaret Cousins's papers is in the Harry Ransom Humanities Research Center, University of Texas at Austin.

Norman Cousins

(24 June 1915 - 31 November 1990)

Sharon M. Murphy and Eileen Stewart
Marquette University

MAJOR POSITIONS HELD: Education editor, *New York Evening Post* (1934–1935); book critic, literary editor, managing editor, *Current History* (1935–1940); executive editor (1940–1942), editor (1942–1971, 1975–1978), editor emeritus, *Saturday Review of Literature,* retitled *Saturday Review* in 1942 (1980–1982); editor, *World* (1972–1973); editor, *Saturday Review/World* (1973–1974).

BOOKS: *The Good Inheritance; The Democratic Chance* (New York: Coward-McCann, 1942);

Modern Man Is Obsolete (New York: Viking, 1945; London: Falcon, 1946);

Talks with Nehru; India's Prime Minister Speaks Out on the Crisis of our Time: A Discussion Between Jawaharlal Nehru and Norman Cousins (London: Gollancz, 1951);

Who Speaks for Man? (New York: Macmillan, 1953);

The Reality of Human Brotherhood (Boston: Starr King, 1954);

Education for the Freedom Years (Ann Arbor: University of Michigan Press, 1956);

Wanted: Two Billion Angry Men (Stamford, Conn.: Overbrook, 1958);

Dr. Schweitzer of Lambaréné (New York: Harper, 1960; London: Black, 1961);

In Place of Folly (New York: Harper, 1961; revised edition, New York: Washington Square, 1962);

Profiles of Nehru: America Remembers a World Leader (Delhi: Indian Book Company, 1966);

Present Tense: An American Editor's Odyssey (New York: McGraw-Hill, 1967);

The Improbable Triumvirate: John F. Kennedy, Pope John, Nikita Khrushchev (New York: Norton, 1972);

The Celebration of Life: A Dialogue on Immortality and Infinity (New York: Harper & Row, 1974);

Anatomy of an Illness as Perceived by the Patient: Reflections on Healing and Regeneration (New York & London: Norton, 1979);

Human Options (New York: Norton, 1981);

Norman Cousins

The Healing Heart: Antidotes to Panic and Helplessness (New York & London: Norton, 1983);

Albert Schweitzer's Mission: Healing and Peace (New York: Norton, 1985);

The Pathology of Power (New York: Norton, 1987).

OTHER: *A Treasury of Democracy,* edited by Cousins (New York: Coward-McCann, 1942);

The Poetry of Freedom, edited by Cousins and William Rose Benet (New York: Modern Library, 1945);

Writing for Love or Money: Thirty-Five Essays Reprinted from the Saturday Review of Literature, edited by Cousins (New York: Longmans, Green, 1949);

"In God We Trust": The Religious Beliefs and Ideas of the American Founding Fathers, edited, with commentary, by Cousins (New York: Harper, 1958);

Great American Essays, edited by Cousins and Frank Jennings (New York: Dell, 1967);

Profiles of Gandhi: America Remembers a World Leader, edited by Cousins (Delhi: Indian Book Company, 1969);

Memoirs of a Man, Grenville Clark, collected by Mary Clark Dimond; edited by Cousins and J. Garry Clifford (New York: Norton, 1975);

The Physician in Literature, edited by Cousins (Philadelphia: Saunders, 1982).

SELECTED PERIODICAL PUBLICATIONS – UNCOLLECTED: "Food for the Trust Busters," *Current History,* 48 (February 1938): 26–30;

"Liberal Intellectuals: 4th Century BC," *Saturday Review of Literature,* 24 (4 October 1941): 7–8+;

"Tell the Folks Back Home: Speech at the Cultural and Scientific Conference for World Peace," *Saturday Review of Literature,* 32 (9 April 1949): 20–22; republished in *Vital Speeches,* 15 (15 September 1949): 723–725;

"Hiroshima, Four Years Later," *Saturday Review of Literature,* 32 (17 September 1949): 8–10+;

"Whole Man," *National Education Association Journal,* 39 (April 1950); 264–265;

"Free Press and Free Enterprise," *Saturday Review of Literature,* 34 (2 June 1951): 20–21;

"Blueprint for Better Schools," *Parents' Magazine,* 26 (September 1951): 40–41;

"The UN's Road to Survival," *UN World,* 7 (May 1953): 38–41;

"Address in Moscow, with Marginal Notes," *Saturday Review,* 42 (25 July 1959): 10–12+;

"The World, the Individual, and Education," *National Education Association Journal,* 49 (April 1960): 10–12;

"Report from Laos," *Saturday Review,* 44 (18 February 1961): 12–14+;

"Nuclear War," *Saturday Review,* 44 (23 September 1961): 24+;

"Shelters, Survival and Common Sense," *Saturday Review,* 44 (21 October 1961): 30+; (28 October 1961): 26–27; (4 November 1961): 28+; (25 November 1961): 30–31;

"Community of Hope and Responsibility: excerpts from an Address, June 2, 1962," *Saturday Review,* 45 (16 June 1962): 12–14;

"Cuba," *Saturday Review,* 45 (6 October 1962): 28+;

"Douglas MacArthur," *Saturday Review,* 47 (2 May 1964): 18–19;

"Notes on a 1963 Visit with Khrushchev," *Saturday Review,* 47 (7 November 1964): 16–21+;

"The Writer as a World Citizen," *Saturday Review,* 49 (13 August 1966): 14+;

"Uncharted Worlds on the Face of a Tree," *Home Garden and Flower Grower,* 54 (November 1967): 35–37;

"Does the US Department of Commerce Know America?," *McCall's,* 95 (May 1968): 5;

"Vietnam: the Spurned Peace," *Saturday Review,* 52 (26 July 1969): 12–16+; republished as "How the US Spurned Three Chances for Peace in Vietnam," *Look,* 33 (29 July 1969): 45–48;

"Linus Pauling and the Vitamin Controversy," *Saturday Review,* 54 (15 May 1971): 37–40+;

"Final Report to the Readers," *Saturday Review,* 54 (27 November 1971): 32–33;

"Truth in Government," *Today's Education,* 63 (January/February 1974): 20–22;

"Watergate on Main Street," *Saturday Review/World,* 1 (18 May 1974): 8;

"Musings on a Golden Anniversary," *Saturday Review/World,* 1 (10 August 1974): 4–7;

"Last Chance for Peace in the Middle East?," *Saturday Review,* 2 (22 March 1975): 10–19;

"Where Is the News Leading Us?," *Today's Education,* 66 (March/April 1977): 26–27;

"Medical Mystery of the Placebo," by Cousins and S. Schiefelbein, *Reader's Digest,* 112 (March 1978): 167–169;

"Hope Can Heal," *Ladies' Home Journal,* 97 (November 1980): 93+;

"Hutchins Believed that History Was a Succession of Open Moments," *Center Magazine,* 14 (January/February 1981): 10–14;

"Writers I Have Known," *Saturday Review,* 8 (April 1981): 24–26;

"Why Writers Matter," *Saturday Review,* 8 (June 1981): 7–8;

"Healing and Belief," *Saturday Evening Post,* 254 (April 1982): 30–32+;

"The Mind's Power Can Be Enlisted to Heal the Body," *Center Magazine,* 16 (January/February 1983): 43–46;

"A Postmortem of the *Saturday Review,*" *Center Magazine,* 16 (May/June 1984): 33–39;

"Smoke Alarm (I)," *Saturday Evening Post,* 256 (May/June 1984): 30–32+;

"Smoke Alarm (II)," *Saturday Evening Post,* 256 (July/August 1984): 36+;

"Science," *Center Magazine,* 18 (November/December 1985): 46–47.

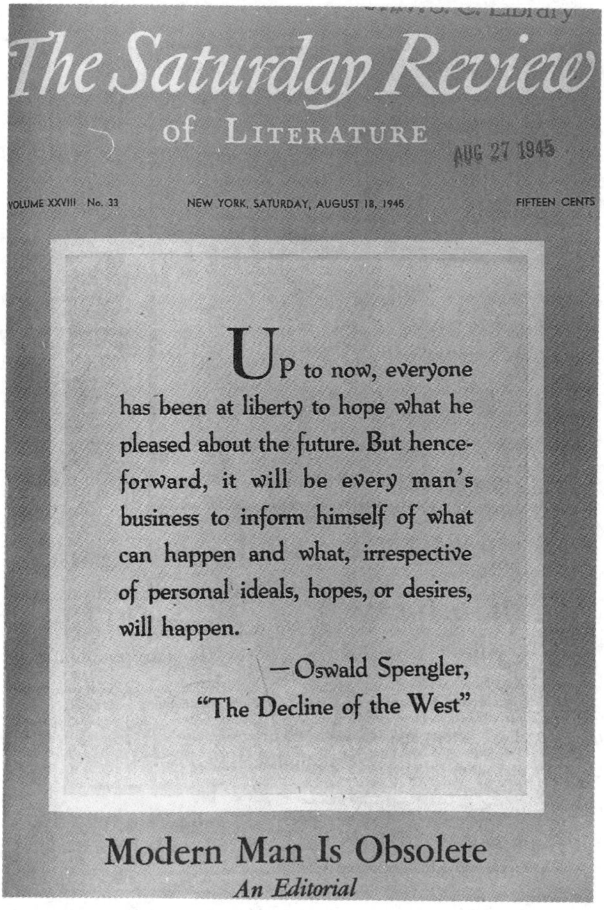

Cover of the issue including Cousins's editorial calling for practical, peacetime use of atomic energy

"Human beings cannot live fully or joyously unless their sense of beauty is exercised and proclaimed," Norman Cousins wrote in the June 1981 issue of *Saturday Review*. "It is the writer's job to deal with these things of beauty in order to provide not necessarily a joy forever but a touch of loveliness that will last as long as society's capacity for beauty will last." Cousins did this job and many others. He was an author, photographer, syndicated columnist, editor, diplomat, negotiator, philosopher, medical humanist, and professor. He tried out most of his hunches on himself and wrote books and articles in which he admitted his own frailties and fears. In "Healing and Belief" (April 1982), an autobiographical essay, he wrote, "I can imagine no greater satisfaction for a person, in looking back on his life and work, than to have been able to give some people, however few, a feeling of genuine pride in belonging to the human species and, beyond that, a zestful yen to justify that pride." His books, beginning in 1942, show this zest as well as an eclectic interest in life.

His book *Anatomy of an Illness as Perceived by the Patient: Reflections on Healing and Regeneration* (1979), which won him an Author of the Year Award in 1981, is a good introduction to Cousins's thought. Along with *The Healing Heart: Antidotes to Pain and Helplessness* (1983), it is an examination of the ways in which patients can and must take charge of their lives and their illnesses. The two books are a challenge to members of the medical profession to look in more-human and -humane ways at the people they treat.

Norman Cousins was born on 24 June 1915 in Union Hill, New Jersey, to Samuel and Sara Miller Cousins. He married Ellen Kopf on 23 June 1939, and they had four daughters. Cousins attended Columbia University Teacher's College and began his journalistic career in 1934 as education editor for the *New York Evening Post*. There followed, in quick succession, posts as book critic, literary editor, and then managing editor of *Current History* (1935–1940). In 1940, as executive editor he began an almost four-decade-long "love affair with the readers" of the *Saturday Review of Literature,* renamed *Saturday Review* in 1942. In 1942 he became editor, a post he held until 1971, when he resigned in objection to major changes planned by the magazine's new owners. At the time of his death in 1990, he was a professor of medical humanities, affiliated with the Brain Research Institute. He was also a vice-president and director of the McCall's Corporation, a post he accepted in 1961.

The *Saturday Review of Literature* was founded in 1924 by Henry Seidel Canby. Because the *Current History* offices were housed in the same building as the *Saturday Review of Literature,* Cousins developed strong friendships among the literary-review staff. Asked to join the magazine as executive editor in 1940, Cousins found it a financially troubled publication with a circulation of about 20,000, hardly enough to sustain it. Never one to be intimidated by the odds, he moved boldly to broaden the scope of the relatively conservative magazine and eventually took it to a circulation of 650,000. Named editor in chief in 1942, Cousins shortened the title to *Saturday Review,* thus reflecting his desire to broaden its scope to encompass current events, sciences, the arts, travel, education, and general concerns. New columnists, including Bennett Cerf, Cleveland Amory, and Joseph Wood Crutch, were hired, and supplements in music, science, education, and communications were introduced. Cousins was discovering a reality about the publishing life: "I learned . . . that you have to edit and publish out of your own tastes, enthusiasms, and concerns, and not out of notions or guesswork about what other people might like to read," he wrote in the 27 November 1971 issue of *Saturday Review.*

The people liked what they read, and they liked the editor. Observers have called *Saturday Review* as much a Cousins cult as a magazine. Readers enthusiastically responded to the content and to Cousins's articles and editorials, signed simply "N.C." He wrote of books and writers; of the human condition and the options open to the human race; and of war and peace and the quest for security. He wrote of healing and healers, and he argued forcefully and consistently for recognition of the powerful role of patient-physician communication in the healing process. Cousins believed that his magazine was closely allied to the human struggle, and he led *Saturday Review* into campaigns against pollution, against indifference to television violence and cigarette advertising, for government support of space exploration, and against American intervention in Indochina. In an August 1945 editorial, "Modern Man Is Obsolete," which was expanded into a book later that year, he urged reconsideration of the uses of atomic energy and called for its practical, peacetime use. Cousins personally carried the message around the world in over two thousand speeches. Two books, *Who Speaks for Man?* (1953) and *In Place of Folly* (1961), further develop his argument in favor of international efforts for peace and nuclear nonproliferation.

An activist as well as a thoughtful writer and editor, Cousins involved *Saturday Review* readers in his crusades. He began a "moral adoption" program, eliciting the support of readers for 440 Japanese children orphaned when Hiroshima was bombed. With reader support, those children were cared for and educated all the way through their college years. He also brought twenty-four "Hiroshima maidens," disfigured by atomic radiation, to the United States for treatment, and later he did the same for the "Ravensbrück Lapins," thirty-five Polish women who were victims of Nazi medical experiments. Readers were also instrumental in the training of Japanese plastic surgeons and, through them, in the treatment in Japan of thirty-seven thousand Hiroshima and Nagasaki survivors. Cousins also traveled extensively to meet and interview the movers and shakers of the world: Soviet prime minister Nikita Khrushchev, President John F. Kennedy, Pope John XXIII, Indian prime minister Jawaharlal Nehru, the humanitarian physician Albert Schweitzer, and Palestine Liberation Organization leader Yassir Arafat. Later Cousins compiled the insights these people shared in his book *Human Options* (1981). His work as editor, author, and lecturer expanded into membership in Americans United for World Organization, which became the international organization United World Federalists, dedicated to the concept of global government. In 1964 he became president of the World Association of World Federalists. After a visit to the Soviet Union in 1960, he helped initiate the Dartmouth Conferences, a series of exchanges between Soviet and American scientists, writers, and scholars. These unofficial, civilian dialogues on common concerns were held in Hanover, New Hampshire, in 1960; in the Crimea in 1961; in Andover, Massachusetts, in 1962; and in Leningrad in 1964.

In 1962 Cousins used his considerable diplomatic skills as he shuttled among President Kennedy, Prime Minister Khrushchev, and Pope John. At issue were the release of an imprisoned Catholic prelate and, ultimately, the entire question of nuclear proliferation. The prelate, Archbishop Josef Slipyi of the Ukraine, who had been imprisoned for eighteen years, was released. And the shuttling be-

Cover for the first issue (11 September 1973) published after Saturday Review *merged with Cousins's magazine,* World

tween the Vatican, the White House, and the Kremlin led to the Soviet-American Nuclear Test Ban Treaty. At Kennedy's request Cousins helped establish the Citizens Committee for a Nuclear Test Ban, a ban that was ratified by the U.S. Senate in September 1963. In recognition of this effort and others toward world peace, Cousins was awarded the Eleanor Roosevelt Peace Prize in 1963, the Family of Man Award in 1968, and the United Nations Peace Medal in 1971.

His life with *Saturday Review* took several twists, and although he had made the magazine popular, he made some mistakes, one of which was especially costly. The owner of *Saturday Review,* Everette De Golyer, had shortly before his death in 1956 transferred ownership of the magazine to Cousins, who in turn distributed all but a controlling 51 percent of the stock to staff members. Three years later the stockholders sold out to the McCall's Corporation, publisher of *McCall's* and *Redbook.* In 1971 *Saturday Review* was sold to the young entrepreneurs John J. Veronis and Nicholas J. Charney, who had founded *Psychology Today.* They announced their plans to divide *Saturday Review* into four separate monthlies on society, education, the arts, and science. "I didn't think it was a sound editorial idea, and therefore not a sound business idea," Cousins told *Business Week* (28 April 1973), and so he resigned as editor. Not content to rest quietly, he founded in 1972 a new biweekly, *World,* that strongly resembled the former *Saturday Review* and quickly attracted many of his loyal subscribers. The four-publication *Saturday Review* plan did not succeed, and in September 1973, following the bankruptcy of Saturday Review Industries, a merged publication under Cousins's leadership appeared as *Saturday Review/World.* His comment at that time, as he assumed the role of editor and chairman of the board of editors, was, "They are giving me back thirty years of my life."

The focus on book reviews and coverage of book publishing was restored. Within a year *Saturday Review/World* was again a profitable venture, and the Magazine Publishers Association recognized that feat by naming Cousins publisher of the year for 1973. The magazine was renamed *Saturday*

Review in January 1975. The financial problems growing out of the Veronis/Charney experiment never fully disappeared, however. In 1977 Cousins sold the magazine to Carll Tucker, a young millionaire, who in turn sold it in 1980 to Robert I. Weingarten, a former stockbroker and owner of the magazine *Financial World*. Cousins became editor emeritus. The magazine finally folded in autumn 1982.

Cousins had long been interested in medicine and the relationship between illness and stress. His own life had given him ample content for study. In 1964 he was diagnosed as having ankylosing spondylitis, a disintegration of the connective tissue in the spine. He was told he had one chance in five hundred for survival, but he rejected the idea of dying and became involved in his healing. The tale of the ensuing odyssey was greeted with both skepticism and joy when it appeared in the *New England Journal of Medicine,* and it was followed by many more observations by Cousins on health and healing. He became known as the patient who laughed himself back to health because of the emphasis he placed on humor in dealing with pain and enhancing his body's restorative powers. He also attracted attention because of his unorthodox self-prescribed regimen of mass doses of vitamin C. Not content with his own cure, Cousins did far more in promoting an understanding of the power of the will to live. "I have learned," he wrote, "never to underestimate the capacity of the human mind and body to regenerate – even when the prospects seem most wretched." *The Healing Heart* grew out of his experiences with a nearly fatal heart attack. He realized that, in responding to heart attacks, treating panic is one of the first and most important tasks. He attributed his recovery, in this situation as in his earlier illness, to "an active partnership with his physician and large doses of love, hope, faith, laughter, confidence and the will to live."

When he left *Saturday Review* for the last time in 1982, Cousins became a consultant and a lecturer at the University of California, Los Angeles, Medical School. He left New York City and resettled in Los Angeles, where he taught medical humanities, discussing medicine and values with medical students. He also participated in a research project with cancer patients, studying the role of attitude in influencing the autonomic nervous system. His hypothesis was that the relaxation of stress and tension connected with laughter can stimulate the healing process. Perhaps even more important than this research on laughter and humor in freeing patients from the inhibiting power of fear was his continuing stress on the role of patient-physician communication. Cousins died on 31 November 1990.

Interviews:

A. P. Sanoff, "A Conversation with Norman Cousins," *U.S. News & World Report,* 96 (23 January 1984): 61–62;

Sara Pacher, "The Plowboy Interview: Norman Cousins: A Spokesman for the Human Race," *Mother Earth News,* 90 (November/December 1984): 14–16+.

References:

"Cousins Quits," *Time,* 98 (29 November 1971): 58;

"Cousins' Second Coming," *Time,* 102 (16 July 1973): 82;

"*Saturday Review,* Back with Cousins, to Stress Books," *Publishers Weekly,* 203 (7 May 1973): 31;

"The *Saturday Review* Goes Home to Cousins," *Business Week* (28 April 1973): 46;

"Son of *Saturday Review,*" *Time,* 99 (24 January 1972): 42+;

John J. Veronis, "Report to the Readers," *Saturday Review,* 54 (4 December 1971): 32–33.

Gardner ("Mike") Cowles, Jr.

(31 January 1903 – 8 July 1985)

Terry Hynes
California State University, Fullerton

See also the Gardner Cowles, Sr., entry in *DLB 29: American Newspaper Journalists, 1926–1950* and the Gardner Cowles, Jr., entry in *DLB 127: American Newspaper Publishers, 1950–1990.*

MAJOR POSITIONS HELD: City editor (1925), news editor (1926), associate managing editor (1926–1927), managing editor (1927–1931), executive editor, *Des Moines Register* (1931–1939); vice-president (1934–1939), associate publisher (1939–1943), president, the Register and Tribune Company (1943–1973); chairman of the board, Minneapolis Star and Tribune Company, president, Iowa Broadcasting Company, president, South Dakota Broadcasting Company, president, Cowles Magazines, Inc., president, Cowles Magazines & Broadcasting, Inc., editor in chief, chairman, and chief executive officer (1937–1971), honorary chairman, Cowles Communications, Inc. (1971–1983); honorary chairman, Cowles Broadcasting Company (1983–1985).

PRINCIPAL MAGAZINES OWNED OR CONTROLLED: *Look* (1937–1971), *Quick* (1949–1953), *Flair* (1950–1951), *Family Circle* (1962–1970), and *Venture* (1964–1971).

BOOK: *Mike Looks Back* (N.p.: Privately published, 1985).

Gardner ("Mike") Cowles, Jr., 1921

Perhaps most widely known as publisher of the mass-circulation, general-audience picture magazine *Look,* Gardner ("Mike") Cowles, Jr., was chief executive officer of a media conglomerate that included newspapers, book publishing, and broadcast outlets as well as several magazines. In newspaper journalism Cowles pioneered the use of opinion polling in the 1920s, when he hired George Gallup to do readership surveys for the Des Moines family-owned newspapers. In the late 1920s he introduced to the *Register* a series-photograph technique for the Sunday rotogravure section. (Most roto sections of the time ran single news items or feature shots of events.) The success of these picture series generated a syndicated-photo company and inspired Cowles to begin *Look* in the late 1930s. He and his older brother John expanded the family's holdings from those in Des Moines to others in Minneapolis and New York and, at their peak, included examples of almost every mass medium of communications. In the tradition begun by his father, Mike Cowles infused into his publications a perspective that was liberal or moderately liberal on national issues and that encouraged audiences to develop an internationalist perspective in order to understand the impact of events on the world.

The sixth child and youngest son of Gardner and Florence Call Cowles, Gardner, Jr., was born in his mother's hometown of Algona, Iowa, on 31 January 1903. Other children included the oldest son, Russell, who later became a successful artist; John, who also joined the family newspaper business; and three daughters, Helen, Florence, and Bertha. According to family legend, his father thought the young Gardner looked Irish and thus nicknamed him Mike, a name that also served as a convenient means of distinguishing him from his father and became the name by which Gardner, Jr., was most commonly known throughout his life.

In November 1903 Gardner Cowles, Sr., and Harvey Ingham purchased controlling interest in the *Des Moines Register and Leader,* which resulted in the family's move in 1904 to the state capital, about sixty miles from Algona. Through the subsequent purchase of the *Des Moines Tribune* and the creation of a newspaper monopoly, Cowles, Sr., created a vigorous newspaper environment that Mike and his brother John would continue and enlarge, beginning in the late 1920s.

As a child Mike Cowles spent much of his time at the newspaper office, in the cashier's cage at age five and reading editorials for twenty-five cents at age eight. He followed his brother John to Phillips Exeter Academy, where, like his brother before him, he became editor of the weekly student paper, the *Exonian.* After graduation in 1921 Cowles again followed John – this time to Harvard – where, also like his brother, he served as editor of the *Crimson.* He was also treasurer of his class. In addition, while a college student, he worked summers as a reporter for the *Des Moines Tribune.*

Cowles was awarded his B.A. from Harvard in 1925 and returned to Des Moines as city editor of the *Register.* When he joined his brother John on the newspaper that year, their father and Ingham had a near monopoly on daily newspaper publishing in Des Moines with the morning (including Sundays) *Register* and the evening *Tribune.* After the *Tribune* merged with the *Capital* in 1927, the monopoly was complete.

With John successfully based on the business side of the papers, Mike worked on the editorial side. He moved quickly through the ranks from news editor (1926) to associate managing editor (1926–1927), managing editor (1927–1931), and executive editor, a position he held for eight years (1931–1939).

Most chroniclers of the accomplishments in mass media of the Cowles family, including biographer George Mills, credit Mike Cowles with hiring George Gallup in the mid 1920s to conduct reader-interest surveys for the *Register* and *Tribune.* Regardless of which family member hired Gallup, a systematic approach to determining reader interests certainly fit with the elder Cowles's traditional concern with circulation. At the time Gallup was hired, he was working on his doctoral dissertation and serving as a journalism instructor at the University of Iowa. Gallup's survey results indicated a strong preference among readers for pictures over words. Thus the *Register* and *Tribune* began to experiment with a greater use of pictures, especially in the Sunday rotogravure section of the *Register.*

The picture layouts were designed to appear as a series that told a story visually in a readily comprehensible manner. For Mike Cowles, the rotogravure section became the experimental forerunner of *Look* magazine. Vernon Pope, then of the Sunday staff of the *Register* and later the first editor of *Look,* was a key leader in designing these series. The photo series were one factor in the newspaper's circulation growth during the Depression. By the mid 1930s the picture formula included series that ran for a dozen weeks or more. In addition, the newspaper's picture series were sufficiently successful that, in 1933, the paper established a roto-picture service and began syndicating its pictures to twenty-six other newspapers.

Look magazine, with its worldwide scope, was an outgrowth of the success of the Cowles family's rotogravure sections and their picture syndicate. While *Look* was still in the planning stages in 1936, Mike heard of *Time* owner Henry Luce's new national picture-magazine project, to be called *Life.* Since the Cowles brothers knew Luce and Roy Larsen, another *Time* official, the four met to discuss their plans. They exchanged experimental dummies of their respective magazines and realized the two were fundamentally different: *Life* was to be a weekly news-picture magazine, and *Look* was to be a monthly publication focusing on feature photographs. Luce initially anticipated a limited audience, while Mike Cowles, from the outset, sought mass circulation.

The immediate success of *Life,* after its appearance in November 1936, persuaded Cowles to proceed with his own project. *Look,* "the monthly picture magazine," first appeared in early January 1937, with a February cover date. Its first cover fea-

Cowles and his wife Fleur on a honeymoon trip to Europe in 1933

tured Hermann Göring, identified as "Germany's strange bridegroom," in an almost-full-page photograph, with smaller photographs of others, including President Franklin D. Roosevelt and Joan Crawford, each with a caption promoting, respectively, stories on a psychologist's assessment of the president's popularity and on the actress's rise as a Hollywood star; in addition there was a major story on the "Parole Racket – America's Shame." The forty-page issue, which promised "200 pictures . . . 1001 facts," sold for ten cents per copy. A one-year subscription cost one dollar.

A promotional advertisement on page 2 of the first issue featured a picture of a bull biting a matador in Spain and touted *Look* as "an educational picture magazine for EVERYONE." The ad stated further, "It is the belief of the editors of *Look* that the news of the world can best be told today in well edited pictures, not in long columns of type. *Look* will bring current events, science, sports, beauty, education, all in interesting pictures, to both the Colonel's Lady and Mrs. O'Grady (and their respective husbands and children) to make them better informed on what's happening in the world." The language of this ad promised content akin to that of *Life,* but the two magazines, especially in their early years, remained distinctively different. *Life* was printed on higher-quality slick paper and emphasized news, culture, and science. *Look,* imitating the rotogravure printing of the Sunday *Register,* was published on cheap paper and featured personalities, animals, beauty, fashion, travel, sports, curiosities, and oddities – all in a somewhat sensational style.

Cowles kept costs down in the early years of *Look* by locating its headquarters in Des Moines and using the *Register* and *Tribune* rotogravure processes, plant, and personnel to produce the magazine. In 1940 Cowles moved the *Look* editorial and advertising offices to New York. By 1947 those headquarters occupied five floors of prime real estate on Fifth Avenue. Beginning in 1950 the *Look* staff shared space with that of *Esquire* magazine.

Look remained a monthly only until April 1937, when Cowles switched publication to every two weeks, with the magazine appearing on Tuesdays. The first issue sold more than seven hundred thousand copies, but he refused to accept advertising until he could estimate circulation with some certainty. After ten months circulation reached 1.7 million, and Cowles accepted the first ads for *Look.* In the interim Cowles had continued to increase the editorial budget and to apply the profits from each issue (about ten thousand dollars) to a promotional campaign. Circulation slipped in 1938, and in 1939 advertising revenues fell below one million dollars. After that, however, revenues rose every year for the next decade. Cowles credited the success of *Look,* especially in the postwar years, to its varied content, with material appealing to every member of the family.

Generally regarded as liberal Republicans for most of their careers, John and Mike Cowles supported some New Deal policies, especially those related to international expansion. They also were among Wendell Willkie's first supporters for the presidency in 1940 and were considered two of his closest advisers. Mike campaigned strenuously on Willkie's behalf prior to the 1940 Republican national convention in Philadelphia. In the month before the convention, he traveled with Willkie throughout the Midwest and mountain states, introducing him to convention delegates and influential newspaper people. Cowles was among the group who accompanied Willkie on his "One World" global trip from late August to mid October 1942. Cowles also helped Willkie get *One World* (1943), the book celebrating his trip, ready for publication and was sole trustee of the One World Foundation, which gave Cowles complete discretion in spending proceeds from Willkie's book. In addition Cowles supported Willkie in his unsuccessful bid for the 1944 Republican presidential nomination and remained a friend to Willkie until the latter's death in October 1944. Cowles would also support John F. Kennedy for president in 1960, after years of giving press breaks to the Kennedy family members who were friends of the Cowleses.

From summer 1942 until May 1943 Cowles served under Elmer Davis as deputy director of the Office of War Information (OWI) in charge of its domestic division. Under Cowles's leadership this division, with its approximately one thousand employees, produced many pamphlets; but preferring to rely on newspapers for disseminating government information, he limited agency-produced material. Public attention was called to the work of the domestic division in April 1943, when fifteen of its writers resigned in opposition to OWI policies they perceived as restricting their ability to provide accurate information when the content was unfavorable to the government. The controversy was exacerbated late in April when the OWI *Information Guide,* which had been prepared for the agency's writers under Cowles's direction, appeared. It forbade writers from crusading "for social, political, or economic reforms" or engaging "in controversy or pleas for reformation" and stated instead that writers should stick to "the facts . . . the truth above all." Cowles resigned in May amid rumors that he would become press agent for Willkie's return bid for the presidency in 1944. In October 1943 one of the issues of *Look* featured Willkie on the cover and in a story running several pages; promotional ads for the issue touted Willkie as "another Lincoln."

Additional expansion of the Cowles media conglomerate in the early 1940s included publication of three pictorial books – *Woodrow Wilson* (1944), *Air Power* (1943), and *How to Be Attractive* (1943) – based on the *Look* approach of creating text to parallel illustration, and six movie shorts, similar to the "March of Time" series, dramatizing subjects treated in the magazine.

During World War II the circulation of *Look* was limited to 2 million copies because of paper shortages. Consequently advertising revenue was constrained – to about $5.25 million during the war years. By 1946 circulation was more than 2.4 million, and advertising revenue reached $6 million. In the same year, Cowles fired approximately sixty staff members and eliminated the book, visual-research, and readers-research departments in order to regain control over costs, which had become exorbitant during the war.

One of the staff members dismissed in 1946 was editor and general manager Harlan Logan, who had earlier been an editor for *Scribner's* and had directed the *Look* operations since 1942. Logan had supported the visual-research department's innovations in combination photo-and-sketch stories (such as the war-hero series) and off-guard pictures (including that of a pickpocket plying his trade on crowds in Times Square). The readers-research department provided audience-response information through polls roughly comparable to those Gallup had conducted for the Des Moines newspapers. The picture-rich productions of the book department had never been profitable, and in the face of costs that had increased by $2 million in 1946 alone, Cowles decided major surgery was necessary to restore the news and reporting focus of *Look.* He assumed Logan's titles of editor and general manager, while Dan Mich remained as executive editor in charge of a staff totaling 103, then the largest in the history of *Look.* By 1949 circulation was almost three million, and advertising revenues were approximately $15 million.

Initial criticism of *Look* focused on the sensational style. A writer for the *New Republic,* for example, chastised it as "a morgue and dime museum on paper." As the editors of *Look* became more comfortable with their ability to attract readers, however, they gave more space to social issues. By October 1937 the *New Republic* was praising *Look* for publishing "the best pictorial study of civil liberties in the United States we have seen anywhere." In later years *Look* abandoned much of its earlier sensationalism, although even in the late 1940s it was criticized for the relatively high proportion of content devoted to death, violence, blood, and sex. In 1963 Cowles acknowledged to a *New York Times* reporter that "During the first fifteen years of *Look,* I greatly underestimated the intelligence and taste of the American public." As twentieth-century-magazine historian Theodore Peterson has noted, "By the early fifties, [*Look*] had worked out a pattern of articles dealing with national and world affairs, health and science, sports and entertainment, fashion and beauty, and foods and home living. Later in the decade it became serious without being dull."

In 1946, after several years of absentee management of *Look,* Cowles moved to New York to supervise the magazine more closely. He maintained oversight responsibility for the Des Moines holdings through the 1960s, while his brother John con-

Cover of the magazine published by Gardner Cowles and edited by Fleur Cowles

tinued to be responsible for the Minneapolis newspapers. The brothers maintained a close personal contact over the years through frequent telephone conversations (as many as two or three half-hour calls each week) in which they coordinated policy for their media holdings.

Mike Cowles was sometimes described as affable but irresolute, as well as restless and creative. Dale Kramer, writing for the *New Republic* (1 December 1947), commented, "As an executive he is something like a prince who neither knows nor cares much about ruling. The result is that he is condescending toward his minor subjects, and indecisive and captious with top advisers. . . . Mike has trouble making up his mind and avoids personal collisions."

After a lengthy period of planning and experimentation, which began during World War II, Cowles began publishing *Quick,* a pocket picture-news magazine, measuring about four by six inches, in 1949. *Newsweek* called the new ten-cent weekly magazine an "ultra-abbreviated news digest . . . which dehydrates the news into capsule summaries." The motto of *Quick* seemed to be, "You give us six sentences, we'll give you the world." Its first, sixty-eight-page issue covered most news items in just one sentence each. *Quick* and the other miniature picture-news magazines that appeared briefly in the 1950s were in some ways a natural outgrowth of earlier efforts to condense text (as in *Time*) or visual presentation of news (as in *Life* and *Look*).

The somewhat sudden appearance of *Quick* in 1949 may have been due to the fact that early that year the owner of a small Baltimore advertising agency, S. J. Lichtman, sent to several magazines (including *Newsweek, Time,* and *Look*) a proposal for a news weekly with a tiny format to include pictures and very short stories covering news of the week. Lichtman claimed he sold the idea to Cowles on a cash-and-retainer basis, with the only change being the name Cowles gave the magazine. Cowles said the basic idea was his, although his own plan had been to have a slightly larger format, closer to that of *Reader's Digest.* Within the first three months Cowles claimed a circulation of five hundred thousand for his new venture (about 35 percent below the break-even point needed without advertising). Just as he had done with *Look,* Cowles did not accept advertising for *Quick* until he was sure of its circulation. Advertising began appearing in seven pages of the news weekly in January 1950, but it was difficult to attract advertisers to an off-size magazine in an era when most magazines were standardizing their sizes to reduce advertising-production costs. Critical reactions to *Quick* generally stated that its news summaries were too abbreviated. After four years, during which production costs outstripped income, Cowles folded the magazine with the 1 June 1953 issue. By then circulation had reached more than one million, still too small to justify separate printing plates, according to most potential advertisers. (Walter Annenberg, publisher of *TV Guide,* bought the *Quick* title from Cowles in 1953 and published it briefly in a larger format as a biweekly without advertising. He gave it up in March 1954, although others began using the title in conjunction with their own publications – as in the case of *Tempo* and *Quick.*)

On 27 December 1946 Cowles married Fleur Fenton, his third wife. His first marriage, to Helen Curtiss of Ames, Iowa, daughter of an Iowa State University professor, lasted from 5 November 1926 until about one year later. His second marriage was to Lois Thornburg, on 17 May 1933. He had met her when she was a student in a journalism class he taught at the University of Iowa. Afterward she was a reporter on his staff at the *Register.* The couple had three children, Lois (born in 1934), Gardner (born circa 1937), and Kate (born circa 1941). The couple divorced on 29 August 1946. (According to some sources, they had a third daughter, who was retarded and who died in a mental institution at age eighteen.)

Fleur Cowles, whom Dale Kramer described in the *New Republic* as "a successful and slightly fabulous advertising executive," had been co-owner (with her first husband, Atherton Pettingill) and executive vice-president of the Dorland International Pettingill and Fenton Advertising Agency from 1936 to 1946. She was a woman of high energy and strong will. In a 1949 *Time* interview she described herself as "rough, uncut, and vigorous" – comparing herself to the large, Russian emerald ring she frequently wore. S. J. Perelman satirized her reputedly capricious and vindictive management style in a 1 July 1950 article in the *New Yorker*. She began working at *Look* early in 1946 as creator of the women's department. She contrasted *Life* and *Look* by describing the former as an "example of glittering objective reporting." She introduced sections on food, fashion, and family problems and served on the executive editorial board. In 1947 she became associate editor of *Look* and later was made associate editor of *Quick*. In the early 1950s she was the only woman on the board of directors of Cowles Magazines.

Fleur Cowles was at the center of planning for the magazine *Flair*, which appeared in January 1950. Her advertising agency had specialized in selling expensive clothes and luxury cars, a background that she felt equipped her to shepherd the development and marketing of the new magazine. Former *Esquire* editor Arnold Gingrich was hired in January 1949 as general manager for *Flair*. An editorial office opened in Paris. Mrs. Cowles served as editor and, from April to June 1949, she worked with associate editor George Davis to create a one-hundred-page-magazine prototype of what would be a lavishly pictorial, elegant fifty-cent monthly (five dollars per year by subscription), designed to cover fashion, literature, travel, art, decor, and entertainment for an upper-middle-class audience.

Innovative production methods for what Mrs. Cowles called the "spectacularly different, completely unconventional" *Flair* included a new method of binding that eliminated staples and permitted pages to lie flat (thus making all facing pages seem to be centerfolds), pages differing in size and texture, and a double cover that gave viewers a preview of the full picture on the second cover. The sample issue unveiled in September 1949 also had an accordion-style pullout on interior decoration, a pocket-sized book insert, a swatch of cotton fabric, and a page written in invisible ink that could be read when heated by a lighted match. Some of these techniques were used in early issues of the magazine when it began regular publication. These expensive production techniques and the decline of similar class magazines caused some magazine publishers to be skeptical of *Flair* even before its first issue. Their judgment was sustained when *Flair* was discontinued after its thirteenth issue (dated January 1951) appeared in December 1950. Although the magazine had reached a circulation of approximately two hundred thousand copies per issue, it carried only 180 pages of advertising during the entire year.

Mike and Fleur Fenton Cowles were divorced in 1955; she left her position at *Look* at the same time. On 1 May 1956 Cowles married Jan Streate Cox, former wife of James Cox of the Cox newspaper family. Mike and Jan Cowles had one daughter, Virginia (born circa 1959).

In spring 1959 Cowles began *Insider's Newsletter*, a kind of private weekly report to subscribers, which sold for eighteen dollars per year and promised to take no more than twelve minutes a week to read. By mid 1962 it was published in two versions – "For Him" and "For Her" – and had more than one hundred thousand subscribers. Five years later, with circulation at 190,000, profits from the newsletter were so small that increased postal and printing costs forced Cowles to discontinue it.

Also in 1959 Cowles founded the *San Juan Star*, the only English-language daily in Puerto Rico. It won a Pulitzer Prize for editorial writing in 1961 and was running at a profit by 1962. (Cowles was a member of the Pulitzer Prize Advisory Board from 1947 to 1958.)

In 1960 Cowles's broadcasting stations and magazines were combined into Cowles Magazines and Broadcasting, the predecessor to Cowles Communications. In 1961 company stock began to be traded publicly. By the time Cowles bought his next magazine, *Family Circle*, in 1962, he also owned another newspaper, the *Gainesville* (Florida) *Sun;* a television station; an encyclopedia company; and a system of magazine subscription/distribution agencies in addition to his other media holdings. He also controlled a Florida land company.

When it was founded in 1932, *Family Circle* was one of the earliest store-distributed magazines in the country. (Store-distributed magazines such as *Family Circle* were sold to the food companies and shipped to their warehouses just like any other product, then sent to each store – a very efficient and economical system as compared with subscription-

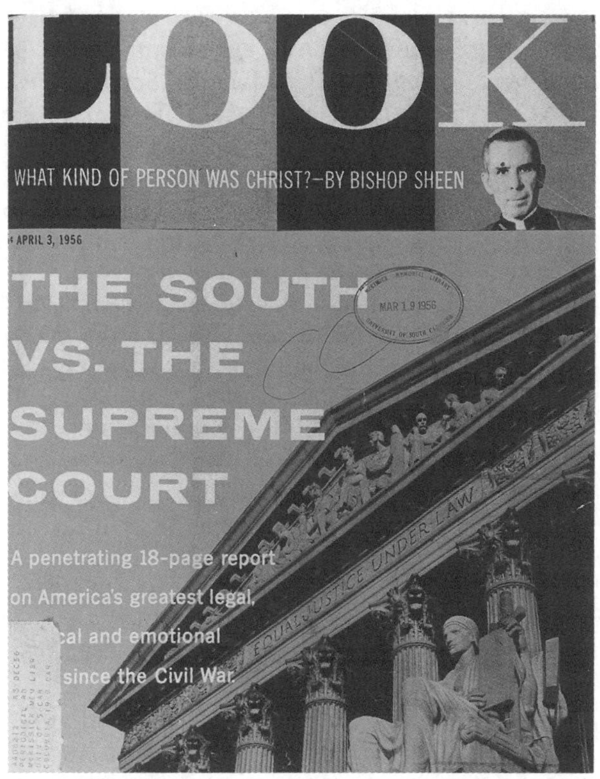

Cover and page from a 1956 issue of Cowles's pictorial magazine featuring a report on racial segregation in the United States

based circulations.) As a women's service magazine *Family Circle* was in one of the most competitive magazine categories of the early 1960s. But its attractions to Cowles were obvious: it had always been profitable; with a monthly circulation of seven million in 1962 it had the largest single-copy sales of any magazine; and it sold in supermarkets, thus eliminating the costs associated with increasing and keeping subscriptions. In 1966, however, *Family Circle* suffered a 10 percent drop in advertising revenue. Cowles responded by cutting circulation and raising the magazine's price, but critics complained that the real changes needed to come from improved editorial content. By 1970 *Family Circle* was operating again at a profit.

When *Collier's* magazine died in 1956, Cowles Magazines bought the title and unexpired subscriptions, hoping to pick up a million new subscribers for *Look. Woman's Home Companion,* the other Crowell-Collier magazine, folded at the same time, and Cowles Magazines bought the company's subscription-selling subsidiary and its educational division. By 1962 the circulation of *Look* was at 7.3 million, making it fourth in circulation among U.S. magazines (after *Reader's Digest, TV Guide,* and *McCall's*). Credit for its growth and continued success was often given to Cowles's unusual ability in the mass-magazine arena to achieve circulation growth by sometimes exhaustive editorial coverage of issues and to promote the increased circulation to advertisers while increasing advertising rates. The highest annual average circulation for *Look,* 7.75 million, was achieved in 1967; the best advertising year was 1966, when total revenues for the magazine were $80 million.

In the post–World War II era at *Look,* when Cowles worked hard to make it a more serious, ambitious magazine than its sensational early issues, the magazine published some significant pieces on national and international affairs, including an interview by Elliott Roosevelt with Joseph Stalin in 1947, an issue on "The South v. the Supreme Court" in 1956, and "The Blacks and the Whites" in 1969. The magazine produced dramatic and timely stories on Vietnam and poverty in the United States. *Look* frequently purchased first serial rights to books and thus helped contribute to the popularity of such books as William Shirer's *Rise and Fall of the Third Reich* (1960). In 1967 the magazine serialized William Manchester's *The Death of a President* (1967), over the objections of Robert Kennedy and Jacqueline Kennedy Onassis. *Look* achieved its record circulation of 9.5 million with the publication of the four installments from

Manchester's book. The last issue of *Look,* in 1971, featured an excerpt from Allen Drury's *Inside the White House,* and it bought, but did not survive long enough to run, excerpts from Lyndon B. Johnson's memoirs, *The Vantage Point: Perspectives of the Presidency, 1963–1969* (1971). When Cowles turned eighty, more than a decade after the demise of *Look,* he told a *New York Times* reporter, "I'm very proud of the fact that *Look* devoted pages and pages to trying to improve relations with blacks, which I think is almost the No. 1 problem in the country. . . . I'm also proud that *Look* was first among national magazines to come out for birth control, for which we were roundly criticized."

Venture, Cowles's travel magazine, began in 1964. Initial plans called for limiting its circulation to 250,000 and restricting subscriptions to American Express credit-card holders. Circulation was expanded, however, and the magazine remained a successful part of the company until the breakup of Cowles Communications in 1971.

According to some industry analysts, Cowles Communications reached its peak, both in number of properties owned and in earnings (almost $4 million on revenues of $150 million) in 1966. In that year the company bought Magazines for Industry (MFI), publisher of eight business magazines, for an estimated $2.5 million. The specialized publications included, for example, journals in the fields of bottling, glass, candy, ice cream, and packaging. Don Gussow, owner of MFI, had studied media corporations carefully when he decided to sell his magazine group, and Cowles had been his first choice for a company that would buy MFI and make it the nucleus of a business-magazine division that Gussow himself would run. At first Cowles's diversification strategy seemed to be working. By 1968 the company was publishing twenty special-interest magazines. Gussow's dream turned into a nightmare, however, as Cowles Communications went into a swift decline in the late 1960s. Three years after Cowles purchased MFI, a bitter, disillusioned Gussow bought his company back, hoping to salvage it.

Also in 1966 Cowles purchased from Sunrise Newspapers the circulation and advertising lists (but not the printing plants) of three small, weekly newspapers in Suffolk County, New York (the *Babylon Town-Leader, Bay Shore Sentinel,* and *Islip Press*), with the intention of closing them to form a new daily, the *Suffolk Sun.* The *Sun,* pitted against Long Island's *Newsday,* lost approximately $15 million during its three-year-existence and was shut down in October 1969. Cowles reportedly regarded the *Sun* as his biggest mistake in publishing, a mistake exacerbated by the economic recession at the end of the 1960s.

In 1967 Cowles Communications announced plans to publish a biweekly education magazine, *Education News,* directed to administrators of public and private schools. By 1968 Cowles's broadcast holdings were in Des Moines, Memphis, and Daytona Beach, and he also owned a newspaper in Lakeland, Florida.

By 1970 Cowles Communications consisted of *Look* and two other magazines, five television and radio stations, three newspapers, thirty-two business and professional magazines, and two book-publishing companies, but *Look* was in trouble. The magazine had had acute financial problems during the preceding year and in 1970 suffered a series of high-level defections from its editorial staff, including the departure of editor in chief William Attwood, who left the magazine to become publisher of *Newsday,* and executive editor Patricia Carbine, who left to become editorial director of *McCall's.* In all about sixty staff members quit or were fired from the magazine in 1970; the San Francisco office was closed; and plans were made to cut circulation from 7.7 million to 6.5 million (with a corresponding advertising-rate cut). For the first time in more than two decades, the magazine lost money.

To replenish his reserves, Cowles sold the successful *San Juan Star* for $11 million to the Scripps-Howard chain during the summer of 1970. On 14 September, when the crisis seemed resolved, Cowles was quoted in *Newsweek* as saying, "There *is* a place for the mass general magazine in the future, particularly if it's a magazine of personal advocacy, of in-depth investigation of the issues that affect us all – a magazine like *Look.* Sometimes we've annoyed readers from the less urbanized parts of the country, but often we've made an impact there. If *Look* should ever become bland, it'll die – and I won't let that happen. . . . Any time you get a wave of gossip about mass magazines being in trouble, and then an economy drive gets going, a lot of people below the top level get anxious. But that is all behind us. I do not foresee any more economy cuts. We've done what we've had to do. . . . My heart is in *Look* – it's my baby. I founded it 33 years ago. I'd sell everything to keep it going." He almost did just that.

A few weeks later Cowles sold some of his most profitable holdings to keep his company alive. In late October 1970 Cowles and *New York Times* publisher Arthur Ochs "Punch" Sulzberger announced a "friendly swap" in which Cowles Com-

Cover for the issue featuring the first installment of an early account of the assassination of President John F. Kennedy

munications acquired approximately $50 million in *Times* stock (about 23 percent of the newspaper's common stock), and the *Times* took over Cowles's $15 million debt. The Times Company also gained *Family Circle;* Cowles's Memphis television station (WREC-TV); three small Florida newspapers (the *Lakeland Ledger, Gainesville Sun,* and *Ocala Star-Banner*); the Cambridge Book Company, which published textbooks; and the Modern Medicine group of seven professional magazines in the medical, dental, and nursing fields. The deal left Cowles debt free and also gave him a seat on the board of directors of the Times Company. He remarked at the time, "I have no thought of disposing of anything else, and certainly, no intention of selling *Look*" (*Newsweek,* 9 November 1970). A few months later he sold Cowles Book Company to the Henry Regnery Company of Chicago. Cowles's company fit well with the general trade and juvenile emphasis of Regnery. The travel magazine *Venture* ceased publication with its July–August 1971 issue; Cowles's *Comprehensive Encyclopedia* had already been sold to the Los Angeles Times-Mirror Company.

The protracted, extraordinary efforts to keep *Look* alive came to an end with the 19 October 1971 issue. Rising production costs, the recession of the late 1960s and early 1970s, and television's drain on magazine advertising revenues all contributed to the magazine's demise, but when he announced the impending suspension of *Look* in September 1971, Cowles cited a planned increase in second-class postal rates as the determining element in his decision to terminate his "baby." The rate increase would have more than doubled the postal bill of *Look,* from $4 million to $10 million in a five-year period. After more than two decades of profitability, *Look* lost approximately $10 million in its last two years of existence, and with no turnaround in sight Cowles was trying to cut his losses before the magazine became further mired in debt. About 260 editorial and advertising staff members lost their jobs when *Look* folded, along with 800 personnel at the subscription center in Des Moines (the center itself was subsequently sold to Time).

At least one insider blamed Cowles himself, however, for the decline of both *Look* and Cowles Communications. MFI owner Gussow argued in his 1972 account of the decline that the diversification program in the 1960s was ill conceived, that the company was poorly managed, and that the docile board of directors simply rubber-stamped what he considered to be Cowles's impulsive, shortsighted decisions.

The death of *Look* left Cowles Communications with four radio stations, three television stations, a small marketing service, a three-dimensional photography venture (Xograph), and a contract to produce *Travel News* for the American Society of Travel Agents. Cowles remained president of the *Des Moines Register* and *Tribune.* He also continued to own two small papers, in Leesburg and Palatka, Florida. (In February 1979 *Look* was revived briefly by *Paris Match* publisher Daniel Filipacchi, but it ceased publication again with the August issue in the same year.)

Cowles served in a wide variety of organizations during his career. By the early 1940s he had been director of the Bakers Life Company and of the Iowa–Des Moines National Bank and Trust Company, president of the Gardner Cowles Foundation, a trustee of Drake University, a member of the Des Moines Chamber of Commerce and the Harvard Fund Council, treasurer of the Des Moines Public Welfare Bureau (1931–1933), and board member of the American Society of Newspaper Editors. He was at one time a director of United Air Lines. He was a pleasant companion with a good sense of humor and was regarded as a good raconteur, especially when the subject was a famous person. He was known to smoke any brand of ciga-

Cowles and his brother John

rette, and he enjoyed Scotch. His chief hobbies as a young man were airplane piloting, golf, and squash. He was also self-effacing and shy. He spoke in a monotone, slowly and deliberately, partly to compensate for a painful stuttering problem, which affected him into late middle age.

Cowles received honorary LL.D. degrees from Drake University (1942), Coe College (1948), Long Island University (1955), Grinnell College (1957), and the Colleges of Hobart and William Smith (1968). He received honorary L.H.D. degrees from Bard College (1950), Cornell College (1951), and Mundelein College (1968); honorary Litt.D. degrees from Iowa Wesleyan College (1955) and Morningside College (1958); and an honorary Sc.D. degree from Simpson College in Indianola, Iowa (1955). He also served on many university boards of trustees during his lifetime, including those of Harvard University, Columbia University Teachers College, the University of Miami, and Drake University.

After *Look* folded in 1971, Cowles gradually gave up his business responsibilities. In 1978 he tried to dissolve Cowles Communications, but the process was slowed because of the potential tax problems involved in the liquidation. It took until 1981 to complete the dissolution. By then Cowles no longer owned any stock in either the Minneapolis or Des Moines family operations. As part of the dissolution, New York Times Company stock was dispersed to Cowles Communications stockholders. In the end all that was left was the broadcasting subsidiary – with Cowles as a principal shareholder – headquartered in Daytona Beach, Florida. This company owned two television stations, one each in Daytona Beach (WESH) and Des Moines (KCCI).

Also in 1981 the Minneapolis and Des Moines branches of the Cowles family empire announced plans to merge. The proposed merger was aborted, however, reportedly because executives of the *Register* and *Tribune* believed the Des Moines holdings would suffer from a merger with the larger Minneapolis group. Shortly before Cowles died in 1985, the Register and Tribune Company was sold to the Gannett Company, leaving Cowles Media, the company formed around the family's Minneapolis newspapers, as the only remaining branch of the family empire.

By the late 1970s Cowles was giving most of his attention to the Cowles Charitable Trust, which had a net worth of $11 million and which gave out approximately $250,000 a year to what he called "fairly conventional" causes, such as museums and colleges. In his last years Cowles suffered from cancer, and on 8 July 1985 he died of cardiac arrest in a hospital near his summer home in Southampton, Long Island.

During his professional career Gardner ("Mike") Cowles, Jr., used his initiative and talent to develop a prominent twentieth-century media conglomerate. In just a few decades he saw it reach its apex, then plummet and decline precipitously until the work of three generations, beginning with his father, was irreversibly scattered. He took risks in magazine publishing, many of which did not succeed. The most successful of them, however, *Look,* fulfilled Cowles's highest – and sometimes not consistently followed – ideal, namely to create a publication that would simultaneously inform and entertain a mass audience about issues of national and international significance.

References:

"Between Friends," *Newsweek,* 76 (9 November 1970): 69;

"The Cash in the Register," *Newsweek,* 104 (26 November 1984): 74;

"The Cowles Boys," *Newsweek,* 34 (4 July 1949): 52+;

"Cowles Buys 10 Magazines and 3 Weekly Newspapers," *Publishers Weekly,* 190 (19 September 1966): 46;

"Cowles Consolidates to Survive," *Business Week* (7 December 1981): 100–101;

"Cowles Empire – A Magazine Phenomenon," *Business Week* (8 October 1949): 26+;

"Cowles Finds Running Mate for Look," *Business Week* (15 September 1962): 33–34;

"Cowles: Iowa Publishers Hitch Evening Star to Their Wagon," *Newsweek,* 5 (29 June 1935): 22;

"Cowles of the Times," *Time,* 96 (9 November 1970): 41;

"Cowles to Publish New Education Magazine," *Library Journal,* 92 (15 May 1967): 1985;

"The Cowles World," *Time,* 72 (8 December 1958): 55+;

"Dynasty in Radio," *Business Week* (4 November 1944): 81–84;

"Fleur's *Flair,*" *Newsweek,* 34 (12 September 1949): 59;

"Fleur's *Flair,*" *Time,* 54 (12 September 1949): 63;

William Barry Furlong, "The Cowles Empire Expands," *Saturday Review,* 51 (11 May 1968): 71–73;

"Girl with Roses," *Time,* 55 (30 January 1950): 57;

Don Gussow, *Divorce Corporate Style* (New York: Ballantine, 1972);

"Inside Look," *Newsweek,* 76 (14 September 1970): 73–74;

"Iowa Formula," *Time,* 26 (1 July 1935): 26+;

N. R. Kleinfield, "Looking Back at Look," *New York Times,* February 1983, p. F6;

Dale Kramer, "Don't Made 'Em Mad," *New Republic,* 117 (1 December 1947): 19–23;

"The Last *Look,*" *Time,* 98 (27 September 1971): 55;

"Look Homeward," *Newsweek,* 28 (9 December 1946): 71–72;

"Look, No Fringe," *Time,* 48 (9 December 1946): 47;

"*Look* Suspends Publication after 34 Years," *Publishers Weekly,* 200 (27 September 1971): 42–43;

George Mills, *Harvey Ingham and Gardner Cowles, Sr.: Things Don't Just Happen* (Ames: Iowa State University Press, 1977);

Thomas Moore, "Trouble and Strife in the Cowles Empire," *Fortune,* 107 (4 April 1983): 156–158+;

S. J. Perelman, "The Hand that Cradles the Rock," *New Yorker,* 26 (1 July 1950): 20–22;

Theodore Peterson, *Magazines in the Twentieth Century* (Urbana: University of Illinois Press, 1964);

"Regnery, Chicago Firm, Buys Cowles Book Company," *Publishers Weekly,* 199 (8 March 1971): 49;

"Times Acquiring Substantial Cowles Properties," *Publishers Weekly,* 198 (9 November 1970): 34;

"What Finally Crippled the Cowles Empire," *Business Week* (25 September 1971): 122–123+;

Lewis H. Young, "Inside the Boardroom," *Business Week* (13 May 1972): 16+.

Papers:

Cowles's papers are in the Cowles Library at Drake University, Des Moines, Iowa.

Frederic Dannay

(20 October 1905 – 3 September 1982)

and

Manfred B. Lee

(11 January 1905 – 3 April 1971)

(Ellery Queen)

Garyn G. Roberts
Michigan State University

MAJOR POSITIONS HELD (jointly by Dannay and Lee, as Ellery Queen): Editors, *Mystery League* (1933–1934); writers, *Adventures of Ellery Queen* [radio series] (1939–1948); editors, *Ellery Queen's Mystery Magazine* (1941–1971).

BOOKS: *The Roman Hat Mystery* (New York: Stokes, 1929; London: Gollancz, 1929);

The French Powder Mystery (New York: Stokes, 1930; London: Gollancz, 1930);

The Dutch Shoe Mystery (New York: Stokes, 1931; London: Gollancz, 1931);

The Greek Coffin Mystery (New York: Stokes, 1932; London: Gollancz, 1932);

The Egyptian Cross Mystery (New York: Stokes, 1932; London: Gollancz, 1933);

The Tragedy of X, by Dannay and Lee together as Barnaby Ross (New York: Viking, 1932; London: Cassell, 1932);

The Tragedy of Y, by Dannay and Lee together as Barnaby Ross (New York: Viking, 1932; London: Cassell, 1932);

The American Gun Mystery (New York: Stokes, 1933; London: Gollancz, 1933); republished as *Death at the Rodeo* (New York: Spivak, 1951);

The Siamese Twin Mystery (New York: Stokes, 1933; London: Gollancz, 1934);

The Tragedy of Z, by Dannay and Lee together as Barnaby Ross (New York: Viking, 1933; London: Cassell, 1933);

Drury Lane's Last Case, by Dannay and Lee together as Barnaby Ross (New York: Viking, 1933; London: Cassell, 1933);

The Chinese Orange Mystery (New York: Stokes, 1934; London: Gollancz, 1934);

The Adventures of Ellery Queen (New York: Stokes, 1934; London: Gollancz, 1935);

The Spanish Cape Mystery (New York: Stokes, 1935; London: Gollancz, 1935);

Halfway House (New York: Stokes, 1936; London: Gollancz, 1936);

The Door Between (New York: Stokes, 1937; London: Gollancz, 1937);

The Devil to Pay (New York: Stokes, 1938; London: Gollancz, 1938);

Ellery Queen's Big Book (New York: Grosset & Dunlap, 1938);

The Four of Hearts (New York: Stokes, 1938; London: Gollancz, 1939);

The Dragon's Teeth (New York: Stokes, 1939; London: Gollancz, 1939); republished as *The Virgin Heiress* (New York: Pocket Books, 1954);

The New Adventures of Ellery Queen (New York: Stokes, 1940; London: Gollancz, 1940; revised as *More Adventures of Ellery Queen* (New York: Spivak, 1940);

Calamity Town (Boston: Little, Brown, 1942; London: Gollancz, 1942);

The Detective Short Story: A Bibliography (Boston: Little, Brown, 1942);

There Was an Old Woman (Boston: Little, Brown, 1943; London: Gollancz, 1944); republished as *The Quick and the Dead* (New York: Pocket Books, 1956);

Ellery Queen's Mystery Parade (Cleveland: World, 1944);

Manfred Lee and Frederic Dannay, circa 1942 (Courtesy of Graphic House, Inc.)

The Murderer Is a Fox (Boston: Little, Brown, 1945; London: Gollancz, 1945);

The Case Book of Ellery Queen (New York: Spivak, 1945);

Ten Days' Wonder (Boston: Little, Brown, 1948; London: Gollancz, 1948);

The Case Book of Ellery Queen (London: Gollancz, 1949);

Cat of Many Tails (Boston: Little, Brown, 1949; London: Gollancz, 1949);

Double, Double (Boston: Little, Brown, 1950; London: Gollancz, 1950); republished as *The Case of the Seven Murders* (New York: Pocket Books, 1958);

The Origin of Evil (Boston: Little, Brown, 1951; London: Gollancz, 1951);

Queen's Quorum: A History of the Detective-Crime Short Story as Revealed by the 106 Most Important Books Published in This Field Since 1845 (Boston: Little, Brown, 1951; London: Gollancz, 1953; revised edition, New York: Biblo & Tannen, 1969);

The King Is Dead (Boston: Little, Brown, 1952; London: Gollancz, 1952);

Calendar of Crime (Boston: Little, Brown, 1952; London: Gollancz, 1952);

The Golden Summer, by Dannay as Daniel Nathan (Boston: Little, Brown, 1953);

The Scarlet Letters (Boston: Little, Brown, 1953; London: Gollancz, 1953);

The Glass Village (Boston: Little, Brown, 1954; London: Gollancz, 1954);

QBI: Queen's Bureau of Investigation (Boston: Little, Brown, 1954; London: Gollancz, 1955);

Inspector Queen's Own Case (New York: Simon & Schuster, 1956; London: Gollancz, 1956);

The Wrightsville Murders (Boston: Little, Brown, 1956);

The Hollywood Murders (Philadelphia: Lippincott, 1957);

In the Queen's Parlor, and Other Leaves from the Editors' Notebook (New York: Simon & Schuster, 1957; London: Gollancz, 1957);

The Finishing Stroke (New York: Simon & Schuster, 1958; London: Gollancz, 1958);

The New York Murders (Boston: Little, Brown, 1958);
The Bizarre Murders (Philadelphia: Lippincott, 1962);
The Player on the Other Side (New York: Random House, 1963; London: Gollancz, 1963);
And on the Eighth Day (New York: Random House, 1964; London: Gollancz, 1964);
Queens Full (New York: Random House, 1965; London: Gollancz, 1966);
The Fourth Side of the Triangle (New York: Random House, 1965; London: Gollancz, 1965);
Ellery Queen's International Case Book (New York: Dell, 1964);
A Study in Terror (New York: Lancer, 1966); republished as *Sherlock Holmes Versus Jack the Ripper* (London: Gollancz, 1967);
The Woman in the Case (New York: Bantam, 1966); republished as *Deadlier Than the Male* (London: Corgi, 1967);
Face to Face (New York: New American Library, 1967; London: Gollancz, 1967);
QED: Queen's Experiments in Detection (New York: New American Library, 1968; London: Gollancz, 1969);
Cop Out (Cleveland: World, 1969; London: Gollancz, 1969);
The Last Woman in His Life (Cleveland: World, 1970; London: Gollancz, 1970);
A Fine and Private Place (Cleveland: World, 1971; London: Gollancz, 1971).

PLAY PRODUCTION: *Danger, Men Working,* by Dannay, Lee, and Lowell Brentano, Baltimore and Philadelphia, 1936.

MOTION PICTURE: *Ellery Queen, Master Detective,* screenplay by Dannay, Lee, and Eric Taylor, Columbia, 1940.

OTHER: *Challenge to the Reader,* edited by Dannay and Lee (New York: Stokes, 1938);
101 Years' Entertainment: The Great Detective Stories 1841–1941, edited by Dannay and Lee (Boston: Little, Brown, 1941; revised edition, New York: Modern Library, 1946);
The Misadventures of Sherlock Holmes, edited by Dannay and Lee (Boston: Little, Brown, 1944);
Best Stories from Ellery Queen's Mystery Magazine, edited by Dannay and Lee (Roslyn, N.Y.: Detective Book Club, 1944);
To the Queen's Taste: The First Supplement to 101 Years' Entertainment, Consisting of the Best Stories Published in the First Five Years of Ellery Queen's Mystery Magazine, edited by Dannay and Lee (Boston: Little, Brown, 1946; London: Faber, 1949);

Dust jacket for Dannay and Lee's 1933 book with a photograph of Lee wearing his "EQ mask"

The Queen's Awards [annual story collection], edited by Dannay and Lee (Boston: Little, Brown, 1946–1955; London: Gollancz, 1948–1955; New York: Simon & Schuster, 1956–1957; London: Collins, 1956–1959); series continued as *Mystery Annuals* (New York: Random House, 1958–1961; London: Collins, 1960–1961; London: Gollancz, 1961–1962);
20th Century Detective Stories, edited by Dannay and Lee (Cleveland: World, 1948; revised edition, New York: Popular Library, 1964);
The Literature of Crime: Stories by World-Famous Authors, edited by Dannay and Lee (Boston: Little, Brown, 1950; London: Cassell, 1952); republished as *Ellery Queen's Book of Mystery Stories* (London: Pan, 1957);
To Be Read Before Midnight, edited by Dannay and Lee (New York: Random House, 1962; London: Gollancz, 1963);
Mystery Mix, edited by Dannay and Lee (New York: Random House, 1963; London: Gollancz, 1964);

Cover for a 1952 issue of Dannay and Lee's magazine

Double Dozen, edited by Dannay and Lee (New York: Random House, 1964; London: Gollancz, 1965);

20th Anniversary Annual, edited by Dannay and Lee (New York: Random House, 1965; London: Gollancz, 1966);

Crime Carousel, edited by Dannay and Lee (New York: New American Library, 1966; London: Gollancz, 1967);

All-Star Lineup, edited by Dannay and Lee (New York: New American Library, 1966; London: Gollancz, 1968);

Mystery Parade, edited by Dannay and Lee (New York: New American Library, 1968; London: Gollancz, 1969);

Murder Menu, edited by Dannay and Lee (Cleveland: World, 1969; London: Gollancz, 1969);

Grand Slam, edited by Dannay and Lee (Cleveland: World, 1970; London: Gollancz, 1971);

Headliners, edited by Dannay and Lee (Cleveland: World, 1971; London: Gollancz, 1972);

The Golden 13: 13 First Prize Winners from Ellery Queen's Mystery Magazine, edited by Dannay and Lee (Cleveland: World, 1971; London: Gollancz, 1972);

Mystery Bag, edited by Dannay and Lee (Cleveland: World, 1972; London: Gollancz, 1973);

Crookbook, edited by Dannay and Lee (New York: Random House, 1974; London: Gollancz, 1974);

Murdercade, edited by Dannay and Lee (New York: Random House, 1975; London: Gollancz, 1976);

Crime Wave, edited by Dannay and Lee (New York: Putnam, 1976; London: Gollancz, 1976);

Searches and Seizures, edited by Dannay and Lee (New York: Davis, 1977);

A Multitude of Sins, edited by Dannay and Lee (New York: Davis, 1978);

Circumstantial Evidence, edited by Dannay and Lee (New York: Davis, 1980);

Crime Cruise round the World, edited by Dannay and Lee (New York: Davis, 1981);

The Best of Ellery Queen, edited by Dannay (London: Hale, 1983).

Dannay and Lee in 1967 (Courtesy of Marc and Evelyn Bernheim)

Ellery Queen was the pseudonym of cousins and collaborators Frederic Dannay and Manfred B. Lee and the name of detective they created. As Queen, they wrote mystery novels and edited two magazines and many story collections during a period of approximately forty years. They also wrote original radio plays under that name and about that character. The cousins were both born in Brooklyn in 1905, and their initial collaborative work as Queen was undertaken in 1928, when Dannay was a copywriter and art director for a Manhattan advertising agency and Lee was a publicity agent for the New York branch of a film studio. That first collaboration was *The Roman Hat Mystery*. Dannay and Lee had responded to a contest sponsored by *McClure's* which offered a prize of seventy-five hundred dollars for the best detective novel submitted. Their manuscript won the contest, but *McClure's* went bankrupt (the assets being bought out by *Smart Set*), and the cousins never collected their prize. However the next year, 1929, found their novel accepted for publication in hardcover by the reputable Frederick A. Stokes Company of New York. Dannay's experience in advertising might have inspired the idea to make the pseudonym of the authors and the name of their series sleuth the same. Whatever the case, the idea was a stroke of genius. Books by and about Ellery Queen sold well from the start.

Frederic Dannay was born Daniel Nathan in Brooklyn on 20 October 1905 and grew up in Elmira, New York. He was educated at Boy's High School in Brooklyn. Manfred Bennington Lee was the older of the pair by ten months. Like Dannay, he was born in Brooklyn and was educated at Boy's High School and like Dannay, changed his original Jewish name. Lee was born Manford Lepofsky. Dannay was married three times: to Mary Beck (1926), with whom he had two sons; to Hilda Wisenthal (1947), with whom he had one son; and to Rose Koppel (1975). Lee married former radio actress Kaye Brinker in 1942. They had four daughters and four sons.

In their *101 Years' Entertainment: The Great Detective Stories 1841–1941* (1941) Dannay and Lee reinforced the common belief that Edgar Allan Poe

Dannay in 1973 (courtesy of Santi Visalli)

and his early stories of French detective C. Auguste Dupin represented the origins of the classic detective-story formula. Other sources celebrate other authors, characters, and stories. Most agree that Sir Arthur Conan Doyle's tales of Sherlock Holmes provided the archetype or fundamental model for what constituted the classical detective. In the 1920s England provided the enduring detective-fiction authors Agatha Christie, Margery Allingham, Dorothy Sayers, John Dickson Carr, and others. However, in American detective fiction of that decade, S. S. Van Dine (the pseudonym of Willard Huntington Wright), with his stories of Philo Vance, was the dominant figure. The early Ellery Queen stories are most like the tales of Van Dine.

During the first four stages in the development of Queen, Dannay and Lee modeled their sleuth most closely after the likes of Vance. (Francis Nevins, Jr., elucidates the four distinct periods in his *Royal Bloodline: Ellery Queen, Author and Detective,* [1974].) Hence, Queen in *The Roman Hat Mystery* is brilliant and often arrogant, much like Vance. The classic tradition in which Ellery Queen, author and detective, emerged is today, for all practical purposes, extinct. The stories from this mystery formula center around the solution of a puzzle presented in the form of a crime perpetuated in limited confines such as a locked room, with a fixed number of suspects and helpless characters alike who are held accountable for, and saved from, the evil by the one person of extreme intelligence in the story capable of the puzzle's solution – the detective hero. These locked-room mysteries are best described as puzzles and follow a rigid pattern. Authors are bound by an unwritten code, which says the writer must play fair with the reader. The allure of these stories is found in the solution as opposed to the action of hard-boiled mystery fiction, such as that by Dashiell Hammett and Raymond Chandler.

In the stories by Dannay and Lee, Ellery Queen is a professional mystery writer and amateur sleuth who works with his father, Inspector Richard Queen, whenever the police need assistance solving a murder mystery. After three novels about Queen, the cousins developed another pseudonym, Barnaby Ross, and began a series of four mysteries about detective Drury Lane, a retired Shakespearean actor. The first of these novels was *The Tragedy of X* (1932). After *Drury Lane's Last Case* (1933) Queen was the detective of all the authors' novels and stories that followed, except the novels *The Glass Village* (1954) and *Cop Out* (1969) and the novelette *Terror Town* (1957). Nevins notes that the early Queen stories were rich in plot and character and were in this sense even superior to the earlier works of Van Dine. Bizarre circumstances, conflicting testimonies, and strange clues mark these early Queen works. In the best tradition of the classic detective story, each also presents the clues to the ultimate solution fairly, if trickily. *The Greek Coffin Mystery* and *The Egyptian Cross Mystery,* both from 1932, are prime examples of what the early exploits of Queen were all about.

By 1936 the Van Dine qualities of the Queen stories began to fade. Slick-paper magazines began to influence and prescribe form for the two cousins. The success and popularity of the novels of Dannay and Lee brought them movie contracts with Columbia, Paramount, and M-G-M. During the 1930s the pair worked in Hollywood but did not receive any screen credits until 1940. In 1939 they began scripting programs for what was to become their popular radio-mystery series, *The Adventures of Ellery Queen.* Detective Queen, during this second stage, began to become less arrogant and more human. In some instances he is found writing for the big screen, reflecting the experiences of Dannay and Lee. Nevins claims that most of the Queen stories that appeared in the late 1930s were thinly plotted and obviously designed for motion-picture adaptation. But Nevins adds that the best Queen book of the period, *The Four of Hearts* (1938), is a multifaceted discussion of Hollywood in its peak years. In the early 1940s Dannay and Lee's creative efforts were largely consumed by the burden of the weekly scripts for the radio series, which lasted until 1948.

In 1933 they began the first of their magazine-editing endeavors. The pair (particularly Dannay) had been interested in publishing a magazine to showcase a variety of mystery-fiction forms. In that year, they edited the first of a short-lived series titled *Mystery League.* After four issues the magazine was discontinued when the publisher went bankrupt. Progress on creative endeavors came to a standstill in 1940 while Dannay recovered from a near-fatal car accident. But in 1941 the pair published their *101 Years' Entertainment,* still considered the single most important overview of the mystery genre; the book was compiled from the editors' large collection of mystery fiction amassed over the years. In the fall of 1941 the cousins convinced Lawrence E. Spivak of Mercury Press to publish the first issue of *Ellery Queen's Mystery Magazine.*

Until his death in 1982, Dannay was the primary editor behind the project. In 1942 the cousins returned to writing and began the third distinguishable period in the Queen canon. That year saw the publication of *Calamity Town,* and, according to Nevins, the novel ushered in the richest period of writing by Dannay and Lee. During a sixteen-year time frame, they produced twelve novels, two short-story collections, and Dannay's autobiographical novel *The Golden Summer* (1953), written under his given name, Daniel Nathan. In-depth character developments, moods, and atmospheres mark the Queen stories from this period. Theological, historical, and psychological topics were explored, and the themes were reminiscent of *Alice in Wonderland,* the Bible, and Darwinian theory, claims Nevins. At the same time, in *Ellery Queen's Mystery Magazine,* Dannay was drawing from his extensive collection of mystery short stories for material for the new magazine. Early issues of *EQMM* reprinted obscure, hard-to-find mystery stories to which Dannay felt the public needed exposure, and stories by new talents Dannay felt were also worthy of public attention. Established authors submitted stories, and *EQMM* provided contests for all authors. There were thirteen annual contests in all, from 1946 to 1957 and in 1962.

The last Ellery Queen novel of the third period was *The Finishing Stroke* (1958), which recounts the life of the young detective after his first case, detailed in *The Roman Hat Mystery.* Dannay and Lee, from all practical appearances, intended on retiring from writing at this point. However, five years later the fourth period for Queen began with the publication of *The Player on the Other Side* (1963). The final Queen novel by the cousins was published in 1971, almost simultaneously with the death of Lee. It was titled *A Fine and Private Place.* Dannay wrote no novels after this point. The fourth period identified by Nevins was characterized by highly stylized plots and character types. Some early themes and motifs from the Queen canon were reused during this time. Lee's fatal heart attack marked the end of an era in mystery fiction and literature. Dannay carried on, until his final illness, as editor of *Ellery Queen's Mystery Magazine.* While several English talents excelled in the field of the classic mystery, Ellery Queen alone was seen by readers and critics as the supreme American practitioner of the form.

The magazine that emerged from the fertile imaginations and hard efforts of Dannay and Lee should not be underestimated in its significance to the genre. Virtually every mystery writer of importance had a story published in *EQMM* at one time or another. The editors had a flair for identifying and nurturing new talent and possessed a respectability that lured to *EQMM* established, famous authors – authors of mystery stories and nonmystery stories alike. According to Chris Steinbrunner and Otto Penzler, approximately thirty Pulitzer Prize and twelve Nobel Prize winners were published in the magazine. Among these were John Steinbeck, Sinclair Lewis, Bertrand Russell, and Pearl S. Buck. A noteworthy feature of *EQMM* was introductions or prefaces to the stories. These essays became an important body of early scholarship on the mystery genre; some were collected in the 1957 book *In the Queen's Parlor.*

Dannay and Lee (as Ellery Queen) were two of the premier anthologists in the history of the mystery story. Their *101 Years' Entertainment* may be the finest collection, but was only one of more than seventy such anthologies they edited. One of their most interesting, and now collectible, anthologies is the 1944 book *The Misadventures of Sherlock Holmes,* which has a variety of Holmes parodies and pastiches; it was suppressed quickly after publication because of fear of legal action by the estate of Doyle.

The novels, short stories, anthologies, radio plays, and the screenplay produced by Dannay and Lee as Queen were all timely and socially conscious. Within the confines of the mystery story, Dannay and Lee provided a forum in which issues of politics, theology, philosophy, and the nature of crime and punishment were addressed in an entertaining package. Dannay and Lee were educators and public speakers themselves, and they employed a story form that praised intelligence as the ultimate virtue. *Ellery Queen's Mystery Magazine* published stories – mysteries and nonmysteries alike – which addressed important social issues.

Good friends and collaborators from the start, the cousins did possess contrasting personalities. Dannay was best described as a quiet, scholarly, introverted perfectionist. Lee was aggressive, assertive, and explosive, according to Steinbrunner and Penzler; both Dannay and Lee believed that their clashing personalities actually improved their writing. Dannay once said, "We're not so much collaborators as competitors."

References:

Armchair Detective, special Ellery Queen issue, 12 (Summer 1979);

Elliot L. Gilbert, *The World of Mystery Fiction* (Bowling Green, Ohio: Bowling Green State University Popular Press, 1983);

Ron Goulart, *The Dime Detectives* (New York: Mysterious Press, 1988);

Ordean A. Hagen, *Who Done It?: A Guide to Detective, Mystery and Suspense Fiction* (New York: Bowker, 1969);

Francis M. Nevins, Jr., *Royal Bloodline: Ellery Queen, Author and Detective* (Bowling Green, Ohio: Bowling Green State University Popular Press, 1974);

Chris Steinbrunner and Otto Penzler, eds., *Encyclopedia of Mystery and Detection* (New York: McGraw-Hill, 1976).

Papers:

A collection of Dannay and Lee's manuscripts is held at the Harry Ransom Humanities Research Center, University of Texas at Austin.

Theodore Dreiser

(27 August 1871 - 28 December 1945)

Edd Applegate
Middle Tennessee State University

See also the Dreiser entries in *DLB 9: American Novelists, 1910–1945*; *DLB 12: American Realists and Naturalists*; and *DLB Documentary Series 1.*

MAJOR POSITIONS HELD: Editor, *Ev'ry Month* (1895–1897); editor, *Smith's* (1905–1906); editor, *Broadway Magazine* (1906–1907); editor, *Delineator, Designer,* and *New Idea Woman's Magazine* (1907–1910); editor, *American Spectator* (1932–1934).

SELECTED BOOKS: *Sister Carrie* (New York: Doubleday, Page, 1900; abridged edition, London: Heinemann, 1901);
The Financier (New York & London: Harper, 1912; revised edition, New York: Boni & Liveright, 1927; London: Constable, 1927);
The Titan (New York: Lane, 1914; London: Lane/Bodley Head, 1914);
The "Genius" (New York: Lane, 1915; London: Lane/Bodley Head, 1915);
Free and Other Stories (New York: Boni & Liveright, 1918);
Twelve Men (New York: Boni & Liveright, 1919; London: Constable, 1930);
Hey, Rub-a-Dub-Dub! (New York: Boni & Liveright, 1920; London: Constable, 1931);
A Book About Myself (New York: Boni & Liveright, 1922; London: Constable, 1929); republished as *Newspaper Days* (New York: Liveright, 1931);
The Color of a Great City (New York: Boni & Liveright, 1923; London: Constable, 1930);
An American Tragedy (New York: Boni & Liveright, 1925; London: Constable, 1926);
Moods: Cadenced and Declaimed (New York: Boni & Liveright, 1926; enlarged, 1928); enlarged again as *Moods Philosophical and Emotional, Cadenced and Declaimed* (New York: Simon & Schuster, 1935);
Notes on Life, edited by Marguerite Tjader and John J. McAleer (University: University of Alabama Press, 1974);
Theodore Dreiser: A Selection of Uncollected Prose, edited by Donald Pizer (Detroit: Wayne State University Press, 1977);
Selected Magazine Articles of Theodore Dreiser, edited by Yoshinobu Hakutani (Cranbury, N.J.: Associated University Presses, 1985).

PLAY PRODUCTIONS: *Laughing Gas,* Indianapolis, Ind., Masonic Temple, 7 December 1916;
The Girl in the Coffin, Saint Louis, Saint Louis Artists' Guild, 28 January 1917;
The Old Ragpicker, San Francisco, Colony Ballroom, 30 January 1918;
The Hand of the Potter, New York, Provincetown Playhouse, 5 December 1921.

SELECTED PERIODICAL PUBLICATIONS – UNCOLLECTED: "Review of the Month," "We Others" (sketch), "The Gloom Chasers" (sketch), "The Literary Shower: 'Out of India,'" and "The Drama," *Ev'ry Month,* 1 (December 1895): 2–9, 15–16, 16–17, 18, 22–23;
"Reflections," "Dramatic," and "The Literary Shower," *Ev'ry Month,* 1 (January 1896): 2–11, 16–17, 21–22;
"Reflections," "The Literary Shower: A Daughter of the Tenements," and "Wintry Landscapes" (sketch), *Ev'ry Month,* 1 (February 1896): 2–6, 10–11, 18;
"Reflections," "Literary Notes: As to the Jucklins," "Cometh in as a Lion" (sketch), and "Dramatic," *Ev'ry Month,* 1 (March 1896): 2–6, 10–11, 16, 22;
"Reflections," "Literary Notes: The Day of Their Wedding," and "Dramatic," *Ev'ry Month,* 2 (April 1896): 2–7, 11, 22;
"Reflections," "Literary Notes: A Singular Life," "I Shall Pass Through This World But Once" (poem), "Conditioned Ones" (poem), and "The Drama," *Ev'ry Month,* 2 (May 1896): 2–6, 11–12, 17, 18, 22;

Theodore Dreiser, circa 1900 (Lilly Library, Indiana University)

"Reflections," "The Madding Crowd" (poem), "The Literary Shower," and "Dramatic," *Ev'ry Month,* 2 (June 1896): 2-6, 17, 21-22, 26;

"Reflections," "Some Notable Women in New York Society," "Chevalier," and "The Literary Shower," *Ev'ry Month,* 2 (July 1896): 2-6, 10-11, 18, 24-25;

"Reflections," "Woes of Cats" (sketch), "Forgotten" (story), and "The Literary Shower," *Ev'ry Month,* 2 (August 1896): 2-7, 10-11, 16-17, 21-22;

"Reflections," "A Royal Abdication," and "The Literary Shower," *Ev'ry Month,* 2 (September 1896): 2-7, 16-17, 22-23;

"Reflections," *Ev'ry Month,* 3 (October 1896): 2-7;

"Reflections" and "A Metropolitan Favorite," *Ev'ry Month,* 3 (November 1896): 2-7, 22;

"Reflections" and "Caricatures and a Caricaturist," *Ev'ry Month,* 3 (December 1896): 2-7, 10;

"Reflections," "William Gillette," and "The Woman Journalist," *Ev'ry Month,* 3 (January 1897): 2-7, 17, 24-25;

"Reflections," *Ev'ry Month,* 3 (February 1897): 2-7;

"Reflections," "Where Grant Is to Rest," "Mary E. Tillinghast: Stained Glass Artist," and "A Social Samaritan: Rose Hawthorne Lathrop's Mission to the Afflicted," *Ev'ry Month,* 3 (March 1897): 2-6, 18-19, 20-21, 25;

"Portia Come Again," *Ev'ry Month,* 4 (May 1897): 8;

"A Finished Farce-Comedian," *Ev'ry Month,* 4 (August 1897): 27;

"The City of Crowds," *Smith's,* 2 (October 1905): 97-107;

"*Smith's:* The Magazine of Ten Million. What It Will Do During the Coming Year," *Smith's,* 2 (January 1906): unpaginated;

"New York and 'The New Broadway'" (editorial) and "The Beauty of the Tree" (sketch), *Broadway,* 16 (June 1906): vii-ix, 130;

"$5,000 for Short Stories!" (editorial) and "The Problem of Magazine Building," *Broadway,* 16 (July 1906): iv, v-vi;

"We Are Building This Magazine Along New Lines," *Broadway,* 16 (August 1906): v-vi;

"As New As New York Itself," *Broadway,* 16 (September 1906): vii-viii;

"Concerning Us All," *Delineator,* 70 (October 1907): 491-492;

"Your Magazine in 1908," *Delineator,* 70 (December 1907): 864-865;

"Just You and the Editor," *Delineator,* 70 (January 1908): 5-7;

"Summer-Time: A Conference," *Delineator*, 71 (April 1908): 508–509;
"At the Sign of the Lead Pencil: The Man on the Sidewalk" (essay), "At the Sign of the Lead Pencil: In the Matter of Spiritualism" (essay), "At the Sign of the Lead Pencil: The Day of the Great Writer" (essay), "At the Sign of the Lead Pencil: The Defects of Organized Charity" (essay), "The Cruise of the Idlewild," and "The Flight of Pigeons," *Bohemian*, 17 (October 1909): 422–423, 424–425, 426–427, 429–431, 441–447, 494–496;
"The Waterfront," *Bohemian*, 17 (November 1909): 633–636;
"At the Sign of the Lead Pencil: Our National Literary Debt," "At the Sign of the Lead Pencil: Pittsburgh," and "The Red Slayer," *Bohemian*, 17 (December 1909): 705–707, 712–714, 793–795;
"The Day of Surfeit," *American Spectator*, 1 (November 1932): 2–3;
"The Great American Novel," *American Spectator*, 1 (December 1932): 1–2;
"A Writer Looks at the Railroads," *American Spectator*, 1 (March 1933): 4;
"The Child and the School," *American Spectator*, 1 (April 1933): 2;
"Townsend" (sketch), *American Spectator*, 1 (June 1933): 2;
"Birth Control" and "Winterton" (sketch), *American Spectator*, 2 (December 1933): 1, 3–4.

Dreiser in 1894. He would become editor of Ev'ry Month *the following year.*

Theodore Dreiser's position in American literature is undeniably secure, primarily based on his novels *Sister Carrie* (1900) and *An American Tragedy* (1925). However, in addition to Dreiser the novelist there is Dreiser the editor – a side of his career that has been mentioned by biographers but seldom discussed in depth. Dreiser's work as a magazine editor is worthy of fuller treatment, as it plays an important role in his eventual rise to critical acclaim.

Theodore Herman Albert Dreiser was born into a poor Catholic home vibrating with three boys and four girls in Terre Haute, Indiana, on 27 August 1871. His father, John Paul, had emigrated from Germany and toiled his way west to Sullivan, Indiana; his mother, Sarah Schanab, had met John Paul, who was working in a woolen mill, and they married in 1851. The family was financially comfortable until John Paul's woolen mill burned and he was later injured. Since John Paul was disabled, Sarah and several of the children had to find jobs. From Sullivan to Terre Haute to Vincennes to Sullivan to Evansville to Warsaw, Indiana, the family moved, trying to earn enough to survive. Complicating matters was the constant gossip about the promiscuity of Dreiser's older sisters, Emma and Mame, who were said to be more than flirtatious with men. The Dreisers were not in any sense the typical midwestern American family – John Paul was stern, perhaps too much so; he forced his children to attend parochial schools until he could no longer afford the cost.

When the family moved to Warsaw, young Dreiser was allowed to attend public schools, where he grew emotionally as well as physically. His older brothers and sisters left home, leaving him to face his father's superstitious fanaticism. When Dreiser was sixteen, his desire to escape his poor surroundings became a reality; he moved to Chicago where he lived with his sisters, who had lived up to their reputations by having several affairs. Dreiser grew infatuated with city life, for he was excited by the bustling traffic on the sidewalks and streets; he enjoyed the marquees over theaters, the noise inside and outside restaurants, the music from stage productions, and, of course, the naive belief that he could earn enough to shake the dispiriting existence he had so long endured.

Cover for an issue of the first magazine Dreiser edited (Special Collections, Van Pelt Library, University of Pennsylvania)

He failed in this ambition, however; jobs, as he soon learned, were not plentiful in Chicago. Mildred Fielding, his high school English teacher, encouraged Dreiser to attend Indiana University for which she would pay his fees. Dreiser, apparently, did not appear to be college material; within a year he returned to Chicago and labored at a series of jobs. He worked for a real-estate agent, drove a laundry wagon, collected on overdue bills for an installment firm, and washed dishes in a restaurant.

In 1892, at the age of twenty-one, he gained employment as a reporter for the *Chicago Daily Globe.* He enjoyed reporting but gained more satisfaction from the camaraderie among reporters and editors. Within six months he moved to Saint Louis; his skills as a journalist had improved sufficiently for him to work as a reporter for the prestigious *Saint Louis Globe-Democrat,* then for the *Republic.* Dreiser grew as a skillful journalist by writing practically every type of story: for example, he reported catastrophes, murders, and robberies; he wrote personality sketches and interviews with celebrities; and he wrote various kinds of reviews – from books to plays.

His stay in Saint Louis was eventful. In 1893 he met Sara "Sallie" Osborne White, whom friends called Jug. They became engaged but did not marry until six years later. Although some biographers give credit to Dreiser's older brother Paul, a successful songwriter and entertainer known as Paul Dresser in New York City, for steering his younger brother eastward, the fact that Dreiser was reared in an environment of constant change was probably the cause of his move. At any rate, Dreiser left Saint Louis; he first stopped in Grand Rapids, Michigan, then moved eastward to Toledo, Ohio, where he found employment on the *Toledo Blade.* There he met Arthur Henry, who would exert a strong influence on Dreiser's career. The city editor of the newspaper, Henry hired Dreiser to cover a streetcar strike, which lasted four days. Within those four days the two had discussed their ambitions to be writers of fiction. Dreiser had met someone who had similar interests, but without a job he had to leave Toledo. He traveled first to Cleveland, then Buffalo, then Pittsburgh, where he was employed as a columnist by the *Dispatch.* Dreiser realized he had an easy task compared to reporting; most days he completed his column hours before deadline and devoted his time to reading books written by Thomas Henry Huxley, John Tyndall, Herbert Spencer, and Honoré de Balzac. The philosophy of Spencer and the realism of Balzac influenced Dreiser's beliefs and work.

In the fall, perhaps as a result of having been assigned to write a column that failed to inform or, in his opinion, serve any major purpose other than to entertain, Dreiser moved to New York City in search of practicing what he knew best – reporting. It seemed to Dreiser that every reporter had the same goal: full-time employment with a newspaper, and such positions were rare. When he grew destitute, he tried working as a stringer for the *New York World.* The pay, which was by inch of space, was too low; Dreiser soon realized he needed help, so he searched for Paul, his successful brother, at the office of the newly formed music publishing company Howley-Haviland and Company, of which Paul was part owner.

Dreiser overheard Frederick Benjamin Haviland tell one of the three owners, Patrick Howley, that their firm needed a magazine to sell songs. Haviland had worked for the music publishing firm Oliver Ditson and Company before founding his own firm and realized that Ditson's *Musical Record* had helped sell songs. Dreiser had never worked as an editor but nonetheless seized the opportunity. He informed Howley and Haviland that he could create a better, more widely read magazine than

Ditson's. Howley and Haviland agreed, and Dreiser was paid ten dollars a week until the first issue of *Ev'ry Month* appeared in September 1895. Thereafter he earned fifteen dollars a week.

Ev'ry Month reflected Dreiser's editorial interests and talents. Although the magazine was published at a nominal cost, Dreiser used every editorial device he could to make the magazine appealing. Promotional photographs submitted by agents or studios graced the covers. Inside, articles written by Dreiser and others filled some twenty-eight to thirty-two pages, depending on how many songs were included.

The extent of Dreiser's contributions was unmatched by most magazine editors at the time. He wrote the regular columns "Review of the Month," "The Gloom Chasers," "The Literary Shower," "We Others," "The Drama," and more than likely "For Those Who Love Flowers." He wrote the fashion column and the captions for the various illustrations. Most readers failed to realize that Dreiser wrote most of the columns because he used various pseudonyms. "Edward Al," for example, reviewed books. "S. J. White," which was taken from his fiancée's name, wrote the literary calendar. "Th.D." wrote some features but was responsible for the monthly review of plays. "Theodore Dreiser" wrote "Forgotten," his first short story to see print, and two poems.

In the column "Reflections," "The Prophet" wrote three to four thousand philosophical words on various subjects. The column began with an emotional presentation of a current crisis of national or international magnitude, then discussed one or more societal problems such as poor housing conditions for immigrants, corrupt politicians and financiers, and the probability of war. Dreiser eventually led the reader into the most important section of the column – his Spencer-based philosophy of man and his environment. Morality as an issue was the heart of this column, while other subjects were mere dilations. He wrote,

> Man is not exactly the sport of the elements in the same sense with rocks, trees and the countless creatures of the air and forest. Nothing can withstand him, for he is working in harmony with great laws which place splendid powers in his hand and assist him to rise. A great maker of stars above is his master, and these, His laws, though cruel in their precision, will do an obedient follower no harm. To-day they sweep the heedless and unthinking from their path, but tomorrow they will aid students and disciples to rise to the highest point of physical and mental power. As a student and disciple of such masterful laws man needs no pity; as a victim of error and misunderstanding regarding them, he deserves none. This is the order of the universe, the plan of irresistible progress, and as an earnest part of it man is safe.

Sara Osborne White "Jug" Dreiser, whom Dreiser married in 1898. The couple permanently separated in 1914 but never divorced.

"Reflections" was Dreiser's most important literary contribution to the magazine. In it he explored the conditions invariably created by man and nature. His philosophy, though sometimes presented in fragments, nonetheless informed the reader that "The Prophet" cared about man's and nature's laws. To Dreiser, neither could survive without order.

For a dime readers – primarily women – were entertained with fiction, poetry, music, and illustrations and informed with personality sketches, editorials, and articles. According to Dreiser, a typical issue of *Ev'ry Month* had sixty-five thousand readers. In October 1896 George Jenks was hired to review books, while fiction by such writers as Stephen Crane and Bret Harte was purchased. Dreiser selected fiction that appealed to women. Such fiction was sentimental and emotional: if a story brought tears to readers' eyes, it was undeniably worth publishing, he thought.

When Dreiser left in the fall of 1897 after quarreling with his employers over the editorial policy of

Ev'ry Month and his low salary, he had learned how to create a magazine that would sell to a specific audience. How he had achieved this at the age of twenty-four with no editing experience was simple: he identified with as well as understood his audience.

For the next several years Dreiser wrote many features on well-known personalities, including artists, musicians, lawyers, inventors, writers, industrialists, and financiers; such features discussed Joseph Choate, Anthony Hope, William Dean Howells, Thomas Edison, John Burroughs, Philip D. Armour, Chauncey Depew, Marshall Field, George M. Pullman, Andrew Carnegie, and Alfred Stieglitz. Dreiser also wrote articles about science, transportation, education, poetry, and the ills of society. Such work not only supported him but provided insight into those who had achieved either artistic and literary recognition or wealth. This information, which appeared in such popular magazines as *Metropolitan, Puritan, Truth, Munsey's, Success, Demorest's, Ainslee's, Cosmopolitan, Collier's, Saturday Evening Post, New Voice, Harper's Monthly, Pearson's, Everybody's, McClure's, Era,* and *Tom Watson's Magazine,* served Dreiser well because he later incorporated into his fiction what he had learned from this writing.

Dreiser as editor in chief at Butterick Publications, 1907–1910

This ability to write popular material, coupled with his friendship with Charles Agnew MacLean of Street and Smith, brought Dreiser the editorship of the new popular monthly *Smith's Magazine* in 1904. Dreiser had suffered a physical and emotional breakdown in 1902 after his novel *Sister Carrie* had been published but not distributed by Doubleday and failed to sell. As he began his duties at *Smith's Magazine,* he was again suffering emotionally, this time due to problems in his marriage.

Smith's Magazine was printed on pulp paper stock, and the fiction Dreiser published had analogous cheap qualities. Most was syrupy and seldom original. Whether Dreiser wanted to publish romantic serials is questionable. Since Street and Smith published hundreds of nickel and dime novels, it is probable that he was asked by the publisher to include similar formularized fiction in the magazine. The nonfiction articles, on the other hand, were informative. Dreiser felt that the magazine promised "something new, fresh and vivid.... This is the biggest, newest and most interesting country in the world, and to produce a big, new and interesting magazine we must reflect American manners and customs, thought and feeling."

Dreiser hoped *Smith's* would appeal to the same audience as *Munsey's,* a highly successful general interest monthly published by the man who had ushered in the era of the pulps, Frank A. Munsey. Apparently it did. Published in April 1905, the magazine's circulation grew to more than one hundred thousand within a year. Dreiser realized that if he followed the editorial practice of identifying with the reader, which he had learned at *Ev'ry Month,* he could not fail. Again he produced what his audience desired. The magazine published serious in-depth articles, personality profiles, and essays.

Dreiser's writing for *Smith's,* though similar in style to his freelance work, was slight. Productivity declined because he, together with MacLean, tried to form a publishing company to reissue *Sister Carrie* and because he grew despondent over his troubled marriage. What he produced, however, concerned his undeniable primary interest: the forgotten man and woman who had been thrust into a society where success was measured by wealth instead of deeds.

In April 1906 Benjamin Hampton offered Dreiser the editorship of *Broadway* magazine, which targeted a male audience with suggestive illustrations of women and titillating articles. Hampton recognized Dreiser's gift as an editor and informed him that he wanted the controversial magazine refined so people would not only purchase it but leave it out for others to see. Dreiser accepted. To change a "spicy" magazine into a journal that women would buy was undoubtedly challenging. To change it into a publication that published material other than muckraking articles when such was in vogue was even more challenging.

In the June issue Dreiser wrote, "It is, to all intents and purposes, a new publication, blessed right now with entirely new and refreshing ideals and rid once and forever, of the cheap, the vulgar, and the commonplace policy which once guided it. No one need to work here any longer for anything but that which is sweet and refreshing, and clean."

With this policy, Dreiser watched the magazine's circulation grow from twelve thousand to more than one hundred thousand within several months, and caused the *New York Standard* to rejoice in 1908, "The job was an Augean one. . . . He turned in a river of good literature and snappy special articles, changing the magazine completely, except in name. People began to sit up and take notice. . . . Instead of sneaking around the corner to read it they carried it in the sunlight and were proud of it. Circulation began to grow, and advertisers gave up real money for its pages. It was the prettiest piece of transformation work seen in New York for many a day. . . ."

Broadway prospered under Dreiser's editorship. Besides regularly contributing editorial essays about the magazine, Dreiser also wrote a few articles about life in Manhattan and one or two poems, though few of these contributions were of any literary significance. Nonetheless, he enjoyed his position, except for the criticism he received from Thomas McKee, who owned less than 50 percent of the magazine. McKee believed Dreiser was derelict in his duties; Hampton believed the opposite.

Though Dreiser was a capable editor, contrary to what McKee thought, his interest in seeing *Sister Carrie* reissued by another publisher propelled him into not only financially supporting B. W. Dodge and Company but working there as an editor in his spare time. Hampton, of course, was unaware of his outside editorial activities. Dreiser, with Ben W. Dodge, advertised his realistic novel heavily before it was reissued. He received endorsements from many writers, and when the novel was published it was reviewed favorably by critics in the *New York World*, the *New York Sun*, and the *New York Times*.

Sister Carrie was controversial because its author did not condemn the major characters; in other American novels characters who broke the law – whether moral or social – paid the price. Yet in Dreiser's novel Carrie, who is involved in extramarital affairs, robbery, and other immoral activities, is rewarded with fame and fortune in show business.

Dreiser thought of submitting a second novel, but his work as an editor came first. He enjoyed putting his philosophy into *Broadway*, but Hampton, who was probably influenced by McKee, began to interfere with Dreiser's editorial decisions. In June 1907 he was offered a salary of between five thousand dollars and seven thousand dollars by George W. Wilder, president of the Butterick Publishing Company, to direct the *Delineator*, the *Designer*, and *New Idea Woman's Magazine*.

In accepting, Dreiser took on an enormous workload. The *Delineator* alone had a circulation of more than four hundred thousand, and the three magazines together attracted more than forty thousand manuscripts a year. Though Dreiser was responsible for the editorial decisions of each publication, he surrounded himself with men and women who had years of editing and publishing experience.

The primary purpose of the "Butterick Trio" was to sell patterns to women. Among the various feature articles that dealt with fashion appeared many illustrations of underwear, bathing suits, dresses, and other garments to entice women to order patterns costing ten to fifteen cents each. Few articles and short stories appeared, and those that did never risked offending the reader with references to drinking, smoking, or sex. All three magazines, especially the *Delineator*, were morally righteous, almost to the extent that they were spiritually uplifting. The Dreiser who had written *Sister Carrie* and who had argued with his previous employers over editorial policy immensely enjoyed his position, even if he had become, in the words of his biographer W. A. Swanberg, "one of the nation's greatest whoremasters of letters."

The *Delineator*, according to Dreiser, had two goals: to increase in circulation and to help humanity by first helping women to learn how to improve their lives. Dreiser tried to achieve these goals first by improving his staff. Charles Hanson Towne was hired as the magazine's fiction editor, though he had to follow Dreiser's extremely conservative editorial policy. Dreiser reorganized the editorial boards of all three magazines by giving each its own staff. Katherine Leckie was hired to head the *New Idea Woman's Magazine*.

Dreiser also instituted various campaigns through the Butterick magazines; one such project, based on Mabel Daggett's tearful human-interest article for the *Delineator*, "The Child Without a Home," was concerned with the placing of institutionalized orphan children into homes. For the first time the magazine had another purpose besides selling patterns. Dreiser promoted the "Child Rescue"

THE DELINEATOR CHILD-RESCUE CAMPAIGN · · FOR THE CHILD THAT NEEDS A HOME, AND THE HOME THAT NEEDS A CHILD

Since November, 1907, THE DELINEATOR has been conducting an educational campaign in the interests of the child without a home and the home without a child. It has strongly advocated the family home in preference to an institution as the best place to care for the normal dependent child, and has urged the cottage-plan institution for the temporary care of children. Largely through its efforts President Roosevelt called the recent remarkable White House Conference which unanimously indorsed everything that has been advocated by THE DELINEATOR on the subject. Much good has been accomplished. In addition to the children whose stories have been told, hundreds of children have been placed in excellent homes directly through the influence of this campaign, and many institutions have modified their methods. Thousands have enrolled as members of the National Child-Rescue League and are effectively working in the interests of dependent children. In response to many suggestions, arrangements have been made whereby, in addition to applications for the specific children whose stories and photographs are presented as types of hundreds of other children available for adoption, THE DELINEATOR will receive and refer to the proper agencies applications from any one desiring to take a child. Applications will be received from all parts of the United States. If you are willing to give some child an opportunity, please tell us of your wishes and we will give the matter immediate personal consideration.

THE EDITOR.

Charlie

An editorial in which Dreiser describes one of the most popular campaigns sponsored by the Delineator

campaign in the pages of the *Delineator,* in newspapers, and in speeches at women's clubs. He received endorsements from Mrs. William Jennings Bryan and Edith Rockefeller McCormick. Dreiser even persuaded President Theodore Roosevelt to hold a national conference. As a result, the National Child Rescue League was organized.

The articles and short-short stories that appeared in the Butterick magazines were written in a personal style. Dreiser maintained that if an article concerned an abstract subject, it had to be personalized so the reader could relate to it. Even the illustrations had to be personalized by portraying characters who were representative of the magazine's readers.

Although the *Delineator* had started as a fashion magazine, Dreiser was determined to change it. He fought for text space and won. In addition to publishing more poetry, he published more articles and short-short stories. H. L. Mencken ghostwrote several medical articles for the magazine. Dreiser repeatedly published pieces that urged women to become more actively involved in society. For example, "What Jane Addams Has Done for Chicago" advised women that they could change their communities if they desired. Other articles, such as "What's the Matter with the Public Schools?," claimed that various problems existed and that women could eliminate the problems if they would act responsibly. Whether Dreiser and the *Delineator* were attacking woman suffrage or explaining the hardships of prisoners and their families, the articles concerned societal evils few readers knew existed. To enlighten, Dreiser believed, was the reason for the magazine's existence. Unfortunately, Dreiser's position conflicted with that of the business and advertising departments. Money came first – from selling patterns and advertising – and editorial matter was secondary.

In 1909, in addition to his successes at Butterick Publishing – the *Delineator* alone now had a circulation of more than one million – Dreiser, with William Smith, secured the *Bohemian,* a defunct magazine. Wilder was not informed of Dreiser's venture, and to keep the matter confidential Dreiser hired Fritz Krog to serve as editor. The *Bohemian* had been a coarse gazette that had published mediocre publicity photographs and articles concerning the theater. Dreiser was determined to publish material with "a big catholic point of view, a sense of humor, grim or gay and an apt realistic perception of things as they are."

The *Bohemian* had a brief life – only four issues. William Sydney Porter (O. Henry) contributed, and although Dreiser wrote several minor pieces for the magazine, including at least three that were later published in *The Color of a Great City* (1923), his primary interest was focusing the reader's attention on the grim realities of city life. In the *Bohemian* Dreiser also revived the Spencerian philosophy that he had spilled onto the pages of *Ev'ry Month.*

When the *Bohemian* died, Dreiser focused on the *Delineator,* which, beginning in October, had to share its facilities with a Butterick purchase, *Everybody's Magazine.* A successful investigative periodical, it was headed by Erman J. Ridgway and had a staff of notable muckraking writers including Lincoln Steffens. At first Dreiser was not intimidated by Ridgway's presence; after all, the *Delineator* had twice the circulation of *Everybody's.* However, when Ridgway started writing a column for the *Delineator* that countered Dreiser's editorial philosophy and competed for budgetary allocations for *Everybody's,* Dreiser realized a confrontation was inevitable. In addition, Dreiser had become infatuated with Thelma Cudlipp, a daughter of Annie Cudlipp, an assistant editor at Butterick. Mrs. Cudlipp confided in Dreiser's wife, who was ill with rheumatic fever. Together, they planned to thwart the affair. Jug was determined not to grant a divorce.

Mrs. Cudlipp discussed the matter with Dreiser several times to no avail; finally, after leaving Thelma in North Carolina, she revealed the affair to George Wilder and Erman Ridgway. If Dreiser was not fired, she said, she would release the story to the newspapers. In late September 1910 Dreiser was told to vacate his office by October. After this episode Dreiser ended his relationship with Jug.

In the *Delineator,* Dreiser had revealed his skills as an accomplished editor. His writing, which appeared in the editorials "Concerning Us All" and "Just You and the Editor," frequented the magazine's pages. However, most of his contributions lacked the philosophical spark that infused his freelance work, which he later collected and published in *The Color of a Great City* and *Twelve Men* (1919), as well as the work he contributed while serving as editor of *Ev'ry Month, Smith's Magazine, Broadway,* and the *Bohemian.*

From 1911 until 1932 Dreiser lived by writing realistic novels and short stories, realistic plays, philosophical and polemical essays, candid articles, and intrinsic poetry. Although Dreiser had several relationships after he left Jug, he lived with Helen Richardson first in New York City and then in Los Angeles, where she pursued a career as an actress. They returned to New York City after three years, in 1922, and Dreiser wrote his memorable realistic novel *An American Tragedy,* which was published in 1925.

In 1932 Dreiser became one of the founding editors – nominally, at least – of a new publication. Although seven founding editors were named, George Jean Nathan and Ernest Boyd were the real editorial forces behind the *American Spectator,* a tabloid-size monthly periodical filled with intellectual and political comment. The first issue came off the press in November of that year. America was suffering from the Depression; intellectuals, as a result, were seeking solutions. Dreiser wanted the *American Spectator,* through its commentary, to work toward ridding society of its problems, or at least to cause the reader to think about something other than his misfortune.

Dreiser thought the *Spectator* would be an excellent publication in which to air the ideas of writers who agreed with his political philosophy; however, most of the work submitted to him for publication never saw print. Nathan and Boyd refused to publish material they believed to have been written years earlier. Nonetheless, Dreiser encouraged contributions from Diego Rivera, Arthur Davison Ficke, and George Ade. He secured an in-depth article concerning life in prison from Tom Mooney, who was in San Quentin, and seriously attempted to obtain an article from Joseph Stalin. The experiment in Russia apparently was not working as well as some editors, including Dreiser, had thought, and Dreiser now realized that Franklin D. Roosevelt's ideas about societal reform were a possible solution to the nation's problems.

In September 1933 Dreiser and the other editors of the *American Spectator* published the controversial "Editorial Conference (With Wine)," in which each editor expressed his opinion as to what should be done with the Jews. Some of the comments, including Dreiser's, were considered by many to be anti-Semitic. Dreiser favored Hitler's National Socialism. To his way of thinking, the Jews should have their own nation. Although the "conference" had never occurred – indeed, the editors had merely expressed sometimes exaggerated opinions – the piece offended many readers and drew letters of protest.

Dreiser received criticism from some of his contributors as well. They disliked writing articles for a cent a word only to have them rejected

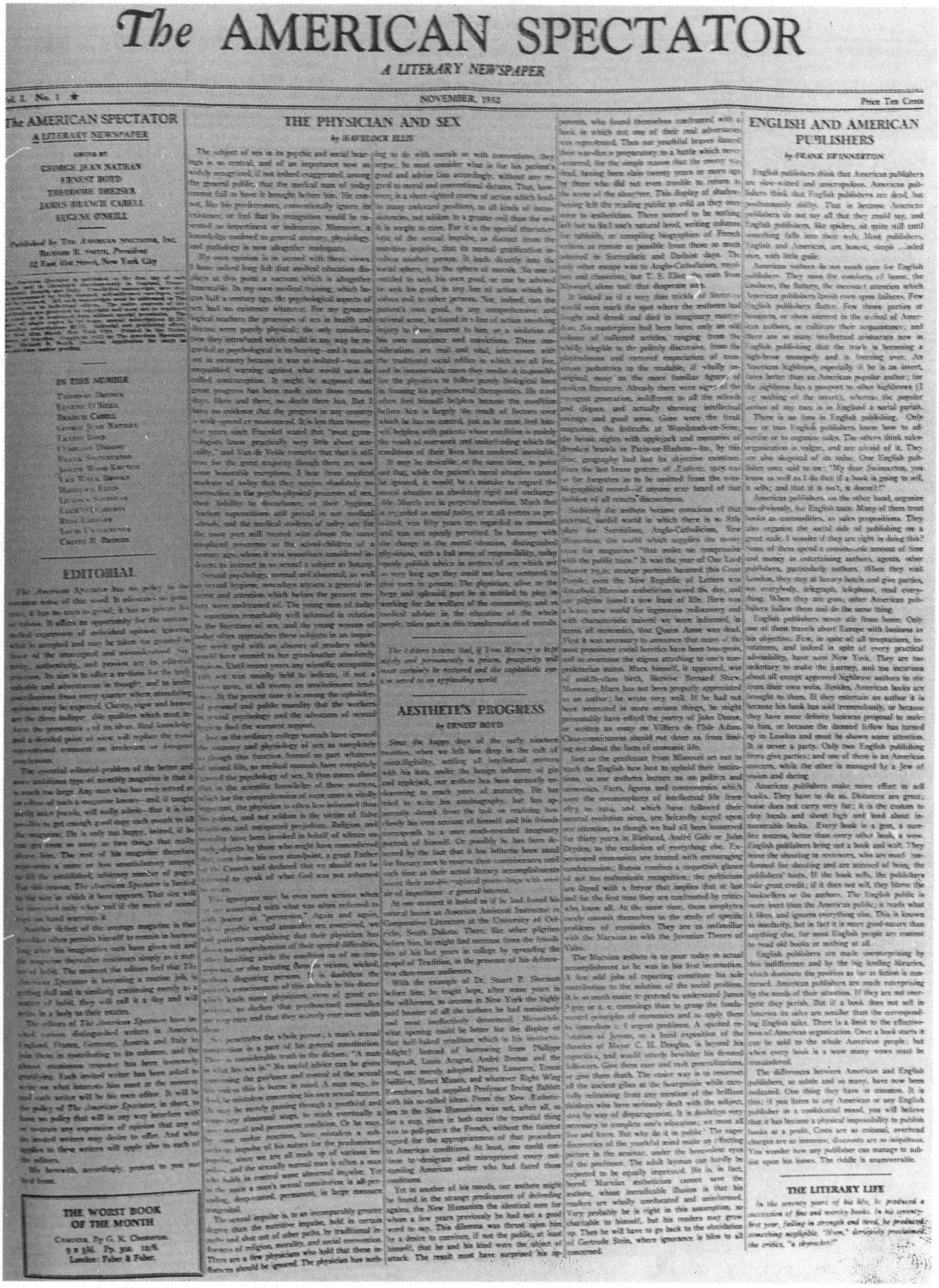
The AMERICAN SPECTATOR

A LITERARY NEWSPAPER

NOVEMBER, 1932

Price Ten Cents

THE PHYSICIAN AND SEX

by HAVELOCK ELLIS

ENGLISH AND AMERICAN PUBLISHERS

by FRANK SWINNERTON

EDITORIAL

AESTHETE'S PROGRESS

by ERNEST BOYD

THE WORST BOOK OF THE MONTH

THE LITERARY LIFE

First page of the first issue of the literary periodical which listed Dreiser as one of its founding editors by Nathan and Boyd. Dreiser attempted to fill the periodical with serious sociological essays and articles; Nathan and Boyd, on the other hand, preferred lighter material. Finally, in January 1934, Dreiser resigned. Too many problems plagued him, such as his book publisher going bankrupt and his increasing annoyance with Nathan and Boyd.

Dreiser's writing for the *American Spectator* included poetry, candid articles, sociological essays, and personality sketches. He discussed such topics as railroads, public schools, and birth control. As always, his philosophy intertwined with the subject discussed, providing the reader not only an insight into the topic but into the author.

In 1938 Dreiser and Helen left New York City and moved to Los Angeles where he circulated pro-Soviet Union broadsides which he had printed. He married Helen on 13 June 1944 in a private ceremony in Stevenson, Washington. Dreiser died of a heart attack on 28 December 1945 at his home in Hollywood.

Though Dreiser's reputation will undoubtedly live as a result of his realistic novels, his nonfiction, much like his best fiction, "contains two complementary themes," according to Donald Pizer. "He was preoccupied with his role as artist and seer, as a 'genius' seeking both fame and truth in an inhospitable world, and he sought to describe the truth and the world as he had found them." The philosophy that guided his writing also guided his editorial decisions. Suggestions of that philosophy can be found even in his upbeat editorial policy for the *Bohemian:* "I want some good interviews with big people, some clever take-offs on current political conditions, some truthful interesting pictures of current day society, and jobs and skits of all sorts. I want bright stuff. I want humor. And above all I want knowledge of life as it is, broad, simple, good natured."

Letters:

Letters to Louise, edited by Louise Campbell (Philadelphia: University of Pennsylvania Press, 1959).

Bibliographies:

Hugh C. Atkinson, *Theodore Dreiser: A Checklist* (Kent, Ohio: Kent State University Press, 1971);

Donald Pizer, Richard W. Dowell, and Frederic E. Rusch, *Theodore Dreiser: A Primary and Secondary Bibliography* (Boston: G. K. Hall, 1975).

Biographies:

Dorothy Dudley, *Dreiser and the Land of the Free* (New York: Beechhurst, 1946);

William Andrew Swanberg, *Dreiser* (New York: Scribner's, 1965);

Ellen Moers, *Two Dreisers* (New York: Viking, 1969);

Robert H. Elias, *Theodore Dreiser: Apostle of Nature* (Ithaca, N.Y.: Cornell University Press, 1970);

Yoshinobu Hakutani, *Young Dreiser: A Critical Study* (Cranbury, N.J.: Associated University Presses, 1980).

References:

Harold Bloom, ed., *Twentieth Century American Literature,* volume 2 (New York: Chelsea House, 1986): 1124–1154;

Wilbur M. Frohock, "Theodore Dreiser: 1871–1945," in Leonard Unger, ed., *American Writers: A Collection of Literary Biographies, volume 1, Henry Adams to T. S. Eliot* (New York: Scribners, 1974), pp. 497–520;

Yoshinobu Hakutani, "Theodore Dreiser's Editorial and Free-Lance Writing," *Library Chronicle,* 37 (Winter 1971): 70–85;

Joseph Katz, "Theodore Dreiser's *Ev'ry Month,*" *Library Chronicle,* 38 (Winter 1972): 46–66.

Hugo Gernsback

(16 August 1884 - 19 August 1967)

Garyn G. Roberts
Michigan State University

See also the Gernsback entry in *DLB 8: Twentieth-Century American Science-Fiction Writers.*

MAJOR POSITIONS HELD: Editor and publisher, *Modern Electrics* (1908-1912), retitled *Electrical Experimenter* (1913-1920), retitled *Science and Invention* (1920-1931); *Experimenter* (1921-1926); *Amazing Stories* (1926-1929); *Everyday Mechanics* (1929-1932), retitled *Everyday Science and Mechanics* (1933-1936); *Science Wonder Stories* (1929-1930), *Air Wonder Stories* (1929-1930), combined as *Wonder Stories* (1930-1936); *Scientific Detective Monthly* (1929-1930), retitled *Amazing Detective Tales* (1930-1935); *Sexology* (1933-1953); *Science Fiction Plus* (1953); writer and publisher, *Forecast* (1957-1965).

BOOKS: *The Wireless Telephone* (New York: Modern Electrics, 1910);

Wireless Hook-ups (New York: Modern Electrics, 1911);

Radio for All (Philadelphia & London: Lippincott, 1922);

Ralph 124C 41+ (Boston: Stratford, 1925);

How to Build and Operate Short Wave Receivers (New York: Short Wave Craft, 1932);

Evolution of Modern Science Fiction (New York, 1952);

Ultimate World, edited by Sam Moskowitz (New York: Walker, 1972);

Official Radio Service Manual and Complete Directory of All Commercial Wiring Diagrams, 1930 (New York: Vestral, 1984).

OTHER: "The Prophets of Doom," in *The Science Fiction Roll of Honor,* edited by Frederik Pohl (New York: Random House, 1975).

SELECTED PERIODICAL PUBLICATIONS – UNCOLLECTED: "I Make A Wireless Acquaintance," *Electrical Experimenter,* 3 (May 1915);

"How Munchhausen and the Allies Took Berlin," *Electrical Experimenter,* 3 (June 1915);

Hugo Gernsback

"Munchhausen on the Moon," *Electrical Experimenter,* 3 (July 1915);

"The Earth As Viewed from the Moon," *Electrical Experimenter,* 3 (August 1915);

"Munchhausen Departs for the Planet Mars," *Electrical Experimenter,* 3 (October 1915);

"Munchhausen Lands on Mars," *Electrical Experimenter,* 3 (November 1915);

"Munchhausen Is Taught 'Martian,'" *Electrical Experimenter,* 3 (December 1915);

"Thought Transmission on Mars," *Electrical Experimenter,* 3 (January 1916);

"The Cities of Mars," *Electrical Experimenter,* 3 (March 1916);

"The Planets at Close Range," *Electrical Experimenter,* 3 (April 1916);
"Martian Amusements," *Electrical Experimenter,* 4 (June 1916);
"How the Martian Canals Are Built," *Electrical Experimenter,* 4 (November 1916);
"Martian Atmosphere Plants," *Electrical Experimenter,* 4 (February 1917);
"The Magnetic Storm," *Electrical Experimenter,* 6 (August 1918);
"10,000 Years Hence," *Science and Invention,* 9 (February 1922);
"The Electric Duel," *Science and Invention,* 11 (August 1923);
"Evolution on Mars," *Science and Invention,* 12 (August 1924).

Hugo Gernsback, one of the most important editors and publishers of science fiction and a founder of the genre (along with Edgar Allan Poe, Jules Verne, and H. G. Wells), was born on 16 August 1884 in Luxembourg. At this time Poe had been dead thirty-five years, Verne's *Twenty Thousand Leagues Under the Sea* (1869–1870) was some fourteen years old, and its sequel, *The Mysterious Island* (1874–1875), was barely nine. Wells's first science-fiction classic, *The Time Machine* (1895), was yet to be published. Hugo was the son of Maurice Gernsback, a wealthy wine wholesaler, and Berta Durlacher Gernsback. His early education was supplied by private tutors, and he later attended the Ecole Industrielle of Luxembourg and the Technikum of Bingen, Germany. Gernsback's primary language was German, but he spoke and read both English and French also.

At age nine Gernsback discovered a German translation of *Mars as the Abode of Life,* by the American astronomer Percival Lowell. The story so profoundly affected him that he literally developed a fever, which may have been psychosomatic in nature. He raved about fantastic places, strange creatures, and life on Mars. This continued into the night, and the following day Gernsback was sent home from school in a state of delirium. This experience profoundly affected his subsequent intellectual pursuits. An accomplished technician, scientist, and inventor, Gernsback was never satisfied with the limits of existing scientific knowledge; he was enamored with pursuits of the imagination. By age thirteen he was accepting installation jobs for telephone and electrical communications systems, forms of communication that were in their infancy. In *Explorers of the Infinite* (1960), Sam Moskowitz relates how "the mother superior of the Carmelite

Cover for the issue of Gernsback's magazine which included the first installment of his serialized novel Ralph 124C 41+

convent in Luxembourg City obtained a special dispensation from Pope Leo XIII, so that Gernsback could equip that institution with call bells." He then busied himself with a variety of projects, including the invention of a new form of battery. Moskowitz notes that this battery was similar to the present-day layer battery. When both France and Germany refused him patents, the young entrepreneur took his accumulated savings from his electrical-installation work and left for the United States in February 1904.

After his immigration to the United States, Gernsback began a career as editor and publisher, yet this had not been his original intention. He had come to America with the hope of marketing his

Cover for a 1927 issue of Gernsback's first magazine devoted exclusively to science fiction, featuring an illustration for H. G. Wells's War of the Worlds

new battery, but he soon discovered that even though his invention provided three times the amperage of any existing American battery, it was impractical since it could not be developed for mass production. Even though he had an unsalable product, Gernsback possessed the technical knowledge he had acquired as a result of his invention. He sold his services to William Roche, a New York manufacturer who had a contract to produce dry-cell batteries for the navy. The inventor was to be head of research at thirty dollars a week. Moskowitz recounts, however, that upon leaving Roche's office Gernsback remembered some details of the employment that had been left unsettled. He returned to Roche's office to find his employer gone. Waiting for the man to return, Gernsback began examining some sample envelopes of battery chemicals that he found on Roche's desk. Roche reentered and, believing the young inventor to be an agent of a competing firm, paid him one week's salary and fired him.

Gernsback went into a partnership and formed Gee-Cee Dry Battery Company, for which he developed and built storage batteries. Business was good, but little money came in – his partner was intercepting the checks. Gernsback dissolved the partnership, recovered the money from his partner's father, and then made an agreement to produce batteries for the largest distributor of motorcar equipment in New York. This arrangement proved successful for Gernsback until the depression of 1907, when his employer lost its contract with Packard, and the company had to be dissolved.

During this period of time Gernsback lived at a boardinghouse on Fourteenth Street in New York. Here he met Lewis Coggeshall, a telegraph operator on the Erie Railroad. The pair formed a company to import experimental and research equipment not generally available in the United States, including X-ray tubes, Geissler tubes, and specialized scientific electric equipment. Gernsback operated the Electro Importing Company while he also pursued other endeavors. Although one of Gernsback's less fortunate ventures, the Electro Importing Company was the first mail-order radio house in the world and produced the first home radio set, called the

Cover for an issue of the science-fiction magazine Gernsback founded after he was forced to sell Amazing Stories

Telimco Wireless. The set was advertised in the *Scientific American,* and Moskowitz notes that the unit included both a transmitter and a receiver, since no commercial radio stations existed at that time. Gernsback also produced the first operating walkie-talkie, based on the Telimco Wireless. The apparatus was described, with photographs, in the January 1909 issue of *Modern Electrics* and was sold in department stores, including F. A. O. Schwartz, Macy's, Gimbel's, and Marshall Field. A replica of this device was placed in the Henry Ford Museum in Dearborn, Michigan, in 1957, the same year the Michigan Institute of Radio Engineers and the American Radio Relay League honored Gernsback for his work.

Yet Gernsback's wireless radio set was not the only revolutionary new product to emerge from the inventor's efforts in the first years of the twentieth century. The catalogue he began to publish in 1905 to promote this radio set became in 1908 the world's first radio magazine, *Modern Electrics.* In 1909 Gernsback opened the world's first radio store at 69 West Broadway, New York, and introduced the word *television* to the American public in a *Modern Electrics* article entitled "Television and the Telphot." By early 1910 Gernsback had formed, through his popular and profitable magazine, a society of ten thousand wireless-radio amateurs. He issued the *Wireless Blue Book* (the first book on radio broadcasting), in which he predicted the formation of radio networks.

Gernsback is chiefly recognized today for his contributions to the formation and definition of the science-fiction genre and for his career as editor of several science-fiction pulp magazines. Yet his novel *Ralph 124C 41+,* serialized in *Modern Electrics* from April 1911 to March 1912 (at that time the magazine had a circulation of about one hundred thousand copies) and published as a book in 1925, has remained a landmark of original craftsmanship in the history of the genre.

In this significant early work of science fiction, the title character is a scientist and one of the ten most intelligent men of the twenty-seventh century, hence the "+" at the end of his name. Since he has such high levels of knowledge and analytic ability, it follows (according to Gernsback) that Ralph is one of the world's greatest humanitarians and resources. His lifework primarily takes place in a New York City skyscraper – Ralph's laboratory and home – in which every room is circular in shape. (Only the magnet-powered elevators are angular.) The government provides the hero with the most luxurious, comfortable living environment possible and all the scientific advances and resources known to man at this time. Yet there is one thing that all of this intelligence and technology cannot give to Ralph, and he discovers that he wants it (love) more than anything else in the world. Love comes to Ralph in the form of Alice 212B 423, who is beautiful, intelligent, and virtuous.

Ralph 124C 41+ was more than the standard fare for pulp magazines deemed "scientific romances," however. The romance aspect of the novel, evident in its fantastic, flowery prose as well as the love relationship between Ralph 124C 41+ and Alice 212B 423, was really nothing new or innovative. But the scientific facet, which predicted future lifestyles and technologies based on existing knowledge, would prove to be of enormous influence in the development of science fiction. Gernsback again employed this technique in *Baron Munchhausen's Scientific Adventures,* serialized in the *Electrical Experimenter* (a 1913 retitling of *Modern Electrics*) from May 1915 to February 1917. Considerably more humorous than *Ralph 124C 41+,* these stories revived a character originated by Rudolf Erich Raspe in *The Adventures of Baron Munchhausen* (1785). In Gernsback's version the eighteenth-century, tall-tale-telling Baron is revived from suspended animation in 1906, and he becomes an inventor extraordinaire and space traveler.

The popularity of these stories led Gernsback to publish "scientifiction," as he called it, by other authors, and *Science and Invention* (another retitling, from 1920) soon amassed a growing backlog of unpublished science-fiction stories. As a result, Gernsback published a special "Science Fiction Number" of *Science and Invention* in August 1923. This issue profoundly affected the editorial policies of the pulp magazines *Weird Tales* and *Argosy.* These leaders in the field of popular fiction altered their policies to include stories with a better basis in science. Moskowitz writes of this change that the "beginning of the end of the scientific romance which had been popularized by Edgar Rice Burroughs was brought nearer. The pattern of modern science fiction was in the process of formation." In 1924 Gernsback sent out twenty-five thousand flyers soliciting subscriptions for a new type of magazine based on traditions established by Poe, Verne, and Wells. The publication was to be entitled "Scientifiction." The reaction to the flyer, however, was not encouraging, and Gernsback did nothing with the idea for two more years. *Amazing Stories* appeared, without advance notice, in April 1926.

If one person is to be given credit for more than abstractly defining science fiction, that individual is Gernsback. In the first issue of *Amazing Stories* Gernsback wrote, "By 'scientifiction' I mean the Jules Verne, H. G. Wells and Edgar Allan Poe type of story – a charming romance intermingled with scientific fact and prophetic vision." His definition has ever since warranted respect, criticism, and scrutiny. A few years later, "scientifiction" became "science fiction" in the June 1929 issue of Gernsback's *Science Wonder Stories.* Soon thereafter, according to Anthony Frewin, "SF spent its formative years in American magazines with such names as *Amazing* and *Astounding,* all of which had a wide circulation that, initially, was restricted to the lower middle classes, manual and semi-skilled workers, and the teenagers." These fiction magazines, deemed "pulps" because of the pulpwood paper on which they were printed, were the predecessors of the mass-market paperback book. Many pulps had circulations in the hundreds of thousands per issue in the 1930s. Yet *Amazing Stories* reached a circulation of one hundred thousand in the mid and late 1920s, a remarkable feat considering the then-extravagant price of twenty-five cents an issue.

Yet Gernsback and his Experimenter Publishing Company did more than just set forth definitional boundaries for the genre. *Amazing Stories* launched a whole new era in popular literature. That first issue contained stories by Poe, Verne, and Wells and, as Robert Sampson notes, "was an inch taller and wider than most other magazines of the time; it measured eight-and-a-half by eleven-and-three-quarters inches, and contained 96 pages (as opposed to the 115 pages of most pulps) of thick, rather soft, pulp paper stock." The magazine was printed on paper of such heavy stock that it was more than half an inch thick. The edges were trimmed, unlike those of most pulps. Its covers by artist Frank R. Paul were brightly colored and depicted detailed, fantastic mechanisms. Gernsback named Dr. T. O'Connor Sloane, an inventor and science writer, as the magazine's managing editor. *Amazing Stories* was subtitled "The Magazine of Scientifiction," and the science-fiction pulp magazine was born.

Three months later, in an editorial titled "Fiction Versus Facts," Gernsback further clarified his editorial policy: "We reject stories often on the ground that, in our opinion, the plot or action is not

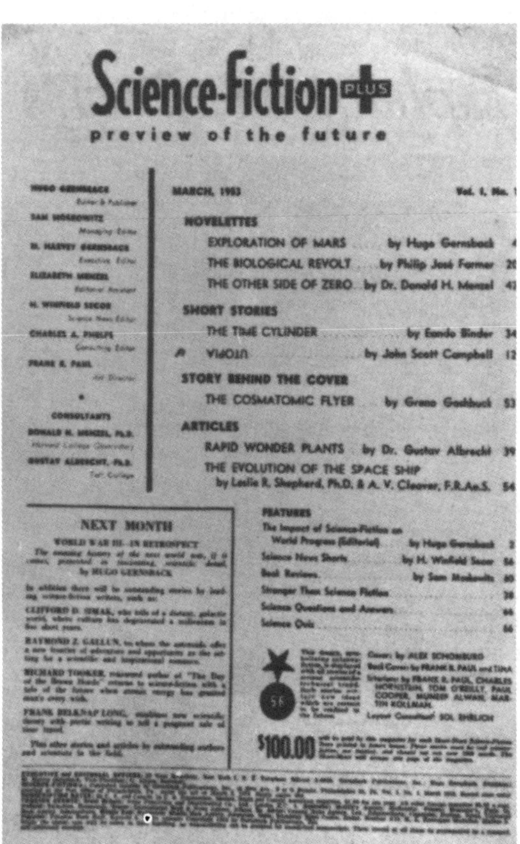
Science-Fiction PLUS
preview of the future

MARCH, 1953

NOVELETTES
EXPLORATION OF MARS by Hugo Gernsback
THE BIOLOGICAL REVOLT by Philip José Farmer
THE OTHER SIDE OF ZERO by Dr. Donald H. Menzel

SHORT STORIES
THE TIME CYLINDER by Eando Binder
UTOPIA by John Scott Campbell

STORY BEHIND THE COVER
THE COSMATOMIC FLYER by Greno Gashbuck

ARTICLES
RAPID WONDER PLANTS by Dr. Gustav Albrecht
THE EVOLUTION OF THE SPACE SHIP by Leslie R. Shepherd, Ph.D. & A. V. Cleaver, F.R.Ae.S.

FEATURES
The Impact of Science-Fiction on World Progress (Editorial) by Hugo Gernsback
Science News Shorts by H. Winfield Secor
Book Reviews by Sam Moskowitz
Stranger Than Science Fiction
Science Questions and Answers
Science Quiz

NEXT MONTH
WORLD WAR III—IN RETROSPECT
by HUGO GERNSBACK

Cover by ALEX SCHOMBURG
Layout Consultant SOL EHRLICH

$100.00

Cover and contents page for the premier issue of Gernsback's final science-fiction periodical

keeping with science as we know it today. For instance, when we see a plot wherein the hero is turned into a tree, later on into a stone, and then back again into himself, we do not consider this science, but rather, a fairy tale, and such stories have no place in *Amazing Stories*. He continued, "beauty lies only in the things that are mysterious . . . scientifiction goes out into the remote vistas of the universe, where there is still mystery and so still beauty." Romantic science fantasy had been published in a variety of dime novels and pulps – Gernsback successfully deviated from that trend. The stories he published and encouraged authors to write were based on "real," "possible" scientific achievements, or so he believed. There were times, according to Sampson, that these stories were "fantasy lightly powdered with science, as in the Ray Cummings and A. A. Merritt serials."

Almost immediately Gernsback discovered that there was a ready-made market for the stories he published. He called the market "Scientifiction Fans," and, surveying his readers, the editor and publisher found that a more frequent publication schedule was desired by the majority. In 1927 he published the *Amazing Stories Annual*. For this special issue Gernsback hired Edgar Rice Burroughs to write a new novel, *The Mastermind of Mars,* for which the author was paid twelve hundred dollars. The one-hundred-thousand-copy printing run of the *Annual* was virtually a sellout, despite its fifty-cent cover price. In 1928 *Amazing Stories Annual* became *Amazing Stories Quarterly*.

Technologically accurate or not, many of those first "amazing" stories were, or became, classics of popular fiction. Luther Trant, the first scientific detective in American fiction, was created by Edwin Balmer and William MacHarg and premiered in Gernsback's publication. At least three of these gadget-oriented tales found their way into *Amazing Stories* between 1926 and 1928. A few years later, in Gernsback's *Scientific Detective Monthly,* five more of these stories would appear. E. E. (Edward Elmer) "Doc" Smith had part of his "Skylark" series serialized in the August, September, and October 1928 issues of *Amazing Stories*. Smith had been working on this epic space opera since World War I. After several submissions of this manuscript to, and subsequent rejections from, magazine publishers,

Smith found a sympathetic audience in Gernsback. The serial met with immediate public approval and has remained a popular science-fiction work. Many of the authors from the early days of *Amazing Stories* and *Scientific Detective* became significant names in the world of science fiction. Among them are David H. Keller, John W. Campbell, Philip Francis Nowlan, Stanton A. Coblentz, A. Hyatt Verrill, Harl Vincent, Bob Olsen, Miles J. Breuer, and Jack Williamson.

Gernsback was also busy with other projects. In 1927 and 1928 he released several humor publications, including a weekly magazine titled *French Humor,* a monthly called *Tidbits,* and several one-shot magazines with such titles as *1,001 Laughs* and *Oi! Oi! I'm Leffing.* He operated radio station WRNY out of New York, which began to broadcast primitive television pictures of its performers to experimental sets as early as 1928, and Gernsback also published at least two issues of *Television* magazine that year. He also began in 1928 a quarterly, general interest health magazine called *Your Body.*

However, nothing could save Gernsback's empire from liquidation in early 1929. Bernarr MacFadden, health expert and publisher of such magazines as *Physical Culture* and the *New York Evening Graphic,* found the scientific approach in *Your Body* (which was edited and written chiefly by medical professionals) too much competition. Gernsback's offer of ten thousand dollars to any medium who could actually contact the dead, and his subsequent use of famed magician Dunninger to reveal such frauds, threatened the existence of another MacFadden publication, *Ghost Stories.* The competition went on, often with Gernsback the more successful of the two competitors, until MacFadden offered to buy Gernsback and his properties out entirely. Gernsback refused the offer. Suddenly, on 20 February 1929, apparently at McFadden's instigation, Gernsback was sued for payment by three creditors, which could force a company into bankruptcy under contemporary New York law, regardless of the company's ability to pay. Gernsback went to the authorities, claiming conspiracy, but was unable to prove MacFadden's involvement. The Father of Science Fiction lost his Experimenter Publishing Company, but MacFadden, still under scrutiny for conspiracy, was unable to purchase the Gernsback properties. The bankruptcy law was changed a week later – too late to help Gernsback.

Although Gernsback's established properties, including all publications, were divided among several purchasers, the inventor and publisher was back in business before 1929 was over. He founded the Stellar Publishing Company, and *Everyday Mechanics* (later retitled *Everyday Science and Mechanics*) and *Science Wonder Stories* premiered in June of that year. In his editorial for the first issue of the latter Gernsback coined the term *science fiction.* In July 1929 *Air Wonder Stories* appeared and then merged with *Science Wonder Stories* to form *Wonder Stories* in June 1930. In December 1929 another Gernsback publication was launched, titled the *Scientific Detective Monthly.* In the familiar Gernsback format, measuring eight-and-a-half by eleven-and-three-quarter inches, the magazine contained ninety-six pages of text printed in double columns on pulp paper, and it sold for twenty-five cents. In the lead article, "Science and Crime," Gernsback wrote, "I confidently believe that in the not-so-distant future the professional criminal will become practically extinct." He reasoned that science would make detection and treatment of crooks flawless endeavors.

The January 1930 issue of *Scientific Detective Monthly* featured the first of a series of stories by Arthur B. Reeve featuring the scientific detective, Craig Kennedy. The stories originally appeared in *Cosmopolitan* between 1910 and 1912, but Gernsback's magazine provided a new market for Reeve's detective hero. Each issue of *Scientific Detective* featured a reprint of a Craig Kennedy story, and Reeve was deemed the "Editorial Commissioner" on the magazine's masthead. Another series character appearing in *Scientific Detective* was Dr. John Thorndyke, the fictional detective created by R. Austin Freeman. The Thorndyke stories, which had debuted in *Pearson's Magazine* in 1908, returned to print in the June 1930 issue of *Amazing Detective Tales* (a retitling of *Scientific Detective*).

Gernsback was once again ahead of his time with his next project, another health-oriented magazine. In 1933 he founded *Sexology,* a digest-size monthly devoted to educational and self-help articles on sexual matters. Like his earlier health publication, *Your Body,* the new magazine was largely edited and written by health professionals. *Sexology* proved to be one of the most successful of Gernsback's publishing ventures, continuing publication under its original title until February 1977 and, after various title changes, ceasing publication in December 1983.

His last attempt at publishing a science-fiction title was with *Science Fiction Plus.* Gernsback hired Moskowitz as the managing editor of the new publication, and the first issue appeared in March 1953. Its format was lavish – the large-size of the early *Amazing Stories;* five-color covers and two-color interior illustrations; "slick," coated paper stock throughout;

and no advertisements. The magazine's sales were less than overwhelming, and Gernsback was soon forced to switch to pulp paper. *Science Fiction Plus* ceased publication after seven issues.

In his remaining years Gernsback turned his publishing energies to the production of annual Christmas cards. Collectively titled *Forecast,* these "cards" were actually digest-sized parodies of popular contemporary magazines – they featured four-color covers and two-color interior illustrations. Gernsback died in New York City on 19 August 1967.

Renowned also as "The Father of the Science-Fiction Magazine," Gernsback helped define and create a popular literary genre which has thrived ever since. The most prestigious fan award in science fiction, and one of the most sought-after trophies among writers of this genre, is named for this influential editor and publisher. Gernsback had been guest of honor at the 1952 World Science Fiction Convention in Chicago; beginning with the 1953 convention in Philadelphia, achievement awards presented at these fan gatherings were declared "Hugos." Gernsback was presented with his namesake award at the Eighteenth World Science Fiction Convention in 1960.

References:

Brian W. Aldiss and David Wingrove, *Trillion Year Spree: The True History of Science Fiction* (New York: Atheneum, 1986), pp. 202–205;

Amazing Stories, special issue, 61 (March 1987);

Isaac Asimov, "Introduction: Amazing Stories and I," *Amazing Stories: 60 Years of the Best Science Fiction* (Lake Geneva, Wis.: TSR, 1985);

Anthony Frewin, *One Hundred Years Years of Science Fiction Illustration* (1840–1940) (New York: Pyramid, 1975);

James Gunn, *Alternate Worlds: The Illustrated History of Science Fiction* (New York: Prentice-Hall, 1975), pp. 117–128;

Sam Moskowitz, *Explorers of the Infinite* (Cleveland, Ohio: World, 1960), pp. 225–242;

Moskowitz, "The Ultimate Hugo Gernsback," in *Ultimate World,* by Gernsback (New York: Walker, 1971), pp. 7–18;

Fletcher Pratt, Foreword to Gernsback's *Ralph 124C 41+* (New York: Crest/Fawcett, 1958);

Robert Sampson, *Yesterday's Faces: A Study of Series Characters in the Early Pulp Magazines,* 2 volumes (Bowling Green, Ohio: Bowling Green University Popular Press, 1983, 1984);

Darrell Schweitzer, "Keeper of the Flame: A Different View of Hugo Gernsback," *Algol,* 15 (Winter 1978): 23–27;

Mark Richard Siegel, *Hugo Gernsback, Father of Modern Science Fiction* (San Bernardino, Cal.: Borgo, 1988);

Robert Silverberg, Introduction to *Amazing Stories: Visions of Other Worlds* (Lake Geneva, Wis.: TSR, 1986).

Arnold Gingrich

(5 December 1903 - 9 July 1976)

A. J. Kaul
University of Southern Mississippi

MAJOR POSITIONS HELD: Editor (1933-1945), editor/publisher/senior vice-president (1952-1974), editor in chief (1974), founding editor, *Esquire* (1975-1976); editor, *Coronet* (1936-1945); editor, *Verve* and *Ken* (1938-1939); vice-president and general manager, *Flair* (1949-1951).

BOOKS: *Cast Down the Laurel* (New York: Knopf, 1935);
The Well-Tempered Angler (New York: Knopf, 1965);
Toys of a Lifetime (New York: Knopf, 1966);
Business and the Arts: An Answer to Tomorrow (New York: P. S. Eriksson, 1969);
A Thousand Mornings of Music: The Journal of an Obsession with the Violin (New York: Crown, 1970);
Nothing But People: The Early Days at Esquire, A Personal History, 1928-1958 (New York: Crown, 1971);
The Joys of Trout (New York: Crown, 1973);
The Fishing in Print: A Guided Tour through Five Centuries of Angling Literature (New York: Winchester, 1974).

OTHER: *The Bedside Esquire,* edited by Gingrich (New York: McBride, 1940);
Esquire's 2nd Sports Reader, edited by Gingrich (New York: Barnes, 1946);
The Esquire Treasury, edited by Gingrich (New York: Simon & Schuster, 1953);
The Armchair Esquire, edited by Gingrich (New York: Putnam, 1958);
The Esquire Reader, edited by Gingrich (New York: Popular Library, 1961);
F. Scott Fitzgerald, *The Pat Hobby Stories,* introduction by Gingrich (New York: Scribners, 1962), pp. ix-xxiii;
Theodore Gordon Flyfishers, *The Gordon Garland,* edited by Gingrich (New York, 1965);
Flyfishers, *American Trout Fishing,* edited by Gingrich (New York: Knopf, 1966).

Arnold Gingrich (Gale International Portrait Gallery)

A forty-four-year career with *Esquire* magazine led to Arnold Gingrich's reputation for being among the nation's "most imaginative editors" and a "headhunter of famous authors." His editorial exuberance and willingness to take risks gave the Depression-born men's magazine a brash, sophisticated sauciness that showcased full-page color pinups of girls alongside stories by twentieth-century America's major writers. The magazine's penchant for elegance and fashion coupled with a flippant style – a prototype for *Playboy* magazine years later – sometimes disguised the remarkable ability of *Esquire* to mix commercial success with literary distinction.

Born 5 December 1903 in Grand Rapids, Michigan, Arnold Gingrich was a son of John Hembling and Clara Alice Speare Gingrich. He attended public schools in his hometown, then earned a bachelor's degree and Phi Beta Kappa key from the University of Michigan in 1925. After graduation Gingrich became an advertising copywriter and acting advertising manager for the Chicago-based men's clothing manufacturer B. Kuppenheimer and Company.

In 1928 Gingrich joined Men's Wear Service Corporation, the publishing partnership of David A. Smart and William H. Weintraub that produced men's fashion booklets and trade papers. An entrepreneurial salesman, Smart was born in Omaha in 1892, grew up in Chicago, and began working while still in high school. He sold record amounts of classified-advertising linage for the *Chicago Tribune,* his huge commissions drawing the attention of *Tribune* publisher Robert McCormick, who promoted him to a position that effectively cut his commission earnings by 90 percent. The so-called promotion coupled with his personal dislike of McCormick prompted Smart to resolve never to work for anyone but himself. After World War I Smart lost a fortune in the sugar business in Michigan, a misadventure that prompted another resolution never to engage in a business whose inventories could suddenly depreciate. According to Gingrich, Smart was a loner who distrusted partnerships. His stormy partnership with Weintraub ended in 1940.

Smart and Weintraub early in 1931 had generated the idea for a publication to compete with *Men's Wear,* a rival trade magazine, telling Gingrich to dream up a periodical modeled on *Fortune* magazine. Gingrich's dream-child was called *Apparel Arts,* an effort to endow a trade paper with sophistication. The first issue of *Apparel Arts* appeared on 15 September 1931, its 148 pages including 90 full-page advertisements and 56 Gingrich-written pages of editorial copy. On the last editorial page of the inaugural issue, Gingrich told readers that the viewpoint of *Apparel Arts* was both commercial and cultural. *Time* took notice of the new magazine under the heading "After Fortune." Using untranslated French phrases for editorial panache and quoting the entire text of a poem in advertisements were deliberate ploys to bolster the arts motif of *Apparel Arts.* The production of *Apparel Arts* was undertaken with an informality that was exhilarating, Gingrich recalled in *Nothing But People* (1971).

The idea for *Esquire* had its origins in an offhand comment by Scandinavian fashion artist C. F. Peters, who told Smart, Weintraub, and Gingrich that their discontinued fashion booklets were missed. Merchants wanted something to replace them, Peters told them, something along the lines of *Apparel Arts* that could be given away or sold. The three men immediately began cutting and pasting old copies of *Apparel Arts* fashion pages into a dummy to get an idea of what the new magazine might look like. Nearly a year of tinkering and fine-tuning would pass before the magazine would take its final form.

Gingrich with David A. Smart, the publisher of Esquire *(Chicago Historical Society)*

Esquire, The Quarterly for Men made its debut at fifty cents a copy – five times the price of typical popular magazines during the early days of the Great Depression – on 15 October 1933, proclaiming itself to be devoted to "the improvement of the art of living and the new leisure." The 124-page first issue sold quickly. When 5,000 newsstand copies sold out within five hours, 95,000 of the 100,000 copies presold to men's stores were recalled for newsstand sales. The second number of *Esquire* ("Now Issued Every Month"), dated January 1934

Gingrich valued good writing, and covers of Esquire *during the 1930s listed the names of some of the most prominent writers of the time.*

with the dapper, pop-eyed trademark figure of "Esky" on the cover, sold 60,983 copies. (Actually, the second issue appeared on Gingrich's thirtieth birthday, a date memorable also for the repeal of Prohibition; the Esky figure was portrayed on the cover celebrating the event with a champagne glass.) The total circulation of *Esquire* doubled by the end of its first year, newsstand sales alone climbing to 90,302 in March, 121,812 in September, and 136,350 in December. Within three years *Esquire* was selling nearly 700,000 copies a month – seven times the 100,000 for many other monthlies – and in January 1938 the magazine's circulation touched 728,000 – nearly four times as high as any fifty-cent magazine had ever climbed.

Between 1934 and 1937 sales of more than ten million copies of *Esquire* had earned the magazine's publishers an estimated $5 million. Gingrich claimed he never knew the exact amount of his own salary. Whenever his bills piled up, Gingrich recalled, his salary was adjusted to liquidate them. Gingrich once bought a town house for $42,500 cash, never pausing for a moment to consider where the money would come from to pay for it. His boss, David Smart, simply told Gingrich that his earnings from the business were enough to cover it. When Gingrich fell behind on the house's upkeep, Smart decided that his editor's $19,000-a-year salary had been set too low, immediately increased it to $30,000, and made it retroactive far enough back to wipe out Gingrich's bills. After the day in 1928 when he joined Smart in the publishing business, Gingrich said he never discussed salary with his boss. These salaries were substantial, invariably more than even Gingrich thought they were.

The profitability and skyrocketing sales of *Esquire* were based on boldly unorthodox marketing pitches to advertisers. A promotional booklet issued in 1933 under the title *The Art of Living and the New Leisure,* another Gingrich innovation, told advertisers that *Esquire* was designed to improve the "new leisure" available to middle-class men that he likened to knights cavorting about the twentieth-century urban landscape. To tap into the new leisure-class market of men, Gingrich wrote, *Esquire* promised to answer the most pressing questions of these modern knights, including what to eat, drink, wear, play, and read. Another Gingrich-written promotional pamphlet, *The Third New Year, An Etude in the Key of Frankness,* declared that *Esquire* was intended to be an adult magazine, admittedly amusing, cynical, flippant, superficial, and brashly sophisticated.

When advertising linage dropped 18 percent and circulation slipped 20 percent in 1938, Gingrich issued an inspired promotional booklet, *The Sixth New Year,* to reassure advertisers that the magazine would survive the business downturn. In Gingrich's promotional rhapsody, *Esquire* was a child of the Depression married to economic recovery. The magazine's four-year-long honeymoon with Recovery, personified as a fickle woman, ended when she abandoned the magazine to take up with Recession. *The Sixth New Year* booklet announced a turning point in the brief history of *Esquire.* The magazine found itself, for the first time, in an overextended circulation position, facing a question that had confronted *Esquire* for a long time: does the magazine want to be a class magazine emphasizing quality or a mass magazine geared to quantity? Gingrich told advertisers that *Esquire* had consciously chosen to be a quality, class magazine.

The new quality-over-quantity editorial policy of *Esquire* meant no departure from the editorial formula that made the publication America's most successful sophisticated-men's magazine. Gingrich held few illusions about what made *Esquire* unique: car-

August, 1936 — 5

Edited by Arnold Gingrich

Esquire
THE MAGAZINE FOR MEN

Publishers: David A. Smart, Wm. H. Weintraub

Contents for August, 1936

Art Director: Eric Lundgren

A Successor to S. Choirboy As soon as we learned of the duplicity of S. Choirboy, our late critic of dramatic critics, we went to work on George Jean Nathan, to see if we couldn't persuade him to take over the fort that was not merely left vacant but split wide open by the presumably unlamented Potter's departure. We had hoped by this issue to be able to announce that Nathan would be our new critic. But as this is written the great George Jean is in one of those redoubtable pouts, and we don't know for sure whether we'll ever be able to kid him out of it. We tried to reopen negotiations with him where they were broken off last January by S. Choirboy's bolt-out-of-blue advent, but this time they were strained by an added handicap. Nathan, it seems, is perhaps no more, but certainly no less, vain than the average critic, and we found him smiling through tears, as it were, in trying to laugh off some of the cracks that were made about him during those few months that seemed like forever in which the hand of the Potter was against all and sundry of the nation's play-reviewers. We tried to be casual about it, and to point out that inclusion in Potter's casualty lists was in itself something of a certificate of merit and card of competency, signifying membership in good standing among the critics who count. But that seemed to sound better to us than it did to Nathan. Then, too, he wasn't sure but what the Critics' Circle might boycott Esquire for Potter's didoes, in which event he couldn't very well take over the job even if he were finally to decide that he wanted to. It went on like that for quite awhile. In fact, that's where the matter stood when he left to go down to visit Eugene O'Neill at Sea Island. O'Neill was to help him brood about it. We can't remember ever having done anything either to or for O'Neill, so we don't know what effect that may have on the outcome. So, anyway, about all we've got to announce for this issue is the fact that we've thought about getting Nathan to be our drama critic. We thought of him first because it seems to us that he is to the world of the theatre what Burton Rascoe is to the world of books. And, second, we're sort of fed up on the idea of employing home-grown unknown talent for a spot like this, after what happened with our last venture in that direction. If this sounds like the burnt monkey's lecture on the unsavoriness of hot soup, well, let it. Because, after the S. Choirboy episode, that's about what it is.

The Trend to go "Light in August" *Light in August* is a Faulkner novel title. But it might well be an annual slogan for the magazine trade in general. Every year, come the dog days, magazines undergo a strange shrinking process. Not only are there fewer ads, but the editorial content, too, is put on a strenuous reducing diet. Esquire, for the third successive summer, has reversed the field by making the August issue bigger than ordinary issues. This time, with a hundred and ten editorial features, we touch our all-time high in magazine money's worth. You don't believe there are a hundred and ten editorial features in this issue? Count, as we list them: fourteen articles, two personality sketches, twelve pieces of fiction, two of semi-fiction, four of sports, four of satire, four poems, two portfolios of artwork, four pictorial features, eight departments, eight fashion pages—that's sixty-four features so far—and twenty-nine cartoons in full color and seventeen in black and white makes a total of a hundred and ten.

Tune of "Sue and be Damned" In an issue containing such high spots as *The Snows of Kilimanjaro, Last Land of Liberty, Afternoon of an Author, A Day of Pleasure, Now It Can be Sold,* and five-star features by Rascoe and Seldes, it seems hardly fair to single out one story for special mention, but there's so much more truth than fiction in Edwin Baird's story, *Lawyers Laugh Last*, concerning the great American pastime of sue-me-sue-you, that we can't resist the temptation to take time out to try our utmost to get you to put it at the head of your list of required reading. Just as nobody wins in modern wars, with the exception of the munition magnates, nobody wins in modern lawsuits, nobody, that is, but the lawyers. Esquire, like almost all other magazines, has enriched many lawyers with no profit to itself. It has been sued some six times in its young life, and has itself sued once. One or two other suits seem to be shaping up on the horizon. Esquire has so far won all suits that have come to their conclusion and is an odds-on bet to win those still pending. Yet nothing has been, or will be, settled by those suits that couldn't have been settled much more quickly and economically without them. The curious thing about people who sue magazines is that almost invariably their basis for suit is that they have suffered in heart and mind, with injuries to their health or happiness through alleged loss of standing in the esteem of their fellows. These wounds having allegedly been made only by the printed word, it would seem logical that their cure could be accomplished by the same agency. But no. The patient always insists that his wounds of heart and mind, caused by print, can be cured only through the purse. Enough of that, though. We're beginning to digress. Turn to page 64 and see why lawyers laugh, and how.

ESQUIRE August, 1936 T. M. Reg.

Esquire is published monthly by Esquire, Inc. David A. Smart, President; Arnold Gingrich, Vice-President; Alfred Smart, Secretary and Treasurer. Editorial, Circulation, Business and Production Departments, 919 North Michigan Avenue, Chicago, Illinois. Entered as second class matter at Post Office at Chicago, Illinois, Dec. 15th, 1933, under the Act of March 3rd, 1879. Manuscripts and drawings must be accompanied by postage or by provision for payment of carrying charges if their return is desired in the event of non-purchase, but no responsibility will be assumed for loss or damage to unsolicited materials. Advertising offices, 366 Madison Avenue, New York, N. Y. Subscriptions for one year payable in advance, in the United States and possessions, Cuba, Mexico, Central America and South America, $5.00; Canada, $5.50; elsewhere, $7.50. Notices of changes of address must be received one month before they are to take effect. Both old and new addresses should be given.

Vol. VI, No. 2 Whole No. 33 T. M. Reg.

Contents for the most famous issue of Esquire, *which includes Ernest Hemingway's "The Snows of Kilimanjaro," with its notorious reference to "poor Scott Fitzgerald," as well as an autobiographical article by Fitzgerald*

toons and first-rate writers. Full-page color cartoons that began with the first issue were an important factor in the magazine's success, giving it a dimension that few, if any, other magazines possessed. The magazine's pert, fashionably risqué dimension derived in large measure from the work of three artists whose work Gingrich acquired for the magazine. E. Simms Campbell, a Harlem-based artist-illustrator and originator of Esky, drew cartoons that appeared in every *Esquire* issue until his death in 1971. George Petty, a photo retoucher whose airbrush gave the magazine much of its graphic impact, produced pinup-girl illustrations that came to be a regular *Esquire* feature known simply as the "Petty Girl." Petty's pinups adorned countless college dormitories, barbershops, and lockers of American GIs during World War II. Alberto Vargas succeeded Petty with a series of scantily clad pinups for *Esquire,* contributing to its reputation for being a girlie magazine.

But full-page cartoons and pinup girls often deflected attention from the magazine's legitimate claim to literary distinction. "*Esquire* has been much more widely looked at than read," Gingrich lamented in his introduction to *The Bedside Esquire* (1940), even though the magazine led its competitors in publishing distinguished stories. Setting a standard that *Esquire* would maintain for decades,

The digest-size magazine became popular during the 1930s, and Coronet *was an attempt to produce an art magazine in this format.*

contributors to the first issue included Dashiell Hammett, Gilbert Seldes, Ring Lardner, Jr., John Dos Passos, Erskine Caldwell, Douglas Fairbanks, Jr., Bobby Jones, Gene Tunney, George Ade, and Ernest Hemingway.

Hemingway's role in helping Gingrich quickly establish a literary dimension for *Esquire* was pivotal, beginning with the first issue. Gingrich met the novelist in a bookstore and seized the opportunity to ask Hemingway to contribute letter-style columns about his outdoor sporting activities. Hemingway agreed, suggesting other writers the editor could approach. Gingrich's proposal to pay the novelist double the magazine's standard rate of one hundred dollars an article struck a responsive chord in Hemingway, whose only condition was that the magazine pay him without making him feel servile.

In 1936 Gingrich paid two advances to Hemingway of five hundred dollars each, which had become his going rate with *Esquire,* as payment for one piece – a short story sent in place of the regular "Letters from Africa" installment. The story was "The Snows of Kilimanjaro." When Gingrich reminded his boss, David Smart, how much the magazine owed to Hemingway for its success, the publisher agreed to give the novelist a thousand shares of *Esquire* stock as a bonus.

In a retrospective published on the magazine's fortieth anniversary titled *Esquire: The Best of Forty Years* (1973), the magazine's editors boasted that sixteen Nobel Prize winners had appeared in *Esquire,* including Albert Camus, William Faulkner, and Luigi Pirandello. In addition to Hemingway, who had appeared thirty-three times (thirty in the first thirty-three issues), the magazine had published forty-five pieces by F. Scott Fitzgerald, the second most frequent contributor, and seventy-nine pieces by Jesse Stuart, the most frequent contributor.

Gingrich was fond of Fitzgerald and had a high opinion of his literary talent. In 1966 *Esquire* published Gingrich's reminiscences of Hemingway and Fitzgerald. "Ernest was always the sore loser, blustering when he couldn't be first in anything and everything," Gingrich recalled, "while Scott with a certain jaunty blend of insouciance and despair was always both gracious and graceful in defeat, perhaps because Scott was always fascinated by failure and Ernest always enamored of success."

Esquire published several minor masterpieces in addition to Hemingway's "The Snows of Kilimanjaro." In 1950 Ray Bradbury's celebrated short story, "The Illustrated Man," appeared in its pages, as did Truman Capote's "Breakfast at Tiffany's" eight years later. A partial list of *Esquire* contributors, compiled by the magazine's editors, included many of the twentieth century's major literary figures: John Steinbeck, Norman Mailer, André Maurois, Erskine Caldwell, Dos Passos, William Styron, Gabriel García Márquez, Kurt Vonnegut, John Updike, Langston Hughes, Joyce Carol Oates, John Cheever, Brendan Behan, Thomas Wolfe, Richard Wright, Nelson Algren, Flannery O'Connor, W. Somerset Maugham, Robert Penn Warren, Gore Vidal, Isaac Bashevis Singer, Graham Greene, Theodore Dreiser, D. H. Lawrence, Yukio Mishima, William S. Burroughs, Joseph Heller, Thomas Pynchon, Vladimir Nabokov, and Thomas Mann. Gingrich even negotiated with Leon Trotsky, then living secretly in France, and the latter's article on Soviet-Japanese relations appeared in August 1934.

The "most notorious piece" in the history of *Esquire,* according to the magazine's editors, was "Latins are Lousy Lovers," written by Helen Lawrenson and published anonymously in 1936. "There were two reasons for this, one bad, one understandable," wrote the editors of *Esquire* in 1973. "The bad one – and it didn't seem as bad then as it does now – was that a woman writer's place certainly wasn't in a man's magazine. The understandable one – and it seemed more understandable then than it does now – was the feeling that the author's name had to be suppressed to protect her innocence." "Latins are Lousy Lovers" was humorous and risqué, especially "the point of the piece" under the subhead "The Latin in Bed." The Latin man devotes his life to sex, Lawrenson wrote: "He talks it, dreams it, reads it, sings it, dances it, eats it, sleeps it – does everything but do it." She contemptuously dismissed the "amatory skill" of "a noted Casanova" as "Amateur College Boy, Class G-6," concluding, "I would swap you five Cubans, three South Americans and two slightly used Spaniards for one good Irish-American any night of the week. . . . I thought that our own home boys might like to know they've been severely underrated and they no longer need tremble before foreign competition in the most popular of indoor sports."

Esquire, Incorporated, emboldened by its success, expanded its publishing activities between 1936 and 1939 with three new magazines. Appearing in 1936, *Coronet* was a pocket-size arts publication offering, as its subtitle stated, "Infinite Riches in a Little Room." Gingrich edited *Coronet* between 1936 and 1945. *Verve* was the retitled name of the defunct *Minotaur* magazine that Smart had bought during a visit to Paris, France. Gingrich served briefly as the editor of *Verve* for its eighteen-month existence in 1938 and 1939, working with its French art editor who had enticed Pablo Picasso, Henri Matisse, and Marc Chagall to produce the magazine's covers. *Ken* was designed to be a political opinion magazine that was both anticommunist and anti-Fascist and against authoritarian dictatorship of any ideological persuasion. *Ken* lasted only a year (August 1938 to August 1939), a victim of low circulation and pressure brought against the magazine's advertisers who received organized mail protests from a variety of highly vocal minority groups. Gingrich later admitted that one error of judgment, the publication in the third issue of an article discussing the professional life of a Los Angeles prostitute, drew protests of indecency and complicated the precarious existence of *Ken.*

During World War II *Esquire* became embroiled in a protracted dispute with the United States government that cost the magazine its second-class mail privileges. In an effort to secure a favorable wartime paper allotment from the War Production Board,

Cover for the first issue of Ken, *a magazine in* Esquire *format but with a strong political component representing the concerns of the 1930s*

Esquire had begun straining to show that larger percentages of its pages were geared to improving troop morale. The morale-boosting content included double-page spreads of pinup girls and even a close-to-life-size, fivefold Petty Girl. In spring 1942 the Post Office Department began questioning the moral content of *Esquire,* prompting Gingrich to make monthly trips to Washington, D.C., with the magazine's dummies in hand, to get the post-office solicitor's prepublication clearance for each page and illustration. Postmaster General Frank Walker, then Democratic National Committee chairman and a Roman Catholic, was unsatisfied with the editor's efforts, and he cited *Esquire* in September 1943 to show cause why its second-class mailing privileges should not be revoked. When the hearing board of three assistant postmasters general agreed that *Esquire* should keep its mailing privileges, Walker overruled the decision. *Esquire* took the case to court, challenging an individual's right to rescind a government mail privilege that could force the demise of many magazines. After weeks of hearings and several court trials, Judge Thurmond Arnold of the United States Court of Appeals reversed the

A 1938 advertisement soliciting subscriptions and featuring a "Petty Girl"

postmaster general's ruling on 4 June 1945. The *Esquire* case raised "the age old question [of] when a scantily clad lady is art," Arnold wrote, "and when she is highly improper." The judge found only "confusion" in the trial transcript to this "vexing riddle." Moreover, the judge estimated that revocation of second-class mailing privileges would cost *Esquire* five hundred thousand dollars a year, a competitive disadvantage that could mean the magazine's demise. In reversing the judgment of the postmaster general, the appellate judge told post-office officials to limit their activities to "the more prosaic function" of "the swift completion of their appointed rounds."

In July 1945 Gingrich left the United States to live in Switzerland, serving as European editor of *Esquire* and *Coronet* and writing articles and translating stories. Gingrich had visited Lake Geneva in 1938, vowing to return after the impending war had ended. Gingrich believed he had done a lifetime's work between the ages of twenty and forty, and he was ready to retire to a Swiss villa at the close of World War II. By summer 1946 Gingrich not only stopped working on *Esquire,* but he even stopped reading it and entirely ended his relations with the magazine. In a transatlantic telephone call Gingrich offered his resignation, and Smart accepted it. Gingrich collected his pension benefits, kept his *Esquire* stock, and ended all contact with the *Esquire* organization. After his departure *Esquire* was edited by Frederic A. Birmingham, who had started at the magazine as a copywriter.

Gingrich ended his European sojourn in 1949, returning to join Cowles Magazines, Incorporated, as vice-president and general manager of the magazine *Flair*. In 1951 Gingrich next went to work for the William H. Weintraub Company, an advertising agency established in 1940. But Smart lured Gingrich back to *Esquire* in 1952, promising to stick to the business side of the operation and to let Gingrich handle the magazine's editorial content.

The postwar boom caught *Esquire* unprepared to tap into the new prosperity and in desperate need of rejuvenation to fend off competition from *Sports Illustrated, Holiday,* and *Playboy* magazines. Gingrich resisted the urge to make sudden major changes in *Esquire,* though he broadened its content and revamped the layout and design to give the magazine wider appeal and a more fashionable appearance. Gingrich learned that repetition of past successes does not assure another round of success when the reintroduction of the Petty Girl failed to make a demonstrable difference in circulation; he let the feature lapse.

The arrival of *Playboy* and its imitators further de-emphasized the pinup phase of *Esquire* after the war years. The centerfold pinups featuring partial nudity that had become the cardinal feature of *Playboy* prompted Gingrich to replace the "Lady Fair" in *Esquire* with "Great Moments in Sports." According to Gingrich, *Playboy* was less an imitation than a caricatured and exaggerated extension of the pinup-girl side of *Esquire.* Hugh Hefner, the editor of *Playboy,* had in fact once worked for *Esquire.*

Under Gingrich's editorship *Esquire* began to stress fashion and youth to position the magazine for the postwar boom that began in the 1950s and soared through the next decade. In keeping with this emphasis on youth, Gingrich recruited young editors to help him rejuvenate the magazine. Rust Hills became the magazine's new fiction editor and added a new list of authors to an already-distinguished roster: James Baldwin, Saul Bellow, John Barth, Truman Capote, Philip Roth, and J. D. Salinger, among others. Other editorial Young Turks recruited by Gingrich later went on to their own commands: Clay Felker to *New York,* Ralph Ginsburg to *Eros* and *Avant-Garde,* and Dave Solomon to *Downbeat.*

The young editors were only partly responsible for the magazine's dramatic turnaround. Gingrich's editorial prowess as "one of the major innovative forces in American magazines" was demonstrated, according to Clay S. Felker in "Life Cycles in the Age of Magazines" (1969), "by a feat that probably no other editor of his time accomplished: the successful rescue of his own magazine. Other magazines have been saved by new editors being brought in, but Gingrich engineered a major editorial shift after years of early success with a somewhat different formula."

The new formula added literary nonfiction or New Journalism to the distinguished fiction *Esquire* had published for decades. *Esquire* virtually defined the New Journalism genre in the 1960s with Tom Wolfe's offbeat article about a custom-car show, "There Goes (Varoom! Varoom!) That Kandy-Kolored (Thphhhhhh!) Tangerine-Flake Streamline Baby (Rahghhh!) Around the Bend (Brummmmmmmmmmmmmmmm. . . .)" (November 1963), and Gay Talese's celebrity profiles "Joe Louis: The King as a Middle-aged Man" (June 1962), "The Soft Psyche of Joshua Logan" (April 1963), and "Frank Sinatra Has a Cold" (April 1966). John Sack's "When Demirgian Comes Marching Home Again (Hurrah? Hurrah?)" and Michael Herr's "Hell Sucks" appeared in 1968, giving *Esquire* two of the Vietnam era's memorable examples of war reportage.

The resurgence of *Esquire* meant that Gingrich could become less involved with the magazine's daily editorial duties, freeing him to pursue his passionate hobbies – toys of a lifetime, he called them. He took up the violin and practiced daily ("He was Godawful," an *Esquire* colleague commented), collected four of the finest violins ever made, and wrote a book, *A Thousand Mornings of Music* (1970), about his "obsession." His other avocation was fly-fishing – aficionados considered him one of the century's master anglers – and he would rise at four each morning to fish for an hour in a stream behind his New Jersey home. He extolled the sport's civilized virtues in several volumes, including *The Joys of Trout* (1973). He reached the mandatory retirement age of seventy at the end of 1973 and was subsequently listed on the masthead as "Founding Editor." Gingrich died of cancer at his Ridgewood, New Jersey, home on 9 July 1976, leaving his second wife, Jane Gingrich, and three sons, John, Rowe, and Michael Gingrich, by his first wife, Helen Rowe Gingrich, who had died in 1955.

In 1968 the Magazine Publisher's Association gave Gingrich its highest accolade for individual achievement, the Henry John Foster Award. In his acceptance speech, Gingrich said that "a continuing sense of wonder" was an indispensable trait for an editor. Harold T. P. Hayes, a former editor at *Esquire,* wrote that Gingrich's editorial style could best be characterized as laissez-faire. He would warn zealous young editors, "For Christ's sake, don't kill it with improvements." Gingrich summed up this style in an early issue of *Esquire* when he proclaimed, "He edits best who edits least."

References:

Deidre Carmody, "Arnold Gingrich, 72, Dead; Was a Founder of Esquire," *New York Times,* 10 July 1976, p. 26;

B. D. Cohen, "Arnold Gingrich of Esquire Dies," *Washington Post,* 11 July 1976, p. B6;

Clay S. Felker, "Life Cycles in the Age of Magazines," *Antioch Review,* 29 (Spring 1969): 7–13;

Harold T. P. Hayes, "Arnold Gingrich, Esquire," *New Republic,* 175 (14 September 1976): 33–37;

Smiling Through the Apocalypse: Esquire's History of the Sixties, edited by Harold Hayes (New York: McCall, 1969);

"Some Words and Pictures about Arnold Gingrich, Founding Editor of Esquire, 1903–1976," *Esquire,* 86 (October 1976): 65–70.

Hugh M. Hefner

(9 April 1926 -)

Donald Allport Bird
Long Island University, Brooklyn

MAJOR POSITIONS HELD: Sales promotion manager, Publishers' Development Corporation (1952); circulation manager, *Children's Activities* (1953); president, HMH Publishing Company (1953–1971); publisher, (1953–1989), editor in chief, *Playboy* (1953–1990); publisher, *Trump* (1957); president and publisher, *Show Business Illustrated* (1961–1962) and *Oui* (1972–1981); chairman of the board and chief executive officer (1971–1989), chairman emeritus, Playboy Enterprises (1989–).

BOOKS: *That Toddlin' Town: A Rowdy Burlesque of Chicago Manners and Morals* (Chicago: Chi Publishers, 1951);

The Playboy Philosophy (Chicago: HMH Publishing, 1963; enlarged edition, 1965).

OTHER: *The Bedside Playboy,* edited by Hefner (Chicago: Playboy Press, 1963);

The Twelfth Anniversary Playboy Reader, edited by Hefner (Chicago: Playboy Press, 1965);

The Twentieth Anniversary Playboy Reader, edited by Hefner (Chicago: Playboy Press, 1974).

Hugh M. Hefner

By creating one of the biggest success stories in American magazine publishing, entrepreneur and editor Hugh M. Hefner has wielded a major influence on both the publishing industry and the mores of his native country as well as the fantasy lives of millions of males. The controversial founder of *Playboy* has been described variously as a philosopher, a philanthropist, a reformer of "remarkable social conscience," the founder of a "new puritanism," the creator of an adult Disneyland, and a crusader against censorship and repressive sex-related laws. One commentator even called *Playboy* a twentieth-century version of John Stuart Mill's *On Liberty* (1859). More-critical observers have called Hefner a male chauvinist, an aging hippie and a perpetual flower child, a hedonist, a "guilt killer," and a pornographer bereft of social conscience who publishes a dehumanizing and exploitative magazine.

Hefner's depiction of unclothed females and his expressed attitude that sex should be not only salubrious but readily available have changed American sexual ideals. Writer Joyce Carol Oates once remarked that this adoration of youth, flesh, and a limited kind of beauty is now typically American. Hefner's publication has also had a strong role in influencing the middle-class male to aspire to "the good life" and an acquisitive upper-class lifestyle. The London *Sunday Times* once chose Hefner as one of the most influential persons of the twentieth century because he "struck an answering chord in the young urban American male. His fantasies became their fantasies." In providing what William Masters called the best available medium of sex education, Hefner was able to link sex with upward mobility.

Once the producer of his own grade-school newspaper, called the *Pepper,* the self-confident and versatile Hefner might have succeeded in other kinds of enterprise or publishing as well, although he since has admitted that he had the right idea at the right time in the right place. He remarked that when he began the *Playboy* venture, he had no idea of the odds against its success. A rare individual who has actually been able to live his own fantasy life, Hefner reports that he enjoys the public's fantasies about him. He has said that *Playboy* represents both fulfillment and projection of an adolescent dream, and he once defined success as "how close you get to fulfilling your childhood dreams" and proclaimed, "In my world I'm king." A devoted fan of the British television series "Pennies from Heaven," Hefner's favorite music verse is, "Somewhere there's a place where all the songs are real." Many writers are reported to have spent months with Hefner trying to capture his essence, but no official biography has been published.

Hugh Marston Hefner was born on 9 April 1926 to Glenn and Grace Hefner. They would have another son, Keith, and the two brothers were reared by their accountant father in a strict household. Hugh served as student-council president at Chicago's Steinmetz High School, where he wrote a joke column for the school paper and was voted "Class Humorist" as well as "One of the Most Likely to Succeed." In 1944 he was graduated 45th in a class of 212. After graduation Hefner joined the army, where he served until 1946. In two-and-a-half years he earned a bachelor's degree in psychology from the University of Illinois, where he contributed articles and cartoons to student publications and founded a campus humor magazine. Hefner married his high-school classmate Millie Williams in June 1949, and they would have two children, Christie, born in 1952, and David, born in 1955. Hefner and his first wife were divorced in 1959.

The 1948 Kinsey report fascinated Hefner and inspired him to study sex and various magazines. In 1950 he enrolled for graduate study at Northwestern University. For one of his courses he submitted a term paper examining sex laws in the United States.

Early in his career Hefner worked as an advertising copywriter in a Chicago department store, published a book of cartoons titled *That Toddlin' Town: A Rowdy Burlesque of Chicago Manners and Morals* (1951), served as a subscription-promotion copywriter with *Esquire,* and was the circulation manager of *Children's Activities* magazine. Although various "girlie" magazines, such as *Eyeful* and *Giggles,* and nudist magazines were available, Hefner began planning a new men's magazine with a different approach. Hefner apparently wanted to blend the quality of *Life* and *Esquire,* the explicit pictures of *Modern Sunbathing,* and the sensibility of *Wink* and *Flirt.*

In 1953 Hefner managed to accumulate $10,600 to invest in a magazine that he put together on a table in his small Chicago apartment with the help of artist Arthur Paul. Hefner originally named the publication *Stag Party,* and the cover pictured a stag in front of a fireplace. This title and cover were soon changed, however, and the undated first issue of *Playboy,* depicting Marilyn Monroe on its cover, containing forty-eight pages, and costing 50 cents, appeared in December 1953. It sold more than fifty-three thousand copies – enough to support another issue. Hefner stood near Chicago newsstands to watch customer reactions to his new publication. In his book *Thy Neighbor's Wife* (1980), Gay Talese recounted those reactions, noting that prior to *Playboy* few American males had seen a color photo of a woman without clothes "and they were overwhelmed and embarrassed as they bought Hefner's magazine at the newsstand, folding the cover inward as they walked away."

Hefner regards his magazine as an extension of himself, and he has remarked that at times he feels he is an extension of his magazine. Much of its content, which Hefner rigidly controlled until 1991, reflects his philosophy and his lifestyle.

Subtitled "Entertainment for Men," the inaugural issue contained fiction, nonfiction, photography, art, and humor and concentrated on the female sex and "the great indoors." This formula has been followed with careful elaboration for forty years. Inside the first edition were a rabbit cartoon and a statement of purpose. Hefner said he planned to target the city male and those of "masculine taste." He promised to concentrate on entertainment, apartment life, cocktails, hors d'oeuvres, art, history, music, and sex. While Hefner vowed to avoid serious topics, such as nuclear tensions, and to attempt to make the American male laugh, he tried to legitimize *Playboy* by saying that the need filled by his publication was "only slightly less important than the one just taken care of by the Kinsey Report." Opposite the statement of purpose was a cartoon of a library with liquor bottles and a roaring fire, with a rabbit attired in a smoking jacket and carrying a cigarette holder in the foreground. On the mantle, alongside a trophy cup and a sculpture of a topless woman, are pipes and books enclosed by nude-women bookends. Gracing Hefner's editorial state-

Cover for the first issue of Hefner's most successful magazine

ment was an illustration of a woman wearing a bathing suit.

Opposite the contents page was "The Men's Shop," which listed seven essential items, including a home fire alarm, a clotheshorse, and a thermoplastic ice bucket. Pictures of the *Playboy* dream car would follow in the seventh issue. Other items in the first issue included a ribald classic, "Tales from the Decameron," a humorous account of adultery, and "Playboy's Party Jokes," most of which derive their humor from that which was suggested rather than said. Later ribald classics included Boccaccio's "The Queen and the Stable-Boy" and Ben Franklin's "Advice on the Choice of a Mistress," with an accompanying comment that the advice was still timely.

Monroe was dubbed as the issue's "Sweetheart of the Month," with the promise that a "beautiful, full color unpinned pinup" would appear in succeeding issues. An article titled "What Makes Marilyn?" detailed her publicity successes and measurements. Pictures included a shot of Monroe with low cleavage and the famous full-figure calendar pose, which Hefner said he had selected from two calendar poses taken in 1949 that had helped her become a star.

The lead article in the inaugural issue sided with men in detailing problems of marriage breakup and the cost of alimony. The flapper days were better, the piece argued: "When a modern-day marriage ends, it doesn't matter who's to blame. It's always the guy who pays and pays, and pays, and pays." Although thirteen separate features were listed on the contents page, smaller features were scattered throughout the first issue. A piece on a Parisian parlor game contained a description of the rules and a picture of the game being played, including a frontal shot of a topless lady.

Hefner relished wordplay and voyeurism. "An Open Letter from California" included three pictures of a woman with high breasts, flat tummy, and large hips in a bathing suit with accompanying narrative about the "pool pal" and California life. Her clothes are shed in a series of photos as the reader turns the pages. Other materials selected by Hefner were a history of Jimmy and Tommy Dorsey, material by Ambrose Bierce, jokes, modern desk designs, a sports piece, news of good food and drink, and full-page cartoons and drawings. The sensuous "Matanzas Love Affair" extolled the satisfaction of drinking and eating.

The early issues of *Playboy* combined these hedonistic themes with materials from men's adventure magazines, complete with violence; for example, an early Erskine Caldwell story titled "New Cabin" contained a two-page painting of a man fighting with a woman whose breast was partially exposed. The description read, "He caught her with both hands. Her dress tore like a sheet of newspaper."

The second issue contained "Miss January" – the first "Playmate of the Month." An article by Sir Arthur Conan Doyle included an illustration of Sherlock Holmes injecting himself with cocaine with the caption, "Holmes pressed down the tiny piston." Seasonal emphasis began in the second issue with a Christmas-party cartoon bylined "By Hef" – Yuletide and other seasons would continue to be emphasized in *Playboy*.

Hefner's original formula continued, and innovations appeared gradually. The centerfold grew until the third issue boasted a full-color, double-page *Playboy* Playmate. The third issue still was bereft of advertising, which did not begin until the second year. "Playbill," a new department, started in the sixth issue, and the definition of a playboy appeared in the April 1956 issue.

Hefner is recognized as the originator of the nude centerfold. Critics Richard A. Kallan and Robert D. Brooks have described Hefner's monthly

Playmate as being unmarried, morally admirable, uncomplicated, generally wholesome, happy-go-lucky, and sexually available. Hefner's early centerfold quickly grew to two full pages, and soon props became more elaborate. As social conditions changed, the individuality of each Playmate began to be stressed rather than her all-American qualities. Well-known stars also appeared in celebrity pictorials for *Playboy,* including Brigitte Bardot, Kim Novak, Catherine Deneuve, Raquel Welch, Jane Fonda, Sharon Tate, Anita Ekberg, and Ann-Margret. Even Marlene Dietrich was shown in a revealing costume.

Many of the early articles published by Hefner advised the reader to work hard, play hard, and enjoy the good life. One chart of the Playboy's penthouse detailed his progress on returning from the theater to taking off his date's wrap, to moving on to the bedroom. More-serious discussion centered on protecting the rights of the individual in a free society and the separation of church and state. Man, because of "the inhibitions of cold-weather puritan morality," asceticism, and the promises of religion, has been kept from reaping earthly pleasures, Hefner wrote, and added that since the world has so many women, polygamy may be acceptable. "One Man's Meat" discussed four basic types of females preferred by men. The bachelor life depicted by Hefner in the 1950s reportedly paralleled the bachelorhood Hefner and his colleagues were enjoying.

The acceptability of voyeurism was suggested early by Hefner through photos of Bob Hope looking at women in bathing suits. Later the reader becomes the voyeur in "Photographing a Playmate," a story about the photographic session, from the model's arrival at the studio fully clothed to her taking off her sweater. Other early articles promote voyeurism and legitimization of sexual practices, making *Playboy* something like a *National Geographic* of sex. The magazine reported that women bared their breasts in a Paris nightclub and that Japanese females were allowed to perform erotic entertainment. An article on degrees of nudity, containing a bare-breasted sequence in a circus filmed for a French audience, hinted that freedom was greater outside the United States. The reader was told that no words exist in the native Hawaiian language for jealousy, chastity, or adultery. Hefner's pictorials frequently depicted studio sessions, with Playmates both in front and in back of the camera. The reader/voyeur was invited, both pictorially and in the copy, to become a partner in the shooting – "Joanne peels off brassiere, slip, and stockings and Adams tries several shots of her entirely nude except for transparent panties."

Humor was a regular part of the early *Playboy,* as well, and would continue to be so. Both written and visual puns frequently appear: one issue included an underwater photograph of a woman, taken at an oblique angle beneath her so that her buttocks appear to be next to her head; another featured an illustration of a bare-backed model lying face down on the sand, with an untanned patch of skin in the shape of the magazine's rabbit mascot on her back. An advertisement that ran in some early issues, in which the Springmaid sheet company pictured an exhausted Indian in a hammock watched over by an Indian maid with the caption: "A buck well spent on a Springmaid sheet," fit in perfectly with the magazine's tone. Few stronger sexual references than this can be found in the early *Playboy,* which was consistently implicit, rather than explicit, on sexual matters. The inference and the tease were preferred to the dirty word. Mother Goose rhymes were printed with selected words blackened out, so that the result suggested sexual situations, and a cartoon in the first issue depicts a man sitting on a couch over a woman lying on her back – in full dress.

Another regular theme of the early issues of *Playboy* is that of self-improvement. One bettered oneself by answering an advertisement and enrolling in a music-appreciation course and listening to the works of Ludwig van Beethoven and Franz Schubert. Readers could study the penthouse apartment in which the playboy lives and strive to become "a man who enjoys good living, a sophisticated connoisseur of the lively arts, of food and drink and congenial companions of both sexes. A man, very much, perhaps, like you."

Hefner said that although many general magazines had died, his magazine continued to publish short stories, and he claimed that the nonfiction it published made *Playboy* become "one of the most thought-provoking magazines in the world." One early issue featured work by John Steinbeck, Caldwell, and Ray Bradbury, whose *Fahrenheit 451* (1953) was serialized in three issues. Hefner published many of the most important American writers: John Updike, Saul Bellow, Henry Miller, John Cheever, Bernard Malamud, and Kurt Vonnegut, Jr. Commentators who have appeared in *Playboy* include William F. Buckley, Jr., Garry Wills, and Murray Kempton. Interviews with Germaine Greer, Stanley Kubrick, George Lincoln Rockwell, and Martin Luther King, Jr., have also appeared in Hefner's magazine. Part of Bob Woodward and

A meeting of the early staff of Playboy: *art director Arthur Paul, art assistant Voe Paczek, Hefner, and editors Ray Russell (standing) and Jack Kessie*

Carl Bernstein's *All the President's Men* (1976) was published first by Hefner. He also published work by such influential British writers as W. Somerset Maugham, Graham Greene, and Ian Fleming.

Hefner's self-promotion is one of his most striking characteristics. As early as the second issue of *Playboy* readers were informed that letters had poured in from all over the country. A former newspaperman praised the bon vivant tone of the publication, while another writer reported that he threw out his two hundred automobile magazines to gain space for his *Playboy* collection. When a reader threatened to cancel his subscription because of slow delivery, Hefner responded that processing backlogs were due to circulation success. Correspondence concerning Marilyn Monroe was still pouring in and being published in the fifth issue; model Marie Stinger was heralded as "the Marilyn Monroe of Miami" in the sixth issue.

Hefner's connection to Monroe was long lasting and proved important for the success of both. Hefner had purchased exclusive rights to some of her pictures, and *Playboy* published a pictorial in December 1960 titled "The Magnificent Marilyn" and a fourteen-page piece titled "MM Remembered" in the January 1964 issue. More than two decades later Hefner was still promoting Monroe – and himself – when in January 1987 he unveiled eight "never-before-published" seminude pictures of Monroe, taken in the late 1940s in the studio of Earl Moran, prior to her calendar posing sessions with Tom Kelley. Hefner has observed commonalities he shares with Monroe: that both were born the same year and grew up in a sexually repressive culture, that nudity played a major role in both of their lives, and that from the start, "the future of both the actress and the publication seemed assured and were forever after interconnected."

Hefner's efforts at promoting his magazine began early and covered a wide spectrum. In the first anniversary issue he announced that circulation had more than doubled, from 70,000 to 175,000 copies, and that the December 1953 and January 1954 issues were almost sold out. To acquire respectability, *Playboy* boasted that subscription orders had been received from the New York Public Library, the Library of Congress, the Institute for Sex Research at Indiana University, and even the chaplain of the Ohio Penitentiary. The eighth issue reported that the original *Playboy* was known to sell for three times the original price. A sense of tradition was forged for the one-year-old magazine when the twelfth issue advertised "The Best from *Playboy.*" While no advertisements appeared in the magazine before 1956, goods and services were plugged in copy. During the third year a *Playboy* cover announced that one million copies were being printed, and "handsome cordoba simulated-leather" binders designed to store back issues of *Playboy* were offered.

But one of the strongest promotional campaigns was reserved for subscription manager Charlene Karalus, later renamed Janet Pilgrim. A "Miss July" and "Playboy's Office Playmate," Pilgrim was photographed just about ready to powder her face in her boudoir, wearing earrings and a silk negligee with her breasts exposed. "Is it possible that a girl as beautiful as Miss July actually works in your circulation department? It seems much too good to be true," wrote one admiring reader. In another issue Pilgrim spends a holiday evening lounging in her pajamas. The reader sees her undressing, getting into more-comfortable clothes, and wearing only a shirt as she wraps Christmas gifts. Hefner also ran pictures of Pilgrim on a date at Dartmouth College. A fuzzy image lurking in the background of one of her centerfolds was rumored to be Hefner. As late as January 1979, *Playboy* would run another picture of Pilgrim, crediting her with the "all-time record" number of appearances as a *Playboy* centerfold. Pilgrim even sent out cards to readers announcing *Playboy* gift subscriptions. For the cost of a $150 lifetime subscription the reader was promised a personal phone call from Pilgrim.

In addition to promoting Playmates as starlets and celebrities, Hefner began covering their activities and reporting news of a sexual nature. For example, Simone Silva was pictured topless and dancing with veils, with an accompanying caption that combines exhibitionism, voyeurism, titillation, reader service, and international spice: "When English starlet Simone Silva pulled off her brassiere at the film festival in Cannes, France, she exposed actor Bob Mitchum to more than a pair of breasts." Much later "Forum Newsfront: What's Happening in the Sexual and Social Areas" would become a regular feature.

The organization grew, and by mid 1955 the company was making a profit and had a dozen employees on the payroll. *Playboy* was enjoying a circulation of more than three hundred thousand. Hefner decided to risk a new publishing venture. He was an admirer of William M. Gaines's satiric cartoon magazine, *Mad* (which had started as a color comic book in 1952 but changed to a black-and-white magazine format in 1955), and he approached Harvey Kurtzman, the editor of the magazine, with the idea of starting a new, all-color competitor. Hefner could offer Kurtzman a bigger budget, more editorial autonomy, and a more lavish forum than was available to him at *Mad.* Kurtzman was convinced and brought many of the most gifted cartoonists on his staff to the new enterprise. *Trump* premiered in January 1957 and drew praise from readers for its production values and the quality of its artwork. Though sales were encouraging, the costs involved in reproducing the full-color art were higher than Hefner had anticipated. In addition Kurtzman's small staff soon found that they were unable to meet deadlines and became frustrated with Hefner's perfectionism. By the time the second issue of *Trump* appeared in March, its losses were already estimated at three hundred thousand dollars, and Hefner decided to cease publication.

In 1959 Hefner moved into a sixty-room mansion on Chicago's North Side that had once belonged to a partner of Robert Todd Lincoln. Hefner's fully equipped private quarters were in the mansion's center. His bathtub could hold twenty-four people, and, according to one observer, on the headboard of his 8.5-foot-diameter bed were "four white Magic Wand vibrators by General Electric, all plugged in and ready to go."

During the mid 1960s Hefner became more reclusive, and his weight dropped from 175 to 135 pounds. During one two-year period he reportedly left the Chicago mansion only nine times. On one of those forays he tried to enter the Palmolive Building, for which he had signed a ninety-nine-year lease, but the guard did not recognize Hefner and initially refused him admittance. While Hefner was successfully creating his private universe, which included women, fame, and power, critics viewed the multimillionaire as overworked and melancholy, an individual with few close friends and who was reluctant to delegate responsibility.

Hefner's work habits were reported to include working from thirty-six to forty-eight hours at a stretch, taking Dexedrine, and drinking two or three dozen bottles of Pepsi brought on a silver tray by a butler. His executive meetings were said to last as long as twenty-six hours. Hefner's hobbies included tennis, volleyball, Ping-Pong, and collecting 78-RPM recordings.

At the start of the 1960s Hefner established the first Playboy Club in Chicago. The girlfriend of Hefner's partner, Victor Lownes, suggested dressing the waitresses as Playboy rabbits, with the bottoms of the costume raised to reveal the thighs. The "Look but don't touch" bunny policy in Hefner's

Hefner and models, 1961 (photo by Art Shay)

clubs was strictly enforced, and by the end of the first year the Chicago Playboy Club claimed 106,000 keyholders and sold more food and drink than any food establishment in that city. Many members who attended the clubs throughout the country turned out to be blue-collar and not at all like the playboy portrayed in the magazine.

Critics charged that organized crime in Chicago was involved in club services such as garbage collection, parking, and hat checking. A fifty-thousand-dollar extortion "fee" to an inspector of the New York State Liquor Authority delayed the opening of a club in New York City until 1963. The incident resurfaced later when Hefner was asked to resign and give up his interest in Playboy Enterprises in order to obtain a license for Playboy's Atlantic City casino. He refused, and he failed to receive the license.

Hefner loved celebrities and invited them to star at his parties and on his television shows. "Playboy Penthouse" was a weekly syndicated television show originating in Chicago during the 1959 and 1960 seasons; "Playboy After Dark" was produced in Los Angeles in 1969 and 1970. Luminaries included Mick Jagger, Jerry Lewis, and Sammy Davis, Jr. More pretty girls attended than men, and witnesses reported that there generally were few handsome males among the five hundred Friday-night guests. Columnist Mike Royko said that not much really went on at Hefner's parties; others said they were populated by middle-aged lechers.

Hefner's fascination with show business and celebrities also found an outlet in another publishing venture. In autumn 1960 entertainer Frank Sinatra urged Hefner to launch an entertainment-industry trade paper to compete with such publications as *Variety* and the *Hollywood Reporter*. Though not interested in publishing a trade paper, Hefner was intrigued by the idea of a magazine that would focus on show business. Inspired by Henry Luce's *Sports Illustrated,* Hefner developed the concept of a colorful consumer magazine that would cover the entertainment industry. He even based its title on that of Luce's magazine; it would be called *Show Business Illustrated.* Frank Gibney, formerly with the news magazines *Time* and *Life,* was hired as editor of the new periodical, and an experienced editorial team was recruited from New York. The first issue of *Show Business Illustrated* appeared on 23 August 1961; more than 250,000 copies were sold on the newsstand, and the magazine received 40,000 subscription orders.

But conflicts quickly developed over the editorial direction of the new publication. Hefner wanted a slick, commercial magazine – a show-business version of *Playboy*. Gibney, on the other hand, pushed for a more sophisticated, literary magazine – a *New Yorker* with an entertainment-industry focus. Circulation and advertising gradually slipped, and after twelve issues *Show Business Illustrated* was showing a loss of $1.5-2 million. Hefner sold the title to Huntington Hartford, the publisher of a competing title, *Show* magazine (which in turn ceased publication soon after).

Hefner later regretted abandoning the project, noting that Luce had poured $25 million into *Sports Illustrated* before it showed a profit. He became convinced that the staff of *Show Business Illustrated* had failed to understand the entertainment industry and hence the unique needs of the magazine; as Hefner described it: "I discovered I had hired a lot of square people to run a hip magazine." But Hefner's attraction to show business and celebrities could again be discerned in a new regular feature of *Playboy* which would experience considerable success: an ongoing series of interviews with popular personalities.

The first "Playboy Interview" appeared in 1962 with Alex Haley's piece on jazz musician Miles Davis. Haley went beyond musical questions to talk with Davis about racial unfairness in America. The interview forum in *Playboy* was designed to discuss the private conduct of public figures and to raise unusual topics. The importance of some of these interviews became fully apparent only after the fact. Martin Luther King, Jr., was awarded the Nobel Peace Prize after his interview. A Haley interview with Malcolm X appeared in the May 1963 issue and was the catalyst for their collaboration on *The Autobiography of Malcolm X* (1965). John Lennon and Yoko Ono's session was published a week before Lennon's death, and Jimmy Hoffa gave Hefner's magazine his last interview in 1975. Jimmy Carter's statement during his *Playboy* interview about adultery grew into a campaign issue, harming his election efforts.

Hefner's social commentaries were published in a series called "The *Playboy* Philosophy," which began in the magazine in December 1962 and ran through May 1966. Self-described as a "direct, organized approach" to a "living statement of our beliefs," it focused on individual rights in a free society. Hefner's philosophy has been called "muddled," and a critic once wryly suggested that "The *Playboy* Philosophy" "measures human worth by bustline and genital energy." In 1963 Hefner's "*Playboy* Advisor" was joined by the "*Playboy* Forum," a section designed to offer readers' comments on issues raised by "The *Playboy* Philosophy." The "*Playboy* Advisor" credited itself with the "decontamination" of sex in the 1960s. Hefner's favorite editorial topics included civil injustices, drug laws, abortion laws, homosexuality, and criminal acts. Sexual questions and answers ran a full spectrum, ranging, for example, from abortion to penis envy to sodomy.

In 1965 Hefner founded the Playboy Foundation, the activist bough of the *Playboy* philosophy. The foundation supported civil liberties and controversial positions involving individual rights. One of its first acts was to provide legal aid for a man serving time in jail for heterosexual fellatio. Funding also has been used to support attempts at sex-law reform, woman's rights, censorship, drug-law reform, government surveillance, and capital punishment. In 1988 a "Hugh M. Hefner First Amendment Award" went to a librarian who alerted individuals of the Federal Bureau Investigation's Library Awareness program, which sought to have librarians watch people who obtained suspicious material.

Playboy and its affiliated enterprises remained profitable in the 1960s, with the magazine grossing nearly $28.5 million in 1965, the eighteen Playboy Clubs generating nearly $20 million, and Playboy Products adding another million or so. Other ventures included a Jamaican hotel, a modeling agency, a book division, a Chicago movie theater, and multimillion-dollar resorts in Lake Geneva, Wisconsin, and Great Gorge, New Jersey. In 1969 Hefner's magazine was selling about 4.5 million copies a month, with no competitor selling more than 110,000 a month. In the 1970s, Playboy Enterprises embarked on foreign editions in Germany, France, Italy, Brazil, Japan, Mexico, Spain, and Australia, and the magazine has been available in braille in North America since 1970. Hefner's first Playboy Jazz Festival in Chicago drew more than seventy thousand fans for the five-day fest in 1969, and it has been held yearly since 1979. The company also began opening various clubs, resorts, and casinos, which included construction at Great Gorge. New clubs were opened in the Philippines and in Manchester and Portsmouth, England.

In 1968 Hefner paid more than $5 million for the "Big Bunny," a DC-9 airplane which included a round bed (with a bedspread made from the fur of Tasmanian possums) and an executive shower for two. Hefner also purchased a mock Gothic-Tudor stone mansion in the Holmby Hills section of Los Angeles for just over $1 million. He then added to the five-and-a-half acre estate a lagoon, waterfalls, and nearly two hundred species of caged birds. In

Hefner composing one of his "Playboy Philosophy" columns, circa 1965

1971 Hefner moved into Playboy Mansion West, which soon became another "salon for celebrities."

Playboy achieved its highest circulation in September 1972: 7,012,000 copies. Yet throughout the 1970s Hefner and *Playboy* were attacked by feminists, who found the magazine's depiction of women to be insulting. On the other hand, increasingly explicit nudity was being offered by such competitors as Bob Guccione's *Penthouse,* which featured full frontal nudity in its August 1971 issue, and some critics began to mock *Playboy* as passé. In addition to these troubles, Hefner believed that he was added to President Richard Nixon's "enemies list" and that he subsequently became a target for politically motivated prosecutors.

Hefner responded to the changing market by introducing a new title. Intended to compete with *Penthouse,* the first issue of *Oui* magazine appeared in September 1972. The new publication was to be a younger, more sophisticated version of *Playboy* with a European flavor in its humor and photography, and its basic concept was adapted from the successful Italian men's magazine *Lui,* published by Daniel Fillipachi.

Oui proved to be a success. By the middle of 1973 it was selling 1.75 million copies per month and had become the only monthly magazine to run $2 million worth of advertising during its first year. But this success was a mixed blessing for Hefner, for *Oui* began to compete with *Playboy,* and it inspired a proliferation of other new titles in the men's magazine market. With so many competing titles, *Oui* began to decline in circulation, until it dropped to 825,000. Hefner sold the title to Goshen Litho in July 1981 for $1.5 million.

Meanwhile, Hefner's Playboy Enterprises had gone public in 1971 and was listed on the Pacific Stock Exchange and the New York Stock Exchange. Its certificate featured a picture of a reclining nude. The stock failed to attract conservative investors and tumbled sharply – 45 percent in one year. The 1975 annual report was delayed, and the U.S. clubs were losing money. The nude was eventually dropped from the stock certificate.

Pulitzer Prize winner Derick Daniels of the Knight-Ridder newspapers was hired in 1976 to solve Playboy Enterprises's financial problems. His reorganization of the company included the firing of Hefner's partner Lownes, who had begun as special projects director in 1955. Lownes, who was at one time the second-largest *Playboy* stockholder, has been called the personification of the Playboy image. He lived in his English country house, Stocks, in imitation of Hefner, and he directed the lucrative British gaming operations. Lownes claims that even the mobsters respected the British operation for its cleanliness and that the London Playboy Club had a larger profit than Caesar's Palace in Las Vegas. Lownes's claim that his efforts made a $32 million profit in 1981 is contested by Playboy officials.

On 28 April 1982 Hefner announced that his daughter, Christie, would take over from Daniels as president of Playboy Enterprises. A summa cum laude Brandeis University graduate with a B.A. in English and American literature, Christie Hefner had worked on the *Boston Phoenix* and had been a *Playboy* editorial trainee in the summer of 1970, an assistant Bunny Mother in Boston, a special assistant to her father, a *Playboy* assistant editor, and a member of a group that evaluated and developed new concepts for future company publications.

Recently Hefner's publications have become the object of organized conservative pressure groups. As a result more than eight thousand stores banned *Playboy, Forum,* and *Penthouse,* as companies such as Southland Corporation, the nation's largest convenience-store

Christie Hefner, Hefner's daughter, who became president of Playboy Enterprises in 1982

company, People's Drug, and Revco refused to stock them. Hefner responded with an editorial charging that Attorney General Edwin Meese and the Commission on Pornography had become the tool of evangelical terrorists, and later he successfully sued Meese and members of the commission for alleged violations of the First Amendment in pressuring stores not to sell the magazine.

Playboy had sparked controversy in the 1960s, causing a heated debate among the clergy and academics on college campuses about the magazine's morality. Nearly twenty-five years after "One Man's Meat" first appeared, the discussion continued when in January 1987 Hefner printed in his "Forum Feedback" section a letter from Andrew Greeley, a Catholic priest, author, and sociologist, arguing that God made the female body creation's loveliest object and that failure to appreciate its beauty was an insult to the Almighty.

Hefner relinquished his bachelorhood on 1 July 1989, when he married Kimberley Conrad, the January 1988 Playmate and the 1989 Playmate of the Year. Their first son, Marston Glenn Hefner, was born 9 April 1990; they had another son, Cooper, on 4 September 1991. Hefner is now the chairman emeritus, owns 70 percent of the company stock, and works full-time on the creative side of *Playboy*. The recipient of various awards, Hefner spends much of his time with his family and is working on his autobiography. He has not traveled to Chicago for seven years, and he has been quoted as saying that the Bunny has become "a symbol of the past." The Chicago mansion was leased for ten dollars a year to serve as a student dormitory.

Hefner views himself as a reformer and thinker: "I'm a romantic, a sensualist, a humanist and a rationalist." He believes that, due to the influence of his unique publication, he has freed readers from puritanism and reintroduced fun into their lives. But many critics have viewed him as a male chauvinist and exploiter of women's bodies, and Hefner became a symbol that helped fuel the women's liberation movement.

Hefner believes his publication to be "a paradigm of entrepreneur publishing success and a metaphor for three decades of social change" in America. He has saved each piece of his writing and drawing and everything written about him by others in more than four hundred scrapbooks kept by trained archivists. In some ways *Playboy* was ahead of its time, as an article published in the fourth issue illustrates. Titled "Trouble in Tobacco Land," the article discussed rodent tests linking cigarettes to cancer more than a decade before a 1964 surgeon general's report made such a connection official. While the exact amount of credit – or blame – due to Hefner for changing American society and mores may be debated, his important place in the history of publishing, in entrepreneurship, and in fighting censorship laws and repressive sexual legislation is clear.

Biographies:

Frank Brady, *Hefner* (New York: Macmillan, 1974);

Victor Lownes, *Playboy Extraordinary* (London & New York: Granada Publishing, 1982).

References:

"Aging Playboy," *Newsweek,* 108 (4 August 1986): 50–54, 56;

Jill Bettner, "After the Centerfold," *Forbes,* 133 (26 March 1984): 43–44;

Ray Bradbury, *The Art of Playboy* (New York: Van der Marck, 1985);

Richard Brookhiser, "The Hilarious Badness of Playboy," *National Review,* 32 (17 October 1980): 1257;

William F. Buckley, Jr., "Come Undressed," *National Review,* 32 (3 October 1980): 1221;

Buckley, "Playboy Needs Your Help," *National Review,* 37 (9 August 1985): 55;

"The Bunnymaster and His Many Mistresses," *Newsweek,* 108 (4 August 1986): 55;

"Cupcake v. Sweet Tooth," *Time,* 99 (20 March 1972): 53–54;

David Halberstam, *The Fifties* (New York: Villard, 1993), pp. 564–576;

Mark Hosenball, "Like a Virgin," *New Republic,* 198 (4 January 1988): 10–12;

"In a Huff About Hef," *Life* (April 1988): 7;

Richard A. Kallan and Robert D. Brooks, "The Playmate of the Month: Naked but Nice," *Journal of Popular Culture,* 8 (Fall 1974): 328–336;

J. Anthony Lukas, "The 'Alternative Life-Style' of Playboys and Playmates," *New York Times Magazine,* 11 June 1972, pp. 72–76, 82–85;

Russell Miller, *Bunny: The Real Story of Playboy* (New York: Holt, Rinehart & Winston, 1985);

"Mrs. Bunny: Luscious Kimberley Fay Conrad becomes Hugh Hefner's Lawfully Wedded Playmate," *Life* (September 1989): 102–106;

"A Pornography Report that Stirs Passions," *Business Week* (9 June 1986): 34;

Lee D. Rossi, "The Whore vs. The Girl-Next-Door: Stereotypes of Woman in *Playboy, Penthouse,* and *Oui,*" *Journal of Popular Culture,* 9 (Summer 1975): 90–94;

Gay Talese, *Thy Neighbor's Wife* (Garden City, N.Y.: Doubleday, 1980), pp. 25–92.

Papers:

Hugh Hefner's personal archives in the Playboy Mansion in Los Angeles contain more than four hundred scrapbooks. These include a compendium of Hefner's writings as well as other materials that he has selected and edited.

Ben Hibbs

(23 July 1901 - 29 March 1975)

Nora Baker
Southern Illinois University at Edwardsville

MAJOR POSITIONS HELD: Managing editor, *Arkansas City* (Kansas) *Daily Traveler* (1927-1929); associate editor (1929-1934), fiction editor (1934-1940), managing editor (1940), editor, *Country Gentleman* (1940-1942); editor (1942-1961), senior editor, *Saturday Evening Post* (1961-1962); senior editor, *Reader's Digest* (1963-1971).

BOOKS: *Two Men on a Job* (Philadelphia: Curtis, 1938);
Targets for an Editor, anonymous (Philadelphia: Curtis, 1943);
Some Thoughts on Magazine Editing (Lawrence: University of Kansas, William Allen White Foundation, 1959).

OTHER: *Great Stories from the Saturday Evening Post, 1947,* edited by Hibbs (New York: Bantam, 1948);
MacKinlay Kantor, *Story Teller,* preface by Hibbs (Garden City, N.Y.: Doubleday, 1967);
White House Sermons, edited by Hibbs (New York: Harper & Row, 1972).

Ben Hibbs

SELECTED PERIODICAL PUBLICATIONS - UNCOLLECTED: "Water to the Sea," *Reader's Digest,* 31 (July 1937): 80-83;
"The Dust Bowl Can Be Saved," *Saturday Evening Post,* 210 (18 December 1937): 16-17;
"The *Saturday Evening Post* Reaffirms a Policy," *Saturday Evening Post,* 214 (16 May 1942): 18;
"Credo," *Saturday Evening Post,* 214 (20 June 1942): 4;
"Journey to a Shattered World," *Saturday Evening Post,* 217 (9 June 1945): 20-22;
"This Business Needs More Men Like Fred Healy," *Saturday Evening Post,* 220 (8 November 1947): 184;
"What's Ahead for Fiction?," *Writer,* 67 (July 1954): 223-224;
"Why I Believe in Magazines," *Rotarian,* 98 (January 1961): 24-27;
"Let's Stand Up on Our Hind Legs and Be Americans," *Saturday Evening Post,* 234 (30 December 1961): 102;
"Happy Birthday Herbert Hoover," *Saturday Evening Post,* 235 (28 July 1962): 66-67;
"Boys' Home on the Range," *Saturday Evening Post,* 235 (24 November 1962): 73-77;

"Progress Goes Marching Through Georgia," *Saturday Evening Post,* 236 (16 February 1963): 69–73;

"Mr. Ford's Busy Billions," *Saturday Evening Post,* 236 (16 March 1963): 68–72;

"Where the Boys Are at Home on the Range," *Reader's Digest,* 82 (April 1963): 112–117;

"California Builds Big for Education," *Reader's Digest,* 83 (July 1963): 164–166;

"Writing Lawyer of Rancho del Paisano," *Reader's Digest,* 83 (August 1963): 160–162;

"Bill Scranton: Champion of States' Rights and States' Responsibilities," *Reader's Digest,* 84 (April 1964): 103–108;

"The Lord Helps Charly, and Vice Versa," *Reader's Digest,* 85 (August 1964): 140–144;

"Boyhood on the Prairie," *Reader's Digest,* 85 (November 1964): 111–113;

"Treasure House on the Prairie," *Reader's Digest,* 90 (May 1967): 146–152;

"Behind the Lines," *Reader's Digest,* 91 (August 1967): 7–8;

"Some Thoughts on Magazine Editing," *Quill,* 56 (March 1968): 10–13.

When Ben Hibbs became editor of the *Saturday Evening Post* in 1942, he initiated changes in content, philosophy, and appearance that not only restored the ailing magazine to its former glory but profoundly affected the character and philosophy of the American people. During his nearly twenty years at the *Post,* Hibbs molded the publication to fit his own beliefs and to appeal to a mass audience, which he instinctively identified as traditional, family oriented, God-fearing, hardworking, patriotic, middle-class, and mostly Republican. Hibbs's instincts were right. During his tenure *Post* circulation climbed from 3.5 million to more than 7 million; advertising revenues soared to all-time highs. Hibbs produced a quality publication, and in the process the *Saturday Evening Post* became as much a symbol of the American way of life as the flag, apple pie, and motherhood.

Benjamin Smith Hibbs was born in Fontana, Kansas, on 23 July 1901 and was the second of the three children of Russell and Elizabeth Smith Hibbs. Shortly after his birth the family moved to Pretty Prairie, Kansas, near Wichita, and Hibbs spent most of his childhood there. His father was an accountant and manager for a lumber company; his mother had taught mathematics in a Fayette, Missouri, boys' school. Growing up in the early years of the twentieth century in a small (population five hundred) midwestern rural community forever shaped Hibbs's values and ideas about America and the world. It was a happy childhood spent playing with his older brother, Russell Robert, and later with his sister, Elizabeth Eugenia, nearly ten years his junior. Ben Hibbs's father exacted obedience and respect from his children but tempered his discipline with basic kindness and a sense of humor and by never being too busy to spend time with his children. Mrs. Hibbs instilled ambition in them and provided them with an understanding of the value of education. Although she had been raised a Baptist and her husband had been brought up a Quaker, the family joined the Methodist church in Pretty Prairie, actively participating in that denomination. There were not many luxuries in the Hibbs household, but there were always books. The family subscribed to the *Kansas City Star,* the *Saturday Evening Post,* and other magazines. Both parents talked to the children about what they had read.

Ben and his brother worked to earn money for their bicycles, baseball gloves, and hunting rifles. They always managed to find odd jobs around town or on nearby farms. When Ben was ten years old, he got his first job with a newspaper, working with his brother in the print shop of the *Pretty Prairie Times* for twenty-five cents a week. The boys were fired for rowdiness. It was also when he was ten that the same paper published Ben's first article, complete with byline, an announcement of his soon-to-be-held fourth-grade class picnic.

After graduation from high school, where he was editor of the school newspaper, Hibbs went to work for a year for the hardware-and-lumber business managed by his father. Then, having earned enough money for his immediate college expenses, he enrolled at the University of Kansas in the fall of 1919. He worked his way through college as a janitor and cafeteria worker but also worked for the university newspaper, the *Daily Kansan,* eventually becoming editor. He wrote for the campus literary magazine and was a member of the Sigma Delta Chi journalism fraternity, the Quill literary society, and Sachem, an honorary society. He was elected to Phi Beta Kappa. Hibbs dropped out of school for a semester at the end of his sophomore year to earn money to further his education. His first newspaper job as an adult was with the *Fort Morgan* (Colorado) *Evening Times* as a reporter during the summer between his junior and senior years. He graduated with his bachelor's degree in February 1924, and in April 1942 he received a distinguished service award from the university. After graduation he

Hibbs in 1942, the year he took over the Saturday Evening Post

went to work as a reporter for the *Pratt* (Kansas) *Daily Tribune.*

After a year Hibbs quit and accepted an offer to teach English and journalism classes at Fort Hays (Kansas) State College. Although the salary was a great deal more than he had earned in Pratt, he missed working in journalism and continued to report and write for the city newspapers in his free time, but it was not enough; after two years of the academic life, he returned to journalism full-time to work for the *Goodland* (Kansas) *News Republic.* In 1927 he was offered a job as managing editor of the *Daily Traveler,* a newspaper in Arkansas City, Kansas. It was there that Hibbs's work began to be noticed by other papers, and soon other midwestern newspapers, including the *Kansas City Star,* were quoting him.

Because of exposure in the *Star,* in 1929 he received an offer to join the staff of *Country Gentleman* as an associate editor. *Country Gentleman,* a magazine for people who lived in rural areas, was published by the Curtis Publishing Company. Acceptance of the position would necessitate a move to Philadelphia, headquarters of the Curtis empire, and Hibbs was initially reluctant to leave his beloved Kansas. But the salary offered was too good to turn down, so with great misgiving he ended his newspaper career and entered the world of magazine journalism. Of his departure William Allen White wrote: "Philadelphia is taking from us the white-headed boy of Kansas journalism" and added that Hibbs was able "to produce a greater volume of first-rate stuff than any other man in the state."

At first Hibbs hated his job and Philadelphia. He considered the work dreary and routine and, because he was unused to city life, felt the people were aloof and cold. He seriously considered returning to Kansas and hunting for another newspaper job. Eventually, as he was given less-boring work to do, he began to enjoy his job and even to become reconciled to living in Philadelphia. A contributing factor to this change of heart was probably his marriage, on 3 June 1930, to Edith Kathleen Doty, a schoolteacher he had met in Arkansas City. In 1935 their only child, Stephen Doty Hibbs, was born.

As time passed, Hibbs began writing general and agricultural articles for the *Country Gentleman* and traveling across America to research them. He loved travel and, over a period of five years, wrote nearly sixty articles for the magazine. His roving days ended, however, when he was promoted to fiction editor in 1934; his duties included seeking and buying material from some of the best-known authors of the time, including Stephen Vincent Benét, Clarence Budington Kelland, and Ben Ames Williams. Two of the writers with whom he worked became lifelong friends – Jesse Stuart and Erle Stanley Gardner.

Hibbs was elected a director of the Curtis Publishing Company in April 1940 and in September of that year became editor of *Country Gentleman.* He immediately began making changes. Editorially he repudiated the isolationist stance that had been the magazine's previous platform. Graphic changes included the use of color photography and more effective display of black-and-white photographs. He rearranged the contents so as to make each page more attractive, tightened the copy in order to make it livelier and more readable, and offered the readers a greater variety of topics than ever before. Circulation in the 1930s had been about 1.5 million; in the two years Hibbs was editor it reached and surpassed 2 million.

Although *Country Gentleman* was doing well, another Curtis magazine, the *Saturday Evening Post,* was in serious difficulty. When George Horace Lorimer retired as editor of the *Post* in 1936, many agreed that he had held the position too long – since March 1899. In his younger days, when he understood his readers and his advertisers, Lorimer was an outstanding editor. He published works by such writers as Rudyard Kipling, Stephen Crane, Jack London, Bret Harte, Edna Ferber, Edith Wharton, Ring Lardner, Sinclair Lewis, Thomas Wolfe, William Faulkner, and F. Scott Fitzgerald. He introduced color paintings to the covers of the *Post* in 1899 and began buying the work of Norman Rockwell in 1916. Lorimer was also an astute businessman. In 1902 the average circulation of the *Post* was 314,761 and advertising revenue was $360,125. Twenty years later circulation had increased to 2,187,024 and advertising revenue had surged to $28,278,755. The magazine reflected its editor, with an emphasis on free enterprise, conservatism, America first, isolationism, and big business. For a while these policies found a sympathetic audience, but then came the Depression, President Franklin D. Roosevelt, and the New Deal. Lorimer stubbornly fought the tides of change in the pages of the *Post,* but it was a losing battle; the magazine had remained the same, while the audience had not. Advertising revenue had peaked at $73 million in 1929, but it stood at $18 million by 1933 and did not achieve the former high again until 1946.

When Lorimer retired, his handpicked successor was Wesley W. Stout, as conservative as his predecessor. He had been with the *Post* for fourteen years and saw no reason to change the philosophy and format that had been in existence since the turn of the century. Although Stout permitted the innovation of an occasional photographic cover, the magazine continued to rail against Roosevelt and the New Deal, organized labor, social reform, and social security. Advertising revenues sank from $26.6 million in 1937, Stout's first year, to $22.3 million in 1938, then inched up to $28 million by 1942. Curtis shareholders were in an uproar.

The final blow was due to a misleading headline, "The Case Against the Jew," placed on an article in the issue of 28 March 1942. People who read no further than the headline perceived the article to be anti-Semitic; actually it was not, but it could be misunderstood and was. Concerned about anti-Semitism in Europe, Stout had felt that by rationally discussing the causes of this prejudice, he could keep it from infecting the United States. He commissioned three articles, all written by Jews, to discuss the issue. The offending article, the last in the series, was written by Milton Mayer, an assistant to Robert Hutchins at the University of Chicago. Mayer denounced American Jews for abandoning their culture and religion in an attempt at assimilation. Although the piece was written with goodwill, it was completely misunderstood, and the resulting furor was tremendous: Jewish readers canceled subscriptions and advertising, and some Jewish-owned newsstands boycotted the magazine for years to come. Coupled with the general decline (the *Post* being in the red for the first quarter of 1942), the uproar over the article prompted Stout's resignation. Curtis directors decided they needed a change quickly. Looking within their own organization, they decided on Hibbs, the successful editor of *Country Gentleman.*

Hibbs became editor of the *Saturday Evening Post* in the spring of 1942. One of his first tasks was to write an editorial, "The *Saturday Evening Post* Reaffirms a Policy," an apologetic attempt to lay to rest the charges of anti-Semitism. He wrote that Stout had thought the series of articles "would be considered as a whole – that they would afford an

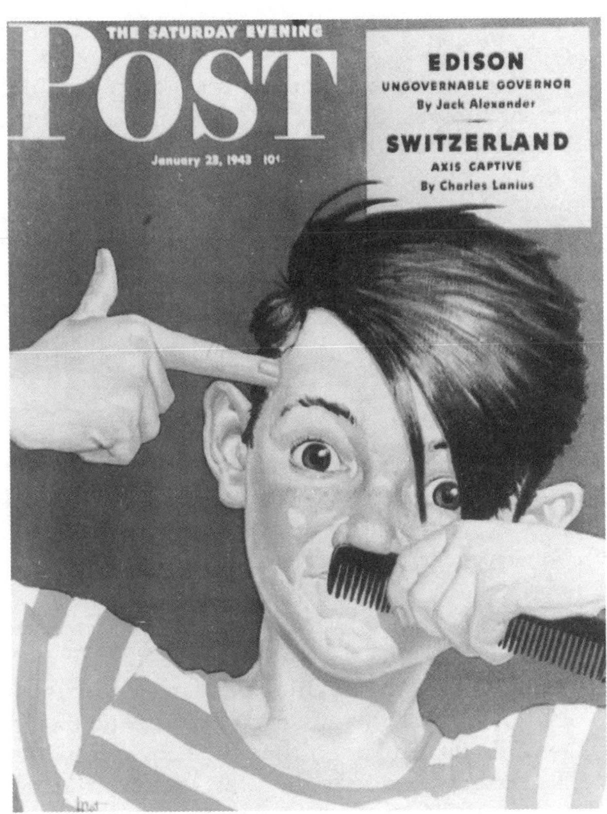

Covers for two wartime issues of Hibbs's magazine, reflecting its characteristically patriotic tone

intelligent basis for discussion on a question . . . [and] a frank airing of the whole question would serve to clear the atmosphere in this country and perhaps help prevent anti-Semitism from gaining a foothold here."

Many of the *Post* staff members were dismayed when they learned of Hibbs's appointment. Some were upset that they had been passed over for the position in favor of Curtis's "farm" editor; they predicted imminent disaster. It did not help that Hibbs was tall and lanky (slightly more than six feet, one inch) and, according to Joseph C. Goulden, had a "boyish, just-from-Kansas face." Hibbs also wore off-the-rack clothes and daily rode the commuter train to work from his home in suburban Narberth. One associate later said, "Frankly, we didn't know what to expect. Here was a newcomer from a farm magazine. It took us about half an hour to realize that we were lucky – that our new boss had the heart of a human, the brains of a Phi Beta Kappa and the energy of a wheat thresher." Norman Rockwell described the new editor as "easygoing and quiet but with iron in his soul."

Although Hibbs never showed it, he was extremely unsure of himself in those early days. Faced with a troubled magazine, a hostile staff, and a Curtis management decision to raise the price of the *Post* from a nickel to a dime, the task before him seemed insurmountable. He brought in Robert Fuoss from the Curtis promotion department as managing editor, and the two men began rebuilding, redesigning, and redefining the *Post* page by page and section by section. Hibbs, Fuoss, and the staff worked seven days a week and at night for three months, changing the format and content and transforming the *Post* into a general family magazine. Although the changes were gradual, they still upset many readers. The moving of the picture of Benjamin Franklin (the Curtis Publishing Company liked to claim Franklin as the founder of the *Post*) from the cover to the contents page was especially irksome. According to Goulden, one reader wrote to complain of Hibbs as the "disgusting young upstart and a barbarian from the Western frontier." Hibbs redesigned the cover by emphasizing the word *POST* in capitals nearly two inches high instead of spreading the full name across the cover as had been done previously. This helped give the *Post* greater visibility on newsstands. He also banished a typeface designed by Lorimer in 1904 for headlines and titles, and known to printers as "Post Old Style." The staff, typographers, and editors worked unceasingly to develop new headline styles and illustrations for articles and stories that would encourage readership of the text and to redesign the standing heads for the various departments, such as "Post Scripts" and "Keeping Posted."

Editorially the *Saturday Evening Post* of Lorimer and Stout had been narrowly focused as a magazine for American businessmen. Hibbs sought an audience that would include the entire family. He compared the table of contents to a restaurant menu, saying that no one expected the average reader to read every item in the magazine, any more than a chef would expect patrons to eat their way through a menu.

In order to expand *Post* readership, Hibbs planned a magazine that would also appeal to women and young people without alienating male readers. In the new *Post* women readers were attracted by personality profiles of movie stars, opera singers, and other notables of the day, while sports stories lured younger readers. In the *Post* of Lorimer's day, articles and short stories could ramble on for eighty-five hundred words; that ended when Hibbs became editor. Hibbs wrote in *Targets for an Editor* (1943): "Perhaps the greatest single factor in helping us gain women and young readers without sacrificing our traditional male following is the fact that *Post* articles are on the average a good deal shorter than they used to be. We insist these days that our writers write compactly, and when they fail to do so, if we want the piece badly, we do the condensing in our own offices." This shortening of copy also enabled the magazine to publish approximately 400 pieces a year; before Hibbs the number was closer to 250.

The most apparent content change, however, was the decrease in the amount of fiction used and the increase in factual articles. Hibbs considered World War II "the greatest news story of our time." His predecessor, Stout, had made no plans to cover the war, which was then in progress. In an interview with Deryl R. Leaming, Hibbs would recall, "Despite the fact that the war was already flaming on many fronts throughout the world, I found we had only one foreign correspondent – and he was in New York." Hibbs immediately organized a team of war correspondents to cover the battlefronts for *Post* readers. These included Demaree Bess, MacKinlay Kantor, and Edgar Snow. Hibbs later said, "Things were happening in the world more exciting than what fiction writers could dream up." The war articles (and later other nonfiction pieces) were moved to the front of the magazine; fiction occupied only about 38 percent of the content.

Recruiting an overseas press corps was only one of the new editor's responsibilities. Another was to stir up patriotic emotions in the American spirit and to provide a promise of hope to sustain those emotions throughout the war. In his "Credo" of 20 June 1942 Hibbs wrote: "We shall try always to keep a note of sound hopefulness in the *Post*. These are grim days, and I am keenly aware that the problems which confront the American people are staggering; yet I am not one of those who believe that civilization is on its way to collapse. I have profound faith in the capacity and the guts of the American people to work and fight their way through these dark years and emerge with a way of life that is still fine and American. . . . If ever this country needed a two-fisted faith in the future, it is now."

As editor, Hibbs knew that factual accounts of the battles were only a portion of the mission of the *Post;* to touch the emotional heart of patriotism would require human interest articles and illustrations. To this end he enlisted the help of Rockwell. The result was the "Willie Gillis" series, which depicted a typical young American soldier – peeling potatoes on KP, spending Christmas away from home, and returning home at war's end to a jubilant neighborhood welcome. Hibbs was proud of Rockwell's interpretation of the human aspect of the war as exemplified by Willie Gillis, but then came Rockwell's "Four Freedoms" series, which made Rockwell and the *Post* immortal. The four paintings, inspired by the Atlantic Charter proclamation by Roosevelt and Winston Churchill, were published as inside features in 1943, each accompanied by a short essay. "Freedom of Speech" was represented by a farmer speaking out in a town meeting, "Freedom from Want" by a family around a Thanksgiving table, "Freedom from Fear" by a sleeping child watched over by parents, and "Freedom of Worship" by two elderly ladies kneeling to pray.

In 1943 Hibbs was one of a panel of editors selected to advise the Office of War Information; later President Harry S Truman nominated him to the U.S. Advisory Committee on Information. During the war years Hibbs continuously warned his staff to consider postwar problems that would affect the United States. Some of these were becoming apparent as early as 1943, when Demaree Bess wrote an article outlining what Russia expected as a reward after the war. It was an eerie prophecy of the cold war, then three years in the future. Although Russia was an ally in 1943, Hibbs courageously stuck his editorial neck out and published the piece. In spite of paper shortages and the scarcity of the products advertised in the *Post,* circulation steadily increased and by 1947 passed four million. The scarcity of paper may actually have helped the magazine, as Clay Blair, one of Hibbs's successors, later pointed out. In *Decline and Fall* (1969) Otto Friedrich quotes Blair as saying, "when [Hibbs] took over, in the middle of World War II, you couldn't lose because of the paper restrictions. The advertisers were begging for space. Then, after the war, you couldn't lose because the big advertisers had to get their message across to the public. So for eight years, any idiot could make money in the magazine business."

During the postwar period the emphasis on nonfiction continued. Hibbs engaged in a circulation war with *Life* and *Look* magazines, a move that later proved to have been unwise since the *Post* spent more to gain a new subscription than the subscription was worth. The *Post* began running a series of the "now-it-can-be-told" variety of memoirs by generals and statesmen associated with the war. Later serials focused on movie stars and celebrities. Hibbs paid a then-unprecedented $175,000 for "My Three Years with Eisenhower," written by the general's aide, Capt. Harry C. Butcher. Hibbs spent $125,000 on the memoirs of Casey Stengel and $100,000 for a biography of Gen. Douglas MacArthur. The MacArthur biography was never published because the quality was so poor; according to Friedrich, Hibbs, in a private office memorandum, referred to it as "my worst mistake in twenty years." Whittaker Chambers was paid only $75,000 for the eight-part "I Was the Witness" in early 1952, but it was one of the most read of that type of series.

The serials proved to be popular with the readers, but they were also a shrewd business maneuver. By serializing Hibbs insured high newsstand sales over a period of time, and because advertising rates are based on circulation, higher rates could be charged. A *Post* serial on Arthur Godfrey, originally assigned to writer Pete Martin but eventually written by Hibbs when Godfrey proved difficult, sold two million copies on the newsstands in the mid 1950s. One of the most successful series was "Adventures of the Mind," an idea conceived and developed by Fuoss and wholeheartedly endorsed by Hibbs in an attempt to balance the preponderance of light pieces with more serious fare. The basic idea was to present articles by scholars and thinkers to a mass audience. These articles were later anthologized in several volumes as *Adventures of the Mind from the Saturday Evening Post,* beginning in 1959.

Hibbs was not afraid of controversy. During his editorial tenure the *Post* dealt with the population explosion, provoking angry protests from Catholic readers. "The Ugly American" made his first appearance in the pages of the magazine, and southerners exploded in outrage when the *Post* tackled the civil-rights issue. Although frequently threatened with libel suits, Hibbs refused to back off, especially when his writers had documented their findings. Goulden notes that Hibbs once said, "When we regard a topic as important, we don't tuck it under the rug simply because some lawyer may make a muscle."

Hibbs had an excellent working relationship with writers, treating them with respect and honesty. Although Lorimer had formulated the *Post* policy of "payment on acceptance," rather than on publication, Hibbs insisted on giving regular contributors an answer within twenty-four hours and believed that every article purchased should be published, unlike the philosophy at some other magazines that regularly bought more manuscripts than they could possibly use. Still, Hibbs was a demanding editor, requiring the best from *Post* writers. He also was that rare editor who could identify the weaknesses in the work and suggest improvements or new angles. Some people felt that Hibbs would have preferred being a writer rather than an editor. During his years at the magazine unsolicited manuscripts were accepted, and Hibbs was always delighted when new talent was uncovered.

However, there was criticism from some staff members that Hibbs was too softhearted and kept people on the payroll long after their usefulness had ended, that he had a weakness for "cornball" fiction, and that he and his magazine were old-fashioned. Blair suggested that Hibbs had lost his audience, much as Lorimer and Stout had lost theirs. As quoted by Friedrich, Blair explained that "television came along, and the advertisers could buy a bigger audience for a lower cost per thousand, and Ben Hibbs was in trouble, and all the other people like Hibbs were in trouble. Because now the question was: Who are your readers, and what have you got to say to them, and are they really listening? And Ben Hibbs didn't have the answers." However, according to Leaming, Ernest Hauser echoed the feelings of most of the writers: "The magazine, and individual journalism, are as dead as engraving on copper. It could not last.

Hibbs and Robert Fuoss, his successor as editor of the Saturday Evening Post, *in 1961*

Steamroller teams of editors were about to move in and take over the medium. The mere fact that the *Post,* in its old form, did last as long as it did, is Ben's greatest accomplishment."

Two years before he stepped down as editor, Hibbs expressed similar feelings about the vanishing days of personal journalism, remarking that a Lorimer or an Edward Bok would be out of place in the modern world of publishing. Although Hibbs was sometimes criticized because he failed to exercise his authority with Curtis management, the problems with the *Post,* which led to the disaster of the 1960s, began before he became editor. One of these was the decision made by Curtis authorities in the 1930s, when they were determined to change the company from a publishing company to a printing company. They began acquiring the paraphernalia required for the endeavor – the presses, buildings, paper mills, and delivery trucks – on a grand scale.

By 1960 the people working for Curtis magazines on the creative level numbered only a tiny fraction of those engaged in printing. A total of about 11,000 people worked for the entire corporation; the *Post* staff stood at about 125 people, the employees in the printing division at 2,600. Curtis owned a $40 million printing plant, three paper mills, 262,000 acres of timberland, and a magazine-distribution company. All of these buildings, the machines, and the salaries of accountants, printers, and promotion people were paid for by the *Post,* the only successful Curtis enterprise. When the magazine began to falter under this heavy burden, when it began showing losses despite high circulation and advertising revenues, Curtis executives decided to change the magazine. This move was doomed from the start because they attempted to make cosmetic changes without changing the content. The "new" *Post* of 16 September 1961 was a mishmash of old and new with some bizarre typefaces and flashy layouts but with much of the trivia that had begun to represent the "old" *Post.* Readers were infuriated, and advertising fell from $104 million to $86 million in that year alone.

Hibbs had planned to retire at the end of 1961, but when he saw the plans for the new *Post,* his initial instinct was to quit before the issue came out. He was talked into staying but said later he had made a mistake by doing so. When he did resign, he named Fuoss as his successor. Hibbs stayed on as senior editor, writing a few articles and doing a little editing, until the end of 1962, when he accepted (from his friend DeWitt Wallace) a position as senior editor at *Reader's Digest.*

The terms of his employment were exactly what he needed at this time, enabling him to work out of an office in his home in Narberth and to have a lighter workload. He was able to do what he loved best – write – and the shorter workdays gave him the opportunity to travel. However, he was considered a full-time employee of the *Digest.* In his capacity as senior editor, Hibbs also edited the work of many of the contributors to the monthly magazine and found himself working once again with former president Dwight Eisenhower, as he had at the *Post.* The two men had a great deal in common, with their rural Kansas upbringings and shared beliefs, and Hibbs was delighted with his friendship and his work with Eisenhower.

Ben Hibbs resigned from the *Reader's Digest* at the end of 1971. When he died of leukemia at his home in Narberth on 29 March 1975, he was a man who had earned professional recognition and the respect of many by his hard work, talent, and basic decency. He was a representative of the average American of his generation, and because he had molded the *Saturday Evening Post* into the kind of magazine he enjoyed, it attained a popularity and mass appeal that few magazines have ever equaled. The *Post* championed free enterprise and the American way; yet, despite Hibbs's deep love for his country, he believed in pointing out shortcomings and working to correct them. His detractors felt that he could have saved the *Post* in the 1960s if he had modified it to satisfy the advertising executives who were pushing for change yet still not modified it so much as to make readers unhappy. Others believed Hibbs was a genius who chose not to change the *Post* because he believed he was right. His judgment was based on circulation figures being at a record high and readership polls that supported him rather than those indicating that the magazine was old-fashioned. In addition to his phenomenal success in increasing circulation, Hibbs will be remembered for exemplifying the editor's skill and maintaining high journalistic standards; for insisting on compact, well-written prose anyone could understand; for instinctively comprehending the needs of a mass audience; for engineering a remarkable editorial turnabout in 1942; for nurturing a loyal and dedicated staff over nearly twenty years; for his editorial independence from advertisers; and for producing a magazine people still remember with affection.

Biography:

Deryl R. Leaming, "A Biography of Ben Hibbs," Ph.D. dissertation, Syracuse University, 1969.

References:

Matthew J. Culligan, *The Curtis-Culligan Story: From Cyrus to Horace to Joe* (New York: Crown, 1970), pp. 54–57, 59;

Otto Friedrich, *Decline and Fall* (New York, Evanston, Ill. & London: Harper & Row, 1969);

Joseph C. Goulden, *The Curtis Caper* (New York: Putnam, 1965), pp. 53–65, 89–91, 100–103, 106–109;

"Hibbs and the *Saturday Evening Post:* A Happy 10-Year Marriage," *Business Week* (15 March 1952): 66–82;

B. R. Manago, "The *Saturday Evening Post* Under Ben Hibbs: 1942–1961," Ph.D. dissertation, Northwestern University, 1968;

"*Post* Shake-Up," *Newsweek,* 19 (23 March 1942): 60–61;

"Return of the Native," *Newsweek,* 53 (23 February 1959): 89;

"Shiny New *Post,*" *Time,* 49 (26 May 1947): 71–72;

Richard Thruelsen and John Koblar, eds., *Adventures of the Mind from the Saturday Evening Post* (New York: Knopf, 1959).

Papers:

The papers of Ben Hibbs are in the archives of the Spencer Research Library at the University of Kansas.

John H. Johnson

(19 January 1918 -)

Patt Foster Roberson
Southern University, Baton Rouge

MAJOR POSITIONS HELD: President and publisher, Johnson Publishing Company (1942-).

PRINCIPAL MAGAZINES OWNED OR CONTROLLED: *Negro Digest* (1942–1951, 1961–1970), retitled *Black World* (1970–1976); *Ebony* (1945-); *Tan Confessions* (1950–1952), retitled *Tan* (1952–1971), retitled *Black Stars* (1971–1981); *Jet* (1951-); *Ebony Jr!* (1973–1985); *EM: Ebony Man* (1985-).

BOOK: *Succeeding Against the Odds* (New York: Warner, 1989).

Heading the wealthiest black business in the United States and generally considered the most powerful black businessman in the nation, John H. Johnson is an entrepreneur. His family-owned business empire currently includes *Ebony, Jet,* and *EM: Ebony Man* magazines; a book-publishing company specializing in black culture and history; WJPC-AM, Chicago (acquired in 1972 as WGRT, Chicago's first and only black-owned radio station), WLNR-FM, Lansing, Illinois (acquired in 1985), and WLOU-AM, Louisville, Kentucky (acquired in 1982); the *Ebony/Jet Showcase* television series (premiered in 1983); Fashion Fair Cosmetics, sold in more than fifteen hundred U.S. department stores and abroad; Supreme Beauty Products for the hair (Duke for men, Raveen for women); and Ebony Fashion Fair, the world's largest touring fashion show with a mail-order fashion catalogue, begun in 1959. His cosmetics line began when he discovered that makeup in shades suitable for Fashion Fair models did not exist, and he could not interest Revlon or Estée Lauder in its manufacture. Both have since reconsidered. Johnson also owns 19 percent of the stock in *Essence* magazine and runs its subscription advertisements in *Ebony*. In his other career he rose from part-time office boy to chairman and chief executive officer of Supreme Life Insurance Company. Johnson has been instrumental in getting major white corporations to advertise in black media and to use black models in their advertising layouts. There were no major black models before *Ebony* began. Johnson has experimented with a book club and a travel club and has considered French and Spanish international editions of *Ebony*.

His wife, Eunice Walker Johnson, is secretary-treasurer and director of Ebony Fashion Fair. Her background includes interior decoration, journalism, and social work. President Richard Nixon appointed her a special ambassador to the 1972 Liberian presidential inauguration. The Johnsons' daughter, Linda (Mrs. S. Andre Rice), who holds an M.B.A. degree from Northwestern University, is vice-president and assistant to the publisher. After determining she had the emotional and intuitive instincts for the job, Johnson created a training program. She sits in on all decision-making meetings and receives copies of important correspondence with his replies, and her opinion is sought in planning. About 95 percent of the time, their opinions are the same. Favorable comparisons have been made between her and Christie Hefner, daughter of Hugh Hefner. The Johnsons' adopted son, John, Jr., died at twenty-five of sickle cell anemia in 1981. He was a staff photographer for *Ebony* and *Jet* magazines, and a eulogy for him by his father was published in *Ebony* in March 1982.

John Harold Johnson was born in poverty in Arkansas City, Arkansas, on 19 January 1918. His father, Leroy Johnson, was killed in a sawmill accident when young Johnson was six, and his mother, Gertrude Jenkins Johnson, remarried when he was fifteen. Because there was no high school for blacks in Arkansas City, his mother worked as a cook for two years to save enough money for train tickets to Chicago. When her husband refused to move north, she took her son and left. Johnson's stepfather soon joined them, but they lived on welfare for almost two years. At DuSable High School, Johnson edited the school paper, was business manager of the yearbook, and excelled academically. He was

Johnson with his wife, Eunice, the secretary-treasurer of the Johnson Publishing Company, and his daughter, Linda, the president and chief operating officer (photograph by James L. Mitchell)

also a member of the debating team and president of the student council and of his class.

His mother was strong, supportive, and self-sacrificing. She taught him that he had to earn success, work hard, and believe things are possible. He became persistent, determined, and persuasive but not threatening.

The turning point in Johnson's life came in 1936, when he met Harry H. Pace, president of the Supreme Life Insurance Company of America, then the largest black business in the North. Johnson had graduated from high school with honors and won a tuition-only scholarship to the University of Chicago. Pace offered him a job so he could accept the scholarship. He earned twenty-five dollars a month as a part-time office boy and was able to enroll in college part-time. Johnson attributes part of his early success to having practically memorized Dale Carnegie's *How to Win Friends and Influence People* (1936), which taught him his favorite motto: "Don't get mad, get smart." His first job was to read and clip articles of black interest from the white press for the *Supreme Liberty Guardian,* a monthly newsletter Pace sent to clients. Johnson also worked as a political secretary for another Supreme Life officer, Earl B. Dickerson, an attorney, pioneer black activist, and Chicago alderman. At Supreme, for the first time in his life, Johnson experienced dignified, secure black people's making decisions and running a business, which inspired him to believe he, too, could be a success in business. After two years in college he quit classes, but he returned to the Northwestern School of Commerce in 1938 and studied an additional two years.

The work with Pace, combined with perusing *Reader's Digest,* gave Johnson the idea for his first magazine, *Negro Digest,* which would present news reprints and feature articles. While the First National Bank told him it would not make loans to blacks, it did refer him to a loan company. He pawned his mother's furniture for five hundred dollars to pay for printing and mailing twenty thousand letters, which he sent to Supreme policyholders offering them a two-dollar charter subscription to his new, though nonexistent, magazine. Responses came from three thousand, and with that six thousand dollars he published his first issue in November 1942, taking a leave of absence from Supreme that would last until he bought controlling interest about twenty years later.

In introducing volume one, number 1, he wrote, "*Negro Digest* gives you a complete survey of current Negro life and thought . . . dedicated to the development of interracial understanding and the

The second office of the Johnson Publishing Company in 1943

promotion of national unity. It stands unqualifiedly for the winning of the war and the integration of all citizens into the democratic process." When no distributor would take his magazine, claiming there was no market, Johnson recruited thirty fellow Supreme employees to make the rounds of South Side newsstands, ask for the publication, buy it, and convince dealers of a demand. Dealers finally provoked a distributor into handling it. Johnson reimbursed his friends with funds intended for the printer. He then resold the magazines and repeated the exercise in Detroit, New York, and Philadelphia. Within a year circulation rose to fifty thousand. Johnson would be in business for more than ten years before a bank would make him a loan. One fund-raising idea he used was to sell lifetime subscriptions for one hundred dollars, a technique later used by *Ms.* and *Playboy* magazines. Johnson told interviewer Dan Rottenberg, "Of course, we're paying for that now. No one tells us when they die."

The monthly *Negro Digest* measured 5 3/8-by-7 3/4 inches, contained one hundred pages, had no advertising, and sold for twenty-five cents a copy or three dollars a year. Circulation jumped from 50,000 to 150,000 when Eleanor Roosevelt contributed a feature titled "If I Were a Negro." Marshall Field III and Edward G. Robinson also contributed to this feature series. All were paid a writer's fee of fifteen dollars. Another popular feature was Johnson's imitation of the *Reader's Digest* "Embarrassing Moments" series, which he called "My Most Humiliating Jim Crow Experience." *Negro Digest* was discontinued in 1951 because of its similarity to *Jet.* Popular demand resurrected it in 1961, and in May 1970 the name was changed to *Black World* because of growing hostility among blacks toward the word *negro.* In the final issue of the publication as *Negro Digest* (April 1970), Johnson wrote, "The magazine will continue its focus on Black ideas, fiction, poetry and the arts, and it will redouble its efforts to bring clarity and insight into the problems and prospects of the children of Africa wherever they happen to be."

Black World premiered in May 1970 with Hoyt W. Fuller as managing editor. Fuller wrote, "*Black*

World will routinely publish articles which will probe and report the condition of peoples and their struggles throughout the Black World . . . publishing the thoughtful essays, the fiction and the poetry of both known and unknown writers, reporting on the arts, educational movements and innovations, and guarding against the opportunists and charlatans who would exploit Black Art and Literature for their own gain and for the spiritual and artistic colonization of Black people."

Special issues of *Black World* ran 130 pages. The format was similar to that of *Negro Digest,* but a copy cost fifty cents (five dollars a year). Number 12 featured a yearly index. According to James Speigner, "Of all Johnson's publications, *Black World* was the only one to be identified as militant. In its glory days – circa 1969 to 1975 – the magazine was a hotbed of black intellectual discourse and controversy. Some of the era's most provocative writing appeared there." According to some critics it was discontinued in April 1976 because of its militant tone. Johnson scorned this notion, pointing out that circulation had dropped from more than one hundred thousand to fifteen thousand and that he was in business to make a profit.

Ebony is a general monthly picture magazine patterned after *Life* and *Look* and named by Eunice Johnson after the fine, black, tropical hardwood. The first press run in November 1945 was 25,000, with an estimated readership of 125,000. The masthead of the fifty-page first issue shows Johnson as editor and publisher, Ben Burns as executive editor, and Jay Jackson as art editor. In his "Backstage" column Johnson wrote, "*Ebony* will try to mirror the happier side of Negro life – the positive, everyday achievements from Harlem to Hollywood. But when we talk about race as the No. 1 problem in America, we'll talk turkey." The contents of this first issue were divided under subject headings of race, youth, personalities, culture, entertainment, and humor. Copies sold for twenty-five cents, subscriptions for three dollars a year. Newsstand sales dropped off during the 1954 recession, and Burns attempted to revive the magazine with more and more sensational articles and art. Johnson opted for a more conservative format directed toward subscribers. His strategy proved successful as church groups began conducting subscription drives as fundraisers. Burns was fired.

The "Publisher's Statement" in the thirtieth-anniversary issue of November 1975 stated that *Ebony* was founded to "provide positive images for blacks in a world of negative images and non-images. It was founded to project all dimensions of the black personality in a world saturated with stereotypes. We wanted to give blacks a new sense of somebodiness, a new sense of self-respect. We wanted to tell them who they were and what they could do."

In 1982 at the announcement reception for WLOU-AM in Louisville, Kentucky, which was attended by one thousand people, including the mayor and governor, Johnson said, "What we're trying to do with Johnson Publishing Company, over the years, is give Black people pride in themselves, to give them the feeling that accomplishment is within their reach; to give them examples of people who have done it. Basically, *Ebony* is the same magazine it was 39 years ago. It is a magazine of how to get ahead in life; a magazine of how not to give up; a magazine that says if you get a good education, if you try hard, if you believe in yourself, it is possible to succeed in spite of the odds."

The fortieth-anniversary special issue (November 1985) contained 364 pages, the largest in the history of the company, and had a press run of 2.3 million, with readership estimated at 9 million. A million-dollar advertising campaign was undertaken to commemorate it; the slogan was "Nothing sells black consumers better." In his publisher's statement Johnson said, "A child of hope and a herald of hope, it was founded to give Black Americans faith in their potential and confidence in their destiny. We believed then – and we believe now – that you have to change images before you can change acts and institutions. This, in brief, was the *Ebony* idea. In a world of despair, we wanted to give hope. In a world of negative Black images, we wanted to provide positive Black images. In a world that said Blacks could do few things, we wanted to say that they could do everything. . . . For we know from experience that if Black people and their allies could change what they changed in the old world of the '40s, then there is no limit to what we can hope and achieve in the 1980s and beyond."

In 1984 single copies cost two dollars, and a year's subscription was priced at sixteen dollars. Johnson attributes his success to good timing, a ready market, and his ability to learn from his mistakes. In his *Ebony* interview of November 1985 he said, "If you are going to travel a long distance, you can't burden yourself with a new load."

In its coverage of the fortieth anniversary of *Ebony,* the *New York Times* reported a major criticism, attributed to Luther P. Jackson, Jr., a journalism professor at Columbia University, that *Ebony* is "heavily weighted towards things that are relatively frivolous." When critics say the magazine is too en-

Johnson with Henry Luce, the publisher of Time *and* Life

tertainment oriented, Johnson responds, "There has not been a single burning issue or a single major event that *Ebony* has not touched. I must confess that I was afraid to deal with some of them, but – the record shows – I dealt with them." In *The Communications Revolution: A History of Mass Media in the United States* (1977), George N. Gordon writes that, during the 1960s, the Johnson empire "changed its orientation from mere imitation of white magazines to a number of publications reflecting the new ethnic identity of the American Black. . . ."

Johnson persuaded advertisers that black consumers are a distinct, viable market. But the going was not easy. It took six years to sell space to Procter and Gamble. Johnson sent an advertising salesman to Detroit by train every week for ten years before getting the first major automobile account. The first national advertiser in *Ebony* was Zenith, an account obtained in 1946. Johnson was able to meet with Cmdr. Eugene McDonald, president of Zenith Radio, only after Johnson convinced him, "As president of a company, I had certain protocol rights in calling on presidents of other companies."

Johnson did his homework and learned that McDonald had gone on an Arctic expedition to the North Pole with Adm. Robert Peary in 1909. Matthew Henson, a black explorer, was also on the expedition and had given McDonald a pair of snowshoes, which McDonald kept on display in his office. Thus Johnson came armed with an issue of *Ebony* containing an article on Henson's arctic adventures and with an autographed copy of Henson's biography personally inscribed to McDonald. McDonald was so impressed that he not only became an advertiser but also persuaded Elgin Watch, Quaker Oats, and Swift, among others, to buy advertising. McDonald died in 1958, but Zenith has remained a major *Ebony* advertiser. Johnson had selected Zenith because many blacks owned that brand of radio, and his mother's ten-year-old Zenith radio was still in good working condition. While most newsstand and subscription sales are made to blacks, 90 percent of advertising sales of *Ebony* are made to corporate white America. In 1986 a full-page color advertisement sold for $25,198, for a single insertion.

Outstanding literary and artistic contributions have been made over the years by Lerone Bennett, Jr., a senior editor and noted historian; Dr. Martin Luther King, Jr., who regularly wrote a column, "Advice for Living," in the 1950s; and Moneta Sleet, Jr., a photojournalist, the first black photographer to win a Pulitzer Prize. Sleet won in the feature-photography category in 1969 with a picture of Coretta Scott King and daughter Bernice at the funeral of Dr. King.

In March 1982 the size of *Ebony* was reduced to 8 1/8-by-10 7/8 inches. Circulation at this time was 1.3 million copies per month, with readership estimated at 6.5 million. Another change since 1945 is that success, as defined by *Ebony*, has been redefined. In 1945 success was equated with material things. Since 1987 any accomplishment or positive goal that is set and met is seen as a success.

Johnson has wrought gradual improvements in style, design, and presentation, with the type content remaining the same. He intends to continue his leadership role of anticipating and defining new trends, and he sees the future of *Ebony* as secure because it is giving people something they cannot get anywhere else. Since 1986 the contents have included articles on art, business, civil rights, education, entertainment, history, literature, music, personalities, politics, social events, and sports. Regular monthly departments have included "Speaking of People," "Backstage" (editorial), "Fashion Fair," "Sounds" (music review), "Ebony Book Shelf," "The Ebony Advisor," and "Date with a Dish" (culinary art). The editorial staff averages twelve people, and freelancers contribute about 15 percent of published material.

As to *Ebony's* future, Johnson says, "If we somehow reach a point in this country when race will no longer be a factor and there will not be a need for Black magazines and White magazines, then *Ebony* will simply serve all the people. And, as I have often said, I think *Ebony* would be a greater success than any of its White competitors simply because Black people have had more experience studying and meeting the needs of Whites than White people have had studying and meeting the needs of Blacks."

Tan Confessions was established in November 1950 in standard format, similar in content to *True Romance* or *True Story*. It underwent two name changes (*Tan*, November 1952; *Black Stars*, November 1971) before it ceased publication in July 1981. In his opening statement in 1950, Johnson called *Tan Confessions* "a unique new venture . . . to reflect a side of Negro life that is virtually ignored in most publications today. It is that part of everyday living concerning the happiness and triumphs, the sorrows and suffering of the troubled heart. Love and romance, marriage and the family are vital concerns of every colored man and woman . . . and only are discussed in most Negro publications in terms of tension and violence that get into police and court records. *Tan Confessions* will also include a magazine within the magazine devoted to home service features. This magazine will include the most extensive homemaking coverage in the Negro field with articles on hair, beauty, child care, health, cooking, interior decoration, party giving, fashions and shopping."

Of *Tan*, one editor stated succinctly, "The formula is basically moral: sin, suffer, and repent. But of course anything can happen along the way." In his "Publisher's Statement" of November 1971, regarding the change of title to *Black Stars*, Johnson explained, "Audience feedback and research findings now indicate that the majority of our readers desire a national, black-oriented magazine which touches on all fields of entertainment. The tastes and preferences of our readers have always been treated as mandates by us. This is why we have changed the name of *Tan* to *Black Stars*, and we will be offering a wider range of entertainment features in subsequent issues of the magazine. *Black Stars* will be entertaining, informative, factual, intimate and lively and will deal almost exclusively with the lives and careers of great, living black entertainers." Circulation rose to 250,000 in 1974.

Jet was established on 1 November 1951 as "The Weekly Negro News Magazine." Under the headline "Why *Jet?*" Johnson wrote, "To give Negroes everywhere a weekly news magazine in handy, pocket-size form. Each week we will bring to you complete news coverage on happenings among Negroes all over the United States . . . as well as features on unusual personalities, places and events. For quick reading and an orderly organization of news you'll find everything you want each week in *Jet*. I am confident you will enjoy *Jet* as much as you like its sister magazines – *Ebony* and *Tan Confessions*."

The first issue, 4-by-5 3/4 inches, with Ben Burns as executive editor and Edward T. Clayton as managing editor, sold for fifteen cents, and a subscription was seven dollars a year. A partial list of contents included national and foreign news, religion, people, crime, business, education, sports, books, entertainment, and medicine. Dimensions were enlarged to 5 1/2-by-7 3/8 inches on 1 October 1971. In that issue Johnson said he recognized that many leaders and organizations sought the support of the 30 million black Americans. The responsibility of *Jet* was "to allow these varied voices a medium to offer their views to our readers in the hope that superior viewpoints will survive and ultimately help Blacks become secure in the exercise of freedom, equal opportunity and equal justice." With more news and less time to read, with advances in four-color printing, and with the demand for black studies, Johnson had decided to expand the size of *Jet* and the news coverage of black people everywhere. A charter subscription to the new "Super" *Jet* was eight dollars; the newsstand price was thirty-five cents. With a weekly circulation of nine hundred thousand, it is the top black-oriented news magazine in the world, second only to *Ebony* in circulation. In addition to basic news, in 1986 *Jet* articles dealt with education, entertainment, health, people, sports, and television. A full-page color advertisement cost $12,109.

Ebony Jr! was established in May 1973, primarily to provide positive black role models for children aged six to twelve. It is published monthly, except the bimonthly issues for June–July and August–September. By 1974 its circulation was 250,000. The magazine was heavily and colorfully illustrated, with few advertisements. In his publisher's statement, Johnson wrote to black children, "You deserve a magazine that reflects the sounds and sights and colors of your community. *Ebony Jr!* is about learning and exploring. It is based on the idea that learning is fun. It is based on the idea that reading is the door to opportunity. It is based on the idea that exploring – exploring new games, exploring new places, exploring new words – is half the fun of growing up committed and productive. For these reasons, *Ebony Jr!* will be a magazine of action.

Cover for an issue of Johnson's newsmagazine

It will be filled with things to do. *Ebony Jr!* will also be a magazine of opportunity. It will challenge you and remind you of the great tradition of which you are a part."

The contents included stories, features, games, and other things to do. Poetry- and story-writing contests awarded cash prizes up to fifty dollars, wristwatches, books, and clock radios. Features covered African life, animals, childhood diseases, children's books, current events, etiquette, geography, the metric system, music, young celebrities, phonics, sportsmanship, and travel. Things to do included art, crossword puzzles, holiday playscripts, riddles, and simple recipes. For lack of advertising and declining circulation, *Ebony Jr!* ceased publication in October 1985.

EM: Ebony Man was established in November 1985 in the same size as *Ebony*. It is directed primarily toward black men from twenty-five to forty-nine. In the first publisher's statement Johnson welcomed readers to "the first and only fashionable living magazine for black men. . . . *Ebony Man* will follow trends, anticipate trends, and make trends. . . . Now, at last, 13 million black men have their own common-sense approach to fashion, health, and style." With a monthly circulation of two hundred thousand, it is the most widely read black men's magazine in America. Beyond fashion, fitness, and grooming, *EM* speaks to black men's needs concerning careers, connections, family, home life, male-female relationships, music, nutrition, personal finance, sports, and travel, as well as issues such as the national economy and South Africa.

In the November 1986 first-anniversary issue, Johnson called *EM* "the leading fashionable living magazine for black men" and said, "Fashion is our primary focus. . . . *EM* wants to stimulate pride among black men in what they do and how they look while doing it." Special issues have been planned and international distribution begun. In the first-anniversary issue Alfred R. Fornay, executive editor, also wrote of the "combination of black pride, masculinity and excellence" that the magazine documents, and he reiterated the commitment toward "celebrating the brilliance of black men."

In announcing *EM,* the *New York Times* wrote that it was founded "in hopes of wooing the growing cadre of upwardly mobile black men" and noted that 22 percent of *Esquire* readers and 17 percent of *GQ* readers are black. The *Times* also noted, "Johnson expects *EM* to succeed and has the deep pockets necessary to publish long enough to become a fixture on newsstands, develop wide circulation and attract advertisers."

Personally Johnson enjoys grocery shopping and cooking as forms of therapy and relaxation: "It goes back to the self-sufficiency my mother taught me. She wanted me to be independent, so she taught me to cook, to wash clothes, to iron, to clean up behind myself." In stature Johnson is short and stocky; he prefers conservative business suits. He has no hobbies, does not drink or smoke, and never learned golf. "I've always been interested in getting ahead," he says, "in watching for new opportunities, in reading books on how to improve myself, books on how to be a public speaker and on how not to be afraid of the things that I'm afraid of." He describes himself as compassionate and fair, though sometimes a tough taskmaster; he finds himself running scared all the time, never quite sure of anything until it happens, remembering the shame of being on welfare, and wanting to live up to his mother's expectations. He told Jonathan Greenberg of *Forbes* magazine, "I think there is no such thing as security. There is no such thing as permanent success."

Among his greatest moments was his selection as one of the Ten Outstanding Young Men of the

Year in 1951 by the U.S. Junior Chamber of Commerce; he was the first black man to be so honored. In 1966 he received the Springarn Medal from the National Association for the Advancement of Colored People "for outstanding contributions to black America through enterprise, ingenuity and imagination in publishing." In the same year he was honored with the John Russwurm Award from the National Newspaper Publishers Association and the Horatio Alger Award, because, as the certificate stated, he had gone "from poverty to riches in the traditional sense, not as a black or white but as an American businessman."

He received the University of Chicago Alumni Association's Professional Achievement Award in 1970. In 1972 he became the first black publisher to be named Publisher of the Year by the Magazine Publishers Association, which awarded him its Henry Johnson Fisher Award for his "significant contributions to the publishing business." (*Ebony* was the first black publication to reach two hundred thousand in circulation and the first to carry more than one million dollars in advertising in a single issue.) In his acceptance speech Johnson discussed "responsible daring" in business: "It is scarcely necessary to remind publishers that magazines must entertain as well as inform. But the danger here is that the publisher will blunder into the sin of dullness by mistaking his own limitations for the limitations of the public. We have to anticipate what the reader will want tomorrow by walking a step ahead of him. In fact, we have to anticipate the reader's desires and wishes by leading him, step by step, to what he really wants."

On 16 May 1972 dedication ceremonies were held for the $8 million, eleven-story Johnson Publishing Company building on Michigan Avenue overlooking Grant Park, the first Chicago Loop building exclusively designed and constructed by a black-owned corporation. The building houses a large collection of paintings and sculpture by black artists from around the world as well as a special library of more than eight thousand books by, about, or relating to blacks. The penthouse executive suite includes a private gymnasium and barbershop. About five hundred visitors a day tour the facility.

At the dedication Johnson said, "From the beginning I considered the company as a vehicle for building and projecting the image of black people in America, an image that had been distorted by media oriented primarily to nonblacks. I felt then that America could never take its rightful place in the front ranks of the struggle for human dignity as long as millions at home were shackled by the crippling effects of damaged self-images. I felt then, and I feel now, that every man must have a wholesome image of himself before he can demand respect from others. . . . Black Americans have become assertive in all areas of American life, and our company has broadened its format and its physical facilities in order to reflect more accurately the contemporary aspirations of its readers." Today, 350 people work at the headquarters; most are black women, all are nonunion, and all were interviewed for their jobs by Johnson. The company functions like an extended family. He firmly believes in looking out for the interests of his employees and then demanding that they look out for the interests of the company. His management shrewdness and toughness is exemplified in the anecdote he tells about one of his managers: "We gave him a big office. We paid him a big salary. We gave him a beautiful secretary. And then we threatened to take it all away from him. You'd be surprised how much we got out of him."

In 1974 Johnson received the Communicator of the Year Award from the University of Chicago Alumni Association and the Columbia Journalism Award. He was named to the Academy of Distinguished Entrepreneurs, Babson College, in 1979. He was one of the first ten businessmen to be enshrined at the Museum of Science and Industry in Chicago, receiving a hand-cut crystal flame symbolizing the spirit of free enterprise. In accepting he said, "Only in America could a Black youth move from a frame house in Arkansas to the circle of great names represented here. Only in America could a youth of any color rise in one generation from a city's welfare rolls to the honor roll of its Business Hall of Fame."

In 1984, for the first time in its eighty-two-year history, the Chicago Boys Clubs, the largest boys-clubs organization in the world, honored a black man. The mayor and governor presented proclamations declaring John H. Johnson Day. Johnson said, "This award is a recognition not of the distance I have traveled alone but the distance we have traveled together and of the obstacles we have overcome together." He was presented the 1985 Robie Award because his "achievement in industry is as an individual whose approach to business and to life gives testament to the most fundamental values of the Jackie Robinson Foundation," memorializing the late Hall of Fame baseball star. At the 1986 National Press Foundation meeting, Johnson received the Distinguished Contributions to the Quality of Journalism Award for making *Ebony* "a beacon of hope for Black Americans and then steering it through civil rights storms of the 1960s, staunchly

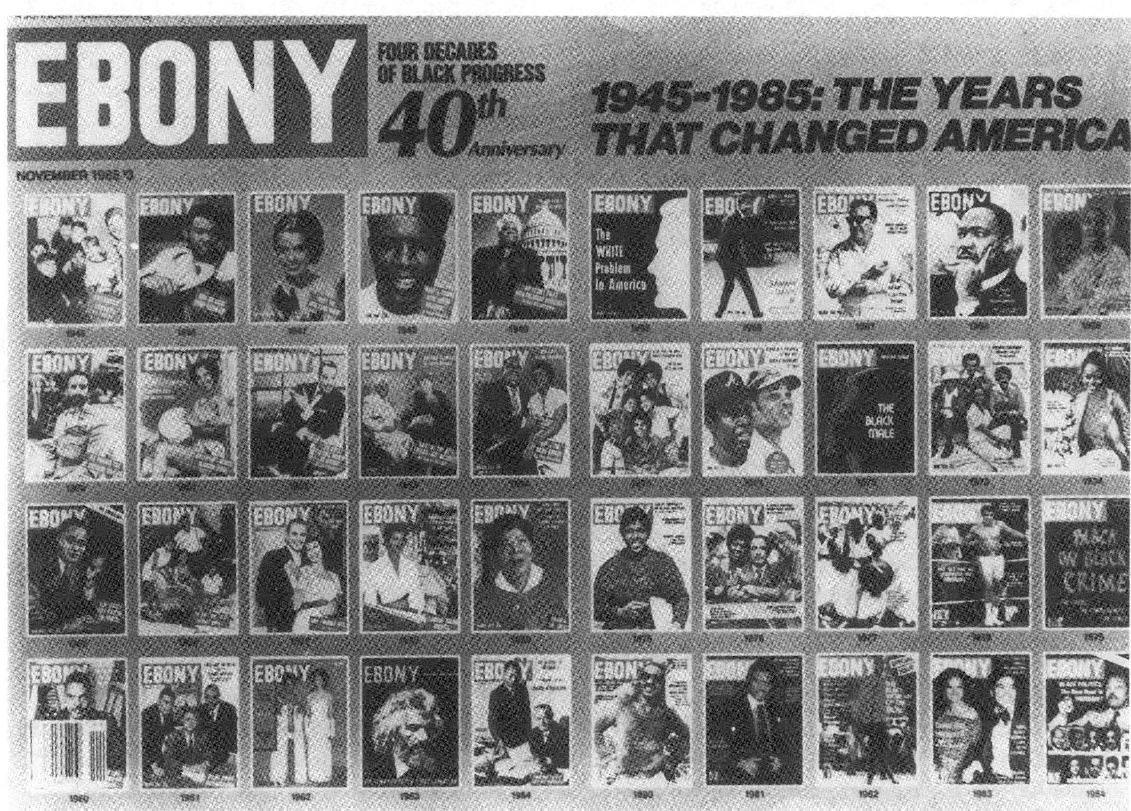

Display celebrating the fortieth-anniversary issue of Johnson's most successful publication

advocating Black rights without succumbing to racial passions."

On the federal level he has attended functions at the White House under six presidents. He was a member of the President's Commission for the Observation of the 25th Anniversary of the United Nations. In 1957 he accompanied Vice-president Richard M. Nixon on goodwill trips to nine African countries and in 1959 to Poland and the Soviet Union. President John F. Kennedy named Johnson one of four special ambassadors representing the United States at the Ivory Coast independence ceremony (1961). President Lyndon B. Johnson named him a special ambassador to the Kenya independence ceremony (1963). John H. Johnson became a fellow of the Society of Professional Journalists/Sigma Delta Chi in 1970 and is a director of the Magazine Publishers Association. He is also a trustee of the United Negro College Fund.

Honorary degrees have been presented to him from Benedict College, Carnegie-Mellon Institute, Central State College, Chicago State University, Eastern Michigan University, Hamilton College, Lincoln University, Malcolm X College, Morehouse College, North Carolina A and T State University, North Carolina College, Northwestern University, Northeastern University, Pratt Institute, Shaw University, Syracuse University, Upper Iowa College, Wayne State University, and Wilberforce University. He was presented the Distinguished American Award for "contribution to leadership and service" by South Carolina State College in 1986.

Despite his multitude of awards, Johnson remains a compulsive man who arrives at work at 8:30 A.M. (the office does not open until 9:00), works weekends, takes work home at night, and does not take vacations. He reads the final proofs of *Jet* magazine and sits in on *Ebony* editorial meetings, having the final say on pictures and copy. A man of seemingly boundless energy, he is not averse to accompanying an advertising salesman on a call on a client or to stopping by a newsstand to see if a distributor is keeping the stand serviced with copies of Johnson publications. An omnivorous reader, he knows what is happening in the business world, with his competitors and with other publications.

For over fifty years Johnson has been improving the image many black people have of themselves, giving them faith and confidence, and telling them about their heritage. To corporate America, he says, "You can't sell successfully to the black consumer market without me." He has brought to life great black leaders of the past through historical articles in his magazines and the books his firm has published. Johnson had an idea, believed in it, and refused to accept failure: "I guess my formula for success is picking attainable goals, then achieving them. Once you have achieved one goal, the success will give you the confidence to reach the next."

He once discussed black capitalism in the *New York Times,* saying "Success in business is a time-honored process involving hard work, risk-taking, money, a good product, maybe a little bit of luck, and most of all, a burning commitment to succeed. I do not believe that this overriding desire to succeed has reached the desired intensity in minority business." On the thought of increasing his own holdings, he is constantly looking for the proper opportunity. He also feels obligated to give back to the community through education, through community groups and organizations, and through politicians who do not have the normal support that would come from the white corporate community. He says, "I'm not giving for them as much as I am giving for myself, for an inner feeling of peace and satisfaction, for the knowledge that I have given back some of what has been given to me."

Interviews:

A. James Reichley, "How John Johnson Made It," *Fortune* (January 1968): 152–180;

"John H. Johnson of *Ebony:* Setting a Goal and Reaching It," *National Business* (April 1974): 854–859;

Eliza G. C. Collins and Wanda A. Lankenner, "Failure Is a Word I Don't Accept': An Interview with John H. Johnson," *Harvard Business Review,* 54 (March–April 1976): 79–88;

James Speigner, "John Johnson Says Get Smart, Not Mad," *Madison Avenue Magazine* (December 1984);

Dan Rottenberg, "Atop the *Ebony* Empire," *United Magazine* (January 1985);

Lerone Bennett, Jr., "*Ebony* Interview with John H. Johnson," *Ebony,* 40 (November 1985);

Paul Lindsey Johnson, "Interview: John H. Johnson," *Crisis,* 94 (January 1987): 32–48.

Bibliography:

George H. Hill and Michael Nelson, "John Harold Johnson: Publishing Magnate," *Bulletin of Bibliography,* 42 (June 1985): 89–94.

References:

C. P. Alexander, "*Ebony's* Man," *Time,* 126 (9 December 1985): 68;

"*Ebony's* Johnson," *Newsweek,* 34 (7 November 1949): 60;

"A $500 Loan Started Him on the Road to Success," in *The Ebony Success Library,* volume 2: *Famous Blacks Give Secrets of Success* (Nashville: Southwestern, 1973), pp. 132–137;

Jonathan Greenberg, "It's a Miracle," *Forbes* (20 December 1982): 104, 106, 110;

"John H. Johnson," in *The Ebony Success Library,* volume 1: *1,000 Successful Blacks* (Nashville: Southwestern, 1973), p. 178;

Carl T. Rowan, "Words That Give Us Strength," *Reader's Digest,* 66 (April 1987): 49–58.

Papers:

John H. Johnson's correspondence, papers, and family archival materials are housed at Johnson Publishing Company headquarters, 820 South Michigan Avenue, Chicago.

Ray Long

(23 March 1878 - 9 July 1935)

Michael D. Applegate
University of Northern Colorado

MAJOR POSITIONS HELD: Reporter, *Indianapolis News* (1900–1905); managing editor, *Cincinnati Post* (1905–1908), *Cleveland Press* (1908–1910); associate editor, *Hampton's* (1910–1911); editor, *Hampton-Columbian* (1911–1912), *Red Book, Blue Book,* and *Green Book* (1911–1918), *Cosmopolitan* (1918–1931), *Photoplay* (1934); editor in chief (1918–1931), president, International Magazine Company (1926–1931; including *Cosmopolitan, Good Housekeeping, Harper's Bazaar, Motor, Motor Boating, McClure's Town and Country, Smart Set,* and *International Studio*); chairman of the board of directors, Ray Long & Richard Smith, Inc. (1931–1935); western editor, *Liberty* (1935).

BOOK: *An Editor Looks at Russia: One Unprejudiced View of the Land of the Soviets* (New York: Ray Long & Richard R. Smith, 1931).

OTHER: *My Story that I Like Best,* edited by Long (New York: International Magazine Company, 1924);

As I Look at Life, edited by Long (New York: International Magazine Company, 1925);

My Favorite Story, edited by Long (New York: International Magazine Company, 1928);

20 Best Short Stories in Ray Long's 20 Years as an Editor, edited by Long (New York: Ray Long & Richard R. Smith, 1932);

"Puppy Love," in *Coal Dust on the Fiddle: Songs and Stories of the Bituminous Industry,* edited by George Korson (Hatboro, Pa.: Folklore Associates, 1965), p. 90.

SELECTED PERIODICAL PUBLICATIONS – UNCOLLECTED: "Why Are Manuscripts Rejected?: A Symposium," *Bookman,* 43 (May 1916): 264–265;

"James Oliver Curwood and His Far North," *Bookman,* 52 (February 1921): 492–495;

"A Meeting in Paris with a Ghost from My Boyhood," *Cosmopolitan,* 78 (March 1925): 15;

"Success – You All Want It. How Many Know What Makes It Worthwhile?," *Cosmopolitan,* 78 (April 1925): 17;

"This Woman Should Interest the Show-Offs," *Cosmopolitan,* 78 (May 1925): 17;

"Just How Much Do You Believe in Luck," *Cosmopolitan,* 78 (June 1925): 21;

"This Man Irritates Me – But I Like Him," *Cosmopolitan,* 79 (July 1925): 23;

"A Lesson I've Learned from a Boy of Nine," *Cosmopolitan,* 79 (August 1925): 25;

"A Letter to a Young Man with an Urge to Edit a Popular Magazine," *Bookman,* 64 (January 1927): 556–560;

"Jim Curwood," *Bookman,* 66 (November 1927): 288–291;

"A Fine Human Document by a Very Human Being," *Cosmopolitan,* 86 (April 1929): 23;

"A Story of a Man," *Cosmopolitan,* 87 (September 1929): 27;

"A Farewell to Legs," *Cosmopolitan,* 88 (January 1930): 17;

"We Tried It on a Dog," *Cosmopolitan,* 88 (February 1930): 17;

"What's Under a High Hat?," *Cosmopolitan,* 88 (March 1930): 15;

"This Is My Ideal for an Epitaph," *Cosmopolitan,* 88 (May 1930): 23;

"Powder Puffs for Men," *Cosmopolitan,* 89 (July 1930): 27;

"A Man Who Studied Men," *Cosmopolitan,* 89 (September 1930): 25;

"By a Homely Man, about a Homely Woman, for Other Homely Folks," *Cosmopolitan,* 89 (November 1930): 19;

"Don't Crowd That Little Fellow – He May Be a Big Man Some Day," *Cosmopolitan,* 90 (February 1931): 15.

Ray Long has been called the editor's editor. A speed reader who by his own estimation consumed nearly three hundred million words in search of the most palatable reading for American tastes, he was renowned for exhibiting uncanny precision in satisfying those tastes. As president of *Cosmopolitan* under owner William Randolph Hearst, Long became the highest-paid magazine editor of his day, and his regular contributors made up a virtual Who's Who of novelists and short-story writers of the early twentieth century.

Long was widely known for the brevity and precision of his communications. He owned five automobiles but did not drive any of them for fear of having an accident. His forty imported suits were all tailored to be too small for him, lest he become overweight. He loved cigarettes, fish chowder, and Scotch, and Irvin S. Cobb called him the greatest poker player in the world. Above all Long was an aggressive idealist. He believed in heroes and in hard work, and his own success story reads like a tale from Horatio Alger, of whose gospel Long was a tireless evangelist. Forced to quit school at an early age in order to help support a fatherless family, Long nevertheless knew what he wanted from life, and he pursued his future vigorously and with calculated single-mindedness. From the time he begged his way onto the staff of the *Indianapolis News* at age eighteen, his life was defined by the goals he set and methodically reached first in the newspaper business, then in magazines, and finally in book publishing.

Ray Long

Ray Long was born on 23 March 1878 in Lebanon, Indiana, the youngest of the three children of John H. Long, a retail store clerk, and Mary Allice Humes Long, whose family were farmers and had been among the original settlers of central Indiana. John and Allice were married in 1870, when he was twenty-four and she eighteen. They settled in Lebanon, where John went to work for the J. H. Perkins and Company dry-goods store. Their first two children, daughters Daisy and Bessie, were born in 1872 and 1875. In 1879, when Ray was a year old, the family moved to nearby Sheridan, where John secured a position similar to the one he had held at J. H. Perkins. They had not been long settled in Sheridan, however, when John died, leaving Allice to provide for the family (which now included her widowed mother as well as the three children). She moved them all to Indianapolis, where she opened a millinery shop, and it was here that Ray was to receive the whole of his brief formal education.

Even as a young boy, Long had a strong sense of responsibility toward his family and began early on to channel his energies toward contributing to their support. He sold newspapers and delivered packages after school, but these activities added only nominally to the household funds, so at the age of thirteen Long quit school and took a job delivering telegrams for Western Union for fifteen dollars a month. During his teen years he also worked as a shoe salesman and a professional bicycle racer, and he even held for a time a minor political post.

Cover for an issue of the popular general-fiction magazine edited by Long from 1911 to 1918

In 1891, while he was thus employed, he encountered on the street one day the sports editor for the *Indianapolis News* and was much impressed to note that the man went about his business wearing a checkered suit and carrying a cane. It was then and there that Long determined to be a newspaperman. He took as his hero and role model Richard Harding Davis, a portrait of whom he obtained and placed over his bedroom dresser. Long endeavored to become just like Davis, even to the extent of emulating his physical appearance. He also became an insatiable reader of everything he could get his hands on, from Russian novels to travel pamphlets. Throughout his career Long would remain a believer in reading for reading's own sake and in the virtue of reading for diversity. Having set his sights on the newspaper business, he began to pester Charles R. Williams, editor of the *Indianapolis News,* for a job. For nearly four years Long made a constant nuisance of himself, hounding Williams with story ideas and editorial suggestions, until finally Williams acquiesced and added Long to his staff at a salary of eight dollars a week.

Indianapolis was at that time something of a melting pot of successful journalists and writers, and while he worked for the *News* Long established some of the most important relationships of his life, both personally and professionally. In his first days as a reporter, he met and befriended Roy W. Howard, who had also just come to the paper. Howard went on to become president of Scripps-Howard Newspapers, and he and Long were to remain lifelong friends. Kin Hubbard, an artist who later gained fame as the creator of "Abe Martin," was also one of Long's contemporaries on the paper. Hubbard was at least partially responsible for giving Long a healthy and enduring respect for illustrators. Those who later worked for Long at *Cosmopolitan* found themselves among the best paid in the business. In Indianapolis Long also met Meredith Nicholson and George Ade, both of whom would become regular writers for *Cosmopolitan.* Others in the Indianapolis literary crowd included Gen. Lew Wallace, James Whitcomb Riley, Charles Majors, Maurice Thompson, George Barr McCutcheon, and Booth Tarkington. Long drew inspiration from his exposure to this elite group, and it may have been their influence that sparked his interest in magazine journalism, which began at about this time. Long was particularly fascinated with *Cosmopolitan.*

John Brisben Walker had acquired *Cosmopolitan* in 1889 and, with the help of assistant editors Edward Everett Hale and Murat Halstead, turned the publication into a powerhouse in terms of both circulation and influence. Long described it as "a publication which was startling in its vigor and enterprise. I determined then and there that some day, somehow, I must be editor of a magazine like *Cosmopolitan.*" Having thus established a new career goal, Long updated his hero as well. Down came the picture of Davis and up went one of Walker.

In 1905 Long left the *Indianapolis News* to become managing editor of the *Cincinnati Post.* He remained at the *Post* for three years, at which time he was offered the editorship of the *Cleveland Press.* While in Cleveland he met and fell in love with Pearl Dillon Schou, whom he married in September 1910. The marriage was childless and ended in divorce ten years later. On 25 July 1922 Long would be married to Lucy Virginia Bovie of Gallipolis, Ohio. They would have one son, Ray, Jr., born in 1926.

In 1910 Long left the *Press* to edit a small paper in Syracuse and, while there, decided upon *Hampton's* magazine (then at the height of its popularity) as his ticket into the magazine business. He proceeded to assail owner Ben Hampton with a flurry of mail full of unsolicited editorial advice, until Hampton sent a telegram inviting Long to New York for a talk. At their first meeting Hampton said, "Well, young fellow, when are you going to quit trying to run this magazine from Syracuse and come down here and try it in New York?" Less than a week later Long was installed as Hampton's assistant.

Hampton's became the *Hampton-Columbian* and Long became its editor, but the publication was clearly moribund (it folded the following year), so Long sought other opportunities. He contacted William Randolph Hearst's general manager George D'Utassy to ask for a job but was told there were no openings, so on 18 December 1911 Long accepted an offer from Louis Eckstein to edit his magazine group, which consisted of *Red Book*, *Blue Book*, and *Green Book*. Shortly after Long went to work for Eckstein, D'Utassy approached him with an offer to edit Hearst's newest acquisition, *Vanity Fair*. Long rejected D'Utassy's offer, naming a higher figure of his own which the Hearst people in turn declined. Six months later Long was again contacted by D'Utassy, who advised him that Hearst was now ready to accept Long's figure. Long's salary had in the meantime increased, however, and so did his asking price. Hearst again demurred. A game of financial tag thus developed between the two which was to go on for seven years.

Meanwhile, Long was developing his editorial style and philosophy at the helm of *Red Book* and winning wide acclaim in the process. In his first year there he introduced serials by Rupert Hughes and H. G. Wells (the magazine's fare had previously been confined to short stories). He also altered the physical format of *Red Book* to match that of *Cosmopolitan* and the *American Magazine*. His reputation as an exceptional judge of popular fiction grew rapidly, and so did the circulation of *Red Book,* which went from 225,000 in 1911 to over 600,000 when Long left in 1918.

Hearst had by now decided that Long was a commodity he could no longer do without. On 11 November 1918 Long was invited to the Hearst residence for a luncheon which, as it turned out, took place on the last day of World War I. The meal was interrupted every few minutes by the arrival of armistice bulletins, and while Hearst was talking business with Long, he was also directing the activities of his own editors. Long was to say later that this meeting "made an indelible impression upon me. I had never met an individual whose mind seemed so amazingly compartmentalized, able to handle many

VOL. LXVIII APRIL, 1920 NO. 4

COSMOPOLITAN

America's Greatest Magazine

This Month

Cover: A Tea-time Reverie
Harrison Fisher

Tolerance 13
Meredith Nicholson

The Grate Fire 14
Edgar A. Guest
Decoration by W. T. Benda

In Chancery 16
John Galsworthy
Illustrated by W. D. Stevens

The Animal That Laughs 25
Rupert Hughes
Illustrated by T. D. Skidmore

Bill the Boob 31
Gouverneur Morris
Illustrated by G. Patrick Nelson

Star-Dust 36
Fannie Hurst
Illustrated by James Montgomery Flagg

Until To-morrow 43
Frank R. Adams
Illustrated by John Alonzo Williams

The Stage To-day 49
Photographs in Artgravure

Poor's Partner 53
Will Payne
Illustrated by Harrison Fisher

Good Men for Bad 59
Jack Boyle
Illustrated with Photographs

Kindred of the Dust 62
Peter B. Kyne
Illustrated by Dean Cornwell

The Scarlet Shoes 69
Thomas Burke
Illustrated by G. Patrick Nelson

The Other Man 75
Dana Gatlin
Illustrated by Grant T. Reynard

Reading Your Dreams To Trace Your Ills 81
Harvey O'Higgins
Photographic Illustrations by A. P. Milne

Sticky Fingers 85
Harris Dickson
Illustrated by Edward L. Chase

Next Month

This is Archie—in New York

"The Man Who Married a Hotel," about whom moves the most ridiculously delightful series of short stories Pelham Grenville Wodehouse has ever written—the first in MAY COSMOPOLITAN.

Side by side comes a feature of tremendous scientific and speculative interest—Thomas A. Edison's entirely startling and novel views on ***What is Life—And Where Does It Come From?*** This is one of the big articles of the year.

And you will not want to miss—among other brilliant works in AMERICA'S GREATEST MAGAZINE for May—the beginning of a two-part story by Rupert Hughes, ***The Kicker.***

The world's greatest writers and artists appear regularly in COSMOPOLITAN. In the May issue, you will find them at their best—making a magazine for America's best intellects.

COSMOPOLITAN'S circulation is sky-rocketing. We cannot supply each month's full increase. To make sure of getting your copy at the news-stands, order it now!

$3.00 A YEAR ***25 CENTS A COPY***

Published monthly at 119 West 40th Street, New York, N. Y., by International Magazine Company. Entered as second-class matter, September 8, 1905, at the Post-Office, New York, N. Y., under the Act of March 3, 1879. Entered on July 1, 1918, at the Post-Office, Atlanta, Ga.; Boston, Mass.; Chicago, Ill.; Los Angeles, Calif.; San Francisco, Calif.

Cosmopolitan, 119 West 40th Street, New York

The Harrison Fisher cover of this issue without lettering mailed on receipt of 25 cents

Contents page illustrating Long's practice of "teasing" upcoming features in order to encourage readers' interest

matters at once, and with perfect ease and mastery. Our ideas in magazines traveled pretty much the same paths. So there was no real difficulty in reaching an understanding."

Hearst's vice-president, Joseph Moore, and Long immediately went to the offices of *Cosmopolitan* (which Hearst had acquired in 1905) and signed a two-year contract. Four months later Hearst tore it up and wrote a new one giving Long a 33 percent raise. The new agreement was for two years as well, but after the first year Hearst wired Moore, ordering him to destroy it and give Long another 25 percent raise. In thirteen years Hearst never waited for Long's contract to expire before replacing it with one substantially more favorable to the editor. By the time Long left the Hearst group in 1931, his annual salary was $185,000 – the highest in the business.

Long had shown at *Red Book* that he knew what sold magazines, and he had made clear to Hearst that while he was at *Cosmopolitan,* he intended to be its absolute ruler. He believed fervently that the success of any publication was a function of its

Cover for the May 1919 issue in which Long is first credited on the masthead as editor

"personality," which depended in turn upon a single individual exercising total editorial control. He had inherited this credo from his hero Walker, and it was confirmed by his observations of other publications. *McClure's, Everybody's,* and the *American Magazine* had all prospered as autocracies but foundered under committee rule. Accordingly, Long not only read and approved every line that was printed, but he chose the illustrators and laid out most of the magazine's typography himself. Even when he was away from his office (which was often), he stayed in touch with his staff daily to hand down command decisions.

In addition to being a forceful administrator, Long possessed keen marketing sense and was aggressive in soliciting material. He liked to attribute his usefulness to the fact that he was simply the average American reader with average American tastes, but there was much more to it than that. To begin with, the average American reader did not, over an average weekend, consume two to three novels, more than thirty short stories, a dozen magazines and trade papers, and every major Sunday paper in the country. Speed reading (to which he had been introduced by Theodore Roosevelt) was crucial to Long's editorial philosophy. Knowledge was power, and Long knew that it was not enough merely to understand the public's tastes. One must be able to anticipate them and, when possible, shape them.

Upon assuming control of *Cosmopolitan,* Long promptly dubbed it "America's Greatest Magazine" and began the practice of regularly teasing the readers with mentions of upcoming features to hold their interest. He later applied the teaser concept to his contributors as well. Promotional pieces on the title page were accompanied by photos, enhancing each author's currency as a celebrity, while creating a sense of intimacy between reader and writer.

Long abandoned the practice of using the same small group of writers in favor of tapping a much broader spectrum of contributors, traveling extensively and spending freely in the process. Under his stewardship *Cosmopolitan* spent nearly a million dollars annually to maintain its reputation as a showcase for the literary elite. From *Red Book* Long brought with him James Curwood and Peter B. Kyne. In the grand Hearst style he stole Irvin S. Cobb, Ring Lardner, and Montague Glass away from the *Saturday Evening Post.* Other regular American contributors included Stephen Vincent Benét, Edna Ferber, Damon Runyon, Rex Beach, Fannie Hurst, Jack London, Theodore Dreiser, and Booth Tarkington. From abroad he imported Rudyard Kipling, H. G. Wells, Bernard Shaw, W. Somerset Maugham, P. G. Wodehouse, Rafael Sabatini, and (later on) an assortment of Russian authors previously unknown to American readers. Long was tireless in his quest for material from new and unexpected sources. One of his most famous coups was the publication of Calvin Coolidge's memoirs in 1929. In addition, *Cosmopolitan* in the 1920s carried articles by Amelia Earhart, Henry Ford, Winston Churchill, Arthur Ponsonby, Lillian Russell, and Benito Mussolini.

Long was not above "ordering up" literature to his own specifications. No sooner had he taken the helm of *Cosmopolitan* than he was off to England to convince war correspondent Sir Philip Gibbs that he ought to be writing fiction. Long had already converted nonfiction writer Jack Boyle and playwrights Laurence Stallings and Frank R. Adams to the short-story genre, and it was while sharing a bottle of Scotch with Long one evening that Albert Payson Terhune found his calling as one of the premier writers of stories about dogs.

Long took an even more hands-on role with some writers. When Rupert Hughes bogged down halfway through a serial, Long finished it for him. Cobb developed the habit of sending lists of his story ideas to Long, who simply checked off the ones he wanted written. Once, when Kyne was running late with several stories, Long took a train from coast to coast and abducted Kyne, locking him in a hotel room for a week until he produced the promised manuscripts.

Long's marketing acuity can be seen in the deftness with which he promoted *Cosmopolitan* to advertisers. In his thirteen years as editor the magazine's full-page ad rates rose from two thousand dollars to over forty-eight hundred dollars. Much of that increase came during the 1920s, when the economy was vigorous and *Cosmopolitan* was regarded as the magazine of the elite. But in 1930, when the Depression forced Long to drop the magazine's price to maintain circulation figures, it became a more difficult proposition to convince advertisers that the readers of *Cosmopolitan* still consisted of those Americans most possessed of what Long had called "buying temperament." To prove his point, Long dispatched his advertising department to Middletown, New York, to conduct a detailed study (from which he produced a promotional film) of 300 *Cosmopolitan* subscribers and 300 nonsubscriber neighbors. Among other things, the results showed that 113 subscribers belonged to the local country club, as opposed to only 97 of the nonsubscribers. The society column of the Middletown *Times Herald* mentioned subscribers 473 times that year, but the names of their neighbors appeared only 301 times. Ten of the *Cosmopolitan* families had brand-new cars, and 57 of them drove 1929 models. In the garages of nonsubscribers, on the other hand, were to be found only one new model and just thirty-two from the previous year. By parading statistics such as these past his advertisers, Long was able to keep them in the fold through hard economic times and actually posted an increase in ad revenues through the difficult first year of the Depression.

Long and Hearst got along well. Hearst, well known for being an autocrat himself, nevertheless left Long completely alone to run his magazines as he saw fit. It is a tribute to Hearst's tremendous respect for Long that it was Long's personality, and not Hearst's, which dominated *Cosmopolitan* throughout the 1920s. On only one occasion is there any record of a disagreement between the two. *Cosmopolitan* had contracted for a novel by an English woman to whom Hearst felt he owed a favor. Upon reading it, Long was dissatisfied and refused to use it. When Hearst insisted, Long wired him in California:

> I do not in any way question your right to order into your magazine any feature you wish, but I think you will be willing to grant me the right to decline to edit a magazine containing something in which I do not take pride. Therefore I must ask you to permit me to resign.

Hearst in turn sent Long a telegram which read, "After all, you and I should not quarrel about a girl at our age – and hers. Don't publish the serial if you feel so strongly about it, but please write her a letter which will soften the blow."

Toward the end of the 1920s Long began to be fascinated with what was happening politically in Russia. He traveled there in the fall of 1930 to attend the celebration of the thirteenth anniversary of the Bolshevik revolution and made the acquaintance of a variety of Russian writers, including Boris Pilnyak, Alexander Yakovlev, Gleb Alekseyev, and Valentine Kataev. He returned to the

Long's office at Cosmopolitan, *circa 1931. The portrait is of William Randolph Hearst, the publisher of the magazine.*

United States a month later with a wealth of manuscripts and with a lasting fondness for things Russian. He began to write and speak widely on Russia and in particular on the advantages (not to say urgency) of normalizing relations and opening trade avenues with the Soviets. Speaking to the Association of National Advertisers in Detroit on 27 April 1931, he admonished Americans to "quit kidding" themselves about Russia, which he called the "greatest potential market in the world." Shortly after leaving the Hearst organization, Long would again travel to Russia, returning with the rights to Joseph Stalin's first book, which Long promised would tell the Russian story from "the inside."

There are conflicting accounts of Long's departure from the Hearst organization. When his resignation was announced in September 1931, the reason given was his eagerness to pursue a career in book publishing. Long had been connected with this aspect of the business since 1929 as a silent partner of Richard Smith, and, after leaving Hearst, he became active in the partnership as chairman of the board. Nevertheless the magazine world was astonished by the news. Long had been one of Hearst's favorites. He had been paid handsomely, and he had enjoyed a degree of freedom in running his shop which was enviable. There were rumors among company insiders that Long had quarreled with Hearst and been forced out. When a power struggle developed between Long and Richard Berlin, head of Hearst's new magazine board, some observers took it as a sign that Long had lost favor with Hearst. Theories arose that Hearst might have come to resent Long, whose reputation was getting to be considerable. Certainly Long had never been shy about accepting credit for his accomplishments. If such resentment was indeed a source of trouble, it can hardly have been ameliorated by the appearance in *Fortune* magazine of an article titled "The *Cosmopolitan* of Ray Long." It is even possible that Hearst had become impatient with Long's growing preoccupation with Russia.

Nevertheless William Lengel, Long's chief assistant, maintained that Long and Hearst had parted company amiably and that Hearst had in fact gone to some lengths to convince Long to stay. Long was in ill health at the time of his resignation, and he may simply have felt that he had outlived his usefulness. There is no evidence of any lasting rancor between the two, and in later references to Hearst, Long was quite generous in praising his former boss.

The book-publishing partnership with Smith seemed to be prospering at first. Long's reputation supplied some momentum, and he scored some early successes, most notably the signing of the deal with Stalin in 1932. But the firm was hard hit by the Depression, which had already claimed Long's personal savings. In addition there were rumors of personality conflicts between Long and Smith. Less than a year after becoming active in the firm, Long, on the verge of a nervous breakdown, walked out of his office and sailed to Tahiti, vowing never to return. In April 1933 the publishing house went into bankruptcy, with nearly fifty thousand dollars in judgments outstanding. Long did return to the United States later that year but never recovered from his setbacks. Settling in Hollywood, he edited *Photoplay* for a short time and then got into motion pictures as a script supervisor – first at Columbia studios, then Fox, and finally M-G-M. At the time of his death he had just been named western editor of *Liberty* magazine, and he was engaged in contract negotiations with an undisclosed, newly formed company, a spokesman for which described Long's mood at the time as "somewhat beaten down."

In Beverly Hills in the early evening of 9 July 1935, Long's housekeeper was taking a telephone message when she heard a gunshot. Running to Long's bedroom, she found him unconscious on the floor, clad in silk pajamas and with a small bore rifle lying nearby. He had shot himself in the mouth. Long was taken to a hospital and into surgery but died without regaining consciousness. His body was cremated and the ashes spread upon the Pacific Ocean by Kyne, Roy Howard, and Ray Long, Jr.

Long had once written that his own ideal epitaph would read, "Here lies Ray Long, a man who minded his own business." If he failed to warrant that inscription, he wrote, it would be because he was too weak to live as he wanted to live. But weakness was a feeling with which he was totally unfamiliar and unprepared to cope. His entire life had been measured by the strength of his achievements. When he sensed that those were all behind him, weakness became not only his epitaph, but his killer as well.

References:

"The *Cosmopolitan* of Ray Long," *Fortune* (March 1931): 41–55;

Frank L. Mott, *A History of American Magazines,* volume 4: *1885–1905* (Cambridge, Mass.: Belknap Press of Harvard University Press, 1957), pp. 497–503;

Alan Nourie and Barbara Nourie, eds., *American Mass Market Magazines* (New York: Greenwood Press, 1990) pp. 79–80;

W. A. Swanberg, *Citizen Hearst: A Biography of William Randolph Hearst* (New York: Scribners, 1961), p. 430;

John K. Winkler, *W. R. Hearst: An American Phenomenon* (New York: Simon & Schuster, 1928), pp. 248–250;

Winkler, *William Randolph Hearst: A New Appraisal* (New York: Hastings House, 1955), pp. 175, 176.

William D'Alton Mann

(27 September 1839 - 17 May 1920)

Alf Pratte
Brigham Young University

MAJOR POSITIONS HELD: Publisher, *Mobile Daily Register* (1868–1871); editor and publisher, *Town Topics: The Journal of Society* (1891–1920) and *Tales from Town Topics* (1891–1905); owner, Town Topics Financial Bureau (1891–1920); publisher, *Smart Set* (1900–1911), *Fads and Fancies of Representative Americans* (1905), and *Tom Watson's Magazine* (1905–1906); editor and publisher, *Transatlantic Tales* (1905–1908); publisher, *Snappy Stories* (1908–1920).

BOOKS: *The Raiders: A Scheme for Improving the Mobility and Efficiency of Troops* (London: Waterlow & Sons, 1876);

Fads and Fancies of Representative Americans at the Beginning of the Twentieth Century (New York: Town Topics Publishing, 1905).

Magazine publishing and editing were only two of the several occupations of William D'Alton Mann, a former Civil War soldier best known for his publications that helped revolutionize society journalism and which were sometimes used by Mann for subtle blackmailing techniques. Although he is remembered by many for his notorious libel suit against *Collier's* magazine in 1905 (which he lost), he is also known for his part in founding the *Smart Set,* attracting such writers as O. Henry, Jack London, H. L. Mencken, and George Jean Nathan, and for producing one of the top-flight literary publications at the turn of the century. Mann's *Town Topics: The Journal of Society* has been described by magazine historian F. L. Mott as "the best-known urban weekly in America" during the period between 1891 and 1920. Sometimes forgotten in the wake of his publishing career and numerous lawsuits are Mann's contributions to railway-car innovation and his part in the development of the transportation industry in Europe.

William D'Alton Mann

Mann was born in Sandusky, Ohio, on 27 September 1839, of Puritan stock. His father, William R. Mann, a descendant of the Mann family that arrived in Massachusetts in 1627, was a native Pennsylvanian who moved to Ohio after the War of 1812. (It is not known where the middle name D'Alton originated; Mann later dropped it and used the letter *D* in some of his columns.) Altogether the senior Mann and his wife, Eliza Ford Mann, had six children. William D'Alton Mann's younger brother Eugene also went into magazine journalism and was responsible for attracting William to New York after William's earlier endeavors as a soldier, inventor, government official, newspaper editor, and politician.

In his midteens William moved with his family thirty miles across the state border to Adrian, Michigan, where he studied engineering. He also served as the manager of a run-down hotel left to him by a relative. There he married the first of three wives and fathered a daughter. At the outbreak of the Civil War, Mann was awarded a captain's commission in the First Michigan Cavalry, which arrived in Washington in the fall of 1861 to help defend the capital.

In 1862 Mann organized at Detroit the first Mounted Rifles, which afterward became the Fifth Michigan Cavalry and Daniel's Horse Battery. It was known in the Army of the Potomac as the Michigan Cavalry Brigade, which had a good reputation under Gen. Philip Henry Sheridan. In a pamphlet called *The Raiders,* published in 1876, Mann wrote that he had been among a group of Union soldiers who recommended that the North use mounted riflemen to fight similar soldiers used for reconnaissance by the South. He claimed that he had been instrumental in whipping Confederate cavalry leader John Mosby "like the devil." Mann was recognized during the Battle of Gettysburg, when he led his regiment in a famous battle on Rummel's Farm three miles east of Cemetery Ridge, as part of the Michigan Brigade under the command of Gen. George Armstrong Custer. According to some historians, the battle provided the margin of victory at Gettysburg. Mann also devised valuable improvements in the accoutrements for troops, including a yokelike device that balanced the equipment carried by troops on their cartridge belts. After receiving patents for the inventions, he resigned from the army and by the end of 1864 had made more than fifty thousand dollars on his improvement ideas. His concepts were extensively adopted by the U.S. and Austrian armies.

After the war Mann dabbled in other business enterprises before becoming involved in an oil-development scheme near the world's first productive oil well in Titusville, Pennsylvania. Using funds from his Civil War inventions as well as from his former inn property, Mann began to sell questionable stock to his old army associates, including Maj. Gen. Winfield Scott Hancock. When Mann failed to meet his promises, some of the trusting, dollar-a-share investors sued him for his part in selling the oil-well stock. After a well-publicized trial involving two thousand pages of testimony and described as one of the first – if not the first – of the major oil swindles, the case was dismissed. The twenty-six-year-old Mann moved to Mobile, Alabama, as the federal assessor of internal revenue.

Despite his previous work, eventually as a colonel, for the northern armies and his new assignment, which authorized him to confiscate property of southern soldiers, Mann was able to adapt to the society of the growing commercial center and cotton port. Using funds he had acquired in his oil-stock scheme, Mann joined with a group of three newspaper editors who in 1868 began to publish morning and evening editions they called the *Mobile Daily Register*. As publisher, Mann not only supervised business activities but occasionally wrote *Register* editorials. On one occasion, biographer Andy Logan says, one of Mann's editorials helped to incite local citizens to riot against a group of northerners. Mann later claimed that the well-known Atlanta newspaper editor Henry Grady had once told him that Mann's Mobile newspapers had been the inspiration for Grady's going into the newspaper business. Mann also used to boast that Mark Twain had written for the *Register* and that the experience eventually culminated in Twain's article "How I Edited An Agricultural Paper" in *Galaxy* magazine in 1870. Twain is not named as the agriculture editor in any surviving copies of the *Register,* however.

According to other accounts, Mann also got into the lumber business, set up a large cottonseed-oil plant, joined the Ku Klux Klan, and even acquired a southern accent. Mann commented later that he considered himself half a southerner because of his residence in Alabama, and he often referred to the fact that, by a special dispensation, he had even been admitted to exclusive membership in the local branch of the Southern Society.

Active in politics, Mann was in 1869 the first candidate of the Democratic party for Congress from the Mobile District. Although he received a large majority of the votes, he was not allowed to assume office by the Reconstruction state government. By 1871 he had become a full-fledged railroad promoter and inventor. In January 1872 he was granted a patent for what he called a "boudoir car" – or sleeper – which was divided by transverse partitions.

Because of the inroads made into the development and sale of "sleeping cars" by George Pullman of Illinois the previous seven years, Mann left the United States to promote his invention in Europe for the next decade. In 1873 he organized the Mann Railway Sleeping Carriage Company, with a factory two hundred miles north of London, to manufacture his boudoir cars and lease them to railroads. He introduced a similar service in Paris and in vari-

Cover for the first issue of Mann's most influential periodical, which began as a literary magazine aimed at an upper-class audience

ous cities between Munich and Vienna – the first such services available to the public on the eastern side of the Atlantic. By 1876 fifty-eight other such companies were operating in countries such as Russia, Germany, and Belgium. In addition to his sleeping car, a car-to-car vestibule, and a refrigerator car, one of Mann's European companies began building cars for the famed Orient Express. Despite Mann's elegant designs and inroads into the European market, his inventions were no match for Pullman's greater carrying capacity and economy. By 1888 Mann, losing money, returned to the United States.

In 1891 Mann became part owner of *Town Topics: The Journal of Society,* a magazine published at the time by his brother Eugene. The publication had been founded originally in 1879 as a biweekly called *Andrews' American Queen: A National Society Journal,* by W. R. Andrews, who manufactured dress patterns. The reading matter in early *American Queen* issues consisted mainly of the lists of guests at social functions and the clothes they wore. It was succeeded in 1883 by the *Social Register,* which was later changed to *Town Topics*. The latter was acquired by Eugene Mann in 1885.

Eugene and William Mann developed the techniques that helped bring about a revolution in society journalism. Although daring accounts of society had been reported as early as 1837 by James Gordon Bennett, the style of the writing and the nature of the content were inhibited greatly until the arrival of the Manns on the New York scene. As early as 1886 Eugene had described his gossipy "Saunterings" column as an "*olla podrida* of gossip, comment, and anecdotal paragraphs of contemporaneous interest . . . not for babes, prudes, idiots or dudes." Among the early accounts that attracted readers were features on strip parties at the beach and lavish social gatherings. Eugene eventually turned his publication over to his brother after writing about the prevalence of abortion and being convicted under the Comstock Postal Law of sending obscene matter through the mails.

Under the direction of Colonel Mann, the circulation of *Town Topics* rose from 60,000 to what he estimated as around 140,000. A weekly appearing every Thursday and selling for ten cents, it had from twenty-four to twenty-eight ten-by-thirteen-inch pages printed on glossy paper; contents included well-written fiction, light verse, politics, and reviews of music and books. Mann was a stickler for good grammar and high-quality writing. He boasted about the enthusiastic description of his weekly by the *Journalist* (later to be taken over by *Printer's Ink*), which described *Town Topics* as "the best-written paper in the English language."

Much of this praise, however, was not due only to Mann's painstaking editing but to the talented or controversial writers who contributed to his publication. Although the pay ranged from only one halfpenny a word to five dollars a column, he was able to attract a great deal of talent because of the freedom *Town Topics* provided for such writers and critics as James Huneker and Percival Pollard, the later of whom wrote as "The Ringmaster." Ludwig Lewisohn later wrote that, until the end of World War I, *Town Topics* served as "a continuing school for critics and short-story writers." Charles Hanson Towne, editor in chief of the *Smart Set* from 1904 to 1908, claimed in his autobiography *Adventures in Editing* (1926) that Colonel Mann described his editorial staff and favorite contributors as his "family." "And we were literally that," Towne said, "as I have never known an organization that worked in such complete harmony."

The major attraction of *Town Topics,* however, was not just the literary contributions that gave the magazine a sense of respectability. Rather, the hidden appeal continued to be "Saunterings," the column sometimes described as America's first gossip column, a potpourri of nearly every social, moral, political, and economic subject, as well as gossip and innuendo. Logan tells of how the Saunterer's world in New York, as well as in Philadelphia, Boston, Baltimore, and Charleston, was populated by "persons who gave receptions, tea dances, and tennis parties and got engaged and married much as they did in Manhattan's other society pages, but who were also branded as adulterers (frequently incestuous), transvestites, nymphomaniacs and homosexuals (male and female)." Walter Davenport and James C. Derieux relate how Mann's stylistic devices such as the "keyed paragraph," hinting at connections between famous people, were used to titillate as well as intimidate socialites:

> A keyed paragraph would tell *Town Topics* readers that an enchanting young society matron, unnamed, had been seen "by the sea" having one of the numerous times of her life with an equally young and handsome scientist. In the third paragraph following there would be the innocent announcement that the young Mrs. (Name) was in Long Branch under the care of Dr. (Name), the rising young heart specialist.

In addition to his magazine, Mann and his associates, including Joseph M. Deuel, justice of the Court of Special Sessions of New York City, published *Fads and Fancies of Representative Americans* (1905), planned as an annual volume of biographical puffs about status-seeking financiers, industrialists, U.S. senators, and top-flight Wall Street men. Davenport and Derieux write that no duller collection of designed inaccuracies ever rolled off anybody's press, but for a minimum of fifteen hundred dollars a copy one could buy the publication and be left alone, unless one did something suspicious and got another visit from the colonel's book agents.

Encouraged by the growing profits of *Town Topics* and the quarterly *Tales from Town Topics* (later transformed into *Transatlantic Tales*), in 1900 Mann launched the *Smart Set.* As a monthly magazine of general literature, it was aimed generally at the same type of upper-middle-class audience attracted to *Town Topics.* The difference, however, was in its larger size and even greater efforts to experiment with forward-looking literary contributions. In the first issue, which set the pattern for the early *Smart Set,* Mann included a one-thousand-dollar-prize novelette; a "true-story" scandal; a one-act play; a travel article; and poems, sketches, and witticisms. In all, 160 pages of text and 20 pages of advertising were bound together in a striking, bluish-gray cover. The price was twenty-five cents, and Mann was later to claim a circulation of one hundred thousand .

The first editor of the new magazine was Arthur Grissom, a poet and free-lance writer who had once collaborated with George Creel in publishing a weekly magazine in Kansas City. After Grissom's death in 1901 the *Smart Set* was edited by Marvin Dana and Towne, who helped maintain the same content formula for the first decade.

Among the many well-known writers whose bylines appeared in the early *Smart Set* were Mary Austin, Ambrose Bierce, James Branch Cabell, Theodore Dreiser, Justus Miles Forman, Henry Snyder Harrison, Kate Masterson, Barry Pain, Max Pemberton, and William Sidney Porter (O. Henry). In 1907 Dreiser persuaded H. L. Mencken to begin submitting a monthly theatrical review to Mann's *Smart Set.* Thus began a relationship that was to continue for fifteen years. It was from this series that Mencken's *Prejudices* books evolved and with them the cult of "Menckenism" that swept through the United States during the 1920s and early 1930s.

Along with *Town Topics,* the *Smart Set* prospered for several years. Mann later declared that he made one hundred thousand dollars a year with the magazine, and, using it as a base, he began a London edition in 1901. By 1908 the American edition reached a circulation of 160,000, though after that high point it gradually declined. In the spring of 1911 Mann sold the *Smart Set* to John Adams Thayer, an advertising man who had also been a publisher of *Everybody's Magazine.* Mencken later frequently asserted that, before he and Nathan took control in 1914, the magazine had dealt only in "perfumed pornography."

Still another of Mann's publishing endeavors was his short-lived experiment (1905–1906) with radical socialism in *Tom Watson's Magazine.* In spite of an aversion to populism, Mann saw the possibility of picking up some of the 117,000 voters who had supported Watson as the Populist candidate for vice-president in 1896; Mann approached the politician from Georgia to edit his own magazine, which Mann would publish. After the initial run of one hundred thousand copies sold out in a day, Mann pushed socialist principles for a year before the economic strain triggered by libel suits and public disclosure of his blackmailing operations wounded portions of his publishing projects, as well as his credibility. The fact that he never paid the nine

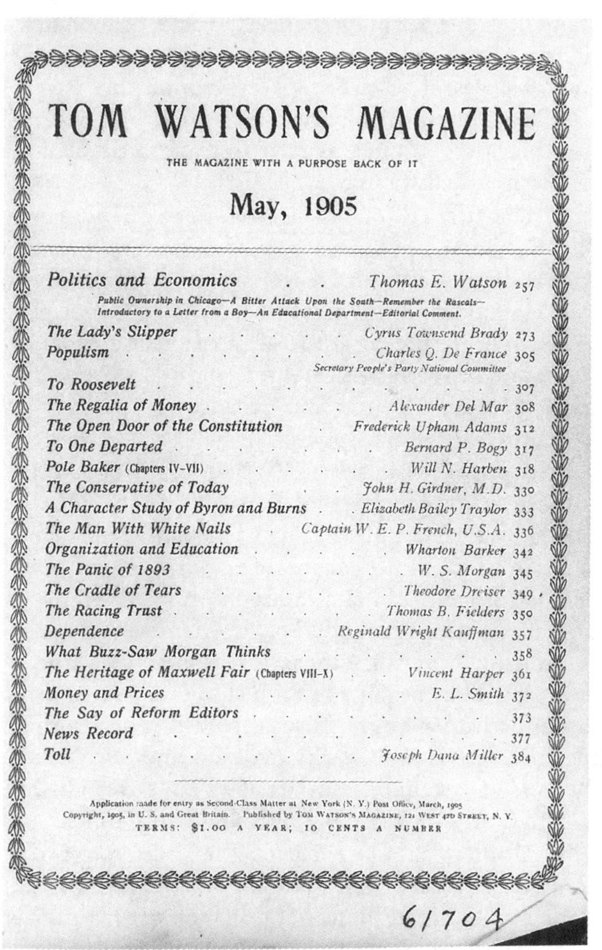

TOM WATSON'S MAGAZINE

THE MAGAZINE WITH A PURPOSE BACK OF IT

May, 1905

Application made for entry as Second-Class Matter at New York (N. Y.) Post Office, March, 1905
Copyright, 1905, in U. S. and Great Britain. Published by Tom Watson's Magazine, 121 West 42d Street, N. Y.
TERMS: $1.00 A YEAR; 10 CENTS A NUMBER

6/704

Cover for an issue of Mann's magazine named for and edited by the 1896 Populist candidate for vice-president

thousand dollars owed to Watson for his editing efforts did not improve his image with the populists or the capitalists to whom he catered.

The decline of Mann's publishing projects, as well as his credibility as an editor, had begun even before his sale of the *Smart Set.* It had started years earlier as *Town Topics* became bolder and its gossip, slander, and libel more audacious, all couched in an Old Testament form of morality in Mann's "Saunterings" column and throughout his own publications.

"My ambition," Mann told a reporter for the *New York Times* (1 August 1905), is to "reform the Four Hundred by making them so deeply disgusted with themselves [as not] to continue their silly empty way of life." Mann said that, in addition to his reporting and criticism, he was also "teaching the great American public not to pay attention to the silly fools. If I didn't publish *Town Topics,* someone else without moral responsibility would do it. I am really doing it for the sake of the country."

One journalist who did not believe Mann was really publishing for the sake of his country was Norman Hapgood, the editor of *Collier's* magazine and an ardent admirer of then-president Theodore Roosevelt and his family. After Mann had made some unflattering remarks about the president's daughter Alice, following her participation at a social event at Newport in the fall of 1904, Hapgood, at the urging of owner Peter Collier, let go with a blast at *Town Topics:*

> The most degraded paper of any prominence in the United States is a weekly of which the function is to distribute news and scandal about society. The mind which guides such a publication tests credulity and forces one to take [Jonathan] Swift's Yahoo as an unexaggerated truth. There have been several of these creatures in our day. One of them used to ride in a closed carriage which carried a strong man to protect him from anticipated horsewhips.

Hapgood went on to describe the attack on the president's daughter by the "sewer-like-sheet": "It uses her first name only. It charges her with all the errors that hurt a woman most and it makes these charges in the most coarse and leering way. We can hardly imagine that many decent men would consent to meet the editor. His standing among the people is somewhat worse than that of the ordinary forger, horsethief or second-story man." The *Collier's* article not only came out sharply against Mann but attacked Judge Deuel, the part owner and legal adviser to the *Smart Set,* for breach of statutes, conflict of interest, and association with the scandal sheet: "Every day he sits upon the bench is a disgrace to the State that endures him."

For the next year both publications hurled insults at each other before Collier and the state district attorney conspired to bait Mann and Deuel to sue *Collier's* for criminal libel in order to get Mann on the witness stand. An associate of Mann's publishing company had already been charged with blackmail in July 1905, but government officials were not confident that Mann could be implicated in the case. As a result Hapgood, who had been writing anonymous attacks on Mann, replaced them with the colonel's name. In Hapgood's 19 August issue he printed "in compact form for the colonel's convenience" all of the attacks *Collier's* published on *Town Topics.* Although Mann was reluctant to take the bait, Deuel was furious and in October filed a suit for criminal libel. Although the pair were able to obtain an indictment against Hapgood, the court case itself turned into a spectacle of revelations against Mann and the questionable use of his publications to

Three editorial cartoons, circa 1905, accusing Mann of using his magazine Town Topics *and his book* Fads and Fancies *for blackmail*

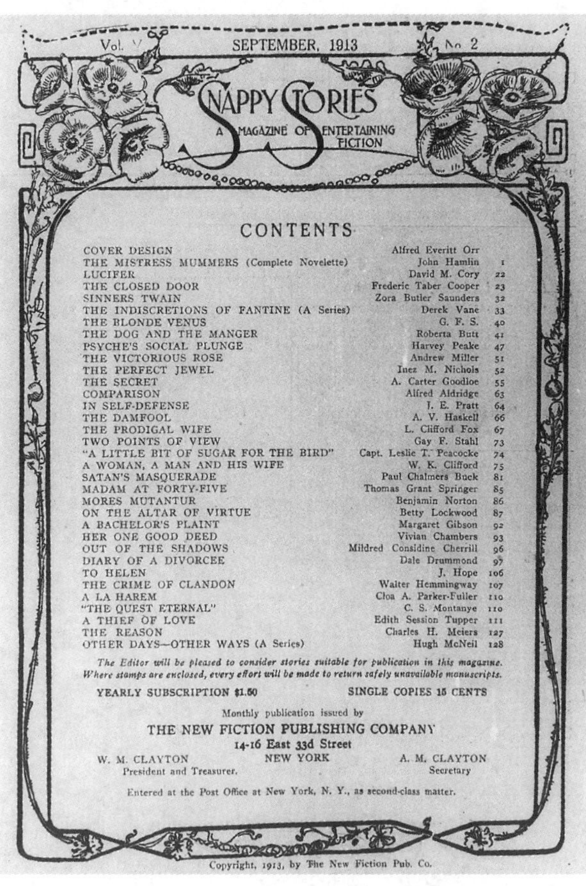

Vol. V SEPTEMBER, 1913 No. 2

SNAPPY STORIES
A MAGAZINE OF ENTERTAINING FICTION

CONTENTS

The Editor will be pleased to consider stories suitable for publication in this magazine. Where stamps are enclosed, every effort will be made to return safely unavailable manuscripts.

YEARLY SUBSCRIPTION $1.50 SINGLE COPIES 15 CENTS

Monthly publication issued by
THE NEW FICTION PUBLISHING COMPANY
14-16 East 33d Street
NEW YORK

W. M. CLAYTON, President and Treasurer. A. M. CLAYTON, Secretary

Entered at the Post Office at New York, N. Y., as second-class matter.

Copyright, 1913, by The New Fiction Pub. Co.

Contents page for an issue of Mann's final publishing venture, a magazine featuring mildly titillating short fiction

extort money from New York high society. Following the introduction of a letter written by U.S. senator Dryden into the case, a writer for the *Nation* (7 December 1905) wondered how such things could be: "There were our hardest-headed men of business, our keenest speculators, our grimmest promoters, our coolest brokers, our most matter-of-fact railroad and insurance men – all classed as ready dupes of a transparent bunko game."

In fairness to members of this idle leisure class, who were mocked almost as much as Mann, there were other prominent officials and socialites, such as Henry Frick, Andrew Carnegie, Cooper Hewitt, and the Rockefellers, who refused to be blackmailed by Mann or his agents. It took the jury only seven minutes to return a verdict acquitting Hapgood. Within twenty-four hours Mann was arrested on a perjury charge.

For the next few years he was forced to spend much of his fortune defending himself and keeping himself out of prison. At his perjury trial the public learned how Mann had managed to extort loans from such prominent New Yorkers as Howard Gould, James R. Keene, John Pierpont Morgan, and William K. Vanderbilt. Mann's attorney, unable to come up with a defense against the evidence, relied primarily on an emotional appeal to the jury: "Send this gallant old hero from this courtroom a free man."

Despite his acquittal on the perjury charge, the fortunes of Mann's magazines were never the same after the revelations of his blackmailing operations and the gullibility of New York high society. For many years Mann continued to blame his faltering advertising revenues and other problems on "the Roosevelt-*Collier's* conspiracy." Mann also tried to regain some stature by expanding his *Transatlantic Tales* into an international belles-lettres magazine by pirating the material of such authors as Anton Chekhov, Ivan Turgenev, and Maksim Gorky. But this too failed, and in 1908 Mann initiated *Snappy Stories,* with tales primarily about good and bad women and other saucy subjects. The publication lasted ten years beyond Mann's death. In contrast to the decline of Mann's fortunes, the celebrated trial helped boost *Collier's* to a new prestige. According to F. L. Mott, "few periodicals in America have ever exerted as strong and direct an influence on national affairs as that of *Collier's* during the Hapgood era."

In 1916 the state of New York evicted Mann from Saunterer's Rest, the island in Lake George where he had held ostentatious house parties. The once-wealthy, white-bearded publisher, compared to Saint Nicholas for his generous habit of handing out dollar bills to visitors to his office, was also forced to sell his holdings on West Fortieth Street, as well as the property on West Thirty-eighth Street that he had once tried to force government officials to purchase as the site for the main post office in New York.

Throughout Mann's declining years his old friend Deuel continued to assist him by reading proofs for *Town Topics* and other publications. Mann kept active in social activities and in the Democratic Club, where he was an enthusiastic supporter of Al Smith for governor. He also attended the fiftieth reunion of the Blue and Grey at Gettysburg. After he died on 17 May 1920 from complications resulting from pneumonia, his coffin was draped with an American flag. On it lay the saber he had carried at Gettysburg.

Even after his death the legal battles that had characterized his life continued to plague his estate. Despite erroneous reports of "Mann's millions," a final accounting showed his debts to be more than his assets. Members of his family, including his third wife, Sophie Hartong Mann, and daughter Emma Mann-

Vynne, appeared in the courts for several years to try to preserve Mann's estate. Little money was left, however. *Town Topics* passed through various hands before its last issue in January 1937. Although Mann was not always acknowledged for his role in founding the *Smart Set,* the publication became one of America's best-known literary publications.

Mann's reputation in magazine history remains scarred because of the libel and perjury trials that exposed him and his enterprises to ridicule and a loss of credibility that contributed to his financial decline. Throughout his later years Mann continued to stress that it was not his publication that was sued for libel but *Collier's,* which had, he said, libeled *Town Topics,* Deuel, and himself. As for the perjury trial, Mann had to continue to remind readers that he had been acquitted.

Not all historians have allowed his crude attempts at extortion under the guise of imposing morality on the Four Hundred to blind them to Mann's other contributions to magazine and literary history. Mott has been generous in praising *Town Topics* and the *Smart Set,* as was Lewisohn, a former employee of *Town Topics* and author of *Expression in America* (1932). An editorial in the *Mobile Register,* one of the few newspapers to comment on the death of Mann, praised the former Mobile entrepreneur and inventor for his contributions to that city and to Alabama.

Biography:

Andy Logan, *The Man Who Robbed the Robber Barons* (New York: Norton, 1965).

References:

Walter Davenport and James C. Derieux, "Dirty Dollar Mann," in their *Ladies, Gentlemen and Editors* (Garden City, N.Y.: Doubleday, 1960), pp. 281–293;

"Fads and Fancies: A Rich Man's Book: 105 Immortals Have Subscribed $200,000 to Be in It and Get It – What They Received for Their Thousands," *New York Times,* 10 December 1905, p. 1;

Ludwig Lewisohn, *Expression in America* (New York & London: Harper, 1932);

"Mammonical Possession," *Nation,* 7 (December 1905): 457, 458;

"Mann Would Reform the Four Hundred," *New York Times,* 1 August 1905, p. 1;

F. L. Mott, *A History of the American Magazine,* volume 5, *1905–1930* (Cambridge, Mass.: Harvard University Press, 1968), pp. 252–278;

Richard O'Connor, "The Terrible Colonel," in his *The Golden Summers: An Antic History of Newport* (New York: Putnam, 1974);

"Oh, Roosevelt Forgot, Col. Mann Declares," *New York Times,* 25 July 1905, pp. 1, 2;

"Preying on the Rich," *Outlook: A Weekly Newspaper,* 82 (3 February 1906), pp. 249, 250;

Robert R. Rowe, "Mann of Town Topics," *American Mercury,* 8 (July 1926): 272–274;

Charles Hanson Towne, *Adventures in Editing* (New York: Appleton, 1926).

Orison Swett Marden

(1850 – 10 March 1924)

J. Douglas Tarpley
CBN University

MAJOR POSITIONS HELD: Founder (1897) and editor, *Success* (1897–1912, 1918–1924).

BOOKS: *Pushing to the Front: Success Under Difficulties* (Boston: Houghton, Mifflin, 1894);
Architects of Fate; or Steps to Success (Boston: Houghton, Mifflin, 1895);
How to Succeed (New York: Christian Herald, 1896);
Rising in the World (New York: Crowell, 1897);
Success: A Book of Ideas, Helps and Examples for All Desiring to Make the Most of Life (Boston: Wilde, 1897);
Secrets of Achievement (New York: Crowell, 1898);
Character: The Grandest Thing in the World (New York: Crowell, 1899);
Cheerfulness as a Life Power (New York & Boston: Crowell, 1899);
Good Manners: A Passport to Success (New York: Crowell, 1900);
The Hour of Opportunity (New York: Crowell, 1900);
Economy: The Self-Denying Depositor and Prudent Paymaster (New York: Crowell, 1901);
How They Succeeded: Life Stories of Successful Men Told by Themselves (Boston: Lothrop, 1901);
An Iron Will (New York: Crowell, 1901);
Talks with Great Workers (New York: Crowell, 1901);
Stepping Stones: Essays for Everyday Living (Boston: Lothrop, 1902);
Little Visits with Great Americans (New York: Success, 1903);
The Young Man Entering Business (New York: Crowell, 1903);
Stories from Life (New York: American Book, 1904);
Choosing a Career (Indianapolis: Bobbs-Merrill, 1905);
The Making of a Man (Boston: Lothrop, 1905);
Every Man a King (New York: Crowell, 1906);
Success Nuggets (New York: Crowell, 1906);
The Consolidated Library (New York: Bureau of National Literature & Art, 1906);
The Power of Personality (New York: Crowell, 1906);
The Optimistic Life (New York: Crowell, 1907);
He Can Who Thinks He Can (New York: Crowell, 1908);
Do It to a Finish (New York: Crowell, 1909);
Lecture on the Deformity of the Civilized Foot (Battle Creek, Mich.: United Schools of Physical Culture, 1909);
Not the Salary But the Opportunity (New York: Crowell, 1909);
Peace, Power & Plenty (New York: Crowell, 1909);
Why Grow Old? (New York: Crowell, 1909);
Be Good to Yourself (New York: Crowell, 1910);
Dickson's How to Speak in Public (Chicago: Dickson School of Memory, 1910);
Getting On (New York: Crowell, 1910);
The Miracle of Right Thought (New York: Crowell, 1910);
Self-Investment (New York: Crowell, 1911);
The Exceptional Employee (New York: Crowell, 1913);
The Joys of Living (New York: Crowell, 1913);
The Progressive Businessman (New York: Crowell, 1913);
The Uplift Book of Child Culture (Philadelphia: Physical Culture, 1913);
Training for Efficiency (New York: Crowell, 1913);
Hints for Young Writers (New York: Crowell, 1914);
I Had a Friend (New York: Crowell, 1914);
Keeping Fit (New York: Crowell, 1914);
Everybody Ahead; or, Getting the Most Out of Life (New York: Crowell, 1914); republished as *Heading for Victory; or, Getting the Most Out of Life* (New York: Morrison, 1920);
The Crime of Silence (Philadelphia: Physical Culture, 1915);
Women and Home (New York: Crowell, 1915);
Making Life a Masterpiece (New York: Crowell, 1916);
Selling Things (New York: Crowell, 1916);
The Victorious Attitude (New York: Crowell, 1916);
How to Get What You Want (New York: Crowell, 1917);
Love's Way (New York: Crowell, 1918);
Thrift (New York: Crowell, 1918);

Orison Swett Marden

Ambition and Success (New York: Crowell, 1919);
Cheerfulness as a Life Power (London: Rider, 1919);
Success Fundamentals (New York: Crowell, 1920);
You Can, But Will You? (New York: Crowell, 1920);
Masterful Personality (New York: Crowell, 1921);
Prosperity, How to Attract It (New York: Success, 1922);
Round Pegs in Square Holes (New York: Crowell, 1922);
Self-Discovery: Why Remain a Dwarf? (New York: Crowell, 1922);
Making Yourself (New York: Crowell, 1923);
"It Won't Last": A Message for the Time (New York: Crowell, 1924);
The Conquest of Worry (New York: Crowell, 1924);
Making Friends with Our Nerves (New York: Crowell, 1925);
The Secret of Achievement (New York: Crowell, 1926).

According to biographer Margaret Connolly, Frank A. Munsey, the well-known American magazine publisher, said of his friend and colleague Orison Swett Marden, "If Doctor Marden had not written his first book he would have been a millionaire. He had a genius for hotel making." Marden was a man of paradoxes. While he was a visionary who tried to bring about a better world for himself and others, he was also a pragmatist who knew the value of a dollar and how to make money. And while he was a man of letters, founding a magazine and authoring many best-selling books, he was respected as a successful businessman. Although he was socially awkward and uncomfortable for much of his life, he eventually won honors for his oratory skills and became a community leader. Marden was a man with many skills and aptitudes, who would have been successful in any one of several vocations, and although he did successfully pursue a career in hotel management for several years, he ultimately left the ranks to launch his career in journalism. He founded *Success* magazine in 1897, authored scores of books, created a radio broadcast, and gained many devoted followers of his success philosophy.

Marden was born in Thornton, New Hampshire, in 1850 and was the second of three children born to Louis and Martha Cilley Marden. His mother died at the age of twenty-two, when Orison was only three years old; his father, a robust and athletic man, worked hard to provide for the family after Mrs. Marden died. He farmed, hunted, and trapped in the rugged New England backwoods until he was badly injured in an accident. He only partially recovered, and he died four years later, leaving the children under the guardianship of a fellow Grafton County farmer, Herod Fifield.

Fifield sent them to live with their grandmother in a little log house located in a remote area of the same community. Unable to provide for the children because of her feebleness and limited resources, she agreed to their being separated from each other and "bound out" by the guardian into several homes for the next several years.

Marden had many vivid and unpleasant memories of his experiences with the five different families with which he was boarded in the New Hampshire backwoods. He recalled always feeling like an "outsider," never enjoying the benefits and relationships of family life. He remembered the hard work of twelve- and fourteen-hour working days, the lack of affection, the loneliness, and the homesickness. Often he was referred to as the "hired boy." Marden generally was called on to assume the workload of a man, missing out on the typical boyhood experiences and opportunities for play and recreation. Late in his life he said of these early years, "I had to work very hard, and forgot what it was to be a child with other children."

In one home with a Baptist minister and his wife, Marden saw the cruelty of church people to the old minister, and this generated in Marden a lifelong suspicion of organized religion and "empty creeds." He hated the "gloomy and depressing" atmosphere of the parsonage and the frightening hellfire sermons he heard weekly. In more than one home he observed people's selfish and violent behavior. With each family with which he stayed, he learned to live with hunger. As he later said, "a bound-out orphan did not seem to have any rights to speak of. His duty was to work. He had no other use and got very little sympathy, very few favors."

However, through these experiences he learned of his inner strength to sustain himself and a love for the beauty and peace of the countryside. While with one family, he learned to appreciate the loyalty and affection of a dog. With another family he learned the value of being a wise manager of limited resources of money and time. In another home he learned the value of real friendship, "that relationship which brings out the best in people." Throughout his experiences in the rough but pristine New Hampshire countryside, he had one refuge from misery – his "unborn love of Nature," to which he turned for joy, peace, and solace, feelings denied him by most people with whom he came into contact.

The fullness of his experiences presented him with the material for later books and articles, and the book by Samuel Smiles titled *Self Help* marked a turning point in Marden's life by helping him clarify his desires and focus on education as a means of achieving his goals. Having come upon the book by chance in an attic, Marden later declared (as Connolly reports): "I felt like a poor man who had just by accident discovered a gold mine. . . . Boys and girls of today, living in the midst of great opportunities, surrounded by schools, libraries, all sorts of books and reading, and a multiplicity of educational facilities, can hardly understand what Smiles' wonderful pages meant to a backward, green country boy. I knew nothing whatever of the great world outside the hills of my native state. Up to that time I had not seen, perhaps, more than fifty different people at any one time, and not more than half a dozen books."

To Marden's surprise he received permission from his guardian to attend Colby Academy, a preparatory school in New London, New Hampshire, for a term. He had to work to earn money for various school expenses, so for the next several years he did various jobs, including kitchen work in a boardinghouse, lumbering, and "barbering" his classmates. He even opened his own school and taught "problem boys" for two years. Learning about himself through these experiences, he later said, "You will be amazed to find how, the moment you cut off all outside assistance, you will be reinforced by a new power which you never before dreamed you possessed. But it will never come to your aid until you stop learning and depending – until you throw away all crutches and stand erect on your own feet."

After meeting with some limited academic success at Colby, he entered New Hampton Institute of New Hampshire, where several students and faculty recognized his talents and encouraged him. Conquering a debilitating fear of public speaking through the encouragement and understanding of a teacher, he eventually won awards in speech competitions, including one designated for the student recognized as most outstanding in public speaking.

Between his first and second terms at New Hampton he secured a summer position as a waiter in the Crawford House, a well-known hotel complex. It was there that he met Munsey, who was also

Cover for an issue of Marden's magazine, with illustration by J. C. Leyendecker

working as a waiter. The men developed a lasting friendship.

When Marden returned to his second term, he opened an eating club for students. The venture was so successful that years later, while attending Boston University, he used his club as a model when he opened a successful eating club for faculty and students: the Boston University Club.

After graduating from the New Hampton Institute in 1873, he became a student in the Theological Seminary at Andover, Massachusetts, where he spent one year. Having obtained some knowledge about "the science of theology," he applied to and was accepted at Boston University in 1874. To fund his academic career he opened and operated his eating establishment. The venture brought him such notoriety that he accepted an invitation from Harvard University president Charles W. Eliot to set up a similar restaurant for Harvard.

His successes in managing people, schedules, and money brought him many invitations to operate everything from hotels to an asylum. In 1877 Marden began to work as a clerk in the front office of Ocean View Hotel, Block Island, Rhode Island. He was quickly made manager because of the success of his suggestions for expanding the business, attracting new clientele, and developing a first-class image of the property. His Boston University classmates had begun to call him "Lucky Marden" because he was winning awards in college, earning the respect of school administrators, and distinguishing himself as a successful and competent hotel manager.

In 1877 he graduated from Boston University with B.S. and A.B. degrees. In 1879 he earned an A.M. degree there. He received his M.D. two years later and in 1882 his LL.B., both from Harvard. By the time he graduated he had been so successful in hotel management and catering that he had saved several thousand dollars. He used part of the money to finance a trip to Europe in 1882. After returning to America, he bought his own hotel, the Manisses at Block Island. He also became proprietor and manager of other well-known hotel properties in other parts of the country. At one time four hotel properties in three different states were under his control. All the while, however, he continued to work on manuscripts for inspirational pieces that he had begun while a university student.

Investing heavily in hotel and other commercial properties in the Kearney, Nebraska, area during an economic boom, he moved there and became a leader in the community, holding the office of president of the board of trade. His philanthropy earned him the admiration and affection of many townspeople. He regularly helped the needy, feeding at his hotel those who were unable to prepare their own meals on special holidays, and assisted young men in bettering themselves socially and educationally. When a drought of three years bitterly and completely broke the area's economic boom and when a fire destroyed some of Marden's property in the East, he lost heavily and could do no more than just survive. The fire not only destroyed his building, it destroyed several thousand pages of his manuscripts and notes.

He later saw this as a momentous time in his life, for it presented him with two options: the possibility of continuing in the hotel business in response to several invitations to manage top-quality resorts across the country and the possibility of embarking on a writing career. He is reported to have said that he felt that he had been divinely led, step by step, to his new career. Although he had devoted a great part of his time and energy to making a success of business, material success was not the main goal of his life. He later said, "There is a divinity within us which speaks . . . its message in the silence. There are many times of storm and stress and doubt when about all we can do is to hearken to that inner voice, which bids us hold to the hand of the Divine guide." He rejected the invitations to the world of business and began a writing career.

In a short time he completed *Pushing to the Front: Success Under Difficulties* (1894). About the same time he completed his second manuscript, *Architects of Fate; or Steps to Success* (1895). Anxious about how the three publishers to whom he submitted his first manuscript would react, he evidently was genuinely surprised when all three wanted to publish it. Houghton, Mifflin published his first book, which was praised by reviewers. The book went through additional printings, becoming a best-seller and an inspirational classic.

Marden felt that the title of his 1894 volume had a lot to do with its success. The book was hailed as "a veritable romance of success." In the book Marden talked about men and women rising to high positions of honor and service from humble backgrounds. He told the life stories of great men, showing their lowly beginnings, frequent discouragements, and repeated failures. Coming from Marden's own experience, the basic theme spoke to many people who needed to be told that success could be realized by all people who discovered the latent strength and power within themselves to "perform the impossible." The book was soon translated into several languages.

Inspired by his success, Marden founded *Success* magazine in 1897 "to reach the largest number of people to give them a new philosophy of life." He said that the demand for *Pushing to the Front* was the immediate origin of *Success.* He had received so many letters from all sorts of people, old and young, telling of the encouragement and inspiration they had received from the book that "it gave birth to the new idea." The more he thought about it, he said, the more convinced he became that such a magazine was needed.

Acknowledging criticism of his effort by "highminded men and women" who saw the publication as too mercenary, he is reported to have declared that the magazine was to be one "which should stand for the only real success in life – the complete development of the man, of the woman, that God made, for service to mankind, and for making a life as well as making a living." Louis Klopsch, publisher of the *Christian Herald,* became a partner in the enterprise and furnished the necessary capital.

Forming the Success Company, the men worked out of New York and Boston to produce the magazine. It ran as a monthly publication through 1897 to November 1898, as a weekly from December 1898 through 1899, and as a monthly again from 1900 through 1912. Regularly published between 1897 and 1912, eventually it was a product of the Success Company's own printing plant, had expansive editorial offices, and at one time employed a workforce of nearly two hundred employees. *Success* claimed a growing circulation but failed when it "was dealt a staggering blow" by bankers and other financial backers who "smarted" when the magazine's editorial formula was altered to move it into line with popular muckraking publications of the day, a move Marden opposed (unsuccessfully since others had taken control of the company). The magazine ceased publication in 1912.

In 1905, when the magazine was enjoying tremendous success, Marden married Clare L. Evans of Louisville, Kentucky. The daughter of an old southern family, Clare was a devoted wife and mother, although she was his junior by many years; three children were quickly born to the two, who made their home in Glen Cove, Long Island. The couple's first child was a son, named for his father, and the other two children were daughters, Mary Newell and Laura Fletcher. The children are reported by Connolly to have characterized their parents' relationship as "Heavenly."

Marden was devoted to his children and took great pride in their affection and accomplishments. Probably because of his unhappy years as a child, "he enjoyed his own children immensely and often talked about the "nature and needs of a child." In his book *The Joys of Living* (1913) he wrote:

> The first duty we owe a child is to teach him to fling out his inborn joy and gladness with the same freedom and abandon as the bobolink does when it makes the meadow joyous with its song. Suppression of the fun-loving nature of a child means the suppression of its mental and moral faculties. Joy will go out of the heart of a child after a while, if he is constantly suppressed.... Children who are encouraged in the expression of their play-instinct will make better business men, better professional men. They will succeed better and have a better influence than those who are repressed.

According to Connolly, in a letter to his son Marden instructed him, "You can be a very much bigger man in the world.... There are possibilities in you and you must keep climbing, growing, improving at every opportunity." He instructed him to "live up to the level of your highest gift" and to "follow through the years of your struggles and watch the glorious future."

Maintaining editorial offices and continuing to write after *Success* ceased operations, Marden dreamed of resurrecting the magazine. In 1917 he arranged for financial support from a man who had been inspired to success through the magazine and who understood the "political nature" of the problems of the earlier venture. The new *Success* magazine was launched with its first edition in January 1918.

In spite of the war effort and the fact that many established publications failed during World War I, the new magazine increased in circulation and went on to be a success that surprised even Marden. One newspaper editorial praised its success as a symbol of the credibility of Marden's philosophy. After realizing the magazine was a financial and editorial success, the elderly Marden retired in January 1924 because of failing health. He also ceased doing the radio program *Bedtime Stories for Grown-Ups,* which had been broadcast evenings since May 1923 over WBZ in Springfield, Massachusetts.

In an effort to rest and restore his health, Marden and his wife traveled to Los Angeles in 1924. Suddenly taken ill soon after his arrival there, he was taken to Clara Barton Hospital, where he later died on 10 March 1924.

His passing was noted around the country. The *Chicago Evening Post* published a short, poignant editorial in which it was noted that with Marden's death Americans lost "a man whose name is known and loved by many an American to whom came the first clear vision of the value of character and the worth of hard work from Dr. Marden's writings." He was referred to as an "optimist of the true type," as one who believed in the "inherent good of human nature and in the beneficent purpose of the universe." He was praised for his influence for good in the lives of many young men and boys. Marden's obituary in the *New York Times* reported that even his last words, which it quoted, were positive and inspiring: "Death is not the end. For in the miracle of Resurrection Life has triumphed over Death. On this Easter season, I extend my greetings. May it be your resurrection and mine."

The message of his writing was one of hope that was illustrated by the example of his life. The message powerfully inspired many people and garnered something of a cult following for this "prophet of success."

The cornerstone of his philosophy of life was a belief that God intended for each person to rise to the highest state of existence of which he was capable through his own efforts. In 1910, in his *Miracle of Right Thought,* he declared that if a man "holds the right mental attitude, and struggles earnestly, honestly toward his goal, he will reach it." This miracle generated self-development and character and concern for and sensitivity to other people. While Marden believed poverty to be one of the world's greatest curses, he believed it could be overcome. He said, "If we are to progress as a race, as a civilization, we must drive this crushing poverty disease from our midst. It is our duty to get away from it and to help others to do so. Every human being on this earth could be living in comfort if he knew the powers locked up within himself and were willing to work and make the best use of them."

His theme of inner strength and self-reliance was reinforced by his aggressive and clear call for determination. Choosing "No surrender!" as a slogan, he said,

> The one who loses heart when he finds the way to his goal unexpectedly blocked – who waits for smooth conditions and favorable circumstances – will not go far in this world. Conditions will never be such that success in any field will be a walk-over. It is he who, at the start, makes up his mind to win in spite of adverse conditions – the man who, instead of surrendering to obstacles, rides over them – that succeeds in life. The very struggle to overcome the obstacles in his way develops the power that carries him step by step to his goal.

His love of nature was another of his recurring themes, again growing out of his own experience. Rejecting organized religion and "empty creeds," Marden said that the forest was his cathedral and the trees his altars.

In her biography Connolly declares, "It was the humanness of the message he gave to the world, this recognition of the divinity and the fundamental oneness of mankind, regardless of differences of race, creed, or color, that won it enthusiastic acceptance." In addition, a reader is struck with the strong sense of constructive energy provoked by it. As Connolly says,

> Everything he wrote was constructive. In all his writings, spread over a period of half a century, there was not a line of pessimism or gloom. He was no careless, unthinking optimist, however. . . . He called attention to evils, – only to show how they may be remedied, – how society as well as the individual, may triumph over everything tending to hinder progress.

And as she and Marden's peers recognized, he practiced what he preached, becoming almost an illustration, "an active application," of his philosophy.

Biography:

Margaret Connolly, *Life of Orison Swett Marden* (New York: Crowell, 1925).

Reference:

Obituary, *New York Times,* 11 March 1924.

Herbert R. Mayes

(11 August 1900 - 30 October 1987)

Howard Price
Eastern Illinois University

MAJOR POSITIONS HELD: Editor, *American Druggist* (1927–1934); editor, *Pictorial Review* (1934–1937); managing editor (1938–1939), editor, *Good Housekeeping* (1939–1958); editor, *McCall's* (1958–1962); president, McCall's Corporation (1961–1965).

BOOKS: *Alger: A Biography Without a Hero* (New York: Macy-Masius, 1928);
Editor's Choice: 26 Stories from Good Housekeeping (New York: Random House, 1956);
The Magazine Maze: A Prejudiced Perspective (Garden City, N.Y.: Doubleday, 1980).

OTHER: *Twenty-Five Stories from Good Housekeeping,* edited by Mayes (New York: Hearst Magazines, 1945);
An Editor's Treasury: A Continuing Anthology of Prose, Verse, and Literary Curiosa, edited by Mayes (New York: Atheneum, 1968).

SELECTED PERIODICAL PUBLICATIONS – UNCOLLECTED: "Good Words," *American Artist,* 28 (December 1964): 73–74;
"Notes on Creative Editing," *Writer,* 78 (February 1965): 18–19;
"Henry R. Luce," *Saturday Review,* 50 (18 March 1967): 16–17;
"Oh, What A Lovely Way to Run An Election," *Saturday Review,* 55 (11 March 1972): 23–27;
"Hoy Horatio!," *Time,* 103 (10 June 1974): 18.

Herbert R. Mayes

Although he is best known for the four years he spent as editor of *McCall's,* Herbert Mayes's career in magazine editing actually spanned approximately forty-two years, including twenty as editor of *Good Housekeeping.* During this time he displayed an extraordinary ability to transform the fortune of declining women's magazines through his selection of articles that would appeal to his readers and through his scrupulous attention to layout and appearance. Mayes considered himself a born editor and began his autobiographical work, *The Magazine Maze* (1980), by stating that editing is what he had always wanted to do.

Herbert Raymond Mayes was born in New York City on 11 August 1900 to Herman and Matilda Hutter Mayes. In September 1915 Mayes was enrolled in the prestigious Townsend Harris High School but had to drop out after only three months to help support his family when his father died. After working at a series of odd jobs, Mayes secured his big break in 1920 when he learned that the *In-*

land Merchant, a trade magazine for small-town general stores, needed a new editor. Mayes obtained several issues of the publication, drew up a sample layout, and convinced the publisher he was the right man for the job. He ran a one-man operation for four years but decided to resign in 1924 when the publisher asked him to add the *Corset and Underwear Review* to his duties.

Mayes was not unemployed for long, however. The Western Newspaper Union hired him to edit *Good Looks Merchandising,* a magazine the union was starting for people engaged in the selling of cosmetics. For his first issue Mayes wrote the lead article, "How to Be Ugly," and illustrated it with a photograph of Lon Chaney in the role of the monstrous Quasimodo in *The Hunchback of Notre Dame.* For a byline Mayes obtained the movie studio's permission to use Chaney's name. In *The Magazine Maze* many years later, Mayes wrote, " . . . it seemed clever then. It doesn't seem so bad even now." The stunt apparently did not anger the union, for Mayes was to remain with the publication for more than two years.

On 4 February 1927 Mayes left the cosmetics magazine, and three days later he went to work for William Randolph Hearst at Hearst's recently acquired monthly pharmaceutical magazine, *American Druggist.* This date is significant in Mayes's career because it marked the beginning of his almost thirty-two-year association with Hearst's publishing empire. While editing *American Druggist* Mayes also began to issue a weekly newsletter called *The Drug Whirl.*

In what free time he had, Mayes decided at the suggestion of a friend to write in 1927 a biography of the novelist Horatio Alger. Rather than base *Alger: A Biography Without a Hero* (1928) on facts, Mayes admitted in *The Magazine Maze* that he falsified most of the details of Alger's life. While not germane to Mayes's magazine career, the book does provide another look at his work. It was greeted with mixed reviews, but no one questioned its authenticity, and many biographical dictionaries later would use details from the book as basic source material.

Meanwhile, stories in Mayes's pharmaceutical publications were occasionally causing commotions by revealing previously unpublicized information about the pharmaceutical industry. This had the effect of bringing Mayes to the notice of Hearst executives, including Richard Berlin, head of Hearst's magazine division. Thus, when in 1934 Hearst acquired *Pictorial Review,* one of the "Big Six" women's magazines of the period, Mayes was appointed editor. *Pictorial Review* had been founded in 1899 by William Paul Ahnelt, a German immigrant who set up a dress-pattern business in the United States with thirteen dollars in capital. The magazine dealt mainly in fashions until 1908, when its editor, Arthur Vance, started attracting writers of quality fiction away from general magazines. The switch was successful, and in the 1920s *Pictorial Review* ranked among the top women's magazines in both advertising revenue and circulation. However, by the time Hearst acquired it, *Pictorial Review* was losing large sums of money due to a loss of advertising during the Depression.

The January 1935 issue was the first one edited by Mayes. Thinking the magazine needed a new look, Mayes hired T. M. Cleland, a respected typographer of the period, to redesign it. To help set the magazine apart, Mayes introduced the "complete-in-one-issue" book-length novel to the magazine. He sought to provide his readers with features not available elsewhere and hired Max Trell to write what was billed as the autobiography of six-year-old child star Shirley Temple. Alwine Dolfuss, widow of the chancellor of Austria, wrote a graphic account of her husband's assassination, and Edith Wharton wrote a sequel to her Pulitzer Prize–winning novel *Age of Innocence* (1920).

Mayes also wanted to ensure that some of the short stories that appeared in *Pictorial Review* would be selected by Edward J. O'Brien for his prestigious annual *Best Stories* anthology. So Mayes hired O'Brien as a consultant with the understanding that he would find at least one story each month that would appear both in *Pictorial Review* and be featured in his collection. Mayes also prevailed on muckraker Ida Tarbell to write about her feelings concerning the Standard Oil Company and John D. Rockefeller many years after her exposés of the two early in the century.

Mayes missed one important opportunity, however. He had a chance in 1935 to obtain rights to serialize *Gone with the Wind,* the novel that would in a few years become a huge best-seller and win author Margaret Mitchell a Pulitzer Prize. Mayes passed up the opportunity because, as he recalled in *The Magazine Maze,* he did not think readers of *Pictorial Review* would be interested in a period novel about the Civil War.

The redesigned and reworked *Pictorial Review* won critical acclaim under Mayes. One year into his editorship the magazine boasted that it had gained fifty thousand more new newsstand buyers than the total of its contemporaries put together. Advertising, however, continued to lag, and *Pictorial Review*

Cover for the first issue to list Mayes on the masthead as publisher and editor

still lost money, even after absorbing *The Delineator,* another highly ranked women's magazine, in 1937 and pushing its circulation above the three million mark. In the face of these steady losses, Hearst decided in January 1939 to fold *Pictorial Review.*

Mayes, however, was not around for the closing. The Hearst organization had decided some months earlier that his talents would be more valuable elsewhere. In 1938 he became managing editor of *Good Housekeeping* with the understanding that, within two years, he would replace William F. Bigelow as editor in chief. Although Bigelow had made *Good Housekeeping* a power in publishing circles, Berlin told Mayes that the magazine was regarded as old-fashioned. Mayes was therefore needed to transform it into a more contemporary publication. Until he took over the editor's job in August 1939, Mayes kept a low profile at the magazine after a preliminary clash with Bigelow, who was resentful of the innovations suggested by Mayes when he arrived there and protested his presence to Hearst.

At *Good Housekeeping* Mayes was successful in altering the stodgy image of the publication which had been described in magazine circles as an "old ladies' magazine." Aware of the declining interest in the late 1930s in magazine fiction, Mayes began to reduce the magazine's traditionally generous offerings in this field. In the 1940s two-part stories began to replace long serials, and novelettes and condensed novels complete in one issue started finding their way into the magazine's pages. Eventually the fictional fare would consist of one long story and three short ones. Contributions to *Good Housekeeping* under Mayes included some of the best-known writers of the day, such as Sinclair Lewis, Christopher Morley, William March, Evelyn Waugh, Daphne du Maurier, and John P. Marquand, who later would rank Mayes as one of the best editors for whom he had worked.

Under Bigelow, *Good Housekeeping* had offered stories on a variety of topics, but the range was broadened by Mayes. The table of contents soon contained articles on such topics as Hollywood, home furnishings, babies, books, food, hairstyles, and fashions. But despite its diversity, *Good Housekeeping* remained a home magazine. World affairs, politics, economics, and social problems were generally ignored except as they directly affected the home; nor did Mayes devote much attention to such subjects as gardening, horticulture, or landscaping.

Under Mayes's two decades of stewardship, *Good Housekeeping* came to be regarded as one of the three or four most valuable magazine properties in the country. It was the bright star in Hearst's magazine division, leading other Hearst magazines not only in circulation but in profits. As a result, Hearst accorded Mayes a great deal of freedom in the operation of the magazine, something he did not do with his newspaper editors. "The nearest thing to a directive (from Hearst)," Mayes wrote in *The Magazine Maze,* "I heard only as a statement attributed to him: 'I do not expect my editors to support or even agree with my political views. I would only wish that in their magazines, they would not openly oppose them.'"

Because of the success of *Good Housekeeping,* Mayes, at various times during his tenure with the magazine, was asked also to take over the editorial side of *Cosmopolitan* or *Town & Country,* other Hearst properties. His assistance was invariably needed because problems had cropped up and someone was needed to smooth them over. When he ran the other magazines, Mayes declined to take on the title of editor and refused to have his name appear in the publications at all, so it is difficult to date these periods accurately.

In 1951 Hearst died, and Berlin, then president of the Hearst Corporation, tightened his control of the publishing empire. Unlike his predecessor, Berlin started sending Mayes messages on how to run *Good Housekeeping.* Friction quickly developed when Berlin, a follower of Wisconsin senator Joseph McCarthy, wanted Mayes to run a story attacking Robert Hutchins, then chancellor of the University of Chicago, whom Berlin contended was a Communist. Despite intense pressure over a period of several weeks, Mayes refused to run the article.

Mayes also was at odds with Richard Deems, Berlin's choice as vice-president of the Hearst magazine division. Mayes rejected many of Deems's recommendations on layout and quarreled with him on budget decisions and remuneration to writers. The editor believed in paying authors as much as possible as a way of ensuring their loyalty with regard to their future work. This did not please Deems, who believed in estimating budgets conservatively and then, according to Mayes, scrutinizing every expenditure from postage to messenger services.

When Mayes sought to add to a series of special takeouts he had instituted in *Good Housekeeping,* he again clashed with Deems. The sections had included a thirty-six-page cake cookbook, a twenty-four-page sewing manual, a home course in manicuring, and a home course in interior decorating, and now Mayes was proposing a regular supplement to be patterned after *Changing Times,* a magazine devoted to such topics as taxes, education, insurance, and banking. The supplement in *Good Housekeeping* would be called "The Better Way" and contain an average of twelve tightly written short articles on similar subjects. It would be produced by recent college graduates hired specifically for the task. When Deems rejected the proposal for budgetary reasons, Mayes decided to reduce the magazine's regular departments by sixteen pages to make space and provide funds for the supplement, which proved to be popular with readers. Deems's response to the success of "The Better Way" was to inform Mayes that the supplement was not so much a new idea as something that Mayes had copied from *Changing Times.* Mayes contended, however, that few ideas in editing are ever original, and most are adaptations of what others are doing, but with new twists.

Mayes also was thwarted by Deems in his plan to run a story about birth-control pills several years before they were made available to the public. Mayes had learned about an experiment in Puerto Rico in which pills were being used and had assigned the magazine's medical reporter to investigate. Deems, however, ordered the article to be removed from the publishing schedule, contending that it would be found objectionable by the Catholic church.

The continuing friction between Mayes, Deems, and Berlin resulted in the editor's dismissal in mid October 1958, after thirty-two years with the company. In 1980 Mayes conjectured that he had been too much of a loner in the opinions of Berlin and Deems. "Nonetheless," he wrote, "there had been no intimation of impending action. When it came, it took even members of the Hearst family, as well as all segments of the publishing industry, by surprise."

Again, Mayes's period of unemployment did not last long. Although according to Roland Wolseley's *Understanding Magazines* (third edition, 1969) *McCall's* hired Mayes the next day, it was actually a few weeks before he was hired by *McCall's* to replace longtime editor Otto Wiese. In late 1958, in a dispute with new management, Wiese and several key staffers had resigned in protest. Mayes agreed to take over but announced that he intended to run the magazine in his own fashion. To fill vacancies created by the departure of key staffers, Mayes brought his top editorial executives

Without portfolio

a monthly commentary

by Clare Boothe Luce

Could a woman be nominated for the Presidency? Should a woman be nominated? Is there today any woman who is qualified? Can she be nominated? Will any woman, even though qualified, ever be nominated either to the Presidency or Vice-Presidency of the United States?

In nine months, we will all be witnessing, and many of us will also be involved in, that chaotic—and orderly; bewildering—and clarifying; passionate—and practical; emotional—and logical; familiar—and awesome; absurd—and glorious upheaval of a free people called a Presidential election.

At the beginning of each Presidential year, for a quarter of a century now, my secretary has laid an empty folder on my desk, which she has chosen to label, somewhat cabalistically, "WOMP" (Woman President). And at just about this time, the WOMP file begins to bulge with letters from all parts of the country. Their authors, who are not infrequently male, wistfully inquire or angrily demand my views on one or more of the above questions.

They are, of course, different questions. But each is so related to the rest that all must be considered, in order that the fundamental question that prompts them can be answered. That question is: *"Are women, in politics, the equals of men?"*

Could a woman be nominated? The answer, as most of the readers of this magazine know, is yes. There is nothing in the Constitution that forbids a woman to hold any elective or appointive office in the land. The only qualifications explicitly set forth by the Constitution are that a President must have reached the age of thirty-five, be native born, and have resided in the United States for fourteen years.

Even the fact that a person is not eligible to vote does not disbar that person from running for the Presidency. Three[a] women have, in fact, been nominated and have run for the Presidency—two of them before the passage in 1920 of the Amendment that gave women the right to vote. Since the passage of that "Suffragette Amendment" forty years ago, women have been proposed in great number for political office—and disposed of, by men, in numbers almost as great. Still, it is percentages that count. And each passing year, an ever higher percentage of women candidates is nominated and elected. The spirit of Susan B. Anthony may be less than satisfied, but has no reason to be utterly disconsolate.

The American voters have so far elected 2 women Senators;[b] 60 women Representatives; 2 women Governors.[c] American Presidents have appointed 2 women Cabinet members[d] and 6 women Ambassadors and Ministers.[e]

In this year 1960, 41 women are serving in State elective posts, besides 347 sitting in State legislatures, 17 in the Congress of the United States; and, according to the G.O.P.'s 1959 report in *Women in Public Service*, 218 women hold "high level" appointments in Federal offices.

In 1952, at the G.O.P. Convention, in one of those very smoke-filled rooms, where a woman's name seldom falls from masculine lips until the last "man who . . ." has been chosen, a modicum of consideration was given to putting the name of Senator Margaret Chase Smith of Maine into nomination for the Vice-Presidency. No doubt this was because that able and astute lady sent supporters to Chicago with pledges of about 200 delegates in their pockets.

Later, at the Democratic Convention, two women were actually put in nomination as "Veep": Mrs. India Edwards, Vice-Chairman of the Democratic National Committee, and Judge Sarah T. Hughes of Texas, President of the Business and Professional Women's Club.

If politics is the "art of the possible," the historical record shows that however great the mathematical and political odds against it, it is certainly *possible* for a woman to be nominated for high office—including the highest in the land.

Should a woman be nominated? Put this way, the question has no more validity than "Should a man be nominated?" or "Should a Jew or a Catholic?" The plainest common garden variety of patriotism suggests that who *should* be nominated is the person best qualified for the Presidency, regardless of sex, color, or creed. Therefore, before we can honestly evoke the WOMP question, we will do well to ask ourselves what we mean by "best-qualified person."

We mean (do we not?) a person who is known or believed to possess certain specific qualifications that our customs, traditions, and the practical politics and political practicalities of our democracy deem necessary for the highest post in the land, which has also become the toughest job in the history of the world.

It seems to me that there are *four basic Presidential qualifications.* They have to do with worldly experience, or know-how.

First, the person should have had considerable personal experience in practical politics. That generally means one with a record of faithful and prestigious affiliation with one of the two big parties that dominate the political life of our country.

This basic requirement is well met by seasoned Senators and Governors, especially those from the larger states of the Union. (In modern times, Ohio, Pennsylvania, New Jersey, California, and New York tend to produce the heaviest crop of Presidential hopefuls.) A high-level and operative experience of government administration and bureaucratic procedures is also essential. That may be why many Cabinet members are regarded as possible "Presidential timber"—or, anyway, plywood.

The second basic requirement is actual military experience; failing that, wide practical association with the Military and related issues, such as disarmament and armament, the production of war materiel, and the control of nuclear weapons. In a nation that has fought two terrible world wars this century, and lives in terror of a third, the proven ability to lead other men in times of military danger cannot be exaggerated.

The third basic qualification for a White House candidate is *continued on page 153*

[a] MRS. VICTORIA CLAFLIN WOODHULL, IN 1872; MRS. BELVA BENNETT LOCKWOOD, IN 1884; MRS. LINEA W. JENSEN, IN 1952
[b] HATTIE CARAWAY; MARGARET CHASE SMITH
[c] NELLIE TAYLOE ROSS, WYOMING; MIRIAM FERGUSON, TEXAS
[d] "MA" PERKINS, SECRETARY OF LABOR; OVETA CULP HOBBY, SECRETARY OF HEALTH, EDUCATION, AND WELFARE
[e] AMBASSADORS: CLARE BOOTHE LUCE (ITALY); EUGENIE ANDERSON (DENMARK); FRANCES WILLIS (SWITZERLAND AND NORWAY); MINISTERS: MRS. J. BORDEN HARRIMAN (NORWAY); PERLE MESTA (LUXEMBOURG); RUTH BRYAN OWENS (DENMARK)

16

Page from Luce's first column in the February 1960 issue of McCall's. *Mayes added the column to balance the liberal views expressed in the monthly column written by Eleanor Roosevelt, who had been hired by Mayes's predecessor.*

from *Good Housekeeping,* much to the annoyance of Hearst officials.

Mayes wasted little time in leaving his imprint on the magazine and transforming *McCall's* into the leading women's periodical of the time. Billing the magazine as the "First Magazine for Women," Mayes set about to alter the image of connubial "togetherness" the magazine had been promoting for several years to a more general concept of togetherness. Changes in content and appearance made by Mayes were credited to a large extent for increases in circulation and advertising revenue. Within a few years the magazine would pass its rivals in these areas, with circulation soaring from 5.35 million in 1958 to 8.221 million in 1963, and advertising revenues increasing from $18.391 million in 1958 to $41.868 million in 1963.

Seeking to alter the content of *McCall's* to keep it more in tune with his readers, Mayes threw out hundreds of thousands of dollars worth of manu-

THE BETTER THE BREAKFAST THE BRIGHTER THE DAY

The rich aroma of coffee, a whiff of frying bacon, the ping of the toaster, the gentle clatter of dishes, cheerful good-mornings. These are the comfortable, comforting signs and sounds of breakfast—the interlude we should all learn to use to the full to prepare ourselves for our day's occupations.

Still, Americans of all ages are shortchanging themselves every day in every way by a juice-and-coffee or no-breakfast routine—the equivalent of expecting an automobile to run without gasoline.

The word "breakfast" comes from two Anglo-Saxon words, "brecan" and "fasten," meaning to break a fast. When you sit down to breakfast—and a substantial breakfast is the only way to fortify yourself for the busy morning ahead—you are usually breaking a fast of more than ten hours, the time between your last meal of the night before and your first meal of the new day. It's the longest period in twenty-four hours in which you do not eat a meal. Refueling your motor at this time of day, with a breakfast high in protein, rich in vitamins and minerals, offers you rewards in energy, efficiency, and a sense of well-being that will carry you triumphantly through to lunchtime. *continued on the following page*

Miss America Lynda Lee Mead, of Natchez, Mississippi, is a young lady with brown hair, green eyes, a twenty-four-inch waist, and the awesome responsibility of personifying American beauty, charm, and decorum for the current year. Lynda was swept to celebrity by a board of contest judges at Atlantic City last September, has spent the intervening months touring the country, making public appearances. Here and on the following pages we show her wearing a collection of brilliant cottons designed for her from McCall's patterns and photographed by four top-ranking photographers.

Wingate Paine

Francesco Scavullo

Left: Twenty-year-old Lynda loves all kinds of fun under the sun, here models a charming sun dress calculated to catch eyes and beaux wherever it goes. It's of a soft cotton crepe, flamboyantly striped in orange and pink. McCall's pattern 5313. This picture was taken by Wingate Paine. Above: She's gaily informal in an engaging coverall of splashily printed poplin. We added a matching kerchief. McCall's pattern 5338. Photographed by Francesco Scavullo. Miss America's Everglaze wardrobe by McCall's patterns in fabrics by Everfast. McCall's Patterns

Pages from the November 1959 (top) and February 1960 issues of McCall's, *showing Mayes's lavish use of illustration and the technique of "page bleeding," whereby the photograph extends to the edges of the page*

scripts on file and pursued features he thought his readers would prefer. Increasing the number of pages, he tried to give his readers more editorial matter than they were getting from any of the competitors. One of his first decisions in this regard was to get Clare Booth Luce to write a monthly column to balance the liberal views of former First Lady Eleanor Roosevelt, who had been hired by Wiese to write a monthly column. Luce was a former ambassador to Italy and in 1959 was probably the best-known Republican woman of the period.

But Mayes did not stop there. He succeeded in getting the duchess of Windsor to contribute a column and John Steinbeck to write fiction. Substantial portions of current nonfiction were excerpted as Mayes tried to keep the general level of the magazine above the merely popular. Authors whose works graced the pages of *McCall's* under Mayes included Allen Drury, John Steinbeck, Ogden Nash, Phyllis McGinley, Herman Wouk, and Anne Morrow Lindbergh.

Contending that a magazine for women must be primarily a service organ, he improved and expanded the fashion and homemaking sections of *McCall's* and added new features. He thought women were bored with cooking so he tried to glamorize food with pictures and stories. One 1962 issue featured articles on hairstyles, chastity, and diet and a story on Hollywood gossip columnist Hedda Hopper.

To alter the magazine's appearance, Mayes made lavish use of photos and illustrations. Top photographers were hired to illustrate features on such topics as fashions, food, and decorating while staff photographers were given a range and freedom they had never known at *McCall's*. Painter Salvador Dali was paid six thousand dollars for a two-page illustration for a story. Production men helped devise a method for page bleeding, the process by which pictures are made to extend to the edge of a page. The result of these changes was a high, wide, and striking use of color photography and illustrations that filled page after page. According to Helen Woodward in *The Lady Persuaders* (1960), the impact of these innovations began to be noticeable in the November 1959 issue, which exhibited "flash, brash, splash."

Mayes's direction of *McCall's* earned him honors and accolades in 1960. The Magazine Editors Council presented him with its "Editor of the Year" award. The University of Southern California presented a distinguished achievement award to him for his work in the field of periodicals, and the New York Art Directors Club presented him a medal. Meanwhile, John Tebbel in an article in *Saturday Review*, "The Remarkable Mr. Mayes," discussed the resurgence of *McCall's*. "For the last several months, people involved with the magazine business have been watching – some with amusement, others with admiration, all with fascination – the remarkable renaissance of *McCall's* under Mayes." In less than two years, according to Tebbel, Mayes had moved *McCall's* from near the bottom of the women's magazine field to the top, ahead of both *Good Housekeeping* and the *Ladies' Home Journal*.

Mayes's success earned him a promotion to president of the McCall's Corporation in August 1961. The position included the overseeing of all corporate operations, including not only the publication of *McCall's* but also the direction of *Redbook* and several business publications. In 1962 McCall's Corporation added the *Saturday Review* to its holdings. For more than a year Mayes continued to serve also as editor of *McCall's*, but in late 1962 he decided to relinquish that post to John Mack Carter, later the editor of *Good Housekeeping*. Despite his experiences in his final years with Hearst, Mayes was unwilling to give Carter autonomy because he still wanted to be the editor of the magazine instead of the president of the corporation. He later admitted in his autobiography, "Nominally [Carter] was editor, but I restricted authority, stuck my nose in his plans, upset them, criticized too much, complimented too little."

In 1965 Mayes stepped down as president, but three years later he returned to *McCall's* as a consultant at the behest of publisher Norton Simon. In this capacity Mayes directed the production of the March and April 1969 issues in an effort to revive the lagging fortunes of the magazine, then being run unofficially by Norman Cousins, the editor of *Saturday Review*. The issues were "stunning," according to Mayes, who was ready to direct several more but was prevented from doing so by Edward E. Fitzgerald, the new president of *McCall's*, who indicated he wanted to rely on new editors to direct future issues and did not want to approve the additional expenditures Mayes sought. Neither Fitzgerald nor the editors he selected lasted long, and Simon, within a few years, had divested himself of his magazines and sold them to others.

Mayes, meanwhile, decided he would like to live in London for six months and made his final departure from *McCall's* and magazine editing. "It was the end of an era, and I knew there could be no inducement attractive enough to make me work again at a regular job," Mayes recalled. Instead of spending six months in London, however, Mayes and his wife, Grace, whom he had married in 1930, spent six years there. From 1970 to early 1972 he contributed an occasional column to *Saturday Review,* writing about the British scene. Homesickness and a longing to see more of his daughters and his grandchildren resulted in his decision in late 1975 to return to the United States.

After his return Mayes formed a partnership with Edward R. Downe, who at one time had owned a stake in several publications. For about a year Downe and Mayes studied magazine properties in need of new capital with the aim of possibly acquiring one. "Nothing that we examined was what we wanted. Everything we saw was what we didn't want. So we sold our partnership and came out, astonishingly, with a profit," Mayes wrote in *The Magazine Maze.*

When he died in 1987, Mayes was described by the *New York Times* as a man "who built a reputation as one of the country's most respected magazine editors." In his years at *Good Housekeeping* and *McCall's,* Mayes revolutionized the field of women's magazines. He said he had always wanted to be an editor, and he always seemed to know how to make successes of the magazines he edited. Unlike others in the field, Mays did not pay much attention to readership research, remarking once, "I'll gamble a hunch against a statistic anytime." Although Mayes's genius was recognized during the twenty years he spent at the helm of *Good Housekeeping,* it was not until he took over *McCall's* in 1958 that he made his greatest mark. With a radical transformation of the magazine's content and layout by Mayes, circulation increased by 53 percent, and advertising revenues more than doubled.

References:

Theodore Peterson, *Magazines in the Twentieth Century,* third edition (Urbana: University of Illinois Press, 1964);

William H. Taft, *American Magazines for the 1980s* (New York: Hastings House, 1982);

John Tebbel, "The Remarkable Mr. Mayes," *Saturday Review,* 43 (8 October 1960): 63-64;

"Turnabout for Togetherness," *Time,* 74 (14 September 1959): 53;

Roland Wolseley, *Understanding Magazines,* third edition (Ames: Iowa State University Press, 1969);

James Playsted Wood, *Magazines in the United States,* third edition (New York: Ronald, 1971);

Helen Woodward, *The Lady Persuaders* (New York: Obolensky, 1960).

Carey McWilliams

(13 December 1905 - 27 June 1980)

Ralph Engelman
Long Island University

MAJOR POSITIONS HELD: Contributing editor (1945–1951), associate editor (1951–1952), editorial director (1952–1955), editor, *Nation* (1955–1975).

BOOKS: *Ambrose Bierce: A Biography* (New York: Boni, 1929); republished with a new introduction by McWilliams (Hamden, Conn.: Archon Books, 1967);

Louis Adamic and Shadow America (Los Angeles: Whipple, 1935);

Factories in the Field: The Story of Migratory Farm Labor in California (Boston: Little, Brown, 1939);

Ill Fares the Land: Migrants and Migratory Labor in the United States (Boston: Little, Brown, 1942; London: Faber & Faber, 1945);

Brothers under the Skin (Boston: Little, Brown, 1943; revised, 1951, 1964);

Prejudice: Japanese-Americans, Symbol of Racial Intolerance (Boston: Little, Brown, 1944);

Southern California Country: An Island on the Land (New York: Duell, Sloan & Pearce, 1946); republished as *Southern California: An Island on the Land* (Santa Barbara, Cal.: Peregrine Smith, 1973);

A Mask for Privilege: Anti-Semitism in America (Boston: Little, Brown, 1948);

North from Mexico: The Spanish-Speaking People of the United States (Philadelphia: Lippincott, 1949);

California: The Great Exception (New York: Current Books, 1949);

Witch Hunt: The Revival of Heresy (Boston: Little, Brown, 1950);

The Education of Carey McWilliams (New York: Simon & Schuster, 1979).

OTHER: *The California Revolution*, edited by McWilliams (New York: Grossman, 1968).

SELECTED PERIODICAL PUBLICATIONS – UNCOLLECTED: "Los Angeles," *Overland*, 85 (May 1927): 135–136;

Carey McWilliams

"Ambrose Bierce," *American Mercury*, 16 (February 1929): 215–222;

"Writers of California," *Bookman*, 72 (December 1930): 352–359;

"Farmers Get Tough," *American Mercury*, 33 (October 1934): 241–245;

"Upton Sinclair and his EPIC," *New Republic*, 80 (22 August 1934): 39–41;

"Hollywood Plays with Fascism," *Nation*, 140 (29 May 1935): 623–624;

"Once Again the Yellow Peril," *Nation*, 140 (26 June 1935): 735–736;

"Joads on Strike," *Nation*, 149 (4 November 1939): 488–489;

"Civil Rights in California," *New Republic*, 102 (22 January 1940): 108–110;

"Moving the West-Coast Japanese," *Harper*, 185 (September 1942): 359–369;

"Hitler To Franco To Us," *New Republic,* 109 (9 August 1943): 203–204;
"Cults of California," *Atlantic,* 177 (March 1946): 105–110;
"Earl Warren: A Likely Dark Horse," *Nation,* 165 (29 November 1947): 581–583;
"Shangri-la of the Atom," *Nation,* 169 (31 December 1949): 639–640;
"Loyalty in California: Sign or Resign," *Nation,* 170 (4 March 1950): 197;
"Witch Hunt and Civil Rights," *Nation,* 174 (28 June 1952): 651–653;
"Disarmament Standstill," *Nation,* 178 (17 April 1954): 319–320;
"Senator McCarthy's Sixth Column," *Nation,* 178 (22 May 1954): 434–436;
"Taps for the 1930's," *Nation,* 182 (7 April 1956): 269–270;
"Anti-Americanism Updated," *Nation,* 186 (31 May 1958): 488–489;
"Kennedy's Take Over," *Nation,* 191 (23 July 1960): 43–45;
"Time for a New Politics," *Nation,* 194 (26 May 1962): 460–466;
"Puerto Rico: Plebiscite for Identity," *Nation,* 195 (15 September 1962): 123–128;
"Goldwaterism: The New Ideology," *Nation,* 199 (24 August 1964): 68–71;
"100 Years of *The Nation,*" *Journalism Quarterly,* 42 (Spring 1965): 189–197;
"How We Bungled Our Way In," *Commonweal,* 82 (23 July 1965): 537–538;
"Ethics in an Affluent Society," *Christian Century,* 83 (22 June 1966): 797–802;
"Protests, Power and the Future of Politics," *Nation,* 206 (15 January 1968): 71–77;
"Bitter Legacy of LBJ," *Nation,* 207 (9 September 1968): 198–201;
"Man, A Place, and A Time," *American West,* 7 (May 1970): 4–8;
"Campaign '72: Politics of Anti-Busing," *Nation,* 214 (6 March 1972): 290–291;
"Mr. Nixon in Peace and War," *Commonweal,* 99 (23 November 1973): 206–208;
"Campaign '76 – Crisis Ahead," *Commonweal,* 103 (3 December 1976): 775–779;
"Milestones of Civil Rights," *Current,* 210 (February 1979): 18–24;
"Figurehead Presidency for an Authoritarian Establishment," *Progressive,* 44 (September 1980): 9.

Carey McWilliams was editor of *Nation,* the oldest continuously published weekly in the United States, from 1955 to 1975. During that tumultuous two-decade period spanned by the cold war and the Vietnam War, McWilliams refashioned *Nation* as the leading journal of opinion of indigenous American radicalism. As editor of *Nation* he drew upon his earlier involvement in California in the literary ferment of the 1920s, the struggles of migrant workers in the 1930s, and the racial conflicts of the 1940s. Fred J. Cook, a longtime associate, stressed how throughout his career McWilliams "seemed to inhale with every breath a sense of developing national issues that others hadn't yet discovered." Studs Terkel called him "a contumacious American radical, who was merely the best muckraking editor of his time."

McWilliams was born on 13 December 1905 in Steamboat Springs, Colorado, to Jerry and Harriet McWilliams. His father owned a large cattle ranch, but lost it when the cattle market collapsed after World War I, and he died a broken man shortly thereafter. McWilliams later attributed the origins of his radicalism to the circumstances surrounding his father's loss of the business.

McWilliams moved to Los Angeles in 1922. California would remain his base of operations until 1951, when he came east to work on *Nation.* McWilliams received a law degree from the University of southern California in 1927, after which he entered law practice in Los Angeles. As a student and young lawyer, McWilliams was drawn to the cultural ferment of the 1920s. He dated his interest in cultural revolt to his reading of F. Scott Fitzgerald's *This Side of Paradise* (1920). McWilliams gravitated to a southern California literary milieu which included Paul Jordan Smith, the literary editor of the *Los Angeles Times;* Phil Townsend Hanna, the editor of *Westways* magazine; poets Louis Adamic and Hildegarde Flanner; and the musicologist José Rodriguez. This was a period in which Los Angeles was being hailed as the city of the future for its pioneering role in the development of broadcasting and film as well as of automobile and airplane transportation. McWilliams and his circle cast a critical eye on the storybook version of frontier growth in southern California in the 1920s, behind which loomed what he termed "the American dream in disarray." McWilliams regularly contributed articles and reviews to California magazines such as the *Overland Monthly,* the *Argonaut,* and the *San Francisco Review* as well as to the *Los Angeles Times* and the *San Diego Union.*

Two important influences on McWilliams during the 1920s were H. L. Mencken and Ambrose Bierce. Mencken appealed to McWilliams because of the breadth of his interests and his focus on the

American scene, in contrast to Ezra Pound, Ernest Hemingway, and other expatriots of the "lost generation" of American writers. Mencken, a mentor for McWilliams, was the first to give the young writer national exposure. In 1929 Mencken published an article by McWilliams on Bierce in *American Mercury*. McWilliams viewed both Bierce and Mencken as part of the "maverick and outlaw" tradition of dissenters in American history. But he recognized in Bierce, the gadfly of the Gilded Age who disappeared mysteriously covering the Mexican Revolution in 1914, a journalist and man of letters who was a more serious and passionate social critic than Mencken. McWilliams's well-received book on Bierce was published in the same year, and was a turning point in McWilliams's development.

In addition to Mencken's magazine, McWilliams's early articles appeared in *New Republic* and *Nation*. He was drawn to the former for its coverage of the arts, the latter for its political and social reportage. McWilliams was an admirer of Edmund Wilson, the associate editor of the *New Republic;* after becoming a contributor to *New Republic* he would have lunch with the staff – which also included Bruce Bliven, Malcolm Cowley, and George Soule – on visits to New York. McWilliams's first link to *Nation* was through correspondence with Joseph Wood Krutch, the magazine's drama critic and associate editor. McWilliams's semiannual visits to New York included regular meetings with editor Freda Kirchwey and her staff at the offices of *Nation* at 20 Vesey Street.

McWilliams would later write that "the cultural rebellion of the 1920s was a necessary first step to the radical criticism of the 1930s." In the early years of the Depression McWilliams's law practice frequently involved bankruptcies and foreclosures reminiscent of his father's difficulties, reinforcing his distrust of the economic system. In the course of the Depression his literary interests receded as he wrote increasingly about social-protest movements in California for the *Baltimore Sun*, *New Republic*, and *Nation*. A key event in McWilliams's politicization was Upton Sinclair's campaign for governor on a platform to End Poverty in California (EPIC). McWilliams came to know the novelist and socialist and covered every phase of his grassroots campaign. Although Sinclair lost, many EPIC-endorsed candidates were elected to state office, among them Culbert L. Olson, who went on to win the governorship in 1938, the first Democratic governor in forty years.

McWilliams's interest in the problem of migratory farm labor was prompted by the strikes by

Freda Kirchwey, publisher of Nation, *in 1944. McWilliams became a contributing editor of the magazine the following year.*

Mexican, Filipino, and other farmworkers throughout California in the early and mid 1930s. These farm strikes, the most extensive in American history, prompted mass arrests and other repressive countermeasures by the farm industry. Adding to the problem of farm labor was the influx of migrants from the Dust Bowl. *Factories in the Field,* McWilliams's book on migrant labor, came out in 1939 and became a best-seller. Jean-Pierre Berlan, the French agricultural economist, later wrote, "When I discovered *Factories in the Field,* I quickly realized that there was more theoretical depth in this book than in all the doctoral dissertations of the Department of Agricultural Economics of the University of California! It was so true that in the 1930s the book was burned in the countryside of California, libraries were forbidden to carry it, [and] the author was threatened with the same fate as the 'boll weevil.' "

The same year *Factories in the Field* appeared, Governor Olson appointed McWilliams as head of the California Division of Immigration and Housing. His hearings on the exploitation of farm labor were the first of their kind to be held in the state. In addition to working to secure better housing and wages for migrant workers, McWilliams sought to expose violations of civil liberties in California labor disputes. McWilliams's appointment in 1939 marked the end of his career as a practicing lawyer and the beginning of full-time activism and journalism. After Earl Warren was elected governor of California in 1943 with the support of the farming industry, he called a press conference and announced that his first official act would be the dismissal of McWilliams from his state post. "In the 1920s I was a rebel," McWilliams wrote; "in the 1930s I became, and remained, an unreconstructed, unapologetic radical."

During the 1940s McWilliams focused his attention on the impact of World War II on questions of race. In 1943, a year in which race riots occurred across the nation, McWilliams published *Brothers under the Skin.* In this comprehensive examination of the status of minorities in the United States, McWilliams identifies race as a major national problem with international implications and advocates far-reaching civil-rights legislation. *Prejudice: Japanese-Americans, Symbol of Racial Intolerance* (1944), about the evacuation of over one hundred thousand Japanese-Americans on the West Coast after Pearl Harbor, was an outgrowth of McWilliams's involvement in the controversy and his visits to the detention camps. *A Mask for Privilege* (1948) treats anti-Semitism, and *North from Mexico* (1949), the plight of Mexican-Americans. McWilliams, in his series of books on discrimination in the 1940s, was one of the first to anticipate the racial revolution of the postwar years.

In 1945 McWilliams, who had contributed articles to *Nation* for the past decade, was named its contributing editor for the West Coast. McWilliams's increasing involvement with *Nation* coincided with the advent of the cold war and McCarthyism. As a *Nation* correspondent he covered the case of the Hollywood Ten, the group of film writers convicted of contempt in 1948 for refusal to cooperate with the House Committee on Un-American activities. He criticized the blacklist and Truman's loyalty program as infringements of the First Amendment. In 1950, the year in which Sen. Joseph R. McCarthy launched his anti-communist crusade, McWilliams wrote *Witch Hunt: The Revival of Heresy,* which addressed the growing crisis in civil liberties.

In 1951 Kirchwey, the publisher and editor of *Nation,* invited McWilliams to come to New York City for a month to edit a special issue on civil liberties. But while he was there, McWilliams became involved in one of the periodic political-financial crises of *Nation:* radical support fell off over the magazine's refusal to support the third-party candidacy of Henry Wallace at the same time that liberal subscribers were offended by the attacks on Truman's policies. When the managing editor resigned, McWilliams assumed his responsibilities and by the end of the year found himself locked into the position. For McWilliams, a month-long visit turned into a twenty-five-year commitment.

During this period *Nation* remained an independent radical weekly, but it denounced anti-communism, which it saw as a vehicle for suppressing dissenting views on American domestic and foreign policy. Among established journals, *Nation* was virtually alone in its uncompromising opposition to the cold war and McCarthyism; other dissenting publications such as *I. F. Stone's Weekly* and *Guardian* were founded in the 1950s. As a result of the independent stance of *Nation* on cold-war issues, including the Alger Hiss and the Ethel and Julius Rosenberg cases, the magazine became the target of what McWilliams considered "cold war liberals," anti-Communist intellectuals who wrote for magazines like *Commentary* and *New Leader.* Moreover, a series of articles on the Catholic church caused *Nation* to be banned from libraries of the New York City school system, a ban which lasted fifteen years and involved costly litigation.

The year 1955 marked a time of transition for *Nation.* The magazine had survived the worst years of McCarthyism, but its financial predicament remained unresolved. Kirchwey, having failed to find a publisher to succeed herself, asked McWilliams if he would assume the position of editor and take responsibility for recruiting a publisher who would put the magazine on a solid financial basis. McWilliams accepted, and he found George Kirstein, a retired executive, who became publisher for a decade.

Kirchwey had first worked at *Nation* in 1918; in 1937 she purchased the magazine and remained its owner/publisher/editor until 1955. Kirchwey was a New Yorker with ties to the "old left" of the East Coast. McWilliams saw himself in the tradition of the less ideologically inclined and more issue-oriented radicalism of the West Coast. The new editor dismissed foreign editor J. Alvarez del Vayo, a former war commissar and minister of foreign affairs in Spain during its civil war. He also indicated his intention of relying less on articles by staff members and of seeking out new contributors. Andrew Roth, a former *Nation* contributor, complained that "all the radical 'Kirchweyites' had been given the cold shoulder." In fact, as Victor S. Navasky said in an unpublished interview, McWilliams sought to make *Nation* a more bicoastal and national publication.

During the "Kirstein Years," from 1955 to 1965, McWilliams brought together a brilliant group of writers to expose the complacency, sacred cows, and continuing inequities and abuses of power of the period. McWilliams was determined to cover social, cultural, and technological changes as well as political developments. McWilliams, the Mencken protégé, used the satiric writings of David Cort, Kenneth Rexroth, and Wade Thompson to take aim at what was being hailed as "the affluent society." McWilliams, the admirer of Bierce, sent Carleton Beals to Latin America to write the first reports in the American press of preparations for the Bay of Pigs invasion. Jacob Bronowski was recruited to write about science and human values, Theodore Roaszak to cover the emerging counterculture. The emergence of the civil-rights and peace movements received extended coverage. Alexander Werth, Geoffrey Barraclough, and Edgar Snow wrote about international relations. During this period *Nation* introduced the writings of William Appleman Williams and other revisionist historians to the general public, a body of work that would provide a foundation for a broad critique of American foreign policy.

Nation revived the muckraking tradition through a new emphasis on special-issue journalism. Fred J. Cook, originally a reporter on the *New York World-Telegram and Sun,* authored or co-authored a series of groundbreaking special issues devoted to such subjects as the Hiss case (1957), the FBI (1958), political corruption in New York (1959), the CIA (1962), the New Right (1962), and the Jimmy Hoffa trial (1964). The special issues on the FBI and the CIA in particular, which provide critical perspectives on institutions previously regarded as untouchable, are landmarks in pre-Vietnam, pre-Watergate American journalism.

To celebrate a century of publication McWilliams wrote an article in the spring 1965 issue of *Journalism Quarterly* charting the fundamental editorial continuity of *Nation.* He stressed founding editor E. L. Godkin's commitment to the freedman and anti-imperialism, his desire to play the role of gadfly and press critic, and his willingness to forsake mass circulation and target a smaller group of opinion makers. McWilliams viewed *Nation* as a miracle of American journalism, its stewardship as a public trust:

> It is an idea, a spirit, a name without an address; it is fragile, without physical assets, but it is free and so it lives. It is of the past as well as the present; it belongs to all those who have read it, quoted it, written for it or helped it; to those who have reviled it no less than to those who have respected it.

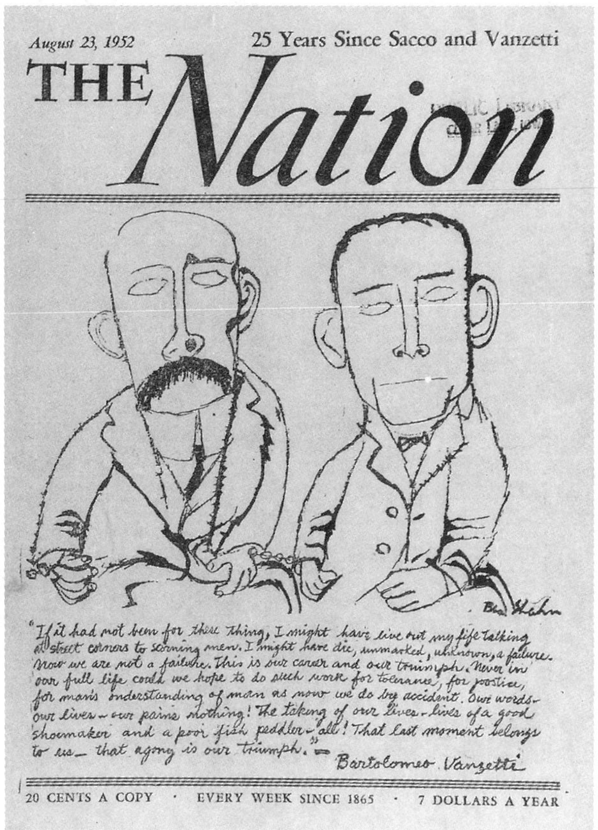
August 23, 1952

25 Years Since Sacco and Vanzetti

THE Nation

20 CENTS A COPY · EVERY WEEK SINCE 1865 · 7 DOLLARS A YEAR

Cover for an issue commemorating the 1927 trial and execution of the anarchists Nicola Sacco and Bartolomeo Vanzetti. In 1952 McWilliams was promoted from associate editor to editorial director of the magazine.

In 1965 *Nation* published a special 335-page one hundredth anniversary issue edited by James J. Storrow, Jr., who replaced George Kirstein as publisher. McWilliams termed the last ten years of his tenure as editor of *Nation* "The Vietnam Decade." He brought together a distinguished group of writers to cover all the ramifications – political and diplomatic, social and cultural – of that conflict. For McWilliams, the war in Vietnam and the Watergate scandal "marked a climactic phase in the Cold War." Following the resignation of President Richard M. Nixon and the end of the Vietnam War, as the country approached its bicentennial, McWilliams stepped down as editor of *Nation* in 1975.

Terkel wrote of McWilliams's modus operandi as editor of *Nation:* "the financial arrangements of McWilliams's assignments were almost comic. He worked out of a hat: a hunch, a phone call, a fee of two figures. He called upon writers who had never done their stuff for *The Nation* before, nor, in some notable cases, for any magazine. . . ." McWilliams was a nurturing editor continually on the lookout for new talent and topics – James Baldwin

McWilliams, circa 1975

and Ralph Nader, for example, were unknowns when their first publications appeared in *Nation.* He often assembled a file on a subject and sent it to an author to suggest an article, and he made it a point to reply personally to any writer who submitted a manuscript. McWilliams would later recall that during a quarter-century at *Nation* he had dealt with an army of contributors, ranging from heads of state and Nobel Prize winners to revolutionaries and avant-garde artists.

After stepping down as editor, McWilliams continued to write a column for *Nation* titled "Second Thoughts." In 1979 he published his memoirs, titled *The Education of Carey McWilliams.* In the political credo at the end of the book, McWilliams reaffirms his brand of pragmatic American radicalism. "As a journalist," he writes, "I have learned to take all ideological projections with a grain of salt." He adheres to the socialist critique of capitalism while expressing reservations about socialism in practice, especially in regard to civil liberties. McWilliams reiterates his commitment to radicalism, socialism, democratic principles, and Christian humanism and to the autonomy of art, ideas, and values. Reactions to the autobiography were predictably partisan. Arthur Schlesinger, Jr., faulted McWilliams for being insufficiently critical of the Soviet Union and excessively critical of anticommunism. Schlesinger characterized McWilliams's memoirs as self-righteous: "He seems to have been right about everything. He records no mistakes and no regrets."

When McWilliams died a year later, in 1980, Navasky, editor of *Nation,* emphasized that McWilliams was a "small-d democrat," adding that his critics could not understand someone whose goal was to expose the power structure rather than to climb it. McWilliams, who edited *Nation* at the height of the cold war, was a radical in the sense in which Hannah Arendt used the word: a person who goes to the root of things while avoiding single-minded dogma, whose cheerful "negativism" makes him immune to the lure of *Realpolitik.* As Navasky observed, the result of McWilliams's lifetime pursuit of this calling was ironic: "after a lifetime as an iconoclast, a self-styled 'Western radical,' fighting institutional injustices, he became something of an institution himself."

References:

Sara Alpern, *Freda Kirchwey: A Woman of "The Nation"* (Cambridge, Mass.: Harvard University Press, 1987);

Jean-Pierre Berlan, "Carey McWilliams," *Monthly Review,* 32 (January 1981): 57;

Fred J. Cook, *Maverick: Fifty Years of Investigative Reporting* (New York: Putnam, 1984);

Kenneth S. Lynn, "A Social 'Humanist,' " *National Review* (20 July 1979): 926–927;

Victor S. Navasky, "Afterword," in Katrina Vanden Heuvel, *The Nation 1865–1990: Selections from the Independent Magazine of Politics and Culture* (New York: Thunder's Mouth Press, 1990), pp. 513–530;

Navasky, "Carey McWilliams," *Nation,* 231 (12 July 1980): 35–36;

Arthur Schlesinger, Jr., "The Making of a Social Conscience," *New York Times Book Review,* 24 June 1979, p. 3;

James Storrow, "The Years with Carey," *Nation,* 231 (12 July 1980): 34;

Studs Terkel, "A Contumacious Radical," *Nation* (30 June 1979): 793–794.

Papers:

The principal collection of Carey McWilliams's papers is housed in the Special Collections Section of the University of California, Los Angeles. A collection of his manuscripts is in the Bancroft Library, University of California, Berkeley.

H. L. Mencken

(12 September 1880 - 29 January 1956)

Vincent Fitzpatrick
Enoch Pratt Free Library, Baltimore

See also the Mencken entries in *DLB 11: American Humorists, 1800-1950; DLB 29: American Newspaper Journalists, 1926-1950;* and *DLB 63: Modern American Critics, 1920-1955.*

MAJOR POSITIONS HELD: Coeditor, *Smart Set* (1914-1923); coeditor, *Parisienne* (1915-1916); coeditor, *Saucy Stories* (1916); coeditor, *Black Mask* (1920-1921); contributing editor, *Nation* (1921-1932); coeditor (1924-1925), editor, *American Mercury* (1925-1933).

PRINCIPAL MAGAZINES PARTIALLY OWNED: *Smart Set* (1914-1923), *Parisienne* (1915-1916), *Saucy Stories* (1916), *Black Mask* (1920-1921), *American Mercury* (1924-1933).

BOOKS: *Ventures into Verse* (Baltimore: Marshall, Beck & Gordon, 1903);

George Bernard Shaw: His Plays (Boston & London: Luce, 1905);

The Philosophy of Friedrich Nietzsche (Boston: Luce, 1908; London: Unwin, 1908);

Men versus the Man: A Correspondence between Robert Rives La Monte, Socialist, and H. L. Mencken, Individualist (New York: Holt, 1910);

The Artist, A Drama Without Words (Boston: Luce, 1912);

Europe After 8:15, by Mencken, George Jean Nathan, and Willard Huntington Wright (New York: John Lane, 1914);

A Book of Burlesques (New York: John Lane, 1916; revised edition, New York: Knopf, 1920; London: Cape, 1923);

A Little Book in C Major (New York: John Lane, 1916);

A Book of Prefaces (New York: Knopf, 1917; London: Cape, 1922);

Pistols for Two, by Mencken and Nathan, as Owen Hatteras (New York: Knopf, 1917);

H. L. Mencken, "the Baltimore Antichrist"

Damn! A Book of Calumny (New York: Philip Goodman, 1918); republished as *A Book of Calumny* (New York: Knopf, 1918);

In Defense of Women (New York: Philip Goodman, 1918; revised edition, New York: Knopf, 1922; London: Cape, 1923);

The American Language: A Preliminary Inquiry into the Development of English in the United States (New York: Knopf, 1919; revised and enlarged edition, 1921; London: Cape, 1922; revised and enlarged edition, 1923; corrected, enlarged, and rewritten edition, New York: Knopf, 1936; London: Paul, 1936); *Supplement I* (New York: Knopf, 1945); *Supplement II* (New York: Knopf, 1948);

Prejudices: First Series (New York: Knopf, 1919; London: Cape, 1921);

The American Credo: A Contribution Toward the Interpretation of the National Mind, by Mencken and Nathan (New York: Knopf, 1920);

Heliogabalus: A Buffoonery in Three Acts, by Mencken and Nathan (New York: Knopf, 1920);

Prejudices: Second Series (New York: Knopf, 1920; London: Cape, 1921);

Prejudices: Third Series (New York: Knopf, 1922; London: Cape, 1923);

Prejudices: Fourth Series (New York: Knopf, 1924; London: Cape, 1925);

Prejudices (London: Cape, 1925); republished as *Selected Prejudices* (London: Cape, 1926) and *Selected Prejudices: Second Series* (London: Cape, 1927);

Notes on Democracy (New York: Knopf, 1926; London: Cape, 1927);

Prejudices: Fifth Series (New York: Knopf, 1926; London: Cape, 1927);

Prejudices: Sixth Series (New York: Knopf, 1927; London: Cape, 1928);

James Branch Cabell (New York: McBride, 1927; revised, 1928);

Selected Prejudices (New York: Knopf, 1927);

Treatise on the Gods (New York & London: Knopf, 1930; revised edition, New York: Knopf, 1946);

Making a President: A Footnote to the Saga of Democracy (New York: Knopf, 1932);

Treatise on Right and Wrong (New York: Knopf, 1934; London: Kegan Paul, Trench, Trubner, 1934);

The Sunpapers of Baltimore, 1837–1937, by Mencken, Gerald W. Johnson, Frank R. Kent, and Hamilton Owens (New York: Knopf, 1937);

Happy Days, 1880–1892 (New York: Knopf, 1940; London: Kegan Paul, Trench & Trubner, 1940);

Newspaper Days, 1899–1906 (New York: Knopf, 1941; London: Kegan Paul, Trench & Trubner, 1942);

Heathen Days, 1890–1936 (New York: Knopf, 1943);

Christmas Story (New York: Knopf, 1946);

The Days of H. L. Mencken: Happy Days, Newspaper Days, Heathen Days (New York: Knopf, 1947);

A Mencken Chrestomathy (New York: Knopf, 1949);

The Vintage Mencken, edited by Alistair Cooke (New York: Vintage, 1955);

A Carnival of Buncombe, edited by Malcolm Moos (Baltimore: Johns Hopkins University Press / London: Oxford University Press, 1956);

Minority Report: H. L. Mencken's Notebooks (New York: Knopf, 1956);

A Bathtub Hoax, and Other Blasts & Bravos from the Chicago Tribune, edited by Robert McHugh (New York: Knopf, 1958);

Prejudices, A Selection, edited by James T. Farrell (New York: Vintage, 1958);

H. L. Mencken on Music, edited by Louis Cheslock (New York: Knopf, 1961);

H. L. Mencken: The American Scene, a Reader, edited by Huntington Cairns (New York: Knopf, 1965);

H. L. Mencken's Smart Set Criticism, edited by William H. Nolte (Ithaca, N.Y.: Cornell University Press, 1968);

On Being an American and Other Essays (Kenkyusha Modern English Reader 7), edited by Shigehisa Narita (Tokyo: Kenkyusha, 1973);

The Young Mencken: The Best of His Work, edited by Carl Bode (New York: Dial, 1973);

A Gang of Pecksniffs, and Other Comments on Newspaper Publishers, Editors and Reporters, edited by Theo Lippman, Jr. (New Rochelle, N.Y.: Arlington House, 1975);

Mencken's Last Campaign: H. L. Mencken on the 1948 Election, edited by Joseph C. Goulden (Washington, D.C.: New Republic Book Company, 1976);

A Choice of Days: Essays from Happy Days, Newspaper Days, *and* Heathen Days, edited by Edward L. Galligan (New York: Knopf, 1980);

H. L. Mencken's Un-Neglected Anniversary, edited by Phillip Jerome Wingate (Hockessin, Del.: Holly Press, 1980);

On Mencken: Essays, edited by John Dorsey (New York: Knopf, 1980);

The Editor, the Bluenose, and the Prostitute: H. L. Mencken's History of the "Hatrack" Censorship Case, edited by Carl Bode (Boulder, Col.: Roberts Rinehart, 1988);

The Diary of H. L. Mencken, edited by Charles A. Fecher (New York: Knopf, 1989);

The Gist of Mencken: Quotations from America's Critic, edited by Mayo DuBasky (Metuchen, N.J. & London: Scarecrow Press, 1990);

The H. L. Mencken Baby Book: Comprising the Contents of H. L. Mencken's What You Ought to Know About Your Baby *with Commentaries,* edited by Howard Markel, M.D., and Frank A. Oski, M.D. (Philadelphia: Hanley & Belfus, 1990);

Tall Tales and Hoaxes of H. L. Mencken, edited by John W. Baer (Annapolis, Md.: Franklin Printing, 1990);

The Impossible H. L. Mencken: A Selection of His Best Newspaper Stories, edited by Marion Elizabeth

Rodgers (Garden City, N.Y.: Doubleday, 1991);

My Life as Author and Editor, edited by Jonathan Yardley (New York: Knopf, 1993).

OTHER: Henrik Ibsen, *A Doll's House,* edited, with an introduction, by Mencken (Boston & London: Luce, 1909);

Ibsen, *Little Eyolf,* edited, with an introduction, by Mencken (Boston & London: Luce, 1909);

Friedrich Wilhelm Nietzsche, *The Gist of Nietzsche,* compiled by Mencken (Boston: Luce, 1910);

Nietzsche, The Antichrist, translated, with an introduction, by Mencken (New York: Knopf, 1920);

Americana, edited by Mencken (New York: Knopf, 1925);

Menckeneniana: A Schimpflexikon, edited by Mencken (New York: Knopf, 1928);

James Gibbons Huneker, *Essays,* selected, and with an introduction, by Mencken (New York: Scribners, 1929; London: Laurie, 1929);

Sara Powell Haardt, *Southern Album,* edited, with a preface, by Mencken (Garden City, N.Y.: Doubleday, 1936);

A New Dictionary of Quotations on Historical Principles from Ancient and Modern Sources, edited by Mencken (New York: Knopf, 1942);

"The American Language," in *Literary History of the United States,* volume 1, edited by Robert E. Spiller, Willard Thorp, Thomas H. Johnson, and Henry Seidel Canby (New York: Macmillan, 1948), pp. 663–675.

SELECTED PERIODICAL PUBLICATIONS – UNCOLLECTED: "The Dreiser Bugaboo," *Seven Arts,* 2 (August 1917): 507–517;

"Editorial," *American Mercury,* 1 (January 1924): 27–30;

"Testament," *Review of Reviews,* 76 (October 1927): 413–416;

"Ten Years," *American Mercury,* 30 (December 1933): 357–387;

"Illuminators of the Abyss," *Saturday Review of Literature,* 11 (6 October 1934): 155–156;

"Four Glad Years," *College Humor,* 1 (November 1934): 8–9, 66;

"The South Astir," *Virginia Quarterly Review,* 11 (January 1935): 47–60;

"Three Years of Dr. Roosevelt," *American Mercury,* 37 (March 1936): 257–265;

"That Was New York: The Life of an Artist," *New Yorker,* 24 (17 April 1948): 64–71.

Mencken in 1904, as managing editor of the Baltimore Morning Herald

During a career that encompassed several roles and lasted for nearly fifty years, Henry Louis Mencken was above all else a libertarian. He saw freedom of speech as the most valuable attribute of any society, and he insisted, throughout some long and bloody battles, upon the need for civil liberty for all people regardless of color, gender, origin, or social class. One of the most articulate members of America's adversary culture, he reveled in his iconoclasm. "The liberation of the human mind has never been furthered by . . . learned dunderheads," he thundered in *Prejudices: Fourth Series* (1924), "it has been furthered by gay fellows who heaved dead cats into sanctuaries and then went roistering down the highways of the world, proving to all men that doubt, after all, was safe – that the god in his sanctuary was finite in his power and hence a fraud." As both writer and editor, he heaved many a dead cat and knocked many a false icon from its shaky pedestal. If little proved sacred to Mencken, then it was for the simple reason that, as he saw things, little deserved to be.

Mencken's career generated huge disagreement and controversy during his lifetime, and the uproar has continued into the present day. In the cities, some worshiped Mencken as a demigod; in the American hinterland, others reviled him as the devil incarnate. For the distinguished critic Joseph Wood Krutch, "Mencken's was the best prose written in America during the Twentieth Century." He reigns as America's most frequently quoted author, and some readers rank him as the country's finest humorist after Mark Twain. Others, however, have judged Mencken a defectively educated bully desecrating the American language. He was likened, rabid at his typewriter, to a dog shaking a snake.

In 1926 Walter Lippmann called Mencken "the most powerful personal influence upon this whole generation of American people." His laughter has been celebrated as salubrious, and he has been extolled for his efforts to make America a saner, more civilized country. On the other hand, he has been scorned as an anti-Semite and racist. *The Diary of H. L. Mencken,* published in late 1989, caused pandemonium on the American literary scene. Long in his grave, Mencken remains adept, to borrow one of his favorite images, at stirring up the animals all over America.

Writing in the *New York Review of Books,* Murray Kempton chose an appropriate image for this career: Mencken as whale, immense and powerful and difficult to capture. To the present age of literary specialization, he indeed seems gargantuan. In fact, he had careers in three mediums: an author of books, a newspaperman, and both an editor of magazines and a frequent contributor to them. Those careers ran concurrently and were often intertwined. The time demanded by one clearly affected his work with the other two. Moreover, as he acknowledged candidly, he would share material among them: what was written for a newspaper column was often revised for a magazine article and then reworked once again for inclusion in a book.

During his lifetime he wrote thirty books and contributed to twenty more, and collections have continued to appear posthumously. He wrote about whatever interested him, for he recognized early on that a writer's worst sin was silence. *The American Language* ran to four volumes (1919, 1921, 1923, 1936) and two supplements (1945, 1948). This subject retained Mencken's interest longer than any other one, and he concluded, quite wrongly, that he would be remembered best as a philologist. His *Prejudices* series of six volumes began primarily as literary criticism but expanded to embrace the many absurdities of the American scene. He always relished controversy; *In Defense of Women* (1918), detailing the bumpy passage of men and women through this vale of sorrow, continues to delight some and outrage others. One of his final enterprises, the *Days* trilogy (1940, 1941, 1943), has proven one of the most engaging autobiographies ever written in America.

If these books are generally the most enduring genre in Mencken's canon, then his journalism contains much of his most ephemeral writing. He knew all too well the transience of this form – today's copy, goes an old joke, wraps tomorrow's fish – but this situation diminished neither his enthusiasm nor his expertise. He always considered himself foremost a journalist, and, by Marion Rodgers's estimate, he wrote about three thousand columns over six decades. He wrote, at different times, for the New York *Evening Mail,* the *Chicago Sunday Tribune,* and the New York *American.* Early in his career he served as the American correspondent for papers in Japan, China, and Ceylon.

By long odds, though, his most important association was with the Baltimore *Evening Sun,* where he served as both editor and columnist during the paper's heyday. During President Franklin D. Roosevelt's New Deal, Mencken concocted an editorial that remains notorious to this day. Consisting of one million closely set dots, it was designed to demonstrate graphically the preposterous scope of the public dole. From 1911 to 1915 he used his daily "Free Lance" column to mock all sorts of visionaries and charlatans. With his flair for neologism, he dubbed the censors and moralists "smuthounds" and "snouters" and "virtuosi of virtue." His Monday Articles, which ran weekly from 1920 to 1938, proved equally uproarious. With no innate respect for America's highest elected official, Mencken entitled a column "Gamalielese" (a spoof on President Warren Harding's middle name) and likened the oratory of the 1921 inaugural address to "dogs barking idiotically through endless nights." In 1929 one of Mencken's colleagues, John W. Owens of the Baltimore *Sunpapers,* called him America's most brilliant newspaperman. The next decade Mencken refused to be considered for the Pulitzer Prize. Beyond argument, his name merits inclusion in any discussion of America's most consequential newspaper writers.

As a magazine journalist, Mencken served as both writer and editor. The range and expertise of his copy are as evident in his magazine work as they are in his books and newspaper columns. Working both for free and for sizable fees, he saw his writing appear primarily in American magazines, but it was also published, among other places, in England, Germany, and Cuba. Everyone, it seems, wanted Mencken's articles; they appeared in such ethnic publications as the *Jewish Tribune* and *Opportunity: Journal of Negro Life* and such special-interest periodicals as *American Speech* and *Birth Control Review*. He contributed to popular magazines like *Cosmopolitan* and *Reader's Digest* and to more highbrow journals such as the *Saturday Review of Literature, Yale Review,* and *Virginia Quarterly Review*. His conservative politics hardly suited the *Nation* and *New Republic,* but both printed his essays. Some of his finest writing, the nostalgic pieces late in his career, graced the *New Yorker*. Much to Mencken's credit and to the benefit of American readers, his magazine writing reached a widely diverse audience.

Mencken's editing of magazines accomplished many things, the most obvious for him being the huge increase in notoriety during the 1920s, the decade of his greatest fame. It is significant that Mencken viewed this role only as an avocation and that, initially at least, he never planned to assume it. Mencken coedited the *Smart Set* from 1914 to 1923. With the *American Mercury,* which he helped to establish in 1924 and edited until 1933, Mencken found a forum that allowed him to cavort on the national level as he never had before.

Mencken's career as a magazine journalist falls into three distinct periods. During the first, which lasted from 1899 to 1908, the fledgling author hustled his poetry, short stories, and essays. The second, and by far the most important, ran from November 1908 until December 1933. This began with Mencken's initial book review for the *Smart Set,* carried through his coeditorship of this magazine and his years with the *Mercury,* and ended with his resignation from the second magazine – an event lamented by his friends and gleefully celebrated by his enemies. The final period, 1934 to 1948, found Mencken writing frequently and with considerable expertise for a variety of periodicals. In fact, his sixth and seventh decades generated some of his finest prose. Much changed in America during those forty-nine years. Mencken saw his reputation rise, plummet, and then ascend once more. His ideas, however, remained remarkably consistent. For Mencken as both man and public figure, his end lay in his beginning.

"I, unfortunately, did not come up from that log cabin," he remarked during a recorded interview in 1948. "My misfortune was that my father was relatively well-off. It has been a curse to me all my life. Nobody will believe me on that ground. It seems to be the idea in America that no man is worth listening to unless he has had some experience in sweat-shops." Despising guilt as misguided and unproductive, Mencken refused to turn on the bourgeoisie that had nourished him. Rather, he celebrated it at every opportunity.

In 1848, a year of revolution in Europe, Mencken's paternal grandfather, Burkhardt Ludwig Mencken, left Germany. His ancestor immigrated to Baltimore, Mencken remarked in the first volume of his autobiography, "to escape a threatened overdose" of democracy. Burkhardt's first son, August, was born in 1854. In 1875, with thirty-five dollars in capital, he and his brother established a successful cigar factory. In late 1879 August married Anna Margaret Abhau, another first-generation German-American, and in September 1880 Henry Louis was born.

In 1883 the family moved to 1524 Hollins Street. A typical Baltimore row house in the southwest part of the city, this three-story building with the red-brick front and white-marble steps would become one of the most famous literary addresses in America. With the exception of the six years during and right after his marriage, Mencken would live here the rest of his life. Unpretentious, efficient, and comfortable, the house stood as the objective correlative of Mencken's values.

His childhood was idyllic – "happy days," he called this period in his memoirs. He and his siblings, two bothers and a sister, "were encapsulated in affection and kept fat, saucy and contented." August Mencken was a benevolent and highly competent *paterfamilias*. "There never was an instant in my childhood," Mencken recalled in *Happy Days* with a mixture of gratitude and irony, "when I doubted my father's capacity to resolve any difficulty that menaced me, or to beat off any danger. . . . I never heard of him being ill-treated by a wicked sweat shop owner, or underpaid, or pursued by rent collectors. . . ." In almost every respect, Mencken proved his father's son.

August was a successful capitalist, a high-tariff Republican who paid good wages but refused to run a union shop. He was also an agnostic who sent his children to Sunday school not out of piety but rather because he wanted to nap undisturbed. He despised all reformers and believed that the personal conduct of one's fellow citizens was best left alone. All of these matters – the business acumen, political conservatism, agnosticism, contempt for reform, and insistence upon personal freedom – were passed on to August's oldest son. Although the cigar maker would not live to see it, his values would be trumpeted all across America.

Mencken in 1913 (photograph by Henderson)

The youthful Mencken proved intellectually curious, articulate, and determined to succeed. His formal education began in 1886, when he enrolled in F. Knapp's Institute in downtown Baltimore, a private elementary school catering largely to pupils of German heritage. Mencken entered the Baltimore Polytechnic Institute, a public high school, in the fall of 1892. In 1894, drawing upon his interest in photography, he wrote an article describing the effects of a platinum toning bath upon photographic prints. Several magazines rejected the piece. The following year, he began to write poetry – the first effort was fittingly entitled "Opening Chorus" – and carefully preserved his efforts. In late March of the following year he completed in one evening his first short story, titled "Idyll." Much later, he joked that it was strongly influenced by the school of fiction represented by the *Ladies' Home Journal.*

That same year, he made his first attempt at reporting – he covered a baseball game – and was delighted when the newspaper account approximated his own. He also managed to draft a comic-opera libretto. During that summer, prior to his sixteenth birthday, he finally managed to break into print with another piece about baseball, a poem titled "Ode to the Pennant on the Centerfield Pole" that ran in the Baltimore *American.* "The appearance of these lines in print," he would reminisce in *My Life as Author and Editor* (1993), "naturally gave me a great thrill, and I set to work at once to write more."

Still prior to his sixteenth birthday, Mencken graduated, first in his class, from the Polytechnic in the spring of 1896. He never sat in a classroom again – in fact, no Mencken male in America ever attended college – and over the years he missed few opportunities to mock the formal education that he had spurned. He could be caustic, or he could draw upon his considerable skill as an ironist. "Some boys go to college and eventually succeed in getting out," he wrote in the *Smart Set.* "Others go to college and never succeed in getting out. The latter are called professors." The professors would return fire – few if any, though, could write as well as Mencken – and his battles with the academy would enliven his work as columnist, essayist, and magazine editor.

Upon his graduation Mencken wanted to begin a writing career, but August expected his oldest son to enter the family business. Mencken obeyed unenthusiastically and labored as a cigar maker, an office clerk, and a salesman; he grew so depressed that he contemplated suicide. The following year he resolved to write a poem a day. In 1898 he took a correspondence course in writing from the Cosmopolitan University in Irvington, New York.

In January 1899 August Mencken died of kidney failure. Now the head of the household, Mencken continued at the cigar factory by day and, every evening for four weeks, presented himself at the office of the Baltimore *Herald.* He was finally given an unpaid assignment, and the paper ran a short news item with no byline. The editor, Mencken recalled, only grunted at this copy, and no one else told the young writer: "I greet you at the beginning of a great career."

In June, Mencken went on salary, seven dollars per week, and never looked back. If the whaling ship proved Herman Melville's Harvard and Yale, then the newspaper served the same function for Mencken. Much later, in *Newspaper Days,* he extolled this "maddest, gladdest, damndest existence ever enjoyed by mortal youth." Despite Mencken's increasing workload at the *Herald,* this year saw his first magazine publication. "To Rudyard Kipling," a poem, appeared pseudonymously in the December *Bookman;* Mencken received ten dollars. The small fee meant nothing; a professional newspaperman and published magazine author at nineteen, Mencken was on his way.

The nineteenth century's final year found Mencken, resourceful and industrious, expanding his literary market. Three poems appeared in three different magazines. "The Cook's Victory," his first published short story, ran in the August issue of *Short Stories;* the fee was fifteen dollars. The story's material was generated by Mencken's experiences as a reporter on the docks of Baltimore. Set on the Chesapeake Bay, "The Cook's Victory" details the conflict between Captain Hiram Johnson, the odious commander of the oyster boat *Sally Jones,* and his black cook, Windmill.

"The Cook's Victory," a rather inconsequential tale, is important mainly because it is Mencken's first published story. However, Mencken exhibits two rudimentary abilities that would become far more pronounced later. His narrator is not loquacious; for the most part, the story moves along briskly. This early sense of pace prefigures Mencken's considerable ability to manage a narrative; he would become one of America's most skillful raconteurs. Second, Mencken shows a good ear for dialect. In time, this aural acuity would increase to the point where he could write American English that on occasion rivals Mark Twain's.

Mencken estimated that he published twenty-five short stories during these early years. He even began an abortive novel set in Elizabethan England. *The Mencken Bibliography* accounts for fifteen short stories published between 1900 and 1906. Douglas Stenerson provides a judicious assessment: "Some of the stories are competent enough to be plausible and entertaining, others are mediocre, none have much literary merit." *Short Stories* magazine remained Mencken's most lucrative market. Other of his stories appeared in *Criterion, Red Book Magazine,* the *Monthly Story Magazine,* and *Frank Leslie's Popular Magazine.*

His contact with the last periodical and its editor proved the most valuable. He made the acquaintance of Ellery Sedgwick, later the editor of the *Atlantic Monthly.* "I got my first real leg up," Mencken explained in *My Life as Author and Editor,* "when Ellery Sedgwick bought a story . . . and there began a friendly association that . . . was very stimulating and useful to me. . . . My other editors had been polite, but that was all. Sedgwick went further, and I began to glow with the feeling, so pleasant to a young author and so stimulating, that an editor was really interested in me." Later, when he was editing the *Smart Set* and the *American Mercury,* Mencken would treat many young authors as Sedgwick had treated him.

As Stenerson explains, Sedgwick had another, more important effect on the young man. Sedgwick suggested that Mencken try to write prose nonfiction. Three articles appeared pseudonymously in Sedgwick's magazine in 1903 and 1904, and he was sufficiently impressed to offer Mencken a position as his assistant. Mencken said no – the first of numerous occasions when he declined to live outside Baltimore. But he also made a decision that changed the direction of his career: at the age of twenty-four Mencken decided that prose nonfiction was his forte.

Mencken never wrote poetry again after 1903, the year his first book, *Ventures into Verse,* was published. Several of the forty poems in this modest venture of forty pages had appeared previously in the *Herald* and various magazines. One hundred copies were printed. Twenty-five went out for review; two sold. Rudyard Kipling's influence permeates this volume, and the poems range from the mediocre to the truly grotesque. Later, when Mencken became famous, rumors circulated that he was so embarrassed by the book that he bought copies to destroy them. He always denied this story.

Two years later, Mencken had more success with *George Bernard Shaw: His Plays,* the first book about Shaw published in America and a volume that Mencken, in *Newspaper Days* (1941), assessed as his own "first real book." This modest volume of 130 pages is most important for what Mencken, through his discussion of Shaw, said about himself. The iconoclasm of this "wild Irishman," then notorious for the discussion of prostitution in *Mrs. Warren's Profession,* clearly attracted Mencken, as did the playwright's belief in mimetic art. Mencken applauded the author who, in *Man and Superman,* makes "a dent in the cosmos with a slapstick." Later, when he acquired greater expertise, Mencken would do likewise as both author and editor.

In 1906 Mencken began a collaboration that effected the most important literary relationship of his career. He teamed with Leonard K. Hirshberg, a Baltimore physician with literary ambitions, to write an article titled "Popular Medical Fallacies." This piece ran under Hirshberg's name in the October issue of *American Magazine,* and a second piece about cancer, also under Hirshberg's name, appeared in February 1907. These pieces were read by Theodore Dreiser, who was then editing the *Delineator* and serving as editorial director of B. W. Dodge and Company.

Cover for the first issue edited by Mencken and George Jean Nathan

As Howard Markel and Frank Oski tell the story, Dreiser contacted Hirshberg and asked him to write articles on child care. In his position for Dodge, Dreiser contacted Mencken and asked him to put together a popular edition of Arthur Schopenhauer. Because of prior commitments, Mencken declined, but he did submit "The Slaughter of the Innocents," a piece on child care that he had ghosted for Hirshberg. Dreiser purchased the piece; eight in all ran under the general title "What You Ought To Know About Your Baby" in 1908 and 1909. A book of this title appeared under Hirshberg's name in 1910.

Kindred spirits in many ways, Dreiser and Mencken broadened their correspondence and met in New York City during the spring of 1908. Years later, Dreiser wrote to Isaac Goldberg that Mencken "beamed on me with the confidence of a smirking fox about to devour a chicken." Dreiser was sufficiently impressed to ask the Baltimorean to contribute to the *Bohemian* magazine; nine humorous pieces, including "The Fine Art of Conjugal Bliss" and "The Psychology of Kissing," would appear the following year. Dreiser also offered Mencken a position on the *Delineator,* which was politely refused, and suggested in 1908 that the *Smart Set* hire Mencken as its book reviewer, a position that proved the biggest break of Mencken's career up to this point.

The year also proved happy because of the publication of *The Philosophy of Friedrich Nietzsche,* a 325-page study that was Mencken's most ambitious undertaking to date. The philosopher had been dead only eight years, and Mencken had to struggle through much of his writing in the original German. Nietzsche's gospel according to Mencken spotlights their mutual opponents: democracy, universal manhood suffrage, and religion. An advanced culture, Mencken explains through his subject, endorses an aristocracy of intellect and expertise, and the ideal government leaves its citizens alone.

With three books behind him, a national forum awaiting his reviews, and certainty about the type of writing he did best, Mencken had completed his literary apprenticeship. The qualities which marked these early years – the industry, versatility, resiliency in the face of setbacks, and objectivity about his own writing – would continue to serve him well during the next period, when he would edit two magazines, terrorize the puritans, pedagogues, and philistines, and write with such power and wit that his name would become known all across America.

The magazine that so greatly influenced both Mencken's magazine journalism and his career had itself a colorful history. In March 1900 Col. William D'Alton Mann began the *Smart Set* as the "literary twin sister" of *Town Topics,* a New York City weekly of social gossip. Mann subtitled the *Smart Set* "A Magazine of Cleverness." Mencken preferred the bizarre and the earthy to the clever and the smart, and this coupling of man and magazine marked one of the more humorous incongruities in the Baltimorean's career. He seemed unsuited for a monthly that worked so hard to be chic and sported a cover on which a masked Mephisto dangled hearts before Cupid's bow. The first issue of the *Smart Set* cost twenty-five cents and sold more than 100,000 copies. Circulation reached 165,000 by 1905. The initial issue published the writing of poet Bliss Carman and of Nathaniel Hawthorne's son Julian. Frank Norris appeared later, as did Jack London, James Branch Cabell, and the young Sinclair Lewis. In November 1908, with the first of what amounted to 182 book-review articles, Mencken joined some fashionable company.

"Write what you damn well please," Mencken was told by the editor, "as long as it's lively and gets attention!" He was paid fifty dollars for eight pages of copy that did not come easily. Mencken had yet to discover his authentic voice, and the first paragraph of his first review shows the clumsy overwriting of a young man trying too hard to be literary:

> Platitudes have their uses, I have no doubt, but in the fair field of imaginative literature they have a disconcerting habit of denouncing and betraying one another. Separate a single platitude from the herd, and you will find it impeccable, inviolable and inevitable; comforting, amiable and well-mannered. But then lead out another, and try to drive them tandem; or three more, and try to drive them four in hand, and you will quickly land in the hospital. . . .

He had gotten stage fright, he acknowledged many years later.

However, the review improves as Mencken discusses novels by Upton Sinclair, Mary Roberts Rinehart, Marie Corelli, and Henry Blake Fuller. And finally, in a capsule review of Henry James's *Views* and *Reviews,* Mencken confidently scoffed, "Early essays by Henry James – some in the English language." Within a few months these reviews began to attract attention, and, to Mencken's delight, his enemies increased.

It was during his first ten or eleven years with the *Smart Set* that Mencken wrote his best literary criticism. He estimated that he read four thousand books and reviewed half that number. Mencken ranged across the continents and among the genres. He discussed the plays of Henrik Ibsen and George Moore, the novels of H. G. Wells and Arnold Bennett, the philosophy of Nietzsche and Henri Bergson. Among American authors, Mencken reviewed the criticism of Van Wyck Brooks, the poetry of Sara Teasdale, and the prose fiction of Dreiser, Willa Cather, Hamlin Garland, Sinclair Lewis, and F. Scott Fitzgerald – such a listing could be continued at great length. Despite the press of his other duties, Mencken ignored little of consequence during these years.

Mencken never considered himself primarily a literary critic. But he showed a remarkable consistency of thought; he recognized that his writing was of one piece, no matter what particular subject he happened to be discussing. The traits that most affected Mencken's response to the American scene – his nationalism, autodidacticism, iconoclasm, fatalism, and rationalism – definitely influenced, for better and for worse, his *Smart Set* reviews. He discussed some writers with considerable perception. On other occasions he seemed uninformed and parochial.

His lust for literary combat could hamper him, and his iconoclasm sometimes led him to treat unfairly figures honored by the literary establishment – James and William Dean Howells are the most obvious examples. He loved the majestic euphony of the universal statement and made embarrassing generalizations. As a critic of poetry, he can be dismissed outright. He viewed poetry as only a literature of escape and thought that T. S. Eliot's *The Waste Land,* with its numerous languages and portentous use of myth and allusion, was some sort of elaborate joke. Too often he allowed his enthusiasm to cloud his judgment and served as cheerleader and press agent instead of a disinterested evaluator.

Perhaps most important, Mencken's thoroughgoing rationalism severely limited his ability to deal with modern literature. He was best at discussing mimetic prose fiction, realism, and naturalism. But modernism, as many critics have pointed out, is neo-Romantic. Mencken proved unable or unwilling to deal with many of the complexities – stream of consciousness and interior monologue, for example, and the movement of a narrative according to psychological time – that entered prose fiction as the century progressed. Some writers came to view Mencken as a critical dinosaur.

Overall, however, his strengths superseded his weaknesses. For Mencken, the true literary critic was an artist himself. Offering both information and entertainment, this critic as catalyst was obligated, Mencken explained in *Prejudices: First Series,* "to provoke the reaction between the work of art and the spectator." After Mencken developed his mature style, his audience was never bored. Mencken's *Smart Set* reviews, frequently discussing authors long since forgotten, are still remarkably vibrant with their wealth of invention and gusto and laughter.

Mencken's review of *The "Genius"* serves as a characteristic example of his approach. He did appreciably more for Dreiser than any other individual ever did, but he found this patently autobiographical novel, published in 1915, Dreiser's least distinguished book. In a December review, titled "A Literary Behemoth," Mencken does not merely say that the novel is verbose; rather, he speaks of a "novel so huge that a whole shift of critics are needed to read it. . . . I read only the first and last paragraphs of each chapter. The rest I farmed out to my wife, to my cousin Fred, to my pastor and my beer man." With his flair for analogy, he calls this volume "as shapeless as a Philadelphia pie woman."

Rather than say that Dreiser's prose is turgid, the parched beer drinker gasps that "a greater regard for fairness of phrase and epithet would be as the flow of Pilsner to the weary reader in his journey across the vast deserts, steppes and pampas of the Dreiserian fable."

Finally, the value of Mencken's reviews lay more in what they accomplished than in their stylistic facility. He always argued that literary criticism should be neither constructive nor didactic. However, he did much good himself and helped to teach both his contemporaries and subsequent critics what is most important: the writer's need to function freely.

When Mencken began his reviews, American literature was not even taught in many of this country's colleges and universities. Long before it became fashionable, he stressed the need for originality rather than imitation, the need for a distinctively American canon rather than, as he remarked in his review of March 1919, "an out-house of English literature." Decades before Ernest Hemingway's *Green Hills of Africa* (1935), Mencken celebrated Mark Twain as the father of American literature. Moreover, he praised the peculiarly American qualities of Dreiser's writing. As much as any other critic of his age, Mencken helped to foster the growth of an indigenous American literature.

Of at least equal importance was his tireless battle with the censors. "I am absolutely against all censorships," he explained in "Autobiographical Notes – 1925." "It seems to me to be far better that indecencies should go unchallenged by law than that gangs of fanatics and perverts should police the rest of us. I believe that every form of censorship . . . falls inevitably into the hands of such fanatics and perverts." Even though Mencken had lampooned *The "Genius,"* he spent three hundred dollars of his own money and considerable time and effort on Dreiser's behalf after the novel was suppressed in 1916. During the next decade he would fight just as ardently for a pedestrian essay in the *American Mercury;* he also defended James Branch Cabell and James T. Farrell when censors turned their attention upon these novelists.

In December 1923, in his final review for the *Smart Set,* Mencken would recall the situation confronting him in 1908: "No novel that told the truth about life as Americans were living it, no poem that departed from the old patterns, no play that had the merest ghost of an idea in it had a chance." Censorship was hardly dead by 1923, but Mencken's determined efforts had definitely gained American authors greater freedom of speech. A grateful Dreiser celebrated the Baltimorean as a literary pathfinder.

During the spring of either 1908 or 1909 – scholars disagree about the exact date – Mencken was summoned to the *Smart Set* office for a meeting. Like his encounter with Dreiser, this meeting would appreciably affect Mencken's career. He was introduced to George Jean Nathan, a theater critic from Indiana two years his junior, who would be taking over the magazine's drama column. After the meeting the men went to the Beaux Arts, drank cocktails, and, as Carl Dolmetsch recounts the event, discussed "everything under the sun." They agreed that the people running the *Smart Set* were "a pack of asses" and that there was little money to be made, but they could still have a lot of fun. This began, as Dolmetsch says, a "friendship and collaboration that would eventually transform not only the *Smart Set* but certain aspects of American literary culture as well."

In several respects, they were an odd couple. Nathan, a graduate of Cornell, dressed impeccably; Mencken wore his clothes, his fiancée later remarked laughingly, as if they were made of tin. Nathan was short and thin; Mencken was taller and shaped, to borrow Carl Bode's highly appropriate image, "like a Michelob keg." Nathan maintained a rather narrow focus on the theater; Mencken's interests were far more extensive at this time and would increase. Nathan kept a bachelor apartment in Manhattan; Mencken, as we have seen, opted for the family's home fire in Baltimore.

On the other hand, both men were agnostics and iconoclasts. Gadflies in their respective fields, they wrote prolifically and shared a sharply honed sense of the absurd. In time, these two would cavort as perhaps America's most famous literary duo. Professionally, they would coedit magazines and write together. Personally, they would laugh and play and drink together and sometimes fight. Their professional relationship would end with considerable bitterness on Mencken's part, but their personal friendship would endure, despite long periods of silence and acrimony, until Mencken's death.

In 1911 Mann sold the *Smart Set* to John Adams Thayer, whose success with *Everybody's* magazine had made him wealthy. He offered Mencken the position of editor, but the Baltimorean refused. In April of the following year Mencken and Nathan began "Pertinent and Impertinent," a provocative feature published under the pseudonym "Owen Hatteras" (the surname derived from the stormy cape off North Carolina). In 1917 *Pistols for Two,* a mock biography of Mencken and Nathan, appeared under this pseudonym.

In January 1913 Thayer named a new editor, Willard Huntington Wright. He is better known to posterity as S. S. Van Dine, the pseudonym under which he would later write the highly successful Philo Vance detective stories. Wright boldly went to work. "A widespread critical awakening has come," he proclaimed in his March essay "Something Personal," "and with it a demand for better literary material. The demand for pious uplift, for stultification, and for fictional avoidance of the facts of life, has diminished. The reader of today demands truth." D. H. Lawrence contributed to the magazine under Wright, as did Frank Harris, George Moore, and W. B. Yeats. However, advertising and circulation declined, and Thayer was convinced that the magazine was growing too bold.

Thayer was also unhappy about the *Blue Weekly,* an abortive project concocted by Mencken, Nathan, and Wright. This periodical, Mencken recalled in *My Life as Author and Editor,* "was to be violently against virtually everything that the right-thinking Americans of the time regarded as sacred, from Christianity to democracy." Wright had a dummy made up and sent the sixty-five-dollar bill to Thayer, who paid it very reluctantly. This conflict between the timid owner and the controversial editor ended predictably. Wright was dismissed in early 1914. Mencken complained in his letter of 18 March to Dreiser that the *Smart Set,* after Wright's firing, was "as righteous as a decrepit and converted madame." Soon afterward, Mencken refused another offer of the editorship.

In August 1914, hurt by the panic on Wall Street that followed the beginning of World War I, Thayer sold the *Smart Set* to his chief creditor, Col. Eugene R. Crowe. Eltinge F. Warner, who had been successful with *Field & Stream,* became publisher of the *Smart Set* as well. He needed an editor and recalled a chance encounter during the previous month. He and Nathan had been returning from Europe on the same ship and struck up a conversation. Warner contacted Nathan and offered him the position.

Nathan telephoned Baltimore and said that he would take the job only if Mencken joined him. Finally – this was the third time that the job had been offered – Mencken accepted. However, he insisted upon two conditions: that he be allowed to continue living in Baltimore and that he and Nathan each be given, without cost, a one-sixth interest in the magazine. It was also understood that the new editors would be given a free hand; the editorial and business offices would be kept separate.

Cover for an issue including a story by F. Scott Fitzgerald, who had received his first commercial fiction publication in the June 1919 issue, under Mencken and Nathan's editorship

A contract was signed on 15 August, and Mencken and Nathan became editors of a magazine approximately twenty-four thousand dollars in debt and losing two thousand dollars a month. They were supposed to receive one hundred dollars per month for their editorial work, but they would not draw this until the magazine became solvent. Advertising was declining and postal rates increasing. From the beginning Mencken was dissatisfied with the magazine's title, its format, the quality of its paper, and its readership; over the years these matters would increasingly frustrate him. On the bright side, Mencken at thirty-four was coeditor of a national publication. On the other hand, he and Nathan were captains, as Dolmetsch remarks, of a "sinking ship."

Immediately, they had to make decisions about two pressing concerns: the position of the *Smart Set* on World War I and the magazine's deteriorating finances. The men handled both with considerable skill that belied their inexperience, and the magazine was saved.

Nathan was essentially apolitical. Mencken, on the other hand, was a strident Anglophobe who believed that England was using the United States for its own self-interest. "England gave us puritanism," he remarked on 31 December 1914 in the Baltimore *Evening Sun.* "Germany gave us Pilsner. Take your choice." He despised President Woodrow Wilson as a hypocrite. (In time, Wilson would enter Mencken's triumvirate of shame with William Jennings Bryan and Franklin D. Roosevelt; they were, in the Baltimorean's eyes, liar, fool, and thief, respectively.) Once the war began Mencken quickly saw what many of his fellow citizens either failed to recognize or refused to acknowledge: that the pro-British press colored the news, that America's professed neutrality was a sham.

Mencken used his column for the *Evening Sun,* "The Free Lance," to present the side of the opposition and bludgeoned his readers almost daily. After the *Lusitania* was sunk in 1915, moral indignation grew. But Mencken insisted coolly that because the ship was an armed vessel carrying munitions, the Germans were not culpable. Understandably, he alienated many readers and found himself at odds with the management of the *Sunpapers,* which supported England. Mencken gave up "The Free Lance" on 23 October 1915, but not without a parting shot: "The truth that survives is the lie that is pleasantest to believe."

It would have been disastrous for Mencken to use the *Smart Set* as a forum for his polemics. Very sensibly, he and Nathan kept all discussion of the war out of the magazine. However, he used other forums to scorn what he saw as the credulity and jingoism of the American masses. The *Smart Set,* he wrote laughingly to Louis Untermeyer on 3 November 1916, was being bombarded by "at least 50 war poems a day from the hog-meat and hominy belts."

Mencken and Nathan responded with equal sense to the magazine's debt. They found a cheaper office and wrote a sizable amount of the copy themselves under various pseudonyms. Moreover, they continued the low rate of pay instituted by Mann. Authors received either one or two cents per word for prose contributions – different sources give different figures – and either twenty-five or fifty cents per line for poetry. Whatever the exact figure, nobody got rich writing for the *Smart Set.*

In addition, Mencken and Nathan founded pulp magazines to help keep the *Smart Set* afloat. "If the broken-down hacks who were operating the most successful of them could get away with it," Mencken asked rhetorically in *My Life as Author and Editor* (1993), "then why not such smart fellows as Warner, Nathan, and me?" In July 1915 the first issue of the *Parisienne* appeared. Some manuscripts rejected for the *Smart Set* were reworked for publication here. However, Mencken and Nathan also sent out a call for original contributions, and manuscripts poured in.

The editors insisted that each piece have a European, preferably French, setting, with wealthy heroes and lovely ladies. Costing fifteen cents, the magazine sold well over one hundred thousand copies and cleared four thousand dollars an issue. Perhaps Mencken was thinking in part of the *Parisienne* when he made one of his most frequently quoted remarks in the *Chicago Sunday Tribune* on 19 September 1926: "No one in the world, so far as I know – and I have searched the records for years, and employed agents to help me – has ever lost money by underestimating the intelligence of the plain people." Mencken and Nathan experienced similar success with *Saucy Stories,* which appeared in August 1916. In October of that year they sold their shares in these magazines to Crowe and Warner. What had begun as a rescue effort made Mencken more money than he had ever possessed before.

The November 1914 *Smart Set,* the first edited entirely by Mencken and Nathan, sported a bold motto on the cover: "One civilized reader is worth a thousand boneheads." Hiding behind such noms de plume as Raoul Della Torre, George Weems Peregoy, and William Fink, the editors wrote more than half the copy themselves. The other contributor most recognizable today was Edna St. Vincent Millay. The typical *Smart Set* contained 160 pages (plus twenty pages of advertising) offering a novelette, a short play, a mixture of short stories and poems, and a variety of aphorisms and short dialogues that sometimes succeeded in being funny.

From the beginning the editors' purpose was as they set it forth in the October 1921 issue. Above all they wanted "to discover new American authors as they emerge, and to give them their first chance to reach an intelligent and sophisticated audience." They also wanted "to present the point of view of the civilized minority," to introduce foreign authors, and "to leaven the national literature with wit and humor." The editors helped their cause by being quite open-minded; according to S. N. Behrman, "You could send them things you couldn't possibly hope to get in anywhere else." Moreover, their handling of manuscripts generated considerable good feeling among the writers.

Remaining in Baltimore – he took the train to New York City for a few days every third or fourth week – Mencken read all manuscripts first. His veto killed a submission. If Mencken liked the manuscript he sent it back to Nathan, whose approval was also necessary for acceptance. There were few disagreements. Response was prompt; more often than not, letters of rejection contained encouragement and incisive criticism. The *Smart Set* paid upon acceptance rather than upon publication, and authors retained the copyright to their work. The editors generally overcame the penury of the *Smart Set* through their charisma, competence, and courtesy.

In the words of Behrman, Mencken and Nathan were "true incubators." Fitzgerald's first published story appeared in the *Smart Set,* and the editors also bought manuscripts from such other young writers as Eugene O'Neill, Dorothy Parker, and Zoë Akins. Among the more established authors who wrote for the magazine were Dreiser, James Huneker, Cather, and Cabell. English authors such as Aldous Huxley, W. Somerset Maugham, and Hugh Walpole appeared in the *Smart Set.* In 1915 the magazine printed two short stories from *Dubliners* – James Joyce's first appearance in an American periodical. In his definitive history, Dolmetsch calls the *Smart Set* a magazine of "inestimable value to literary history as the proving grounds, between 1900 and 1924, of more illustrious literary careers . . . than any other journal ever published in America." Although they edited the *Smart Set* for less than half this period, Mencken and Nathan still figured prominently in the magazine's distinguished literary history.

While the *Smart Set* was a critical success, its operations never became stuffy. Mencken loved the garish ambiance of the magazine's office, which sported a hideous red carpet, posters showing the effects of alcohol upon various organs in the body, college pennants, and several stuffed fish. Mencken served a free lunch on a marble slab and, as reading material for his visitors, put out journals from undertakers and plumbing suppliers. After receiving a love letter that obviously failed to warm him, he returned it with a rejection slip. Taking himself too seriously was never one of Mencken's faults, and he and Nathan clearly had a good deal of fun with their new venture.

When Mencken and Nathan looked back, they pointed to the period from the spring of 1915 to the summer of 1916 as their happiest time with the magazine. In December 1916 Mencken went to Germany to cover World War I for the Baltimore *Sunpapers.* When he returned in March, he found himself showing markedly less interest in the *Smart Set.* He would continue as coeditor but, as he recalled in *My Life as Author and Editor,* "in a state of gradually augmenting reluctancy."

This reluctancy was due in part to his inability to shape the magazine more to his liking. Also, after more than eight years he was growing tired of reviewing books. Moreover, his interests were expanding from literary matters to the American scene at large. Finally, his mind was surely diverted from the *Smart Set* by the uproar over the publication of *A Book of Prefaces* in October 1917.

Consisting in some measure of material reworked from the *Smart Set, Prefaces* offers essays on Joseph Conrad, Dreiser, and Huneker and concludes with "Puritanism as a Literary Force." The final essay, one of Mencken's longest, most caustic, and most skillful, bemoans the effect of puritanism upon all of American life. He goes so far as to dub his native land the "culture of the intellectually disinherited." A German-American of unpopular views during World War I, Mencken uses all four essays to shout "I accuse" at the American public.

Surely he anticipated what was coming. Mencken was excoriated more than he ever had been before – as much for his German heritage as for his literary and cultural views – but during the war he was unable to fight back. His opponents merely wrapped themselves in the flag, and free exchange ceased. When the war ended and Mencken could speak freely, he more than got even with his detractors, and he found an audience, grown tired of Wilsonian grandiloquence, far more receptive to his views. In all, the war marked the most obvious watershed in his career.

During the next two years three more books drew in varying degrees upon his *Smart Set* material. In 1918 the uproarious *In Defense of Women* was published. The following year was marked by the appearance of the first edition of *The American Language.* This "preliminary inquiry," as Mencken modestly describes the volume in its subtitle, actually offers more than three hundred pages of text, thoroughly documented, as well a substantial bibliography and a long list of words and phrases. Besides discussing such matters as pronunciation, euphemism, vulgarity, and platitudes, Mencken uses the image of "diverging streams" to depict British and American English. The first volume of the *Prejudices* series appeared the same year as the philological study. "It is light stuff," Mencken wrote to Fielding H. Garrison on 28 September, "chiefly rewritten from the *Smart Set.* . . . Such books are mere stinkpots, heaved occasionally, to keep the animals perturbed."

Nathan and Mencken in 1923, after leaving the Smart Set

In April 1919 Mencken and Nathan heaved another stinkpot in the *Smart Set* when they instituted the feature "Répétition Générale." They laughed uproariously and perturbed many an animal. "[T]here were some things in it," Mencken recalled in *My Life as Author and Editor,* "that grossly violated the pruderies, and especially the patriotic pruderies, of the first post-Armistice year."

During their six years of steering the *Smart Set,* Mencken and Nathan had grown quite notorious. In December 1920 they found themselves lampooned in Berton Braley's "Three – Minus One" in the *New York Sun*:

There were three that sailed away one night
Far from the madding throng;
And two of the three were always right
And everyone else was wrong.
But they took another along these two,
To bear them company,
For he was the only One ever knew
Why the other two should Be.
And so they sailed away, these three –
Mencken
Nathan
And God.

Nathan's and Mencken's bank accounts grew along with their notoriety. Recalling their success with the *Parisienne* and *Saucy Stories,* they founded in 1920 the *Black Mask,* a monthly mystery magazine. Sales climbed to 250,000, and the editors sold the magazine to Crowe the following year. Mencken estimated that the *Black Mask* earned him twenty-five thousand dollars.

Surveying his workload in 1921, Mencken was appalled. On 21 May he joined the *Nation* as a contributing editor. He was coediting both the *Smart Set* and the *Black Mask* and advising Emily Clark about her *Reviewer* in Richmond. He was reworking *The American Language* and putting together *Prejudices: Third Series* (1922). There were his weekly articles for the *Evening Sun* and his monthly book reviews for the *Smart Set.* Moreover, he contributed articles to the *Freeman,* the *Outlook* in London, the *New Republic,* and *Vanity Fair.* He was an author approaching the height of his powers who had a huge range of contacts and loved a challenge and wanted to do nothing so much as write. Retrenchment was impossible; Mencken might as well have promised to stop smoking his cigars or to drink only one beer.

He was writing so prolifically and with such convincing skepticism that he became by 1922, as he expressed it in *My Life as Author and Editor,* "the symbol and to some extent the leader, however designed and unwilling, of the revolt of post-war youth against the Old American certainties." The iconoclast had become, much to his embarrassment, an icon himself.

Happily for both Mencken and Nathan, 1923 marked the end of their association with the *Smart Set.* On 10 July Mencken informed Sara Haardt, whom he would marry in 1930, that "I am making plans to start a serious review – the gaudiest and damndest ever seen in the Republic." This endeavor, of course, was to be the *American Mercury.* Although the circulation of the *Smart Set* had fallen below twenty-five thousand, Mencken and Nathan were willing to continue the magazine as an all-fiction counterpart to the new monthly, but an incident with Warner would prevent this arrangement.

In August the publisher broke his promise to keep out of the magazine's editorial affairs. After the death of President Harding, the editors planned to run a satiric story about the funeral train. Warner forbade publication; Mencken and Nathan resigned.

In their broadside of 10 October, they said nothing of Warner's meddling. Rather, they announced that they were stepping aside because they had accomplished what they had set out to do ten years earlier: "That purpose was to break down some of the difficulties which beset the American imaginative author . . . above all, to do battle for him critically, attacking vigorously all the influences which sought to intimidate and regiment him. This work is obviously no longer necessary." This final, self-congratulatory comment was premature, as were Mencken's remarks on the same subject in his final review in December. In any event, Mencken had had enough of the *Smart Set;* as far as he was concerned, the magazine was yesterday's news. (The *Smart Set* would continue for another six and one-half years before the Depression killed it in June 1930.) He was free to move on to the project that interested him far more. It was his association with the *American Mercury* that contributed most to his notoriety during the 1920s – a notoriety that would be very difficult to exaggerate.

Mencken believed that a man frolicked most knavishly in his forties, and the 1920s in America belonged to the Baltimorean more than to any other individual. The *New York Times* suggested that Mencken was the most influential private citizen in his native land. With its childlike optimism and frantic quests for all sorts of gratification, this decade eminently suited the writer who, as he admitted in *Prejudices: Third Series,* had a "medieval but unashamed taste for the bizarre and indelicate [and a] congenital weakness for comedy of the grosser varieties."

Many tropes have been used in retrospect to capture the American experience during the 1920s: the party before the long hangover, the night of revelry before the harsh light of dawn, the period of favor before the fall from grace. Mencken at this time chose a far different image. "No other country," he exclaimed in the *Bookman* in October 1928, "houses so many gorgeous frauds and imbeciles as the United States. . . . I love this country as a small boy loves the circus."

Not surprisingly, similar thinking colored his conception of the new magazine. Dreiser had suggested several flashy titles. "What we need," Mencken responded in his letter of 10 September 1923, "is something that looks highly respectable outwardly. The American Mercury is almost perfect for that purpose. What will go on inside the tent is another story. You will recall that the late P. T. Barnum got away with burlesque shows by calling them moral lectures." For a decade "Mencken" and "the *Mercury*" would be synonymous. This coupling would raise the magazine to immense prominence and would also prove a central factor in its fall from favor.

Mencken had first met Alfred A. Knopf, then a young publisher of twenty-one, in 1913. With Knopf's publication of *Prefaces,* the men had begun a long, friendly, and mutually beneficial relationship. As publisher of the *Mercury,* Knopf initially wanted Mencken as sole editor, but the Baltimorean insisted that Nathan join him. The men were each given twenty-five shares of stock – the remaining one hundred were divided among Knopf, his wife, and father – as well as full editorial control. Mencken's name was to come first on the masthead, the reverse of the order on the *Smart Set,* and he was to receive five thousand dollars per year.

The *Mercury* was directed at the intelligent, solvent, and urbane American. In his letter of 17 Au-

Mencken in 1923 at Alfred Knopf's summer house in Portchester, New York. Knopf would soon begin publishing Mencken and Nathan's American Mercury.

gust 1923 to Haardt, Mencken called the magazine "an organ of educated Toryism." The *Mercury,* Mencken explained in his first editorial, "is entirely devoid of messianic passion. The Editors have heard no Voice from the burning bush. They will not cry up and offer for sale any sovereign balm, whether political, economic or aesthetic, for all the sorrows of the world." Mencken hoped that the magazine would solace the "outcasts of democracy." It would proceed, he promised, "without indignation on the one hand and without too much regard for tender feelings on the other."

Unlike the *Smart Set,* the *Mercury* confined itself to the editors' native land. Mencken promised "a realistic presentation of the whole gaudy, gorgeous American scene," and the magazine discussed not only the fine arts but also politics, government, and the natural and social sciences. As M. K. Singleton explains in his detailed history of the magazine, the *Mercury* carried about seven times as many essays as short stories, and approximately one-third of those essays tended to be satiric. Some of Amercia's more vulnerable targets were assaulted repeatedly: pedagogy, chiropractic, homeopathy, Christian Science, Prohibition, puritanism, and the sad credulity of rural America.

As Mencken wished, the magazine's controversial content was decorously clothed by its respectable title and distinctive Paris-green cover. The magazine was printed on expensive Scotch featherweight paper, and the Garamond type was set in double columns. There were no illustrations in each issue of 128 pages. Like Knopf 's books, long celebrated for their appearance, the *Mercury* was thoroughly first-rate. Mencken now had a magazine whose understated elegance set it apart from many of its competitors.

The first issue of the *Mercury* in January 1924 had an initial printing of five thousand copies. A second printing was necessary, then a third. By the end of the year, circulation had climbed past forty-two thousand. This number far surpassed even the most optimistic expectations.

This first issue carried over several features from the *Smart Set.* Nathan's "The Theatre" was the penultimate essay, and Mencken's "The Library" closed the magazine. Initially, Mencken farmed out some of the book reviews, and Cabell, Ernest Boyd, and Goldberg contributed to this first issue. Mencken soon decided, though, that this plan was unworkable and wrote the entire "Library" himself. Both Mencken and Nathan contributed to "Clinical Notes," which approximated the "Répétition Générale" department of the *Smart Set.*

Far more lively, though, was "Americana," which had first appeared in the *Smart Set* in May 1923 and was ostensibly compiled by Owen Hatteras. It consisted of items gleaned from newspapers and magazines; separated according to states, this material was reprinted with brief commentaries. As he explained in his introduction to the book published in 1925 under the same title, Mencken wanted to familiarize his readers "with what is going on in the minds of the masses – the great herd of undifferentiated, good-humored, goose-stepping superstitious, sentimental, credulous, striving, romantic American people."

The first issue of the *Mercury* contained a list of distinguished contributors. The editors published two poems by Dreiser, a prose piece by the poet John McClure, an essay by Carl Van Doren about Stephen Crane, and a lively collection of letters by Huneker. Boyd's "Aesthete: Model 1924," a trenchant satire in the best Menckenian vein, stirred up the self-proclaimed artistes in Greenwich Village. The editors also planned to run a scathing indictment of the Ku Klux Klan by Gerald W. Johnson, the distinguished journalist then teaching at the University of North Carolina at Chapel Hill. This piece had to be bumped to the February issue; there simply was not room.

As time passed, distinguished authors continued to submit manuscripts. Mencken published prose by Dreiser, Fitzgerald, Sinclair Lewis, Sherwood Anderson, William Faulkner, and Farrell. Carl Sandburg, Edgar Lee Masters, and Vachel Lindsay contributed poetry. Dorothy Parker also wrote for the *Mercury.*

The magazine's pages were enlivened by some of the more controversial figures of the day. Emma Goldman, the political radical, appeared in the *Mercury,* as did Margaret Sanger, the advocate of birth control. Mencken had an open mind and the good editor's sense of a story; he also knew how to turn a query from an inexperienced writer into a polished piece. He cultivated material from a variety of figures not actively courted by most commercial magazines. Physicians, clergymen, lawyers, and soldiers wrote for the magazine, as did hoboes, dishwashers, taxi drivers, and outdoorsmen. Beyond argument, the eclectic nature of its contributors was one of the magazine's strengths.

Mencken also published pieces by several black authors, and this association proved mutually beneficial. Mencken had attacked segregation and lynching in many forums for decades, but he used the *Mercury* to make his most representative statement about race relations. "Personally," he remarked in May 1931, "I hate to think of any man as of a definite race, creed, or color; so few men are really worth knowing that it seems a shameful waste to let an anthropoid prejudice stand in the way of free association with one who is."

According to Charles Scruggs in *The Sage in Harlem: H. L. Mencken and the Black Writers of the 1920s,* discussion of "every possible aspect of Negro culture" was included in the pages of the *Mercury.* By Fenwick Anderson's count, Mencken ran fifteen editorials about racial issues as well as fifty-four articles, split almost equally between black and white authors. With nine contributions, George Schuyler was the black author who appeared most frequently. James Weldon Johnson and Langston Hughes also wrote for the magazine, as did W. E. B. Du Bois and Walter White (later head of the NAACP) and the poet Countee Cullen. As Scruggs remarks, "More than any other critic in American letters, black or white, Mencken made it possible for the black writer to be treated as a fellow laborer in the vineyard." Black writers recognized the editor's expertise and courage; for Cullen, the Baltimorean was "the intrepid Mr. Mencken."

Unfortunately for their friendship, dealings between the two coeditors proceeded far less smoothly than Mencken's dealings with contributors. Within the first six months of the founding of the *Mercury,* so much tension developed that the partnership was finally dissolved.

Mencken found Nathan's interests too narrow for the new magazine. Moreover, Mencken grew irritated because he thought he shouldered too great a share of the editorial duties. As he recalled this conflict decades later, Mencken remarked that it was during the summer of 1924, while he was covering the Democratic National Convention in New York City, that he decided the situation was hopeless. Friendship aside, he pushed for a quick resolution.

On 15 October 1924 he wrote to Nathan that "the scheme of the *American Mercury* as it stands is full of defects, and . . . to me at least it must eventually grow impossible." The Baltimorean offered two alternatives: he would assume complete editorial control and hire a managing editor, or he would retire as editor and become a mere contributor to the magazine. Later that month Mencken argued that "divided counsels make for too much irresolution and compromise. In particular I doubt that you and I could carry it off together. Our interests are too far apart. We see the world in wholly different colors." Nathan was willing to try to resolve their differences, but for Mencken the arrangement was clearly doomed.

The Baltimorean prevailed, and Nathan agreed in February to step down as coeditor; he would remain as contributing editor. This change was announced in the August 1925 issue. For a while, Nathan continued to write "Clinical Notes" and "The Theatre." Between 1929 and 1931 Nathan sold his shares in the magazine for twenty-five thousand dollars. In 1930 he ceased contributing to the *Mercury*.

Publicly, Nathan gave no hint of the disagreement; he withdrew, he announced, because he wanted "to be free from the technical details of editing." Hence, the rift was kept from the magazine's readership. Mencken hired an assistant, Charles Angoff, in early 1925, and the reputation of the *Mercury* continued to grow. Clearly, Mencken had won the struggle for control, but there were to be costs that he could not then foresee. Understandably, Nathan harbored resentment about the way he had been treated, and he would turn on Mencken and the *Mercury* in late 1932. Angoff waited much longer. It was not until after Mencken's death that Angoff released the most derogatory book written about the Baltimorean.

During 1925 the rise of Mencken's personal reputation paralleled the ascent of the *Mercury*. In this year marked by the publication of Boyd's *H. L. Mencken* and Isaac Goldberg's *The Man Mencken,* the first two books devoted entirely to Mencken's life and art, Burton Rascoe would call the *Mercury* "the most talked-about magazine of the time." The year's major event was Mencken's coverage of the trial of John Scopes in Dayton, Tennessee. This "Tennessee Circus," as he lampooned the event in the *Evening Sun* on 15 June, generated some of Mencken's finest newspaper columns and led to an essay that is among the most skillful that he ever wrote.

In March of that year the Tennessee legislature made it unlawful to teach the theory of evolution in any public school. A high-school biology teacher, Scopes volunteered to test the law and was subsequently arrested. William Jennings Bryan, then almost thirty years past his impassioned "Cross of Gold" speech, volunteered to serve as the prosecuting attorney. Mencken helped to recruit Clarence Darrow, the celebrated defense attorney. The *Sunpapers* sent a cartoonist and four columnists to cover this highly publicized battle between science and religion, this age-old struggle, as Mencken saw it, between knowledge and superstition.

The events both disgusted and delighted him. He was appalled that such an event could take place in a supposedly civilized country during the twentieth century. On the other hand, he was amused by the bewildered judge and the court that opened each day with a prayer. He laughed at the figure wearing a sandwich board that proclaimed him the "Bible champion of the world," at the atheist parading a mangy chimpanzee throughout the town, at the spurious messiahs who descended upon Dayton, and at the meeting of fundamentalist Christians in the hills beyond that culminated in the speaking of tongues and a writhing heap of bodies. These proceedings so inflamed some of the youngsters, Mencken joked, that they snuck off to make love and returned with sparkling eyes. In short, this Tennessee circus proved a windfall for Mencken, and he was grateful. Toward the end of the trial, Darrow called Bryan to the stand and asked about his interpretation of the Bible. The man nominated three times for the presidency of the United States thundered that man is not a mammal. By this time, pressed by other duties, Mencken had returned to Baltimore. Bryan died of a stroke shortly after the trial.

Mencken's obituary of the Great Commoner, simply entitled "Bryan," ran in the *Evening Sun* on 27 July. Substantially revised, it appeared in the October *Mercury*. Mencken's first sentence leaves no doubt about the tone or direction of the essay: "Has it been marked by historians that the late William Jennings Bryan's last secular act on this earth was to catch flies?" One of the cruelest things that Mencken ever wrote, the essay skillfully mixes images of dirt, sweat, grease, hair, and excrement to make Bryan seem scarcely human. This staunch opponent of the theory of evolution appealed not to enlightened Americans but rather to those of arrested development: "gaping primates" who spoke in "simian gabble." Dayton is the site of another witch trial, Mencken concluded, with Bryan "[bawling] for the fagot and the stake."

This essay proved as much an indictment of rural America as an ironic elegy of a person whom Mencken loathed. "Wherever the flambeaux of Chautauqua smoked and guttered," Mencken scoffed, "and the bilge of Idealism ran in the veins, and Baptist pastors dammed the brooks with the saved, and men gathered who were weary and heavy laden . . . there the indefatigable Bryan set up his traps and spread his bait." Through the vivid image of the human dam formed by the baptism of immersed hordes, Mencken divided America into two camps: those sophisticated readers entertained by such grotesquerie, and the mindless souls participating in it.

Some of Mencken's columns about the trial were picked up throughout the South. However, with the appearance of this essay in the *Mercury,* he reached a different audience and showed the considerable extent to which the magazine could solace America's enlightened minority. In 1944, when Lawrence E. Spivak and Charles Angoff constructed *The American Mercury Reader,* there was room for only one Mencken piece, and the editors chose "Bryan."

Like the previous year, 1926 marked a bad time for Mencken's friendships. During the past decade his relationship with Theodore Dreiser had grown increasingly strained. Mencken ridiculed what he viewed as Dreiser's promiscuity and argued that the novelist was wasting his considerable talents on various types of experimental writing. Dreiser, in turn, found Mencken officious and narrow-minded.

In December 1925 Dreiser's *An American Tragedy* was published, and Mencken wrote the author that his review, which was to appear in the February 1926 *Mercury,* contained a mixture of praise and censure. Enraged, Dreiser wrote Mencken a letter so insulting that the men remained estranged for more than eight years. Like his unperceptive review of Fitzgerald's *Great Gatsby* the previous year, Mencken's wrongheaded analysis of *An American Tragedy* showed that his acuity as a literary critic had declined as his interest in fiction diminished.

The spring of that year was enlivened by the uproar over "Hatrack," a pedestrian essay about a small-town prostitute that appeared in the April *Mercury.* This publication generated the most significant censorship case in Mencken's career; the *New York Times* likened the event to a "second Scopes trial." A chapter from Herbert Asbury's forthcoming autobiography, *Up from Methodism,* "Hatrack" is set in Farmington, Missouri, that American hinterland which Mencken so loved to deride. Asbury criticizes the hypocrisy of the clergy, who attack vice for personal gain, and the prurience of small-town life. Called "Hatrack" because of her scrawny figure, the protagonist is shunned in church by her supposed fellow Christians. She retires to the graveyard on Sunday nights to practice her trade. She expects little from her customers; to the stranger who offers her a dollar, she replies with the sincere remark that closes the piece: "You know damned well I haven't got any change."

The first issue of the periodical that was conceived by Mencken as a satiric review of American culture. He took over as sole editor in 1925 and continued in that capacity until 1933.

"Hatrack" seems as tame as it is undistinguished. Asbury does not titillate his readers, nor does he morally affirm his protagonist. In his indictment of moral hypocrisy, Asbury says nothing that had not already been said far more scathingly. However, the Reverend J. Franklin Chase, a Methodist minister and secretary of the Boston Watch and Ward Society, found the piece "immoral" and "full of filthy and degrading descriptions." On 30 March a magazine vendor in Harvard Square sold the April *Mercury* to one of Chase's agents and was arrested. A more timid editor might well have ignored the insult – financially it meant next to nothing – but Mencken decided to challenge Chase and thereby placed himself at considerable personal risk. If found guilty of publishing obscenity, he could be jailed for two years.

On 5 April Mencken went to Brimstone corner of Boston Commons, sold the magazine to Chase, and was arrested. He was tried the next day and acquitted the day after that. Before a cheering crowd at Harvard, Mencken proclaimed that the moralists could be run out of Massachusetts as they had been vanquished in the Maryland Free State. His exuberance was premature, for he had underestimated his opponent's resources.

Chase succeeded in having the April *Mercury* barred from the mail. This time the editor was given no chance to defend his magazine. "We wondered why action was taken without a hearing," Arthur Garfield Hays, the distinguished lawyer for the *Mercury*, later wrote scathingly. "Murderous cancer cures circulate, sometimes for months, before they are barred from the mails. But then, they are not obscene – merely fatal." The magazine's May issue, containing another innocuous piece with the provocative title of "Sex and the Co-ed," was already with the printer. If this issue were also banned, then the *Mercury* would lose its second-class mailing privilege, a potentially catastrophic situation. It cost Mencken eight thousand dollars to recall the issue and substitute a piece on playing the cello. In all, the "Hatrack" affair cost the magazine twenty thousand dollars in cash and a substantial loss of advertising revenue. Moreover, for the first time with either the *Smart Set* or the *Mercury,* the moralists had forced Mencken to withdraw a piece that he had accepted for publication.

Mencken staunchly defended free speech, the cause that he valued above all others. In 1928 the Baltimorean published *Menckeniana: A Schimpflexikon,* a collection of abuse. He made certain to include the most violent denunciations of him and his magazine. He undoubtedly laughed when Mencken the editor was called a "putrid public pest." But he had to take considerable satisfaction when the *Mercury* was reviled as "the greatest single danger that exists in American life today." He could hardly have asked for a better testament that the magazine had indeed accomplished what it had set out to do.

By the end of 1927 the circulation of the *Mercury* had reached eighty thousand; it peaked at about eighty-four thousand in early 1928. This period marked the magazine's zenith under Mencken's editorship. At the age of forty-eight Mencken had succeeded, far beyond his own and Knopf's expectations, with the journal designed to console the country's civilized minority. Even those who despised Mencken acknowledged his stature. Few men of letters have achieved such prominence in America. Mencken's reign and the magazine's success, however, could not last indefinitely. Just as several matters effected the ascent of Mencken and his monthly, other issues contributed to their decline. Beyond argument, the king had erred, but he also found himself powerless, watching his kingdom disappear.

As a cultural critic, Mencken was victimized by his own expertise. While the Depression hastened the decline of the *Mercury,* it did not initiate it. The magazine's popularity had begun to slump more than a year and a half before. Mencken's satire had run its course. He had written and edited so proficiently that there was less need for the social commentary of the *Mercury.*

Moreover, his response to the Depression made the magazine seem increasingly archaic. Initially, Mencken, like many other Americans, underestimated the importance of the stock-market crash in October 1929. As conditions worsened, Mencken retained his belief in laissez-faire capitalism. He believed that the economy would naturally correct itself, just as it had after the hard times in 1893 and 1894. This individualist never doubted that the strong person's gain necessitated the weak person's loss and that to destroy the threat of failure was also to destroy incentive. For Mencken, the prototypical underdog in America was not one of life's unfortunates but rather that individual who acquired competence at a trade, paid the bills, and refused to yell for help during bad times.

It was not until 1932 that Mencken discussed the Depression in the *Mercury.* "We have all lost something," he acknowledged in March, "but not many have really lost everything. In actual value the country is still rich, and any man who owns any honest part of it still has that part, and will see it making money when the clouds roll by." The clouds never rolled; instead, unemployment swelled to thirteen million, and the Bonus Army camped in Washington that summer. When Mencken saw the bread lines in Times Square, he was so appalled that he stripped off his overcoat and gave it to a stranger. Once so palatable, the magazine's iconoclasm did not sit well on an empty stomach. By the end of the year, circulation had fallen to forty-two thousand.

The establishment of the *American Spectator* in November hardly brightened Mencken's mood. This monthly was edited by Boyd, Dreiser, Nathan, Cabell (whose *Jurgen* [1919] Mencken had defended against the censors), and O'Neill. As Singleton points out, the *American Spectator* imitated the *Mercury* by drawing upon "The Theatre," "The Library," and "Americana." The first issue ran an editorial that, although it did not refer specifically either to Mencken or the *Mercury,* disparaged both. Moreover, the magazine's second issue carried Dreiser's "The Great American Novel," a harsh and lengthy commentary attempting to discredit Mencken as a literary critic. Even Herbert Asbury wrote for this competitor of Mencken's magazine. Mencken remained unperturbed. In his correspondence, he argued that the *American Spectator* was not to be taken seriously and would not last long. He was right, at least on the second count, for the magazine was marked by considerable editorial squabbling and folded after only four and a half years.

In the presidential election of 1932 Mencken voted for Franklin D. Roosevelt. In Mencken's view, Prohibition, not the economy, was the central issue, and Roosevelt had promised to end this national embarrassment. Obviously, Mencken could not then foresee the sweeping changes that Roosevelt would initiate during the controversial Hundred Days. From the spring of 1933 until America's entry into World War II, Mencken would use the *Mercury* and every other available forum to scorn the New Deal.

Mencken never doubted that once the mentality of the dole was established, continued expectations of public assistance would erode the American work ethic. Believing in self-reliance, he argued at length that the New Deal robbed people of their self-respect. "Divide the wealth; deal the cards anew, again and again" was always the gist of Mencken's rejoinder to Roosevelt's euphonious scheme. "But you will find, if you let the game naturally run its course, that the competent player will leave the table with more money than was brought, and that the incompetent person will be a chronic loser. You may mean well, but you are misguided and destructive. You cannot restructure American society because you cannot restructure the nature of man." Such an attitude was hardly fashionable during the Depression.

By the summer of 1933 the *Mercury's* circulation had declined to thirty thousand. It was time to move on, and on 6 October the *New York Times* announced Mencken's forthcoming retirement. "Ten Years," in the December issue, was Mencken's farewell. "I am firmly convinced," he explained, "that magazines, like governments, are benefited by rotation in office," and he proceeded to praise the qualifications of Henry Hazlitt, his successor. Remarking that ten years is long enough on any one enterprise, he said that he wanted more time to devote to his books and to travel. He left open the possibility that he might contribute later to the magazine – he would – and expressed thanks that he would have to do no more book reviewing. "It is now time," he closed mischievously, "for other, and perhaps even worse critics to take over the job." Mencken offered neither apologies nor complaints, and the implicit message throughout this final essay is both affectionate and a bit melancholy: it was a lot of fun while it lasted. So ended the most significant period of Mencken's magazine journalism, which had stretched from his twenty-eighth through his fifty-third year.

America had changed immensely – Mencken, not at all. He would never again edit a magazine. Surely, he suspected that he would never again have a national forum that would give him the freedom to write as the *Mercury* had. Here as elsewhere he reacted demonstrably to neither triumph nor disaster. At the end of *Treatise on the Gods* (1930) he spoke of man's need for a "proud imperturbability." Mencken lived what he wrote, and he endured. No circus could run forever, and during the final fifteen years of his career the former ringmaster would assume two new roles. Discussing the contemporary scene, Mencken was America's Jeremiah. Recalling a past that he found far more attractive, he was America's winsome elegist. For many readers, this mellow Mencken proved the most endearing character of all.

Freed from editing the *Mercury,* Mencken had far more time to write, and 1934 proved one of his most productive years as a magazine journalist. In fifteen magazines he published thirty-two articles that showed his usual wide range of subject matter and tone. The *New Yorker* ran nine travel pieces generated by his and Sara's trip to the Mediterranean. On 6 October the *Saturday Review* published "Illuminators of the Abyss," his scathing attack upon proletarian literature. Mencken scorns the *New Masses* and "the revolutionists who now tell us in such shaky English that only bad writers can really write, and only the low-down are really worth writing about." Mencken always believed that the artist does the most good by writing well.

He chose a much different tone for "Four Glad Years," which appeared in *College Humor* in November. After praising the superior professor, the autodidact laughs at "the rabble of quacks and racketeers" who have chosen pedagogy. "[S]uperior men would be wasted on the job of trying to educate the uneducable," he continues in his best Menckenese, "and maybe be driven insane. The best professor for an idiot is a quack – and that is what American colleges provide for him, whether deliberately or by natural law. The two understand and esteem one

Mencken (center) after his arrest for selling on Boston Common a copy of the April 1926 issue of the American Mercury, *with "Hatrack" (courtesy of the Mencken Room, Enoch Pratt Free Library)*

another. What the one can't teach is precisely what the other doesn't want to learn. They are happy together in a perfect symbiosis." For Mencken, "mass education" was always an oxymoron.

Unfortunately, the following year generated no such laughter. Sara's health, always precarious, continued to decline, and she died on 31 May, at age thirty-seven, from tubercular meningitis. "Now I feel completely dashed and dismayed . . . ," the usually stoic Mencken lamented in his letter of 7 June to Sedgwick. "What a cruel and idiotic world we live in!" But Mencken persevered once more.

The fourth edition of *The American Language* appeared in 1936. Receiving considerable acclaim, the book made the best-seller list for nonfiction. The reception of this fourth edition marked, in Charles Fecher's phrase, "the beginning of [Mencken's] critical rehabilitation." The same month, the *New Yorker* published "Ordeal of a Philosopher," the first of the autobiographical sketches later collected in the *Days* trilogy, comprising *Happy Days, 1880–1892* (1940), *Newspaper Days, 1899–1906* (1941), and *Heathen Days, 1890–1936* (1943).

With these narratives, Mencken discovered a form perfect for his abilities as a comic raconteur. They are not "sober history but yarning," he explained in *Heathen Days,* "and [they are] thus devoid of any purpose save to entertain." He had the space to frolic as he pleased – to create, embellish, shock, and sigh – and discovered a wealth of material that he found relatively painless to write. The success of these pieces genuinely surprised him; they came too easily, he thought, to be considered so good.

Between February 1941 and September 1943 the *New Yorker* published eighteen more sketches under the highly appropriate general title of "Days of Innocence." In "The Girl from Red Lion, Pa.," a widely anthologized story, Mencken tells the tale of an anonymous farm girl seduced by her beau Elmer. Religion tells her that she is condemned to a life of sin, so she takes the train to Baltimore to seek work in a brothel. Mencken's agent of salvation, named Peebles, guides his young charge to the house of Miss Nellie d'Alembert, a madame with the proverbial heart of gold. A visiting journalist, who clearly knows his Mark Twain, delivers the sermon: "I advise you to go home, make some plausible excuse to your pa for lighting out, and resume your care of his cows. At the proper opportunity take your beau to the pastor. . . . It is the safe, respectable, and hygienic course. Everyone agrees that it is moral, even moralists." As he had done twenty-four years before in "Puritanism as a Literary Force," Mencken scorns the odious effects of moral convention. Humor, however, has now replaced vituperation. The sage clown, Mencken turns the world of conventional virtue upside down.

In the sixty sketches filling the *Days* trilogy, Mencken leaves a cache of Americana and says hail and farewell to a better day. "We were lucky to have been born so soon," he remarks in the collected edition (1947). Mixing irony with regret, he explains what his country has lost but what his art can preserve: "As the shadows close in we can at least recall that there was a time when people could spend weeks, months, and even years without being badgered, bilked or alarmed. . . . The human race had not yet succumbed to the political and other scoundrels who have been undertaking of late to save it, to its infinite cost and degradation." He speaks fondly of his youth, of his salad days as a newspaperman, and of the lively times after World War I. "I enjoyed myself immensely," he concludes, "and all I try to do here is to convey some of my joy to the nobility and gentry of this once great and happy Republic, now only a dismal burlesque of its former self." In this elegy for a once-remarkable country now irrevocably lost, Mencken plays a part that would have seemed unthinkable twenty-five years before: Prospero waving his wand.

Mencken knew that the shadows were edging closer to himself as well. He suffered a slight stroke in 1939, but retrenchment again proved unthinkable, and his seventh decade proved remarkably productive. He stopped writing for the *Sunpapers* in early 1941 – not to diminish his workload but rather because he abhorred the paper's favorable response to President Roosevelt's foreign policy. Mencken was convinced that Roosevelt, because of the abject failure of the New Deal, planned to lead America into a war not its own in order to resuscitate the economy. In addition to the *Days* trilogy, the decade was marked by the publication of *A New Dictionary of Quotations* (1942) and the two supplements to *The American Language.*

In August 1947 he and Nathan met at the Stork Club in New York City. They were getting old – this was almost forty years after that initial lively meeting about the *Smart Set.* Dreiser had died in December 1945, and in April 1948 Mencken took the opportunity, again for the *New Yorker,* to look back in laughter upon events that had previously made him rage. In the century's second decade Mencken had excoriated Dreiser for acquiring the signatures of a number of radicals on the document protesting the suppression to *The "Genius."* More than thirty years later, Mencken joked that "not a few of the hand-painted-oil-painted signatories were being pursued by the indignant mothers of runaway daughters." Mencken had admonished Dreiser about his companions in Greenwich Village. Chuckling about the plethora of inarticulate writers and inept painters who had descended upon his friend, Mencken recalled that he once found Dreiser at his desk "surrounded by a breastwork of [unsalable manuscripts] at least three feet high, and in a corner was a stack of canvases, showing women with purple hair, the jaws of hell [and] gem-set umbilici." The fire was out, and Mencken could laugh about the absurdity of it all.

He rejoined the *Sunpapers* during the summer of 1948 to cover, with his usual irreverence, the three presidential conventions. Beginning in August he wrote sixteen columns, mostly political in nature. His final piece, which ran on 9 November, concerned something far more important than the follies of the electoral system. Blacks and whites had been arrested for playing tennis together in a municipal park. Disgusted by such bigotry in the Free State, Mencken proclaimed that "it is high time that all such relics of Ku Kluxry be wiped out in Maryland."

Two weeks later this man of extraordinary energy and immense gifts suffered a stroke that robbed him of his ability to read and write. Thereafter Mencken spoke of 1948 as the year of his death. His old friends were there when he needed them. Knopf proved boundlessly generous, and Nathan telephoned faithfully. When Dolmetsch interviewed the Baltimorean in August 1955, he remarked of Nathan: "I'm not sure that we treated George fairly." On 29 January 1956, about twenty weeks past his seventy-fifth birthday, Mencken died in his sleep of a coronary occlusion. He had written his epitaph decades before for the December 1921 *Smart Set:* "If, after I depart this vale, you ever remember me and have thought to please my ghost, forgive some sinner and wink your eye at some homely girl."

"[N]o man whose name is so constantly before the public," Mencken remarked in *Vanity Fair* in February 1934, "is so thoroughly obscure as a magazine editor." His tenure with both the *Smart Set* and the *Mercury* belied his generalization. He was alternately extolled and vilified, but he was never obscure. As Dolmetsch states, the Baltimorean's coeditorship of the *Smart Set* "marks one of Mencken's finest and most enduring achievements and the area of his greatest impact upon American literary history." It was here that Mencken learned his trade as a literary critic, and he influenced the course of American letters in this century. Moreover, he gained the expertise as editor that led to the foundation and huge success of the *Mercury*. With this Paris-green monthly, Mencken, as William Manchester points out, was "the last of the great cultural editors."

What he wrote for magazines proved as important as how he edited them. Mencken was never motivated primarily by money. Unlike many other American authors, he found it easy to make a living – his estate totaled some three hundred thousand dollars – but he always scorned what William James called "the bitch-goddess SUCCESS . . . the squalid cash interpretation put on the word. . . . " For half a century he never ignored what interested him merely because he could have gotten a larger check for writing something else. He never courted public approval. "I don't give a damn," he wrote to Dreiser on 8 November 1919, "what any American thinks of me." This healthy indifference to wealth and approbation gave him the freedom to say exactly what he thought.

His beliefs are set forth most succinctly in "Testament," which appeared in the October 1927 *Review of Reviews*. His creed, he explains, is "that it is better to tell the truth than to lie, that it is better to be free than to be a slave, [and] that it is better to have knowledge than to be ignorant." These tenets, he remarks, seem innocuous and obvious enough, "but they are inordinately offensive to the overwhelming majority of Americans." The average American, he complains, is timid, and "no man can be dignified as long as he is afraid." It is in this celebration of candor and freedom and knowledge, this contempt for hypocrisy and debasement and mindlessness, that Mencken spoke most forcefully to his age and continues to speak so convincingly to ours.

Letters:

Letters of H. L. Mencken, edited by Guy J. Forgue (New York: Knopf, 1961);

The New Mencken Letters, edited by Carl Bode (New York: Dial, 1977);

Letters from Baltimore: The Mencken-Cleator Correspondence, edited by Philip E. Cleator (Rutherford, N.J.: Fairleigh-Dickinson University Press, 1982);

Dreiser-Mencken Letters: The Correspondence of Theodore Dreiser & H. L. Mencken, 1907–1945, 2 volumes, edited by Thomas P. Riggio (Philadelphia: University of Pennsylvania Press, 1986);

"Ich Kuss Die Hand": The Letters of H. L. Mencken to Gretchen Hood, edited by Peter W. Dowell (University: University of Alabama Press, 1986);

Mencken and Sara, a Life in Letters: The Private Correspondence of H. L. Mencken and Sara Haardt, edited by Marion Elizabeth Rodgers (New York: McGraw-Hill, 1987);

Fante/Mencken: John Fante & H. L. Mencken, a Personal Correspondence, 1930–1952, edited by Michael Moreau, consulting editor Joyce Fante (Santa Rosa, Cal.: Black Sparrow Press, 1989).

Bibliographies:

H. L. M.: The Mencken Bibliography, compiled by Betty Adler, with the assistance of Jane Wilhelm (Baltimore: Johns Hopkins University Press, 1961);

Man of Letters: A Census of the Correspondence of H. L. Mencken, compiled by Adler (Baltimore: Enoch Pratt Free Library, 1969);

H. L. M.: The Mencken Bibliography, A Ten-Year Supplement, 1962–1971, compiled by Adler (Baltimore: Enoch Pratt Free Library, 1971);

H. L. M.: The Mencken Bibliography, a Second Ten-Year Supplement, 1972–1981, compiled by Vincent Fitzpatrick (Baltimore: Enoch Pratt Free Library, 1986);

H. L. Mencken: A Research Guide, compiled by Allison Bulsterbaum (New York: Garland, 1988).

Biographies:

Isaac Goldberg, *The Man Mencken: A Biographical and Critical Survey* (New York: Simon & Schuster, 1925);

Edgar Kemler, *The Irreverent Mr. Mencken* (Boston: Little, Brown, 1950);

William Manchester, *Disturber of the Peace: The Life of H. L. Mencken* (New York: Harper, 1950; second edition, Amherst: University of Massachusetts Press, 1986);

Carl Bode, *Mencken* (Carbondale: Southern Illinois University Press, 1969);

References:

Fenwick Anderson, "Black Perspectives in Mencken's *Mercury*," *Menckeniana,* no. 70 (Summer 1979): 2–6;

Charles Angoff, *H. L. Mencken: A Portrait from Memory* (New York: Thomas Yoseloff, 1956);

Irving Babbitt, "The Critic of American Life," *Forum,* 79 (February 1928): 161-176;

Randolph Bourne, "H. L. Mencken," *New Republic,* 13 (24 November 1917): 102-103;

Ernest Boyd, *H. L. Mencken* (New York: McBride, 1925);

Alistair Cooke, *Six Men: Charles Chaplin, H. L. Mencken, Humphrey Bogart, Adlai Stevenson, Bertrand Russell, Edward VIII* (New York: Knopf, 1977), pages 83-117;

Carl Dolmetsch, "'HLM' and 'GJN': The Editorial Partnership Re-Examined," *Menckeniana,* no. 75 (Fall 1980): 29-39;

Dolmetsch, "Mencken as Magazine Editor," *Menckeniana,* no. 21 (Spring 1967): 1-8;

Dolmetsch, *The Smart Set: A History and Anthology* (New York: Dial, 1966);

John Dorsey, ed., *On Mencken* (New York: Knopf, 1980).

George H. Douglas, *H. L. Mencken: Critic of American Life* (Hamden, Conn.: Archon Books, 1978);

Douglas, *The Smart Magazines: 50 Years of Literary Revelry at* Vanity Fair, The New Yorker, Life, Esquire, *and* The Smart Set (Hamden, Conn.: Archon Books, 1991), pp. 55-91;

Joseph Epstein, "H. L. Mencken: The Art of Point of View," *Menckeniana,* no. 71 (Fall 1979): 2-11;

Charles A. Fecher, *Mencken: A Study of His Thought* (New York: Knopf, 1978);

Vincent Fitzpatrick, "The *American Mercury,*" in *American Literary Magazines: The Twentieth Century,* edited by Edward E. Chielens (Westport, Conn.: Greenwood Press, 1992), pp. 7-16;

Fitzpatrick, *H. L. Mencken* (New York: Continuum, 1989);

Fitzpatrick, "The *Smart Set,*" in *American Literary Magazines: The Twentieth Century,* edited by Chielens (Westport, Conn.: Greenwood Press, 1992), pp. 333-341;

Guy Jean Forgue, *H. L. Mencken: l'Homme, l'Œuvre, l'Influence* (Paris: Minard, 1967);

Michael Gold, *The Hollow Men* (New York: International Publishers, 1941), pp. 11-25;

Fred C. Hobson, Jr., *Serpent in Eden: H. L. Mencken and the South* (Chapel Hill: University of North Carolina Press, 1974);

Gerald W. Johnson, "Reconsideration: H. L. Mencken," *New Republic,* 173 (27 December 1975): 32-33;

Alfred Kazin, "Mencken and the Great American Boob," *New York Review of Books,* 34 (26 February 1987): 8-11;

Kazin, *On Native Ground* (New York: Reynal, 1942), pp. 198-204;

Murray Kempton, "Saving a Whale," *New York Review of Books,* 28 (11 June 1981): 8, 10-12, 14;

Alfred A. Knopf, "H. L. Mencken, George Jean Nathan, and the *American Mercury,*" *Menckeniana,* no. 78 (Summer 1981): 1-10;

Joseph Wood Krutch, "This Was Mencken: An Appreciation," *Nation,* 182 (11 February 1956): 109-110;

Walter Lippmann, "H. L. Mencken," *Saturday Review of Literature,* 3 (11 December 1926): 413-414;

Edward A. Martin, *H. L. Mencken and the Debunkers* (Athens: University of Georgia Press, 1984);

Sara Mayfield, *The Constant Circle: H. L. Mencken and His Friends* (New York: Delacorte, 1968);

Frank Luther Mott, "*The American Mercury,*" in his *A History of American Magazines,* volume 5 (Cambridge, Mass.: Belknap Press of Harvard University Press, 1968), pp. 3-26;

Mott, "*The Smart Set,*" in his *A History of American Magazines,* volume 5 (Cambridge, Mass.: Belknap Press of Harvard University Press, 1968), pp. 246-272;

Robert F. Nardini, "H. L. Mencken's *Ventures Into Verse,*" *South Atlantic Quarterly,* 80 (Spring 1981): 195-205;

Nardini, "Mencken and the 'Cult of Smartness,'" *Menckeniana,* no. 84 (Winter 1982): 1-12;

George Jean Nathan, *The Intimate Notebooks of George Jean Nathan* (New York: Knopf, 1932), pp. 94-121;

William H. Nolte, "The Enduring Mencken," *Mississippi Quarterly,* 32 (Fall 1979): 651-662;

Nolte, *H. L. Mencken, Literary Critic* (Middletown, Conn.: Wesleyan University Press, 1966);

Burton Rascoe and Groff Conklin, eds., *The Smart Set Anthology* (New York: Reynal, 1934), pp. 11-34;

Thomas P. Riggio, "Dreiser and Mencken: In the Literary Trenches," *American Scholar,* 54 (Spring 1985): 227-238;

Louis D. Rubin, Jr., "H. L. Mencken and the National Letters," *Sewanee Review,* 74 (Summer 1966): 723-738;

Gerald Schwartz, "The West as Gauged by H. L. Mencken's *American Mercury,*" *Menckeniana,* no. 89 (Spring 1984): 1-14;

Charles Scruggs, *The Sage in Harlem: H. L. Mencken and the Black Writers of the 1920s* (Baltimore: Johns Hopkins University Press, 1984);

Ellery Sedgwick III, "HLM, Ellery Sedgwick, and the First World War," *Menckeniana,* no. 68 (Winter 1978): 1-4;

Stuart Pratt Sherman, "Beautifying American Literature," *Nation,* 105 (29 November 1917): 593-594;

Frank R. Shivers, Jr., *Maryland Wits & Baltimore Bards: A Literary History with Notes on Washington* (Baltimore: Maclay, 1985), pp. 163-186;

M. K. Singleton, *H. L. Mencken and the* American Mercury *Adventure* (Durham, N.C.: Duke University Press, 1962);

Douglas C. Stenerson, "The 'Forgotten Man' of H. L. Mencken," *American Quarterly,* 18 (Winter 1966): 686-696;

Stenerson, ed., *Critical Essays on H. L. Mencken* (Boston: G. K. Hall, 1987);

Stenerson, *H. L. Mencken: Iconoclast from Baltimore* (Chicago: University of Chicago Press, 1971);

Stenerson, "Short-Story Writing: A Neglected Phase of Mencken's Literary Apprenticeship," *Menckeniana,* no. 30 (Summer 1969): 8-13;

Carl Van Doren, "Smartness and Light, H. L. Mencken, a Gadfly for Democracy," *Century,* 105 (March 1923): 791-796;

Philip Wagner, *H. L. Mencken* (Minneapolis: University of Minnesota Press, 1966);

W. H. A. Williams, *H. L. Mencken* (Boston: G. K. Hall, 1977);

Edmund Wilson, "H. L. Mencken," *New Republic,* 27 (1 June 1921): 10-13;

Wilson, *The Shores of Light: A Literary Chronicle of the Twenties and Thirties* (New York: Farrar, 1952).

Papers:

The Enoch Pratt Free Library, Baltimore, houses the most extensive collection of Mencken papers. Some of this material was given by Mencken during his lifetime; other papers arrived after his death. These holdings include manuscripts, typescripts, proofs, pamphlets, a variety of scrapbooks, Mencken's correspondence to and from Marylanders, and some correspondence with non-Marylanders. The great majority of Mencken's correspondence with non-Marylanders is housed at the New York Public Library. Cornell University owns the books that Mencken inscribed to George Jean Nathan and approximately four hundred letters written to Nathan. In all, Betty Adler's *A Descriptive List of H. L. Mencken Collections in the U.S.* lists thirty-four institutions, libraries, and individuals holding Mencken papers.

George Jean Nathan

(14 February 1882 - 8 April 1958)

Sam Bruce

MAJOR POSITIONS HELD: Drama critic and associate editor, *Bohemian* and *Outing* (1906-1908); drama critic, *Harper's Weekly* (1908-1910); drama critic (1908-1923), coeditor, *Smart Set* (1914-1923); drama critic, *Judge* (1922-1935); cofounder (1924), coeditor (1924-1925), drama critic, *American Mercury* (1924-1930, 1940-1951); drama critic, *Vanity Fair* (1930-1935); cofounder (1932), coeditor, *American Spectator* (1932-1935); drama critic, *Life* (1935-1936), *Esquire* (1935-1946), *Scribner's* (1937-1938), *Newsweek* (1937-1940), *Liberty* (1940-1942), King Features national syndicate (1943-1956).

PRINCIPAL MAGAZINES PARTIALLY OWNED: *Smart Set* (1914-1923), *Parisienne* (1915-1916), *Saucy Stories* (1916), *Black Mask* (1920-1921), *American Mercury* (1924-1930).

BOOKS: *Europe after 8:15,* by Nathan, H. L. Mencken, and Willard Huntington Wright (New York: Lane, 1914);

Another Book on the Theatre (New York: Huebsch, 1915);

Bottoms Up, an Application of the Slapstick to Satire (New York: Goodman, 1917);

Mr. George Jean Nathan Presents (New York: Knopf, 1917);

Pistols for Two, by Nathan and Mencken, as Owen Hatteras (New York: Knopf, 1917);

A Book without a Title (New York: Goodman, 1918);

The Popular Theatre (New York: Knopf, 1918);

Comedians All (New York: Knopf, 1919);

Heliogabalus, a Buffoonery in Three Acts, by Nathan and Mencken (New York: Knopf, 1920);

The American Credo: A Contribution toward the Understanding of the National Mind, by Nathan and Mencken (New York: Knopf, 1920; revised and enlarged, 1921);

The Theatre, the Drama, the Girls (New York: Knopf, 1921);

The Critic and the Drama (New York: Knopf, 1922);

The World in Falseface (New York: Knopf, 1923; London: John Lane, Bodley Head, 1923);

George Jean Nathan

Materia Critica (New York: Knopf, 1924);

The Autobiography of an Attitude (New York: Knopf, 1925);

The House of Satan (New York & London: Knopf, 1926);

Land of the Pilgrims' Pride (New York: Knopf, 1927);

The New American Credo: A Contribution toward the Interpretation of the National Mind (New York: Knopf, 1927);

Art of the Night (New York & London: Knopf, 1928);
Monks Are Monks: A Diagnostic Scherzo (New York: Knopf, 1929);
Testament of a Critic (New York: Knopf, 1931);
The Intimate Notebooks of George Jean Nathan (New York: Knopf, 1932);
Since Ibsen: A Statistical Historical Outline of the Popular Theatre since 1900 (New York: Knopf, 1933);
Passing Judgments (New York: Knopf, 1935);
The Theatre of the Moment, a Journalistic Commentary (New York & London: Knopf, 1936);
The Avon Flows (New York: Random House, 1937);
The Morning after the First Night (New York & London: Knopf, 1938);
Encyclopedia of the Theatre (New York: Knopf, 1940);
The Bachelor Life (New York: Reynal & Hitchcock, 1941);
The Entertainment of a Nation; or, Three Sheets in the Wind (New York: Knopf, 1942);
Beware of Parents, a Bachelor's Book for Children (New York & Toronto: Farrar & Rinehart, 1943);
The Theatre Book of the Year: A Record and an Interpretation, 9 volumes (New York: Knopf, 1943–1951);
The World of George Jean Nathan, edited by Charles Angoff (New York: Knopf, 1952);
The Theatre in the Fifties (New York: Knopf, 1953).
Editions: *The Magic Mirror: Selected Writings on the Theatre,* edited by Thomas Quinn Curtiss (New York: Knopf, 1960);
A George Jean Nathan Reader, edited by Arnold L. Lazarus (Rutherford, N.J.: Fairleigh Dickinson University Press, 1990).

OTHER: Isaac Goldberg, *The Theatre of George Jean Nathan* (New York: Simon & Schuster, 1926) – includes *The Eternal Mystery: Play in One Act,* pp. 231–250; and "Love: A Scientific Analysis," pp. 253–262;
The Critics' Prize Plays, edited by Nathan (Cleveland, Ohio: World, 1945);
Ralph Ginzburg, *An Unhurried View of Erotica,* preface by Nathan (New York: Helmsman, 1958).

SELECTED PERIODICAL PUBLICATIONS – UNCOLLECTED: "Conversations: IV. On Politics," by Nathan and H. L. Mencken, *Smart Set,* 44 (February 1921): 93–98;
"The Editor and His Public," *Bookman,* 61 (May 1925): 275–276;
"The Theatrical Year Ends," *Vanity Fair,* 32 (June 1930): 44, 96.

George Jean Nathan is chiefly remembered as one of the most influential drama critics in the history of American theater. Yet Nathan's influence extended beyond his critical impact on drama – as coeditor of the *Smart Set* from 1914 to 1923 and as a cofounder and coeditor of the *American Mercury* from 1924 to 1925, he and his editorial partner, H. L. Mencken, helped to launch the careers of such important American writers as F. Scott Fitzgerald and Eugene O'Neill and introduced to American audiences the work of Lord Dunsany (Edward John Moreton Drax Plunkett) and James Joyce. Perhaps just as important, the Nathan-Mencken partnership played a key role in forming the context for a literary revolution out of which grew one of the richest periods in American belles lettres.

Nathan was born on 14 February 1882 in Fort Wayne, Indiana, to Charles Naret Nathan, a successful businessman who owned a French vineyard and a Brazilian coffee plantation, and Ella Nordlinger Nathan. George Jean Nathan's maternal grandfather had been among the first settlers in Fort Wayne, and Charles Nathan's international business interests and the Nordlingers' high standing in the community combined to provide an affluent upbringing for George that included studying under highly qualified tutors in languages, history, literature, and the piano.

In 1888 the Nathans moved to Cleveland, where George's maternal uncle Fred Nordlinger-Nixon managed playhouses for a Cleveland-Philadelphia syndicate. The family attended many plays in the late 1880s and the 1890s, doubtless fueling Nathan's interest in the theater. When the acclaimed actress Sarah Bernhardt was a guest at his uncle's house in 1892, she gave Nathan a souvenir ring that he wore for several years.

During summers abroad with his father, Nathan was afforded the opportunity to study at European universities: he enrolled as a special student at the University of Bologna in 1897; while attending the University of Paris in 1898 he wrote a satiric essay, "Love: A Scientific Analysis." He studied at Heidelberg University in 1899.

Nathan entered Cornell University in 1900 because in his opinion it was the closest in spirit to European universities. He edited both the *Cornell Daily Sun* and the *Cornell Widow* and won several prizes for his achievements on the fencing team. He graduated in 1904; his father died the same year.

Nathan's journalistic career began in earnest in 1905 when his uncle Charles Nordlinger, the drama critic for the *New York Herald,* secured his nephew a position as cub reporter for the paper at

Covers for two issues of the literary magazine Nathan coedited with H. L. Mencken from 1914 to 1923

fifteen dollars a week. He began by covering murder trials, was transferred to sports, and then became a third-string reviewer, assigned to plays that none of the other reviewers wanted. Soon Nathan was writing two feature articles a week for the *Sunday Herald;* but he became increasingly unhappy with his job, feeling severely hampered by the paper's timidity. As Nathan later recalled, "There were so many don'ts editorially that it would have taken a vaudeville mind-reader to remember them in composing an article."

At that point Lynn Wright, a fellow former editor of the *Cornell Daily Sun* who was then editor of the Knapp magazines *Outing* and the *Bohemian,* offered Nathan the position of head of the drama departments of both. Thus Nathan left the *Herald* and began his magazine career in 1906.

In 1908 Nathan received national exposure when *Harper's Weekly* began to publish his play reviews on a regular basis. That summer he received an offer that was to be the turning point of his career. In 1900 the colorful and somewhat disreputable Col. William D'Alton Mann had started *Smart Set: A Magazine of Cleverness* with the proceeds from his *Town Topics,* a magazine of gossip about the rich and powerful of New York. With stories and verse written by socialites, the *Smart Set* would be "by, for and about 'The Four Hundred.'" The magazine had passed through various editorial hands and had survived, though with a tarnished reputation, a major scandal in 1906 in which Mann was charged with libel. When Charles Hanson Towne, who had taken over the editorship of the *Smart Set* in 1904, left the magazine in 1908, the publisher took over as editor with Fred C. Splint as managing editor and Norman Boyer as assistant editor. To battle the declining fortunes of their periodical the three decided to imitate their chief competitor, *Ainslee's* magazine, by adding a literary editor to contribute book reviews. In addition, Channing Pollock, the magazine's drama editor, had announced his intention to leave, so that his position would have to be filled as well. Mencken and Nathan were selected as literary editor and drama editor, respectively. There are conflicting reports as to when the two men met for the first time – either they were hired simultaneously in Boyer's office on 8 May 1908, or Mencken was hired first and later summoned to Boyer's office to meet Nathan in May 1909.

Pollock was not yet ready to leave, so Mencken's literary reviews began to appear in the *Smart Set* first, starting with the November 1908 issue. (Though Mencken was now on the staff of the *Smart Set,* his primary residence remained in Baltimore, and he often conducted his business with the magazine through the mail.) Nathan contributed an essay, "Why We Fall in Love with Actresses," to the October 1909 issue, and his first regular article, "The Drama Comes into Season," appeared the following month after Pollock had finally vacated his position.

Nathan and Mencken quickly developed distinctive voices. Nathan would succinctly describe his authorial persona in *The World in Falseface* (1923): "I am the sort that takes nothing very seriously; nor on the other hand do I take it too lightly, for one who takes nothing very seriously takes nothing too lightly." The tone that came across in Nathan's reviews in the *Smart Set* was one of amused, aristocratic aloofness: though his responses were often intense, they were those of one who was above it all.

But though Mencken and Nathan proved popular, the magazine's financial problems continued. In the spring of 1911 Mann sold the *Smart Set* to John Adams Thayer, who had previously acquired *Everybody's* magazine and made it a financial success. Mencken and Nathan had developed an idea for a new periodical that would satirically attack American customs and taboos and would be called the "Blue Weekly" or "Blue Review" (based on the *Blue Weekly,* a periodical created by the hero of H. G. Wells's novel *The New Macchiavelli,* 1911). In 1912 they proposed the idea to Thayer, who, not ready to start a new magazine, suggested a new department in the *Smart Set* that would test reader response to such an approach (Mencken called it "Anti-puritan"). Nathan and Mencken's "Pertinent and Impertinent" column first appeared in the April 1912 issue under the joint pseudonym "Owen Hatteras." The column enjoyed great popularity, and most readers had no idea that Owen Hatteras was a fictional creation. A humorous "biography" of Nathan and Mencken, *Pistols for Two,* appeared under the Hatteras pseudonym in 1917. In time, the name became a house pseudonym.

In 1913 Thayer, at Mencken's urging, promoted associate editor Willard Huntington Wright to the position of editor. Wright instituted radical changes in the *Smart Set,* publishing work that defied what he considered the bland and sentimental conventions of contemporary fiction. Following the lead of Nathan and Mencken's "Pertinent and Impertinent" column, he proclaimed that his intention was to make the *Smart Set* an American version of the German satiric weekly *Simplicissimus,* and he vigorously solicited quality contributions by promising generous pay rates. Wright's editorship drew accolades from the intellectual community, but Thayer began to receive complaints from social contacts and traditional readers and grew increasingly alarmed at Wright's lavish expenditures. He fired Wright in December 1913 after testing the reactions of Nathan and Mencken to the move. Both had clearly favored the new editor's policies and put forward some token objections to his dismissal, but they deferred to Thayer's authority.

Thayer replaced Wright first with Harry Torsey Baker and then with Mark Lee Luther and instituted a return to the magazine's earlier tenor. Thayer published an announcement in the March 1914 issue that confessed, "we have been too serious as regards the relations of literature to life" and promised that the *Smart Set* would in the future contain "a good round measure of romantic and humorous relief." The *Smart Set* continued under this bland editorial policy for several months but succeeded only in alienating readers who had been attracted by Wright's policies without regaining those, "who are not ultra in any respect," whom Thayer had hoped to appease. In the face of dwindling circulation and mounting debts, Thayer signed the magazine over to his paper supplier, Eugene R. Crowe.

Crowe put Eltinge F. Warner, who had turned *Field & Stream* magazine into a success, in charge of the *Smart Set.* Warner had recently met Nathan on a cruise ship, where, noticing that they were wearing identical overcoats that had been sold to them as originals by a London tailor, they had struck up a conversation. Warner had been impressed with Nathan, and upon taking over the *Smart Set* he asked the drama critic to be the magazine's editor. Nathan agreed on the condition that Mencken be brought in as coeditor. Mencken insisted that he would accept the position only if he could remain in Baltimore. The final agreement, promising complete autonomy to Nathan and Mencken on editorial matters and giving each a one-sixth interest in the company in lieu of salary until the magazine's debts were paid, was reached on 16 August 1914.

Under the banner of Nathan and Mencken the *Smart Set* become one of the most influential Ameri-

Richard R. Smith, publisher of the American Spectator, *with three of the journal's founding editors: Ernest Boyd, Nathan, and Theodore Dreiser*

can literary magazines, cherished by thousands of readers for its polished combination of iconoclastic wit and cavalier attitude. The regular departments – such as the highly popular "Répétition Générale," which began in April 1919 – exhibited the erudite and often scathing wit of the two editors, and the features usually presented risqué subject matter and themes through understated comedy and clever wordplay. The *Smart Set* had its share of "serious" pieces, but the overall tone of the magazine was one of sophisticated amusement.

Nathan and Mencken's approach to the business of editorship was extremely efficient but every bit as irreverent and nontraditional as their authorial personae in the pages of their magazine. Twice a week manuscript acquisitions were mailed to Baltimore, where Mencken managed to sort through each lot within a few hours after its arrival. According to *Pistols for Two,* the pieces Mencken deemed interesting were marked with "the Dano-Norwegian word 'bifald,' signifying assent" and returned to Nathan for confirmation; the others were immediately returned to their authors. If Nathan approved the submission it went back to Mencken for another read before being set in type; those Nathan rejected were returned to their authors. Thus, any submission had to be approved by both editors – the veto of either automatically killed the piece. Payment was sent immediately on acceptance, and copyrights reverted to the authors upon publication.

Nathan described his editorial philosophy in a 1925 piece for the *Bookman* that reflects the flippant, indifferent style of his writing for the *Smart Set:* "In so far as I have any talent for editing, that talent consists merely in printing anything that interests me. What interests other people, I do not know. If what interests me happens luckily to interest other people, I am given credit for being an astute and discerning editor which I do not deserve. . . . This is doubtless no way to be an editor. I am very sorry."

The offices of the *Smart Set* included a waiting room with a church pew set up for visitors. Nathan's and Mencken's desks (the latter often empty) were at opposite sides of the inner office, which was decorated with beer posters, pictures of Friedrich Nietzsche, Ludwig van Beethoven, and Otto von Bismarck (all bearing phony autographs to the editors); a tapestry, thrown over a large claw-foot chair, showing a dog rescuing a baby; two saw-horses surmounted with a marble slab that Mencken had stolen from a graveyard; and a huge banner that read "GOD BLESS OUR PRESIDENT!" On a table in the outer office was a large stack of two-page brochures listing twenty-six "Suggestions to Our Visitors," including: "Visitors are kindly requested to refrain from expectorating out of the windows," "The House Surgeon is forbidden to accept fees for the treatment of injuries received on the premises," and "Photographs of the Editors are on sale at the Portier's desk."

Nathan and Mencken at the Stork Club in August 1947

Nathan searched for European contributors; the dark fantasy "The Bureau d'Echange de Maux" in the January 1915 *Smart Set* marked Lord Dunsany's first American publication, and his tales would appear regularly in the magazine during the following three years. Nathan and Mencken received Joyce's *Dubliners* stories through the intercession of Ezra Pound, and "A Little Cloud" and "The Boarding House" appeared in the May 1915 issue. Nathan was responsible for the acquisition of W. Somerset Maugham's "Miss Thompson," published in the April 1921 issue; the story would provide the basis for John Colton's successful play *Rain* (1927).

On their native shores, Nathan and Mencken share responsibility for launching the career of Fitzgerald, who was first published professionally in the June 1919 issue of the *Smart Set* with his story "Babes in the Woods." But the biggest literary "discovery" in the magazine for which Nathan received the majority of the credit was undoubtedly O'Neill. Early in his career O'Neill sent three one-act plays to Mencken for his opinion. Mencken was encouraging and forwarded the pieces to Nathan. Much to O'Neill's surprise, the first of these, *The Long Voyage Home,* appeared in the October 1917 issue of the *Smart Set,* providing the playwright his first national exposure; the other two appeared soon after. Nathan championed O'Neill's work and played no small part in his rise to fame, though he could be the dramatist's harshest critic when he felt the occasion warranted it. In his review of *The First Man* (1921) he wrote that O'Neill "rolls up his sleeves and piles on the agony with the assiduity of a coalheaver. . . . He piles psychological and physical situation on situation until the structure topples over with a burlesque clatter."

Despite a loyal readership and undoubted influence (which extended to Mencken and Nathan's founding of several "louse" publications, as Mencken referred to them: *Parisienne* in 1915; *Saucy Stories* in 1916; and *Black Mask* in 1920), the *Smart Set* continued to experience economic difficulties. When Nathan and Mencken wrote a satiric "Répétition Générale" column about the recent funeral of President Warren G. Harding for the September 1923 issue, Warner learned about the piece while the issue was at press and demanded that it be withdrawn. Nathan and Mencken felt that Warner had broken his agreement to respect their editorial autonomy, and although they gave way to Warner's wishes, they sent out a broadside on 10 October

1923 announcing their resignation from the magazine.

Mencken was less than grieved over the end of his association with the *Smart Set,* which he had come to view as a trivial publication. He revived his and Nathan's "Blue Review" concept of a magazine with a deeper political and sociological consciousness than had been allowed in the "magazine of cleverness." After an abortive attempt by the publisher Alfred A. Knopf to buy the *Smart Set,* Mencken persuaded Knopf to underwrite a new magazine and then convinced a somewhat reluctant Nathan to continue their editorial partnership. An agreement was reached with Knopf whereby the pair would be coeditors and part owners of the publication.

There was some initial disagreement as to the title: Mencken wanted "Blue Review," but Knopf felt that the name was too "arty"; Nathan suggested "American Mercury," but Mencken thought that it would suggest that the magazine was imitative of the *Mercure de France* or the *Mercurio Peruano.* Knopf liked Nathan's suggestion, however, and Mencken warmed up to the title. Manuscripts were solicited, and the first issue of the *American Mercury* appeared in January 1924.

Friction quickly developed between Mencken and Nathan over the direction the new magazine should take: Nathan pushed for a literary emphasis, while Mencken was interested in satiric social and political commentary. These differences in editorial temperament had occasioned good-natured debates between the two men in the pages of the *Smart Set,* but they took on a deeper significance as Mencken tried to forge the *American Mercury* into a forum for his unique style of social commentary. When O'Neill offered *All God's Chillun Got Wings* to Nathan for publication in the *American Mercury,* Nathan considered the manuscript an editorial godsend; but Mencken felt that the play was inappropriate for the magazine. Nathan pushed for its publication, Knopf backed him, and O'Neill's play appeared in the February 1924 issue. This episode infuriated Mencken, who became increasingly critical of Nathan. Mencken claimed that he was performing a larger share of editorial duties than his partner and furthermore felt that Nathan's interests were too narrow for the needs of the *American Mercury.* Mencken finally offered Knopf two options: either he would continue as sole editor or resign his editorial post and continue as a contributor only. Knopf recognized that the *American Mercury* was really Mencken's forum and asked for Nathan's resignation, which was submitted on 8 November 1924 and announced in the February 1925 issue. Nathan continued to write drama criticism and the regular "Clinical Notes" section for the *American Mercury* until he sold his percentage in the magazine back to Knopf and Mencken in March 1930.

Nathan kept busy in the meantime. He began contributing a regular column on the theater to *Judge* in 1922 and to *Vanity Fair* in 1930. Also, in the late 1920s and early 1930s the drama critic was regularly seen in the company of Lillian Gish. He introduced her to many of the literary celebrities of the day, including Fitzgerald, O'Neill, Theodore Dreiser, and Sherwood Anderson. In his *Vanity Fair* column Nathan gave Gish a rave review for her performance as Helena in a production of Anton Chekhov's *Uncle Vanya.* He proposed to the actress on more than one occasion, but she steadfastly turned him down. She later commented in her autobiography, "I will always be grateful that I did not marry George and spoil his life."

The year 1932 was a busy one for Nathan. In March the theater manager M. L. Erlanger, with the help of Congressman William Sirovic of New York, threatened to serve Nathan and other "offensive critics" with subpoenas to appear before a congressional committee. Erlanger blamed Nathan's often-caustic reviews for a serious slump in theater attendance, though the Depression was a more likely culprit. Nathan stood his ground, refusing to soften his reviews, and the incident soon blew over.

Also in 1932, besides writing his regular drama columns for *Vanity Fair* and *Judge,* Nathan became one of the founding editors of the *American Spectator* along with Dreiser, O'Neill, Ernest Boyd, and James Branch Cabell. The tabloid-sized monthly obviously drew on its eighteenth-century British namesake, Joseph Addison and Richard Steele's *Spectator,* for inspiration and was made up of short essays and opinion pieces with a strong literary flavor, written by the periodical's editors as well as by other contributors.

A disdain for partisanship or concern with the topical pervades the opening editorial:

> The *American Spectator* has no policy in the common sense of the word. It advocates no panaceas; it has no axes to grind; it has no private list of taboos. It offers an opportunity for the untrammelled expression of individual opinion, ignoring what is accepted and may be taken for granted in favor of the unaccepted and misunderstood.... Its aim is to offer a medium for the truly valuable and adventurous in thought, and to invite contributions from every quarter where stimulating opinions may be expected. Clarity, vigor and humor are the three indispensable qualities which must inform the presentation of its ideas.

Nathan with Julie Haydon, whom he met in 1944 and married in 1955

The first issue included "Aesthetes' Progress," by Boyd; "The Physician and Sex," by Havelock Ellis; "English and American Publishers," by Frank Swinnerton; "The Lor and the Profits," by Ring Lardner; "The Irish Censorship," by Liam O'Flaherty; "The Theater," by Nathan; and "The Genteel Tradition in Sex," by Cabell. All of the pieces are brief and polished; the vast majority focus on art or literature rather than on social concerns.

Besides the monthly editorial column, the regular "departments" of the *American Spectator* consisted of short, boxed items and squibs. They bore such headings as "Worst Book of the Month," which in the first issue read in its entirety: "CHAUCER. By G. K. Chesterton. 9 x 5 3/4. Pp. 302. 12/6. London: Faber & Faber." Other such filler departments were "Servants of God," brief news items concerning clergy caught in embarrassing or criminal situations; "American Jurisprudence"; "English Men of Letters Series"; and "Literati," quotations of inept comments by the intellectual elite.

The *American Spectator* has sometimes been dismissed by critics as a pale imitation of the *American Mercury;* but, although the satiric aspects and certain departments of the *Spectator* resemble those of its predecessor, the later publication creates a unique tone. A comparison of the *Mercury* with the *Spectator* reveals the related but distinct editorial approaches of Mencken and Nathan: whereas the former magazine usually invokes a literate voice to comment satirically on the foibles of the society and politics of its day, the latter typically uses items in the news – when it deigns to notice them at all – as excuses for irreverent literary composition, as in Nathan's "Motion Picture Censorship" in the October 1934 issue. Though the piece ostensibly addresses a topical issue, Nathan turns it into an aesthetic condemnation of the movie as an art form that is found sadly wanting when held to anything resembling a classical standard: "How the intelligence of a public is to be affronted and how its cultural rights are to be invalidated by eliminating from the movies scenes in which Mr. James Cagney pinches his old grandmother on the bottom . . . I should like the anticensorship crusaders, including those with whom in other directions I am whole-heartedly affiliated, to explain to me." Nathan's argument is overwhelmingly aesthetic rather than ethical in its focus; its central point is that "there is a whale of a difference between reputable literature, reputable drama and even reputable motion pictures on the one hand, and foul money-grubbing dung on the other." Generally speaking, then, the editorial voice of the *American Mercury* focused on the contemporary social context while the *American Spectator* was primarily interested in literary creation, though both positioned themselves in ironic opposition to the status quo.

Nathan would describe his nontopical approach to editing in "On Monthly Magazines," which appeared in *The World of George Jean Nathan* (1952): "The curse of timeliness has laid its heavy hand on magazine editing, with the result that a magazine which in an earlier era could be read with satisfaction some months after its publication date presently becomes flat and stale a few days after it appears . . . a magazine worth its salt should forego the common editorial preoccupation with journalistic immediacy and devote itself instead to those materials of art and life that . . . deepen, whether seriously or lightly, a reader's understanding of his surroundings, of himself, and of his fellows."

The March 1935 issue carried an "Editorial Announcement" noting the cessation of the *American Spectator:* "we told you . . . in our first editorial that when and if we got tired of the job, which . . . had only a little belletristic diversion in view, we would, as we expressed it, 'retire to our estates.' Well, we are tired of the job, although it has been a lot of fun. . . . So we are merrily concluding our performance." The *American Spectator* reappeared in June 1935 under different editorship; Nathan's association with the magazine had ended, and he would never again take on an editorial role in a periodical publication. His drama criticism, however, appeared regularly throughout the late 1930s, the 1940s, and the 1950s in several major magazines, including *Esquire,* the *Saturday Review of Literature, Scribner's, Newsweek,* the *American Mercury, Liberty,* and *Theatre Arts;* he also wrote a nationally syndicated column for King Features from 1943 to 1956. Nathan served as president of the New York Drama Critics Circle from 1937 to 1939 and produced *The Theatre Book of the Year* from 1943 to 1951.

In 1944 Nathan met the actress Julie Haydon at rehearsals of Tennessee Williams's *The Glass Menagerie* at the Chicago Civic Theater, and they began a relationship. In the summer of 1953 he received an honorary doctor of letters degree from Indiana University; with a mixture of irony and delight, he wrote in July to Mencken's brother, August, "You may now address me as Herr Doktor." But balancing such pleasurable experiences was Nathan's worsening health in the late 1940s and early 1950s, when he frequently suffered from the effects of arteriosclerosis. On 19 June 1955 Nathan, who had for many years touted the pleasures of bachelorhood and the miseries of wedded life, married Haydon in a private ceremony on board the Grace Line's S.S. *Santa Rosa.* On 7 April 1958, less than three months after H. L. Mencken's death, Nathan suffered a severe stroke. He requested and received Catholic last rites, and he died in his wife's arms at 12:15 the following morning.

The bulk of Nathan's literary career was devoted to the theater, and he would no doubt be pleased that his reputation rests mostly on his drama criticism and its influence. But his career as a magazine editor, easy to overlook in the more enduring editorial impact of his longtime partner, deserves more than passing attention. In their days at the *Smart Set* Nathan and Mencken were indeed a team – in fact, if either exerted a stronger editorial presence during the latter days of that publication, it was probably Nathan – and the influence of the "aristocrat among magazines" on the literary community of its day was enormous. Nathan proved he could still exert an entertaining editorial presence in the pages of the *American Spectator;* but by that time the "toy" had begun to lose its luster, and Nathan abandoned it to devote his time to writing about theater – the game he loved most. In the final analysis, Nathan's approach to editing, as he summed it up in "On Monthly Magazines," was not so different from his approach to drama criticism: "To view the world of life and art with intelligence and humor, to avoid indignation and platitude, and to keep uppermost in mind good writing – that, as I see it, should be an editor's credo."

References:

Carl R. Dolmetsch, *The Smart Set: A History and Anthology* (New York: Dial, 1966);

George H. Douglas, *The Smart Magazines: 50 Years of Revelry at* Vanity Fair, The New Yorker, Life, Esquire, *and* The Smart Set (Hamden, Conn.: Archon, 1991), pp. 9-91;

Constance Frick, *The Dramatic Criticism of George Jean Nathan* (Ithaca, N.Y.: Cornell University Press, 1943);

Lillian Gish, *The Movies, Mr. Griffith, and Me* (Englewood Cliffs, N.J.: Prentice-Hall, 1969), pp. 338-339;

Isaac Goldberg, *The Theatre of George Jean Nathan* (New York: Simon & Schuster, 1926);

Burton Rascoe, "'Smart Set' History," in *The Smart Set Anthology,* edited by Rascoe and Groff Conklin (New York: Reynal & Hitchcock, 1934), pp. xiii–xliv.

Papers:

The principal collection of George Jean Nathan's papers is the Nathan Collection at Cornell University; others are in the Manuscripts Department of the Library of Princeton University and the Beinecke Library of Americana at Yale University.

George Washington Ochs-Oakes

(27 October 1861 - 26 October 1931)

Whitney R. Mundt
Louisiana State University

MAJOR POSITIONS HELD: Managing editor (1879–1896), general manager, *Chattanooga Times* (1896–1900); publisher, Paris edition of the *New York Times* (1900); general manager, *Philadelphia Times* (1901); publisher and general manager, *Philadelphia Public Ledger* (1902–1915); editor, *Mid-Week Pictorial* (1915–1923); editor, *Current History* (1915–1931).

BOOKS: *Hamilton County, Tennessee, Together with a Brief Resume of the Growth and Resources of Chattanooga, Tenn.* (Chattanooga: Times Printing Co., 1889);

Chattanooga and Hamilton County, Tennessee (Chattanooga: Committee of Chattanooga and Hamilton County, 1897);

The Life and Letters of George Washington Ochs-Oakes, arranged and edited by William M. Schuyler (New York: privately printed, 1933).

PERIODICAL PUBLICATIONS: "Journalism," *Annals of the American Academy of Political and Social Sciences,* 28 (July 1906): 38–57;

"Monroe Doctrine," *Current History,* 5 (October 1916): 54–63;

"Titanic Struggle in Picardy," *Current History,* 5 (October 1916): 16–19;

"Dangerous Plight of Greece," *Current History,* 5 (November 1916): 234–236;

"United States Policy Toward Latin-American Republics," *Current History,* 18 (May 1923): 188–190;

"Is Official Censorship of Books Desirable?" *Congressional Digest,* 9 (February 1930): 52–54.

Though he labored always in the shadow of his brother, George Ochs-Oakes accomplished enough to fill two lifetimes. At various times he served as general manager of the *Chattanooga Times, Philadelphia Times,* and *Philadelphia Public Ledger.* But he excelled as editor of *Current History.* All of these publications were owned by his brother Adolph

George Washington Ochs-Oakes

Ochs, founder in 1896 of the modern *New York Times.*

George Washington Ochs was born in 1861, three years after Adolph. There were three boys and three girls in the Ochs family, sons and daughters of Julius and Bertha Ochs, natives of Germany who had immigrated to America in the 1840s. When George was born, his father was serving with the Union forces guarding the railroad between Cincinnati, Ohio, and Saint Louis, Missouri, and he directed that the newborn child should be named George Washington, after the first president of the United States.

After the war the family moved from Cincinnati to Knoxville, Tennessee, where George, at the age of seven, delivered the *Knoxville Chronicle,* working from 4 until 7 A.M. each day. He supplemented the family income in this way through his junior year at East Tennessee University, when he moved with the family to Chattanooga. He had distinguished himself academically at the university, and in 1880 he was awarded his degree from the newly named University of Tennessee despite having completed only three years of study there.

Adolph Ochs had purchased the *Chattanooga Daily Times* in 1878, and after George completed his third year at the university, he became a reporter at his brother's paper. In his memoirs he relates that newspaper life in Chattanooga was a rough-and-tumble affair in those post–Civil War days when the town's population numbered only twelve thousand or so, about one-third black. Twice he was forced to draw his weapon in self-defense, and on one of those occasions he shot his assailant. Journalistically he acquitted himself well, succeeding his brother as general manager in 1896, when Adolph purchased the *New York Times* and moved to that city to compete with Joseph Pulitzer, Joseph Gordon Bennett, and other press lords in the metropolis.

During his tenure with the *Chattanooga Times,* George Ochs was active politically, reportedly in spite of his brother's objections. In 1891 he was appointed police commissioner of Chattanooga, and the following year he was chosen as a delegate to the Democratic National Convention in Chicago, where he seconded the nomination of Grover Cleveland for president. In 1893 he was elected mayor of Chattanooga, and in 1895 he was reelected for a second two-year term. During this period he was no longer directing news coverage of the *Chattanooga Times;* instead, he had been placed in charge of a biweekly auxiliary publication, an industrial magazine called the *Tradesman.* But in 1896 he became general manager of the *Times* while continuing to serve as mayor. George declined to run for a third term in that office, but a few months after he stepped down, he was elected to the board of education and served as its president until 1900. In 1899 he became president of the Chattanooga Chamber of Commerce, resigning the following year in order to assist Adolph with a plan to promote the *New York Times.*

Adolph Ochs had originally acquired the failing newspaper in an unusual arrangement: he proposed that *Times* stock should be held in escrow, to be given to him if he could turn a profit within four years. By the end of 1899 the stock was released to him. Adolph had turned the paper into a success by introducing a new formula in the world of sensational New York journalism – "All the News That's Fit to Print" – and by cutting the price from three cents to a penny. As a result the *Times* multiplied its circulation by a factor of eight and began turning a handsome profit.

In 1900 Adolph hit upon another scheme to advance the fortunes of the *Times.* He summoned his brother from Chattanooga and proposed that George travel to Paris to publish a daily edition of the *New York Times* at the Paris Exposition. For eight months that year, six days each week, George published a ten- to fourteen-page edition of the paper in the American Pavilion, in full view of thousands of visitors each day. He used an octuple Goss press, the largest on the continent, and six Linotypes, mechanical marvels which had been invented by Ottmar Mergenthaler only four years earlier. The Paris edition was a great success, and after George returned to Chattanooga in December, he learned that he had been nominated by the president of France to receive the Cross of the Chevalier of the Legion of Honor for his efforts at the Paris Exposition.

George had served his brother well in both Chattanooga and in Paris, and a few months after the exposition ended, Adolph asked George to become general manager of the *Philadelphia Times,* which he had purchased on 7 May 1901. The following year Adolph acquired the *Philadelphia Public Ledger,* and he merged the two papers. George became publisher and general manager of the consolidated newspaper. In his memoirs he relates, with apparent pride, that during his fourteen years with the newspapers in Philadelphia he refrained from political activity. Considering George's extensive political involvement in Chattanooga and the intensity of Adolph's opposition to it (he reportedly refused to vote for George in the mayoral election), it is probable that Adolph offered the position in Philadelphia to George on the condition that he stay out of politics. But he used the pages of the *Public Ledger* for political purposes: the paper led a campaign to oust the "machine politicians" from city government in 1911. It wholeheartedly supported a reform candidate for mayor and suffered the loss of considerable advertising revenue as a result.

Under George Ochs's direction the *Public Ledger* was profitable, and in 1911 Cyrus H. K. Curtis approached George with a proposal to buy the paper. He persuaded Adolph to relinquish ownership for $2 million and an agreement that George would remain as publisher for two years. He believed that the enormous resources of the Curtis Publishing Company, which at that time owned the *Ladies' Home Journal* and the *Saturday Evening Post,* would benefit the *Public Ledger.* The sale was com-

THE BOARD OF ASSOCIATES IN CURRENT HISTORY

ALBERT BUSHNELL HART
ALBERT HOWE LYBYER
W. STEARNS DAVIS
WILLIAM R. SHEPHERD
ARTHUR LYON CROSS
HARRY T. COLLINGS
PAYSON J. TREAT
FREDERIC A. OGG
RICHARD H. DABNEY
LILY ROSS TAYLOR
A. PETRUNKEVITCH
CHARLES W. HACKETT

The members of the Faculties of twelve leading American universities forming the group of historians who are contributing to CURRENT HISTORY *the Monthly Survey of World Events*

Page from the November 1923 issue of Current History, *featuring the first appearance of the twelve-member board of associates instituted by Ochs-Oakes*

pleted on 1 January 1913, and immediately thereafter Curtis began a program of expenditure and promotion similar to that with which he had built his magazines. But this kind of spending was alien to George Ochs's nature, and as soon as his two-year contract period had expired, he resigned.

He was not out of work for long: on 1 July 1915, six months after his resignation from the *Public Ledger,* Adolph asked George to come to New York and take charge of two magazines published by the *New York Times:* the *New York Times Current History* and *Mid-Week Pictorial.* George moved to New York with his two small sons to begin another episode in his career. He had married Bertie Gans in 1907, but she had died in 1913 following the birth of their second child. John Bertram Ochs was two when the family moved to New York; George Washington Ochs, Jr., was almost six. Upon the death of their mother, their unmarried aunt Nannie came to care for them. She was the oldest of George's three sisters, one year older than he was.

When George moved to New York in the summer of 1915, he entered the world of magazine journalism – a world vastly different from the daily news gathering he had known. *Current History* had been founded by his brother Adolph in December 1914 under the title the *New York Times Current History of the European War,* and it was intended to provide in-depth coverage of the war that had begun that summer. *Mid-Week Pictorial* had been started in September, as a weekly, in order to provide visual coverage of the war through photographs, maps, and cartoons. Several years after the war it was transferred from George Ochs's control to the Wide World Photograph Department of the Times Company, and it remained a Times Company property until it was sold to Monte Bourjaily in October 1936. Bourjaily apparently was unable to compete with the fabulously successful *Life* magazine, and *Mid-Week Pictorial* met its demise in February 1937.

Current History, on the other hand, is still being published, although it, too, was sold by the Times Company in 1936. A large measure of credit for the magazine's longevity must be given to George Ochs. *Current History* was established as "a repository for the official and authentic records of the War." But when the war ended, Ochs enlarged the scope of the publication so that the magazine became a more comprehensive contemporary historical record, including articles on international politics, sociology, economics, and literature. As editor, Ochs developed a board of associates consisting of twelve historians, each from a different university. Each one was assigned a specific region of the world and wrote an article each month about significant events occuring in that region. This section of the magazine was intended as "an objective, trustworthy, impartial and authoritative survey of the history of the world, month by month," according to Ochs. The rest of the magazine was devoted to articles dealing with other aspects of contemporary history.

World War I was, of course, the most outstanding development in world events during Ochs's tenure as editor from 1915 to 1931. It was especially traumatic to him because of his German descent; he was filled with revulsion that Germans were committing such barbarities as the sinking of the *Lusitania.* In 1917, therefore, he petitioned the court for permission to anglicize his name by adding the suffix "Oakes." Henceforth he was known as George Washington Ochs-Oakes. Other members of the Ochs family were reportedly insulted by George's action. In his petition he stipulated that while he would continue to be recognized by the hyphenated version of his name, his sons were to be known as George Washington Oakes, Jr., and John Bertram Oakes. Ochs-Oakes also attempted to enlist when war was declared by the United States, but at fifty-five he was considered too old for active duty. He managed to enlist in the National Guard and served for the duration of the war as a private, taking part in weekly drills and other military training. He was honorably discharged the day after the armistice was signed.

Under his tutelage *Current History* grew in circulation. Chief among the reasons for this success was Ochs-Oakes's innovative device of the monthly survey of the history of the world. But he was also successful in luring well-known contributors to the sections of the journal: H. G. Wells was published in *Current History,* as were Rudyard Kipling, John Galsworthy, Arthur Conan Doyle, and such journalists as Bruce Bliven, Ernest K. Lindley, and Raymond B. Clapper. The greatest surge in circulation – from about thirty-eight thousand to eighty thousand – took place in 1924 when Ochs-Oakes reduced the price from thirty-five to twenty-five cents per copy.

During the period of the magazine's greatest success, Ochs-Oakes was active in public affairs. He served three terms as president of the Civitan Club of New York, was elected president of the Chattanooga Society in New York, and was elected president of the Tennessee Society in New York. He served four terms as historian of the Camp of Sons of Confederate Veterans. (He was eligible because members of his mother's family had served with the Confederacy.) And New York governor Alfred E. Smith appointed him one of three state commissioners for the Sesqui-Centennial Exposition at Philadelphia. In addition he had enrolled at Columbia University to pursue a Ph.D. in history. He had accumulated fifty-four of the required sixty course credits through study from 1925 to 1931. He had intended to complete the course work and to write his dissertation in 1932 in order to receive his degree before his seventy-first birthday.

On the eve of his seventieth birthday, however, while recovering in the hospital from surgery, Ochs-Oakes suffered an embolism and died suddenly. Funeral services were held on 28 October in the chapel of Temple Emanu-El, with Rabbi H. G. Enelow presiding. His body was buried beside that of his wife in Mount Sinai Cemetery in Frankford, Pennsylvania.

Public tributes testified to the esteem in which Ochs-Oakes was held. President Herbert Hoover wrote that he "prized his friendship and mourned his loss as a friend and a splendid American." Sen. Cordell Hull observed that "No person cherished a more intense devotion to his fellow-men, nor worshiped at the shrine of unalloyed patriotism more devotedly than he." Professor Albert Bushnell Hart of Harvard University called him "the prince of goodfellows" and added, "Editor he was from brain to pencil point." Clark Howell, editor of the *Atlanta Constitution,* called *Current History,* under Ochs-Oakes's editorial hand, "the leading historical digest and commentary of this country." Former senator W. E. Brock focused on his integrity, saying, "His whole life has been an open book and was such that no one could question his motives."

References:

"In Memoriam: George W. Ochs-Oakes," *Current History,* 35 (December 1931): 322–324, 485–500;

Gay Talese, *The Kingdom and the Power* (New York: World, 1969).

Edwin Hill ("Ted") Patrick

(3 September 1901 – 11 March 1964)

Kathryn News
Temple University

MAJOR POSITIONS HELD: Copywriter, Young & Rubicam (1928–1942); chief, graphics section, Office of War Information (1942–1944); vice-president, Compton Advertising (1944–1946); editor, *Holiday* (1946–1964).

BOOKS: *Great Restaurants of America,* by Patrick and Silas Spitzer (New York: Bramhall House / Philadelphia: Lippincott, 1960);

The Thinking Dog's Man (New York: Random House, 1964).

OTHER: *Holiday Book of the World's Fine Foods,* introduction by Patrick (New York: Simon & Schuster, 1956);

World's Fine Food, introduction by Patrick (New York: Simon & Schuster, 1960);

Holiday Guides, introductions by Patrick (New York: Random House, 1960–1964);

Ludwig Bemelmans, *Italian Holiday,* foreword by Patrick (New York: Houghton Mifflin, 1961);

The World of Mankind, introduction by Patrick (New York: Golden Press, 1962).

SELECTED PERIODICAL PUBLICATIONS – UNCOLLECTED: "Tennis Enchanted," *Holiday,* 14 (September 1953): 70–72+;

"Italian Food Afloat," *Holiday,* 25 (June 1959): 98–102+;

"Cairo," *Holiday,* 26 (July 1959): 26+;

"*Holiday* Handbook of American Restaurants," by Patrick and Silas Spitzer, *Holiday,* 28 (July 1960): 107–116;

"Ischia: A Muddy Cure," *Holiday,* 33 (January 1963): 20+.

Ted Patrick

Edwin Hill ("Ted") Patrick, editor of *Holiday* magazine from 1946 until his death in 1964, was respected internationally for his editorial leadership, for his exquisite taste, and for the remarkable success of the handsome travel/lifestyle magazine he created for the Curtis Publishing Company. Patrick combined an astute marketing sense with refined editorial and managerial skills to sculpt *Holiday* into a literary and artistic showcase. Capitalizing on the rapidly expanding travel industry of the postwar era, he presented, to a leisure-hungry American public, the exotic sights and delights a shrinking world could bring. In the nation's eager return to peacetime pursuits, Patrick's vision of "the good life, the good times" (a *Holiday* slogan) portrayed a tasteful, accessible, and rewarding cosmopolitan life; armchair travelers participated vicariously in the charming intellectual and cultural discoveries of V. S. Pritchett, E. B. White, Clifton Fadiman, Laurens Van der Post, and Joyce Cary, while the growing numbers of active globe-trotters found a lavish guide to the finest travel and lifestyle experiences available. Patrick's eighteen-year expedition with *Holiday* charted a new type of publication that presaged the scope of travel magazines to follow.

Patrick's achievements brought this "natty, 44-year-old, slightly greying Manhattan Adman" (as *Time* described him soon after he joined *Holiday*) some rare awards. As early as 1955 the Italian government named him Commandatore Ufficiali dell' Ordine al Merito for "outstanding contributions" to America's knowledge of Italy. France decorated him in 1957 as Chevalier de la Légion d'Honneur. Secretary of Commerce Luther H. Hodges cited the magazine for its "distinguished reputation as an interpreter of the world and its people."

Patrick, world traveler, gourmet, oenophile, and jazz buff, came to Curtis (publisher of *Saturday Evening Post*, *Ladies' Home Journal*, and *Country Gentleman*) after a career in advertising, initially to develop "project X," a pictorial weekly to compete with *Life*. That plan was soon abandoned, and Patrick was assigned to *Holiday*. His personality reshaped the magazine, and the magazine permeated his life. When someone asked how many hours he spent working, Patrick said, "Just about everything I do relates to *Holiday*." His leisure pursuits – travel, fine dining, tennis (he purportedly played a "better than fair" game), breeding champion Airedale terriers, watching baseball, enjoying good company – all translated into his periodical as a portrait for living well. Guided by a sharp eye for quality and a fine talent for visual and print communication, he forged what was then a four-month-old, unfocused travel magazine into a handsome, internationally respected package of superb photography and prose – a sophisticated presentation of the finest artists, writers, and photographers of the time. Names such as Nathaniel Benchley, Ludwig Bemelmans, John Steinbeck, James Michener, Saul Bellow, Truman Capote, Arnold Newman, Slim Aarons, John Lewis Stage, Henri Cartier-Bresson, Al Hirshfield, and James Thurber graced the pages of *Holiday*.

Patrick was born on 3 September 1901 to John and Rita Alyea Hill, into a middle-class Rutherford, New Jersey, family of Irish descent. He had two brothers, Arthur and Garrabrant. He attended public schools and never went to college. But as a young man he played semiprofessional baseball, and that athletic prowess led to a job as sportswriter for the *Rutherford Republican*. In 1928 Patrick was hired by the Young and Rubicam advertising agency – by accident, according to Draper Daniels. Reportedly, Lou Green, manager of the copy department, was in a hurry to leave on vacation and told his assistant to hire "that young man from New Jersey who played ball" – meaning another applicant. Patrick was called in and when asked how much pay he would need, timidly said "sixty-five," meaning dollars per week. Hired at sixty-five hundred dollars a year, he could not believe his first paycheck. It took him three months to figure out what had happened, and he would not mention the matter until years later, after he had become a stockholder and one of the company's better-paid executives.

On 11 February 1929 Patrick married Vera Yereance, a union that would last for thirty-four years. Advancing professionally, he became president of the Ad Council, an organization that contributed public service ads for various nonprofit organizations. During the 1930s Patrick volunteered his skills for World Peaceways, writing emotional pacifist copy for their publicity campaigns: one poster that ran in national magazines showed a steel-helmeted skeleton labeled "Cornfed Kid from the West." But from 1942 to 1944 Patrick was working as chief of graphics for the Office of War Information, responsible for all printed material. He also assisted with setting up British psychological warfare training units and by the war's end had zigzagged across the world. The places he saw and the people he met broadened his views. From 1944 to 1946 he worked as vice-president and director of Compton Advertising, before joining Curtis and beginning his long career with *Holiday*.

As with Harold Ross at the *New Yorker* or Arnold Gingrich at *Esquire*, Patrick's magazine was an extension of the man: handsome, cosmopolitan, engaged in a gentlemanly pursuit of quality, a chronicler of good taste – but with humor, wit, and occasional touches of irony. Patrick simply created a magazine that reflected his own personal interests and aspirations. Garth Hite, a *Holiday* staffer during Patrick's editorship and later publisher of the magazine, related in an unpublished interview that Patrick "never permitted 'packaging' or 'marketing' to enter the editorial prerogative – a rarity then and an unknown dimension now."

The success of *Holiday* was due also to the extraordinary people Patrick gathered around him: art director Frank Zachary (later editor of *Town &*

Cover for the first issue to appear after Patrick's assumption of the editorship

Country), editorial director Harry Sions, picture editor Louis Mercier, assistant to the editor Al Farnsworth, senior editor James Cerruti (later with *National Geographic*), and other prestigious names. Patrick was a creditable writer, but as with other distinguished editors, his greater talent lay in the ability to recognize and attract top professional talent – men and women who generated quality elements to be blended into a many-faceted, finely honed presentation of complementary tones and styles. He gave his staff both the freedom and the support they needed for creative work; in turn they gave the magazine a cohesive, contagious energy.

Patrick and his staff thus obtained work from some of the most notable writers of the period. Steinbeck's *Travels With Charlie* (1962) originated with an assignment from *Holiday. Ten Years of Holiday* (1956) contains "a Nobel Laureate, several Pulitzer Prize winners, and a double handful of the crack stylists of our day," wrote Fadiman in his introduction. The collection includes White's "Here is New York," Cleveland Amory's "High Society, U.S.A.," Cary's "The Heart of England," Roger Angell's "Baseball – the Perfect Game," among other pieces of lasting literary merit. *Holiday* editors found they could elicit authoritative copy with a strong sense of place by commissioning fiction writers to write about their homes, thus creating a series of memorable articles such as Capote on "My Years in Brooklyn," Bellow on "My Illinois Journey," Ernest Hemingway on Cuba, A. B. Guthrie on Montana, and William Faulkner on Mississippi. More surprising, however, was the inclusion of Yukio Mishima, unknown at that time, and many other young, new artists and writers brought into the *Holiday* format by Sions and Zachary.

Holiday became known for developing a personal essay style, a casual, reflective, descriptive response to places, experiences, life – but tempered with a light touch, the wit and charm of lively minds. Fadiman saw in it a "new kind of American journalism in which editor, publisher and advertising manager cheerfully relinquish some of their triune omnipotence . . . to get the writer to produce the best he has in him, on the theory that you must give him his head before you can get him to use it." This appreciation for the process of individual creativity set Patrick apart and, perhaps more than any other attribute, made him distinctive. His modus operandi – a true professional recognizes the professionalism of others – brought him a dedicated staff, passionate in their devotion to their magazine and their editor.

In his editing style, however, Patrick was not, Hite says, as detail-oriented as Gingrich or Ross. He relied largely on his staff for ideas, almost exclusively for manuscript processing and production. In the office Patrick kept somewhat apart, rarely dealing directly with office workers. He often let the staff interpret the magazine to the advertising people and outsiders and refused to permit the magazine to be pigeon-holed as a "travel" publication. This policy position resulted from limited travel-ad revenue potential. Patrick, not a sloganeer, was extremely touchy about promotion efforts and reluctantly approved the subtitle "The Magazine of Constructive Leisure," used mostly in promotional literature. Farnsworth says, "The only slogan we thought came close was 'The magazine of people, places and pleasures.' " Travel, for Patrick, represented much more than a pursuit of personal pleasure. It became a broadening of knowledge and understanding, an appreciation of true values, with considerations of survival hovering overhead – "travel of the mind as well as the body," Patrick called it. In 1963 Patrick wrote that *Holiday* had "evolved tremendously, . . . getting farther and farther away from the image of just a travel magazine.

JAPAN: JOURNEY THROUGH A FLOATING WORLD

BY LAURENS VAN DER POST

PHOTOGRAPHS BY BURT GLINN

● My journey to Japan took me first to its head, Tokyo, then to its heart, Kyoto, and only after that to its body. The historic approach would have been from the south by sea, landing far from Tokyo at one of the ports of Kyushu, the southernmost of the four main islands of Japan. That is the direction from which the Portuguese, the first Europeans to discover Japan, came in 1542, and for nearly four centuries this remained the main route between the West and Japan. What is more, that, too, may have been the way the Japanese, or at least the subtle Yamato core of their race, so mysterious and remote in its origin, came to their land in some dim stone-age day. But time and distance, those terrible enemies of mortal intentions, compelled me to do this journey by air.

I had only one consolation. As these misgivings assailed me in a jet plane, forty thousand feet up in a Bible-black night and approaching Tokyo at a speed of more than 500 miles an hour, I reminded myself that once, many years before, I had followed history to Japan in a way that few people of my generation had done.

Japan was the first country I had known outside Africa. In 1926, just before Emperor Hirohito began his fateful reign, I sailed for Japan in a Japanese ship, the *Canada Maru*. I sailed from Durban, the chief port on that part of the southeast coast of Africa—which the great and terrible Vasco da Gama christened Natal when he first set eyes on it, on Christmas Day, 1497, during his voyage of discovery to India—and many weeks later came to anchor in the roadstead of the straits of Shimonoseki at the entrance to the Inland Sea of Japan. It was then slightly more than two generations after Commodore Perry's black ships had forced Japan to abandon its determined policy of isolation and to open itself to commerce and intercourse with Europe and America.

Continued on Page 56

ON THE INLAND SEA, near Onomichi, a fishing boat drifts in fog. Prawns, octopus and sole are plentiful here. The reeds have been set up to gather seaweed.

IN THE HILLS of Shikoku, the smallest of Japan's four main islands (opposite), wheat fields make a formalized pattern. Some of the terraces are centuries old.

54

Pages from an October 1961 article in Holiday *by one of Patrick's regular contributors*

In this complex world today, everybody is traveling, and we try to tell them about this world from an international, intellectual point of view – whether it's in a story about Iran, the Ford family, or the United Nations."

Patrick and his restaurant critic, Silas Spitzer, were experienced gourmets (most of the finest restaurants worldwide had served them) who wrote enthusiastically about meritorious dining adventures. Their gustatory delights served the magazine financially as well as editorially. In a brilliant move to spark advertising in spare summer issues, they instituted, in 1952 at Spellman's suggestion, the *Holiday* Fine Dining Awards program, an annual listing of top restaurants in America and, later, Europe. A network of "spies" visited recommended restaurants at least three times before those deemed worthy could be included in what became the most prestigious such listing to that time. Restaurateurs vied for the award. Recipients proudly hung the elegant gold-embossed certificate, with the crest of crossed knife and fork under a chef's hat, in the lobbies of their well-appointed establishments. Restaurants achieved instant popularity on receipt of the award; getting dropped from the listing portended dire futures. But award winners or not, they advertised – as did wine and liquor interests. Readers planning trips eagerly awaited the announcements – and ordered thousands of copies of the separately published *Guide to Fine Dining*. Overall, the program became a solid income producer for Curtis and provided immeasurable publicity value that continued long after Patrick's death.

Patrick represents some intriguing paradoxes: a world traveler and bon vivant, he remained a quiet, somewhat introverted man, devoted to his wife Vera, his dogs, and his tennis. While he wrote peace propaganda between the wars, from 1942 to 1944 he worked for the Office of War Information, and assisted with setting up British psychological warfare training schools. A man of exceptional marketing abilities, he forcefully withstood publisher pressures throughout his career. A man who rose up through advertising, he was adamant about maintaining absolute separation of editorial and advertising interests. Of the two positions, he preferred editing. He pointed out that an editor "doesn't have a client – that's the biggest difference

Cover for the fifteenth anniversary issue of Patrick's travel magazine, featuring a selection of previous covers

in the world. Your only client is the reader, and for that reason you can go directly to him."

Whether Patrick knew exactly what his readers wanted, as some claimed, or whether his approach attracted the kinds of readers that responded to his lifestyle, the magazine grew steadily, from four hundred thousand circulation when Patrick arrived, to a guaranteed circulation of one million. In *The Curtis Caper* (1965) Joseph C. Goulden reports that between 1955 and 1960 *Holiday* increased its annual revenue from $5,853,825 to $11,090,176, and its total advertising pages from 888.76 to 1,247.14. In Patrick's latter years *Holiday* was Curtis's only adult magazine to stay in the black, according to *Editor & Publisher* in March 1964.

But Curtis by then was in serious difficulty. When Patrick heard rumors of a reduced promotion budget and new editorial director Clay Blair, Jr.'s plan to dictate policy for all the company's magazines, he responded, "It's taken a lot of hard work and seventeen years to build *Holiday* into the magazine it is today. This is a 24-hour-a-day job. No one can tell me that he can edit the [*Saturday Evening*] *Post* from 9 to 11, the *Ladies' Home Journal* from 12 to 2, and *Holiday* from 3 to 5 and still do any justice to them. This kind of editing would be the kiss of death for *Holiday*." Blair quickly assured Patrick that "*Holiday* is one of the best magazines in the country . . . I don't intend to do anything. . . . *Holiday* is sailing along beautifully."

Patrick's goals translated not only onto the pages of his own magazine but into a lifetime effort for the achievement and protection of editorial integrity. The latter brought him respect in the industry, culminating, in September 1963, in his election as the first chairman of the American Society of Magazine Editors (ASME). It was an organization he had helped establish with Edward Weeks, editor of the *Atlantic Monthly,* and Dan Mich, editor of *Look.* Their goals were to give editors strength among magazine executives, to provide a professional forum and voice, to raise standards and quality of schools of journalism and writing, and to develop public-relations programs of long-range benefit. (ASME continues to thrive as the leading professional organization for magazine editors.)

Nevertheless, the deteriorating financial situation and well-documented corporate contortions and power struggles at Curtis eroded the health of *Holiday* and, perhaps, its editor. Despite his magnificent and often successful efforts to ward off encroachments, efforts that earned him the adoration of his staff, publishing pressures intensified. When Curtis asked Patrick's friend David Ogilvy of Ogilvy, Benson, and Mather to write an advertising tribute to Patrick as a promotional gesture, he grabbed the opportunity. Ogilvy wrote the copy himself, got eleven of the largest ad agencies to undersign it, and on 21 January 1964 placed a full-page "ad-tribute" in the *New York Times,* entitled, "An open letter to Ted Patrick from 12 of *Holiday*'s 3,263,000 readers." It read: "Dear Ted: Holiday is your baby. In 18 years as editor, you have produced 210 glorious issues. They get more glorious every year. We applaud your belief that 'an editor's only boss is the reader.' We applaud your indifference to the pressures of advertisers and the heckling of publishers. Month after month, year after year, you entertain and you enthrall us. You have pursued excellence, and you have achieved it. You are a great editor." Ogilvy intended, Goulden reports, to tell "those stupid, shallow jerks at Curtis . . . that if you fire [Patrick], we are not going to advertise with you. But you know, the people at Curtis were so damned dumb they didn't understand it!"

In October 1963, one month after Patrick's election as chair of ASME, his wife of thirty-four years died suddenly. This, and the bitter struggles at Curtis, some reports say, sapped his spirit, though Farnsworth insists that Patrick was never "a defeated man." On 8 March 1964 Patrick was rushed by ambulance to New York hospital, where he died three days later of infectious hepatitis.

The bitterness at Curtis subsequently intensified, but accolades for Patrick poured in. The publishing industry around the globe mourned his death, and the International Union of Official Travel Organizations, at a March 1964 meeting in Dublin, set aside a moment of silence in his honor. Sen. Hubert Humphrey presented a personal tribute to the Senate, recorded in the Congressional Record of 24 March 1964. The *New York Journal-American* called him a "genie to thousands of people he could never hope to meet. He gave them the magic carpet to faraway places they had neither the time nor the money to visit."

Patrick had overseen 215 issues of *Holiday.* His last signed article appeared in January 1963 and concerned the baths of the Mediterranean island Ischia. An obituary, written by his staff and published in the April issue, concluded, "Ted Patrick had charm, a brilliant and gallant spirit, a great heart and a gentle nature. We of his staff can only say again what others have said of him: he was a great editor."

References:

Martin Ackerman, *The Curtis Affair* (Los Angeles: Nash, 1970);

Matthew J. Culligan, *The Curtis-Culligan Story: From Cyrus to Horace to Joe* (New York: Crown, 1970);

Clifton Fadiman, *Party of Twenty* (New York: Simon & Schuster, 1963);

Otto Friedrich, *Decline and Fall: The Struggle for Power at a Great American Magazine, The Saturday Evening Post* (New York: Harper & Row, 1969);

Bruce and Beatrice Gould, *American Story* (New York: Harper & Row, 1968);

Joseph C. Goulden, *The Curtis Caper* (New York: Putnam, 1965);

"Grolier Gastronomy," *New Yorker,* 37 (26 February 1961): 25–26;

"*Holiday* Life," *Newsweek,* 62 (1 July 1963): 40–41;

"*Holiday* Troubles," *Time,* 48 (8 July 1946): 48;

Obituary in *Holiday,* 35 (May 1964): 37;

"Philadelphia Project," *Time,* 47 (25 February 1946): 58+;

"Portrait," *Business Week* (28 September 1946): 50.

William Phillips

(14 November 1907 -   )

Kenneth A. Robb
Bowling Green State University

MAJOR POSITIONS HELD: Editor, *Partisan Review* (1934-   ); chairman, Coordinating Council of Literary Magazines (1967-1975).

BOOKS: *Mental Health and Education,* by Phillips and Olive A. Wheeler (London: University of London Press, 1961);

A Sense of the Present (New York: Chilmark, 1967);

A Partisan View: Five Decades of the Literary Life (New York: Stein & Day, 1983).

OTHER: "Literature in a Political Decade," by Phillips and Philip Rahv, in *New Letters in America,* edited by Horace Gregory and Eleanor Clark (New York: Norton, 1937), pp. 172-180;

Great American Short Novels, edited by Phillips (New York: Dial, 1946);

The Partisan Reader: Ten Years of Partisan Review 1934-1944: An Anthology, edited by Phillips and Rahv (New York: Dial, 1946);

The Short Stories of Dostoevsky, edited by Phillips (New York: Dial, 1946);

The New Partisan Reader, 1945-1953, edited by Phillips and Rahv (New York: Harcourt, Brace, 1953);

The Berkley Book of Modern Writing, edited by Phillips and Rahv (New York: Berkley, 1953);

Art and Psychoanalysis, edited by Phillips (New York: Criterion, 1957);

The Partisan Review Anthology, edited by Phillips and Rahv (New York: Holt, Rinehart & Winston, 1962);

Literature and Psychoanalysis, edited by Phillips and Edith Kurzweil (New York: Columbia University Press, 1983);

Writers and Politics: A Partisan Review Reader, edited by Phillips and Kurzweil (New York: Routledge & Kegan Paul, 1983);

William Phillips

Partisan Review: The Fiftieth Anniversary Edition, edited by Phillips (New York: Stein & Day, 1985).

SELECTED PERIODICAL PUBLICATIONS – UNCOLLECTED: [As Wallace Phelps] "*Class*-ical Culture," *Communist,* 7 (January 1933): 93-96;

"Three Generations," *Partisan Review,* 1 (September-October 1934): 49-55;

[With Philip Rahv] "Private Experience and Public Philosophy," *Poetry,* 48 (May 1936): 98–105;

"The Esthetics of the Founding Fathers," *Partisan Review,* 4 (March 1938): 11–21;

"Portrait of the Artist as an American," *Horizon,* 16 (October 1947): 12–19;

"The Native," *Partisan Review,* 18 (January-February 1951): 59–65;

"A French Lady on the Dark Continent: Simone de Beauvoir's Impressions of America," *Commentary,* 16 (July 1953): 25–29;

"A Season in the Stands," *Commentary,* 48 (July 1969): 65–69.

So intimate is the connection between William Phillips and the *Partisan Review,* which he cofounded in 1934 and continues to edit over half a century later, that it is impossible to write much about the one without writing about the other. In fact, Phillips's memoir, *A Partisan View: Five Decades of the Literary Life* (1983), is symbolic of this connection; little is revealed about the man apart from his view of the magazine and his relationships with the people who were associated with it at various times. Of the *Partisan Review,* Phillips has said from a relatively recent perspective, "We were clearly partisans of the new, of the tradition of the new, . . . [which was] a fusion of modernist sensibility and radical consciousness." Both the magazine and its editor are also critics of culture, seeking the relation, often the continuity, between old and new, focusing on the humanities, particularly literature and political history.

From his long tenure as editor, his own memoir, and comments by those who know him, it seems clear that Phillips has been instrumental in perpetuating the *Partisan Review,* from its founding as an organ of the John Reed Club (its subtitle on the index page read "A Bi-Monthly of the Revolutionary Literature/Published by the John Reed Club of New York"), to its highly influential status around the time of World War II, to James Burkhart Gilbert's evaluation in 1974: "This combination of cultural, literary, and political criticism has made the *Partisan* a fascinating archive of important intellectual developments" in the twentieth century.

William Phillips was born 14 November 1907, in Manhattan, to Jewish immigrants from Russia, Marie (Berman) and Edward Litvinsky, his father having changed his name to Phillips at the suggestion of friends to suit his new life in America. When his mother and father separated, Phillips accompanied his mother to her home in Kiev, where they lived for three years with her family. When they returned and rejoined his father, the family settled in the Bronx. Soon they were joined by his maternal grandmother from Kiev. Phillips believes his father was not suited to be a lawyer, his chosen profession, and he was not successful at it. He moved the family out to Rockaway at one point in hopes that he would become a judge but then moved back after two years to the East Bronx, which Phillips describes as "the dumping ground then for European immigrants, as it is now for blacks and Puerto Ricans."

In his memoir Phillips describes how his father withdrew more and more, first reading philosophers like Plato and Aristotle, then trying Yoga, "dematerialization," Couéism, Fletcherizing, and, finally, Christian Science. His mother became a hypochondriac and tried various cures and diets, a "self-made victim" who lived to be ninety-six. He sums up his account of their lives rather dryly: "They were certainly not ordinary parents."

Phillips attended the predominantly Jewish P. S. 40 and Morris High School, where he did well, and proceeded to City College (now City College of the City University of New York). He received his real education, however, not in the classroom but from fellow students – friends like Jules Henry and Herbert Ferber and an unnamed older student, who suggested he read T. S. Eliot's *The Sacred Wood* (1920). He did so and thus was introduced to modernism, which would play an immensely significant role in his intellectual life. Another great intellectual revelation occurred, he writes, when he became tired of the standard essays he and his students were supposed to read in an expository writing class he was teaching as a graduate student at New York University. He began to use the *Nation* and the *New Republic* as texts, which had the effect of politicizing both him and his students.

Phillips reports that while he was at NYU he became aware of Greenwich Village and bohemian life. At a party in New Rochelle he met Edna M. Greenblatt, who was majoring in English and philosophy at NYU, and soon they married. There are references to Edna in Phillips's memoir as a companion on later trips abroad or in gatherings at home; she has obviously been an important part of his life. Delmore Schwartz's story "New Year's Eve," first published in the summer 1945 issue of the *Partisan Review,* was inspired by a party at the Phillipses' in 1937 and is dedicated "To Edna Phillips." The "Edna" who plays a central role in Phillips's fine little sketch "The Native" (1951) may be based on her.

Phillips declares in his memoir that, like the *Partisan Review,* "Intellectually speaking, I, too, was

PARTISAN REVIEW

A Bi-Monthly of Revolutionary Literature
Published by the John Reed Club of New York

VOLUME I, No. 3. JUNE-JULY 1934

Contributors

Address all communications to PARTISAN REVIEW, 430 Sixth Avenue, New York City. Subscription: $1.00 for six issues; $2.00 for twelve issues. All manuscripts must be accompanied by stamped, self-addressed envelopes.

Contents page for an early issue of the leftist literary magazine edited by Phillips and Philip Rahv. Phillips co-authored the first article in this issue under the pseudonym Wallace Phelps.

born in the thirties." Alan M. Wald has shown that Phillips, like many of the New York intellectuals, manifests "the politics of memory" in his memoir, particularly concerning his political life in the early 1930s. For various reasons, says Wald in defining "the politics of memory," "individuals sometimes perceive or remember facets of their lives inaccurately for psychological or emotional reasons beyond their conscious control." Wald records, for example, that the January 1933 issue of *Communist* published an essay by Phillips, under the pseudonym "Wallace Phelps," in which he attacked José Ortega y Gasset as a socialist Fascist. But in his memoir Phillips says he first heard of the John Reed Club in 1934 and was surprised to learn of their Communist-party connections after having joined one, conveying an impression that he was much more naive and more of a novice than he actually must have been.

At any rate, Phillips particularly emphasizes the effect of the Depression in causing loss of "faith in the idea of the future," that is, in what had been the "orderly progression from youth to adulthood," and hence the appeal of Marxist ideas to his generation. He was attracted to left-wing groups in the early 1930s, eventually rising to become secretary of the John Reed Writers Club. However, he was also becoming more and more aware of how Communist-influenced aesthetics could distort literary values and judgments. About this time he met Philip Rahv (the pseudonym adopted by Ivan Greenberg), and together they conceived of a magazine that would combine political radicalism and modernist aesthetics.

The latter did not play a large part in the "Editorial Statement" that began the first issue of the first volume of the new bimonthly *Partisan Review,* published for February–March 1934. Rather, the revolutionary movement and concomitant revolutionary art of the 1930s are emphasized as well as the magazine's association with the John Reed Club and the intention to "publish the best creative work of its members as well as of non-members who share the literary aims of the John Reed Club," a bow to the association which had made it possible to raise enough money to start the magazine. Finally the viewpoint of the magazine is firmly stated as "that of the revolutionary working class," and the declaration is made that "the defense of the Soviet Union is one of our principal tasks."

For the first seven issues of this version of the *Partisan Review* Phillips used his pseudonym "Wallace Phelps." It appears in the list of names of the editorial board and on a review of two books by T. S. Eliot, an essay on Malcolm Cowley's *Exile's Return* (1934), two articles co-authored with Rahv, and an essay titled "Form and Content" (separate entries for Wallace Phelps and William Phillips appear not only in Margaret Sader's *Comprehensive Index to Little Magazines, 1890–1970,* but also in the *Partisan Review Index, 1934–1965*). The name William Phillips did not appear until the eighth issue (July–August 1935) when the magazine's association with the John Reed Club was dropped from the masthead and only the descriptive "A Bi-Monthly of Revolutionary Literature" remained. It was declared that the *Partisan Review* would be "edited by a group of young Communist writers, whose purpose will be to print the best revolutionary literature and Marxist criticism in this country and abroad," but Phillips denies that he ever joined the Communist party; nevertheless, Wald says he "was so close to the party in the early 1930s that many radical intellectuals believed he was a member." Phillips describes in detail in his memoir the increasing disillusion with the Communist party that he shared with Rahv.

An announcement on page 2 of the tenth issue (February 1936) explained the new list of editors and masthead, *Partisan Review & Anvil,* and this version continued for five more issues (through October 1936), but Phillips records that the differences between the *Partisan Review* and Jack Conroy and his magazine, the *Anvil,* were too great, and they separated. In fact, as Wald has shown, the Communist party was in considerable turmoil at this time, particularly with regard to its relationship to "the proletarian cultural movement" and associated groups like the John Reed Clubs and the League of American Writers. Rahv and Phillips broke with the Communists and forged new associations with F. W. Dupee, Dwight Macdonald, Mary McCarthy, and George L. K. Morris, and in a little over a year the *Partisan Review* was reborn (December 1937) with "A Literary Monthly" as the subheading on the masthead, all six names listed as editors, and a new "Editorial Statement."

The emphasis in this statement is on independence from political organizations, notably the Communist party, in which a "totalitarian trend is inherent," but a commitment to revolutionary literature, "a literature which, for its origin and final justification looks beyond itself and deep into the historic process," and a commitment to the conception of literary editorship previously developed by the magazines of the tradition of aestheticism but adapted to the new literature. William Barrett, an associate editor from 1945 to 1953, claims in his memoir *The Truants: Adventures Among the Intellectuals* (1982) that the two idols of the *Partisan Review* as he knew it were Marxism and modernism; in an editorial comment on the book, Phillips denies the appropriateness of these terms for the period about which Barrett was primarily writing (roughly 1945–1956) but implies that they might be fitting – if oversimplified – rubrics for a discussion of the early years of the magazine.

In an article in the *Partisan Review* of March 1938, "The Esthetics of the Founding Fathers," Phillips investigates the concept of "Marxist criticism" as promulgated by the Communist party and finds little justification for it in the writings of Karl Marx and Friedrich Engels and nothing of significance to art or art criticism in Joseph Stalin or Georgy Valentinovich Plekhanov. Although Leon Trotsky's insights into literature are often interesting, as is his argument against the concept of proletarian art ("the proletarian revolution . . . is laying the foundations of a culture which is above classes and which will be the first culture that is truly human"), Phillips decides in the end that "Trotsky never made a formal attempt to work out the problems of Marxist criticism." (Nevertheless, the editors of the *Partisan Review* carried on correspondence with Trotsky and published writings by him.) In this article Phillips finds that both literary criticism and Marxism have to do with the evaluation of values and that Marxism is relevant to literary criticism, "for it supplies a method not only for finding the social origins of values but also for determining their contemporary significance." After discussing some examples, such as an article on Gustave Flaubert by Edmund Wilson, Phillips concludes that "an analysis of literary problems or of specific writers which *flows from or is consistent with* a materialistic version of society is a form of Marxist criticism – at least, in its infant stage."

In his memoir Phillips notes that he spent a summer in the 1930s trying to formulate a Marxist aesthetic and criticism that would surpass other contemporary versions of Marxism, and that this task was never completed, but he asserts that, especially in the 1940s, a strength of the *Partisan Review* was its emphasis on the relation of a social context to literary matters. Nevertheless, its pages were always open to other schools or approaches of literary criticism, even though the value of these points of view was frequently questioned by other writers, the editors, or writers of letters that were published in the magazine.

As noted above, Eliot's criticism was responsible for introducing Phillips to modernism, and soon he was reading Charles Baudelaire, Stéphane Mallarmé, Gerard Manley Hopkins, James Joyce, Thomas Mann, and Ezra Pound as well as studying modernist art, criticism, and aesthetics. In retrospect, Phillips would recognize certain inconsistencies between Marxism and modernism, such as the dependency of modernism on an elite group of intellectuals. In some issues of the *Partisan Review* in 1938 and 1939, the descriptive heading under the masthead was "A Quarterly of Literature and Marxism," separating the two interests – quite different from 1935's "A Bi-Monthly of Revolutionary Literature" or 1937's "A Literary Monthly."

In his memoir he says of himself in the 1930s:

> I was a member of five minority groups. I was a disaffected writer and an editor of an against-the-grain publication. I was a Jew. I believed in modernism, which at that time was outside the dominant culture. I had become an anti-Communist after a brief flirtation with the party, which was not very fashionable. I tried to hold on to some radical politics and social ideas, however vague and Utopian they really were, and compromised by the Soviet regime, when the swing was clearly to the right.

Cover for the first issue published with Phillips as sole editor, after Rahv's resignation

And of himself and the *Partisan Review* group he says, "We felt completely outside the literary as well as the political establishment." Apparently intense feelings of isolation, of being on the fringes of society, caused these modernists to gravitate toward fellow isolated spirits and form groups, the most important being, for several of them, the *Partisan Review* group; many of them in retrospect refer to it as a "family."

This group also shared a desire to make European culture available to American audiences, and an obvious example of the European bent of the *Partisan Review* was the frequent appearance of a "Paris Letter" by various writers, from Sean Niall (Sherry Mangan's pseudonym) in 1939 to Cyprien Mormiche to H. J. Kaplan, who contributed many examples after the war. More regularly published was the series "London Letter" by George Orwell during World War II and later by Arthur Koestler and others. In the fall 1945 issue, under the heading "From the Capitals of Europe," were grouped "Rome Letter" by Moses Brown (William Barrett), "London Letter" by Orwell, and "Paris Letter" by Kaplan. The reader experiences shock in the spring 1958 issue to find "Letter from Home" by Kaplan, who has now returned from Paris, and even more of a shock to find "California Letters" in the winter 1968 issue, so fixed eastward had the publication's emphasis traditionally been. But an indication that all the communication has not been one-way is the announcement in the March–April 1947 issue that the *Partisan Review* was being published simultaneously in England and the United States, apparently the first time an American literary magazine had had a concurrent foreign publication.

By this time, indeed, what had been a group of writers and critics on the fringes of American culture had moved to a central importance. The writers had been as notable for their disagreements as for their agreements, as both Phillips in his memoir and Irving Howe in his autobiography, *A Margin of Hope* (1982), point out. Phillips says, "we were friends, but I think we were held together less by friendship than by a sense of common values and purpose." He felt closest to Clement Greenberg, who wrote art criticism for the *Partisan Review,* in the early years and later, among the younger writers, to Schwartz, who joined the staff in 1943 as editor and in 1946 began about ten years of service as associate editor with his friend Barrett, with Phillips and Rahv serving as editors.

In addition to the six writers noted above as editors of the 1937 "reborn" *Partisan Review,* James T. Farrell, Wilson, Sidney Hook, and Horace Gregory were close associates of the *Partisan Review* in its early years. Among the younger generation, in addition to Schwartz, Phillips frequently refers to Harold Rosenberg, Meyer Schapiro, Lionel Abel, Elizabeth Hardwick, Lionel Trilling, Diana Trilling, Saul Bellow, Paul Goodman, and Irving Howe, then Robert Lowell, Leslie Fiedler, Isaac Rosenfeld, Robert Brustein, Steven Marcus, and Susan Sontag – but this is simply a sampling of the reservoir of talent centered in the *Partisan Review.* James Baldwin's "Sonny's Blues" appeared in the summer 1957 issue, a section of Ralph Ellison's then-unfinished novel *Invisible Man* was published in 1963, and, in keeping with its interest in European culture, the magazine published pieces by Koestler, Hannah Arendt, Jean Genet, André Malraux, Jean-Paul Sartre, and Albert Camus. In 1961 a special double number, edited by Patricia Blake and Max Hayward, was devoted to "Dissonant Voices in Soviet Literature."

Phillips and Rahv served the *Partisan Review* together from the beginning until a terse announcement appeared in the double number of late 1969: "Partisan Review announces that Philip Rahv has resigned." Rahv seems to have been the more flamboyant, opinionated, and self-dramatizing of the two, while Phillips seems to have been more devoted to the nuts and bolts of the editorial and financial aspects of the magazine – "it was he who was pushed into the shadow by Rahv's more aggressive and blustering personality," says Barrett. One may suspect that it was Rahv who helped foster the distinctive tone of the early *Partisan Review,* characterized by Phillips as "raucous, impious, and intransigent," and Irving Howe characterizes the style of its essays as "nervous, strewn with knotty or flashy phrases, impatient with transitions, and other concessions to dullness, willfully calling attention to itself as a form or at least an outcry, fond of rapid twists, taking pleasure in dispute, dialectic, dazzle."

In Phillips's opinion, Rahv became less and less involved in the actual work of putting out the *Partisan Review* but maintained the appearance of being vital to its operations. Phillips, Barrett, Schwartz, and Greenberg had a confrontation with Rahv over lunch at a Jewish restaurant on Second Avenue in 1946. They had learned that Rahv was talking negatively about his fellow staffers and friends of the magazine behind their backs, and Phillips felt the situation had become intolerable. Rahv responded nervously and defensively at first, then became evasive and finally managed to smooth matters over temporarily, in part because his opponents were so uneasy over the task they had set themselves.

Until World War II Phillips, Rahv, and most other members of their group were united in Marxist sympathies and their opposition to Stalinism (and liberals who defended it) and fascism. They were also united by having to respond to the frequent attacks upon them by the other groups. When the war came, more-radical members of the staff had a difficult time adjusting. Though they tended toward the Marxist view that wars of the West were fought for economic, not moral, reasons, in the end they did not oppose the war. For Phillips that position "meant the end of traditional radicalism, particularly of the Marxist or Trotskyist variety, which was predicated on the pure idea of internationalism. And it opened the door to the legitimization of nationalist feelings and doctrines." Dwight Macdonald, however, took a firm antiwar position in a debate carried on in the magazine, then gradually shifted toward an anarchist position, and finally published a letter of resignation in the July-August 1943 issue, complaining that social questions were not receiving enough emphasis in the magazine. In reply, the editors wrote, "we could never agree to 'subordinate' art and literature to political interests" and insisted that the magazine's success was owing to "the specific modulation achieved in combining socialist ideas with a varied literary and critical content. This will continue to be the policy of the magazine."

Phillips was the editor who had been most involved in the financial details of the magazine. The difficulty of his position is probably reflected in the many shifts that were made in the frequency of publication of the *Partisan Review* from monthly to quarterly to bimonthly to monthly to quarterly, and so on, with the change sometimes explicitly tied to costs. Phillips relates some of his efforts to gain financial backing from agencies and from individuals – sometimes successful, often not.

In 1963 he was finally successful in finding support for the magazine at an academic institution, Rutgers University, and the relationship was mutually beneficial for fifteen years. However, relationships with his coeditor deteriorated around this time; Rahv seemed unhappy with the move to Rutgers and left most of the actual editorial and financial concerns for Phillips to handle, but he still felt justified in exerting his authority when he wished. Politically, Rahv returned to his earlier Marxism and became more dogmatic in his critical opinions as well as his politics. Barrett relates how Greenberg in conversation once called his attention to "something 'negative' " in the thinking of Rahv and Phillips, and Barrett came to conclude that it existed in modern intellectuals generally. However, after further considerable observation and analysis, he concluded that "Rahv was a Nihilist" – not necessarily in his writing but certainly in his less public behavior. On the other hand one finds little evidence of nihilism in the records of Phillips's relationships with others or in his writings, and the contrast, whether ever explicitly recognized or not, may have underlain the tension in the relationship of the coeditors.

According to Phillips, the editorial board was recognizing the real state of affairs when it voted to make him editor in chief in 1965, and he is listed as such in the summer and fall quarterly issues, with the names of Richard Poirier and Rahv listed in that order under his, followed by Steven Marcus as associate editor. Rahv, however, threatened a lawsuit, which was avoided only by months of negotiations and a settlement preserving what he considered to

1984 $8.00

50TH ANNIVERSARY

PARTISAN REVIEW

Daniel Aaron, Lionel Abel, Kathleen Agena, John Ashbery, Jacques Barzun, Daniel Bell, Peter Berger, Harold Brodkey, Robert Brustein, Eleanor Clark, Barbaralee Diamonstein, James Dickey, Morris Dickstein, Robert Fitzgerald, Helen Frankenthaler, Nathan Glazer, Eugene Goodheart, Juan Goytisolo, Gerald Graff, Clement Greenberg, Geoffrey H. Hartman, John Hollander, Sidney Hook, Irving Howe, Philip Johnson, Alfred Kazin, Irving Kristol, Milan Kundera, Edith Kurzweil, Harry Levin, Dwight Macdonald, Norman Mailer, Bernard Malamud, Mary McCarthy, Daphne Merkin, Leonard Michaels, Robert Motherwell, Vladimir Nabokov, Joyce Carol Oates, Amos Oz, Cynthia Ozick, William Phillips, Norman Podhoretz, Philip Roth, Arthur Schlesinger, Jr., Robert Shattuck, Isaac Bashevis Singer, Deborah Solomon, Muriel Spark, Stephen Spender, George Stade, Diana Trilling, Robert Penn Warren, Rosanna Warren

FROM LIONEL TRILLING'S NOTEBOOKS

Cover marking the first half century of the magazine that was founded as the official publication of the New York John Reed Club

be his rights. He did not, however, resume an active role as editor, nor were the bad feelings overcome, and finally, in 1969, the announcement of Rahv's resignation appeared.

During this period Phillips had begun to emerge from the shadows into which his more flamboyant associate had often cast him. He and Edna first went to Europe for several weeks in the winter of 1949, visiting with leading European intellectuals and American friends in Paris, Italy, and London. He served on the board of the American Committee for Cultural Freedom from 1951 to 1963. In 1962 Phillips went on a world tour under the auspices of the United States Information Agency, starting off in Australia and continuing on to Manila, Tokyo, Hong Kong, Delhi, Beirut, Athens, Rome, and London, conferring with editors of literary magazines and meeting writers, occasionally giving informal talks. In 1989 he returned to Israel, which he had previously visited in 1968, to give a paper at a conference of the International Society of Political Psychology. He was chairman of the Coordinating Council of Literary Magazines from 1967 to 1975. He also took an active though minor part in politics – in the national political campaigns of Robert Kennedy and Jimmy Carter, Richard Hughes's campaign for the governorship of New Jersey, and John Lindsay's campaign to become mayor of New York.

After Rahv's resignation more short pieces by Phillips began to appear in the *Partisan Review,* often comments on pieces appearing in the magazine, such as those by Peter Brooks and by Leo Bersani on the New Left and the Black Panthers in 1970 – which evoked a response from those authors and a riposte from Phillips. Opening remarks by Phillips began to appear more frequently in issues of the magazine, sometimes under the headings "Editor's Note," "Points After," or "Extra Points" but sometimes simply as "Comment" or "Remarks." And he appeared as moderator or presenter or both and certainly always as a discussant at some of the symposia and conferences whose proceedings were printed in whole or in part in the magazine, including "New York and the National Culture" (1977), a *Partisan Review*-sponsored conference on the state of criticism (1979), "Our Country and Our Culture" (1984; Phillips's contribution is printed in the double issue of 1985), and "The Crisis in Our Culture" (1991).

But Phillips underwent a further ordeal when a change in administrators at Rutgers in 1978 led to the ousting of the *Partisan Review* and subsequent lawsuits over possession of its files and other properties. Phillips was eventually able to regain possession of its files and move the magazine to Boston University, where it continues to be based.

Although the *Partisan Review* and Phillips have received university support – Phillips has held the position of professor of English at both Rutgers and Boston – he has in recent years strongly criticized the teaching of the humanities and, more specifically, literary studies in modern higher education. He particularly deplores the rejection of tradition by contemporary schools of criticism that teach students revisionism and has lamented the loss of qualitative judgments in academic criticism. What students in mass education really need, according to Phillips, is "a grounding in the Western tradition." Instead of focusing intensely on literary criticism and literary theory, graduate study "should be revised simply to provide more intensive and wider reading of literary works."

Phillips's denunciation of the arguments of those who reject tradition as "revisionism" is reminiscent of his frequent criticisms of memoirs by former associates or acquaintances, many of whom, like Barrett, Hook, and Norman Podheretz, became neoconservatives. His comments on Lillian Hellman's charge that the *Partisan Review* "took no editorial position against [Joseph] McCarthy himself" are particularly trenchant, and the writing of his memoir was prompted partly by his perception that many events of the past which he remembers clearly are being subjected to revisionism. Although many differences of opinion or acrimonious disputes break out explicitly in the memoir, the uninitiated reader often feels that there are many more swirling just beneath the surface. And one must remember that Phillips is indeed presenting "a partisan view" himself that must be checked against fact and related to the partisan views of others.

In 1967 Phillips's *A Sense of the Present* was published, a collection of a dozen of his major essays, three short stories, and five book reviews. His works give insight into cultural and political history and are often interesting, but, in the end, writing is probably not his forte. However, he has a special talent for nurturing the minds and talents of others. Something of this is caught in his review of Alexander Bloom's *Prodigal Sons: The New York Intellectuals and Their World* (1987), a history of the 1930s:

> The fact is that some of our ideas were quite personal, even though there was a kind of collective consciousness, for many of us were essentially literary, not political, intellectuals. Hence we were sometimes almost as much interested in being original and interesting as in being correct. And I believe it is this combination of political and literary sensibility that has enabled us to have had an intellectual as well as a literary influence – which most students of the period, including Bloom, think we did. We were charged up, excited by incessant arguments, by new ideas, by new works; and for those of us who edited *Partisan Review*, there were the triumphs of creating a new intellectual atmosphere.

As a longtime editor of the *Partisan Review* and a guardian of its tradition, William Phillips has continued to have a remarkable effect on the country's intellectual atmosphere – almost to the end of the century.

References:

William Barrett, *The Truants: Adventures Among the Intellectuals* (Garden City, N.Y.: Anchor/Doubleday, 1982);

Terry A. Cooney, *The Rise of the New York Intellectuals: Partisan Review and Its Circle* (Madison: University of Wisconsin Press, 1986);

James Burkhart Gilbert, "Partisan Review," in *The American Radical Press, 1880–1960,* edited by Joseph R. Conlin (Westport, Conn.: Greenwood Press, 1974), pp. 548–553;

Gilbert, *Writers and Partisans: A History of Literary Radicalism in America* (New York: Wiley, 1968);

Irving Howe, *A Margin of Hope: An Intellectual Autobiography* (New York: Harcourt Brace Jovanovich, 1982);

Alan M. Wald, *The New York Intellectuals: The Rise and Decline of the Anti-Stalinist Left from the 1930s to the 1980s* (Chapel Hill: University of North Carolina Press, 1987).

Gerard Piel

(1 March 1915-)

Jack Colldeweih
Fairleigh Dickinson University

MAJOR POSITIONS HELD: Editorial assistant (1938-1939), science editor, *Life* (1939-1944); assistant to the president, Henry J. Kaiser Company and Associated Companies (1945-1946); president (1946-1984), publisher, *Scientific American* (1948-1987); chairman of the board (1985-1987), chairman emeritus, Scientific American Inc. (1987-).

BOOKS: *Science, Censorship and the Public Interest: A Talk* (New York: Scientific American, 1956);

Consumers of Abundance (Santa Barbara, Cal.: Center for the Study of Democratic Institutions, 1961);

The Illusion of Civil Defense: A Talk at the Commonwealth Club, San Francisco, California, 10 November, 1961 (New York: Scientific American, 1961);

Science in the Cause of Man (New York: Knopf, 1961; revised and enlarged, 1962);

Jobs, Machines, and People, A Conversation, by Piel, Ralph Helstein, and Robert Theobald (Santa Barbara, Cal.: Center for the Study of Democratic Institutions, 1964);

Toward Peace and Quiet on the Campus (New York: Scientific American, 1968);

The Acceleration of History (New York: Knopf, 1972);

Gerard Piel on Arms Control: Science and Economics (Lanham, Md. & London: University Press of America, 1987);

Only One World – Our Own to Make and Keep (New York: Freeman, 1992).

OTHER: "Technology & Democracy," in *Challenges to Democracy: The Next 10 Years,* edited by Edward Reed (New York: Center for the Study of Democratic Institutions, 1963; reprinted, Freeport, N.Y.: Books for Libraries Press, 1971), pp. 45-60.

PERIODICAL PUBLICATIONS: "No. 1 Shipbuilder," *Life,* 12 (29 June 1942): 80-84;

"Narcotics," *Life,* 15 (19 July 1943): 82-84;

"BW," *Life,* 21 (18 November 1946): 118-120;

Gerard Piel

"Powell Crosley, Jr.," *Life,* 22 (17 February 1947): 47-48;

"Your Personality Sits for Its Photo," *Nation's Business,* 35 (April 1947): 51-52; revised as "Machine That Measures Personality," *Science Digest,* 22 (July 1947): 3-6;

"Cancer," *Life,* 22 (21 April 1947): 77-84;

"Army Ant," by Piel and Theodore Christian Schnierla, *Scientific American,* 178 (June 1948): 16-23;

"Mathematics Comes out of the Classroom," *Yale Review,* new series 39 (Spring 1949): 132-141; republished in *Science Digest,* 27 (January 1950): 7-10;

"Forum of Science," *Newsweek,* 39 (31 March 1952): 59;

"Human Want Is Obsolete," *Saturday Review,* 36 (27 June 1953): 9-11;

"Science and the Next Fifty Years," *Bulletin of Atomic Scientists,* 10 (January 1954): 17–20;
"Scientists and Other Citizens," *Science Monthly,* 78 (March 1954): 129–133;
"Need for Public Understanding of Science," *Science,* 121 (4 March 1955): 317–322;
"Planet Earth," *Bulletin of Atomic Scientists,* 11 (September 1955): 238–243;
"Your New Books: Oceanography," *Natural History,* 65 (November 1956): 455;
"Science, Censorship, and the Public Interest," *Science,* 125 (26 April 1957): 792–794;
"Science, Disarmament, & Peace," *Bulletin of Atomic Scientists,* 14 (June 1958): 217–219;
"Revolution in Man's Labor," *Bulletin of Atomic Scientists,* 15 (September 1959): 278–283;
"Economics of Disarmament," *Bulletin of Atomic Scientists,* 16 (April 1960): 117–122;
"End of Toil," *Nation,* 192 (17 June 1961): 515–519;
"On the Feasibility of Peace," *Science,* 135 (23 February 1962): 648–652;
"Can Our Economy Stand Disarmament?," *Atlantic Monthly,* 210 (September 1962): 35–40;
"Advent of Abundance," *Bulletin of Atomic Scientists,* 19 (June 1963): 2–6;
"Abundance & The Future of Man," *Atlantic Monthly,* 213 (April 1964): 84–90;
"Federal Funds & Science Education," *Bulletin of Atomic Scientists,* 22 (May 1966): 10–15;
"World Free of Want?," *Bulletin of Atomic Scientists,* 24 (January 1968): 16–22;
"Support of Science on the University's Own Terms," *Science,* 166 (28 November 1969): 1101;
"Lobbyist for an Age of Reason: C. P. Snow," *Life,* 72 (31 March 1972): 19;
"New Hereditarians," *Nation,* 220 (19 April 1975): 455–459;
"Next 200 Could Be Best," *BioScience,* 26 (July 1976): 431;
"Toward a Steady State Society," *Current,* 185 (September 1976): 10–11;
"Idi Amin and the H-Bomb," *Progressive,* 43 (May 1979): 17;
"Let Them Eat Cake," *Science,* 226 (26 October 1984): 393;
"Development & the Market Process," *Science,* 227 (22 February 1985): 838;
". . . to Thy Jubilee Throng," *American Heritage,* 37 (August–September 1986): 98–101;
"Natural Philosophy in the Constitution," *Science,* 233 (5 September 1986): 1056–1060;
"Human Biology & Public Policy," *BioScience,* 38 (April 1988): 293–294.

Gerard Piel – president from 1946 to 1984 and publisher from 1948 to 1984 of the *Scientific American* and chairman of the board from 1985 to 1987 – has been a proponent of science information and education for the public and one of those most responsible for demystifying science. During the atomic age – even in the years of the cold war – he has been one of the nation's strongest advocates of open science information and opponents of censorship.

With only a few years of experience in magazine journalism, Piel transformed a moribund periodical into the preeminent science magazine of its day. He was able to convince prominent scientists to write for the public as well as for other scientists at a time when public policy questions in the realm of science were freighted with enormous political, military, and environmental significance. Although now retired from active management of the magazine, he continues to work, and he will be remembered for promoting a scientifically enlightened and active citizenry in the best sense of classical liberalism.

Born on 1 March 1915 to William F. J. Piel and Loretto Scott Piel in Woodmere, New York, Piel was the fourth of six children and the grandson of one of the founders of Piel Brothers Brewery. His father had gone to Columbia College intending to be a writer and critic; he had edited the daily campus newspaper and the literary magazine and had even started a literary magazine of his own. William Piel had graduated from Columbia College in 1905 and had attended law school, but the death of his father in 1915 compelled him to leave law school prior to finishing his degree (although he was admitted to the bar) and take over the family business (which was then producing near beer, legal during Prohibition because it contained less than five percent alcohol). He encouraged Gerard to go into journalism.

Piel attended the Jesuit's Brooklyn Preparatory School and Phillips Academy in Andover, Massachusetts, where he had a scholarship. At Andover he wrote for the school paper, the *Phillipian,* and the literary magazine, the *Mirror.* Bored by his physics teacher, he flunked. Determined to show up his instructor, he memorized every formula in the book and its proper application and achieved a perfect score on his college board exam.

He attended Harvard on scholarship, achieving membership in Phi Beta Kappa. Although slim in build, he lettered on the varsity wrestling team. Piel majored in history, believing that academic journalism programs are a waste of time. Oddly, in

Cover for the first issue of Scientific American *to reflect Piel's editorial changes*

view of his later career, he avoided science courses and would eventually graduate without taking a single one. His broad reading and grasp of history were promoted by a series of remarkable tutors, including Michael Karpovich, councillor to the Kerensky embassy in Washington, D.C., and the future sociologist Robert Merton, who was then a graduate student. Piel had taken his father's encouragement and was determined to be a magazine journalist. He got his start as business manager of the *Harvard Advocate* in his freshman year and experienced his first brush with censorship. He and several other members of the staff, including the editor, Cyrus Leo Sulzburger of the *New York Times* family, were arrested for obscenity because some material taken from an Ernest Hemingway story had upset the local police and the Watch and Ward Society; the copies were seized and burned, and the young men had to go through the formality of a public resignation from the publication – though they returned to work on it the next day.

Piel was able to try his hand at commercial journalism in the summer of his junior year by using his family connections. The Victor Ridder family (of the Knight-Ridder newspaper chain), close friends of his parents, provided him with a summer reporting job on the *Grand Forks* (North Dakota) *Herald.* The experience enabled him to see the relationship between a small newspaper and the community it served and cemented his goal of becoming a journalist. He was convinced from his study of history that another world war was about to begin, and he wanted to cover it.

Although Ralph Ingersoll was Piel's neighbor in Salisbury, Connecticut, where the Piel family had a summer place, Piel rejected using his connection in landing a job after being graduated magna cum laude in 1937. Ingersoll, who had been managing editor of the *New Yorker* and then of *Fortune,* had moved upstairs at Time when Piel applied for a job at *Fortune.* Piel's application was treated routinely; he was asked to write a trial article as a test of his employability and was deemed unsuitable.

He got as close as he could to Time by going to work in the mail room of the J. Sterling Getschell Advertising Agency on the ninth floor of the

Chrysler Building; the offices of Time began on the twenty-seventh floor. He soon surmised that the real reason he was hired was that Getschell wanted the Piel Brewery account. Nevertheless, his job was a stroke of good luck: Time founder Henry Luce was a hero to Getschell, who tried to emulate his *Life* magazine by producing a picture magazine of his own titled *Picture,* and Piel was brought from the mail room to the editorial staff of the new magazine. Even before he published the first issue, in January 1938, Getschell had decided that launching the magazine was too big an enterprise, and he shut it down after the publication of the three issues for which he had already gathered material.

Piel offered his services to *Life;* he was the first person hired there who had had prior experience on a picture magazine. Piel was given an office-boy job of sorting pictures, a task at which he claims he was poor because he wanted to look at the pictures rather than read the information on the back. John Billings, the managing editor at *Life,* eventually assigned him to work as an assistant to editorial associate Alexander King, whom Piel considers one of his mentors.

After securing employment at *Life,* Piel was married on 4 February 1938 to Mary Tapp Bird, of Tenafly, New Jersey, who had been his boss at *Picture.* They had two sons, Jonathan Bird and Samuel Bird. The couple divorced in 1955. On 24 June 1955 Piel married Eleanor Virden Jackson, a California trial lawyer; they had one daughter, Eleanor Jackson, Jr. Piel's son Samuel died in a highway accident in September 1964.

Billings was unhappy with the science department of *Life* and invited Piel, at age twenty-four, to edit it. His assumption was that since Piel knew nothing about science, he might be able to learn something about it; if he could then explain it to Billings, then they might be able to explain it to the readers. Piel immediately began to read everything he could find on science. His bigger task, however, was to persuade scientists to trust him. Many scientists had had unpleasant experiences with mass circulation magazines that all too frequently introduced error and hype into their science reporting. But they were pleased by Piel's *Life* stories, for the photographs insured more authenticity even as they attracted readers. Additionally, in consideration of their cooperation in the picture setups, the scientists were allowed to read and correct the captions for the photographs. Piel found it increasingly easy to enlist their collaboration. The reputation Piel built up at this time would serve him well when was ready to begin his own magazine.

A story that Piel likes to tell concerns the question of whether a pitched curve baseball actually follows a curved path. He enlisted Gjon Mili, a student of Prof. Harold Edgerton at the Massachusetts Institute of Technology, to answer the question by using high-speed photography. Mili positioned one camera overhead and one at the batter's end; the flight of the ball was lighted with strobe lights. The pictures demonstrated that there was no horizontal deviation in the ball's flight; the illusion came from the different angles from which the pitcher threw the ball. Piel had the method, text, and pictures reviewed for scientific accuracy; they were certified to be sound. Nevertheless, the conclusion is still commonly rejected by laymen.

The favorable response of scientists to his department in *Life* convinced Piel that they had need for a general science magazine – one that would tell them about work in fields outside their specialty and not covered in the specialized journals they had to read in line of duty. If he were to start such a magazine, however, he had to learn something about business.

In January 1945, after arranging for sports editor Dennis Flanagan to replace him as science editor, Piel quit *Life* and went to work as a personal assistant to the industrialist Henry J. Kaiser. Piel had written what he now describes as "a very miserable" *Life* profile of Kaiser, titled "No. 1 Shipbuilder" and published in June 1942 and aimed at making Kaiser the Paul Bunyan of the industrial war effort. Kaiser stories had become a Piel subspecialty thereafter, and they had become good friends. A year with Kaiser – learning to read a balance sheet and run a cash-flow statement – supplied Piel with the business schooling he needed.

In the autumn of 1945 Piel, Flanagan, and management consultant Donald H. Miller, Jr., began to talk about starting a new magazine of science. After six months of planning, Piel decided that "the idea was good enough, and I had got brave enough" to take the plunge. He offered his resignation to Kaiser, who invited Piel to stay until the magazine's prospectus was ready. At the end of May 1946 Piel took his leave, with Kaiser's blessing and the solid backing of Kaiser's Wall Street lawyer, Leo Gottlieb, who was to be general counsel and a director of the new magazine company for the next thirty-eight years. By June the magazine had the commitment from another Gottlieb client, Lessing J. Rosenwald, of one-third of the estimated start-up capital.

Early in 1946 McGraw-Hill, publisher of many specialized trade journals, announced it

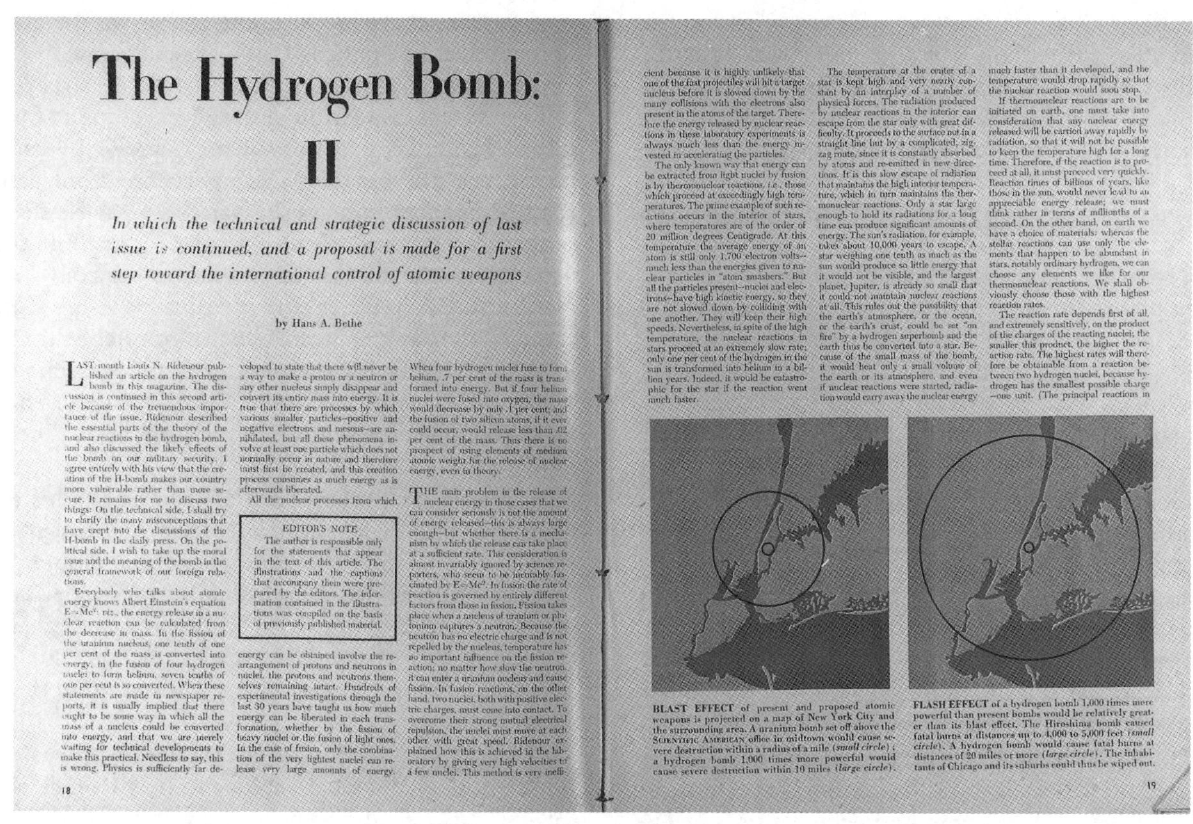
The Hydrogen Bomb: II

In which the technical and strategic discussion of last issue is continued, and a proposal is made for a first step toward the international control of atomic weapons

by Hans A. Bethe

LAST month Louis N. Ridenour published an article on the hydrogen bomb in this magazine. The discussion is continued in this second article because of the tremendous importance of the issue. Ridenour described the essential parts of the theory of the nuclear reactions in the hydrogen bomb, and also discussed the likely effects of the bomb on our military security. I agree entirely with his view that the creation of the H-bomb makes our country more vulnerable rather than more secure. It remains for me to discuss two things: On the technical side, I shall try to clarify the many misconceptions that have crept into the discussions of the H-bomb in the daily press. On the political side, I wish to take up the moral issue and the meaning of the bomb in the general framework of our foreign relations.

Everybody who talks about atomic energy knows Albert Einstein's equation $E=Mc^2$, etc., the energy release in a nuclear reaction can be calculated from the decrease in mass. In the fission of the uranium nucleus, one tenth of one per cent of the mass is converted into energy; in the fusion of four hydrogen nuclei to form helium, seven tenths of one per cent is so converted. When these statements are made in newspaper reports, it is usually implied that there ought to be some way in which all the mass of a nucleus could be converted into energy, and that we are merely waiting for technical developments to make this practical. Needless to say, this is wrong. Physics is sufficiently far developed to state that there will never be a way to make a proton or a neutron or any other nucleus simply disappear and convert its entire mass into energy. […]

EDITOR'S NOTE

The author is responsible only for the statements that appear in the text of this article. The illustrations and the captions that accompany them were prepared by the editors. The information contained in the illustrations was compiled on the basis of previously published material.

18

BLAST EFFECT of present and proposed atomic weapons is projected on a map of New York City and the surrounding area. A uranium bomb set off above the SCIENTIFIC AMERICAN office in midtown would cause severe destruction within a radius of a mile (*small circle*); a hydrogen bomb 1,000 times more powerful would cause severe destruction within 10 miles (*large circle*).

FLASH EFFECT of a hydrogen bomb 1,000 times more powerful than present bombs would be relatively greater than its blast effect. The Hiroshima bomb caused fatal burns at distances up to 4,000 to 5,000 feet (*small circle*). A hydrogen bomb would cause fatal burns at distances of 20 miles or more (*large circle*). The inhabitants of Chicago and its suburbs could thus be wiped out.

19

Opening pages of an article that was blocked by the United States Atomic Energy Commission until Piel agreed to remove sensitive material. The censored version was published in the April 1950 issue of Scientific American.

would launch a new magazine of science for the general reader, under the title *Science Illustrated.* The thought of McGraw-Hill as a competitor almost caused Piel and his partners to give up their plans. They quickly decided the publishing giant would probably aim at a mass circulation of readers not particularly interested in science, leaving the niche they had chosen unoccupied. The first issue, in April, confirmed their prognosis. In fact, *Science Illustrated* was soon in enough trouble that James McGraw asked Piel to come over and run it, saying, "We're trying to do the same thing you're trying to do." Piel drew a diagram and replied, "Here's a pyramid; this pyramid has to do with understanding of science; at the top of it are the people who do it and make it move and advance. At this part of the pyramid are the people who are interested in what they are doing. Down here are the people who are going to get involved someday, but haven't the slightest idea. I don't know how to talk to them, but our interests are the people at the top of the pyramid." Clearly that was not what McGraw was trying to do.

Over the next two years, Piel raised the rest of the estimated $450,000 capital, which proved to be less than half of what was needed for the new magazine to break even. A telling detail of Piel's relationship with scientists is that when he wrote one hundred of them to get their support for his fund-raising efforts, he received one hundred replies endorsing what he was trying to do and offering to write for the magazine. The principal investors, besides Rosenwald, were John Hay Whitney and Frazier W. McCann; smaller backers included such other well-known names as Bernard Baruch, Gerard Swope, and Royal Little.

The original working title of the proposed magazine was "The Sciences"; the publication's aim, according to the prospectus, would be "to serve the need of the scientist, the engineer, the doctor, the educator and the intelligent layman for information concerning the progress of science, engineering, and medicine in all their branches and in their application at the social and economic level to the lives of all men." Piel then discovered that *Scientific American* was for sale; its readership and advertising space had been falling for some time, and Orson Munn, the heir to the magazine, was more interested in patent and copyright law than in publishing. The asking price was one hundred thousand dollars – a thousand for each year of its existence – and Piel bought the magazine at that price in notes and stock for the new company in September 1947. Audit of the circulation and other assets, under the tough terms of the Gottlieb purchase contract, reduced the price paid in cash to forty thousand dollars – one dollar for each unit of guaranteed circulation.

The magazine's circulation of forty thousand proved largely illusory. There were about one thousand direct-to-publisher subscribers, attracted by a column on how to grind a telescope mirror. Some five thousand libraries were there on discounted "catalogue agent" subscriptions. The rest of the subscriptions were sold by door-to-door "field agents" who terrorized housewives and swapped subscriptions for haircuts and hamburgers. On his first day as publisher Piel received notice from N. W. Ayer and Company that Bell Laboratories was canceling the last regular contract the magazine had. The cancellation was reversed when Bell Labs learned of his plans for the magazine.

Piel also discovered that *Scientific American* had been receiving a check for twenty-five hundred dollars from *Reader's Digest* every year for the privilege of planting articles in *Scientific American* that could be condensed in the digest. To the amazement of the editors of the digest, Piel put an end to that source of easy money; he told them that, of course, terms could be worked out for the digesting of original *Scientific American* articles.

In assigning titles for the new staff of the magazine, Piel assumed those of president, publisher, and chairman of the editorial board; Flanagan was editor, and Miller was general manager.

"An Announcement to Our Readers" in the last issue of the "old" magazine (April 1948) stated: "The new *Scientific American* will find a unique place among U.S. magazines. It will serve as a universal medium for communication among men in the sciences, and between them and the public that is best equipped to understand their work and purposes." The readership the magazine was designed to serve, according to Piel, includes those "who are interested in science who turned out to be primarily the people who are engaged in the work of science, either in its advance or its application; then peripherally there are a lot of bright people who are running large corporations who if they were not recruited for the research department, they got there because they knew something about what business their company is in and they know something besides bookkeeping. . . . Our typical reader is the person who knows some part of science and wants to know what is going on in all the rest of it."

The titles of the articles in the first issue of the new *Scientific American* (May 1948) testify to the fulfillment of the promise to cover "five major areas: the physical, biological and social sciences, engineering and medicine": "The Man-Ape of South Africa," "The Future of the Amazon," "Social Physics," "Versalius' History of Science," "The Dust Cloud Hypothesis," "Luminescence of Living Things," "Davisson and Germer," and "Smelting Under Pressure." The sixty-four pages of the first issue also included a book review department, an amateur scientist department, and a news department in the middle called "Science and the Citizen." Piel and his colleagues had wanted to use "Science and Society" for the news department, but the United States Communist party already had that title for its quarterly periodical, and 1948 was not a good year to risk any such confusion. There were almost no advertisements, nor was there an editorial page, a practice maintained up to the present.

The readers to whom Piel was addressing his magazine wanted it so much that they had been picking up the old *Scientific American* at the newsstand and then throwing it away in disgust. The name Piel had bought was actually inhibiting his promotional efforts; his subsequent promotions merely called the periodical "this great new magazine of science." At one point Piel revived the courage of his backers, reluctant to come up with additional funds, with an offer from the American Academy of Arts and Sciences (AAAS) to take over the magazine; impressed that the AAAS would consider doing so, the backers came through with enough money to tide the magazine over. McGraw-Hill had spent millions of dollars building up a subscription circulation of five hundred thousand for *Science Illustrated.* When it went under, Piel obtained its subscription list and picked up about fifty thousand subscribers. That was enough to meet the goal of one hundred thousand with the January 1950 issue. Piel was determined to have "no cut-rate subscriptions, no 'arrears,' all readers fully paid direct to publisher, no dubious channels of sales, etc.," a policy that is firmly maintained to this day. His editorial product was so successful that the AAAS folded its own publication, *Scientific Monthly,* feeling that *Scientific American* was doing a better job at promoting science education.

Piel felt that his magazine's main advertising market was "corporations that do business with other corporations." Madison Avenue still has trouble comprehending that scientists and engineers

Piel (right) with Scientific American *general manager Donald H. Miller and advertising manager Martin Davidson in 1958*

make crucial business decisions. Their industrial clients understood, however. By 1960 the General Electric Company had thirteen divisions running ads in the magazine's pages, bought by sales managers to sell products such as electric motors and silicone plastics to other industries. (It did not hurt that one of the magazine's most enthusiastic investors was Swope, who had been president of GE before the war and had come back to run it during the war, or that Piel had done a piece on GE turboprop engines while at *Life*.) People who make such purchases for corporations have to know what they are buying. That is why, Piel argued, corporations hire scientists and engineers. The magazine reached break-even advertising income with the January 1951 issue and published its first really profitable issue in September of that year. Piel firmly believes that *Scientific American* remade industrial advertising: "what we did was bring out of the woodwork all the guys who were making ads for the little trade papers, and here we gave them a place to shine in the sunlight. *Scientific American* in five or six years transformed and lifted the level of copy of industrial advertising, [which had used] a picture of Atlas or something, instead of putting some intelligent copy on paper. Advertisers had to rise to the level of the readers."

Piel's devotion to popular understanding of science, and his consequent opposition to scientific secrecy, got him into difficulty during the cold war years of the 1950s. Piel says that his "deep, private" reason for starting *Scientific American* was that, as a historian more interested in politics than in science, he wanted to provide a place where rational, reliable, and objective information could be injected into the making of public decisions. He felt that it was the function of the magazine to cover what he called the impact of science on society or the interface between science and society, "all the terms which make the terrible assumption, which is sustained by reality, that science is not a part of the natural culture of our population or of our country." Piel came to realize that the government was about to decide to make thermonuclear weapons – that is, hydrogen bombs. "We thought that this was the raising of the peril of the arms race by a whole order of magnitude. And that it ought to be understood by the public and discussed by the public." A four-part series was designed. The first article was by Prof. Louis Ridenour of the University of Pennsylvania, who explained what conditions were needed to set off a hydrogen bomb. The second was by Hans Bethe of Cornell University, who discussed the reasons for the use of the heavier form of hydrogen and why an atomic bomb was needed to set off a hydrogen bomb. While the issue was being printed, word came from the Atomic Energy Commission (AEC) to cease publication immediately for national security reasons. Piel argued that the information had already been published in one form or another and was now in the public domain. The AEC countered that what was important was who said it, because the source lent confirmatory weight to the information. In the end the AEC let the article be published in the April 1950 issue with the offending passages deleted, as long as the three thousand copies already printed were burned and the original plates and Linotype slugs were destroyed. In deciding whether to fight, Piel had to consider that the magazine was in debt and that there were no resources to conduct what was likely to be a huge legal battle. Piel capitulated but was proven right when his subsequent request for reclassification was granted without question.

In 1950 Piel suffered an additional indignity when an invitation from the surgeon general of the United States to join the advisory board of a journal published by the Public Health Service embroiled him in President Harry S Truman's personnel-security proceedings. A loyalty check produced "evidence" that *Scientific American* had "derided" the evidence presented by the government in the Rosenberg spy trial and questioned the loyalties of certain of Piel's friends. Upon being "cleared," Piel resigned from his only United States governmental appointment.

Piel once contemplated getting involved in politics, and to that end he agreed to serve as chairman on a commission studying the problems of New York City's health services for Mayor John Lindsay. Piel had written on the Kaiser health plan when he was with *Life* magazine and felt that he could make a contribution. The 1968 report, from what became known as the Piel Commission, has become influential in cities around the country; but it was filed away by the Lindsay administration, and Piel gave up his political ambitions.

Meanwhile, the circulation of *Scientific American* was growing out of the reach of advertisers' budgets. When it reached two hundred thousand, the full-page price was twenty-four hundred dollars; multiplied by twelve, or even six, issue placements, the sum was perhaps the annual budget for a product manager at a firm such as General Electric. The industrial advertising market began to decline at about the same time television began to absorb many other types of advertising. Through the 1970s the annual number of advertising pages dropped from sixteen hundred to less than four hundred, while circulation climbed to a little more than five hundred thousand. What saved the magazine was the strong appeal of its editorial content to the subscribers, giving it a record low circulation sales cost. By 1980 *Scientific American* was again carrying more than one thousand pages of advertising, this time in four colors for up-scale consumer products. The magazine's new success attracted competition from Hearst and Piel's alma mater, Time. They made the same mistake as McGraw-Hill – addressing their magazines (*Science Digest* and *Discover,* respectively) to people who were not primarily interested in science. When they had lost enough money, they left *Scientific American* once more in monopoly of its niche.

Piel put the first million dollars earned by the magazine into purchasing in 1964 W. H. Freeman and Company, a college science textbook company that had gone into a joint venture with *Scientific American,* selling to colleges the reprints of its articles. In addition, it published the Scientific American Library, which now consists of more than thirty titles. The magazine, since 1970, has had an international circulation of one hundred thousand, excluding the United States. It is now published in Italian, Japanese, Spanish, French, German, Chinese, Russian, Arabic, and Hungarian; a tenth edition is published in English in India. The magazine has a circulation of one million in all languages combined. Piel's son Jonathan has started a venture called *Scientific American Medicine.*

Nearly all articles in *Scientific American* have been solicited, although some have originated as ideas from outside. Scientists are notably chary about talking to the mass media about their work because their comments frequently come out garbled or sensationalized. Piel and Flanagan were highly successful in getting them to write for the magazine. *Scientific American* has published articles by more than eighty Nobel Prize winners, most of them prior to their receiving the award. The author's payment is now a flat one thousand dollars. Scientists write for the magazine because they share Piel's view of the necessity of a broader understanding of science and trust his handling of the material. "About half of the editorial coverage is given to illustrations," he says, "and the il-lustrations take a lot of the burden off the prose."

During the takeover fervor of the 1980s an unfriendly offer was made to the shareholders of Scientific American, Incorporated, at a quite favorable price. To preserve the integrity of *Scientific American,* Piel asked Salomon Brothers to run an auction for the company. Some thirty-three companies looked at the books, and among those companies Piel found in 1986 the one he was looking for: Verlagsgruppe Georg von Holtzbrinck of Stuttgart,

Piel circa 1958

Germany. It permits Scientific American, Incorporated, to operate as an independent company, just as before. Piel retired as publisher in 1984 and as chairman in 1987 and now holds the title of chairman emeritus. His son Jonathan is the editor.

While shepherding *Scientific American* to stability, affluence, and influence, Piel has spoken out on the necessity for public understanding of science before congressional committees, newspaper editors, scientific bodies, and universities, and he has written articles for a variety of journals – but not for his own magazine; that space, he says, is reserved for people who know what they are talking about. His activities in the promotion of science education earned him the George Polk Award in 1961 for contributions to journalism; the Kalinga Prize from the United Nations Educational, Scientific, and Cultural Organization in 1962 for contributions to the popularization of science; and the Arches of Science Award from the Pacific Science Center in 1969 and the Rosenberger Medal from the University of Chicago in 1973 for contributions to public understanding of science. He was recognized as Publisher of the Year in 1980 by the Magazine Publishers Association and was named president of AAAS in 1985 and chairman in 1986.

Believing that most science and science education are done at universities, Piel has maintained an active association with them, serving as overseer of Harvard University and trustee of Radcliffe College, New York University, and Phillips Academy. He has received many honorary degrees: the Sc.D. from Lawrence College (1956), Colby College (1960), the University of British Columbia (1965), Brandeis University (1965), Lebanon Valley College (1977), Long Island University (1978), Bard College (1979), the City University of New York (1979), the University of Missouri (1985), and Blackburn College (1985); the Litt.D. from Rutgers University (1961) and Bates College (1974); the L.H.D. from Columbia University (1962), Williams College (1966), Rush University (1979), Hahneman Medical College (1981), and Mount Sinai Medical School (1985); the LL.D. from Tuskegee Institute (1963), the University of Bridgeport (1964), the Polytechnic Institute of Brooklyn (1965), Carnegie-Mellon University (1968), and Lowell University (1986); and a doctorate from Moscow State (Lomonosov) University (1985).

Piel devoted the first few years of his retirement to writing a book: *Only One World – Our Own to Make and Keep* (1992). His thesis is that people can decide the future of humanity. He feels that economic development and the consequences of human activity on the environment and human population growth are all "intertwined into one single, horrendous, huge question. . . . I'm trying to do a book that will explain that to people in a way they can understand and make them want to do something about it; and in particular, to get my fellow citizens to think of the need to share our wealth and our knowledge with the poor people of the world and promote their economic development as rapidly as possible."

Piel's importance lies in his perceptiveness in foreseeing the growing impact that science would have in the second half of the twentieth century, the necessity for public education about science, and the ability to do something about it. His timing in launching the revived *Scientific American* was perfect, catching the rise of the professional-technical employment category as a major communication interest and need. His aim was to "present scientific knowledge to the end that science shall occupy the same place in the mind of every thinking citizen that it occupies as an integral part of our modern civilization." His belief that "without such information, modern man has only the haziest idea of how to act in behalf of his own happiness and welfare, or that of his own family and community" has been repeatedly demonstrated. The classic liberal assumption that knowledge would lead to appropriate action has not been so demonstrated. The interested and educated elite to whom Piel's magazine appeals have so far not led the public in the direction he intended. It is unclear, however, that he would have had any more success, or have even survived as a publisher, had he appealed instead to a broader, less educated public.

Piel has, nevertheless, provided for scientific information a forum that had not existed, at a time when it was most needed: a time when the public is either thrilled or threatened by the discoveries, applications, and costs of science.

References:

"AAPT Distinguished Service Citations, 1971," *Physics Teacher,* 10 (May 1972): 260;

Dennis Flanagan, *Flanagan's Version* (New York: Knopf, 1988);

Flanagan, "Gerard Piel: President-Elect of the AAAS," *Science* (27 July 1985): 385–387;

"Gerard Piel of *Scientific American:* The Story of a 'Remarkable Venture,' " *Printer's Ink,* 265 (10 October 1958): 57–60;

David Hollinger, "The Defense of Democracy and Robert K. Merton's Formulation of the Scientific Ethos," *Knowledge and Society,* 4 (1983): 1–15;

"Kalinga Prize," *Nature,* 198 (18 May 1963): 638–639;

Bruce V. Lewenstein, "Magazine Publishing and Popular Science after World War II," *American Journalism,* 6 (Fall 1989): 218–234;

"*Scientific American* – A Case of Clicking," *Tide,* 31 (5 September 1957);

Dael Wolfle, *Running a Scientific Society* (Washington, D.C.: American Association for the Advancement of Science, 1989).

Papers:

Documents concerning Gerard Piel and the *Scientific American* include the Charles W. Gray Papers, Gerard Piel Oral History (1984), and Dennis Flanagan Oral History (26 February 1986), all at Columbia University; Warren Weaver, "The Program in the Natural Sciences" (March 1959) and "Understanding Science," at the Rockefeller Archival Center, North Tarrytown, New York; Gerard Piel Oral History (23 September 1986) at the American Philosophical Society, Philadelphia; and "The Scientific American, Inc., 1949–1955" at the American Association for the Advancement of Science archives, Washington, D.C.

Ken W. Purdy

(28 April 1913 - 7 June 1972)

James S. Featherston
Louisiana State University

MAJOR POSITIONS HELD: Managing editor, *Radio Digest* (1939); associate editor, *Look* (1939-1942); editor, *Victory* (1942-1945); editor, *Parade* (1946-1949); editor, *True* (1949-1954); editor, *Argosy* (1954-1955); contributing editor, *Playboy* (1956-1972).

SELECTED BOOKS: *The Kings of the Road* (Boston: Little, Brown, 1949);

Bright Wheels Rolling, by Purdy and James Melton (Philadelphia: Macrae Smith, 1954);

Wonderful World of the Automobile (New York: Crowell, 1960; enlarged edition, 1963);

All but My Life, by Purdy and Stirling Moss (New York: Dutton, 1963);

The New Matadors, by Purdy and Horst Baumann (Newport Beach, Cal.: Bond 1965);

Motorcars of the Golden Past, by Purdy and Thomas Burnside (Boston: Little, Brown, 1966);

Young People and Driving: The Use and Abuse of the Automobile (New York: John Day, 1967);

Ken Purdy's Book of Automobiles (Chicago: Playboy Press, 1972).

SELECTED PERIODICAL PUBLICATIONS – UNCOLLECTED: "Peace at a Price," *Collier's,* 106 (7 September 1940): 16;

"Window," *Collier's,* 112 (16 October 1943): 52;

"Music that Comes from a Foundry," *Nation's Business,* 37 (May 1949): 70-73;

"Those Bloodcurdling Vanderbilt Cup Races," *Reader's Digest,* 59 (November 1951): 107-110;

"Change of Plan," *Atlantic Monthly,* 190 (September 1952): 35-37;

"What Are Little Boys Made Of ?" *Reader's Digest,* 59 (March 1953): 42-44;

"How not To Go Broke on $10,000 a Year," *Cosmopolitan,* 140 (February 1956): 114-117;

"Blood Sport," *Saturday Evening Post,* 230 (27 July 1957): 26-27;

"U.S. Automobiles Taken for a Ride," *Saturday Review,* 235 (4 October 1958) 16-17;

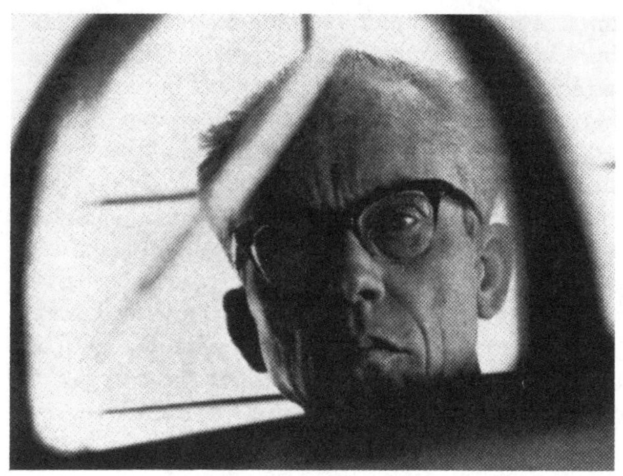

Ken W. Purdy

"Is Fairfield County Part of New England?," *Look,* 24 (22 September 1960): 81-87;

"Karate," *Look,* 25 (14 February 1961): 66-70;

"Bargain at the Price," *Saturday Evening Post,* 235 (22 September 1962): 32-37;

"Motor Sports," *Sports Illustrated,* 15 (23 October 1961): 68-69;

"World's Greatest Automobile Collection," *Atlantic Monthly,* 216 (July 1964): 82-92;

"Depreciation in Reverse," *Holiday* (August 1969): 40-41;

"Far from the Madding Crowd," *Playboy,* 19 (July 1972): 94-98, 172-173.

A prolific writer and gifted editor, Ken W. Purdy was widely known and greatly admired during a journalism career that spanned nearly four decades before his death in 1972. His byline was familiar to millions of readers, as he produced an astounding array of articles and short stories for a wide variety of magazines ranging from the *Atlantic Monthly* to *Playboy*. From 1942 to 1955, he was editor of four magazines, *Victory*, *Parade*, *True*, and *Argosy*. He was a contributing editor for *Playboy* magazine for more than fifteen years, during which time he wrote more than seventy nonfiction and fiction pieces. Purdy was a writer and editor with interests ranging from hypnotism to crossbow archery, but his particular specialty was automotive writing. He wrote numerous articles, short stories, and books about cars and road racing, and he was recognized internationally as an authority on automobiles, both foreign and domestic and both modern and classic. He was considered the Dean of Automotive Writers.

Purdy once estimated that about fifty percent of his articles and short stories dealt with cars and road racing. In a 1970 speech to the Society of Magazine Writers, Purdy said he sold his first automobile piece in 1949 to *True,* before he became its editor. "Because my interest was in exotica, and not in the nuts-and-bolts aspects, I fell into a kind of superspecialty: the great personalities, like Bugatti, Benz, Daimler, Porsche, Sir Henry Royce and so on; the great cars: Bugatti, Rolls-Royce, Hispano-Suiza, Ferrari; and the great drivers. The virtue of this choice lay in the fact that these subjects could be treated in magazines of general circulation, while the other stuff was useful only in the fan magazines, the buff books, where competition is severe and payment minuscule. And almost no one, early on, who was writing about automobiles could write well. The result was that in about ten years I found that I had an international reputation."

Ken William Purdy was born 28 April 1913 in Chicago, Illinois. He was the son of William T. and Mary Helene Purdy. His father, a musical prodigy and a graduate of Hamilton College in Clinton, New York, was a talented pianist, vocalist, and composer who booked musical acts for concerts and other engagements. His father also composed "On Wisconsin," the University of Wisconsin marching song. His father, who had long suffered ill health, died in 1919 at the age of thirty-six, when both Ken and his sister, Marylois, were small children. The children grew up primarily in New York State, and Ken Purdy graduated from high school in Ithaca in 1931. Purdy decided during his childhood that he wanted to be a writer. He was a voracious reader, and by the time he was ten or twelve he was checking out and reading two or three books a week from the public library. He would analyze the elements of good writing. During his senior year of high school, he won a national essay contest by writing on the topic "Is Chemical Warfare Justifiable?"

Ken and Marylois Purdy both attended the University of Wisconsin – Madison where, because their father had written the school song, out-of-state tuition was waived during their first year, and they were given small cash scholarships to defray expenses. Ken Purdy was a brilliant but erratic student: if a class failed to interest him, he would simply stop attending. He began working on the campus newspaper, the *Daily Cardinal,* during his freshman year. At that time the paper had no wire service, and the small staff would fill eight to sixteen pages daily with local news. Later Purdy credited his work on the *Daily Cardinal* with teaching him much of what he knew about journalism.

He also attracted considerable attention with one of his campus pranks. Purdy, who had inherited some of his father's musical talent, had been overcelebrating at a fraternity party when he decided to climb the university tower and awaken the entire campus with a stirring carillon rendition of "Annie Laurie" at three o'clock in the morning. He said the stunt was meant to impress his girlfriend, but it also impressed the daily *Wisconsin State Journal,* which carried a story about the prank on its front page.

During a summer vacation, Purdy worked on the *Athol Daily News* in Massachusetts, and he also interrupted his college career for about a year to edit the *Free Press,* a Progressive party newspaper, in Oshkosh, Wisconsin. In 1936 Purdy left college without graduating to take a magazine job with *Radio Guide,* an Annenberg publication, in Chicago. Purdy's sister would later recall that their mother was upset to learn he was leaving school, but he assured her that he could be successful without a diploma, which was, he told her, "just a piece of paper."

Purdy remained with *Radio Guide* as a writer for about two years before becoming editor of *Click,* another Annenberg magazine. In 1938 he married Jeanne Hale in New York; they would have one son, Geoffrey, who was born on 6 August 1940. In 1939 he became managing editor of *Radio Digest,* still another Annenberg publication, before becoming an associate editor of *Look,* a Cowles publication, later in the same year. In 1942 Purdy was chosen by the Office of War Information to edit a propagandistic picture magazine that appeared in nine languages and was shipped monthly to all accessible parts of Europe, Asia, Africa, Australasia, and territories of the United States. The magazine was in the format of the pictorial newsmagazine *Life* and sought to explain American culture through photographs and articles. Purdy, then only twenty-nine years of age, began with only one full-time and four part-time writers on his staff. His job was a difficult one; not only did he have to meet deadlines, but his stories and pictures also had to be cleared through various censors and government offices.

After the war Purdy served briefly as a consultant for the Crowell-Collier publishing firm before becoming in 1946 an editor of *Parade,* the newspaper supplement magazine owned by Marshall Field. When Purdy took over, *Parade* was a distant third in its field, lagging far behind *American Weekly* and *This Week,* and industry observers believed it would soon fold. Purdy raised the level of the magazine's writing, and its circulation passed the 3 million mark and then zoomed to 5.2 million. Also in 1946 Purdy married his second wife, Lucille von Urff, on 6 January.

Much in demand, Purdy was hired in 1949 as editor of *True,* which billed itself as "The Man's Magazine." Purdy started with a salary of thirty thousand dollars a year, which was considered at the time a fabulous magazine salary. A Fawcett publication, *True* had in ten years evolved from a lurid pulp magazine into a somewhat more sophisticated slick-paper publication that was attracting such big-name writers as Paul Gallico, Quentin Reynolds, and MacKinlay Kantor. When Purdy took over, the circulation was about 1.4 million. Within three years the magazine had picked up an additional five hundred thousand in circulation. Purdy attributed the magazine's success to its guarantee that the articles were true and that it carried escapist fare: "We run *True* like a portable twenty-five cent private study . . . In *True,* the customer gets escapist material . . . no reminders of the sad state the world is in today . . . no whither-are-we-going stories . . . no doom-is-just-around-the-corner stuff." Purdy also credited the magazine's ban on fiction as another reason for its success. "The fact is men don't read magazine fiction anymore," he claimed. "They still want good reading, good stories, but they like them better when they know they are true."

In 1954 Purdy became editor of *Argosy,* a competitor that differed from *True* in that it published both fiction and nonfiction articles. *Argosy* had a long history, dating back to 1882, when it was founded as a children's magazine by Frank Munsey, who in the 1890s transformed it into a pulp magazine filled with adventure stories for men and boys. Eminent writers such as Jack London, Edgar Rice Burroughs, and O. Henry contributed to the magazine at one time or another, but *Argosy* was in decline when Popular Publications bought it from Munsey in 1942. Under the new owners *Argosy* became a slick-paper, all-fiction magazine, but later it became a general men's magazine similar to *True.* Purdy remained at *Argosy* only two years because he wanted to devote more time to writing. For about a year he was editorial chairman of Ziff-Davis Publication Company; this was a consulting job that left him much free time to write.

In 1956 Purdy joined *Playboy,* which was then only three years old and which had earlier tried to hire him as its top editor. At first Purdy was given the title of eastern editor, although in fact he was a staff writer; later he was listed as a contributing editor. Purdy became the most prolific writer in the history of *Playboy,* writing seventy-three articles and short stories. During most of his career Purdy and his family lived in a spacious home in Wilton, Connecticut, which was within commuting distance of New York. During his time with *Playboy,* Purdy traveled widely, and for about three years the family lived mostly in England, a country Purdy loved because he considered it to be "very civilized." He became a legend at *Playboy,* and the other editors had difficulty keeping up with all his activities. His postcards, which became known as Kencards, arrived at the Chicago office at a rate of more than one a day. When editors would query him about a story, Purdy himself sometimes would have difficulty determining which one they meant. Once asked about his ongoing activities, Purdy replied that at the moment he was working on eight articles, two books, one short story, and one screenplay and that he was also planning trips to Ireland and Italy.

Arlene Bouras, then a copy editor at *Playboy,* recalled that Purdy would argue with her over diction and usage. Purdy liked writing for *Playboy,* which he said was about the only market left for short stories except for the formula-written women's magazines. He praised the magazine's "marvelous production" and said in 1970 that he could recall only one typographical error in all the pieces he had done for it. He went on to recount a long-distance phone call he had received in London from *Playboy* asking permission to change two words.

Purdy's love for automobiles was legendary, and in addition to writing about them, he also bought them, restored them, and drove them. Over the years he owned a procession of classic cars, some of which he restored at considerable cost. Purdy also greatly admired and enjoyed the companionship of the great racing riders, and he glorified them in much the same way that Ernest Hemingway did bullfighters. Purdy's first book about cars, *The Kings of the Road,* appeared in 1949, and it remained in print for seventeen years. He was a good friend of the racing champion Stirling Moss, and his book about Moss, *All but My Life* (1963), was a best-seller in Great Britain. All of Purdy's books were about automobiles, but in his articles he wrote about various subjects including acupuncture, bullfighting, karate, hypnotism, baseball, carillons, crossbows, graphology, liqueurs, player pianos, manners, and morals. His magazine output was so great that he sometimes wrote under the pen name of Karl Prentiss.

Purdy also wrote fiction, and this was perhaps his first love. One of his first published magazine pieces was a short-short story titled "Peace at a Price," which he sold to *Collier's* in 1939. During his career he wrote about 150 short stories for various magazines. According to Purdy, "The great thing about short stories is that you don't have to do a lot of research or depend on anyone else. And the creative satisfaction is greater."

Purdy was hired to write the script for a racing car movie but resigned along with the director, John Sturgis, while they were on location in France when a dispute developed between Sturgis and Steve McQueen, who was both producing and acting in the film. The movie, *LeMans,* was released in 1971, but Purdy received no screen credit. In 1972 he wrote the script for *Azzura,* a short documentary picture about bullfighting.

Plagued with ulcers and other health problems and suffering from depression, Purdy shot and killed himself at his home in Wilton on 7 June 1972. Funeral services were private. The September 1972 issue of *Playboy* eulogized Purdy in an unsigned editorial:

> The public image Ken projected was filled with *machismo* – a consuming passion for karate, weaponry, for the artifacts of war and mayhem, for the men, who in their occupations and avocations, accepted death as a possible payoff. He painted himself as a very hard number. But those who were privileged to know him well soon saw beneath the veneer. In his personal relationships, Ken was warm and kind, with a gallantry toward women that was almost Victorian. The truth is that – in spite of what he would have liked everyone to believe – Ken Purdy was a gentle man. The world will be a little lonelier now that he's gone.

The first Ken Purdy Scholarship was awarded on 22 January 1975 at the University of Wisconsin School of Journalism and Mass Communication. Jess Gorkin, who had succeeded Purdy as editor of *Parade* and had also worked with him at *Victory* and *Look,* established the scholarship fund and made the first presentation to Mary Ellen Haskett, an outstanding student from Fond du Lac, Wisconsin. Purdy's sister, Marylois, spoke to an assembly of students and faculty. She discussed her brother's career, his editorial integrity, and his willingness to help young writers. "Ken Purdy always had proteges," she said. "He wanted to help those who were just starting, and many young men and women sought and got his advice. Therefore, I think it's particularly fitting that the Ken Purdy Scholarship has come to pass. In a sense, Mary Ellen Haskett is Ken's latest protege. He would have liked that."

References:

Pat Chappell, "It Is Necessary to Remember Friends – Particularly the Great Ones," *Car Classics,* 9 (April 1977): 116–120;

"Ken W. Purdy," *Playboy,* 19 (September 1972): 44;

"Ken W. Purdy, Writer on Cars for Playboy, Is a Suicide at 59," *New York Times,* 8 June 1972, p. 50;

"A Man's World," *Time,* 55 (6 February 1950): 38, 40;

Theodore Peterson, *Magazines of the Twentieth Century* (Urbana: University of Illinois Press, 1956);

"A Punch for Parade," *Time,* 48 (7 October 1956): 74–75;

"Taxpayers' Victory," *Time,* 41 (1 February 1943): 52, 54;

"True Man," *Newsweek,* 9 (28 February 1949): 55;

"True's Story – It Gives Its Men What They Want," *Tide,* 26 (28 March 1952): 56.

Papers:

Ken Purdy's papers are at the State Historical Society of Wisconsin, Archives Division, Mass Communications Center, University of Wisconsin.

Philip Rahv

(10 March 1908 - 23 December 1973)

James T. F. Tanner
University of North Texas

MAJOR POSITIONS HELD: Coeditor, with William Phillips, *Partisan Review* (1934–1969); editor, *Modern Occasions* (1970–1972); professor of English, Brandeis University (1957–1973).

BOOKS: *Image and Idea: Fourteen Essays on Literary Themes* (New York: New Directions, 1949); revised and enlarged as *Image and Idea: Twenty Essays on Literary Themes.* (New York: Laughlin, 1957);

The Myth and the Powerhouse (New York: Farrar, Straus & Giroux, 1965);

Literature and the Sixth Sense (Boston: Houghton Mifflin, 1969) – includes *Image and Idea* and *The Myth and the Powerhouse*;

Collection: *Essays on Literature and Politics, 1932–1972, by Philip Rahv,* edited by Arabel J. Porter and Andrew J. Dvosin, with a memoir by Mary McCarthy (Boston: Houghton Mifflin, 1978).

Philip Rahv (photograph by Sylvia Salmi)

OTHER: *The Great Short Novels of Henry James,* edited by Rahv (New York: Dial, 1944);

Henry James, *The Bostonians,* edited by Rahv (New York: Dial, 1945);

The Short Novels of Tolstoy, selected, with an introductory essay, by Rahv, and translated by Aylmer Maude (New York: Dial, 1946);

The Partisan Reader: Ten Years of the Partisan Review, 1934–44, edited by Rahv and William Phillips (New York: Dial, 1946);

Discovery of Europe: The Story of American Experience in the Old World, edited, with an introduction, by Rahv (Boston: Houghton Mifflin, 1947; revised edition, Garden City: Doubleday, 1960);

Great Russian Short Novels, edited by Rahv (New York: Dial, 1951);

Selected Short Stories of Franz Kafka, introduction by Rahv, translated by Willa and Edwin Muir (New York: Modern Library, 1952);

The Berkley Book of Modern Writing, edited by Rahv and Phillips (New York: Berkley, 1953);

The New Partisan Reader, 1945–1953, edited by Rahv and Phillips (New York: Harcourt, Brace, 1953);

Literature in America: An Anthology of Literary Criticism, edited by Rahv (New York: Meridian Books, 1957);

The Partisan Review Anthology, edited by Rahv and Phillips (New York: Holt, Rinehart & Winston, 1962);

Eight Great American Short Novels, edited by Rahv (New York: Berkley, 1963);

Modern Occasions, edited by Rahv (New York: Farrar, Straus & Giroux, 1966);
Bernard Malamud, *A Malamud Reader,* edited by Rahv (New York: Farrar, Straus & Giroux, 1967).

SELECTED PERIODICAL PUBLICATIONS – UNCOLLECTED: "The Literary Class War," *New Masses,* 8 (August 1932): 7–10;
"Maxim Gorky and the Cultural Revolution," *Daily Worker* (23 December 1932): 4;
"T. S. Eliot," *Fantasy,* 2 (Winter 1932): 17–20;
Review of Ernest Hemingway, *Winner Take Nothing, Partisan Review,* 1 (February–March 1934): 58–60;
"Marxist Criticism and Henry Hazlitt," *International Literature,* 2 (1934): 112–116;
"For Whom Do You Write?" *New Quarterly,* 1 (Summer 1934): 18–20;
"Problems and Perspectives in Revolutionary Literature," by Rahv and Wallace Phelps, *Partisan Review,* 1 (June–July 1934): 3–10;
"Valedictory on the Propaganda Issue," *Little Magazine* (September–October 1934): 1–2;
"Marxian Criticism," by Rahv and Phelps, *Partisan Review,* 2 (April–May 1935): 16–25;
"Private Experience and Public Philosophy," by Rahv and William Phillips, *Poetry,* 48 (May 1936): 98–105;
Review of William Carlos Williams, *White Mule, Nation,* 144 (26 June 1937): 733;
Review of Louis Celine, *Mea Culpa, Nation,* 145 (21 August 1937): 174–175;
Review of Ilya Ilf and Eugene Petrov, *Little Golden America, Nation,* 145 (25 September 1937): 326;
"Some Aspects of Literary Criticism," *Science and Society* (Winter 1937): 212–220;
"Two Years of Progress," *Partisan Review,* 4 (February 1938): 22–30;
"Trials of the Mind," *Partisan Review,* 4 (April 1938): 3–12;
"Dostoevksy and Politics: Notes on *The Possessed,*" *Partisan Review,* 5 (July 1938): 25–36;
"Munich and the Intellectuals," *Partisan Review,* 6 (Fall 1938): 7–10;
"Two Years of Progress – from Waldo Frank to Donald Ogden Stewart," *Partisan Review,* 4 (Fall 1938): 22–30;
Review of Bertolt Brecht, *A Penny for the Poor, Nation,* 147 (26 November 1938): 571–572;
"Proletarian Literature: A Political Autopsy," *Southern Review,* 4 (January 1939): 616–628;
"'The Death of Ivan Ilyich' and Joseph K.," *Southern Review,* 5 (Summer 1939): 174–185;
"Twilight of the Thirties," *Partisan Review,* 6 (Summer 1939): 6–15;
"Paleface and Redskin," *Kenyon Review,* 1 (Summer 1939): 251–256;
"Franz Kafka: The Hero as Lonely Man," *Kenyon Review,* 1 (Winter 1939): 60–74;
"The Slump in American Writing," *American Mercury,* 49 (February 1940): 185–191;
"What Is Living and What Is Dead," *Partisan Review,* 8 (May–June 1940): 175–180;
"The Men Who Write Our Plays," *American Mercury,* 50 (August 1940): 463–469;
"The Cult of Experience in American Writing," *Partisan Review,* 7 (November–December 1940): 412–424;
"The Artist as Desperado," *New Republic,* 104 (21 April 1941): 557–559;
"The Dark Lady of Salem," *Partisan Review,* 8 (September–October 1941): 362–381;
"10 Propositions and 8 Errors," *Partisan Review,* 8 (November–December 1941): 499–508;
"Notes on the Decline of Naturalism," *Partisan Review,* 9 (November–December 1942): 483–493;
"The Heiress of All the Ages," *Partisan Review,* 10 (May–June 1943): 227–247;
Review of Edmund Wilson, *The Shock of Recognition, American Mercury,* 57 (August 1943): 243–248;
"The Progress of Cultural Bolshevism," *Partisan Review,* 11 (Summer 1944): 361–363;
"The Liberal Fifth Column," *Partisan Review,* 13 (Summer 1946): 279–293;
"Concerning Tolstoy," *Partisan Review,* 13 (September–October 1946): 420–432;
"Disillusionment and Partial Answers," *Partisan Review,* 15 (May 1948): 519–529;
"Religion and the Intellectuals: A Symposium," *Partisan Review,* 17 (March 1950): 237–244;
"Our Country and Our Culture: A Symposium," *Partisan Review,* 19 (May–June 1952): 304–310;
"The Myth and the Powerhouse," *Partisan Review,* 20 (November–December 1953): 635–649;
"Fiction and the Criticism of Fiction," *Kenyon Review,* 18 (Spring 1956): 276–299;
"Literary Criticism and the Imagination of Alternatives," *Michigan Alumnus Quarterly Review,* 63 (Winter 1956): 7–16;
"Dostoevsky in *Crime and Punishment,*" *Partisan Review,* 27 (Summer 1960): 393–426;
Translation of letter from Vissarion Belinsky, *Letters to V. P. Botkin, Partisan Review,* 27 (Fall 1960): 727–736;
"Why a New Magazine," *Modern Occasions,* 1 (Fall 1970): 1–5;

PARTISAN REVIEW

A Bi-Monthly of Revolutionary Literature
Published by the John Reed Club of New York

VOLUME I, NO. I FEBRUARY-MARCH 1934

COVER DESIGN *Elroy Webber*	
EDITORIAL STATEMENT	
TWO SKETCHES *Grace Lumpkin*	3
IN A COFFEE POT *Alfred Hayes*	12
STUDS LONIGAN *James T. Farrell*	16
THE SHEEP DIP *Ben Field*	24
POEM *Edwin Rolfe*	32
DEATH OF A SHOP *Arthur Pense*	35
FOUR POEMS *Joseph Freeman*	44
THE ANATOMY OF LIBERALISM *Wallace Phelps*	47
BOOKS *Obed Brooks, Granville Hicks, Philip Rahv, Waldo Tell*	52
JOHN REED CLUB NOTES	64

Editorial Board:
NATHAN ADLER, EDWARD DAHLBERG, JOSEPH FREEMAN, SENDER GARLIN, ALFRED HAYES, MILTON HOWARD, JOSHUA KUNITZ, LOUIS LOZOWICK, LEONARD MINS, WALLACE PHELPS, PHILIP RAHV, EDWIN ROLFE.

Copyright 1934 by the John Reed Club of New York. Address all manuscripts and other communications to PARTISAN REVIEW, *430 Sixth Avenue, New York City. Subscriptions: $1.00 for six issues; $2.00 for twelve issues.*

Contributors meet with the editors for:
POETRY: Mondays 3:00-5:30
FICTION: Wednesdays 3:00-5:30
CRITICAL ESSAYS: Thursdays 3:00-5:30

Contents for the first issue of Rahv and Phillips's magazine of "Revolutionary Literature"

"Cultural Malaise and Ultimate Capability," *Modern Occasions,* 1 (Fall 1971): 461–469;

"What and Where Is the New Left?" *Modern Occasions,* 1 (Winter 1971): 157–162;

"The Other Dostoevsky," *New York Review of Books,* 18 (20 April 1972): 30–38;

"Dostoevsky: Descent into the Underground," *Modern Occasions,* 2 (Winter 1972): 1–13.

Philip Rahv is chiefly remembered as the cofounder (with William Phillips) of *Partisan Review,* one of the most influential literary journals published in America. Active in the "New York School" of left-wing literati, widely considered a leading Neo-Marxist critic, recognized as an astute book reviewer, respected as an austere copy editor, and active in liberal political causes, Rahv deserved his reputation as an important and influential twentieth-century man of letters.

Philip Rahv was born Ivan Greenberg, the second of three sons, on 10 March 1908 in Kupin, Ukraine. He would adopt the name Philip Rahv when he became a Communist in 1933; Rahv is the Hebrew word for rabbi. His parents were Jewish shopkeepers living in the midst of a peasant population. Rahv's parents were early Zionists, and after the revolution they immigrated to Palestine, where Rahv's father opened a small furniture factory. Rahv came to America in 1922, settling in Providence, Rhode Island, living with his older brother, and attending grade school there. His first job was as a junior advertising copywriter for a small firm in Oregon. Lacking the time and financial resources for a college education, he educated himself in public libraries. He read voraciously – Karl Marx, Lenin, Leon Trotsky, James Joyce, Joseph Conrad, Marcel Proust, and Thomas Mann.

In 1932, during the Great Depression, he migrated to New York City, where he stood in breadlines and slept on park benches. It was in this context that he became a Marxist and moved in influential New York Jewish intellectual circles. Also in 1932 his first important essay was published in the August issue of the *New Masses;* "The Literary Class War" reflects the intensity of his personal suffering and his observations of the class struggle in New York. For the Communist *Daily Worker* he wrote "Maxim Gorky and the Cultural Revolution," but he also wrote sympathetically on T. S. Eliot for *Fantasy.*

In 1933, the year that Adolph Hitler came to power in Berlin and that Franklin D. Roosevelt began his first term as president of the United States, Rahv joined the John Reed Club (a Marxist organization founded in New York in 1929), cultivated literary and intellectual acquaintances, and planned, with William Phillips, to establish a new left-wing literary and intellectual periodical. He and Phillips persuaded the editor of the *New Masses* that a literary journal was needed as an adjunct to the heavily political *New Masses* as a means of reaching literary intellectuals with a Marxist message.

Thus *Partisan Review,* frankly subtitled "A Bi-Monthly of Revolutionary Literature" and coedited by Rahv and Phillips, appeared in 1934 as a forum for the John Reed Club. The first issue carried a February–March cover date. "We were cocky kids," William Phillips wrote years later. "We had the idea of launching a new literary movement, combining older with younger talents, and the best of the new radicalism with the innovative energy of modernism." The magazine was destined to become the leading intellectual focus of liberal and Marxist intellectuals during the 1930s and beyond. In "Problems and Perspectives in Revolutionary Literature" (1934) and in "Marxian Criticism" (1935), Rahv and Phillips struggled to define their objectives in the evaluation of literary works. Rahv's difficulties in dealing with Marxist revolutionary theory is apparent in his review of Tess Slesinger's *The Unpossessed* (1934), a radical work concerned with personal as well as political relationships. According to Rahv, the work lacks "a disciplined orientation for radicalized intellectuals," a view Rahv held mainly because he was not concerned to see the peculiar problems of female intellectual radicals in contrast with their male counterparts; a woman's desire for marriage and children and the consequent sacrifice of intelligence and political ideals seemed to him a frivolous bit of rhetoric, an attitude that the feminist critic Elaine Showalter condemns in her essay "Women Writers Between the Wars."

But from the outset Rahv demonstrated an interest in serious American literature – the first issue of *Partisan Review* contains his appreciative review of Ernest Hemingway's *Winner Take Nothing* (1933). That issue also contained contributions from Delmore Schwartz, James Agee, Edmund Wilson, James T. Farrell, Dwight Macdonald, Mary McCarthy, Sidney Hook, Lionel Trilling, Wallace Stevens, and Pablo Picasso. Already apparent in this list of contributors is Rahv's double commitment to Marxist historical interpretation and his championship of modernism.

In 1935 Rahv worked on the Federal Writer's Project and observed the First American Writers Congress. He also wrote on the Constitution of the Communist Party Popular Front which was adopted in that year. In 1936, in the wake of the first Moscow purge trials, the John Reed Club forced *Partisan Review* to merge with the *Anvil,* another left-wing journal. After six issues the combined magazine (now known as *Partisan Review/Anvil*) closed down, as Rahv and Phillips dissociated it from the John Reed Club and the Communist party. Thereafter Rahv denounced Stalinism and considered himself a Trotskyite. In December 1937 Rahv and Phillips revived their magazine with its original title. Rahv also formally left the Communist party. The *Partisan Review* now devoted itself "to the modern sensibility in literature and the arts and to a radical consciousness in social and political matters." Over the next thirty years the magazine became, in the words of the novelist and magazine writer McCarthy, "the best literary magazine in America."

Although Rahv had condemned Stalinism and had broken officially with the Communist party, Marxism remained his orientation in literary and artistic criticism. More than anything else, he maintained that Marxism alone possessed a true sense of history – the "sixth sense" of which he so often

This Month:

With this issue, PARTISAN REVIEW AND ANVIL are combining to publish a new literary monthly. Though continuing the traditions of its predecessors, the new magazine will be broader in scope and, we believe, more mature. We invite contributions from writers the country over, and letters from readers on their reactions to our policy as well as specific stories, poems and articles.

Grade Crossing is from JOHN DOS PASSOS's work in progress, *The Big Money,* a continuation of *The 42nd Parallel* and *1919.*

ILDEFONZO PEREDA VALDES is the author of numerous books of poetry, fiction and criticism. He is a defense attorney for the International Red Aid, a leading member of the Anti-War Committee of Uruguay, and a professor of Castilian literature at the University of Montevideo.

CARL VAN DOREN's essay is a re-written version of his address at the Book Union dinner. As Mr. Van Doren writes: "I have made a new draft of it for you, keeping close to the original and trying to make it say to the reader what the speech said to its hearers."

JAMES NEUGASS's poems have appeared in two recent anthologies of modern American verse. He lives in New York City.

In the Heart of Darkness is a selection from *Days of Wrath,* ANDRE MALRAUX's latest work, which deals with the imprisonment of a German Communist by the Nazis. The novel has been translated by Haakon Chevalier, and will be published next month by Harrison Smith and Robert Haas, Inc.

KERKER QUINN is an editor of *Direction* and one of the contributors to *Trial Balances,* an anthology of younger poets. He lives in Urbana, Ill.

NEWTON ARVIN was recently awarded a Guggenheim fellowship to write a book on Walt Whitman.

WALDO FRANK is chairman of the League of American Writers. He is now at work on a new novel.

GENEVIEVE TAGGARD's latest book of verse is entitled *Not Mine to Finish.*

BEN FIELD is the instructor of the short story class in the John Reed Writers School, which is held under the auspices of PARTISAN REVIEW AND ANVIL. His stories have appeared frequently in earlier issues of the magazine.

JOSEPH FREEMAN's forthcoming book, *An American Testament,* a narrative of ideas and personalities in relation to the revolutionary movement, will be published in the spring by Farrar and Rinehart.

SAUL LEVITT has contributed stories to the *New Masses, The Magazine, The Anvil, The American Mercury,* and other periodicals. He is now completing his first novel.

CLARA WEATHERWAX's *Marching! Marching!* published last month, won the prize in the *New Masses* and John Day Co. contest for the best proletarian novel. It was also a Book Union choice. She lives in Los Angeles, Calif.

JAMES T. FARRELL and KENNETH FEARING will cover the theatre and the movies every month for PARTISAN REVIEW AND ANVIL.

Due to the large number of contributions received for this first issue, the entire book review section had to be eliminated. However, these reviews—by JACK CONROY, OBED BROOKS, RUTH LECHLITNER, EDWIN BERRY BURGUM, DAVID RAMSEY, and EDWIN SEAVER—will be published next month.

2

CONTENTS

VOLUME III FEBRUARY 1936 NUMBER 1

PARTISAN REVIEW AND ANVIL is published monthly at 430 Sixth Avenue, New York City. Subscriptions $1.00 for 10 issues; foreign rates, $1.50. Copyright by PARTISAN REVIEW AND ANVIL. Manuscripts will not be returned unless accompanied by stamped, self-addressed envelopes.

Editors: ALAN CALMER, JACK CONROY, BEN FIELD, WILLIAM PHILLIPS, PHILIP RAHV, EDWIN ROLFE, CLINTON SIMPSON.

Associates: NELSON ALGREN, J. S. BALCH, ERSKINE CALDWELL, KENNETH FEARING, ALFRED HAYES, JOSEPH KALAR, MERIDEL LE SUEUR, H. H. LEWIS, SAMUEL PUTNAM, HOWARD RUSHMORE, EDWIN SEAVER, WALTER SNOW, WILL WHARTON, RICHARD WRIGHT.

Designed by ROBERT JOSEPHY

Contents for the first issue of the merged Partisan Review *and* Anvil

spoke. He thought that other contemporary criticism, especially the New Critics and the Myth Critics, lacked this sense.

Throughout the 1930s Rahv – even though he was actively engaged with editorial work for *Partisan Review* – frequently contributed insightful articles and incisive book reviews to such periodicals as the *Nation, Kenyon Review,* the *New Republic,* the *New Masses,* the *New Leader,* and the *Southern Review.* His book reviews in particular established him as one of the most important practical critics of the era.

In 1939 three of Rahv's most important essays appeared: a political "autopsy" of proletarian literature in the *Southern Review* and in the *Kenyon Review* a critical introduction to Franz Kafka (the first piece on Kafka to appear in the United States) and his most celebrated essay, "Paleface and Redskin," which describes the "dichotomy between experience and consciousness" in American literature and divides American writers into two opposing camps.

"Paleface and Redskin" is Rahv's best-known pronouncement in literary criticism. The fastidious gentility of authors such as Henry James and Nathaniel Hawthorne is set in contrast to the realism

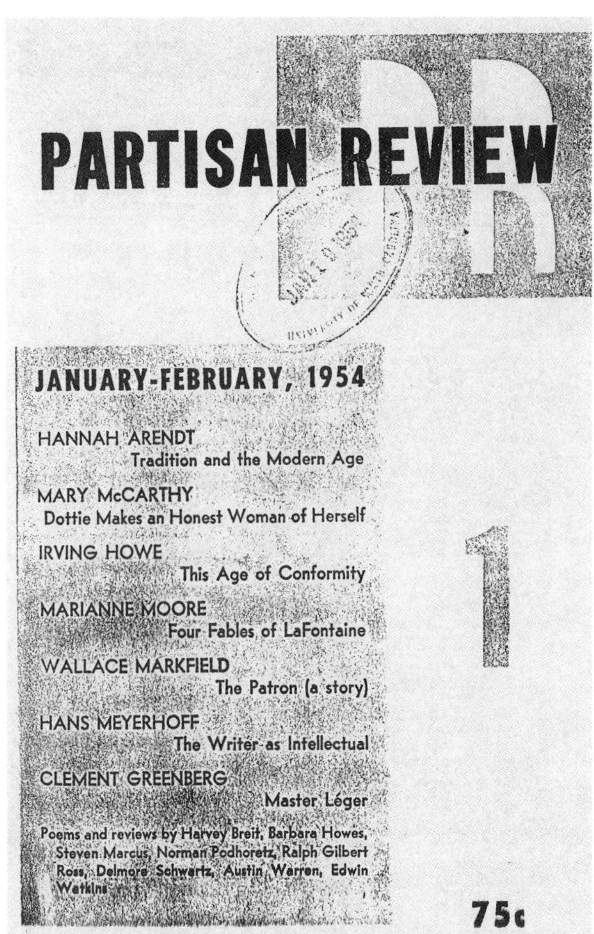

Cover for an issue whose contents illustrate the characteristically literary and intellectual tone of the publication

and anti-intellectualism of writers such as James Fenimore Cooper, Walt Whitman, and Theodore Dreiser. The inadequacy and incompleteness of each category of writers was apparent to Rahv, who thought that American literature had become too fragmented, incomplete, and immature because of this division. His own basically European orientation allowed him to appreciate the strengths and to discern the weaknesses of each group.

In 1941 Rahv married Nathalie Swan, an architect, a union that would last until 1955, when they were divorced. In 1956 he married Theodora Jay Stillman, who died in a fire at their home in 1968, leaving him considerable property and income. Rahv's friends noted that his first two wives had both been heiresses, quite rich, and totally unliterary in outlook. In 1970, late in life, he married Betty McIlvain, a woman much younger than he; this union proved to be an unhappy one.

During World War II, Rahv broke with his former collaborators Macdonald and Clement Greenberg on the issue of whether American radicals should support the war against Hitler. "And yet in a certain sense it is our war," Rahv argued in a long meditative article wherein he rejected his colleagues' arguments that the European war belonged to the Europeans. Aside from all the Marxist theorizing, Rahv was considerably troubled about what he, a Jew, was doing to combat Hitler. *Partisan Review* was, in fact, according to Rahv and Phillips, "both anti-fascist and anti-communist long before it became commonplace to identify the two forms of totalitarianism and to regard them with equal repugnance."

In 1950 Rahv was awarded the Guggenheim Fellowship in Criticism. During the 1950s he voiced his unequivocal opposition to Sen. Eugene McCarthy and the hearings conducted by the House Un-American Activities Committee. In 1953 "The Myth and the Powerhouse" appeared in the November–December issue of *Partisan Review.* In this essay Rahv deplored the myth-criticism that had become all the rage in academic circles and which tended to detach the work of art from its historical contexts. He claimed that Northrop Frye and his followers tended to substitute myth for religion; such doctrines Rahv considered an opiate for intellectuals without the stomach for engagement in politics.

In 1957 Rahv accepted a professorship at Brandeis University, teaching in the English and comparative literature departments. Never a true academic in the traditional sense, he had earlier been known for his contempt of academic intellectuals. Nevertheless he would remain on the faculty at Brandeis for the remainder of his life. A stubborn Marxist, he was also adept in using Freudian psychoanalysis, existentialism, and anthropology when the need for such doctrines arose in the context of the text he had at hand. Yet between the years 1957 and 1962 Rahv actually wrote little.

Rahv was particularly critical of the various "trendy" schools of literary criticism that arose during his academic years. His opposition to the New Criticism was well known. In 1958 he observed that it was "virtually done for." Basically his view was that the New Critics were quite adept in dealing with the text but either ignorant of or indifferent to the context (especially the historical context) of literary works. The right-wing orientation of the New Critics did not go unnoticed by Rahv and other Marxist critics.

Partisan Review was greatly influential in American literary culture largely because of Rahv's cultivation of what has been called "a Jewish-American literary aesthetic." The identification of *Partisan Re-*

view with a distinguished group of New York intellectuals, including Saul Bellow, Paul Goodman, Bernard Malamud, Phillips, Norman Podhoretz, Isaac Rosenfeld, Schwartz, and Trilling, among many others who began their careers in *Partisan Review,* gave the magazine substance and respectability. Perhaps Rahv's greatest strength during the *Partisan Review* years was his willingness occasionally to depart from his Marxist ideology; as Ian Hamilton asserts in his *The Little Magazines* (1976): "*Partisan*'s greatest strength throughout was that it was never as foolish as its principles made it look."

Literature and the Sixth Sense (1969) is a compendium of Rahv's important critical and political essays up to that point in his life. The "sixth sense" to which he refers is the *historical* sense, an awareness that Rahv attributed in his own case to his absorption of Marxist principles. Indeed, the older Rahv was no longer the "cocky" intellectual that Phillips has so well described. Experience had loosened his grip on rigid ideology.

In 1970 Rahv embarked upon a new magazine venture, *Modern Occasions,* with two associate editors, Mark Krupnick and Alan Lelchuk. Rahv himself put up the money for the publication, which was to be radical in its politics while reserving the right to criticize the New Left. Philip Roth's "Salad Days" appeared in the first issue (Fall 1970), and in a later issue a section of *Our Gang* (1970), Roth's book on Richard Nixon, was printed.

Rahv was severely critical of the New Left in *Modern Occasions.* In the editorial introduction to the second issue (Winter 1971), titled, "What and Where Is the New Left?," he attacked the Weathermen and the idealistic "kids" who needed, he thought, a talking to. He was entirely without sympathy for the New Left's notions of university reform. He observed that the New Left had shown "no understanding whatsoever of the first rule of revolutionary strategy, which is the education, build-up, and preservation of its leading cadres."

Modern Occasions failed after only six issues mainly because Rahv found himself in basic disagreement with contemporary trends manifested by the anti–Vietnam War protesters, black militants, pornographers, pop music cultists, and doomsayers of various stripes. He opposed such pop culture heroes as Leslie Fiedler, Norman O. Brown, R. D. Laing, Marshall McLuhan, Herbert Marcuse, Claude Lévi-Strauss, George Steiner, and Norman Mailer; almost instinctively he suspected anything new or trendy. Rahv disapproved of what he saw as the carefree and callow attitudes reflected by these figures and trends, and he felt free to go on the attack against them. According to his associate editor Mark Krupnick, Rahv become attached to "an orthodoxy of negation" and "There was never anything – person, idea or movement – the magazine wholeheartedly supported." Increasingly Rahv seemed old-fashioned and ill-tempered. In her *New York Times* obituary of Rahv, Mary McCarthy observed that "It was as though he came into being with the steam engine: for him, literature began with Dostoevsky and stopped with Joyce, Proust and Eliot; politics began with Marx and Engels and stopped with Lenin. He was not interested in Shakespeare, the classics, Greek city states; and he despised most contemporary writing and contemporary political groups, being grumblingly out of sorts with fashion, except where he felt it belonged, on the backs of good-looking women and girls." During the Vietnam War, Rahv was privately scornful of the idealistic Noam Chomsky and Father Daniel Berrigan, and, according to Krupnick, Roth had a suspicious attitude toward writers: "In his view the poets were worse than novelists, but they were all monsters of self-promotion, log-rollers, puffers, morally retarded."

In 1973 Rahv took a year's leave of absence from his teaching duties at Brandeis ostensibly to work on two book-length studies – one on Trotsky and the other on Fyodor Dostoevsky, but his health declined quickly. He separated at this time from his wife and moved into an apartment in Boston, being careful to rewrite his will so that his estate could be left to the state of Israel rather than to his estranged wife. He drank excessively, overindulged in medications for his various ailments, and behaved erratically. Philip Rahv died on 23 December 1973 in Cambridge, Massachusetts.

McCarthy's obituary summed up the formidable cultural contribution of Philip Rahv: "It would be hard to overestimate the cultural importance of Rahv's and Phillips's decision to break with Stalinism without abandoning the social and political ideals (and analytic techniques) of the Marxist tradition." Indeed, Marxist literary criticism probably survived in America largely due to Rahv and his colleagues associated with *Partisan Review.*

Bibliography:

Andrew James Dvosin, Bibliography, in "Literature in a Political World: The Career and Writings of Philip Rahv," Ph.D. dissertation, New York University, 1977, pp. 226–241.

Biography:

Andrew James Dvosin, "Literature in a Political World: The Career and Writings of Philip

Philip Rahv

Rahv," Ph.D. dissertation, New York University, 1977.

References:

Daniel Aaron, *Writers on the Left: Episodes in American Literary Communism* (New York: Harcourt, Brace & World, 1961);

William Arrowsmith, "*Partisan Review* and American Writing," *Hudson Review,* 1 (Winter 1949): 526–536;

William Barrett, "The Truants: *Partisan Review* in the 40's," *Commentary,* 57 (June 1974): 48–54;

Malcolm Bradbury, "Neorealist Fiction," in *Columbia Literary History of the United States,* edited by Emory Elliott and others (New York: Columbia University Press, 1988): 1126–1141;

Malcolm Cowley, "*Partisan Review,*" *New Republic,* 96 (19 October 1938): 311–312;

Frederick Crews, "The Partisan," *New York Review of Books* (23 November 1978): 3–9;

John P. Diggins, *The American Left in the Twentieth Century* (New York: Harcourt, Brace, Jovanovich, 1973);

Diggins, *Up from Communism: Conservative Odysseys in American Intellectual History* (New York: Harper & Row, 1975);

F. W. Dupee, "Stalinism and Hitlerism," *New Masses,* (26 January 1937): 250–256;

Andrew James Dvosin, "Literature in a Political World: The Career and Writings of Philip Rahv," Ph.D. dissertation, New York University, 1977;

Arthur Edelstein, ed. *Images and Ideas in American Culture – The Functions of Criticism: Essays in Memory of Philip Rahv* (Hanover, N.H.: Brandeis University Press, 1979);

Maxwell Geismar, *Henry James and the Jacobites* (Boston: Houghton Mifflin, 1963);

James Burkhart Gilbert, *Writers and Partisans: A History of Literary Radicalism in America* (New York: John Wiley & Sons, 1968);

Eugene Goodheart, "Philip Rahv and *Image and Idea,*" *Sewanee Review,* 92 (1984): 103–113;

Ian Hamilton, *The Little Magazines* (London: Weidenfeld & Nicolson, 1976);

Elizabeth Hardwick, "Philip Rahv (1908–1974) [*sic*]," *New York Review of Books,* 20 (24 January 1974): 16;

James David Hart, "Philip Rahv (1908–1973)," in *The Oxford Companion to American Literature,* fifth edition (New York: Oxford University Press, 1983), p. 624;

Terry Hoagwood, "The New Historicism," *CCTE Studies,* 54 (1989): 73–76;

Irving Howe, "The New York Intellectuals," *Decline of the New* (New York: Harcourt, Brace, 1970): 211–265;

Howe, "Philip Rahv, A Memoir," *American Scholar,* 48 (1979): 487–498;

Marian Janssen, *The Kenyon Review 1939–1970: A Critical History* (Baton Rouge: Louisiana State University Press, 1990);

Mark Krupnick, "He [Philip Rahv] Never Learned to Swim," *New Review* (London), 2 (January 1976): 33–39;

Christopher Lasch, "Modernism, Politics, and Philip Rahv," *Partisan Review,* 47 (March–April 1980): 183–194;

Francis Carol Locher, "Ivan Greenberg [Philip Rahv], 1908–1973," in *Contemporary Authors: A Bio-Bibliographical Guide to Current Writers in Fiction, General Nonfiction, Poetry, Journalism, Drama, Motion Pictures, Television, and Other Fields,* volumes 85–88 (Detroit: Gale, 1980), pp. 225–227;

S. A. Longstaff, "The New York Family," *Queen's Quarterly,* 83 (Winter 1976): 556–572;

Longstaff, "*Partisan Review* and the Second World War," *Salmagundi,* 43 (Winter 1979): 108–129;

Mary McCarthy, "Philip Rahv, 1908–1973." *New York Times Book Review,* 17 February 1974, pp. 1–2;

Daniel Neil Morris, "The *Anvil* Writers: Oral History and Quantification Conjoined," Ph.D. dissertation, University of Missouri – Columbia, 1988;

New York Times Book Review, 17 February 1974, pp. 1–2;

Newsweek (7 January 1974): 41;

Dorothy Nyren and others, eds., "Philip Rahv (1908–1974 [*sic*])," *A Library of Criticism: Modern American Literature,* volumes 3 and 4 (New York: Unger Publications, 1960, 1976), III: 39–41; IV: 393;

Partisan Review Papers, Rutgers University;

Richard H. Pells, *Radical Visions and American Dreams: Culture and Social Thought in the Depression Years* (New York: Harper and Row, 1973);

William Phillips, "How *Partisan Review* Began," *Commentary,* 62 (December 1976): 42–46;

Phillips, "On *Partisan Review,*" in *The Little Magazine in America: A Modern Documentary History,* edited by Elliott Anderson and Mary Kinzie (Yonkers, N.Y.: Pushcart Press, 1978), pp. 130–141;

Phillips, "What Happened in the Thirties," *Commentary,* 34 (September 1962): 204–212;

Sanford Pinsker, "Philip Rahv's 'Paleface and Redskin' Fifty Years Later," *Georgia Review,* 43 (1989): 477–489;

Norman Podhoretz, *Making It* (New York: Random House, 1967);

Walter B. Rideout, *The Radical Novel in the United States, 1900–1954: Some Interrelations of Literature and Society* (Cambridge, 1956);

Herbert Eugene Shapiro, "*Partisan Review:* The Forging of a Jewish-American Literary Aesthetic," Ph.D. dissertation, University of Rochester, 1980;

Elaine Showalter, "Women Writers Between the Wars," in *Columbia Literary History of the United States,* edited by Emory Elliott and others (New York: Columbia University Press, 1988): 822–841;

Robert Wooster Stallman. "Fiction and Its Critics: A Reply to Mr. Rahv," *Kenyon Review,* 19 (Spring 1957): 290–299;

Stewart R. Sutherland, "Language and Interpretation in *Crime and Punishment,*" *Philosophy and Literature,* 2 (1978): 223–236;

Alan M. Wald, *The New York Intellectuals: The Rise and Decline of the Anti-Stalinist Left from the 1930s to the 1980s* (Chapel Hill: University of North Carolina Press, 1987);

Edmund Wilson, "The Literary Class War: I," *New Republic,* 70 (4 May 1932): 313–322;

Michael Wood, "Literary Criticism," in *Columbia Literary History of the United States,* pp. 993–1018;

Dennis Wrong, "The Case of the *New York Review,*" *Commentary,* 50 (November 1970): 49–63.

Papers:

The principal collection of Philip Rahv's papers is in the *Partisan Review* Collection at Rutgers University in New Brunswick, New Jersey.

Harold Ross

(6 November 1892 - 6 December 1951)

Norman Sims
University of Massachusetts – Amherst

and

Sam G. Riley
Virginia Polytechnic Institute & State University

MAJOR POSITIONS HELD: Managing editor, *Stars & Stripes* (1918–1919); editor, *Home Sector* (1919–1920); editor, *American Legion Weekly* (1920–1924); editor, *Judge* (1924–1925); founder and editor, *New Yorker* (1925–1951).

Harold Ross

Harold Ross created and for twenty-seven years edited one of the most important magazines of the twentieth century, the *New Yorker.* Ross was not a New Yorker by birth or upbringing, and his quirks and lack of sophistication often made him seem an odd character at the helm of the *New Yorker.* Yet his success is attributable to his talents for improvisation, a masterful reading of the marketplace, and, according to some of his contemporaries, a sure sense of taste. The magazine became his enduring achievement, an institution that attracted many of the best writers and employed some of the ablest editors in America.

When Harold Wallace Ross was born on 6 November 1892 in Aspen, Colorado, his father, George, an immigrant in 1881 from County Monaghan, Ireland, was working as a mining technician. The family moved seven years later to Salt Lake City, where George went into the demolition business. A Scotch-Irishman who distrusted organized religion, George Ross liked to engage the local Mormons in theological debate. His wife, the former Ida Martin, a Scotch Presbyterian born in Salina, Kansas, and a former schoolteacher in the Oklahoma Indian Territory, named her son Harold because it meant "leader of men," and she also endowed him with a high moral sense and a squeamishness that later caused him to refrain from swearing in the company of women and to keep sexual references or innuendos out of the *New Yorker.* As a young man he was awkwardly built and had large hands and feet, a pale complexion, squinty gray eyes, and cowlicks in his hair. He fidgeted constantly but was an able student.

At West Side High School, Ross was a staffer on the school paper, the *Red and Black.* His hero was war correspondent Frederick Palmer, and, longing to become a newspaperman, Ross haunted the local papers, the *Telegraph* and the *Tribune,* running errands and tagging after reporters. By now schoolwork interested him little, and frequent arguments with his father caused him to run away from home on several occasions. On one such adventure he stayed in Denver with an uncle who found him a job as an errand boy for the *Post.* In his junior year he dropped out of school and became a full-time reporter on the *Tribune.* In 1910, at age eighteen, he joined the ranks of the "tramp journalists," hopping freight trains from town to town and finding newspaper work where he could. Never showing unusual writing or reporting talent, the young Ross lived a rough-and-tumble life, drinking, playing poker, and developing his lifelong habit of swearing when in the company of men. The first of these transient newspaper jobs was with the Marysville (Cal.) *Appeal.*

In 1911 he was taken on by the Sacramento *Union,* a paper that had once employed Samuel Clemens. His city editor, Kenneth Adams, as a practical joke, sent Ross, via a hopped Southern Pacific freight, across the Sierra Nevada to cover a story in Truckee, then arranged for a sheriff friend to roust the young reporter from his train car and jail him in Auburn, California. By the next morning Ross had recognized the joke and had his fellow inmates convinced that he was wanted in Salt Lake City for three murders. He wrote up this adventure for the *Union,* signing the story as "Hobo Ross," a nickname that stuck for years.

His travels soon justified the nickname. In 1912 he worked at the *Bee* in Needles, California, and at the Panama City *Star and Herald,* going from there to the New Orleans *Item,* where he covered the local courts and worked with eventual Pulitzer Prize-winning biographer Bessie Rowland, then to New York City, where he failed to find work. After brief employment on the Brooklyn *Eagle,* he went south and covered the Leo Frank murder case for the Atlanta *Journal.* From Atlanta he traveled again to New York City, where he tried, once more without success, to get on with a metropolitan daily, though he worked briefly for the Hudson (N.J.) *Observer.*

Ross gravitated in 1916 to San Francisco and the *Call and Post,* where he achieved a colorful reputation covering the Barbary Coast waterfront district. He was called Hal by his friends, sometimes extended to "Roughhouse Hal," and his interests aside from his reporting were women, cribbage, and reading the antiauthoritarian ideas of English philosopher-sociologist Herbert Spencer. He also admired the work of Mark Twain and Jack London.

When the United States entered the war against Germany in 1917, Ross and several other *Call and Post* reporters volunteered, joining the 18th Engineers Regiment as privates. After training at Fort Lewis, Washington, where Ross helped launch a regimental newspaper, Ross and his regiment were among the first twenty-five thousand U.S. soldiers to arrive in France. Ross was sent to an officers training program at Langres, but, according to his first wife, he failed an examination and was slated to become the program's company clerk. When he read an announcement that experienced journalists were needed to staff a new military newspaper in Paris, he applied. Having received no reply after a few weeks' wait, he went AWOL, arriving at the paper's offices in the Hotel Sainte Anne in February 1918. The officer in charge, Lt. Guy "Visk" Viskniskki and his editor, the former *Yale Record* editor Hudson Hawley, had turned out the first issue of *Stars and Stripes* just days before, on 8 February. The project enjoyed the support of Gen. John Joseph "Black Jack" Pershing, commander of the American Expeditionary Forces, and Lieutenant Viskniski was able to get Ross reassigned without punishment.

Within a week, a long, off-again–on-again friendship began for Ross with the arrival of former *New York Times* drama critic Alexander Woollcott. When the two young men were introduced, Ross asked Woollcott where he had worked. Woollcott proudly responded that he had been drama critic for the *New York Times.* Ross, who distrusted all college men and city dwellers, merely laughed. Not to be so easily insulted, Woollcott fired back, "You remind me a great deal of my father's coachman." From this shaky start, the two men became friends, Woollcott admiring Ross's drive and organizational ability, Ross admiring Woollcott's writing and reporting skills; yet this was a friendship between two dominant personalities, which made their relationship a highly competitive one. Other *Stars and Stripes* colleagues were Capt. Franklin P. Adams, former *Springfield Republican* copy editor John Winterich, Ross's old city editor from Sacramento, Ken Adams, and artists Albian Wallgren and Leroy Baldridge.

Eventually Ross became managing editor, and the former itinerant reporter had his first taste of authority, which he found pleasing. A campaign Ross spearheaded raised roughly one million dollars from U.S. military units that "adopted" French children who had been orphaned by the war, and a second Ross campaign used the *Stars and Stripes* as a forum to urge soldiers to write to their fathers. Some credit Ross as the "father of Father's Day."

The *Stars and Stripes* achieved enormous popularity among the troops and provided important so-

Ross with Jane Grant, whom he married in 1920 (photograph by Nicholas Muray)

cial contacts for Ross. His circle of friends included sportswriter Grantland Rice, syndicated writer Ring Lardner, Heywood Broun of the *New York Tribune,* Richard Oulahan of the *New York Times,* Walter Duranty of the London *Daily Mail,* and Jane Grant, a former *New York Times* reporter introduced to him by Woolcott; she would later become Ross's first wife. This journalistic coterie met in off-duty hours in Montmartre at Nini's, a little restaurant where they matched wits; played poker, craps, chemin de fer, gin rummy, and cribbage; and laid plans for what to do after the war. Ross's first inclination was to charter a boat and sail off for an adventure in the South Pacific, but the group's talk of starting a witty, sophisticated New York City tabloid also appealed to him. Meanwhile the *Stars and Stripes* staff successfully contrived to have Lieutenant Viskniski promoted to major and transferred to Germany, and adopted the position that enlisted men should be in charge of the editorial side of the growing paper. Their new commander was Capt. Mark Watson, who had been with the *Chicago Tribune.*

Upon war's end, Ross signed a contract with the Butterick Publishing Company, owner of the fashion magazine *Delineator,* that called for the founding of a new magazine for returning veterans. Ross in turn hired his *Stars and Stripes* colleagues Hawley, Woollcott, Winterich, and Baldridge. Before returning home, however, Ross arranged for the private publication of two joke booklets to be sold to the troops, *Yank Talk* and *More Yank Talk.* The Red Cross bought and distributed fifty thousand copies of the first booklet.

Ross returned to the United States in May 1919, moving into a Manhattan apartment with Winterich as his roommate. His new magazine, the *Home Sector,* identified in its masthead as "A Weekly for the New Civilian" and adding that it would be edited by former *Stars and Stripes* staffers, appeared in September 1919. Ross was editor, with Winterich serving as managing editor. Hawley, who had remained in France, was the weekly's European correspondent. A printers' strike caused an eight-week delay for the ninth issue of the *Home Sector,* and a permanent suspension of the magazine appeared likely. At this juncture the American Legion offered Ross a chance to take over the editing of its house organ, the *American Legion Weekly.* He accepted, and the final *Home Sector* was published on 17 April 1920.

The new job was not at all what Ross would have wished for, yet it paid a comfortable salary of ten thousand dollars a year and enabled the fledgling editor and Grant to marry. According to author Howard Teichmann, it was Grant who proposed to Ross, and most of the wedding arrangements were made by Woollcott, an inveterate matchmaker who delighted in taking charge of such functions. Woollcott selected New York's Little Church Around the Corner for the ceremony, booked the Bellevue-Stratford in Philadelphia for the honeymoon, and even selected the bride's ring, which was purchased at Tiffany's. The newlyweds shared a house with another recently married couple, the rising columnist Heywood Broun and reporter Ruth Hale. Early feminists who took pride in retaining their maiden names, Grant and Hale cofounded the Lucy Stone League to promote women's rights. Teichmann reported that Ross frequently complained about the two women's incessant tirades on the domineering male and the need for women's rights.

Grant kept her job on the *New York Times,* and the couple circulated in a young, sophisticated social set. Known as the Algonquin Round Table, this luncheon meeting group dined at New York's Algonquin Hotel on West Forty-fifth Street. Accounts of how the Round Table originated differ considerably, but apparently the group's original nucleus consisted of three young *Vanity Fair* staffers: Dorothy Parker (drama critic), Robert Benchley (managing editor) and Robert Sherwood (drama editor). Eventually they were joined by Ross and Grant, Woollcott, Adams, Hale, Edna Ferber, Herman Mankiewicz, John Peter Toohey, Ben Hecht, George and Beatrice Kaufman, Laurence Stallings, Deems Taylor, Neysa McMein (who had changed her first name from Marjorie) and others. The Round Table designation came about after the diners were moved from the hotel's Pergola Room to a larger, round table in the center of the Rose Room. According to Margaret Case Harriman, daughter of the hotel's manager (later its owner) Frank Case, the Algonquin Round Table tag was first applied by a *Brooklyn Eagle* cartoonist who signed his work "Duffy." A cosmopolitan, literary bohemian group centered in Greenwich Village, the Round Table regulars, few of whom were native New Yorkers, enjoyed clever repartee and debunking the ways of the bourgeoisie and, due to their barbed humor, sometimes referred to themselves as "The Vicious Circle." Ross revived the card games of his army days, variously calling the group of players the Thanatopsis Literary and Inside Straight Club, The Young Men's Upper West Side Thanatopsis and Inside Straight Club, or the Thanatopsis and Inside Straight Chowder and Marching Society, and making it, in essence, the Round Table's late-night auxiliary.

The Round Table and the Inside Straight Club first became known to many New Yorkers through Adams's *New York World* column "The Conning Tower." Ross took advantage of the notoriety and had letterhead printed that read: "Harold W. Ross – Man About Town." The members of the Round Table struck a smart, cosmopolitan pose and tweaked convention; a sizable segment of postwar America liked what the Tablers wrote. At this point Ross watched and learned about what the sophisticates and would-be sophisticates appeared to want in their reading matter. Generally dissatisfied with being at the helm of a mere house organ, Ross continued to examine the New York publishing scene for just the right opportunity. He and Grant laid plans to start a new periodical of their own, either a trade paper for the shipping industry or a magazine of reporting and humor. The couple paid their day-to-day expenses from Grant's earnings and saved Ross's salary to add to their nest egg. Grant's writing career was progressing well; she had become syndicated and was writing four different weekly columns: on fiction, beauty, actresses, and society figures. With her friend Kate Sproehnle, she also wrote for the *Saturday Evening Post* under editor Thomas Costain, later famous for his historical novels set in England. On one trip to the Philadelphia headquarters of the *Post*, Grant met editor in chief George Horace Lorimer and showed him a copy of the *New Yorker,* which had just been launched. Lorimer predicted an early death for the magazine and threw the copy across his office. In the planning phase of the magazine, other such professional acquaintances as *New York Times* managing editor Carr Van Anda advised them that a successful venture might require as much as five million dollars to capitalize. Even with two substantial salaries, prospects seemed dim until circumstances moved Ross in the desired direction.

He met Frank Crowninshield, the silvery, oldworldly editor of *Vanity Fair,* published by Conde Nast. Crowninshield's magazine, along with *Life, Judge,* and the *Smart Set,* comprised the upper crust of America's witty magazines of that era. Studying these periodicals and their respective appeals convinced Ross that their national circulations lost them certain categories of New York advertising – for department stores, theaters, restaurants, and the like – that would be wasted on readers in other parts of the nation. He also observed that some forms of humor became stale by the time these witty magazines reached their more far-flung subscribers. Slowly he evolved a plan that centered on the advantages of publishing a geographically specialized magazine, and what better market than New York?

In this period Ross and Grant moved several times. A suite at the Algonquin proved too expensive, and the couple spent two years living in a rented walk-up above a shop on West Fifty-eighth Street. Eventually they moved into the rough Hell's Kitchen area of the city in order to become homeowners. Their new home was a sort of modified commune on West Forty-seventh Street which they called "Chinaman's Chance" after the Chinese servants they employed. Other names for the place were "Wit's End" and "The Speakeasy," the latter owing to the constant round of drinking and partying that went on there. In her book *Ross, The New Yorker and Me* (1968), Grant reports that to save money on entertainment costs, she made "bathtub gin" there twenty gallons at a time and on one occasion would have been hauled into court had her boss Van Anda not intervened by calling a friend at the district attorney's office.

It was an active, arty social scene for the Rosses, with frequent visits from the Tablers, poetry readings by Edna St. Vincent Millay, conversation with individuals as varied as F. Scott Fitzgerald, Ethel Barrymore, Helen Hayes, and Harpo

Marx; tunes played on a slightly out-of-tune piano by Irving Berlin; and nightly gambling. A highlight was when George Gershwin previewed *Rhapsody in Blue* (1924)for them before he had completed the piece. The wealthiest of the Rosses' guests was financier Bernard Baruch, who occasionally treated them to trips by private train car to Atlantic City or to Baruch's South Carolina plantation retreat. Co-owned with their friend Hawley Traux, the house (actually two connected brick houses) at 412–414 West Forty-seventh had a shared kitchen and dining room, a room for cards and cribbage, and apartments for the Rosses, Woollcott, who bought into the property, Woollcott's wealthy friend Kate Oglebay, and public-relations man William Powell. Friction soon developed due to lack of privacy and contributed to Ross's first ulcer.

Still, he rose to the occasion when the company that printed both the *American Legion Weekly* and *Judge* bought into the latter magazine and offered Ross its coeditorship. Ross assumed this position in 1924, and his friend Winterich became editor of the Legion's magazine. Though editing *Judge* was a step closer to his true ambition, Ross arrived at that magazine well into its downhill slide, with its humor becoming less and less urbane, and he was embarrassed by the slow, reluctant attitudes of the owners toward payment to contributors. His ambition was not yet satisfied, and, now thirty-two and modestly experienced in New York publishing, he was ready to make his big move.

Early in 1924 Ross prepared a mock-up of an ambitious new humor magazine, as yet unnamed, and showed it to potential financial backers. Raoul Fleischmann expressed interest. Ross and Grant explained that fifty thousand dollars would start the venture, and Fleischmann, heir to a modest yeast and baking fortune, agreed to put up half the amount. The first time Ross visited Fleischmann to make his pitch, he lost his nerve and showed Fleischmann his mock-up for a more practical periodical he had also been planning, a shipping paper to have been titled the *Marine Gazette.* This project held no interest for Fleischmann, as it offered no glamor. It took Ross another week to build up enough nerve to return to his future backer with the plans for his humor magazine. Ross and Grant scraped together another twenty thousand dollars, and on 21 February 1925 the first issue of the *New Yorker* went on sale.

The magazine was headquartered at 25 West Forty-fifth Street in a building owned by the Fleischmann family. Ross's block of offices was sparsely furnished and poorly equipped. His full-time staff was similarly limited, consisting at first of Harvard graduate Tyler Bliss and Ross's old chum Roy Kirk, editorial assistants; aspiring writer Helen Mears, who served as Ross's secretary; all-purpose gofer Philip Wylie; an advertising salesman and his secretary; and a switchboard operator. Ownership was vested in the F-R Publishing Company, with Ross as president and Fleischmann as vice-president.

Part-time employees included James K. McGuinness, the first writer of "The Talk of the Town"; Rea Irvin, who acted as art editor; nightlife writer Charles Baskerville; Howard Brubaker, who contributed a department called "Of All Things"; Herman Mankiewicz, who became a *New Yorker* theater and movie critic; and general-assignment writer Marquis James. Some copy and ideas were contributed by Ross's cohorts from the Round Table, sometimes in exchange for stock in F-R Publishing. James R. Gaines, author of *Wit's End* (1977), a book about the Round Table, suggests that Ross's friends were also repaid through the many favorable reviews of their work and the many friendly accounts of their comings and goings that appeared in the early issues of the *New Yorker*, although the touting of the Tablers was brought to a stop by Ross in mid 1926.

Stock valued at fifteen hundred dollars was offered as a prize for whoever suggested the best name for the new periodical. While most of the Tablers were busy churning out clever, witty titles, Toohey was perfectly direct. Ascertaining that the magazine's primary market was to be New Yorkers, he suggested the obvious: the *New Yorker.* Grant helped set up the magazine's circulation department, and Adams acted as unofficial poetry editor. To lend the venture added credibility, Fleischmann had Ross sign those members of the Round Table who were unencumbered by conflicting job contracts as nominal advisory editors. Those whose names appeared in this capacity in the prospectus were Marc Connelly, Broun, Ferber, Irvin, George S. Kaufman, Ralph Barton, Stallings, Alice Duer Miller, Parker, and Woollcott.

The first issue, selling at fifteen cents, sold fifteen thousand copies. In it appeared Ross's prospectus, which promised rather more than the magazine could deliver in its first year. Ross wrote:

> *The New Yorker* starts with a declaration of serious purpose but a concomitant declaration that it will not be too serious in executing it. It hopes to reflect metropoli-

tan life, to keep up with events and affairs of the day, to be gay, humorous, satirical but to be more than a jester.

> It will publish facts that it will have to go behind the scenes to get, but it will not deal in scandal for the sake of scandal nor sensation for the sake of sensation. It will try conscientiously to keep its readers informed of what is going on in the fields in which they are most interested. It has announced that it is not edited for the old lady in Dubuque. By this it means that it is not of that group of publications engaged in tapping the Great Buying Power of the North American steppe region by trading mirrors and colored beads in the form of our best brands of hokum.

The part of this prospectus that has lived on in public memory is Ross's promise not to edit the magazine "for the old lady in Dubuque." Ross explained elsewhere that he meant no disrespect but that appeals to conflicting tastes and interests hampered most national magazines. The *New Yorker* would be "avowedly published for a metropolitan audience," in New York City and elsewhere.

In assembling ideas for the magazine's format and content, Ross made use of the venerable English humor periodical *Punch,* published since 1841, as well as other humor titles from France and Germany. The first regular department that *New Yorker* readers encountered was "Of All Things," Ross's version of the section "Charivaria" in *Punch*. Next came "The Talk of the Town," done in first-person plural and signed "Van Bibber III," ostensibly someone who knew all the city's "right people" and frequented all the "right places." Some content seemed to find its sophisticated mark, other contributions seemed flip and failed to achieve the urbane tone for which Ross was striving. Overall it was not a prepossessing start, and few advertisers had risked their money on the new magazine. Of the first issue's thirty-six pages, fewer than seven were taken up with advertising. Fleischmann, fearing for his investment, went to magazine consultant John Hanrahan and then began making suggestions to Ross, which led to friction between F-R Publishing's principals. Contributors could be paid little, Ross collected only one hundred dollars of his three-hundred-dollar-a-week salary, and sales declined. Ross recognized that his taste, and the style of the magazine, had to find an audience. "An editor prints what pleases him," Ross said. "If enough people like what he does he is a success." Expenses mounted as the search for readers continued, and by April circulation was eight thousand and the *New Yorker* was losing eight thousand dollars a week. Fleischmann had hoped to interest his even wealth-

Cover for the first issue of the magazine Ross created and edited until 1951. The top-hatted dandy examining the butterfly is Eustace Tilley, the New Yorker *icon*

ier cousin Julius Fleischmann in investing, but soon after the first issue of the *New Yorker* appeared, Julius died while playing polo. Ross could contribute no more money – for one thing he had lost twenty-nine thousand dollars in a Thanatopsis poker game to the wealthy Herbert Bayard Swope, managing editor of the *New York World* – and, in a meeting on 9 May at the Princeton Club, Fleischmann announced that he intended to cut his losses and abandon the venture.

An early death for the *New Yorker* was forestalled at the wedding of Adams and Esther Root, introduced to one another by Millay, who contributed to Adams's column as "Nancy Boyd." The ceremony was attended by both Ross and Fleischmann, and the latter suggested to Ross that they meet and discuss the matter again. The result was that the bakery heir would keep the magazine alive while Ross's friend Traux searched for outside capital. This search bore no fruit, and during the remainder of the magazine's first year Traux and his brother-in-law Lloyd Stryker supplied $15,000 while Fleischmann continued to pump in money, much of which apparently came from his mother, until his contribution reached a reported $195,000.

The paradoxical Ross found himself courting snobs, just the kind of people he had always detested (though his conception of an upscale audience was based not only on social position but on intellectual snobbery as well). New staffers were hired, in part, for their social connections. Examples were Fillmore Hyde and Ralph Ingersoll, young men with moneyed family backgrounds, and artist Peter Arno, a Yale graduate and an orchestral pianist whose real name was Curtis Arnoux Peters and whose father was a well-to-do judge. Well-connected Lois Long, a former *Vanity Fair* theater editor, was hired to do a nightlife column, which she signed as "Lipstick," and later a fashion column titled "Fifth Avenue." Bit by bit Ross was positioning his magazine on the right side of New York City's tracks. Toward this same end, he and Fleischmann decided that the *New Yorker* needed a symbol of some kind that would bespeak class and an attitude of detached, whimsical waggery. They gave young comic artist Corey Ford the job of adapting Irvin's monocled Regency snob; Ford redrew this haughty character, making only minor changes, and named him "Eustace Tilley," whose last name was borrowed from Ford's aunt. Tilley was even given his own listing in the New York telephone book as a publicity stunt. Still, circulation declined and was down to a mere seventy-five hundred by the time the magazine was half a year old.

In an effort to stave off disaster, Ross took out in various New York newspapers a sixty-thousand-dollar series of full-page ads that featured testimonials by such prominent New Yorkers as Mayor Jimmy Walker, financial great Baruch, musical luminaries Jascha Heifetz, Gershwin, and Berlin, and entertainers Al Jolson and W. C. Fields. He also cut the magazine's budget; hired a new managing editor, Joseph Moncure Marsh; and searched for manuscripts that would awaken the kind of audience he wanted. Ellin Mackay, a twenty-two-year-old who would marry Berlin the following year, brought Ross just what he needed: "Why We Go to Cabarets, A Post-Debutante Explains." Mackay's article said debutantes thought most men in their own social set "pretty terrible" and avoided the worst of the stag boys at parties by frequenting nightclubs. Arriving in the midst of the debutante season (in the 28 November 1925 issue), the article drew thousands of new readers and several write-ups in newspapers. A second Mackay article, "The Declining Function: A Post-Debutante Rejoices," lambasted the stiff formality of many society functions and was likewise a big success in attracting new readers from the silk-stocking crowd.

The Round Table had connected Ross to Broadway and the newspaper set; Mackay handed him a stylish Park Avenue readership. The ad campaign, which had appealed to the speakeasy crowd, and Mackay's rebellious article both contributed to healthy growth in the circulation of the *New Yorker.* In addition, B. Altman, Rolls Royce, Cunard Lines, Brooks Brothers, and Saks–Fifth Avenue signed advertising contracts for the coming year. By the end of its first year the *New Yorker* had finally found an audience and the financial support it needed for survival. By 1927 Fleischmann's investment had grown to more than four hundred thousand dollars, yet the magazine was a success.

Having achieved greater financial stability for his magazine, Ross as a "company manager" was ever tinkering, ever changing in a quixotic quest for efficiency. Walls and temporary partitions were frequently moved, and a posh reception room decorated by Fleischmann's wife Ruth was soon eliminated. Ross had his own office soundproofed, then did not like the quiet and had the soundproofing removed. Likewise, a fancy electronic lock on his office door proved to be more trouble than it was worth. Over a period of years one of Ross's great office perplexities concerned how he could get from his office to the men's room without passing the ladies' room or having to stop and talk to staffers. Finally the problem was solved when someone suggested that a new men's room be installed adjacent to the editor's office.

From the earliest days of the magazine Ross sought to surround himself with geniuses. He recognized his own shortcomings and that even his near-boundless energy could not spread itself to cover all matters. Ross imagined a perfect managing editor who could devise systems for handling the endless petty details of magazine publishing. In his book *Here at The New Yorker* (1975), Brendan Gill quotes Ross's eventual successor William Shawn as saying that Ross was "by nature strikingly unsystematic" yet always hopeful of establishing a fail-proof system that would be capable of solving all office problems, keeping track of the heavy, constant paper flow, and instantly ascertaining the whereabouts and progress on assignments of the magazine's entire staff. Such a system, Ross thought, demanded that he find a managing editor who was the very paragon of businesslike organization and who, seated at a centrally located desk, could function as the hub of what Ross viewed as the frantic, disorganized efforts of his talented yet unbusinesslike writers and illustrators. The "genius" Ross hoped to find – the staff transformed the name to "Jesus" – proved elusive. A parade of managing editors came and went, including Joseph March, Oliver Claxton, Stanley Walker, Arthur Samuels, and St. Clair McKelway, some sixteen altogether. Ross hired them all but could not bear to fire them face-to-face, instead leaving the building, or in at least one instance hiding in a coat closet, while someone else did the unpleasant deed. M. B. "Bill" Levick avoided being fired as "Jesus" by becoming the magazine's makeup man for art. The dour Levick, who greeted coworkers with the phrase "One day nearer the grave," eventually resigned after slugging the assistant Ross had sent to criticize Levick's placement of two similar illustrations. Art Samuels's firing as managing editor was practically preordained, as he was a Princeton graduate and an old school chum of Fleischmann. Samuels's *New Yorker* office was lavishly furnished and appointed, in contrast to the masculine plainness of Ross's own. Referring to the Spartan decor of his office, Ross grumbled that he did not want anyone to mistake him for the editor of *Vanity Fair*. Samuels was fired by telegram.

Ross could never seem to explain himself completely when hiring a new managing editor. When James Thurber came to the magazine from a job on the *New York Evening Post,* Ross failed to make Thurber's assignment clear. Every week a secretary would bring the writer a stack of papers to sign. When Thurber asked for an explanation, she said, "It's the payroll. You're managing editor." When the time came for a "Jesus" to leave, Ross was equally vague. He would remove responsibilities, assistants and office furniture ahead of time as gentle hints, always avoiding a personal meeting. Sometimes he would send a letter, then keep away from the office until the deposed executive had departed. As part of dealing with this process, Ross persuaded himself that moving fairly often from one job to another was good for editors', writers', and artists' careers.

Advertising revenue continued to climb, and the first anniversary of the *New Yorker* was celebrated with the publication of a seventy-page issue, which was more than double the size of most earlier numbers and which was fattened by ads for various luxury products. No longer would Fleischmann have to seek out old friends and ask them to take out ads, as he had done with George Washington Hill, who had obligingly bought twelve back covers for Lucky Strikes cigarettes advertisements. Circulation reached forty thousand, most of which was in the city or its immediate environs. As the magazine's business situation improved, Ross continued to pace the editorial corridors, fretting and growling over nearly every possible detail, groping his way toward the tone and content he knew that he wanted but could not quite define.

Rea Irvin's caricature of Ross as Tilley and critic Alexander Woollcott as an insect (from the first-anniversary issue of the New Yorker*)*

Ross's own newspaper reporting experience dictated his desire for factual accuracy, and his personal inclination was for clear, unambiguous use of language balanced by a relaxed, conversational, casual style. Brief prose selections in the *New Yorker* became known, in Ross terminology, as "casuals." Finally, the fretful editor urged his writers and illustrators to strive for a sort of detached, whimsical tone that should avoid being flip but take quiet delight in both reporting on and ribbing the Big City as it became ever bigger. This kidding, slightly superior tone gave *New Yorker* readers the feeling that they were looking at the city from an elevated, privileged vantage point. Gradually the emphasis on humor for its own sake gave way to reporting that was in general more serious yet still done with a wry touch. Ross wanted the writing that appeared in the *New Yorker* to avoid that which was self-consciously literary or intellectual. One of his tenets was that since writers tend to be "writer-conscious," *New Yorker* contributors should focus on content, not on themselves or their literary friends.

The work of former *New York World* writer Morris Markey was important in the early development of *New Yorker* style. His department, at first titled "In the News," a takeoff on Lardner's popular *Chicago Tribune* column "In the Wake of the News," was changed to "Behind the News," possibly to give the reader more of a feeling of being in the know, then to "A Reporter at Large." Markey anticipated the New Journalists of the 1970s by writing factual stories but making use of the narrative structure of the short story.

Adding acid wit to the magazine's pages was Ross's Round Table chum Dorothy Parker, who had already made quite a name for herself before October 1927 when she became the magazine's book reviewer as "Constant Reader." Almost as paradoxical as Ross himself, Parker managed to write copy that was one minute warm and insightful, the next minute darkly cynical and pessimistic, and that often came back to her favorite theme: the battle of the sexes. As a reviewer she pulled no punches and took no prisoners alive. Of all the devastating zingers she delivered in her reviews, one of the best remembered was her comment upon reading A. A. Milne's *House at Pooh Corner* (1928): "Tonstant Weader Fwowed Up." Ross admired her cleverness but kept on guard lest she slip something suggestive past him. A chance meeting in a Manhattan speakeasy produced a quip that at once shows how ill equipped the new magazine was and demonstrates Parker's ready wit. When Ross asked her why she was drinking instead of working at her *New Yorker* desk, she replied that "Somebody else was using the pencil."

The Massachusetts-born, Harvard-educated humorist Robert Benchley became Ross's drama critic in 1929. Gentle in his criticism, Benchley, whom Ross had published in *Home Sector,* and who had been theater critic for *Life,* wrote with wry, upper-crust charm. Eventually he took over Markey's press-criticism column, changed its title to "The Wayward Press," and signed his work "Guy Fawkes." Benchley also wrote profiles under the nom de plume "Searchlight" but in time severed his connection with the magazine in favor of acting in movies and writing humor books.

While the search for a suitable "Jesus" continued, Ross hired four other individuals who would further shape the destiny of the *New Yorker.* Roughly halfway through the magazine's first year came a Bryn Mawr graduate and a former writer for *New Republic* and *Atlantic Monthly,* Katharine Sergeant Angell, who was hired as a fiction editor. Angell's cultivation and taste compensated for what was lacking in Ross's own background. Ross proclaimed from the start that there would be no office romances at the *New Yorker,* yet among the exceptions – Peter Arno and Lois Long, Bernard Bergman and Long's assistant Frances Dellar, and others – was the marriage of Angell to the shy, sensitive hypochondriac Elwyn Brooks White, who had been hired on her recommendation in 1926.

White was a graduate of Cornell, where he had studied under William Strunk, Jr.; White later revised Strunk's *Elements of Style* (1959), one of America's best-selling style guides. White came to know of Ross while working for the Legion News Service at the same time Ross was editing the *American Legion Weekly.* None of White's early jobs had brought him success; he found his natural writing style difficult to fit to the expectations of newspapers. He had gone from job to job, perpetually short of funds and rather a forlorn figure until he found in the *New Yorker* a perfect home for his distinctive brand of sensitive whimsy. His initial duty there, writing punch lines for "Newsbreaks" (short reports of newspaper goofs to which funny afterthoughts were added), brought him to Ross's attention, and soon he moved on to penning casuals and pieces of verse, supplying cartoon captions, and writing stylish "Talk of the Town" and "Notes and Comment" pieces. White came to be one of Ross's inside circle of writer/editors, due both to his talent and his personality. Though a quiet, shy man, he had a taste for occasional devilment, which included joining Ross for practical jokes. One of their most risky pranks was perpetrated when the two men vandalized the sign that hung in front of the offices of the Society for the Prevention of Vice, led by John Sumner, whom Ross and White considered an unbearable do-gooder.

Before applying for a job at the *New Yorker,* Thurber had tried for months to publish freelance in the magazine, but the rejected manuscripts came back, he later recalled, "like a serve in tennis." His stumbling block was editor John Chapin Mosher, the magazine's "rejection machine," as Thurber put it. Finally the ice was broken with the acceptance of a Thurber parody on channel swimming that featured a man setting the world record for going round and round in a revolving door. Thurber arrived in April 1927 as the new "Jesus" and shared an office with White, which began a long friendship marked by mutual admiration. Ross tried unsuccessfully for months to keep Thurber harnessed to the managing editor's desk, but the new arrival

I-1. Insert good but will work only, I think if repeats phrase from previous clause, i.e. "in charge of" should follow an "in charge of" describing someone else.

2. Outside of what. Don't get.

3. Too detailed

4. Where Cutler school. Also, doesn't story get out of sequence here? Must have given his lectre beforeg going Cutler school.

5. Who he?
6. Did they votex sperately in these three categories, Must have, and its am amazing coincidence that he came in fifth in all three, and tied for third at that. Transcends credulence.

7. He means heśs moved to Pennsylvania. Fix wording.

8. Trimming can be done here.

9. Mean she left her husband for a few mos. after marraige?

10. This whole page awfully soft. For God sake, at (a) there's no point to enumerating all these subisidiaries. We haven't space for such, and its dull.

11. What tanks? Explain.
12 Awful lot of words here. Its this kind of thing that gets repetious. Hellman has a dozen examples of such adrbitness before x gets through, probably eight or nin nine of them unneduessary.

~~hm~~ Part II I. Why single out the 100 mil of domestic business just? First part says radio o does $160 mil. Mean Turck just has to do with domestic business, or What. Indirection her anyway.

4. Indirection. There's been no indication Rockefeller was going to work there.

5. Not certain I understand this exactly, but it seems like the same old point again.

6. Has his father the Dr. passed on, or what?

~~7.xxxxxxxxxxxxxxxxxx~~

7. Sheriff who? Who's he?

8. Bushwah.

9. ~~xxx~~ As dull and unconvincing a joke as I've heard in some time.

Editorial queries by Ross for a New Yorker *profile by Geoffrey T. Hellman (from Brendan Gill,* Here at The New Yorker, *1975)* avoided the fate of the earlier "Jesuses" by becoming a valued staff writer and cartoon artist. His whimsical drawings, many of them rescued from the wastebasket by White, became a *New Yorker* trademark. A staff member reportedly remarked in 1934 that though Ross had created the magazine's body, White and Thurber became its soul. Thurber was one of the non-Ivy League additions to the *New Yorker,* having graduated from Ohio State University before working as a reporter for the *Columbus Dispatch,* the Paris edition of the *Chicago Tribune,* and the *New York Post.* He had managed to sell a few manuscripts to the *New Yorker* before White recommended to Ross that Thurber be hired as an editor. The versatile Thurber, like White, became one of Ross's favorites and was allowed to display the full range of his talents. An especially noteworthy contribution by Thurber was the twenty-five-article series "Where Are They Now?," which he signed as "Jared L. Manley." The series examined the current circumstances of people who had at one time been prominently in the news, an idea originally suggested by Elmer Davis.

In 1928 Ross hired native New Yorker Oliver Wolcott Gibbs, who began as a copyreader and later occupied nearly every job except managing editor. His parodies, profiles, rewrites of articles and short stories, reviews, and editing done under Angell's direction contributed to the magazine's consistent tone. Gibbs's background was a curious mix: limited schooling, employment as a railroad brakeman and as a reporter for a small newspaper, yet good family connections that appealed to Ross's desire to surround himself with well-connected people. Thurber credited Gibbs with having been the best of all the magazine's many copy editors, a man blessed with the ability to edit a manuscript heavily without losing the writer's style or tone.

Ross's combative friend Woollcott was initially dubious about the success of the *New Yorker* and in its early years wrote for it only occasionally, though Ross paid him better than any other writer. During this period Woollcott was associated with the *New York World,* then with *Vanity Fair,* and he also wrote for the *American Mercury, McCall's, Collier's, Cosmopolitan,* and *Pictorial Review.* Woollcott's early *New Yorker* contributions were mainly profiles, the first of which was of Van Anda. Other Woollcott profiles, some of which were written under pen names, included E. Haldeman-Julius, the editor of *Appeal to Reason,* Harpo Marx, Frank Lloyd Wright, George Kaufman, and Noel Coward – all individuals he liked. Then in 1929 Woollcott became a *New Yorker* regular. His department, called "Shouts and Murmurs" after the title of a book he had written earlier, filled one page – the magazine's only department written to fit a specified space. During the next six years he wrote between two hundred and three hundred such pages on a considerable variety of subjects.

Knowing that Woollcott would prove difficult to edit, Ross gave the job of overseeing "Shouts and Murmurs" to the diplomatic Katharine Angell White, one of the few editors to whom Woollcott was always polite. Ross thought his old friend a prima donna and referred to him as the "Gila monster" because of that choleric writer's frequent complaints and threatened resignations when so much as a comma was changed in his copy. Adding to the friction, Ross needled him whenever the opportunity arose. According to Howard Teichmann in *Smart Aleck* (1976), after Woollcott's first appearance on Mutual radio in 1929 Ross sent him a telegram that read: "You were wonderful. I lost my dinner." Also, Gaines reported the discovery in Benchley's personal library of a book that Ross had inscribed: "To Alexander W Woollcott, who stole the first dollar I ever earned." Actually, the name was Alexander H(umphreys) Woollcott, but Ross enjoyed mangling the name or its spelling to aggravate his old crony.

Toward the end of the six-year run of "Shouts and Murmurs," its writer grew weary of it and sometimes missed issues. Kramer also reported Ross's displeasure at Woollcott's habit of accepting gifts in exchange for product or business plugs on his page in the magazine. One such exchange brought Woollcott a box of one hundred neckties, which Ross intercepted and distributed among his employees with instructions that they put the ties on prior to the portly writer's arrival. Even "Sterling Finny," a department-store dummy Ross kept in his office, was wearing one. Later, when one of Woollcott's *New Yorker* pages appeared in only slightly altered form in *McCall's,* Ross's patience with his old chum grew thin, though it is not clear whether Woollcott resigned or was fired from his *New Yorker* job. His last appearance in Ross's magazine was a January 1939 profile of the magazine's old supporter, and Woollcott's old school friend, Stryker.

In the early years of the *New Yorker,* Ross also had to feel his way toward the kind of illustrations he wanted, largely accomplished by searching *Punch* and other humor magazines such as Germany's *Fliegende Blätter,* and depending upon art adviser Rea Irvin to translate his general wishes into terms that artists could understand. Having worked at

Ross with Edward Weeks, editor of the Atlantic Monthly, *at Dartmouth College, where they received honorary degrees in 1950*

Life, Irvin had considerable experience with cartoon illustration and was able to convey to artists just how to apply the right urbane, waggish feel to illustrations showing New York and its inhabitants.

Initially, Irvin came to the magazine's offices only one day a week, and on that day from lunch until 5 or 6 P.M., the weekly art conference was held. Interruptions and phone calls were not allowed on these afternoons. The principal figures at these meetings were Irvin and Ross. Editorial assistant Wylie would place all submissions on a table and would hold them up one at a time, beginning with the cover illustrations and proceeding to cartoons and other art, reading captions aloud. Illustrations were immediately separated into acceptances, rejections, and possible acceptances pending changes. Nothing was sent to production unless it bore the ultimate seal of approval, Ross's "R." Irvin would go over needed changes, which Wylie would later pass along to the various artists. Ross would join the discussion, puffing Camel cigarettes, pointing with a knitting needle at what he liked or disliked, fretting over the possibility of phallic symbols or sly sexual connotations that might get by him, demanding clarifications or explanations, and often pushing his preference for one-line captions – something unusual in an era long accustomed to two- or multi-line caption writing. Ross even liked, and sometimes used, cartoons that carried no caption whatever, such as some of the work of illustrators Gardner Rea and Otto Soglow.

An early cartoon favorite in the *New Yorker* was a series by Arno called the "Whoops sisters" that featured a pair of elderly tiplers. Another standout was Helen "Hoky" Hokinson, whose work poked fun at the flapper era of the late 1920s and who came to specialize in drawing whimsical, bemused fat ladies. Also contributing flapper illustrations that suited Ross was Barbara Shermund, who did the magazine's third cover; Mary Petty specialized in drawing the city's upper classes; and Hokinson's friend Alice Harvey pleased Ross with her drawings of children. Petty's husband, Alan Dunn, did news-related illustrations, Carl Rose caricatured foreigners arrived in the city, and Al Frueh, who did the magazine's second cover, drew scenes of the city's theater world. Charles Baskerville, as "Top Hat," was unusual in that he both illustrated and wrote his department, "When Nights Are Bold," the magazine's original nightclub column, which was later taken over by Long and retitled "Tables for Two." Other early artists whose work Ross bought included Reginald Marsh, Johan Bull, Carl Rose, George V. Shanks, Rube Goldberg, and Gluyas Williams. Thurber participated in some of the art meetings, and in 1929 careful records of the magazine's illustrations and of Ross's comments on them began to be kept by Daise E. Terry, sometimes assisted by office boy Truman Capote. By the early 1930s the magazine had purchased and stockpiled enough illustrations to last for roughly two years. Office security became an issue from time to time when Ross suspected that *New Yorker* captions were being leaked to rival magazines before he could run them.

Wednesday mornings were devoted to the weekly "Talk meeting," at which Ross, Katharine Angell White, Thurber, Ingersoll, and other staffers would gather around the conference-room table to go over the copy for the "Talk of the Town" department, which led off the magazine's editorial hole. This department contained bits of this and pieces of that, all of which dealt with the Big City and its denizens, both great and small. For one to three hours Ross would suggest, challenge, and complain, his many idiosyncrasies making themselves known. Sometimes he would perform rewrites on the spot. Thurber reports having occasionally rewritten some of Ross's clumsier efforts, forging the magic "R." During one "Talk" meeting, Ross complained that the department had become too grim, that it did not ever share a single laugh. Thurber pointed out to the editor that he said that every week, to which Ross growled, "Well, there are even fewer this time." The department owed part of its charm, however, to Ross's delight in the little things about human nature as observed in the city, things not likely to be reported in newspapers. The other side of its charm, of course, is attributable to the talent of its writers, most especially Thurber and White but also Russel Crouse, Charles H. Cooke, who wrote some twelve hundred "Talk" pieces, and James Cain, later the author of *The Postman Always Rings Twice* (1934), who liked to do his work on the floor instead of at a desk.

Compensation for "Talk" writers was arrived at by another weekly ritual, in which Thurber would work from a dummy issue, reminding Ross of who had contributed what. Ross would then indicate how much each writer should receive. His weekly "Talk pricing" was done according to the principle that he wanted to pay writers well, yet not too well, lest too much pay eliminate their incentive to work. Pay was generally rather low until the mid 1940s, when Ross began feeling guilty and paid liberal bonuses. Until that time, his writers had to consider that part of their compensation came in having their work showcased in a magazine known for its good writing. To Ross's credit, however, he always bought only first serial rights, allowing writers to enjoy any reprints or subsidiary rights they could arrange.

As the *New Yorker* moved into its more secure second year, Ross, like his magazine, gradually began to look more prosperous and at least slightly more urbane. His wife took him to an English tailor, and later Ross went with Adolph Menjou to that suave actor's tailor. Ross was still gap-toothed, of course, and his brown hair seemed to grow straight up. Worn long, reportedly an inch and a half high in what is usually described as a pompadour, it gave him somewhat the appearance of a Caucasian version of rock 'n' roll singer Little Richard in his early years as a performer. A remark by Ina Claire that she would like to walk barefoot through Ross's hair was quoted in the papers, after which Ross began trying to bring his gravity-defying hairstyle under control. As to Ross's face, Hecht thought it looked like that of a burglar; Margaret Case Harriman thought him clown-faced and wrote about his habit of rubbing his hand across his face in a gesture of mock bewilderment. Stanley Walker thought the editor looked like an American Indian, and Woollcott characterized his appearance as that of "a dishonest Abe Lincoln." Ross began to favor wearing dark business suits, though they never quite appeared to fit, leaving him, in Thurber's words, looking like a "carelessly carried umbrella." A later writer for the magazine, Gill, remembered Ross as "a dark-suited simian figure" that slouched about the offices, and Thurber recalled Long having described Ross by saying that when he walked, he seemed to be "pushing something invisible ahead of him." To Thurber, Ross always appeared to be "in mid-flight" and resembled "a sleepless, apprehensive sea captain pacing the bridge," afraid to rest for fear of imminent disaster. Thurber also said that Ross kept four or five dollars in change in his pockets so that he would have the correct fare for taxi rides, and that as he went about his office rounds, the editor would jingle the coins. Ross was given to growling and grumbling, as though most problems had been sent by an unfriendly providence to afflict him personally, often blurting out such remarks as "God how I pity me!"

Also, Ross was notoriously shy around most women. "It takes two or more women to surround the average man," Thurber wrote, but, he continued, Ross could look "as beleaguered as Custer in the presence of only one." Thurber, in *The Years with Ross* (1959), wrote about how Ross had once fired an editor because the man had brought his wife into Ross's office to meet him. Ross looked up to find her standing there, "seeming to be closing in on him from all sides." Ross's more intimate relationships with women were likewise marked by strain, partly because he was so thoroughly married to his magazine. Ross rented a room at the Webster Hotel across the street from the *New Yorker,* and his marriage to Grant ended after nine years in 1929. Ross played the part of man-about-town for a few years thereafter, renting apartments at the Ritz and on Park Avenue and at one time rooming on East Fifth-seventh Street with stage comedian Ed McNamara. In 1934 he married Marie Francoise "Frances" Elie and moved out of the city to Fairfield County, Connecticut, where the couple had a daughter, Patricia, born on Saint Patrick's Day 1935. This marriage ended in divorce after five years. In 1940, after another brief period of bachelorhood during which one of his lady friends was the actress Ginger Rogers, Ross was married for a third time, to Ariane Allen, a young Texas actress. Ross and his third wife were separated at the time of his death in 1951.

Though Ross was reportedly a fond, loving father, an anecdote related by his trusted friend Thurber shows a side of his nature that no doubt rubbed off on his magazine: his determined machismo. One day Thurber found Ross pacing, frowning, and jingling his pocketful of coins. His immediate problem was that he was concerned that real men should have sons, not daughters, but he brightened when Thurber pointed out that heavyweight boxing champion Jack Dempsey's children were both girls. Even so, Ross slouched off, grumbling that he hated "going around with female hormones in me."

Ross, for all his strange notions, had accurately detected an opportunity for positioning in the magazine marketplace, and his vision helped make the *New Yorker* a financial success. Recognizing that New York businesses would not pay for out-of-town readers, Ross gave advertisers a choice of two editions: the New York circulation for one price or, for a slightly higher figure, a national audience. By 1929 metropolitan circulation was sixty-two thousand – the highest concentration of New York readers available to any magazine advertiser – and the "boonies" added another sixty-three thousand readers. Ross had originally envisioned a circulation of fifty thousand, but the figure had grown to far beyond that, at which point he lost interest. Ross was not very much concerned with commercial considerations, Shawn wrote later, adding that his predecessor had not based his selection of editorial matter on that which would attract advertisers or produce a large circulation. Instead, what interested him most was the quality of the magazine's writing and editing. He firmly believed in the desirability of separating the magazine's editorial functions from its business department, resigning as F-R Publications president and director and eventually selling much of his own stock in the company. He and Fleischmann continued their personal feud, and more than once Ross threatened to quit as editor. Fleischmann, however, realized that most of the better staffers were loyal to their editor and might also resign if Ross left the magazine.

The former tramp journalist, who seemed to enjoy the fallacious rumor that he had read only one book all the way through, had somehow created one of the most urbane, literary, and successful magazines in America. He poured a large percentage of the budget into the editorial department – 14 percent by one estimate, or about four hundred thousand dollars a year in the midst of the Depression – and received in return some of the best writing found anywhere, despite the fact that Ross the editor was a hard taskmaster. Though he eventually paid his writers and editors well, he expected extremely long workweeks from them and in the early years was often less than solicitious about his employees' personal needs and problems. Ross was also given to stopping the presses, newspaper style, to make last-minute changes, to the despair of his makeup and production staff.

Still, Ross showed an increasing ability to hire good people, to recognize latent talent in those who were already his employees, to attract top freelance writing talent, and to let the magazine's content evolve and improve. A distinctive *New Yorker* feature was the personality profile, written in an irreverent, probing style that differed from other magazines' profiles, most of which were aggrandizing to their subjects and/or inspirational in tone. Thurber credited this *New Yorker* innovation to Russel "Buck" Crouse, who served as a rewrite man for "Talk of the Town" and who began two other departments, "That Was New York" and "They Were New Yorkers." Crouse's suggestion to Ross was to profile failures as well as big successes. A Crouse profile of a Bowery bum in the 31 October 1931 issue appealed to Ross, who had initially been skeptical of the idea, and the *New Yorker* profile was born. Another pioneer *New Yorker* profile writer was former *New York Times* Pulitzer Prize winner Alva Johnston, who wrote with great wit as well as with journalistic accuracy.

Many *New Yorker* profiles were of literary figures: Parker on Ernest Hemingway, Maxwell Bodenheim on Eugene O'Neill, Raymond Holden on Robert Frost, W. E. Woodward on Sinclair Lewis, Woollcott on Coward, Griffin Barry on Millay, Hamilton Basso on W. Somerset Maugham, and

Ross on a fishing trip in Aspen, Colorado

John Mosher on Fitzgerald. Other profiles – twelve during the magazine's first twenty years – were on journalists. The first of these was a brief sketch of Van Anda of the *Times*. According to a study written by the late journalism scholar John Drewry, these 112 profiles represented the work of sixty-five writers, both staff and freelance. The profiles grew in length, and some were presented in installments. McKelway's work on syndicated columnist and radio commentator Walter Winchell ran in six installments, John Winkler's account of publishing magnate William Randolph Hearst in five. Also profiled were persons who had succeeded in other fields of endeavor: advertising man Bruce Barton, statesman Franklin D. Roosevelt, cartoon king Walt Disney, pollster George Gallup, publicist Ivy Lee, actress Mae West, comedian Fields, industrialist Henry Ford, and others.

The magazine's "casuals" continued to attract talent and new ideas. Hemingway wrote a parody of English editor Frank Harris, whose 1925 autobiography had recently appeared. Then Thurber did a waggish parody of Hemingway's own macho writing style. John O'Hara contributed satiric pieces. Wolcott Gibbs began writing casuals, the first of which dealt with a pun that he had tried hard to work into a conversation, only to mess it up when his chance finally came.

The "Reporter at Large" department was at first written by Markey. Later, other reporters contributed to it, the first having been Boston writer Karl Schriftgiesser. Joel Sayre, Joseph Mitchell, David Lardner, Richard Boyer, Don Wharton, Jack Alexander, McKelway, and Sanderson Vanderbilt had all begun as reporters before joining the *New Yorker*. Another was Ik Shuman, who metamorphosed from writing "Reporter" pieces to serving a stint as managing editor.

Other talent hired by Ross included Russell Maloney, who wrote for "Talk of the Town," and Charles H. Cooke, who in twelve years authored around twelve hundred "Talk" pieces. Another "Talk" writer was Harvard graduate Ogden Nash, who joined the magazine in 1930 and gained fame as a humor poet. Clifton Fadiman, a Columbia University graduate and one of the magazine's few native New Yorkers, was a book reviewer for ten years; Sally Benson specialized in describing childhood memories. Charles Brackett came aboard as drama critic; Mosher did a movie column; Murdock Pemberton wrote on art; Robert Simon, on music. More attention was directed at sporting activities as well: polo, rowing, motoring, horse racing, horse shows, tennis, and golf.

During the Depression years the work of *New Yorker* humor writers helped lighten the dismal news. Frank Sullivan's characters "Mr. Tattersall" and "Mr. Arbuthnot" were popular. Lardner wrote regularly for Ross's magazine during his last years; another older humorist was Clarence Day. Arthur Kober's contributions, written in Bronx dialect, featured "the Gross family." Quite likely the most talented of the newer humorists to join the magazine during this period was S. J. Perelman, yet another Ivy Leaguer, from Brown University, who had written earlier for *Judge*.

Another development of the Depression years was what became known as "the *New Yorker* short story." The distinctive features of this form were an introspective tone, a near absence of plot, and endings that, in Kramer's words, gave the appearance that the writers "had gone out for a drink and forgot to come back." These sketchlike stories had been done earlier in some of the "little magazines," but the *New Yorker* was able to offer far better payment and a much wider audience. Writers included Kay Boyle, John Collier, Robert Coates, Sally Benson, Parker, Mosher, and O'Hara.

O'Hara was the most prolific of the fiction writers who used the *New Yorker* as a launching pad. By his contemporary Gill's reckoning, O'Hara sold 225 stories to Ross's magazine, having at first freelanced while employed as a reporter on the *New York Tribune,* then gaining his own desk at the *New Yorker* in the 1940s. At the time Gill was counting various writers' contributions to the magazine, John Cheever had sold 119, John Updike 104, and Coates and Benson around 100 each. Salinger was a relative newcomer at that time, as was Capote.

Ross's development of writing talent had another tangible result: the publication of hundreds of books that had their genesis in *New Yorker* stories. Examples are O'Hara's *Pal Joey* (1940), Thurber's *My Life and Hard Times* (1933), Updike's *Pigeon Feathers* (1962), Rachel Carson's *Silent Spring* (1962), and Clarence Day's *Life with Father* (1943). As the magazine historian Theodore Peterson has pointed out, the *New Yorker* under Ross's leadership exerted a remarkable influence on American letters for a magazine of its modest circulation.

As an editor, Ross specialized in long, detailed comments on manuscripts, totaling perhaps millions of words during his twenty-seven-year tenure. His comments and queries were usually numbered, and writers or fact checkers were expected to respond to each. Many of his notations were brief: "Who he?," "What mean?," "When happen?," "Locate," "Tinker," "Fix." The editor was a stickler for grammar, syntax, and punctuation. According to Shawn, Thurber, and other Ross contemporaries, the editor was not at his best working directly with writers and artists. Although he admired them, and though he eventually grew more sympathetic to their professional and personal problems, he felt ill at ease in their presence and could be confusing, awkward, and tactless if he tried to deal with them in person. His associates Katherine White, Gibbs, William Maxwell, Gustave "Gus" Lobrano, and James Geraghty mended relations on these occasions.

Letters to the editor were handled by Kip Orr, who could be feisty at times. When one reader complained that the magazine's copy was putting him to sleep, Orr simply wrote back, "Pleasant dreams." In Ross's search for grammatical and other writing errors, his infallible reference source was H. W. Fowler's *Dictionary of Modern English Usage* (1930). To ensure factual accuracy, he created what many considered the finest fact-checking department ever seen at an American magazine, and he continued to worry that despite the best efforts of himself and his staff, a double-entendre would sneak into the magazine. In every way Ross set the magazine's tone. He wanted to publish the best writers and artists he could find, and once he had located talent, he did his best to encourage it. The magazine was moved two blocks south to 25 West Forty-third Street in the mid 1930s, and the one floor of editorial offices enlarged to two.

Kramer suggests that Ross's change from a hard-nosed, single-minded architect of a new magazine to an editor who took a patronly, patriarchal interest in his writers and artists might have originated with the suicide in 1931 of the illustrator Barton. Thereafter, Ross listened more carefully to his employees' troubles and took care to compliment jobs well done. After the *New Yorker* had become quite prosperous, Ross instituted a complicated drawing-account method for paying contributors in an effort to regularize their income and provide them a sense of financial security. His method was to make regular deposits into their accounts, upon which they could draw on an as-needed basis. These accounts would be reconciled periodically against the person's actual contributions to the magazine. Sometimes the magazine would owe the employee more, at other times the individual would owe the magazine. According to Kramer, many such debts were forgiven by Ross.

After becoming the editor of the *New Yorker,* Ross hardly ever wrote anything of his own. Thurber recalled Ross's occasional attempts at writing "Talk of the Town" pieces. Ross admonished his writers that these pieces should read like dinner-table conversation, but although he was reputedly an entertaining conversationalist, he was unable to produce the same effect in written form, other than in personal letters. Ross was a classic case of the editor who is personally unable to do what he demands of his writers. Perhaps, of course, available time was one of the causes. According to Ross lore, a social acquaintance once found him looking concerned and asked what was wrong. Ross replied nothing serious, he was just trying to finish a book. The friend allowed that he did not know Ross was writing a book. Not writing, Ross corrected him, reading one.

The World War II years gave Ross real reasons to worry. His editorial corps was weakened, Thurber's eyesight was failing, the Whites had moved to Maine, and wartime enlistments scattered his younger writers. Ross was afraid the war would ruin his magazine, but just the opposite happened. A twenty-four-page "pony" edition published without advertising for the troops overseas reached a wartime circulation greater than that of its parent. More important, the magazine's far-flung correspondents produced stunning work. A. J. Liebling, E. J. Kahn, Jr., writing under the heading "The Army Life," and Walter Bernstein reported the war in Europe and the Pacific. Two of Lardner's sons also covered the war for the *New Yorker.* David Lardner was killed in Belgium, and his brother John landed with the troops at Iwo Jima and Okinawa.

A long-time writer for the magazine, and one whose contributions changed and became more important over time, was Janet Flanner, who had been brought to Ross's attention by wife Jane. Flanner had a modest independent income and had decided to live the life of an expatriate in Paris. Her newsy contributions about art, music, and people, signed "Genêt" at Ross's suggestion, was given the headline "Letter from Paris" and began appearing in October 1925. By 1930 she had begun to slip in material on prewar politics in France, and by 1936 Genêt's copy was mainly political, her audience large and appreciative. Her later book *Men and Monuments* (1957) was dedicated to Ross, "For whom over the years we wrote, and for whom we still write." One of the most significant magazine publications of the war era appeared in the 31 August 1946 issue of the *New Yorker,* in which John Hersey's "Hiroshima" took up the entire editorial space, a break with tradition that surprised long-time readers. The issue has become a collector's item.

Ross's search for a "Jesus" who could run the magazine in line with his vision finally paid off during the war in the person of Shawn, who had joined the magazine's staff in 1933. A small, quiet, mannerly man in his mid twenties, Shawn began as a "Talk of the Town" reporter and apparently made little impression on Ross for his first eight years with the magazine. During the latter part of this period the *New Yorker* had what amounted to two managing editors: Shuman over editorial finances and operating systems, and McKelway over story and article content. When the United States entered the war, some of the key *New Yorker* staffers, including McKelway, joined the service. Shuman suggested Shawn as his successor, and the editor agreed to give him a try, knowing that the magazine's veteran reporter Johnston also thought highly of Shawn's abilities. Shawn, who had changed his name from Chon, served as managing editor from 1939 until he succeeded Ross as editor on 21 January 1952. Like Ross, Shawn was an editor, not a writer; he published his own work in the magazine but once, in the 14 November 1936 issue – a fiction story titled "The Catastrophe" about a meteor that struck New York.

By the end of World War II, humor and satire, formerly the bread and butter of the magazine, had been largely supplanted by fiction and substantial nonfiction articles. During these years when Ross and Shawn worked together, the magazine changed in reaction to the war, becoming thicker, more serious in tone and content, and much wider in its scope – far less a city magazine than in its early period. Contributors of long fiction in these years included Salinger, Cheever, Mary McCarthy, and Jean Stafford. By this time many competitors had faded from the scene. *Vanity Fair*, *Life*, *Judge*, and *Smart Set* had died, leaving the *New Yorker* in a preeminent position among periodicals aimed at a literate, wealthy, well-educated audience. By war's end the *New Yorker* and its editor had become quite famous among magazine readers and writers worldwide. By Ross's death in 1951 the magazine's library, which had been originated in 1934 by Ebba Johnsson, contained roughly four hundred books filled with copy and art that had first appeared in the magazine. Also, a good many *New Yorker* stories such as Day's "Life with Father" and Thurber's

"The Secret Life of Walter Mitty" had inspired Broadway plays and Hollywood movies.

For all the success Ross had achieved with his magazine, his life was interrupted and made more difficult by factors quite apart from the war. A financial setback for him came when his private secretary from 1935 to 1941, Harold Winney, swindled him out of seventy-one thousand dollars. The quiet, efficient, unobtrusive Winney was, unknown to Ross, fond of fine clothes and addicted to betting on the horses. To save himself time, Ross had entrusted his bank accounts to Winney, who soon learned to forge Ross's signature. When Ross and his second wife left in 1938 for an extended vacation in France and England, he gave Winney power of attorney over his securities holdings, a tempting target. The thievery was eventually discovered in August 1941 by Fleischmann and Shuman. When word got to Ross, Winney went home, turned on the kitchen gas, and committed suicide. According to Thurber, Ross, whose attention to money matters was such that he never even filled out stubs on the checks he wrote, cared less about the loss of the seventy-one thousand dollars than about the kidding he knew he would receive from his friends.

A much larger loss of funds that angered Ross far more was the drain of roughly three-quarters of a million dollars of company money by Fleischmann, who wanted to score a second triumph in the magazine industry and who backed Hanrahan's unsuccessful magazine venture *Stage* (1932–1939). The dapper, Vienna-born Fleischmann – who was married three times, loved to gamble, owned race horses, and had been nicknamed "Royal Flushman" in his Thanatopsis days – had played fast and loose with F-R Publishing funds. Both Ross and Fleischmann's former wife, then Mrs. Peter Vischer, threatened court action, and there was some talk of replacing Fleischmann as publisher, but a compromise was reached. Fleischmann agreed to put his shares in escrow for a certain period and agreed that the firm would be overseen by lawyer Stryker, stockholder and director Traux, and Ross's confidant and stockbroker Dan Silberberg. After this, Ross and Fleischmann seldom spoke to one another.

Ross too had entertained thoughts of starting another magazine, though he never did so. He liked reading crime copy and laid plans to bring out a magazine titled *Guilty?* that would contain true detective stories, which he envisioned editing personally. Such a magazine might offer him a financial safety net in case his feud with his publisher should ever lead to his dismissal from the *New Yorker,* he reasoned. His friend Silberberg convinced him not to take this gamble, the start-up costs of which would have been more than Ross could risk. Also, timing was bad, as the country was still in the Depression. Another, smaller Ross venture for extra income involved a spray-painting device. Concerned that Ross's attention was straying from his magazine responsibilities, certain staffers, who have since managed to remain anonymous, went to Fleischmann suggesting that he replace Ross. Thurber reports having thrown a tantrum when the publisher broached the subject.

By the early 1950s the *New Yorker* was selling roughly 350,000 copies a week, only a third of which were in New York City. It was fat with advertising, and its reputation was assured. Ross was gratified that his brainchild was being taken seriously on both sides of the Atlantic but was concerned at the magazine's paucity of good humor writing. For humor he had come to depend more than ever on his cartoonists. Irvin was still art adviser, though James Geraghty was art editor. Favorite among the magazine's cartoonists was Charles Addams, apostle of the macabre, followed in popularity by Romanian-born Saul Steinberg.

The job of managing editor was split between Gus Lobrano, who concentrated on fiction, and Shawn, who mainly dealt with nonfiction. Shawn supervised a staff of six other fiction editors. Two of these editors would read each incoming manuscript; either could reject it. If no rejection notice was sent, two more editors would read it, and, as always, Ross had the final say.

For some years prior to his death, Ross had made periodic trips to the Lahey Clinic in Boston for treatment of stomach trouble. In April 1951 a checkup showed bronchial cancer, possibly a result of his cigarette smoking. By this time Ross was separated from his third wife and living in a suite at the Algonquin; his daughter was away at school in New England. Ross went to the Lahey Clinic for surgery, having indicated that if the procedure were unsuccessful, he wanted Shawn to succeed him as editor. Ross died on the operating table of an embolism on 6 December 1951.

Of the several Ross contemporaries who have written about him, only one found his abrasive charm more abrasive than charming. This was Gill, who in 1975 published *Here at The New Yorker.* All who worked with Ross agreed that he was self-taught, but only Gill adds that his learning was "spectacularly hit-or-miss." The picture of Ross that Gill paints is of "an aggressively ignorant man," a belligerent, distrusting, incompetent editor who was condescending to his underlings and whose own attempts at writing read like "Henry James with a tin ear." Ross's quest for accuracy, Gill wrote, resulted in frequent literary mutilations as the "clumsy water buffalo of an editor," from his own lack of education, "clung to facts as a shipwrecked man clings to a spar" while purposely ignoring inconvenient reality. In Gill's book, Ross emerges as prudish and puritanical, yet at the same time loud, profane, and lacking in religious belief – a man for whom "God remained at most a convenient epithet." Ross was, in Gill's view, bigoted, homophobic, and a general boor. Even the editor's Fabian Bachrach portrait that hung in the magazine's offices appeared to Gill like "a small-town crook arrested for having tried to hold up a bank with a water pistol."

Gill was not alone in noting the difficult and deficient sides of Ross's nature. Nash remarked in a letter to Thurber that Ross was nearly impossible to work for and added that the editor was "rude, ungracious and perpetually dissatisfied" with writers' work. Even so, Nash concluded, he found Ross the most admirable man he had met in his entire professional experience, mainly because Ross was, in his own unique way, a perfectionist. Thurber, who clearly loved Ross, wrote about his boss's grotesque spelling and innocence of literature that caused him to approach fiction contributions, in Thurber's words, "with curiosity, respect, and trepidation, the way I once saw a Scottie approach a turtle."

Anecdotes abound regarding Ross's uneven education, the most often repeated of which originated when the editor appeared at the door of the magazine's fact-checking department and inquired whether Moby Dick was the man or the whale. Even his contemporaries were not sure what to make of stories like this one. If Ross's first wife is to be believed, however, the editor took delight in playing the fool, or as she put it, "acting the goon." According to Grant's assessment, her former husband was brilliant, a near-genius. Possibly the truth lies somewhere between the extremes. Certainly Ross was a complex, multisided character with far more to him than met the eye. His friend Charles MacArthur put it nicely when he remarked that Ross "had the charm of gaucherie." For those who never met Ross and must form an image of the man secondhand, perhaps an English painter who visited the editor in 1931 offered the best assessment. After a conversation with Ross, Paul Nash remarked to Ogden Nash and Thurber, "He is like your skyscrapers. They are unbelievable, but there they are."

Ross's was one of the greatest magazine success stories of the century: the creation of a periodical that offered to its public a content of unusually high literary quality, with the additions of wit and sophistication. By trial and error, and by nurturing excellent talent, the irascible, contradictory Ross was able, as the founding editor of the *New Yorker,* to produce a blend of elements that appealed to affluent, educated, urbane readers. He would no doubt be pleased that his magazine can still refer to itself as "probably the finest magazine ever published."

References:

John E. Drewry, "A Study of New Yorker Profiles of Famous Journalists," *Journalism Quarterly,* 23 (December 1946): 370–380;

Susan Edmiston, and Linda D. Cirino, *Literary New York, A History and Guide* (Boston: Houghton Mifflin, 1976), pp. 195–202;

Leslie Frewin, *The Late Mrs. Dorothy Parker* (New York: Macmillan, 1986);

James R. Gaines, *Wit's End: Days and Nights of the Algonquin Round Table* (New York: Harcourt Brace Jovanovich, 1977);

Brendan Gill, *Here at The New Yorker* (New York: Random House, 1975);

Jane Grant, *Ross, The New Yorker and Me* (New York: Reynal, 1968);

Margaret Case Harriman, *The Vicious Circle* (New York: Rinehart, 1951);

Ralph Ingersoll, "The New Yorker," *Fortune,* 10 (August 1934): 73–97;

Dale Kramer, *Ross and The New Yorker* (Garden City, N. Y.: Doubleday, 1951);

Edward A. Martin, *H. L. Mencken and the Debunkers* (Athens: University of Georgia Press, 1984), pp. 184–186;

Howard Teichmann, *Smart Aleck: The Wit, World and Life of Alexander Woollcott* (New York: William Morrow, 1976);

James Thurber, *The Years With Ross* (Boston: Little, Brown, 1959);

George Y. Wells, "Inseparable Phenomena," *Saturday Review of Literature,* 34 (22 December 1951): 18–19;

E. B. White, "H. W. Ross," *New Yorker,* 27 (15 December 1951): 23.

Robb Hansell Sagendorph

(20 November 1900 - 4 July 1970)

Donald R. Avery
Eastern Connecticut State University

MAJOR POSITIONS HELD: Editor and publisher, *Yankee* (1935–1970), *Old Farmer's Almanac* (1939–1970), *Dublin* (New Hampshire) *Opinion* (1950).

BOOKS: *Rain, Hail, and Baked Beans,* by Sagendorph and Duncan McDonald (New York: Ives Washburn, 1958);
America and Her Almanacs: Wit, Wisdom & Weather, 1639–1970 (Dublin, N.H.: Yankee, 1970).

OTHER: *Robb's Cabinet of Curiosities, Being a Collection of Interesting, Amusing, and Instructive Clippings Culled from Old Newspapers and Family Scrapbooks,* compiled by Sagendorph (Dublin, N.H.: Yankee, 1951);
The Old Farmer's Almanac Sampler, edited by Sagendorph (New York: Washburn, 1957);
New England, edited by Sagendorph and Arthur Griffin (Winchester, Mass.: Houghton, 1962);
That New England, edited by Sagendorph and Judson D. Hale (Dublin, N.H.: Yankee, 1966).

SELECTED PERIODICAL PUBLICATIONS – UNCOLLECTED: "What Have You Got To Swap," *American Magazine,* 160 (October 1955): 110;
"Old Farmer's Almanac," *Atlantic Monthly,* 198 (November 1956): 87;
"About Winter," *New York Times Magazine,* 16 December 1956, p. 16;
"Theophrastus Was Right," *New York Times Magazine,* 19 April 1959, p. 54.

Robb Hansell Sagendorph was for thirty-five years the epitome of New England and what it represented. As editor and publisher of *Yankee* magazine and the *Old Farmer's Almanac,* he perpetuated an ideal regarded as the spirit of New England, and he demonstrated to the rest of the nation what it was like to be a "Yankee."

Sagendorph was born in Newton Centre, Massachusetts, on 20 November 1900 to George and Jane Cooper Hansell Sagendorph. He attended the exclusive Noble and Greenough School in Dedham, Massachusetts, where he developed a deep interest in Greek and Latin. He continued his education at Harvard University, receiving his A.B. in 1922. During his undergraduate days he served as business manager of the *Harvard Lampoon,* an experience that would serve him well later in life. Sagendorph went on to study at the Harvard University Graduate School of Business from 1922 to 1923 but did not complete a degree.

Sagendorph worked in his father's business, the Penn Metal Company, from 1923 to 1929. This work took him to New York, where he tried to establish an export market for the company in Latin America. Despite his attempts, he was not successful at the steel business; however, he was diligent and turned his hand to virtually every job from steel handler to vice-president. Nevertheless, Sagendorph did not really enjoy the work, and he was not upset when his father's company merged with a larger firm in 1929. The new Penn Metal Company had no need for a vice-president more interested in writing and literary magazines than in steel fabrication, and Sagendorph was dismissed.

Sagendorph married Beatrix Thorne on 27 October 1928. They would eventually have two daughters, Jane Thorne and Lorna. Neither Sagendorph, who wanted to write and perhaps start a literary magazine, nor his wife, who was an artist and wanted to paint, thought much of a large city as a place to raise a family. As a child, Sagendorph had spent his summers at his father's summer house near Peterborough, New Hampshire, and he returned to the town in 1929 to buy a house. The Sagendorphs ended up in Dublin, New Hampshire, the owners of an old farmhouse that had been converted into a rambling, Italian-style villa, with marble mantels and tile floors. For the next few years Sagendorph lived the life of a writer and gentle-

Robb Hansell Sagendorph

man farmer. He had little success in either endeavor. Sagendorph wrote hundreds of short stories, but by 1935 he had managed to sell only two, for a total of eighty-five dollars.

A chance meeting with an unemployed printer led to the beginning of Sagendorph's career in publishing. For several years Sagendorph had been thinking about starting his own magazine containing poems, stories, and articles about New England. The result was *Yankee* magazine, the first issue of which appeared in September 1935. *Yankee* was illustrated by Beatrix Sagendorph and was in many ways as much her publication as her husband's. In fact, her inheritance from her grandfather George Arthur Thorne, who had been Montgomery Ward's original business partner, carried the publication through its first few years.

Sagendorph occasionally regretted starting a magazine that, financially, seemed to be a bottomless pit. "I discovered that people liked good literature, but that they wouldn't pay for it," Sagendorph said in a 1954 article for the *Saturday Evening Post.* He experimented with all aspects of the publication, but by 1939 he was heavily in debt, and *Yankee* continued to lose money. The magazine would almost certainly have folded had it not been for another publication suffering a similar fall in prospects.

Established by Robert B. Thomas, the *Old Farmer's Almanac* had been published annually for 147 years but had fallen on hard times by the 1930s. Its editors had watched its circulation fall to about eighty thousand despite all their attempts to salvage it by hiring well-known writers and substituting official U.S. Weather Bureau tables for the forecasts written by "Abraham Weatherwise." The publisher, Little, Brown, and Company, cast about for someone who might be interested in purchasing the failing publication. Sagendorph bought and immediately set about salvaging the *Almanac.*

From the beginning Sagendorph believed he knew enough about operating marginal publications to put the *Almanac* back on its feet and in the process save *Yankee.* Properly operated, Sagendorph believed, the *Almanac* could be a profitable title which could see *Yankee* through to better times. He immediately threw out all the updated ideas of the previous editor and returned, as nearly as he could, to the publication's roots. Many of the early departments which had disappeared were restored. In addition, Sagendorph attempted to recapture the bellicose language of the early editors. "I know many men, who are called farmers, that deserve not the name any more than a cobbler does that of a shoemaker . . . in many places the master loves new rum and the mistress is a slut!" Thomas had written in the 1807 issue. It was this sense of the irreverent that Sagendorph tried to emulate.

Sagendorph recognized that the *Almanac* was both a victim and a beneficiary of changing demographic trends in the country. Its sagging fortunes in the 1930s were less a result of the shift from a rural to an urban orientation in American society than an inability of the publication's editors to recognize that nothing fundamental was wrong with the *Almanac*. Assuming that readers would no longer be interested in rural matters once they had abandoned the farm, the editors basically tried to fix that which was not broken. But Sagendorph recognized that in a world growing more complex, the simple kind of life implied by the *Almanac* would have enormous appeal.

It was this widespread desire to return to a simpler time that Sagendorph was able to capitalize upon by returning the *Almanac* to its roots. While the number of farmers was decreasing, the number of those interested in the simpler lifestyle that farming represented was growing among the American population. These readers did not want an almanac filled with modern fiction and poetry; they wanted a publication that would allow them to live vicariously a lifestyle that had all but disappeared. In providing such nostalgic material, Sagendorph saved both the *Almanac* and *Yankee*. From a circulation of about eighty thousand in 1939, the *Almanac* grew to 1.6 million in 1970.

The publication that Sagendorph produced was filled with astronomy tables; weather predictions; old-fashioned recipes; poetry; advice on when to plant and harvest crops and how to mend fences and buildings; listings of holidays and events, both common and odd ("Abe Lincoln conceived, May 7, 1808"); kitchen hints; hunting and fishing laws; postal rates; reproduction and gestation tables; and motor-vehicle laws. One of the most important steps taken by Sagendorph was to reinstate the weather predictions of the pseudonymous Abe Weatherwise. Sagendorph claimed to have made a study of historical records all the way back to the sixteenth century and to have rediscovered the secret weather-predicting formula of the first editor of the *Almanac*. While Sagendorph claimed a better prediction record than the U.S. Weather Bureau (78.5 percent accuracy for the *Almanac* versus 65.5 percent for the Weather Bureau), critics argued that he was highly selective in making his comparisons.

Contemporary newspaper and magazine accounts give Sagendorph credit for writing about two-thirds of the *Almanac*, including all of the

Cover for an issue of the successful regional magazine Sagendorph published from 1935 until his death in 1970

weather predictions. In fact, although he wrote some of the material himself – most notably the weather predictions and the listing of holidays – most departments were actually written by others; the poetry was written by an English teacher, the astronomical tables by a former researcher at the Harvard Observatory, the Farmer's Calendar by an apple grower, and other sections by unknown staff writers.

Over the years people from all over the world turned to Sagendorph for advice and weather tips. From the letters the *Almanac* received, it would seem that the most important aspect of the publication has been its weather predictions and marginal comments about the weather. Sagendorph received letters from the elders of a drought-ravaged village in India (it rained the day Sagendorph's response arrived, and the villagers concluded that he was a holy man); a woman in Washington, D.C., preparing a calendar in the language of the Loma tribe in western Africa; and a stockbroker asking about

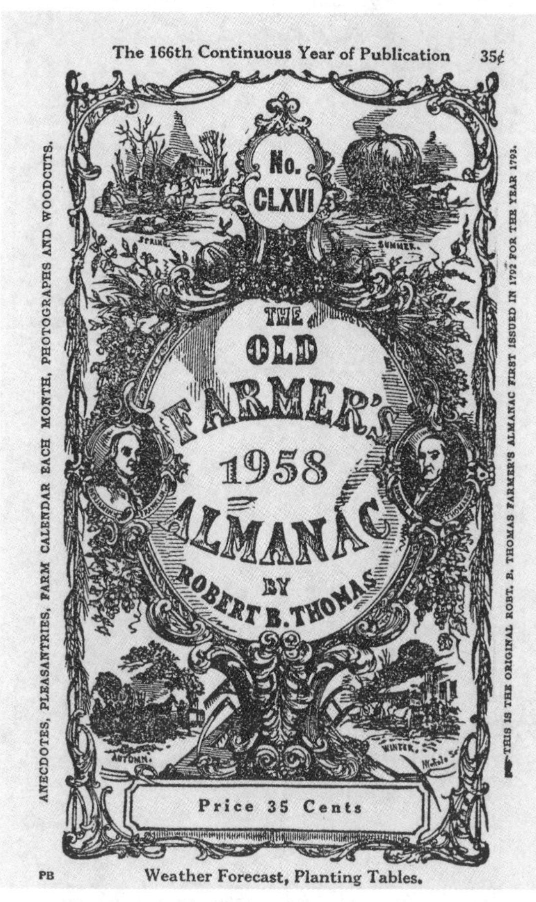

Cover for an issue of Sagendorph's annual miscellany of agrarian-oriented facts, predictions, and anecdotes

summer weather before recommending the purchase of soft-drink stock.

Despite Sagendorph's thirty-one-year association with the *Almanac,* his name never once appeared in its pages. The *Almanac* carried and still carries the signature and picture of Robert B. Thomas, who died in 1846. However, while Sagendorph wanted to maintain the tradition of having Thomas's name associated with the *Almanac,* no such reticence hid his name at *Yankee.* For its first thirty-five years *Yankee* was synonymous with Sagendorph.

Despite Sagendorph's ultimate success with *Yankee,* establishing a publication in 1935 in the midst of the Great Depression would have to be considered poor timing if not foolish. Franklin D. Roosevelt signed the Social Security Act in 1935; people were worried about being unemployed, finding the next meal, and where they were going to sleep. Sagendorph saw the period as a difficult time for the magazine's namesake – the hard-nosed, self-reliant, ornery Yankee was forced to recognize that Social Security might actually be necessary. As Sagendorph wrote in the magazine's first issue: "For the Yankee this is the age of bewilderment. He sees individuality, initiative, natural ingenuity, the things his father and their fathers fought for – about to be sold, to be 'swallered inter a sea of chainstores, national releases, and nationwide hookups.'"

Sagendorph had difficulty defining his magazine, and others have tried and generally failed. "*Yankee* magazine is what it is," Managing Editor Judson D. Hale, Sr., said in 1985 to the Newcomen Society. "It reflects what New England is. It does not analyze New England, but is rather a *part* of the New England others may wish to analyze. *Yankee* partakes of the American spirit as it chooses. And that spirit is what it is."

Sagendorph's successor as publisher, C. Robertson Trowbridge, argues that there are three reasons for the magazine's longevity. First, *Yankee* was an idea, not a product – it had a purpose. Sagendorph in the first issue said that this purpose was "the expression and perhaps indirectly the preservation of that great culture in which every Yank is born and in which every real Yank must live." While products are often imitative and tied to popular trends, as long as *Yankee* succeeded in its aim the publication was free to change.

Second, the personal nature of Sagendorph's publishing practice is such that a publication takes on the personality of the editor: "the magazine has acquired a personality in such a way that people don't talk about *Yankee* magazine; they talk about 'The Yankee' as if it were a person who comes to the home on a regular basis, a friend who is invited to tell its tale once a month, coming in welcome and expected," Trowbridge said.

Third, *Yankee* succeeded because of perseverance. It met the need in Americans to return to their roots, a penchant that became more pronounced in the 1960s, with the country's growing interest in history. However, the publication changed over the years and became less literary, addressing itself to the natural interests of the people of the region it served with stories and articles on New England history, crafts, how-to, antiques, and collecting.

For several years Sagendorph had to subsidize *Yankee* with proceeds from the *Almanac* before the former began to make a profit. A major reason for the eventual success of *Yankee* was the mail-order business. For most of the magazine's formative years the mail-order business was seen by most Americans as little more than charlatans hawking

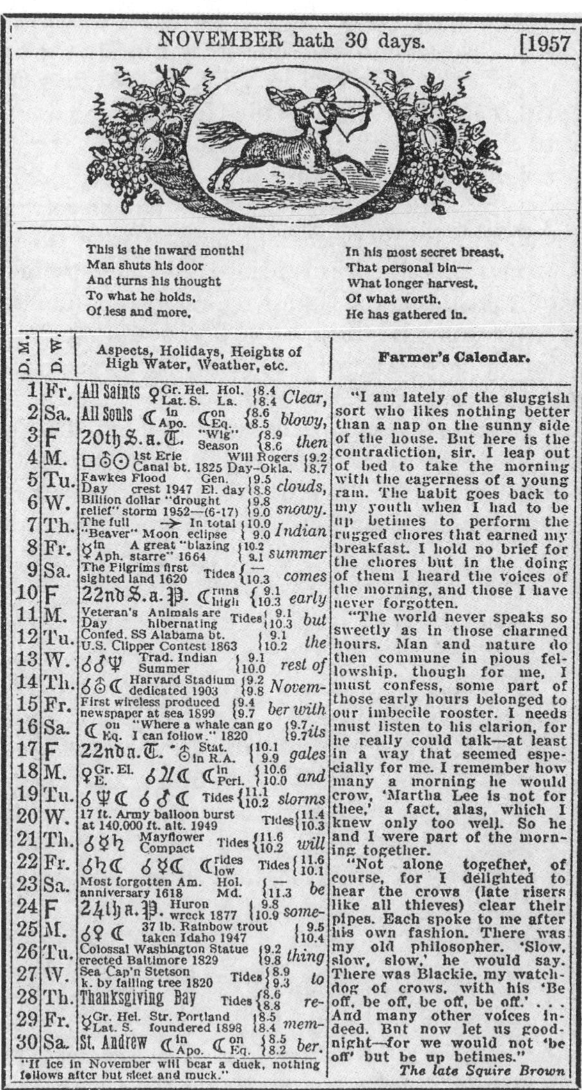

NOVEMBER hath 30 days. [1957

This is the inward month!
Man shuts his door
And turns his thought
To what he holds,
Of less and more,
In his most secret breast,
That personal bin—
What longer harvest,
Of what worth,
He has gathered in.

D. M.	D. W.	Aspects, Holidays, Heights of High Water, Weather, etc.		
1	Fr.	All Saints ♀ Gr. Hel. Lat. S. Hol. La.	8.4 8.4	Clear,
2	Sa.	All Souls ☾ in Apo. ☾ on Eq.	8.6 8.5	blowy,
3	F	20th S. a. T. "Wig" Season	8.9 8.6	then
4	M.	□ ♅ ☉ 1st Erie Canal bt. 1825 Will Rogers Day–Okla.	9.2 8.7	
5	Tu.	Fawkes Day Flood crest 1947 Gen. El. day	9.5 8.8	clouds,
6	W.	Billion dollar "drought relief" storm 1952—(6-17)	9.8 9.0	snowy.
7	Th.	The full "Beaver" Moon → In total eclipse	10.0 9.0	Indian
8	Fr.	☿ in Aph. A great "blazing starre" 1664	10.2 9.1	summer
9	Sa.	The Pilgrims first sighted land 1620 Tides	— 10.3	comes
10	F	22nd S. a. P. ☾ runs high	9.1 10.3	early
11	M.	Veteran's Day Animals are hibernating Tides	9.1 10.3	but
12	Tu.	Confed. SS Alabama bt. U.S. Clipper Contest 1863	9.1 10.2	the
13	W.	☌ ♂ ♆ Trad. Indian Summer	9.1 10.0	rest of
14	Th.	☌ ♅ ☾ Harvard Stadium dedicated 1903	9.2 9.8	Novem-
15	Fr.	First wireless produced newspaper at sea 1899	9.4 9.7	ber with
16	Sa.	☾ on Eq. "Where a whale can go I can follow." 1820	9.7 9.7	its
17	F	22nd a. T. ♅ Stat. in R.A.	10.1 9.9	gales
18	M.	♀ Gr. El. E. ☌ ♃ ☾ ☾ in Peri.	10.6 10.0	and
19	Tu.	☌ ♆ ☾ ☌ ♂ ☾ Tides	11.1 10.2	storms
20	W.	17 ft. Army balloon burst at 140,000 ft. alt. 1949 Tides	11.4 10.3	
21	Th.	☌ ☿ ♄ Mayflower Compact Tides	11.6 10.2	will
22	Fr.	☌ ♄ ☾ ☌ ☿ ☾ ☾ rides low Tides	11.6 10.1	
23	Sa.	Most forgotten Am. anniversary 1618 Hol. Md.	— 11.3	be
24	F	24th a. P. Huron wreck 1877	9.8 10.9	some-
25	M.	☌ ♀ ☾ 37 lb. Rainbow trout taken Idaho 1947	9.5 10.4	
26	Tu.	Colossal Washington Statue erected Baltimore 1829	9.2 9.8	thing
27	W.	Sea Cap'n Stetson k. by falling tree 1820 Tides	8.9 9.3	to
28	Th.	Thanksgiving Day Tides	8.6 8.8	re-
29	Fr.	☿ Gr. Hel. Lat. S. Str. Portland foundered 1898	8.5 8.4	mem-
30	Sa.	St. Andrew ☾ in Apo. ☾ on Eq.	8.5 8.2	ber.

"If ice in November will bear a duck, nothing follows after but sleet and muck."

Farmer's Calendar.

"I am lately of the sluggish sort who likes nothing better than a nap on the sunny side of the house. But here is the contradiction, sir. I leap out of bed to take the morning with the eagerness of a young ram. The habit goes back to my youth when I had to be up betimes to perform the rugged chores that earned my breakfast. I hold no brief for the chores but in the doing of them I heard the voices of the morning, and those I have never forgotten.

"The world never speaks so sweetly as in those charmed hours. Man and nature do then commune in pious fellowship, though for me, I must confess, some part of those early hours belonged to our imbecile rooster. I needs must listen to his clarion, for he really could talk—at least in a way that seemed especially for me. I remember how many a morning he would crow, 'Martha Lee is not for thee,' a fact, alas, which I knew only too well. So he and I were part of the morning together.

"Not alone together, of course, for I delighted to hear the crows (late risers like all thieves) clear their pipes. Each spoke to me after his own fashion. There was my old philosopher. 'Slow, slow, slow,' he would say. There was Blackie, my watchdog of crows, with his 'Be off, be off, be off, be off.' . . . And many other voices indeed. But now let us goodnight—for we would not 'be off' but be up betimes."

The late Squire Brown

1957] NOVEMBER, ELEVENTH MONTH.

ASTRONOMICAL CALCULATIONS.

☉'s Declination. Days.	° ′	Days.	° ′	Days.	° ′	Days.	° ′	Days.	° ′
1	14s. 30	7	16 20	13	18 01	19	19 31	25	20 47
2	14 49	8	16 38	14	18 17	20	19 44	26	20 59
3	15 08	9	16 55	15	18 32	21	19 58	27	21 10
4	15 26	10	17 12	16	18 47	22	20 11	28	21 21
5	15 45	11	17 29	17	19 02	23	20 23	29	21 31
6	16 03	12	17 45	18	19 17	24	20 36	30	21 41

○ Full Moon, 7th day, 9 h. 32 m., morning, W.
☾ Last Quarter, 14th day, 4 h. 59 m., evening, W.
● New Moon, 21st day, 11 h. 19 m., morning, E.
☽ First Quarter, 29th day, 1 h. 57 m., morning, W.

KEY LETTERS REFER TO CORRECTIONS TABLE, PAGES 101-4, FOR ALL POINTS OUTSIDE NEW ENGLAND

Day of Year	Day of Month	Day of the Week	☉ Rises. h. m.	Key	☉ Sets. h. m.	Key	Length of Days. h. m.	Sun Fast. m.	Full Sea, Boston. Morn h.	Full Sea, Boston. Even h.	☽ Sets. h. m.	Key	☽ Souths. h. m.	☽'s Place	Moon's Age
305	1	Fr.	6 17	L	4 38	F	10 22	32	6½	6¾	12 A.M. 30	G	7 P.M. 30	PSC	10
306	2	Sa.	6 18	L	4 37	F	10 19	32	7¼	7½	1 27	H	8 12	PSC	11
307	3	F	6 19	L	4 36	E	10 17	32	8	8½	2 25	I	8 54	ARI	12
308	4	M.	6 21	M	4 35	E	10 14	32	8¾	9¼	3 23	J	9 37	ARI	13
309	5	Tu.	6 22	M	4 34	E	10 12	32	9½	9¾	4 21	K	10 22	ARI	14
310	6	W.	6 23	M	4 32	E	10 09	32	10	10½	5 A.M. 21	L	11 09	TAU	15
311	7	Th.	6 24	M	4 31	E	10 07	32	10¾	11¼	rises	–	11 P.M. 57	TAU	16
312	8	Fr.	6 26	M	4 30	E	10 05	32	11¼	11¾	5 P.M. 22	E	—	—	—
313	9	Sa.	6 27	M	4 29	E	10 02	32	—	0	6 10	D	12 A.M. 49	G'M	17
314	10	F	6 28	M	4 28	E	10 00	32	0½	0¾	7 04	D	1 42	G'M	18
315	11	M.	6 29	M	4 27	E	9 58	32	1¼	1½	8 05	E	2 36	CNC	19
316	12	Tu.	6 31	M	4 26	E	9 55	32	2	2¼	9 09	E	3 30	CNC	20
317	13	W.	6 32	M	4 25	E	9 53	31	2¾	3	10 16	F	4 24	LEO	21
318	14	Th.	6 33	M	4 24	E	9 51	31	3¾	4	11 P.M. 25	G	5 17	LEO	22
319	15	Fr.	6 34	M	4 23	E	9 49	31	4¾	5¼	—	–	6 09	VIR	23
320	16	Sa.	6 36	M	4 22	E	9 47	31	5¾	6¼	12 A.M. 36	H	7 00	VIR	24
321	17	F	6 37	M	4 21	D	9 45	31	6¾	7¼	1 47	I	7 52	VIR	25
322	18	M.	6 38	N	4 21	D	9 43	31	7¾	8¼	2 58	K	8 45	LIB	26
323	19	Tu.	6 39	N	4 20	D	9 41	30	8¾	9¼	4 10	L	9 40	LIB	27
324	20	W.	6 40	N	4 19	D	9 39	30	9½	10	5 A.M. 22	M	10 36	SCO	28
325	21	Th.	6 42	N	4 18	D	9 37	30	10¼	11	sets	–	11 A.M. 32	SCO	29
326	22	Fr.	6 43	N	4 18	D	9 35	30	11¼	11¾	5 P.M. 24	D	12 P.M. 29	SGR	1
327	23	Sa.	6 44	N	4 17	D	9 33	29	—	0	6 21	D	1 25	SGR	2
328	24	F	6 45	N	4 16	D	9 31	29	0½	0¾	7 19	E	2 18	CAP	3
329	25	M.	6 46	N	4 16	D	9 30	29	1½	1½	8 20	E	3 09	CAP	4
330	26	Tu.	6 48	N	4 15	D	9 28	28	2¼	2½	9 20	F	3 57	AQR	5
331	27	W.	6 49	N	4 15	D	9 26	28	3	3¼	10 18	G	4 42	AQR	6
332	28	Th.	6 50	N	4 15	D	9 25	28	3¾	4	11 P.M. 16	H	5 25	PSC	7
333	29	Fr.	6 51	N	4 14	D	9 23	27	4¾	5	—	–	6 07	PSC	8
334	30	Sa.	6 52	N	4 14	D	9 22	27	5½	6	12 A.M. 14	I	6 P.M. 49	PSC	9

Astronomy tables from the Old Farmer's Almanac

worthless nostrums, patent medicines, and shoddy merchandise. For every Sears and Roebuck and Montgomery Ward selling merchandise through a catalogue, there were dozens of smaller companies trying to survive and perhaps expand in direct mail. The industry needed credibility, and one of the best ways of achieving it was to get product and company advertising into successful publications such as the *Progressive Farmer*, *Grit*, or *Yankee* (though Sagendorph steadfastly refused to permit patent-medicine advertising in either *Yankee* or the *Almanac*). If *Yankee* helped such mail-order companies as L. L. Bean, Yield House, and Johnny Appleseed to find new customers, those same companies helped *Yankee* find a substantial revenue base. The publication's circulation grew steadily over the postwar years and reached about five hundred thousand in 1970.

Despite his continuing concern with publishing and writing, Sagendorph's life was filled with other activities as well. From 1942 to 1945 he served as a resident analyst for the U.S. Office of Censorship in New York City. He continued to publish the *Almanac* during the war but was forced to stop publication of *Yankee* due to the logistics of producing a monthly magazine from New York. In a 1956 interview with J. H. Winchester, Sagendorph claimed that the Office of Censorship removed the 1943 issue of the *Almanac* from newsstands because the government feared the publication's weather data might be used by the enemy. Indeed, the only uniformed Germans to invade American soil during

Sagendorph conversing with residents of Dublin, New Hampshire, where the Old Farmer's Almanac *was published, in 1954. He used the wicker basket as a briefcase.*

the war were captured in Long Island, New York, and had in their possession a copy of the 1943 issue of the *Almanac*.

Sagendorph was a one-man civic-improvement association in Dublin. He lived in the town, and all his publications were produced there in a small cottage and its adjoining barn on the main street of the town, which never had more than one thousand people during Sagendorph's lifetime. He served as town moderator and as a selectman (a kind of town council and council president) during the final twenty-five years of his life. Sagendorph owned most of the buildings and was responsible for the erection on the Dublin town square of new buildings such as the post office.

Sagendorph was also involved in a wider region. He was awarded an honorary Litt.D. degree by New England College in 1959. In 1963 he was named Man of the Year by the New England Society of New York. Sagendorph also served as chairman of the board of the Monadnock Regional Association from 1966 to 1968 and was named to the New Hampshire Bicentennial Commission in 1970. At various times he was a member of many organizations, including the National Grange, the American Meteorological Society, the Society for the Protection of New Hampshire Forests, the American Rocket Society, the Century Association, the Harvard Alumni Association, the Harvard Club of New York City, the Hasty Pudding Club of Harvard, and the Country Club of Brookline, Massachusetts. He was also a director of the Penn Metal Company.

Despite a lengthy illness Sagendorph continued to operate his enterprises until a few months before his death. In early 1970 he named his son-in-law, C. Robertson Trowbridge, as president of Yankee Publishing Incorporated. In a speech to the Newcomen Society in 1985, Trowbridge reported Sagendorph's words when he turned over the company and its publications to Trowbridge and a new managing editor: "But, boys, don't grow too much because the johns won't take it." He died 4 July 1970 in Peterborough, New Hampshire.

References:

J. F. Fix, "Weather Eye on Nostalgia," *Saturday Review,* 44 (9 December 1961): 64;

Joe Alex Morris, "The Man Who Guesses Right," *Saturday Evening Post* (20 November 1954): 48;

Obituary, *New York Times,* 6 July 1970, p. 31;

J. Poling, "Wit, Wisdom and Weather," *Collier's,* 126 (25 November 1950): 31;

L. M. Robbins, "Counselor & Friend," *New York Times Magazine,* 9 March 1947, p. 18;

C. Robertson Trowbridge and Judson D. Hale, Sr., *Yankee Publishing Incorporated: Fifty Years of Preserving New England's Culture While Extending Its Influence* (New York: Newcomen Society, 1985);

J. H. Winchester, "Almanack Man," *Scholastic,* 68 (1 March 1956).

Edwin F. Self

(15 June 1920 –)

Michael D. Murray
University of Missouri at Saint Louis

MAJOR POSITIONS HELD: Advertising manager, *La Jolla Light* (1946); editor and publisher, *North Shores Sentinel* (1947–1948); publisher and editor in chief, *San Diego* (1948–).

BOOK: *San Diego: A Portrait of a Spectacular City,* by Self and Syd Love (San Diego: San Diego Magazine Publisher, 1969).

SELECTED PERIODICAL PUBLICATIONS – UNCOLLECTED: "The Civil Service Straightjacket," *San Diego,* 8 (September 1956): 33;

"Operation Eurocom," *San Diego,* 13 (June 1961): 39–42+;

"Cruising the Pleasure Coast of Mexico," *San Diego,* 18 (February 1966): 58–62+;

"To Mendocino, Staying Close to the Coast," *San Diego,* 24 (February 1972): 76–81+;

"The West: A New Mystique of Cruising," *San Diego,* 25 (October 1973): 70–73+;

"Golf, Whiskey and Politics in the Troubled Kingdom," *San Diego,* 28 (March 1976): 60–71;

"Los Angeles in the Time of Tut: Art, Archeology and Cruisine," *San Diego,* 30 (April 1978): 175–176;

"Cruising the Colonies," *San Diego,* 34 (April 1982): 126–129+;

"In Memory of Jack," *San Diego,* 35 (January 1983): 62–68;

"The Battle of Britton – James Britton II, 1915–1983," *San Diego,* 35 (March 1983): 80+;

"No Contest; The McCarthy-Curb Race," *San Diego,* 38 (November 1986): 12–14;

"Publisher's Point: Mayor Maureen and the Soviets," *San Diego,* 41 (June 1989): 10;

"We Were First . . . And Now We're 45," *San Diego,* 45 (October 1993): 58–60.

Edwin Self created the nation's first modern, independent city magazine, *San Diego.* He and his wife, Gloria Winke Self, a former *San Diego* editor, set the standard for the concept of the critical city magazine, unlike promotional chamber-of-commerce–type publications. Under Self 's tutelage, *San Diego* gained notoriety for emphasis on civic improvement and political consciousness. A staff of specialists in such areas as art and architecture, the environment, and local history, along with an emphasis on high-quality graphics and photography, set the magazine apart and made it a prototype publication during the postwar period, one of tremendous growth in San Diego.

The son of Robert Self and Agnes Wilson Self, Edwin Forbes Self was born in Dundee, Scotland, immigrated with his family to the United States the year after his birth, and was naturalized as a citizen twenty years later. As a high-school student Self won first prize in a national contest with thirty-five thousand entrants for best news story. He was editor of his grade-school, junior-high, and high-school newspapers and worked summers as managing editor of an organizational newspaper, the *San Diego Times.* After graduation from San Diego High School, Self went on in 1942 to earn an A.B. degree, magna cum laude with distinction in political science, from Dartmouth College.

Self was admitted to the Harvard School of Public Administration in 1942, but his plans were interrupted by the war. He became a lieutenant senior grade while serving in Okinawa in the U.S. Coast Guard, then returned to the States in 1945, having completed four years of active duty. Back in his home community, Self worked as the advertising manager for the *La Jolla Light.* In 1947 he purchased the *North Shores Sentinel* in Pacific Beach for eighteen thousand dollars in partnership with a boyhood friend. The two partners sold that newspaper for thirty-eight thousand dollars the next year, and in 1949 Self became business manager for *Frontier* magazine in Los Angeles. He also began discussing plans for the start of a magazine to be called *San Diego* with a local broadcaster, Gloria Eileen Winke.

The influence of Winke was undoubtedly a by-product of her experience in the entertainment field and her intimate contact with and commitment to the San Diego cultural and arts community. She began as a child performer on radio station KGB with Art Linkletter and was later heard alongside the Hollywood actress Rita Hayworth. Winke excelled in her schoolwork and entered San Diego State University at the age of sixteen. She gained a wide reputation and respect in the community as director of entertainment for the United Service Organizations (USO) in San Diego County during the war. After the war she was featured on a radio interview program, "San Diego Scrapbook," before becoming a reporter for the *San Diego Tribune*.

In her capacity as news reporter Winke continued to focus her attention on the city and its people, frequently using her background as a broadcaster and former history major to add clarity and perspective to local developments. This attribute would carry over to her work at *San Diego;* she always attempted to give the background to developments, particularly those involving artistic expression. The first issue of *San Diego,* published in October 1948, contained articles on the quality of local radio programming and coverage of an unsolved disappearance in 1844 of a Yankee sea captain from the Old Town jail.

Self 's initial intent was to pattern city interests around an editorial policy which would fuse the approach of some national magazines, namely *Time*, *Harper's*, and the *New Yorker*. Winke argued for a more wide-ranging concept with emphasis on visual elements including both photography and graphics. Winke and Self were married on 18 August 1951, and their partnership of ideas would make a lasting impression on American magazine journalism.

Ed Self's political instincts and Gloria Self's concern with quality graphics are often cited as being key to the success of *San Diego.* When the magazine was founded at the start of the postwar baby-boom period, the city of San Diego had a relatively modest population of 350,000. Since the magazine began publication, that population has increased to more than one million. The Selfs targeted urban growth as an editorial issue and direction – stressing the importance of a balance in civic and cultural affairs as well as planned growth – in their magazine's in-depth reporting on the community.

In the late 1940s and early 1950s *San Diego* presented a series of arguments for local civic improvement. Self emphasized the importance of an enhanced downtown library by taking readers into the deteriorating stacks of the facility, where he interviewed librarians and patrons. Some would say he attempted to embarrass city fathers with a downtrodden public building in an otherwise progressive community. Similarly, he attacked the need for improved rapid transit and a new airport facility for the community to be on a par with the enhanced national standards.

The magazine's coverage of civic issues was achieved with the assistance of respected reporters and commentators on the local scene. Lionel Van Deerlin discussed the local political arena, and James Britton oversaw city-planning issues and wrote about specific projects such as the need for an improved city library. Roberta Ridgely offered readers a regular and careful examination of the role of the arts in the city from the Old Globe Theatre and Starlight Opera, to the star-studded La Jolla Playhouse – focusing especially on such Hollywood artists as Gregory Peck who made the city their home.

San Diego also gained a wide reputation for its coverage of architecture, and preservation of historical buildings became a key area of emphasis – one that paid dividends in terms of community development and later support. Self 's publication also became well known for its attention to and concern for the environment, long before it became a popular issue. The potential threat of offshore drilling was treated by *San Diego,* and the magazine also pushed for pollution control and recognition of environmental effects of dumping hazardous waste.

Self encouraged political recognition for the large Hispanic community and took an active role in fostering cooperation between the United States and Mexico. He frequently traveled to major Mexican cities and out-of-the-way "hidden treasures" in that country, encouraging cooperation, tourism, and cultural recognition south of the border. The magazine offered close coverage of a formal state dinner hosted by then-president Richard Nixon, for example, to honor Mexican president Gustavo Dias-Ordaz at the famed Hotel Del Coronado with such distinguished guests as former president Lyndon Johnson and California governor Ronald Reagan in attendance.

Gloria Self also gave readers an international perspective, traveling to the Soviet Union for a series on cultural differences, with Edwin later focusing on Japan's impact on the local economy. At the same time, the editor and his wife were encouraging the talents of some of the best journalists on the West Coast. Mary Harrington Hall was a popular writer for *San Diego* before moving to *Psychology Today*. She specialized in investigative stories and reported on the academic community which had built up around the Salk Institute, San Diego State University, and the University of California at San Diego.

Hall was followed by Harold Keen, whom Edwin Self referred to as a "walking encyclopedia," a writer who helped to raise the quality of the city through his work at the magazine and in television, first as a reporter and then as editorial director of KFMB-TV. Keen, while covering the academic beat, specialized in some of the social criticism taking place during the 1960s. He became San Diego's best-known television reporter and interviewer, a position which helped him gain access to some of the most interesting stories and people of the period.

San Diego provided competition to the powerful and conservative *San Diego Union-Tribune*. In an investigative piece titled "*Union-Tribune*, The Mute Town Crier," Self chronicled several major news events suppressed or ignored by the major California conservative dailies and contributing to the image of San Diego as a city dominated by "right-wing crackpots" and the navy. In the opening section of the article, Self described how confused citizens of San Diego might have been on the occasion of the Academy Awards, when *Midnight Cowboy,* which had received an X rating from the Motion Picture Association of America (MPAA), won the Academy Award for Best Motion Picture of the year. Since no reviews, advertisements, or any form of publicity for X-rated films was allowed in the Copley newspapers, Self ironically suggested that many local people may have been unaware of the movie's existence.

Self obtained permission from *Newsweek* and *Time* to reprint articles from these national newsmagazines that criticized the management and editorial policies of the *Union-Tribune*. In addition to a review of the treatment of X-rated films, these articles pointed out that the newspaper edited sex out of "Dear Abby" columns and painted pants on nude comic strip figures. There were also more-serious charges of bias, including the failure of the Copley press to report adequately on corruption in the San Diego Police Department, a local story covered more thoroughly by the city bureau of the *Los Angeles Times*.

Concern over local politics and a willingness to speak out on controversial issues in his magazine helped to establish Self as a community leader. He led the movement toward historic restoration in the San Diego and southern California area, as in a "Publisher's Point" essay titled "Restoring the Boulevard of Broken Dreams," in which he presented arguments for the restoration of El Prado, the recreation of a Spanish colonial city first fashioned for the 1915 San Diego Exhibition. Similarly, Self editorialized on the need to appreciate city landmarks such as La Valencia Hotel, built in 1926, a historic refuge for the Hollywood entertainment community. He made a continuing effort to remind *San Diego* readers of their historic heritage and to keep the city at the forefront of contemporary magazine journalism.

Self also worked to develop an awareness of problems accompanying southern California's population growth – a crisis in immigration and abuses by the Border Patrol; the dangers of toxic pollution and nuclear waste; declining water quality; congestion; and drug trafficking. The problem of how to deal with the homeless within a generally affluent city has also received regular attention in *San Diego,* in stark contrast to other local publications, which emphasize tourism, business growth, and society gossip.

As an independent city magazine, Self's *San Diego* has set the tone for other such endeavors, and the publisher has served as a consultant to such aspiring city magazines as the *Washingtonian* and *San Francisco*. In 1965 Self served as an adviser throughout the first year of the nation's capital-city magazine. He has contributed to other magazines, including *Los Angeles*, *Town and Country*, and the *Nation*. From 1949 to 1955 he acted as business manager for *Frontier* magazine, while continuing his regular duties with *San Diego*.

Beginning in 1955 a partnership with John A. Vietor, publisher of the *Point Newsweekly,* added several new writers to the pages of *San Diego*. The two publications shared resources until the partnership dissolved in 1960. Efforts to increase circulation helped *San Diego* achieve status as one of the top five city and regional publications in the nation – a position it continues to hold. Much of this financial success can be attributed to Self's insistence that advertising-copy graphics be of as high a quality as the magazine's editorial content.

San Diego was honored in 1977 with the William Allen White Award for General Excellence by the City and Regional Magazine Association. Self has been recognized by a wide variety of organizations. In 1963 he received the American Institute of Planners' Telesis Award, the California Teachers' Association presented him with the John Swett Award in 1966, and he received a public information award in 1970 from the American Institute of Architects.

Although still editor in chief at *San Diego,* Self is assisted today by his daughters. Winke Self Hill is the magazine's associate publisher, while Corey Self serves as coeditor of the "Dining Out" section. Self 's son-in-law, Martin Hill, worked as an investigative reporter for *San Diego* before becoming editor of the San Diego *Business Journal.* In 1988, on the occasion of the fortieth anniversary of *San Diego,* Robert Myers, former publisher of the *New Republic,* praised Edwin and Gloria Self for the hundreds of stories their magazine covered which were overlooked or perhaps unappreciated by the local newspapers. At the same time, Carey McWilliams, retired editor of the *Nation,* applauded the Selfs for adding a new dimension to their city, describing their good fortune at being in the right place, at the right time, and with the right idea. McWilliams emphasized Edwin Self 's civic responsibility and political instincts as well as Gloria Self 's interest in magazine graphics as major factors in the growth and maturity of the publication and the tremendous reputation for quality it enjoyed. The publication is still emulated across the country, and Self 's vision for an involved, community-focused, action-oriented magazine offers hope for contemporary critics who decry the ever-shrinking marketplace of ideas in the nation's big cities.

References:

Stephen Birmingham, *California Rich* (New York: Simon & Schuster, 1980), pp. 64–79;

Carol Kendrick, "Harold Keen on Local Scene," *San Diego Union,* 25 July 1976, p. B1;

Paul Krueger, "City Currents," *San Diego Union,* 13 December 1978, p. B1;

Richard Louv, "The Harold Keen Phenomenon," *San Diego* (December 1978): 237–278;

Carey McWilliams, "Two Distinguished Opinions," *San Diego* (October 1988): 145;

Roberta Ridgely, "The Way We Were," *San Diego* (October 1988): 144–285.

Joseph T. Shaw

(8 May 1874 - 1 August 1952)

Garyn G. Roberts
Michigan State University

MAJOR POSITIONS HELD: Editor, *Black Mask* (1926-1936); literary agent, Sydney A. Sanders Agency (1942-1951); president, Joseph T. Shaw Associates Agency (1951-1952).

BOOKS: *From Wool to Cloth* (Providence, R.I.: Printed by Livermore & Knight, 1904);

The Wool Trade of the United States: History of a Great Industry; Its Rise and Progress in Boston, Now the Second Market of the World (Washington, D.C.: U.S. Government Printing Office, 1909);

Spain of To-day: A Narrative Guide to the Country of the Dons, with Suggestions for Travellers (New York: Grafton, 1909);

Derelict (New York: Knopf, 1930);

Danger Ahead (New York: Mohawk, 1932);

Out of the Rough (New York: Windward House, 1934);

Blood on the Curb (New York: Dodge, 1936);

It Happened at the Lake (New York: Dodd, Mead, 1937).

OTHER: *The Hard-Boiled Omnibus: Early Stories from Black Mask,* edited by Shaw (New York: Simon & Schuster, 1946);

Spurs West!, edited by Shaw (Garden City, N.Y.: Permabooks, 1951).

SELECTED PERIODICAL PUBLICATIONS – UNCOLLECTED: "Makings," *Black Mask,* 9 (December 1926): 78-100;

"Fugitive," *Black Mask,* 15 (August 1932): 24-47; (September 1932): 42-56; (October 1932): 66-85; (November 1932): 38-68;

"Death Rides Double," as Mark Harper, *Black Mask,* 22 (October 1939): 69-77.

Joseph T. Shaw

As editor of *Black Mask* mystery magazine from 1926 to 1936, Joseph T. ("Cap") Shaw brought the pulp magazine a measure of literary respectability by publishing the early work of such writers as Dashiell Hammett, Raymond Chandler, and Erle Stanley Gardner. In so doing, he helped to establish the characteristics of the distinctively American genre of the "hard-boiled" detective story.

Joseph Thompson Shaw was born in Gorham, Maine, on 8 May 1874 to Milton and Nellie Morse Shaw; an ancestor, Roger Shaw, had immigrated to New England in the 1630s. At Bowdoin College in Brunswick, Maine, Joseph Shaw edited the campus newspaper, was a member of the Alpha Delta Phi fraternity, and led the school fencing team. After graduating in 1895 he worked briefly for the *New York Globe* and a trade journal, then became secretary of the American Woolen Company in Boston. His pamphlets *From Wool to Cloth* (1904) and *The Wool Trade of the United States* (1909) were written for the firm. After a trip to Europe he wrote the travel guide *Spain of To-Day* (1909). In 1916 he was a member of the national championship fencing team, winning the President's Medal in foil, épée, and saber.

When the United States entered World War I, Shaw joined the army; starting out as a bayonet instructor, he served in Europe in the Chemical Warfare Service and rose to the rank of captain – providing the nickname "Cap," by which he was known for the rest of his life. After the war he served for five years with Herbert Hoover's American Relief Administration, distributing food to famine victims in Czechoslovakia and Greece.

After returning from Europe, Shaw spent some time as a "story doctor" for the *Saturday Evening Post.* Before the war he had submitted some pieces to *Field and Stream* magazine and had gotten to know its editor, Ray Holland. In 1926 he learned from Holland that Pro-Distributors, a subsidiary of Warner Publications that published *Field and Stream* and *Black Mask,* was looking for an editor for the latter publication to replace Phil Cody, who wanted to return to the business side of publishing. Shaw, who had never heard of the magazine, applied for the position and received it; he was also allowed to buy stock in the magazine. *Black Mask* was a monthly pulp magazine (so called because it, like others of its kind and the dime novels that had preceded them, were printed on cheap, short-fiber pulp-paper stock to keep the price low) that had been founded in 1920 by H. L. Mencken and George Jean Nathan; its content was described by its subtitle, *An Illustrated Magazine of Detective, Mystery, Adventure, Romance, and Spiritualism.* Mencken and Nathan had started the magazine to help support their sophisticated literary periodical, the *Smart Set.* The title of the new magazine was derived from the line drawing of Satan in a black mask that appeared on the cover of each issue of the *Smart Set,* and its logo was a black pirate's mask in front of a crossed dagger and flintlock pistol. Mencken always despised the *Black Mask* – he called it a "louse" – and neither his nor Nathan's name ever appeared in it. The first editors were Florence Osborne (listed as "F. M. Osborne" to conceal her gender) and Wyndham Martyn, who were associate editors at the *Smart Set.* The stories were generally of poor quality; the detective fiction was written in pale and inept imitation of the classic British school, with melodramatic plots and unrealistic dialogue. Nevertheless, the magazine was successful, rising to a circulation of 250,000 in its first year. Mencken and Nathan, who had invested only $500 in the magazine, sold it in November 1920 to Eltinge F. "Pop" Warner and Eugene Crowe, the publishers of the *Smart Set,* for a sum that has been variously reported as $12,250 and as $100,000. In October 1922 George W. Sutton took over as editor, with Harry C. North as associate editor; Sutton was succeeded by Cody in April 1924. The first issue edited by Shaw was that for November 1926; subtitled *Western, DETECTIVE, and Adventure Stories,* it included work by Gardner, Carroll John Daly, Raoul Whitfield, and Frederick Nebel.

Hammett, with his characters the Continental Op and Sam Spade, was to the hard-boiled detective story in the *Black Mask* in the mid 1920s what Sir Arthur Conan Doyle, with his Sherlock Holmes, had been to the classical detective story in the *Strand* magazine in Britain and *Collier's* in the United States around the turn of the century. Neither writer created the formula with which he worked, but each provided archetypal examples of it. In reading back issues of the *Black Mask* to prepare himself for his new position, Shaw had been particularly impressed with the spare, realistic writing of Hammett, who had written for the *Black Mask* – mainly stories featuring the Continental Op – from December 1922 through March 1926. When Cody was unable to convince Warner to raise Hammett's pay rate by a penny a word, Hammett had quit and gone into advertising, and the circulation of the *Black Mask* had fallen to sixty-six thousand. Shaw lured him back and made Hammett's fiction the standard by which he evaluated all work submitted for publication.

The traditional detective story, as created by Edgar Allan Poe and perfected in Britain by Doyle, R. Austin Freeman, E. C. Bentley, Agatha Christie, and Dorothy L. Sayers, was typically set on a country estate or in a drawing room and emphasized the solving of the puzzle by a genteel, intellectual, often aristocratic amateur sleuth. The world depicted in these stories was a basically orderly one in which crime was a temporary aberration. The hard-boiled, or "tough-guy," detective story, on the other hand, as exemplified for the first time by Daly's "Three Gun Terry" in the 15 May 1923 issue of the *Black Mask* and perfected in Hammett's works, was set in the streets and alleys of a large American city and emphasized action rather than ratiocination; the heroes were cynical, streetwise professionals – usually private detectives but sometimes policemen or newspaper reporters – who used their fists and their guns as well as their wits and were not unwilling to bend or even break the law to achieve what they considered to be justice. The surrounding society was not orderly but irrational, chaotic, and corrupt. Exposition and description were sparse; the plots were advanced largely by dialogue, and the latter was written in a blunt, colloquial American idiom.

AS I WAS SAYING:—

THE following letter is typical of very many being received by *Blask Mask* in almost every mail. Moreover, its inquiry forms such a happy introduction to our editorial purpose, that we cannot do better than reproduce it.

"The Editor,
BLACK MASK:

"I hope you do not think that your readers are tired of Race Williams, Ed Jenkins and the like characters. We are not; for they are supreme in their line.

"Where is Hammett's 'Continental Crook'? Where is 'Mac,' that other sleuth, who was such a super-entertainer?

"You think it well, perhaps, to give us a change once in a while, but you must not let your old actors die, for they have won too firm a footing in the pages of *Black Mask*.

"I have become the bane of Los Angeles and 'Frisco booksellers, worrying them to get me all back numbers of *Black Mask* possible. My worldly troubles are many and varied but I forget them all when I take your excellent magazine in hand.

"E. W. J.........."

And here is our answer:

Not long since we had a roundup with all the old, dependable contributors to *Black Mask*—the early builders of the magazine. We conveyed to them our purpose and inspiration—to make *Black Mask* bigger and better—the best of all. We invited them to sit in with us, take off their coats and accomplish this very thing. We looked around very carefully and asked a few more to join in—men worthy to take their places with this select group.

And their reply?

One and all, from the Atlantic to the Pacific, from the far North to the luring tropics, have sent in the message, in the inspiring words of Stanley Gardner:—"LET'S GO!"

And it would seem that all at once the thing has started, with renewed life, with reawakened interest, with increased virility.

Carroll John Daly has commenced a brand new line for Race Williams, a great, ambitious work.

Erle Stanley Gardner has just sent us the first of a new Ed Jenkins series—a popular favorite in the most thrilling, gripping action we have seen in a long while.

J. Paul Suter, whose delightful style satisfies the most hardboiled critic, is preparing some stiff problems for the Reverend McGregor Daunt to crack.

Dashiell Hammett has called back the Continental detective from his long retirement and is setting him to work anew. Francis James is returning with a harder punch than ever. Tom Curry has injected new fire of life into the old reliable "Mac" and is broadening the scope of his activities. Raoul Fauconnier Whitfield is hitting on all eight cylinders in a new airplane series. Frederick L. Nebel is deep in startlingly realistic tales of the Underworld.

And this is but a mere suggestion of what the old favorites of *Black Mask* readers are at work upon.

Others, newcomers to our pages, are crowding forward and bringing no less enthusiasm than our old reliables who have taken the hunch.

There is much more that we could tell you, but now we will just say that neither E. W. J. nor any other of our reader-friends need seek for past numbers of *Black Mask*, although—and here's more than a promise—you may soon find it advisable to place your orders in advance with your newsdealer for the new ones.

For right now we can see the momentum of this new, concerted effort gathering force and volume.

Already we can add to Erle Stanley Gardner's rallying call, the assurance that—WE ARE ON THE WAY!

THE EDITOR.

107

Shaw's editorial statement of purpose from the January 1927 issue of Black Mask

Hammett returned to the *Black Mask* with "The Big Knock-Over," a Continental Op story, in the February 1927 issue. He, Daly, Gardner, Chandler, Whitfield, and Nebel, all of whom had been writing for the magazine before Shaw arrived, formed the nucleus of what came to be known as "the *Black Mask* School" of detective fiction. Shaw, like Sutton before him, knew that stories with continuing characters would hold reader interest. All of the *Black Mask* school writers had such protagonists, among them Hammett's Op and Sam Spade; Daly's Race Williams; Gardner's Ed Jenkins, Bob Larkin, Black Barr, and Pete Wennick (Gardner's best-known hero, Perry Mason, did not appear in *Black Mask*); Whitfield's Chuck Reddington, Mac, Cary Greer, Mal Ourney, Jo Gar (in stories written under the pseudonym Roman Decolta), Alan Van Cleve, Don Free, and Dion Davies; and Nebel's "Donny" Donohue and the police captain/newspaper reporter team of MacBride and Kennedy.

By 1927 the magazine's circulation had increased to eighty thousand. That year Shaw shortened its title from *The Black Mask* to *Black Mask*. He paid close attention to both the cover art and the illustrations; for the latter he used only one artist, Arthur Rodman Bowker, whose bold and stylized drawings perfectly fit the atmosphere of the stories. Shaw refused to refer to his publication as a "pulp" magazine, because of the negative connotations of the word; he called it a "rough-paper book," in distinction to the "smooth paper" magazines such as the *Saturday Evening Post*.

By such means and by constant encouragement, he tried to instill in his authors pride in their craft; one of them, Lester Dent, would recall: "When you went into his office and talked with Shaw, you felt you were doing fiction that was powerful. You had feelings of stature." Shaw also raised his writers' pay rate from two cents a word to six cents, arranged contacts for some of them with New York book publishers, used the editorial page to promote their works, and established an association with Warner Bros. Studios that led to screen adaptations of stories from the magazine. During the heyday of the pulps in the 1920s and 1930s, there were about thirteen hundred writers providing stories to more than two hundred of the magazines; only 5 percent of those authors were able to break into *Black Mask*.

Among the new writers Shaw introduced in *Black Mask* were Horace McCoy in 1927 and Earl and Marion Scott and Katherine Brocklebank in 1928. With Shaw's encouragement Hammett began adapting his stories for the magazines into novel form; *Red Harvest* (1929), *The Dain Curse* (1929), *The*

Maltese Falcon (1930), *The Glass Key* (1931), and *Blood Money* (1943) were all based on stories that had appeared in *Black Mask* between February 1927 and June 1930. After the great success of *The Maltese Falcon,* which he dedicated to Shaw, Hammett again left the magazine; his last story for it was "Death and Company," published in the November 1930 issue. This time the circulation, which had reached 103,000, did not drop. Paul Cain, Theodore A. Tinsley, and Norbert Davis began contributing in 1932; in that year Shaw finally dropped Western stories from the magazine, making it an all-detective-story publication with the subtitle *Gripping, Smashing Detective Stories.* In an editorial in the April issue Shaw summarized what he saw as the magazine's significance:

> *Black Mask* is unique among fiction magazines, appealing to a wide group of readers ranging from those who like action fiction for action alone, where it is real and convincing, to the most discriminating readers in the professional classes – clergymen, bankers, lawyers, doctors, the heads of large businesses, and the like.
>
> While it is commonly classed as a detective fiction magazine, it has, with the help of its writers, created a new type of detective story which is now being recognized by book critics as inaugurating a new era in fiction dealing with crime and crime combatting.

Among the readers of the magazine in the early 1930s were Presidents Hoover and Franklin D. Roosevelt and the bookman A. S. W. Rosenbach.

In 1933 Thomas Walsh, Roger Torrey, H. H. Stinson, W. T. Ballard, and Chandler made their debuts in the magazine. Shaw thought that Chandler's first submission, "Blackmailers Don't Shoot," was so good that it might be plagiarized; he asked Ballard for his opinion, and Ballard advised him to print it. The story appeared in the December issue; Chandler would write ten more stories for *Black Mask* before leaving in 1937. He was not as prolific as some of the other contributors because he painstakingly reworked his stories through many drafts. Having lost Hammett, Shaw used Chandler as his model of good writing: while chatting with a writer in his office, he would hand over a paragraph by Chandler and a pencil and ask the writer to cut a few words from the copy; the writer would discover that every word was essential. Chandler's series characters, Mallory (no first name) and Ted Carnady, would coalesce into Philip Marlowe in the novels Chandler later based on his *Black Mask* stories. Chandler's collection of five of his *Black Mask* stories, *Five Murders* (1944), was dedicated to Shaw "with affection and respect, and in memory of the time when we were trying to get murder away from the upper classes, the week-end house party and the vicar's rose garden, and back to the people who are really good at it."

Shaw brought Dwight Babcock, John K. Butler, and George Harmon Coxe (creator of "Casey, Crime Photographer") into the magazine in 1934–1935. Shaw had become less and less enchanted with Daly's rather crudely written Race Williams stories, but he had been hesitant to drop one of the magazine's most popular authors – the announcement of a new Race Williams story on the cover would increase sales of an issue by 15 to 20 percent – but in 1935 Daly moved to the higher-paying *Dime Detective* magazine. Dent, who had been writing the Doc Savage series for Street and Smith under the pseudonym Kenneth Robeson, became a contributor to *Black Mask* under his own name in 1936.

By that time, however, the circulation had fallen to sixty-three thousand – about where it had been when Shaw took over as editor – probably because of the Great Depression, even though the price per issue had been cut in 1934 from twenty to fifteen cents. In a salary dispute with Warner, Shaw was relieved of the editorship in November 1936. His writers were shocked; Dent, Nebel, and Chandler left for other magazines, and Cain quit pulp writing. Shaw was replaced by "F. Ellsworth"; as in the case of the magazine's first editor, the initial concealed a woman's name – Fanny Ellsworth had been the editor of the pulp *Ranch Romances. Black Mask* would cease publication, after a total of 340 issues, with the July 1951 number.

While editing *Black Mask,* Shaw had written some adventure stories of his own. "Makings" (1926), a western, and "Fugitive" (1932), a serial set in the Far East, both appeared in the magazine. The detective novel *Derelict* was published in book form in 1930 and serialized in *Black Mask* the following year; his other detective novels were *Danger Ahead* (1932), *Blood on the Curb* (1936), and, after he left *Black Mask, It Happened at the Lake* (1937). He returned to the magazine as a contributor in October 1939 with "Death Rides Double," a story about a motorcycle policeman. Shaw's astuteness as an editor, however, did not translate into talent as an author; his works were throwbacks to the melodramatic sort of writing that had characterized the earliest days of the *Black Mask.* Chandler said that they contained "about the deadliest writing I ever saw on a supposedly professional level." Shaw also wrote a golf instruction book, *Out of the Rough* (1934), that

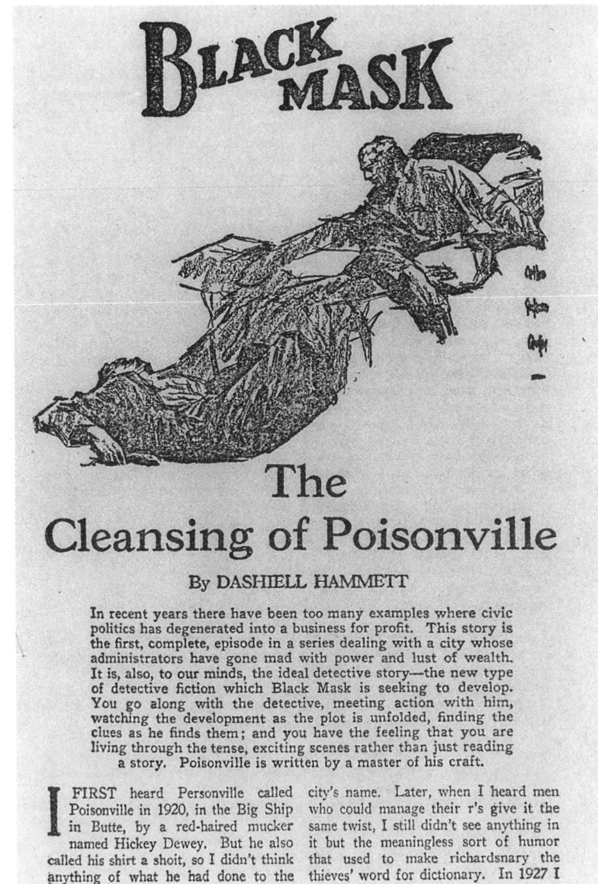

BLACK MASK

The
Cleansing of Poisonville

By DASHIELL HAMMETT

In recent years there have been too many examples where civic politics has degenerated into a business for profit. This story is the first, complete, episode in a series dealing with a city whose administrators have gone mad with power and lust of wealth. It is, also, to our minds, the ideal detective story—the new type of detective fiction which Black Mask is seeking to develop. You go along with the detective, meeting action with him, watching the development as the plot is unfolded, finding the clues as he finds them; and you have the feeling that you are living through the tense, exciting scenes rather than just reading a story. Poisonville is written by a master of his craft.

I FIRST heard Personville called Poisonville in 1920, in the Big Ship in Butte, by a red-haired mucker named Hickey Dewey. But he also called his shirt a shoit, so I didn't think anything of what he had done to the city's name. Later, when I heard men who could manage their r's give it the same twist, I still didn't see anything in it but the meaningless sort of humor that used to make richardsnary the thieves' word for dictionary. In 1927 I

Cover illustration for and opening page of the four-installment novel that Hammett wrote with Shaw's encouragement. It was revised and published in book form as Red Harvest *(1929).*

had some success both in the United States and Australia.

In 1942 Shaw cofounded the Sidney A. Sanders Literary Agency. He selected detective stories from *Black Mask* for a collection titled *The Hard-Boiled Omnibus* (1946); in the introduction he reflected on what he and his contributors had accomplished:

> We meditated on the possibility of creating a new type of detective story differing from that accredited to the Chaldeans and employed more recently by Gaborieau, Poe, Conan Doyle – in fact, universally by detective story writers; that is, the deductive type, the cross-word puzzle sort, lacking – deliberately – all other human emotional values . . .
>
> Dashiell Hammett had his own way of phrasing this: If you kill a symbol, no crime is committed and no effect is produced. To constitute a murder, the victim must be a real human being of flesh and blood.
>
> Simple, logical, almost inevitable. Yet, amazingly, this principle had been completely ignored by crime writers – and still is, in the deductive type of mystery story. . . .
>
> . . . If you read of a thousand aborigines wiped out by earthquake or flood, you are abstractly interested, but you are not disturbed. But let a member of your own family be even remotely threatened and you are at once intensely concerned, emotionally aroused. This is true in real life. Why shouldn't it hold true in fiction, which must create the illusion of reality?
>
> . . . in this new pattern, character conflict is the main theme; the ensuing crime, or its threat, is incidental.

In 1951 Shaw edited *Spurs West!*, a collection of western stories. His partner, Sanders, died that year, and Shaw continued the business under the name Joseph T. Shaw Associates. He died at his desk on 1 August 1952. He was survived by his widow, Hanna Muskova Shaw; two sons; and a daughter.

Although Shaw did not create the hard-boiled writing style and was apparently unable to practice it in his own works, he was largely responsible for the success of this uniquely American genre. He recognized it as something new when he discovered it in Daly and Hammett, he formulated its principles, he encouraged other writers to adopt it, and he disseminated it in the pages of his magazine. The *Black Mask* school, with Hammett and Chandler as its most significant representatives, reinvigorated American crime fiction.

References:

Robert A. Baker and Michael T. Nietzel, *Private Eyes – 101 Knights: A Survey of American Detective Fiction 1922–1984* (Bowling Green, Ohio: Bowling Green University Popular Press, 1985);

Philip Durham, *Down These Mean Streets a Man Must Go* (Chapel Hill: University of North Carolina Press, 1963);

Tony Goodstone, ed., *The Pulps: Fifty Years of American Popular Culture* (New York: Crown, 1970);

Ron Goulart, *Cheap Thrills: An Informal History of the Pulp Magazines* (New Rochelle, N.Y.: Arlington House, 1972);

Goulart, *The Dime Detectives* (New York: Mysterious Press, 1988);

Goulart, *The Hardboiled Dicks* (New York: Pocket Books, 1967);

E. R. Hagemann, *A Comprehensive Index to Black Mask, 1920–1951* (Bowling Green, Ohio: Bowling Green University Popular Press, 1982);

Hagemann, "*The Black Mask,*" in *Mystery, Detective, and Espionage Magazines,* edited by Michael L. Cook (Westport, Conn: Greenwood Press, 1983), pp. 62–68;

Dorothy B. Hughes, *Erle Stanley Gardner: The Case of the Real Perry Mason (A Biography)* (New York: Morrow, 1978);

Diane Johnson, *The Life of Dashiell Hammett* (London: Hogarth Press, 1984);

Richard Layman, *Shadow Man: The Life of Dashiell Hammett* (New York: Harcourt Brace Jovanovich, 1981);

Dave Lewis, "The Backbone of *Black Mask,*" *Clues: A Journal of Detection,* 2 (Fall/Winter 1981): 117–127;

Will Murray, "Lester Dent, The Last of Joe Shaw's *Black Mask* Boys," *Clues: A Journal of Detection,* 2 (Fall/Winter 1981): 128–134;

Francis M. Nevins, Jr., ed., *The Mystery Writer's Art* (Bowling Green, Ohio: Bowling Green University Popular Press, 1970);

William F. Nolan, "The Black Mask Boys Go Legit," *Armchair Detective,* 13 (Winter 1980): 23–24;

Nolan, *Dashiell Hammett: A Casebook* (Santa Barbara: McNally & Loftin, 1969);

Nolan, *Hammett: A Life at the Edge* (New York: Congdon & Weed, 1983);

Nolan, ed., *The Black Mask Boys* (New York: Morrow, 1985);

Herbert Ruhm, ed., *The Hard-Boiled Detective: Stories from Black Mask Magazine 1920–1951* (New York: Random House, 1977);

Julian Symons, *Dashiell Hammett* (New York: Harcourt Brace Jovanovich, 1985).

William Shawn

(31 August 1907 - 8 December 1992)

Janet M. Novey

MAJOR POSITIONS HELD: Reporter, *Las Vegas* (New Mexico) *Optic* (1928); Midwest editor, *International Illustrated News* (1929–1933); reporter (1933–1935), associate editor (1935–1939), managing editor (1939–1952), editor, *New Yorker* (1952–1987); editor, Farrar, Straus and Giroux (1987–1992).

OTHER: Janet Flanner, *Paris Journal,* 2 volumes, edited by Shawn (New York: Atheneum, 1965, 1971; London: Gollancz, 1966);

Mollie Panter-Downes, *London War Notes, 1939–1945,* edited by Shawn (New York: Farrar, Straus & Giroux, 1971).

" . . . he has become famous by eschewing fame and is today one of the best-known unknown men in the country." Thus was William Shawn, editor of the *New Yorker* for thirty-five years, characterized in 1975 by his longtime associate Brendan Gill. While certainly not a recluse in the ordinary sense of the word, Shawn invariably declined to grant personal interviews, and most of his friends and colleagues have declined to discuss him with interviewers. He exemplified the persona of the editor – powerful, eminent, but invisible to the public.

Shawn's personal vision helped mold the *New Yorker* into a magazine that combined literature and journalism in a way that is unique in American publishing. In the magazine's 22 April 1985 "Notes and Comments" section, Shawn wrote of his *New Yorker:* "In an age when television screens are too often bright with nothing, we value substance. Amid a chaos of images, we value coherence. We believe in the printed word. And we believe in clarity. And in immaculate syntax. And in the beauty of the English language." The *New Yorker* also believed, he added, that the truth can emerge from a cartoon, from one of the magazine's covers, from a poem or a short story, from an essay or an editorial comment, from a humorous piece, from a critical piece, or from a piece of reporting. The central consideration, he concluded, was always to try to tell the truth.

William Shawn

Shawn was born William Chon in Chicago on 31 August 1907 to Benjamin W. and Anna Bransky Chon. He attended a prestigious Chicago preparatory school, the Harvard School for Boys, graduating in 1925. For two years he was enrolled at the University of Michigan. The day after his twenty-first birthday he dropped out of college and married Cecille Lyon. They had three children: William, who became an actor and playwright; Allen, a composer and teacher; and Mary, who was mentally handicapped and was placed in an institution. He changed his name from Chon to Shawn so that peo-

A REPORTER AT LARGE

HIROSHIMA

I—A NOISELESS FLASH

AT exactly fifteen minutes past eight in the morning, on August 6, 1945, Japanese time, at the moment when the atomic bomb flashed above Hiroshima, Miss Toshiko Sasaki, a clerk in the personnel department of the East Asia Tin Works, had just sat down at her place in the plant office and was turning her head to speak to the girl at the next desk. At that same moment, Dr. Masakazu Fujii was settling down cross-legged to read the Osaka *Asahi* on the porch of his private hospital, overhanging one of the seven deltaic rivers which divide Hiroshima; Mrs. Hatsuyo Nakamura, a tailor's widow, stood by the window of her kitchen, watching a neighbor tearing down his house because it lay in the path of an air-raid-defense fire lane; Father Wilhelm Kleinsorge, a German priest of the Society of Jesus, reclined in his underwear on a cot on the top floor of his order's three-story mission house, reading a Jesuit magazine, *Stimmen der Zeit*; Dr. Terufumi Sasaki, a young member of the surgical staff of the city's large, modern Red Cross Hospital, walked along one of the hospital corridors with a blood specimen for a Wassermann test in his hand; and the Reverend Mr. Kiyoshi Tanimoto, pastor of the Hiroshima Methodist Church, paused at the door of a rich man's house in Koi, the city's western suburb, and prepared to unload a handcart full of things he had evacuated from town in fear of the massive B-29 raid which everyone expected Hiroshima to suffer. A hundred thousand people were killed by the atomic bomb, and these six were among the survivors. They still wonder why they lived when so many others died. Each of them counts many small items of chance or volition—a step taken in time, a decision to go indoors, catching one streetcar instead of the next—that spared him. And now each knows that in the act of survival he lived a dozen lives and saw more death than he ever thought he would see. At the time, none of them knew anything.

THE Reverend Mr. Tanimoto got up at five o'clock that morning. He was alone in the parsonage, because for some time his wife had been commuting with their year-old baby to spend nights with a friend in Ushida, a suburb to the north. Of all the important cities of Japan, only two, Kyoto and Hiroshima, had not been visited in strength by *B-san*, or Mr. B, as the Japanese, with a mixture of respect and unhappy familiarity, called the B-29; and Mr. Tanimoto, like all his neighbors and friends, was almost sick with anxiety. He had heard uncomfortably detailed accounts of mass raids on Kure, Iwakuni, Tokuyama, and other nearby towns; he was sure Hiroshima's turn would come soon. He had slept badly the night before, because there had been several air-raid warnings. Hiroshima had been getting such warnings almost every night for weeks, for at that time the B-29s were using Lake Biwa, northeast of Hiroshima, as a rendezvous point, and no matter what city the Americans planned to hit, the Superfortresses streamed in over the coast near Hiroshima. The frequency of the warnings and the continued abstinence of Mr. B with respect to Hiroshima had made its citizens jittery; a rumor was going around that the Americans were saving something special for the city.

Mr. Tanimoto is a small man, quick to talk, laugh, and cry. He wears his black hair parted in the middle and rather long; the prominence of the frontal bones just above his eyebrows and the smallness of his mustache, mouth, and chin give him a strange, old-young look, boyish and yet wise, weak and yet fiery. He moves nervously and fast, but with a restraint which suggests that he is a cautious, thoughtful man. He showed, indeed, just those qualities in the uneasy days before the bomb fell. Besides having his wife spend the nights in Ushida, Mr. Tanimoto had been carrying all the portable things from his church, in the close-packed residential district called Nagaragawa, to a house that belonged to a rayon manufacturer in Koi, two miles from the center of town. The rayon man, a Mr. Matsui, had opened his then unoccupied estate to a large number of his friends and acquaintances, so that they might evacuate whatever they wished to a safe distance from the

TO OUR READERS

The New Yorker this week devotes its entire editorial space to an article on the almost complete obliteration of a city by one atomic bomb, and what happened to the people of that city. It does so in the conviction that few of us have yet comprehended the all but incredible destructive power of this weapon, and that everyone might well take time to consider the terrible implications of its use.

—THE EDITORS

Page from the 31 August 1946 issue, with the opening of John Hersey's classic work on the destruction of Hiroshima, Japan, by an American atomic bomb. Shawn persuaded editor Harold Ross to publish the entire piece in a single issue.

ple would not assume that he was Chinese; actually, he was of Russian-Jewish descent. His journalism career began in 1928 with a job as a newspaper reporter for the *Las Vegas* (New Mexico) *Optic*. In 1929 he became Midwest editor for the *International Illustrated News* in Chicago.

In 1933 the Shawns left Chicago for New York, where Shawn made an uncertain living composing music for theatrical groups until he was hired by the *New Yorker* to write for the "Talk of the Town" section and act as a research assistant for some of the magazine's senior reporters. In 1935 he was promoted to associate editor, and from 1939 to 1952 he served as managing editor.

During all those years Shawn had just one bylined story in the magazine, and it was signed only with the initials W. S.: a fiction piece, "The Catastrophe," appeared on 14 November 1936. The wryly humorous story involves a meteor that scores a direct hit on New York City, turning it into a kind

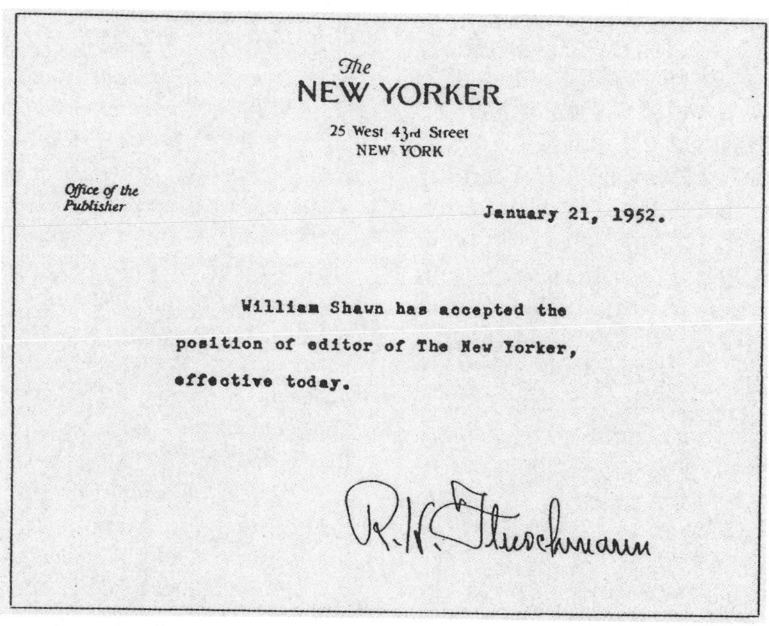
The
NEW YORKER
25 West 43rd Street
NEW YORK

Office of the Publisher

January 21, 1952.

William Shawn has accepted the position of editor of The New Yorker, effective today.

R. H. Fleischmann

The note announcing to the staff Shawn's promotion from managing editor to editor. A single copy was posted on an office bulletin board (from Brendan Gill, Here at the New Yorker, *1975).*

of Pompeii. Eventually, all memory of the Big City vanishes – a concept presumably unthinkable to New Yorkers. Thereafter, Shawn wrote only "Talk of the Town" segments and an occasional obituary for a staffer. Like the magazine's editor, Harold Ross, Shawn displayed far more talent as an editor than as a writer.

Ross died in December 1951, and on 21 January 1952 Shawn was named editor. His promotion was announced to the staff with a brief note on a bulletin board on the twentieth floor of the building at 25 West Forty-third Street in which the *New Yorker* occupies the eighteenth, nineteenth, and twentieth floors. As Gill recalled, "It consisted of a single sentence: 'William Shawn has accepted the position of editor of *The New Yorker,* effective today.'"

Yet Shawn's presence had been felt long before he assumed the top editorial position. Perhaps one of the first instances was in 1946, when the 31 August issue was given over to John Hersey's "Hiroshima." Shawn had persuaded Ross to publish the piece in its entirety in a single issue and had worked with Hersey on its narrative style. The publication of the story and the subsequent book version made publishing and political history. Under Shawn's direction the magazine began to address a wide range of political, social, and environmental issues. Shawn published Rachel Carson's "Silent Spring," James Baldwin's "The Fire Next Time," and many other groundbreaking articles that were markedly more serious than most of the magazine's copy had been under Ross's editorship.

Shawn directed roughly two dozen editors and about 140 writers of fiction and nonfiction who worked under contract to the magazine. A few of the writers, mainly the regular columnists, were on salary; the others, following the system set up by Ross, received a small annual sum that granted the *New Yorker* first refusal of their work, supplemented by cash advances while they researched and wrote. Some took these advances in the form of a weekly check. All such arrangements had to be made directly with Shawn; otherwise, advertising and other monetary considerations remained, as they had been under Ross, at arm's length from the editorial department. It is said that Shawn also gave bonuses to reward writing he thought especially good.

Shawn read every word that went into each issue in typescript, in galleys, and in page proofs. He dealt with many of the magazine's new writers personally, rather than passing them off to other editors. One of the ways in which he set the more serious tone that the *New Yorker* would retain for decades was in his choice of writers. At Harvard, Shawn's son Wallace made friends with a group of young men with strong social and political opinions; George Trow, Hendrik Hertzberg, Daniel Chasan, Jacob Brackman, and Jonathan Schell were all hired by the elder Shawn when they graduated from the university. Schell, for example, having come of age during America's involvement in Vietnam, developed an antiwar outlook that was clearly voiced in such articles as "The Village of Ben Suc" (15 July 1967), a description of the American army's destruction of that village, and the three-part "The Fate of the Earth" (1 February - 15 February 1982), which contemplated the outcome of a nuclear war. Both stories gained widespread attention.

Shawn personally edited such important works as "Silent Spring" and, in 1965, Truman Capote's New Journalism piece "In Cold Blood," publishing them in the *New Yorker* before they appeared as books. Reflecting Shawn's broad interests, other long articles, many running fifty or sixty thousand words, covered some rather esoteric or arcane – some thought tedious – topics: the Swiss army, the history of rice and the soybean in various cultures, and the geologic formation of North America. Similarly, the magazine's covers during the Shawn years were sometimes criticized as bland or boring; Shawn saw them as civilized and aesthetically pleasing. Even so, under Shawn, the *New Yorker* became one of the most prestigious magazines in the history of periodical publishing. Shawn was supported by the magazine's directors, and particularly by its principal owners, the Fleischmann family, in maintaining the course he had set. Shawn once remarked, "We published what pleased us and we ignored the question of whether or not it was fashionable." The arrangement worked: for many years the magazine was as financially successful as it was intellectually acclaimed.

Shawn's appearance was unprepossessing. He was balding, slight of build, with large ears and rosy cheeks. When he was seated his feet barely touched the floor; his hands and feet were long and thin. His speech was slow, deliberate, and formal, his voice thin and high-pitched. He was gentle, self-effacing, and exceedingly diplomatic and polite. Some of his employees, however, saw this manner as a pose that was affected as a means to the end of always getting his way, and they referred to him privately as "the iron mouse." Publicly, virtually everyone, even longtime co-workers, called him only "Mr. Shawn."

Shawn's relationship with writers was that of the quintessential editor. He saw his role as one of providing the best atmosphere to induce creativity. He was supportive and patient, never imposing strict deadlines but allowing writers to work at their own pace. When editing copy he was quick, fastidious, and thorough. He could be as generous in financial matters as he was with his time; many writers were carried with great patience until they found their voices. Unlike Ross, Shawn built an enormous inventory of stories; often, writers who had been paid handsomely for their work would have to wait for years to see it appear. According to Gigi Mahon, the record was a short piece by John Updike that appeared twenty-one years after the *New Yorker* bought it. Shawn preferred to work at home rather than in his office. He disliked parties, receptions, or other large gatherings. Among his only diversions were listening to jazz and hosting occasional musical evenings at his home, where he would play George Gershwin or Richard Rogers tunes on his Steinway grand piano accompanied by his sons, the sons of the writer Philip Hamburger, and *New Yorker* staff members Whitney Balliett and Bruce Bliven.

In 1975 Shawn, mindful of the inevitability of his eventual retirement, named Bob Bingham executive editor but soon decided that Bingham would be unsuitable as his replacement. In 1976 he selected Schell; Schell's editing, however, generated a consensus among *New Yorker* staffers that he was not a worthy successor, and he returned to writing. In 1977 Shawn again gave Schell limited editing duties, but the magazine's directors were no longer willing to consider him as Shawn's heir apparent. Shawn's final choice as successor was Charles McGrath, who had joined the magazine in 1973 as a copy editor. In November 1984 McGrath was made co-managing editor for fiction. Also in November 1984, Advance Publications, headed by S. I. Newhouse, Jr., and his brother, Donald Newhouse, purchased 17 percent of the stock of The New Yorker Magazine.

Raoul Fleischmann, the founding publisher of the *New Yorker,* had died in 1969 and had been succeeded by his son, Peter. "In sixty years, neither man ever made an editorial suggestion, ever commented favorably or unfavorably on anything we published or on any editorial direction the magazine was taking, ever permitted the advertising or circulation or accounting people to bring any pressure to bear on us," Shawn bore witness in his 22 April 1985 "Notes and Comments" piece. His remarks were prompted by the unanimous vote by the board of directors on 2 March to accept the Newhouses' offer to buy The New Yorker Magazine for two hundred dollars per share plus $142 million. The Fleischmann family had at last decided to sell the magazine. Shawn's comments amounted to a public declaration that if the *New Yorker* were to remain the *New Yorker,* its tradition of editorial independence must be maintained. The Newhouses declared that they were not the "barbarians at the gate," that the *New Yorker* would be "operated on a stand-alone

Shawn at his desk at the New Yorker

basis as a separate company," and that Advance wished "to maintain the *New Yorker*'s personnel and their operating practices and traditions," including the tradition of complete editorial independence. At the annual meeting on 7 May, the shareholders voted to accept the Newhouse offer. Newhouse and Steven T. Florio were elected to the board, and Florio was named executive vice-president and publisher of the *New Yorker*.

It was of paramount importance to Shawn that he be succeeded by someone who had been imbued with *New Yorker* traditions. In November 1986 meetings between Shawn and Newhouse appeared to culminate in an agreement that Shawn would retire on 1 March 1987 and that McGrath would be his successor. On 19 January 1987, however, Newhouse came to Shawn's office and informed him that he had offered the position to Robert Gottlieb of Alfred A. Knopf, a company that is part of the Advance conglomerate.

At 2:00 P.M. on 20 January, Shawn gathered his staff in the stairwell between the eighteenth-floor editorial offices and the nineteenth floor, which houses the offices of the writers. The group included office boys, editors, and such well-known writers as Calvin Trillin, Lillian Ross, Roger Angell, and James Lardner. Following Shawn's brief announcement, a committee of writers drafted a letter asking Gottlieb not to accept the job. Others solicited leading American literary figures' signatures, 154 of which were affixed to the letter that was finally delivered. Gottlieb's reply was brief: he was going to accept the position of editor.

Shawn retired from the *New Yorker* on 13 February 1987 and became an editor with the publishing firm Farrar, Straus and Giroux in New York. He also had an office at Broadway Video lent to him by Lorne Michaels, executive producer of the television show "Saturday Night Live."

On the morning of Tuesday, 8 December 1992, Shawn died of a heart attack in his apartment at Fifth Avenue and Ninety-sixth Street; he was eighty-five. His death was followed by an outpouring of tributes, mainly by those who worked with him at the magazine. Thirty-two of these tributes appeared in the 28 December 1992–4 January 1993 issue of the *New Yorker* under the headline "Remembering Mr. Shawn." Far less glowing was Joseph Nocera's "Unslick Willy" in the *New Republic,* which painted a verbal picture of a stuffy, tiresome, pretentious magazine too long presided over by an old-fashioned editor who cared more for his writers than for his readers. The criticism was reminiscent of Raymond Sokolov's 1986 remarks in the *Wall Street Journal* about "the Shawnian twilight" of the *New Yorker* and of Tom Wolfe's comment in the *New York Magazine* Sunday supplement of the *Herald Tribune* in 1965 that depicted Shawn as "the smiling embalmer" of Ross's magazine.

Shawn's champions and detractors alike have always been fascinated by his eccentricities: his painfully ceremonious politeness in insisting that others pass through doorways ahead of him; his refusal to talk while riding in elevators or to ride in self-service elevators at all; his disdain for travel by subway; his "house-rules" that forbade the use in his magazine of the words *balding, photo, wig, intrigued* (for *interested*), *tycoon, promptly, feisty, gadget,* and Yiddish slang in general; and his precise punctuality. Many observations have been made about his handwriting, as placed on manuscripts with his silver mechanical pencil. In "Remembering Mr. Shawn" Charles McGrath characterized it as "tiny, feathery," Gardner Botsford as "crabbed," and Daniel Menaker as "Lilliputian."

Certainly the magazine's attainments were many during the Shawn years: fiction by Updike, John Cheever, Isaac Bashevis Singer, and J. D. Salinger; humor by S. J. Perelman and Woody Allen; nonfiction by Capote, John McPhee, Hersey, Carson, Lillian Ross, A. J. Liebling, and Richard Rovere; essays by Schell, Baldwin, and Hannah Arendt; and criticism by Edmund Wilson, Pauline Kael, and Harold Rosenberg. Updike's assessment in "Remembering Mr. Shawn" was that under Shawn "the magazine's fiction became more avant-garde and its nonfiction more mandarin." Hal Espen wrote of the Shawn-led magazine's "oxymoronic values of lively dignity, active calm, and disinterested engagement." During a period in which most magazines were becoming more lowbrow and televisionlike, Shawn kept the *New Yorker* genteel and civilized. He himself was, wrote Schell in "Remembering Mr. Shawn," "a kind of one-man civilization."

References:

Jonathan Alter, "The Squawk of the Town: A *New Yorker* Revolt," *Newsweek,* 109 (26 January 1987): 83;

Jeremy Bernstein, "Out of My Mind . . . Breaking in at the *New Yorker,*" *American Scholar,* 56 (Winter 1987): 7–10;

William F. Buckley, Jr. "William Shawn, RIP," *National Review* (18 January 1993): 15–17;

Richard Cohen, "Shawn (Yawn) Gone: Unlike *New Yorker* Sentences, an Editor Can't Go on Forever," *Washington Post,* 18 January 1987, p. C2;

Edwin Diamond, "The Fate of the Earth: Hubbub at *The New Yorker,*" *New York,* 20 (26 January 1987): 12–13;

Ron Dorfman, "Next Time, Strike," *Quill,* 75 (April 1987): 33–34;

Brendan Gill, *Here at The New Yorker* (New York: Random House, 1975);

John J. Goldman and Elizabeth Mehren, "Legendary Editor Leaving *New Yorker,*" *Los Angeles Times,* 13 January 1987, p. I4;

Paul Gray, "Anniversary Waltz," *Time,* 105 (24 February 1975): 60;

Don Hausdorff, "Politics and Economics: The Emergence of a *New Yorker* Tone," *Studies in American Humor,* 3 (Spring 1984): 74–82;

William Howarth, "E. B. White at *The New Yorker,*" *Newsweek,* 103 (14 March 1984): 74–82;

Charles Kaiser, "The Talk of *The New Yorker,*" *Newsweek,* 101 (14 March 1983): 67–68;

Stefan Kanfer, "*The New Yorker* Turns Fifty," *Time,* 105 (3 March 1975): 56–57;

William Leary, "Jean Stafford, Katherine White, and *The New Yorker,*" *Sewanee Review,* 93 (Fall 1985): 584–596;

Coleman McCarthy, "Editor and Sage," *Washington Post,* 24 January 1987, p. A23;

Edwin McDowell, "At *The New Yorker,* Time to Change Guard," *New York Times,* 12 February 1987, p. C23;

McDowell, "Shawn Becomes Farrar, Straus Editor," *New York Times,* 14 July 1987, p. C20;

Gigi Mahon, *The Last Days of The New Yorker* (New York: McGraw-Hill, 1988);

"Mr. Shawn," *New York Times,* 18 January 1987, IV: 28;

Joseph Nocera, "Unslick Willy," *New Republic* (25 January 1993): 10, 12;

"Remembering Mr. Shawn," *New Yorker,* 68 (28 December 1992–4 January 1993): 134–145;

Dan Rottenberg, "The Talk of the Town: An Eye-opener for Eustace Tilley," *Quill,* 75 (April 1987): 30–32;

Earl Rovit, "Modernism and Three Magazines: An Editorial Revolution." *Sewanee Review,* 93 (Fall 1985): 540–553;

Craig Unger, "Murmurings at *The New Yorker,*" *New York,* 16 (28 November 1983): 28–40.

David A. Smart

(4 October 1892 - 16 October 1952)

Jack A. Nelson
Brigham Young University

PRINCIPAL MAGAZINES OWNED OR CONTROLLED: *Esquire* (1933–1952), *Coronet* (1936–1952), *Verve* (1937–1939), *Ken* (1938–1939).

In 1933, at the height of the Depression, David A. Smart appeared on the American magazine scene with *Esquire*. When the magazine proved a success, some observers felt he had simply made a lucky guess. As he followed that publishing venture with other profitable magazines, however, it became apparent that Smart had a shrewd sense of the market and a talent for gathering talented people around him to put his ideas into effect.

Unorthodox, brash, and a strong believer in fate, Smart took risks in the magazine business, sometimes on an impulse or a hunch, that other publishers would have avoided. For a time it seemed everything he touched during the depth of the Depression turned to gold. His digest-sized art magazine, *Coronet,* started in 1936, was richly illustrated and began to be collected by appreciative readers. His goal was to produce the world's most beautiful magazine, and some critics think that in the early years of the magazine, when it featured brilliantly reproduced examples of the most acclaimed art on the globe, he came near to that distinction. In 1937 Smart bought *Verve,* another art magazine, on a whim; it featured specially commissioned covers by some of the world's great artists. Smart also experienced failure, however, with *Ken,* a news weekly he started in 1938. The magazine floundered and ceased publication after a short career when the editors found that advertisers did not like their political policies.

Born in Omaha, Nebraska, on 4 October 1892, Smart moved with his parents when he was young to Chicago's West Side. After a two-year try at high school, the outspoken and brash youth started selling hats. A born salesman and entrepreneur, Smart got a job in 1911 selling advertising for the *Chicago Tribune.* Soon he was selling more classified-ad linage for the paper than anyone had ever sold before.

David A. Smart

When his astonishing commissions came to the attention of Colonel McCormick, the owner of the *Tribune,* Smart was put on a regular salary, which had the effect of cutting his pay by nine-tenths. Resolving never to work for anyone but himself again, Smart left the *Tribune* and started his own advertising agency.

During World War I, Smart served in the field artillery with the American Expeditionary Force in France. He returned from the war ready to invest a sizable amount of money in some new venture. He

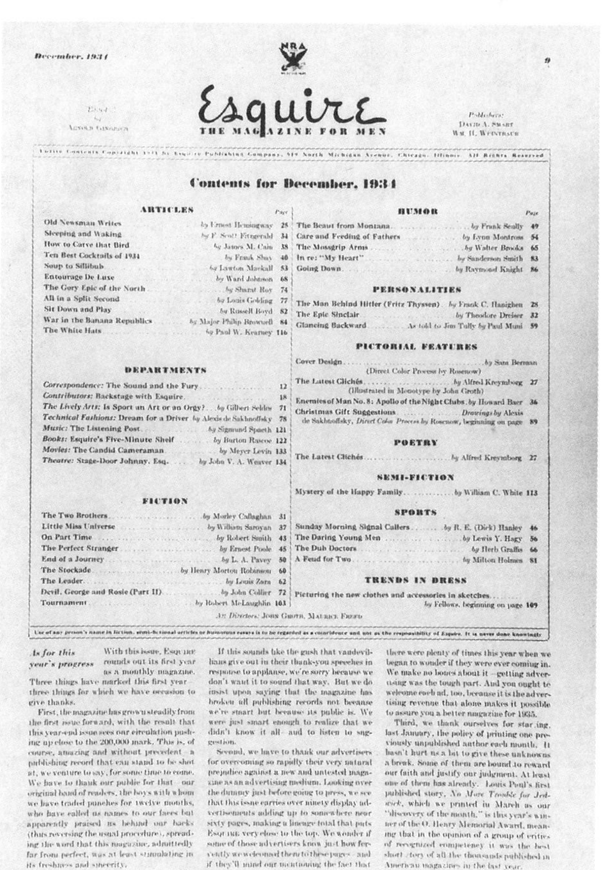

December, 1934 9

Esquire

THE MAGAZINE FOR MEN

Publisher: David A. Smart, W. H. Weintraub

Contents for December, 1934

ARTICLES

DEPARTMENTS

FICTION

HUMOR

PERSONALITIES

PICTORIAL FEATURES

POETRY

SEMI-FICTION

SPORTS

TRENDS IN DRESS

Art Directors: John Groth, Maurice Fried

Use of any person's name in fiction, semi-fictional articles or humorous essays is to be regarded as a coincidence and not as the responsibility of *Esquire*. It is never done knowingly

As for this year's progress With this issue, Esquire rounds out its first year as a monthly magazine. Three things have marked this first year—three things for which we have occasion to give thanks.

First, the magazine has grown steadily from the first issue forward, with the result that this year-end issue sees our circulation pushing up close to the 200,000 mark. This is, of course, amazing and without precedent—a publishing record that can stand to be shot at, we venture to say, for some time to come. We have to thank our public for that—our original band of readers, the boys with whom we have traded punches for twelve months, who have called us names to our faces but apparently praised us behind our backs (thus reversing the usual procedure), spreading the word that this magazine, admittedly far from perfect, was at least stimulating in its freshness and sincerity.

If this sounds like the gush that vaudevillians give out in their thank-you speeches in response to applause, we're sorry because we don't want it to sound that way. But we do insist upon saying that the magazine has broken all publishing records not because we're smart but because its public is. We were just smart enough to realize that we didn't know it all—and to listen to suggestion.

Second, we have to thank our advertisers for overcoming so rapidly their very natural prejudice against a new and untested magazine as an advertising medium. Looking over the dummy just before going to press, we see that this issue carries over ninety display advertisements adding up to somewhere near sixty pages, making a lineage total that puts Esquire very close to the top. We wonder if some of those advertisers know just how fervently we welcomed them to these pages—and if they'll mind our mentioning the fact that there were plenty of times this year when we began to wonder if they were ever coming in. We make no bones about it—getting advertising was the tough part. And you ought to welcome each ad, too, because it is the advertising revenue that alone makes it possible to assure you a better magazine for 1935.

Third, we thank ourselves for starting, last January, the policy of printing one previously unpublished author each month. It hasn't hurt us a bit to give these unknowns a break. Some of them are bound to reward our faith and justify our judgment. At least one of them has already. Louis Paul's first published story, *No More Trouble for Jedwick*, which we printed in March as our "discovery of the month," is this year's winner of the O. Henry Memorial Award, meaning that in the opinion of a group of critics of recognized competency it was the best short story of all the thousands published in American magazines in the last year.

Cover and contents page for an early issue of Smart's most successful magazine. The pop-eyed, mustachioed "Esky" was the cartoon mascot of the publication for many years.

experimented with playing the commodity market, in which he first earned $750,000 in sugar and then quickly lost all but $50,000, and became more wary. With his brother Alfred as secretary-treasurer, he went back into the advertising business, starting the David A. Smart Publishing Company in 1921. Always an idea man, he hired salesmen to sell booklets, calendars, and other advertising gimmicks that would not be printed until after the orders were in, taking no chance of being stuck with inventory – a principle that would account for much of his success during years when other publishers were foundering. He formed an uneasy partnership with William S. Weintraub, a sales genius who ended up promoting and selling the things Smart envisioned. Their first venture was with the *National Men's Wear Salesman,* a mildly successful trade magazine they had modeled after *Printer's Ink.* Shortly afterward they began publishing *Gentleman's Quarterly,* a lavishly illustrated stylebook for men's stores to give away – in effect, a catalogue in the guise of a magazine. Also Smart also produced two series of advertising booklets, one circulated to menswear stores and another aimed at banking institutions.

Neither Smart nor Weintraub were very good at writing, however, and they needed a talented writer to put Smart's ideas into practice. They selected Arnold Gingrich, a young advertising copywriter at Kuppenheimer Clothes. Gingrich was to guide the major magazines of the company as editor for nearly three decades, with a seven-year hiatus which he spent in Europe following World War II.

In 1931 the company began publishing *Apparel Arts,* a lavishly illustrated trade magazine. Expensive to print, it was of such quality that haberdashers reported customers were stealing copies. The episode convinced Smart and Weintraub that there was strong demand for a men's fashion magazine even during the worst of financial times, and they decided to launch one.

Smart and Gingrich spent the night pasting up a dummy that focused not only on fashion but on other topics of interest to men. Thus during the height of the Depression, contrary to the best advice, Smart and his colleagues launched *Esquire,* which appeared on 15 October 1933. A men's fashion magazine was unheard of at that time, and its price of fifty cents per copy brought dire predictions of failure, for almost everyone agreed there was hardly a loose half-dollar in the country. But Smart assured the project's solvency by having Weintraub – who seemed to be able to sell anything – with only a rough dummy of the projected magazine in his hand, visit men's clothing shops across the country to get guarantees for 100,000 copies. In addition, Smart conferred with a retail distributor, who was convinced that there were only a few people willing to lay down fifty cents for a magazine during those tough times and assured Smart that he should expect a maximum of 5,000 newsstand sales, with half of those likely to be returned unsold. Thus with a projection of 105,000 sales, the three men put together the magazine. At that time 100,000 copies was regarded as the norm for outstanding magazines such as the *Atlantic Monthly*, *Harper's*, and *Fortune*. Called *Esquire: The Quarterly for Men,* the initial issue was relatively conservative, with a cover showing two campers emerging from a floatplane on a Canadian lake. But it was oversize, on glossy paper, with about a third of its 116 pages in color.

Within five hours the newsstand copies had sold out, and the distributor who had previously advised Smart called to ask for more copies, urging the magazine to change from quarterly to monthly immediately. Five thousand of the copies remained with the men's stores, but the others were retrieved and placed on newsstands, where they quickly sold. The second issue, dated January 1934, came out as a monthly, appearing on the day Prohibition was repealed. It featured the debut of the puppet figure that came to be associated with *Esquire* magazine – Esky, the little bug-eyed gentleman – climbing over the rim of a champagne glass.

Like much of the first issue, the title was something of a fluke. When the firm's lawyer wrote informing the publishers that all the titles they had proposed were previously taken, he addressed the letter to "Arnold Gingrich, Esq." Upon seeing the envelope, Smart reportedly shouted, "*Esquire,* that's our title!"

Gingrich assembled articles by an impressive group of writers for the first issue: Ernest Hemingway, John Dos Passos, William McFee, Erskine Caldwell, Manuel Komroff, Dashiell Hammett, and sports pieces by Gene Tunney, Bobby Jones, and Ring Lardner. The issue also included full-page color cartoons, which immediately proved extremely popular. Though the *New Yorker* had established the full-page cartoon, they were never in color. But when assembling the first issue of *Esquire,* Gingrich found himself with 13 extra full pages of color to fill, and he happened to have on hand a batch of excellent color cartoons. Of the total of 124 pages in the first issue, 27 of those were cartoons. Smart and Gingrich had found a young artist in Harlem, E. Simms Campbell, whose drawings and cartoons would be featured in color for the next quarter century of *Esquire.*

Perhaps because of his love of art, Smart always insisted on lavish use of color and the best reproduction in his magazine. Probably no American magazine had featured so much color and artwork as the early issues of *Esquire.* Among its regular features, the long-limbed, curvaceous beauty clad in a gossamer gown and known as "the Petty Girl" became as well known as the Gibson Girl of an earlier time. During World War II this aspect of the magazine changed somewhat. To try to get favorable consideration for paper allotments, it courted the servicemen audience with pinups of beautiful women, often double-page spreads. Some *Esquire* supporters even seriously suggested there might be a lowering of soldiers' morale without the Varga girl. This "girly-magazine" image would later be shed as *Playboy* emerged to capture that audience following the war.

Part of the reason for the magazine's success was that it got top writers cheaply because Gingrich was willing to publish almost anything they wrote, which meant accepting things other publishers turned down. Writers were attracted to *Esquire* because they were not forced to fit into the trite fiction formulas then current. At the very first a deal was struck with Hemingway to use his contributions at double the usual rate. Hemingway's name, in turn, attracted other writers. Although the rates were low, Gingrich paid immediately, an important factor when many magazines were on the verge of bankruptcy and left their writers waiting for payment. In 1936, lacking his monthly column, Hemingway sent a story he had recently finished. Recognizing the brilliance of "The Snows of Kilimanjaro," the magazine paid him double his usual five-hundred-dollar rate – the most *Esquire* had paid for a story. The following year, when public stock was sold in the magazine, Smart dealt Hemingway one thousand shares of stock in recognition for his part in its success.

Smart's flamboyant management style was a puzzle to more-traditional publishers. A 1937 article in *Literary Digest* reported that when Smart was con-

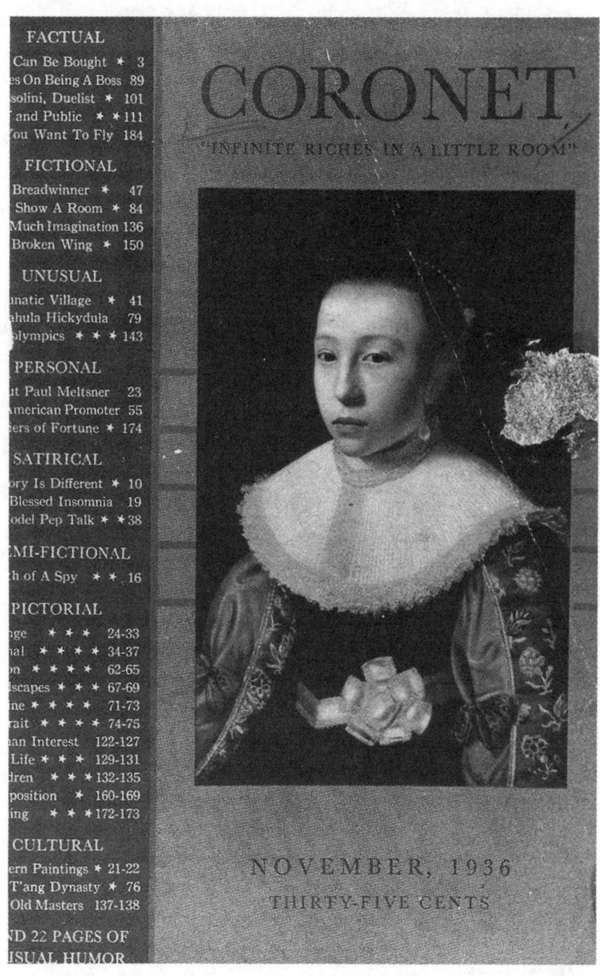

Cover for the first issue of Smart's digest-size art magazine

fronted by a publisher friend and admonished for a lack of editorial policy at *Esquire,* he asked, "Your publications have strong editorial policies and a systematic organization. How are they doing?" When the other publisher replied that they were losing money, Smart retorted, "Then we'll run our publication without policy or system."

His working methods were just as foreign to most magazine journalists. During production time Smart was apt to grab a couple of his favorite artists and head to Florida for a fishing jaunt. From his Florida outpost he would sometimes tear apart an *Esquire* layout to insert an article he had read on the southbound train or some new drawings he had found.

By November of 1936, following the success of *Esquire,* Smart launched into a separate publishing venture on his own. He and Weintraub, always uneasy partners, were copublishers of *Esquire,* but Smart wanted to try an idea – a pocket-size magazine without advertising that would feature outstanding color reproductions of great art. The new magazine was titled *Coronet,* with the subtitle "Infinite Riches in a Little Room." Smart viewed it as something the public ought to like and was not concerned about whether it made money, because it would be offset by the burgeoning profits of *Esquire.* Any losses, he reasoned, would be helpful for tax benefits. He gave his editor orders to make it the most beautiful magazine in the world and to do it in pocket size. *Coronet* was set up as a separate corporation, excluding Weintraub, and its debut was heralded in two elegant gold and black pages in *Saturday Evening Post* that began "Quietly, on November 23, 1936, a new magazine appeared on the nation's newsstands." The promotion added that *Coronet* would seek "recognition as the most beautiful of magazines."

The first issue featured color reproductions of Rembrandt and Raphael paintings, a cover in five colors, and etchings and drawings as well as fiction, nonfiction, and photographs. Magazine critics generally agree that the editors of *Coronet* did not fall far short of Smart's goal. Later issues were filled with classical and modern art, satire, and portfolio studies of various artists. Its early issues were decorated with such things as pictures of Persian miniatures. The covers featured reproductions of old masterpieces, with other art reproductions inside. Smart sent the editor to prowl through the museums of Europe looking for art to feature in the magazines. According to Gingrich, Smart even designed a special *Coronet*-dimension frame through which he could view art objects to be sure they would fit the magazine's shape. It was counted a coup when the editor was able to buy at bargain prices the plates used by the British Museum for the color reproductions of their world-renowned collection of paintings. For three years these provided the majority of the reproductions used by *Coronet.*

Coronet started with an initial sale of more than 250,000, but by 1940 circulation had dropped to only 80,000. The magazine was clearly struggling until Oscar Dystel was installed as its new editor. Smart moved Dystel over from the promotion department of *Esquire* because he seemed to be full of ideas to revitalize *Coronet.* Dystel went to work with a passion, immediately restyling *Coronet* almost beyond recognition. Covers that had once featured the likes of Domenico Ghirlandajo's portrait of a lady of the Sassetti family and Corneille de Lyon's portrait of La Duchesse d'Estampes were suddenly devoted to photographs of Hollywood starlets and models. It ceased to be a unique magazine and became a competitor of *Reader's Digest,* divested of its exclusiveness, originality, and artistic appeal. Articles were the standard formula pieces of other digest-size magazines. At the same time, the company reached an agreement for better national distribution, and circulation shot upward. By using his paper allotment during World War II in a clever way, Smart was able to save *Coronet* during the war. Because *Coronet* did not accept advertising during the war years, its circulation figures are not available for that time, but magazine historian Theodore Peterson says several outsiders estimated its sales at as much as five million for that period. Advertising was added in 1947, when *Time* reported that *Coronet* had been built from a wobbly offspring of *Esquire* into a two-million-plus circulation, larger than its parent.

During the 1950s *Coronet* editors were caught up in a trend by general-audience magazines to push circulations upward to meet the rising competition of television – in spite of dire warnings from some editors that this approach could be fatal. By 1961 the annual losses of *Coronet* had climbed to $600,000. Its publishers negotiated in the same year with *Reader's Digest* to take over that magazine and its assets, including a ten-color press. The October *Coronet* was the final issue. Although another publication using that title subsequently appeared, it had no relation to the original *Coronet.* In a speech to the Association for Education in Journalism in 1963, Gingrich offered an epitaph for *Coronet:* "That lovely little magazine, full of treasures of the world's great museums, was about twenty-five years ahead of the great art boom, on which it might have been ridden like a surfboard. Instead of letting it die a natural death, we chose to make it into something that it wasn't born to be, with the result that it lived all the twenty-five years of its life on the crutch of family support."

An incident in the spring of 1937 explains the mercurial nature of Smart and his impulsive methods in the publishing business. He had gone to Paris to seek acupuncture treatment for recurring migraine headaches, when he met in a friend's apartment a downcast Greek named E. Teriade, who spoke no English. The friend explained that Teriade was devastated because he had just come from an interview with the patron of his struggling art magazine, *Minotaur,* and the patron had brutally thrown him out on the street and withdrawn all funds. On the spot Gingrich told Teriade that he would buy the little magazine, sight unseen. "I've got one art magazine now, so I might as well have two," Smart told the astonished friend, according to Gingrich.

Smart initially got very little for his one-thousand-dollar investment, since the former patron retained the title and all the other properties of the magazine. Gingrich chose *Verve* as the new title for the quarterly because it meant the same in French as in English and lent itself to unusual treatments. Teriade turned out to be a first-rate editor and negotiator. Pablo Picasso, Henri Matisse, and Marc Chagall all did covers for the magazine. Gingrich reported the color plates to be "among the best examples of craftsmanship that have yet appeared." Produced in France and edited in America in both French and English, the rich-looking publication sold for $2.50 and $3.50 an issue. Smart's sponsorship of *Verve* continued until 1939, when he withdrew his support. The magazine suspended publication in 1940 but continued in occasional editions following the war.

In 1937 it seemed that everything Smart and his partners touched turned to gold, leaving the

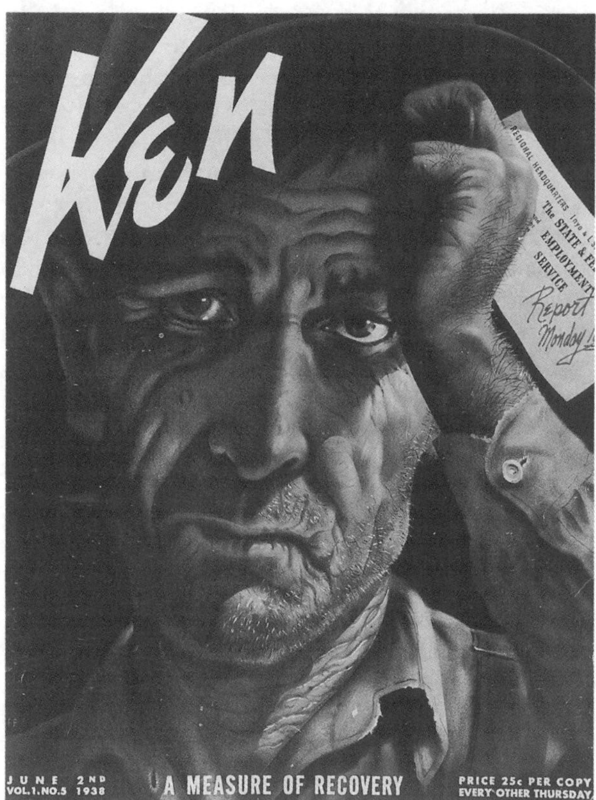

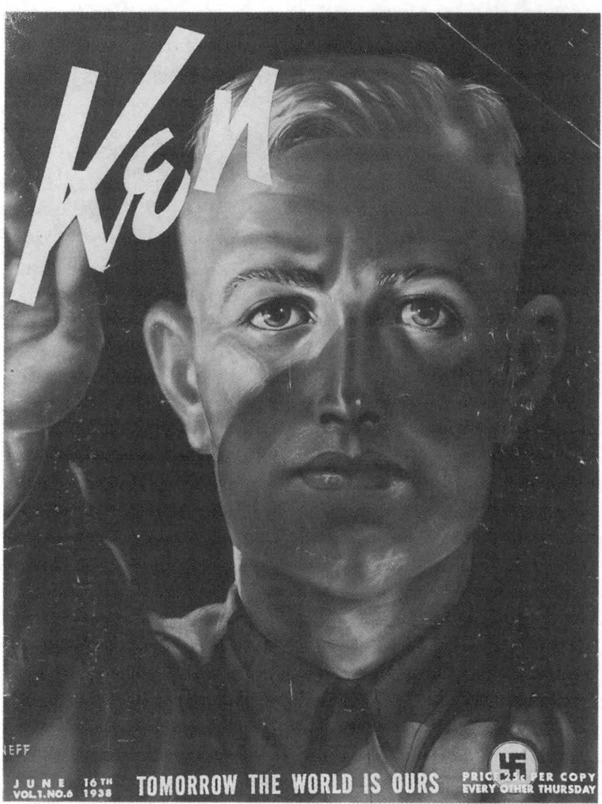

Covers for two issues of Smart's magazine in the Esquire *format, expressing the political concerns of the time*

publisher exclaiming, "This publishing business is a lead-pipe cinch," according to Gingrich. This self-assured attitude lay partly behind Smart's first unqualified failure in the magazine business. Two years after launching *Coronet,* he decided to publish a news magazine with pictures. The partners had noted the public's disillusionment with the press – particularly in the reporting of the Spanish Civil War – and their magazine was to be for those who had lost faith in the integrity of reporting. Smart, Gingrich, and a foreign correspondent for the *Chicago Tribune* named Jay Cooke Allen decided there was a demand for a more liberal reporting of the news, presenting background stories of events as insiders saw them. It was called *Ken: The Insider's World.* Smart saw it as a cross between *Nation* and *Life.*

The first biweekly issue of *Ken* appeared in April 1938, heralded with much fanfare. It was supposed to be antiwar and anti-Fascist, with reports from John Spivak, Paul de Kruif, and Hemingway. Almost at once difficulties arose because of conflicts between editorial policy and potential advertisers. In attacking both communism and fascism it alienated both readers and contributors – including Hemingway, who insisted his name not appear on the magazine's masthead. The magazine did enjoy some successes, however. Hemingway wrote of the war in Spain, John Malone on the sack of Nanking, China, and there were articles about the cotton economy of the South and the plight of migratory workers in California. *Ken* also featured a rich use of photographs in documentary style. The policies of the magazine had little appeal for advertisers, however, and some of them even threatened to pull their ads from *Esquire.*

In a last-ditch effort the format of *Ken* was changed. It became a weekly, and the price was dropped to ten cents. Finally, in August 1939, after losing four hundred thousand dollars, Smart ceased the publication of *Ken.* He simply announced they had "backed the wrong horse." In 1940 the shaky relationship between Smart and Weintraub ended on less-than-amiable terms, with Weintraub leaving to start his own advertising agency. Smart also entered into a romantic relationship at about this time. In 1934 he had met Gaby Dure (Edna Gabrielle Richards), a New York fashion model. According to Gingrich it was the first time the debonair publisher had regarded any woman as other than "just another babe." He married her on the eve of his fiftieth birthday in fall 1942.

Further difficulties arose four years after the demise of *Ken* that threatened the Esquire/Coronet Publishing Company's very existence. In 1943 Smart was forced into a battle with the Post Office Department over the moral tone of *Esquire*. On Labor Day weekend, Postmaster General Frank Walker ordered the owners to show cause why their second-class mailing privileges should not be withdrawn. Walker said that *Esquire* was not, as the law required, "published for the dissemination of information of a public character, or devoted to literature, the sciences, arts or some special industry." Without the favorable second-class rates, the owners of *Esquire* realized they would have had to pay an additional five hundred thousand dollars a year to distribute their magazine – enough to threaten its survival. They took the Post Office to court. After a two-year court battle in which other publications joined in support, a unanimous Supreme Court chastised the postal officials for trying to establish a requirement "that art or literature conform to some norm prescribed by an official," and *Esquire* magazine kept its second-class mailing privileges.

Gingrich left *Esquire* in 1945 to live abroad seven years, and the magazine underwent revisions of content, typography, and makeup. The quality of the fiction and nonfiction declined. But at Smart's request Gingrich returned in 1952, at which time he scrapped hundreds of backlogged manuscripts, selected a new fiction editor and new art director, and set out to recapture the magazine's lost distinction. *Esquire* adopted a new seriousness of purpose, featuring such writers as Philip Roth, William Inge, Norman Mailer, and Arthur Schlesinger, Jr. Arthur Miller wrote *The Misfits* (1961) for the magazine. Gingrich had returned from Europe just in time to renew his association with Smart. Shortly after Gingrich took over *Esquire* for the second time, Smart went into the hospital for surgery to remove a minor polyp on his internal organs, and he died during the operation on 16 October 1952 at age sixty.

Smart's younger brother John moved to the presidency of Esquire and later became chairman of the board. In 1987 *Esquire* was continuing to prosper as perhaps the best monument to the audacity and vision of David A. Smart and Gingrich. But the success in its early years of his tiny magazine *Coronet,* with its little room of infinite riches, also have earned Smart a lasting place in that line of the world's fine magazines produced with passion rather than an account book.

References:

Arnold Gingrich, *Nothing But People: The Early Days at Esquire – A Personal History 1928–1958* (New York: Crown, 1971);

Gingrich and L. Rust Hills, eds., *The Armchair Esquire* (New York, 1958), p. 19;

"Hypodermic for Pageant," *Newsweek* (29 December 1947): 43;

Harold L. Nelson and Dwight L. Teeter, *Law of Mass Communication* (Mineola, N.Y.: Foundation Press, 1978): 390;

Theodore Peterson, *Magazines in the Twentieth Century* (Urbana: University of Illinois Press, 1964);

Henry F. Pringle, "Sex, Esq.," *Scribner's,* 103 (March 1938): 33–39, 88;

"*Scribner's* to the Smoking Room," *Time,* 34 (4 September 1939): 34;

George Seldes, "*Ken* – The Inside Story," *Nation,* 146 (30 April 1938): 497;

"Success Without Editorial Policy," *Literary Digest,* 123 (6 February 1937): 20–21;

"Thirty Years Hath Esquire," *Esquire,* 30 (October 1963): 8+;

Roland E. Wolseley, *The Changing Magazine: Trends in Readership and Management* (New York: Hastings House, 1973).

Lawrence E. Spivak

(11 June 1900 –)

W. J. Hug
Jacksonville State University

MAJOR POSITIONS HELD: Business manager (1933–1935), publisher (1935–1950), editor, *American Mercury* (1944–1950); founder and publisher, American Mercury Books / Mercury Mysteries (1937–1954), Bestseller Mysteries (1940–1954), *Ellery Queen Mystery Magazine* (1941–1954), Jonathan Press (1942–1954), *Magazine of Fantasy and Science Fiction* (1949–1954), *Detective, The Magazine of True Crime Cases* (1950–1954); cofounder, producer, and moderator/panelist, "Meet the Press" (1945–1975).

BOOK: *The American Mercury Reader,* edited by Spivak and Charles Angoff (Philadelphia: The Blakiston Company, 1944).

Lawrence E. Spivak

Though Lawrence Spivak is best known as the creator of NBC television's "Meet the Press," he made important contributions during the 1930s and 1940s to the American print media as well. Between 1933 and 1950 Spivak was business manager, publisher, and ultimately editor of what had been one of America's most controversial magazines: H. L. Mencken's *American Mercury*. Under Spivak's administration, the *Mercury* adopted more-conservative social and political perspectives, while it maintained its reputation for quality writing and incisive thought. To keep his financially ailing magazine afloat, Spivak developed the nation's first successful paperback publishing house in over a quarter century, American Mercury Books.

Lawrence Edmund Spivak was born in Brooklyn, New York, on 11 June 1900, the only son and second oldest of four children of William Benjamin and Sonya (Bershad) Spivak. Though his father was a prosperous manufacturer of nurses' uniforms and ladies' dresses, Lawrence entered the working world through a relatively menial route: as a schoolboy carrying papers for the Brooklyn *Eagle*. Spivak attended Boys' High School in Brooklyn and, upon graduating in 1917, entered Harvard. During college he became an avid and skillful boxer. He lost only one bout, to Francis X. (Dick) Collins, who later represented the United States in the Olympics. Spivak's tenacity in the ring mirrored his tenacity in the classroom: he graduated cum laude in the class of 1921 with majors in English and history.

In the decade that followed, various jobs, most in magazine management, prepared Spivak for his subsequent work with the *American Mercury*. Upon leaving Harvard, he became business manager for *Antiques* magazine and worked as a reporter for the Boston *American* in the evenings. Such a workload was crushing, however, and he was forced to give up his newspaper work. Journalistic responsibilities soon were replaced by familial ones: Spivak and Charlotte Bier Ring were wed in 1924. Over the course of their marriage they would have a daughter, Judith, and a son, Jonathan Martin. In 1930 Spivak left *Antiques* to become circulation manager and assistant to the publisher of *Hunting and Fishing* and *National Sportsman.* Thus by 1933, when he came to the *Mercury* as business manager, he knew the workings of virtually every aspect of magazine operations.

Spivak's acumen would be tested strenuously in his new position, for the *Mercury* was at that time in a tenuous state. Its popularity had been in steep decline since the late 1920s. From a peak circulation of seventy-five thousand in 1927, readership had fallen to sixty-two thousand in 1930, and to thirty-three thousand by 1933. To make matters worse, the magazine's greatest asset, its flamboyant editor, Mencken, had decided to resign, though by this time Mencken's popularity had begun to erode as well. His flashy iconoclasm, so attuned to the jaded sensibilities of the 1920s, seemed to some readers petty and self-centered amid the national poverty of the 1930s. And Mencken, now beyond fifty, was tired. Thus in December 1933 Spivak joined the *Mercury* staff, and Mencken left it, taking with him the brash irreverence that had been the journal's trademark. Although Mencken proclaimed in his editorial farewell that this trait would endure, the two editors who followed him in rapid succession – Henry Hazlitt, a former financial writer, and Charles Angoff, who had been Mencken's assistant – could not rekindle the magazine's uninhibited flair; nor could Spivak revive its ailing finances. Advertising had dropped off, readership continued to decline, and by January 1935 the *Mercury* suffered losses of thirty-eight thousand dollars.

If the magazine was to be saved, clearly it would have to abandon any attempts to rejuvenate the Mencken formula in favor of a perspective attuned to the more somber times of the 1930s. Spivak and a fellow Harvard alumnus, journalist Paul Palmer, developed what they believed could be the right concept – a more conservative review, a combination of *Forum*, *New Yorker*, and *Collier's* – and in January 1935 the two bought the *American Mercury* from Alfred Knopf. With Palmer as editor and Spivak as publisher, the partners set about to implement their notion of the new *Mercury*. Over the next two years they redefined the magazine's identity; a shift to the political right was made almost immediately.

Throughout Mencken's tenure the magazine's hallmark had been its unabashed glee in "belabor[ing] sham as agreeably as possible," particularly in the mores and behavior of the conservative, materialistic middle class – the notorious "booboisie," as Mencken termed them. While it had espoused no definite social or political agendas beyond its mission to root out and puncture hypocrisy, the avowed skepticism of the *Mercury* had frequently allied it with the political Left, and in fact the magazine had published articles by such established leftists as John Dos Passos and even Leon Trotsky. Under Palmer and Spivak, however, all that changed. A staunch conservative agenda, strongly anticommunist and anti-Roosevelt, was established, espoused in a tone of earnest polemic by a new group of contributors, among them William Henry Chamberlin, Harold Lord Varney, and Eugene Lyons. In the later 1930s articles on the failures of communism in Russia, fears of Red expansionism, and the dangers of totalitarian influences in America became customary. The contents of the *Mercury* for 1935–1936 include such essays as "The Sad Fate of World Communism," "Paradise Imagined: The Truth About Soviet Russia," and "Are the Capitalists Asleep?" Roosevelt and the New Deal were severely criticized in such articles as "The WPA Racket in Pennsylvania" and "Wanted: An Honest President." However, the most vitriolic attack on Roosevelt came from the former editor, for Mencken took the same dim view of Roosevelt's domestic policies as did Spivak and Palmer. In his March 1936 article, "Three Years of Dr. Roosevelt," Mencken brought back to the *Mercury* the vicious playfulness with which he had so often attacked his victims: "Quacks are always friendly and ingratiating fellows, and not infrequently their antics are amusing. The Honorable Franklin D. Roosevelt, LL. D. is typical of the species." The essay provides a scarce example of the tone of the old *Mercury* combined with the politics of the new.

Other less drastic changes were implemented as well. Under Mencken the magazine had devoted a substantial portion of each issue to fiction and poetry, as well as commentary on literature, the arts, and ideas, by some of the era's most respected writers, artists, and scholars. Sherwood Anderson, Theodore Dreiser, William Faulkner, Thomas Beer, Mark Van Doren, Grant La Farge, and Oswald Spengler had all appeared in Mencken's *Mercury*. Now, with the conservative political emphasis that Spivak and Palmer introduced, works of artistic and scholarly natures had less prominence. One was apt to find one or two short stories per issue rather than three or four, with fewer poems interspersed throughout the pages and far less discourse on the

Cover for an issue of the magazine Spivak joined as business manager in 1933 and published from 1935 to 1950. From 1944 to 1950 he was also its editor.

arts or on ideas. Still, the magazine maintained a solid standard in its literary and scholarly offerings. During the fourteen years of Spivak's tenure as publisher, the *Mercury* printed items by such contributors as G. K. Chesterton, Philip Rahv, Stanley Kunitz, Loren Eiseley, and Henry Steele Commager. Nevertheless, the arts and ideas had taken a backseat to politics. *Mercury* articles frequently discussed the sexes and sexuality as new side issues. In January 1936 Spivak and Palmer published Havelock Ellis's "Studies in Sex: A History"; over the coming years essays along similar lines followed: "Our Sexual Ethics," by Bertrand Russell; "Utopia by Sterilization," by Mencken; "Common-Law Wives," by Anthony M. Turano; and, after the outbreak of World War II, "Sex is a Nazi Weapon," by George W. Herald.

The inevitable reshuffling of departments and personnel also occurred. Mencken's monthly selection of book reviews, entitled "The Library," was placed in the hands of Lawrence Stallings, and later John W. Thomasson. "The Check List," a catalogue of brief, unsigned reviews, was shifted from the advertising section to the body of each issue; "Open Forum" – a revival of "The Soap Box," which had appeared late in Mencken's tenure – invited comments from happy or irate readers. Meanwhile, the old "Arts and Sciences," a grab bag of comments on virtually any topic from theology to radio, was recast as "The Clinic," brief prognoses of diverse political, social, and economic ailments afflicting the nation and prescriptions for their possible cures. Alan Devoe now contributed a monthly nature essay under the rubric "Down to Earth"; Albert J. Nock provided commentary on national and international affairs; and in 1938 George Jean Nathan, who had been a cofounder and coeditor during the first year of the *Mercury,* returned to do a theater column. Even the look and price of the magazine changed. Spivak and Palmer reduced the *Mercury* from the large octavo to a pocket or digest size; the former price of fifty cents, a somewhat exorbitant amount for a magazine during the 1930s, was cut in half.

All of this revamping produced varied results. Before long the new *Mercury* had more than doubled its circulation, yet it continued to lose advertising. The conservative stance initiated by Palmer and Spivak involved the magazine in two widely publicized imbroglios, though neither had serious or long-lasting effects. In the first, the new owners were accused of illegal labor practices after they dismissed two employees of the *Mercury* staff who had entered the Office Workers' Union only days before. Both Spivak and Palmer denied any knowledge of the employees' union membership, claiming that they were fired because of inefficiency. However, the union called a strike against the *Mercury* which continued for fourteen weeks. Finally, after rulings by the regional labor board and the U.S. Supreme Court, the National Labor Relations Board chose not to pursue a case against the magazine. In an interview published in the 26 June 1935 issue of the *Nation,* Spivak attributed the affair to a "radical group" angered by his magazine's political shift from the Far Left to a more moderate "liberalism."

The second occurred in December 1936. When a *Mercury* article, "Are the Capitalists Asleep," by Varney, accused the American Civil Liberties Union of extravagant sympathies for Soviet Russia, the magazine was charged with libel. Mencken immediately rose to the defense of his former protégé, proclaiming that the suit threatened freedom of the press, an ACLU ideal. ACLU Director Arthur Garfield Hays then suggested that Mencken serve as arbitrator in the dispute. His summation of the case, published in the *Mercury,* was largely inconclusive but highly entertaining: he found both sides to be in error.

The controversies brought substantial publicity to the *Mercury,* and circulation continued to improve, but still it lost money. In 1937 Spivak developed an idea that would not only subsidize the magazine but turn a substantial profit as well: American Mercury Books would be reprints of popular fiction and nonfiction in softcover, at twenty-five cents apiece. In the introduction to the first volume in the series, James M. Cain's *The Postman Always Rings Twice* (1934), Paul Palmer, as series editor, explained the new endeavor: "These books will have . . . a magazine distribution – the newsstand; and a magazine endorsement – THE AMERICAN MERCURY. Presenting both fiction and non-fiction, AMERICAN MERCURY BOOKS will be selected carefully from the hundreds of first-rate volumes published each year. They will be distinguished in style and engrossing in content." The idea proved successful, and Spivak quickly refined and expanded it. By 1940 he had dropped the nonfiction selections and begun to specialize in mystery novels; the series name was now Mercury Mysteries. Spivak introduced another line, Bestseller Mysteries, the same year, and *Ellery Queen's Mystery Magazine* the next. In 1942 yet another *Mercury* offshoot, Jonathan Press, appeared, offering tougher mystery novels than the Mercury and Bestseller series. Spivak would later introduce two additional publications: the *Magazine of Fantasy and Science Fiction* in 1949; and *Detective, The Magazine of True Crime Cases* in 1950. The combined yearly circulation of the *Mercury* subsidiaries would reach six million by 1950. With the profits from these publications, Spivak could cover the debts of the parent magazine, which during the war and postwar years ran as much as one hundred thousand dollars annually.

In these years financial as well as managerial responsibilities for the *Mercury* were solely Spivak's; in 1939 he purchased complete control of the magazine from Palmer and installed Eugene Lyons as editor. Born in Russia and raised in New York, Lyons had become interested in communism while attending City College. After editing *Soviet Russia Pictorial 1922–1923,* he had been assistant director of Tass, the Russian news agency, yet he never joined the Communist party. A six-year stint in Russia as a United Press correspondent had soured Lyons's enthusiasm for the Soviet way, and after Russian authorities demanded his return to the United States in 1934, he became an outspoken critic of communism, frequently publishing articles in the *Mercury* under Spivak and Palmer. As Spivak's editor until 1944, Lyons staunchly maintained the magazine's conservative position. He gave particular emphasis to the international scene, publishing a consistent stream of articles on Soviet Russia and Nazi Germany by the most authoritative contributors. One finds in the *Mercury* volumes of the war years such titles as "Tsars and Kaisers Were Liberals," "Nazi Trade Invades Mexico," "Secret Nazi Instructions on Conquered Peoples," and "Coming: A Totalitarian America." *Mercury* authors of this period included Cordell Hull, Herbert Hoover, Winston Churchill, and Alexander Kerensky. A related issue pursued with particular vigor during Lyons's editorship was the development of the American air force. In a series of *Mercury* articles Maj. Alexander P. de Seversky touted air power as the dominant military force of the future. In addition to their concern with international affairs and America's place in them, Spivak and Lyons also attended to humanitarian matters, especially ethnic and racial issues. Particularly noteworthy was the January 1943 article by Lyons and Ben Hecht, "The Extermination of the Jews"; in close succession, *Mercury* items titled "The Jews Fight Back" and "Jews Who Fight Zionism" appeared as well. Racism at home was also criticized by such distinguished writers as Zora Neale Hurston and Commager.

With Spivak as publisher and Lyons as editor, the readership of the *Mercury* gradually increased. Between 1943 and 1945 the magazine's average circulation per issue rose to around eighty thousand, the largest in its history, though it continued to operate at a deficit, which Spivak covered with profits from the *Mercury* subsidiaries. In 1944 Spivak and Angoff, who had returned the year before as literary editor, compiled *The American Mercury Reader,* an anthology of essays, fiction, drama, and poetry from the magazine's first twenty years. As one would expect, the list of authors is impressive: F. Scott Fitzgerald, Sinclair Lewis, Eugene O'Neill, Edgar Lee Masters, Vachel Lindsay, Thomas Wolfe, Carl Sandburg, and Robert Frost, among others.

This same year Lyons left Spivak's employ to operate a new magazine titled *Pageant,* though he would continue to write *Mercury* articles on Soviet Russia. Spivak assumed the editorial duties and installed Angoff as managing editor. Under this arrangement, relatively few changes in departments and staff occurred. "Open Forum" and "The Check List" continued, as did Devoe's regular nature essay and Nathan's theater column. Arthur Bronson came

Cover for an issue of the magazine founded by Spivak in 1949

to the *Mercury* as music critic, and Bergen Evans contributed a monthly feature on popular superstitions, called "Skeptic's Corner."

However, Spivak did alter the editorial stance of the *Mercury* somewhat, softening its conservative position, perhaps because, with Allied victory in the War now within sight, strong polemic was becoming less pertinent and appealing. Yet the *Mercury* had not abandoned its previous position – in the last years of the war and the years that followed, the magazine maintained its familiar campaign against Soviet Russia, monitored the struggle between Communist and Nationalist China, and decried Communist infiltration in the West. But such issues were now addressed less frequently than before. An increasing number of articles on other topics – elementary and secondary education in America, or the dangers of anti-Semitism and racism, for examples – added leaven to the conservatism of the *Mercury*. More human-interest items began to appear as well and contributed to the diversity. In the later 1940s, essays on such varied topics as human health, humor, and the American clergy gave the magazine greater breadth than it had had in years.

As always, the quality of thought and of writing remained high. With Spivak in the editor's chair, the *Mercury* continued to publish articles by America's most respected statesmen, jurists, scholars, and writers; Arthur Schlesinger, Jr., Learned Hand, Commager, and Faulkner were among the magazine's contributors during Spivak's editorial tenure. In 1949, to commemorate the twenty-fifth year of the *Mercury*, Spivak published an unsigned editorial retrospective, highlighting the magazine's virtues and accomplishments over its quarter century of existence. Chief among these were its independence of thought, limited only "by considerations of truth and the immemorial decencies," and the battle against totalitarianism: "we believe we are simply stating a fact when we say that no other periodical of our class has devoted so much space to it."

But despite the magazine's record of integrity, conviction, and quality, the *Mercury* continued to lose money. Nor did measures that Spivak took in the late 1940s improve the situation. In 1949 he raised the price per copy to thirty-five cents: circulation declined to forty thousand. Then the *Mercury* absorbed *Common Sense,* an anticommunist weekly, but the small increase in readership that resulted did little to allay the problem. Finally, after a seventeen-year affiliation with the *American Mercury,* Spivak decided to sell the magazine – if he could find a buyer willing to carry on his editorial policies. Not only had the chronic deficit become too burdensome, but Spivak increasingly found his time absorbed by a new venture, a weekly radio and television program entitled "Meet the Press," on which prominent and sometimes controversial public figures underwent unrehearsed interviews by a panel of reporters. Ironically enough, Spivak had originated the idea as a means of promoting the *Mercury* on radio, and in 1945 he and radio producer Martha Rountree had convinced the Mutual Broadcasting System to give it a try. The show soon emerged as the prestige program of the Mutual network, and in 1947 it was picked up by the National Broadcasting System's television network. By 1949 *Meet the Press* had become a far more profitable pursuit than the magazine it had been intended to promote.

A half dozen prospective buyers approached Spivak about the *Mercury,* but only one was willing to accept his conditions. Clendenin J. Ryan, a multimillionaire investment banker and former adviser to New York City mayor Fiorello La Guardia, had an abiding interest in politics and the financial resources to keep the *Mercury* going. He purchased the magazine in 1950 for approximately fifty thousand dollars. After Spivak's departure, the *Mercury* went through a succession of owners and editors who took it farther and farther to the political right. As soon as Ryan gained control he installed as editor William Bradford Huie, a lecturer, author, and frequent *Mercury* contributor. As the *New American Mercury,* the magazine under Huie returned to essentially the same staunch conservative position it had taken under Eugene Lyons; a secondary interest in sexual issues reemerged as well.

The shift to the right continued with the next owner, J. Russell Maguire, who controlled the magazine from 1952 to 1960. Under Maguire and the four editors he employed, the concern with sexuality disappeared and the anticommunist campaign intensified, particularly in the defense of Sen. Joseph McCarthy and his crusade against Red infiltrators. By the late 1950s the *Mercury* had become an organ of the Far Right, publishing short items by senators, congressmen, and governors of that faction. In 1960 it was sold once more, to The Defenders of the Christian Faith; it was sold again in 1963 to the Legion for the Survival of Freedom; both were extreme right-wing groups. In 1980 the *American Mercury* ceased publication.

The magazine's movement to the far right disturbed Spivak, even in the late 1950s. In a 1959 letter to Frank Luther Mott, Spivak stated that had he known what would happen to the *Mercury,* he "would have buried it." He continued, "It is a shame that the magazine that contributed so much and earned a great name in its day, should come to its present low state."

If he was saddened at the fate of the *Mercury,* certainly he was gratified at the development of "Meet the Press." After the program had been added to NBC television's Sunday evening schedule, its popularity and prestige continued to increase, and Spivak soon decided to devote himself to it entirely. In 1953 he purchased Rountree's interest in the show; in 1954 he sold American Mercury Books, his magazine and paperback concern, to a business associate, Joseph W. Ferman. By 1955 "Meet the Press" was so solidly established that NBC purchased it from Spivak with the stipulation that he continue as the show's producer and as a panelist and moderator. In the twenty years of his tenure it became one of the most respected and influential news programs on the air, winning two Emmys and two Peabodys and spawning numerous imitators. From its inception the show attracted the most prominent political newsmakers as guests, including J. Robert Oppenheimer, McCarthy, John L. Lewis, Adlai Stevenson, John and Robert Kennedy, Fidel Castro, Richard Nixon, Indira Gandhi, and King Hussein of Jordan. The show frequently made as well as covered the news when, amid the panelists' questions, guests would make revelations of national or international impact. McCarthy's credibility suffered badly when during a 1950 program he repeatedly hedged as Spivak challenged him to name names or provide tangible evidence of Communists in the State Department; in 1961, with tensions running high at the Berlin Wall, Attorney General Robert Kennedy proclaimed during a broadcast that President John Kennedy would "stand up" for West Berlin, even if it meant using nuclear weapons.

As a moderator and panelist, Spivak became something of a celebrity for the aggressive and unrelenting attitude he adopted in questioning the show's guests. A *Newsweek* article from 1962 offers an especially vivid portrait of his manner on camera: "Sitting on two pillows, his feet dangling just above the floor, Spivak, looking up through his glasses like an exasperated baby owl and shooting questions in a voice that is precariously polite, radiates almost total suspicion of his guests." It was, however, a highly effective method of ferreting straight answers out of savvy politicians, as well as a source of pride for Spivak. On the wall of his Washington office, he displayed a *New Yorker* cartoon in which a husband and wife sit together watching "Meet the Press"; "Lawrence Spivak would take that tone with *me* just once," the wife fumes. Throughout his years on the program, this unabashed feistiness was Spivak's hallmark, but since his retirement in 1975 he has kept out of the public eye, returning to it only once, in 1976, as moderator of a symposium on the regulation of American political campaigns. He and his wife, Charlotte, continue to reside in Washington, D.C.

For his development of the unrehearsed panel interview format, originated and refined on "Meet the Press," Spivak will certainly be remembered. Less noted but no less noteworthy is his clear-headed management of the *American Mercury* during his years as publisher and editor, from 1935 to 1950. Though he wrote virtually nothing for the magazine, Spivak redefined its character, transforming the *Mercury* from a well-written and stimulating periodical that was freethinking and essentially literary into a well-written and stimulating periodical that was independently conservative and essentially political. Few other magazines of the time promoted a strong national defense and a wariness of Soviet Russia while castigating ethnic and racial injustice, and all in quality prose, much of it by authorities of national and international repute. Spivak's independence and integrity in recreating the *American Mercury* merit an enduring recognition.

References:

Harry Castleman and Walter J. Podrazik, *Watching TV: Four Decades of American Television* (New York: McGraw-Hill, 1982), pp. 25–26;

"The *Mercury*'s Bills," *Newsweek,* 36 (21 August 1950): 58;

Frank Luther Mott, "*The American Mercury*" in his *A History of American Magazines,* volume 5 (Cambridge, Mass.: The Belknap Press of Harvard University Press, 1968), pp. 2–26;

Hubert Pryor, "Bigwigs Under Fire," *Look,* 17 (10 February 1953): 33–34;

"Question Man," *Newsweek,* 60 (3 September 1962): 68;

John Reddy, "TV's Hot Seat: 'Meet the Press,'" *Reader's Digest,* 102 (March 1973): 49–54;

Frank L. Schick, *The Paperbound Book in America* (New York: R. R. Bowker Company, 1958), pp. 62–65.

Papers:

The Library of Congress has an extensive collection of Lawrence Spivak's materials. It includes transcripts of "Meet the Press" programs during Spivak's years as producer and moderator/panelist as well as reports, articles, and correspondence from his years as publisher and editor of the *American Mercury.*

DeWitt Wallace

(12 November 1889 - 30 March 1981)

and

Lila Acheson Wallace

(25 December 1889 - 8 May 1984)

James S. Featherston
Louisiana State University

MAJOR POSITIONS HELD (by DeWitt Wallace): Cofounder and coeditor (1922-1964), cochairman *Reader's Digest* (1964-1973).

MAJOR POSITIONS HELD (by Lila Wallace): Cofounder and coeditor (1922-1964), cochairman *Reader's Digest* (1964-1973).

BOOK: *Getting the Most Out of Farming: A Selected List of Publications, of Value to the Farmer and Farmer's Wife, Available for Free Distribution by the Government and State Experiment Stations,* compiled by DeWitt Wallace (Saint Paul, Minn.: Webb Publishing Co., 1916 [i.e., 1915]).

DeWitt Wallace (Gale International Portrait Gallery)

Together DeWitt and Lila Wallace founded a magazine that would reach the largest readership in world history and created the world's greatest publishing empire. *Reader's Digest* would gain a circulation of more than thirty million and be read by an estimated one hundred million people in a Babel of languages throughout much of the world. The magazine, in turn, would spawn other enterprises, including a hugely successful book-publishing division and the nation's largest book club. DeWitt and Lila Wallace not only made millions of dollars, they also gave away millions to enrich the lives of others.

Both were approaching their thirty-second birthday when they married after a two-day courtship; then they were together for nearly sixty years until DeWitt's death in 1981 at the age of ninety-one; Lila died three years later at the age of ninety-four. *Time* magazine, in a cover story on the couple for its 10 December 1951 issue, called them a "perfect team" and said each complemented the other despite physical and emotional differences. He was tall, standing an inch over six feet, angular, and bony, and she was small (five feet and three inches), slight, and dainty. "He is a worrier, torn by inner doubts and subject to spells of melancholy; she is self-possessed and an optimist to the bone," the article said. Lila called her husband "Wally," and this nickname caught on among his colleagues. No doubt DeWitt Wallace was the driving force behind the *Reader's Digest,* but Lila Wallace's contributions

Lila Acheson Wallace (Gale International Portrait Gallery)

were considerable; it is doubtful the magazine would have achieved its enormous success without her. Wallace called her his "pillar of strength" and said she was an "incredible and wonderful woman." A close friend put it this way: "Wally's the genius, all right, but Lila unwrapped him."

William Roy DeWitt Wallace was born 12 November 1889 in Saint Paul, Minnesota. He was the fifth child of Dr. James Wallace, a teacher who later would become dean and then president of Macalester College, and Janet Davis Wallace, whose father was the librarian at the College of Wooster in Ohio. James Wallace, who was a Presbyterian preacher as well as a professor of Greek and modern languages, had previously taught at Wooster. The baby grew into an athletic and fun-loving youth and shortened his name to DeWitt. He was reared among books and family prayers.

After showing early scholastic promise, Wallace became a mediocre student at Macalester Academy and was sent to Mount Hermon School for Boys, which was founded by the evangelist Dwight L. Moody in Northfield, Massachusetts. While there, he and a companion took an unauthorized leave, traveling to Boston, to New York, and then on to San Francisco, paying their way by working at construction jobs along the way. In the fall of 1907 Wallace entered Macalester College, excelling at sports though sometimes neglecting his studies. During the summers he did farmwork in Montana and once played semiprofessional baseball at Leeds, North Dakota. After his sophomore year at Macalester, Wallace worked for a year in a bank operated by his uncle, Robert Wallace, in Monte Vista, Colorado.

James Playsted Wood, in *Of Lasting Interest: The Story of the Reader's Digest* (1958), writes that Wallace first began reading widely in current publications while in Colorado. Also at that time, according to Wood, "Wallace began keeping a card file of the high points of what seemed to him to be the best articles. During the fall and winter of 1909–10, DeWitt Wallace began practicing the technique that, after several mutations and tribulations enough, was to lead to *The Reader's Digest* twelve years later."

After his stay in Colorado, Wallace decided to attend the University of California, Berkeley. He again enrolled as a freshman because, as he explained later, "the freshman year is more fun." Tall and handsome, Wallace became a member of the Psi Upsilon fraternity and enjoyed a lively social life. During the Christmas holidays of 1911 an old friend from Macalester, Barclay Acheson, invited Wallace to go home with him to Tacoma, Washington. There Wallace met and was much taken with Acheson's sister, Lila, but discovered that she was already engaged. Back at Berkeley, Wallace continued to neglect his studies, and after his second year he decided to quit. He returned to Saint Paul.

In 1912 he found a job writing sales-promotion letters for the Webb Publishing Company, which produced farm publications and high-school textbooks. While at Webb, Wallace noticed the many helpful free pamphlets on various farm subjects produced by the United States Department of Agriculture and state experiment stations. Wallace suspected that many farmers were not aware that such pamphlets existed, so he compiled a listing of these publications with brief descriptions of each and printed a 120-page booklet titled *Getting the Most Out of Farming* (1915). Wallace established credit with Webb, left his job, bought a Model T Ford, and set out to sell the booklets to banks for free distribution to their farm customers – he had left spaces on the covers of the booklets in which the banks could print their names. Wallace drove throughout North Dakota, Montana, and parts of Oregon and Washington, often sleeping in his car. He sold about one hundred thousand copies before returning to Saint Paul, where he took a job as a manager of the mail-order department of Brown and Bigelow, which published calendars and greeting cards.

When the United States declared war on Germany in April 1917, Wallace, partly because of patriotism and partly because he was bored with his job, immediately enlisted and was among the first twenty-five men in Saint Paul to leave for service. He became a sergeant and instructor at Fort Dodge, Iowa, but took a demotion to private to get overseas. By April 1918 he was again a sergeant and serving in France with the Thirty-fifth Infantry Division in France. During the Meuse-Argonne offensive half of his company had been killed or wounded by 1 October, and the survivors were about to be withdrawn when Wallace was hit by shrapnel in the neck, nose, lungs, and abdomen. He was sent to the army general hospital at Aix-les-Bains, where he spent four months recovering.

The hospital was well supplied with reading material, including many magazines, and during his long convalescence Wallace further developed the idea that had been on his mind since working in his uncle's bank in Colorado – a publication which would present a selection of the best articles from important magazines. Furthermore Wood relates that Wallace believed that the majority of these articles could be condensed by as much as 75 percent without damaging their essential meanings. He began to experiment with this concept, producing edited versions of the magazine articles made available to him at the hospital.

Wallace became convinced that a monthly magazine featuring such condensations of the best articles from current publications would appeal to many readers. When he was discharged from the army in April 1919 at Norfolk, Virginia, he returned to Saint Paul but made no effort to find a job. Instead he spent his days at the Minneapolis Public Library, poring over magazines going back as far as ten years. He practiced incessantly at condensing what he thought were the best articles into briefer and more readable versions, and he discovered that he could make extensive cuts and still retain the substance and the writer's style. He began to believe that most articles could actually be improved through condensation.

In January 1920 Wallace produced the first trial issue of his magazine, which he called *Reader's Digest.* He selected thirty-one articles of "enduring value and interest" and condensed them for printing in two hundred copies of a pocket-sized sample magazine. Wallace mailed copies to leading Manhattan publishers and others he thought might support the venture. He was rejected by all, and only one publisher bothered to offer any encouragement at all. William Randolph Hearst told Wallace that such a magazine might reach a circulation of three hundred thousand but that this was too small an enterprise for Hearst to underwrite. Wallace was bitterly disappointed; he later said he undoubtedly would have given away the magazine to anyone who would have made him editor.

He temporarily abandoned his publishing dream and was working as a salesman for a wholesale grocer in the summer of 1920 when he got some good news to dispel his gloom. Acheson, now a Presbyterian minister in Saint Paul, reported that his sister, Lila, was neither married nor engaged but was doing social work with women in Bridgeport, Connecticut. Wallace immediately wired her: "Conditions among women workers at St. Paul ghastly. Urge immediate investigation." By coincidence she then was temporarily assigned to Minneapolis to establish an industrial center for the Young Women's Christian Association. Wallace proposed marriage on their first date on 15 October; she accepted the following day.

Lila Bell Acheson was born on 25 December 1889 in Virden, Manitoba, Canada, the third of five children of the Reverend T. Davis Acheson and the former Mary Huston. Her father, a Presbyterian minister, soon moved to the United States, and Lila was reared in several small midwestern towns, including Marshall, Minnesota, and Lewistown, Illinois, where he preached. She attended Ward Belmont in Nashville and the University of Oregon, from which she graduated in 1917. She taught two years at a high school in Eatonville, Washington, and helped managed a YWCA summer home on an island in Puget Sound. At the outbreak of World War I she was recruited to work with women who were flocking into industry for the first time. She headed a staff of thirty social workers assigned to the Industrial Service Center at a huge Du Pont munitions plant in Pompton Lakes, New Jersey.

It was a tough job for Acheson, a blue-eyed, delicate-looking but strong-willed woman. The large New Jersey plant was open around the clock, and problems were frequent. Employee turnover was high, and the accident rate was frightening, particularly on the night shifts. The woman workers suffered both fatigue and insomnia. Tense and restless, the night workers would wander around the town after their shifts, and this situation created resentment among the townspeople. Lila Acheson and her staff improved working conditions, counseled workers, organized recreational activities, and improved relations between the woman workers and the community.

Cover for the trial issue DeWitt Wallace mailed to publishers and potential investors

After the war Lila Acheson continued to do the same type of work in other industrial centers. In New Orleans she converted an old home into a social center for woman workers. The center included a small restaurant, parlors, and a dance floor and offered classes in music, language, homemaking, and art. After her stay in New Orleans, Acheson became head of a new social service department started by the Presbyterian Board of Missions. She traveled the nation, making speeches and raising funds. She then was loaned out to the Inter-Church World Movement to work among the migrant families who harvested crops from Mississippi north into New England and New York State. She convinced canners to build centers, schools, and nurseries, and she recruited college girls to work among the migrant workers during the summer.

Although Lila Acheson accepted DeWitt Wallace's proposal on the second day of their courtship, the couple postponed their marriage for a few months. In the interim Acheson went to New York, and Wallace found a job in Pittsburgh, Pennsylvania, with Westinghouse's newly organized international publicity department. A colleague at Westinghouse with mail-order experience read Wallace's sample magazine and told him he thought it could successfully be sold by mail. For the next three months and with four thousand dollars borrowed from his father and brothers, Wallace mailed out thousands of circular letters seeking subscriptions to the yet-unborn magazine. The direct-mail solicitations were sent to public-school teachers, college professors, nurses, and others, and Wallace also solicited subscriptions from women's clubs and professional groups. Although Wallace was discharged from Westinghouse during the economic recession of 1921, the circulars he had mailed began bringing in some responses and remittances, and Wallace was encouraged.

Wallace and Acheson were married on 15 October 1921 in a suburb of Pleasantville, New York. Officiating at the church ceremony was Barclay Acheson. The couple rented a garden apartment in Greenwich Village and a basement room under a nearby speakeasy for office space and storage. They mailed out another round of Wallace's circulars and then traveled to the Poconos for a two-week honeymoon. When they returned, they were delighted to find bundles of letters awaiting them with remittances that totaled nearly five thousand dollars when added to the earlier mailings from Pittsburgh. The couple borrowed another thirteen hundred dollars and hired a Pittsburgh printer to produce five thousand copies of the first issue of *Reader's Digest.* It was dated February 1922 and listed the couple as cofounders, co-owners, and coeditors. Acheson was listed first because Wallace believed that the magazine's principal appeal would be to women. For this reason he also listed as editors Louise M. Patterson and Hazel J. Cubberly, who had nothing to do with the magazine.

During those early days in Greenwich Village the Wallaces would hire customers from the speakeasy upstairs and girls from a nearby community club to wrap and address copies of the magazine; they would then hire a taxicab to take the issues to the post office. Hard-pressed for money, the young couple sublet one room of their small apartment to a New York University professor and his wife, with whom they shared the bath and the kitchen. To save money on magazine subscriptions, Wallace did most of his work in the periodical room of the New York Public Library, a favorite haven for derelicts seeking warmth on winter days. Wallace would condense articles from various magazines in longhand on yellow sheets of paper until he was exhausted, then hurry back to Greenwich Village to see what was in the mail.

Their new magazine caught on quickly with the reading public; the first subscribers liked the *Reader's Digest* and spread the word by mouth. New subscriptions, at twenty-five cents a copy, or three dollars a year, came in steadily. The magazine featured thirty-one articles per issue, and subscribers liked this article-a-day concept. They also approved of the condensations, which provided quick and easy reading. Furthermore there was no advertising and would not be until thirty-three years later. The pocket-size format was also convenient, and many readers began to save their issues for future reading, rather than discarding them after a short time.

By the fall of 1922 the *Reader's Digest* was a small but encouraging success. Subscriptions had reached seven thousand and were steadily rising. Further success seemed assured, and the Wallaces, tired of the noise and distractions of Greenwich Village, longed for a rustic retreat. They found a garage apartment in Pleasantville, a place with fond memories for both, and rented it from Pendleton Dudley, a successful New York public-relations counselor. They agreed to pay twenty-five dollars a month for the twenty-five-by-thirty-foot apartment. They later paid an extra ten dollars a month to rent a pony shed next to the garage for use as an office. The Wallaces moved in, bought a minimum of furniture, and brought with them their other possessions, which consisted mostly of bundles and crates of magazines and letters. After cleaning and painting the apartment, the Wallaces immediately turned their attention to producing the magazine which had become an obsession for them.

They worked from early in the morning until late at night. Lila Wallace read the current magazines and chose the articles she thought were best. DeWitt Wallace reviewed them and did the condensations, sometimes with her assistance. He also wrote magazine editors, asking for permission to reprint and condense articles. The editors almost always were happy to grant permission; they realized their magazines would reap valuable publicity with the reprints which were credited to their publications. Nor did they consider the new magazine competition since it did not carry advertising. One exception was George Horace Lorimer of the *Saturday Evening Post,* who had a long-standing rule forbidding quotations of more than five hundred words from his widely circulated magazine. Wallace traveled to Philadelphia and persuaded Lorimer to make an exception.

As soon as he could afford it, Wallace began to pay editors small sums for reprints, and this practice did much to ensure their ready cooperation. Also Wallace and his wife would sometimes move into a country inn or lodge for a week or ten days and prepare an entire issue in that time from already-selected material. This quick preparation left the rest of the month for Wallace to deal with editors and prepare promotional messages. He stressed the lasting interest of the magazine's articles as well as the compactness and permanence of his publication. He also explained in a promotional flyer, "*The Reader's Digest* is not a magazine in the usual sense, but rather a co-operative means of rendering a time-saving service. Our Association is serving you; it should also be serving your friends."

The Reader's Digest Association had been organized with Wallace owning 52 percent of the stock and his wife the other 48 percent; subscribers automatically became members. Each issue of the magazine printed testimonials from satisfied subscribers, and Wallace offered low renewal rates to readers who obtained new subscriptions from others. The magazine advertised itself as providing "an article a day from leading magazines – each article of enduring value and interest, in condensed, permanent booklet form," and it reprinted articles by H. G. Wells, John Galsworthy, Lincoln Steffens, Bertrand Russell, and other notables on a wide variety of subjects.

By 1925 circulation had reached sixteen thousand, and the *Reader's Digest* had clearly outgrown the pony shed. The Wallaces bought land next to the Dudley estate and built a long, low, Normandy-style house to serve as both a home and an office. They also hired their first employee, Ralph Ernest Henderson, a Harvard-educated son of missionaries. He had taught four years in Burma before joining the Wallaces as their business manager. The *Reader's Digest* was so little known then that, when Henderson arrived in Pleasantville, he had trouble obtaining directions to the Wallaces' house. This situation soon changed, however; the magazine quickly outgrew even its new quarters, and the Wallaces began renting space in Pleasantville, first over the post office and then over two banks. The Wallaces also hired local workers to handle the increasing number of magazines being wrapped and mailed. By 1929 the circulation had reached more than two hundred thousand with gross revenues of six hundred thousand dollars, and the *Reader's Digest* had taken over nearly all of Pleasantville's available office space. The Wallaces hired another significant employee, the Reverend Harold A. Lynch,

Cover for the first issue of the magazine founded by the Wallaces

who left the clergy and succeeded Henderson as business manager. This freed Henderson to take on editorial duties that would eventually lead to his heading the company's successful Condensed Books operation.

Wallace so far had resisted selling his magazine on newsstands for several reasons. He preferred that the *Reader's Digest* be considered a special service by its readers, and this concept would no longer be valid if it appeared on newsstands. He also believed newsstand success might cause resentment among other publishers who then would deny him the reprint rights upon which he depended. Finally, he feared that some publishers with greater financial resources might realize how great his idea was and begin their own digest magazines. Eventually, however, it was competition from several imitators, some with a format and even typeface identical to that of *Reader's Digest,* that forced Wallace to arrange with a distributor to sell single copies of his magazine on the newsstand.

The subsequent newsstand success of his magazine did, indeed, cause some editors to rebel against granting reprint rights to Wallace. Wallace, however, had a staunch supporter and ally in Kenneth W. Payne of the *North American Review.* Payne convinced fellow editors that the *Reader's Digest* was stimulating mass interest in their quality material and that they should continue to provide articles for reprinting. In 1930 Payne became the first experienced professional to join the *Reader's Digest* staff.

Another problem faced Wallace. It was the beginning of the Great Depression, and some of the magazines from which he selected articles were going out of business. Others were in financial trouble. The Wallaces no longer could be sure of obtaining all the articles they needed for their magazine, so Wallace decided to use some original material, proceeding slowly and cautiously. In the April 1930 issue appeared an unsigned item titled "Music and Work" that was billed as "A special compilation for Reader's Digest." Other anonymous articles followed, and finally, in the February 1933 issue, appeared the first signed original article, "Insanity – The Modern Menace," by Henry Morton Robinson, who later became a best-selling novelist. Articles would be written on assignment for the *Reader's Digest* and then first offered to other magazines; if accepted and printed, the articles would appear afterward in condensed form in the *Reader's Digest.* Magazine editors usually were happy with this arrangement; it meant they could obtain quality articles at no cost because the *Reader's Digest* paid the writer for the original manuscript.

An original article appeared in the August 1935 issue of the *Reader's Digest* that was to result in a great deal of publicity for the magazine, and the idea for the piece originated with DeWitt Wallace. He was driving in the countryside one day when he thought about the bad automobile accidents reported in the newspapers. He stopped at a garage and asked the mechanic if he had handled any bad wrecks lately. The mechanic then began to describe some recent accidents in great and gruesome detail. Wallace was aghast, and he quickly assigned a writer named J. C. Furnas to produce an uncompromising article that would dramatize the need for highway safety. Wallace intended to shock the nation into awareness of the numerous accidents, many caused by reckless and careless driving, that occurred with monotonous regularity throughout the nation.

Furnas's article " – And Sudden Death" was graphic in its descriptions of injury and death and was preceded by this editorial warning: "Like the gruesome spectacle of a bad automobile accident itself, the realistic details of this article will nauseate some readers. Those who find themselves thus affected at the outset are cautioned against reading the article in its entirety, since there is no letdown in the author's outspoken treatment of sickening fact." The article pulled no punches; it did indeed translate "dry statistics into a reality of blood and agony" as its opening paragraph promised. Wallace then contacted his former landlord, Dudley, and asked if his firm would publicize the article. Dudley, who later handled all of the publicity for *Reader's Digest,* recognized the national implications and the article's impact and quickly agreed to take the job. Proofs were mailed to five thousand newspapers and other publications, inviting them to reprint some or all of the article after its appearance in the *Reader's Digest.* Many did so, and excerpts from, as well as editorials concerning, the article appeared in periodicals throughout the nation.

The project snowballed; the article was read and discussed on radio programs, syndicated as a comic strip, and made into a short motion picture. The *Reader's Digest* distributed four million reprints of " – And Sudden Death" within three months, giving this article the widest circulation of any article in journalism history. Traffic-court judges read it aloud in their courtrooms; some traffic violators were made to copy it in longhand as part of their punishment. Wyoming issued a copy of the article with every automobile license plate, and New York toll collectors distributed reprints to drivers going over the George Washington Bridge or through the Holland Tunnel. The province of Ontario mailed copies with all of its correspondence. Some credited the article with decreasing the number of accidents; annual traffic deaths during the six years following the article's publication declined by one-third.

By 1936 the *Reader's Digest* had a circulation of about two million and an editorial staff of thirty-two in Pleasantville. Wallace was able to pay generous sums to editors for reprint rights, to writers on *Reader's Digest* assignments, and to his key workers. By this time the magazine's operations were growing too large for available office space in Pleasantville – *Reader's Digest* workers were housed in fourteen separate offices scattered throughout the village. The Wallaces considered moving their offices to New York City but instead decided to build a headquarters on eighty acres of land in a wooded area of rolling hills seven miles north of Pleasantville between Chappaqua and Mount Kisco. Lila Wallace was a great admirer of the restored colonial architecture of Williamsburg, Virginia, and the architects for the new headquarters visited Williamsburg before drawing up their plans. The result was a three-story, white-towered, red-brick Georgian building costing $1.5 million in Depression dollars and providing 185,000 cubic feet of working space. Lila Wallace planned the interior decorations and the landscaping for the original building as well as later additions and acreage. The new *Reader's Digest* offices included soft pink and green pastel walls, patterned linen draperies, eighteenth-century Georgian tables, and leather-topped desks. On the walls were paintings by such masters as Pierre-Auguste Renoir, Marc Chagall, Henri Matisse, Maurice Utrillo, and Vincent van Gogh. The surroundings were idyllic and pastoral, and the *Reader's Digest* complex won a national award for industrial landscaping. Although the grounds included formal gardens, the rural atmosphere also was preserved. The complex resembled a small New England college more than it did a place of business. After the *Reader's Digest* moved to the site near Chappaqua in 1939, it continued to use Pleasantville as its mailing address.

DeWitt and Lila Wallace soon moved into a new home as well, about five miles from the *Reader's Digest.* Lila Wallace drew the sketches for the five-bedroom, castlelike stone structure that they built on a steep hill above Byram Lake in Mount Kisko. The imposing structure, which they named High Winds, overlooked a lake, woods, hills, and a part of the Hudson Valley. The Wallaces frequently visited the hilltop during the construction of the home, and the first party they gave there was for the workmen who built it. Later they occasionally entertained at cocktail parties, and the guests usually were *Reader's Digest* staff members or business associates. Wallace did much of his work in an office in the tower of High Winds, poring over piles of manuscripts until midnight or later.

Many observers have expressed opinions about the phenomenal success of the *Reader's Digest* and DeWitt Wallace's "magic formula." Wallace explained it in these words: "Primarily, we are looking for articles of lasting interest which will appeal to a large audience, articles that come within the range of interests, experiences, and conversation of the average person. The overall emphasis . . . has been a more or less conscious effort to promote a Better America, with capital letters, with a fuller life for all. . . ." Everyone seemed to agree that Wallace was the guiding genius behind the *Reader's Digest* and that he had an unerring instinct for knowing what the masses like to read. Louis Bromfield, the novelist and once a frequent contributor, said that the magazine's main appeal was to "intellectual mediocrity" and that Wallace's own "strictly average mind" accurately reflected the mentality of his read-

Downtown Pleasantville, New York, in 1936. The editorial offices of the Reader's Digest *were on the top floor of the Mount Pleasant Bank and Trust Company building at left (photograph by Wendell MacRae)*

ers who liked the *Reader's Digest* because "it requires no thought or perception." Norman Cousins, editor of the *Saturday Review,* offered a kinder assessment: "The secret of the *Reader's Digest* is editing. I tell my audiences, often to their surprise particularly in academic circles, that the *Reader's Digest* is the best edited magazine in America. Wally himself is the best pencil man, and the result of his technique is clarity – the words lift right off the page into your mind."

During the early years the *Reader's Digest* was produced by what one writer called "gifted amateurs," but as the magazine prospered, Wallace hired more and more professional editors, some of whom had edited their own magazines. Beginning in 1940, Wallace hired writers who were listed on the masthead as "roving editors." These rovers, who lived in various parts of the nation and the world, formed the permanent writing staff of the *Reader's Digest.* They were paid generous annual salaries and received payment for each article they wrote, in addition to bonuses. They were encouraged to travel widely on expense accounts. When one rover, Lois Mattox Miller, asked Wallace if she might take a trip to Georgia, he replied: "What are you asking me for? You can go anywhere in the world." A stock joke at the *Reader's Digest* had four roving editors meeting in the middle of the Sahara and discovering they were all there doing the same story.

The editing process at the *Reader's Digest* has been called "organized chaos." There was no rigid chain of command, and editorial communication was largely carried on through what one writer called "osmosis and contagion." Wallace, of course, was the top boss, but there were many other editors who wielded considerable authority. Edward T. Thompson, the magazine's editor in chief, estimated that a typical article was handled by five different editors and given a total of twenty to thirty hours of attention.

Samuel A. Schreiner, Jr., a former *Reader's Digest* editor, described the editing process in his book, *The Condensed World of the Reader's Digest* (1977): "An article scheduled for publication in the *Digest,* whether it is an original or a reprint, rises from the hands of a first cutter to a more experienced or skilled cutter to an issue editor to a managing editor to the editor-in-chief and/or DeWitt Wallace. Each of these editors is charged with putting the article into what he personally feels is the best length and shape for final publication in the *Digest.* In the process, anything from whole pages to phrases to single words are taken out or restored, according to the preference of the last – and highest – editor working on the piece." To some authors the line of offices in which articles were edited and condensed became known as "murderer's row."

The main ingredient in the *Reader's Digest* formula for success was DeWitt Wallace. It was he who decided what articles were "of lasting interest," and to him this was no complicated task. As Wallace explained it, "I simply hunt for things that interest me, and if they do, I print them." His goal was to print articles that informed, inspired, and entertained. Self-improvement, inspiration, science, youth, sex, and humor were among the subjects of articles in the first issue of the *Reader's Digest,* and this editorial mix continued. Wallace imbued the magazine with optimism, and he kept the articles relatively simple. It was said that a *Reader's Digest* article, no matter how complicated the subject, could be read and understood by the average high-school student. Wallace also conducted crusades, particularly against cigarettes, even though at the time he was smoking two packs of cigarettes a day. The *Reader's Digest* became known for such regular features as "My Most Unforgettable Character" and "Life in These United States" as well as for its humorous fillers. Promotional messages regularly appeared in the magazine, such as the one in the first issue: "When a man stops learning, he stops living. Knowledge means power; the well-informed man is the strong man. Consider the information value of *The Reader's Digest* in the course of a year."

The *Reader's Digest* became an international publication in 1938, when it issued a British edition, which quickly became the best-selling shilling monthly magazine published in the British Isles. Two years later a Spanish-language edition for Central and South America was published. The price was cut in half for the Spanish-language edition because of the low income of the prospective readers, and the magazine accepted advertising to make up the difference. Wallace, in announcing the Spanish-language edition in the August 1940 issue of the *Reader's Digest,* wrote: "Letters from all over the world tell us that *The Reader's Digest* is a most effective interpreter of the United States to those living in other countries. . .

Readers everywhere join in emphasizing the need for extending the interpretative influence of *The Reader's Digest* throughout those countries where a clear conception of the United States of today will promote an alliance of interests in the cause of peace tomorrow." The initial press run of 125,000 copies of *Selecciones del Reader's Digest* sold out, and circulation within two years climbed to 400,000 in Mexico, Colombia, Ecuador, Peru, Chile, and Argentina. Advertising revenue also poured in, and the *Reader's Digest* had no deficit to overcome. Two years later the magazine began publishing a Portuguese edition for other Latin American readers, particularly in Brazil, and within a year the Portuguese edition had a circulation of 300,000, with 37,000 copies each month going to Portugal itself.

Barclay Acheson was made director of the international editions in 1942, and plans were made to publish a Swedish edition. He and an assistant, Marvin Lowes, flew to Sweden and interviewed 150 translators, from whom they picked an editor and a chief translator. A year later, at the height of World War II, *Det Basta Ur Reader's Digest* appeared on Swedish newsstands even though Nazi Germany tried to prevent its publication. The first issue had to be reprinted twice to keep up with the demand. By the end of the war the Swedish edition had a circulation of 235,000, in a country were the total population was only about six million. After the war other international editions were established, and soon the magazine was sold throughout most of the world. Editors discovered that people everywhere more or less liked the same kind of reading material. By 1987, in addition to English, the *Reader's Digest* would be printed in Spanish, Portuguese, Swedish, Finnish, Norwegian, Danish, French, German, Dutch, Chinese, Italian, Korean, Arabic, and Hindi (editions in Japanese and Greek were discontinued). For the visually impaired the magazine was available in a large-type edition, in Braille, and on talking records.

By 1950 the *Reader's Digest* organization had branched out into the book-publishing business. The *Reader's Digest* had published brief versions and excerpts from books as early as 1922, but in 1934 Wallace decided to make book condensations a regular feature on the magazine. With the December 1934 issue the magazine was increased from 112 to 128 pages so that it might include a condensation of Arnold Bennett's *How to Live on Twenty-Four Hours a Day* (1934), described as "a little classic in the science of self-direction, suggesting an infallible antidote to mental flabbiness – a technique which assures adding zest to all one's daily activity." Book publishers and authors discovered that a condensation in the *Reader's Digest* created a wider demand for and in some cases catapulted the unabridged book to the best-seller lists.

The book condensations in the magazine proved highly popular, and readers asked for more. In response Wallace conceived the idea of the Reader's Digest Condensed Book Club. But he delayed before entering the book-publishing business. Wallace worried that he would be risking not only money but the prestige of the *Reader's Digest;* he would also be offering fiction to a nonfiction readership. In 1949 he decided to proceed with the project, and he named Henderson, his first editorial employee, to head the Condensed Books operation.

The pattern of the Condensed Books was established: each of the quarterly volumes would contain about 575 pages and include condensations of four or five books that had not previously been condensed in the magazine. The hardcover books would be attractively bound, clearly printed in large type, and illustrated in color. The first volume appeared in the spring of 1950 to 183,000 charter subscribers, and it contained condensations of *The Show Must Go On,* by Elmer Rice (1949); *The Cry and the Covenant,* by Morton Thompson (1949); *The Autobiography of Will Rogers* (1949); and *Cry, The Beloved Country,* by Alan Paton (1948). Within a year the Reader's Digest Condensed Book Club had 512,000 members, many more than any other such club. Within four years there were 2.5 million members. Some books were published almost in their entirety; others were greatly abridged. The Condensed Books editors maintained close contacts with publishers in New York, Boston, and London and read several thousand books a year in making their selections. Modern fiction was the mainstay of the Condensed Books; nonfiction books were generally reserved for the magazine. Nobel Prize and Pulitzer Prize winners have seen their work appear in the Condensed Books; so have journalists, writers of light fiction, and comparatively little-known authors. The success of the Condensed Book Club in the United States soon led to others being established in Canada, England, and Australia and also in France, Italy, Germany, Sweden, the Netherlands, and Latin America. Later the *Reader's Digest* published entire "general" books, produced records, and ventured into the motion-picture and television business.

For many years the *Reader's Digest* astonished the magazine industry by prospering mightily without accepting advertising. Wallace appreciated the virtues of advertising, but he also was appalled by false and misleading examples; consequently the *Reader's Digest* crusaded against fraudulent practices in the industry. Many advertisers and advertising agencies accused the *Reader's Digest* of unfair attacks, but *Advertising Age,* the leading trade journal, which had long fought false advertising, praised the articles.

Wallace resisted accepting advertising in the United States edition of the *Reader's Digest* for more than thirty years for several reasons. He knew that the absence of advertising had become a trademark of the *Reader's Digest,* and many readers considered it a guarantee of the magazine's courage and im-

Reader's Digest *managing editor Kenneth W. Payne, Wallace, and business manager Ralph Ernest Henderson (photograph by MacRae)*

partiality. He also worried that other magazines might not continue to sell reprint rights to the *Reader's Digest* if it became a competitor for advertising dollars. By 1954, however, rising costs forced Wallace to choose between raising the price of the *Reader's Digest* from its traditional rate of three dollars per year or twenty-five cents per copy, or accepting advertising. He decided in favor of advertising, and an announcement was prepared which explained: "Polls of readers indicate an overwhelming preference for inclusion of advertising rather than an increase in price. Starting with the April '55 issue, therefore, a limited amount of the highest grade advertising will be accepted. For at least one year not more than 32 pages of advertising will appear in any issue. There will be no alcoholic beverage, tobacco, or medical-remedy advertisements.... There will be no reduction in the number of editorial pages, and the budget for editorial material and new talent will continue to be increased from year to year. Under the new program it will be possible to give readers more for their money than ever before." The announcement was delayed, however, until other publishers were notified, and soon the word was spread in publishing and advertising circles, and the *Reader's Digest* was swamped with orders even though its rates, ranging up to thirty-one thousand dollars for a full-color page, were the highest in magazine history. Within two weeks the *Reader's Digest* received orders for 1,107 pages of advertising, three times what it could accept for the entire first year. The first advertisements appeared in the April 1955 issue, which contained 216 pages instead of the usual 168. Later the magazine changed its policy of limiting advertising material to thirty-two pages, but the ratio of advertising to editorial content still remained lower than it was for most mass magazines.

Through it all, the Wallaces, who remained childless, lived unpretentiously and were greatly admired. DeWitt Wallace was a somewhat shy individual whose modesty was legendary. Many of the thousands of employees at the *Reader's Digest* headquarters had no idea who he was. He answered his own telephone and placed his own calls. Although elegantly tailored, he usually drove a battered old car the five miles between his home and the *Reader's Digest* complex. Despite his magazine's efforts to promote highway safety, Wallace drove so recklessly that some of his friends refused to ride with him. He liked to drink socially and enjoyed playing poker. He bought a plane, learned to fly, and sometimes buzzed High Winds to scare his wife; during World War II, when Britain was hard-pressed, Wallace gave the plane to Canada. Wallace was widely liked, although some liberals objected to his conservative political views. A generous employer, Wallace provided an ideal working environment, offered excellent fringe benefits, and paid unusually high salaries plus bonuses for work well done. The Wallaces relinquished their editorial titles in 1964, but remained as cochairmen of the *Reader's Digest* organization. On 28 January 1972 President Richard M. Nixon presented each of them a Medal of Freedom. The couple officially retired in 1973, but continued their involvement in the magazine. DeWitt Wallace died on 30 March 1981 at the age of ninety-one at High Winds.

Lila Wallace, until her very last years, chose the artwork for all the digest covers and over the years played a significant, although usually indirect, role in editorial decisions. She and her husband were a lively and gracious couple who seemed to enjoy a lifelong love affair. On the night he died, the last time she saw him, he kissed her goodnight and promised, "I'll bring you flowers in the morning." One observer said Lila Wallace, even in her eighties, was "flirtatiously feminine," wore the bright colors her husband preferred, and liked to drink martinis and dance. Each night after dinner she and her husband would dance for about fifteen minutes in the rumpus room of High Winds. Her passions were art and gardening, and these interests were sometimes reflected in the way she dispensed millions in donations. She died on 8 May 1984 at the age of ninety-four at her home in Mount Kisco. The editors of *Reader's Digest,* in the July 1984 issue, eulogized her: "Perhaps Lila Wallace's greatest contribution was the loving support she gave her husband. Together, savoring joy, they lived his favorite dictum: 'Never take yourself too seriously.' Their publications, their gifts, their very human caring live as a lasting tribute to this remarkable couple."

DeWitt and Lila Wallace rank among the greatest philanthropists in American history. The Wallaces made donations personally, through the Reader's Digest Association or the Reader's Digest Foundation, of which they were the sole owners. The amounts were kept secret but were estimated to be well in excess of one hundred million dollars. The *Reader's Digest,* in a promotional brochure in 1987, listed these major recipients: Metropolitan Museum of Art, for the Lila Acheson Wallace wing; Memorial Sloan-Kettering, for children's cancer research; Boscobel Restoration, to rebuild a nineteenth-century manor house; New York Zoological Society, for the "World of Birds" and a new Central Park zoo; Juilliard School, for a library and to develop young composers and conductors; New York Public Library, for the new Periodicals Reading Room; Colonial Williamsburg, for the DeWitt Wallace Decorative Gallery; Macalester College, to provide excellence in education; the Hudson Highlands, for preservation of the river and its shorelines; and the Lincoln Center for Performing Arts, for continuing support of new productions. Money was also donated to the University of Oregon, the Northern Westchester Hospital, and other institutions and to restore Claude Monet's magnificent gardens at Giverny and to save the ancient Egyptian temples at Abu Simble.

After Lila Wallace's death, a spokesman noted that she owned all the voting stock of the Reader's Digest Association. A memorandum was distributed to employees, saying that her voting stock would pass, under the terms of her will, to the DeWitt and Lila Wallace Trust, ensuring that the association would continue to be a privately owned company. At the time of her death, the enterprise she and

Lila Acheson Wallace in 1936 (photograph by MacRae)

her husband started beneath a Greenwich Village speakeasy had for many years been a global communications force. In 1987 it employed eight thousand people around the world with annual revenues of about $1.4 billion. The "little magazine" had become a worldwide publishing leader.

References:

John Bainbridge, "Little Magazine," *New Yorker,* 21 (17 November 1945): 33–42; (24 November 1945): 36–47; (1 December 1945): 40–51; (8 December 1945): 38–53; (15 December 1945): 38–59;

Bainbridge, *Little Wonder* (New York: Reynal & Hitchcock, 1946);

"DeWitt Wallace 1889–1981," *Reader's Digest,* 118 (June 1981): 65;

"The Digest Cleans a Rug," *Time,* 60 (6 October 1952): 73–74;

"Dig You Later," *Time,* 46 (14 November 1948): 45;

"The Final Condensation," *Time,* 117 (13 April 1981): 108;

John Heidenry, *Theirs Was the Kingdom: Lila and DeWitt Wallace and the Story of the* Reader's Digest (New York: Norton, 1993);

Donald D. Holt, "Hall of Fame for Business Leadership," *Fortune,* 14 (14 April 1980): 107;

"Indigestion," *Time,* 32 (14 November 1938): 45;

Tom Lashnits, "Treasures from the Reader's Digest Collections," *Reader's Digest,* 127 (October 1985): 153–154;

"Lila Acheson Wallace, 1889–1984," *Reader's Digest,* 125 (July 1984): 56–57;

"Point IV," *Fortune,* 41 (February 1950): 96;

"Public Spirited," *New Yorker,* 48 (25 November 1972): 41;

"The Reader's Digest – A Success in Magazine Publishing," *Fortune,* 14 (November 1936): 121–131;

Samuel A. Schreiner, Jr., *The Condensed World of the Reader's Digest* (New York: Stein & Day, 1977);

George Seldes, "DeWitt Wallace – The Story That Money Couldn't Buy," *Nation,* 232 (23 May 1981): 629–630;

R. A. Tuggle, "New Audiences," *Opera News* (21 November 1970): 21;

George A. Wallis, *Sagas of the Wallace Clans* (Melbourne, Fla.: Wallace, 1977), pp. 124–132;

Simon Winchester, "Road from Pleasantville," *World Press Review,* 28 (May 1981): 45;

James Playsted Wood, *Of Lasting Interest: The Story of the Reader's Digest* (Garden City, N.Y.: Doubleday, 1958).

Edward Augustus Weeks, Jr.

(19 February 1898 - 11 March 1989)

Wallace B. Eberhard
University of Georgia

MAJOR POSITIONS HELD: Assistant editor, *Atlantic Monthly* (1926–1928); editor, Atlantic Monthly Press (1927–1937); editor, *Atlantic Monthly* (1938–1966).

BOOKS: *This Trade of Writing* (Boston: Little, Brown, 1935);
The Schooling of an Editor (New York: New York Public Library, 1950);
Early and Late (Lewisburg, Pa.: Bucknell University Press, 1952);
Mazo de la Roche (Boston: Little, Brown, 1953);
The Open Heart (Boston: Little Brown, 1955);
In Friendly Candor (Boston: Little, Brown, 1959);
Breaking into Print: An Editor's Advice on Writing (Boston: The Writer, 1962);
Men, Money and Responsibility: A History of Lee, Higginson Corporation, 1848–1962 (Boston, 1962);
The Lowells and Their Institute (Boston: Little, Brown, 1966);
Fresh Waters (Boston: Little, Brown, 1968);
The Moisie Salmon Club: A Chronicle (Barre, Mass.: Barre Publishers, 1971);
A. Lassell Ripley: Paintings, by Weeks and Aiden Lassell Ripley (Boston: Guild of Boston Artists, 1972);
My Green Age (Boston: Little, Brown, 1973);
Writers and Friends (Boston: Little, Brown, 1981).

OTHER: *Books We Like: Sixty-Two Answers to the Question, "Please Choose and Give Reasons for Your Choice, Ten Books . . . That You Believe Should Be in Every Public Library,"* preface by Weeks (Boston: Massachusetts Library Association, 1936);
Great Short Novels: An Anthology, edited by Weeks (Garden City, N.Y.: Doubleday, Doran, 1941);
The Pocket Atlantic, edited, with an introduction, by Weeks (New York: Pocket Books, 1946);
Jubilee: One Hundred Years of the Atlantic, edited by Weeks and Emily Flint (Boston: Little, Brown, 1957); republished as *New England Oracle, A Choice Selection of One Hundred Years of the Atlantic Monthly* (London: Collins, 1958);
The Troubled Campus, Prepared by the Editors of the Atlantic, introduction by Weeks (Boston: Little, Brown, 1966);
Louisa May Alcott, *Little Women,* introductory essay by Weeks (Westport, Conn.: Easton, 1976);
Leverett Saltonstall, *Salty: Recollections of a Yankee in Politics,* as told to Weeks (Boston: Boston Globe, 1976);
Selected Letters of James Thurber, edited by Weeks and Helen Thurber (Boston: Little, Brown, 1981).

SELECTED PERIODICAL PUBLICATIONS – UNCOLLECTED: "A Criminal in Every Family," *Atlantic Monthly,* 140 (October 1927): 445–451;
"We Have Read with Interest," *Atlantic Monthly,* 143 (June 1929): 735–744;
"Practice of Censorship," *Atlantic Monthly,* 145 (January 1930): 17–25;
"My Friends the Writers," *Atlantic Monthly,* 147 (January 1931): 32–43;
"Method in Their Madness," *Bookman,* 75 (May–June 1932): 150-155, 225–232;
"Fifty Influential Books," *Publishers' Weekly,* 127 (23 March 1935): 1227–1229;
"Hard Times and the Author," *Atlantic Monthly,* 155 (May 1935): 551–562;
"Authors and Aviators," *Atlantic Monthly,* 172 (November 1943): 58–162;
"Short Stories of Tomorrow," *Writer,* 60 (April 1947): 113–115;
"Editor in London," *Atlantic Monthly,* 182 (December 1948): 25–29;
"An Editor in Orbit," *Vital Speeches,* 26 (15 March 1960): 346–349;
"A Quarter Century: Its Retreats," *Look,* 25 (18 July 1961): 58–59, 61–62;
"Keep the Truth Marching On," *Vital Speeches,* 28 (1 July 1962): 563–565;

Edward Weeks (right) with Charles Morton, associate editor of the Atlantic Monthly, *circa 1945*

"Words and Style," *Writer,* 80 (April 1967): 22–23, 76;

"Curtain Speech," *Atlantic Monthly,* 236 (August 1975): 78–80.

The literary career of Edward Weeks covered a wide spectrum: he was an author, lecturer, and influential literary critic. But undoubtedly the most important aspect of his career was that of editor – first at the *Atlantic Monthly* magazine and then at the book-publishing branch of the company, the Atlantic Monthly Press.

Edward Augustus Weeks's path to editorial prominence was, at the outset, a meandering one. He was born on 19 February 1898 in Elizabeth, New Jersey, the son of Edward Weeks, a cotton factor and merchant who commuted to Manhattan, and Frederica Suydam Weeks. He was a self-confessed slow starter who would later remind the president of Harvard of the inequality of IQ tests and their potential damage to those who bloomed late. Both sides of his family were seventeenth-century arrivals in America, and that tradition seemed to cast a spell of traditional kinship upon him, instilling lasting pride in his family heritage.

Weeks attended the Pingry School and Battin High School in Elizabeth. In writing about his early education, he could not recall any instance of an autobiographer who "professed to be happy about his schooling," and he claimed to be no exception. But if his early education was not entirely satisfying, he gratefully remembered those teachers at Pingry School who pushed him hard and encouraged his abilities. In particular, there was a stern Latin teacher who helped Weeks in his struggle with English grammar by patiently drilling him on the basics.

Admitted to Cornell University as an engineering student in fall 1916, Weeks knew by winter that his promise in that field was limited. He was entranced by a fellow student's tales of life as an ambulance driver in France, and he applied for employment with the American Field Service. Though he had no driver's license, Weeks worked without pay in a Manhattan repair shop in order to learn how to drive. He sailed for France on 9 July 1917. The glamour of a transatlantic voyage and the excitement of France soon faded as he and his colleagues went into action at the front. Fatigue, cold, shellfire, boredom, fear, the close camaraderie of difficult duty – all left their lifelong mark on Weeks as he helped move the human wreckage of war to aid stations and hospitals, first for the French and then for the American army. He and his unit served 322 days at the front, and he returned home in 1919

JANUARY 1946

THE *Atlantic*

THE ATLANTIC REPORT — ON THE WORLD TODAY

1 year $5.00 2 years $9.00 3 years $12.00

Cover for an issue that includes the first installment of a serialized novel by Eudora Welty, her second publication in the magazine

with a Croix de Guerre and a new outlook and maturity.

After a summer of rest and reimmersion into family life, he was admitted to Harvard as an unclassified student. He plunged into the study of English language and literature, supported by a growing circle of friends and a love of language. Jobs as a Midwest harvest hand and, in 1922, a stringer for the *Boston Transcript* sustained him, along with money from home. As a member of the Harvard *Advocate* board he worked with others who would later earn success in publishing, including Roy Larson of Time and John Cowles of the Des Moines *Register*. An issue of the *Advocate* parodying *Atlantic Monthly* earned Weeks a visit with its editor, Ellery Sedgwick, a contact that would prove profitable within a few years. Weeks's Harvard professors helped hone his writing competence, leading to a Fiske Fellowship for a year's study at Trinity College, Cambridge, after graduation in 1922. There, Weeks studied more literature and history and wrote for the *Transcript,* the Associated Press, and various newspapers to make ends meet.

The conclusion of that intellectually charged year and his return to Elizabeth brought Weeks every young graduate's problem: finding a job. Finally, he jumped at an offer from publisher Horace Liveright to sell books. He mastered the salesman's ways on the streets of New York, before moving into screening manuscripts. In 1924 a letter arrived from Boston that directed Weeks into the path in which he eventually achieved national recognition: it was an invitation from Sedgwick to interview for a position at the *Atlantic Monthly*. The interview went well, and Weeks started to work as an assistant editor at the prestigious magazine. Before long, Weeks entered another major commitment when he married Frederica Watriss in 1925. The couple would have two children, Sara Thompson and Edward Francis.

If at first the prospects for success seemed tenuous at the *Atlantic,* Weeks rapidly honed and estab-

A 1957 editorial meeting. Weeks is at the head of the table; seated at the table, from his left, are Morton; Nancy Reynolds, assistant editor of the Atlantic Monthly Press; Curtis Cate, Paris correspondent; Daniel Thompson, reader; Donald Snyder, publisher; Peter Davison, associate editor of Atlantic Books; Phoebe Lou Adams, reader; Priscilla Merritt, assistant copy editor; Penelope Greenough, manuscript reader; Louise Desaulniers; and managing editor Emily Flint. Against the wall are Virginia Albee and an unidentified visitor.

lished his ability to judge good writing and encourage young writers. At Liveright he had perfected the knack of speed-reading, and at the *Atlantic* he used it to work through fifty to seventy-five manuscripts a day. The *Atlantic* was not afraid to take a chance with relative unknowns; on Weeks's recommendation, for instance, a manuscript titled "Fifty Grand" by Ernest Hemingway appeared in the July 1927 issue of the magazine.

In 1927 Weeks's aggressiveness and competence as Sedgwick's assistant editor earned him a promotion. He was asked to become editor of the Atlantic Monthly Press, but it may have seemed to Weeks like taking over the Titanic just after it hit the iceberg. Atlantic Monthly Press was ten years old and had run up a deficit of $110,000 due to its undistinguished and limited publishing list. But a new cooperative agreement with the publishing firm of Little, Brown, and Company wiped out the deficit as Weeks took over. He began his editorship by initiating a ten-thousand-dollar contest for new manuscripts. Weeks's staff consisted of only two other people – a secretary (who doubled as a reader) and a proofreader. Hundreds of contest manuscripts flowed in, from which was chosen a winner: *Jalna* (1927), by Canadian Mazo de la Roche, whose heirs still receive royalties from the book.

In the decade that followed, Weeks's literary sense, vigor, and feeling for the reading public built a list of two hundred published books, an increasing profitability for the Atlantic Monthly Press and Little, Brown, and an elevated reputation for both firms. The titles included many best-sellers and new authors: *Drums Along the Mohawk* (1936), by Walter D. Edmonds; *Good-bye Mr. Chips* (1934), by James Hilton; *Rats, Lice and History,* by Hans Zinsser. Other authors joined the Atlantic stable: Walter Lippmann, Samuel Eliot Morison, and Catherine Drinker Bowen. His success as book editor was summed up by John F. Baker in *Publishers Weekly:* "He saw far more in a publisher's job than the mere function of accepting or declining a manuscript. In the first place, he went out after books instead of waiting for them to drop onto his desk. In his personal equipment he had not only a wide acquaintance among writers but also very definite ideas about what the reading public wanted. The second step was to bring the author and the subject together, and the next, by the soundest of editorial advice and assistance, to make a good book a better book."

During this period Weeks aligned himself with those who sought to eradicate the phrase, "Banned in Boston." Officials of Suffolk County, in which Boston is located, prosecuted what they perceived as obscene material much more zealously than the rest of Massachusetts – frequently, books banned in Boston were available three miles away in Cambridge. Weeks's sympathies were especially with the bookseller, often equipped with only "the vaguest notion of the contents on his counters." If notified by vice watchers of "obnoxious" books, he was faced "with the choice of withdrawing the book from circulation or running the risk of arrest and trial." Either course was difficult. The Massachusetts law was eventually eased and modified, due to the work of Weeks and others who lobbied for broader protection for literature.

Weeks also found time to develop his abilities as a lecturer, thereby promoting himself and Atlantic's books, and continued to review books in his "Peripatetic Reviewer" column of the *Atlantic,* thereby staying in touch with literature and keeping his writing before the public. Even in the depths of the Depression he was optimistic, especially in appraising the state of American letters and the reading public. The economic downturn meant reduced sales of new hardback originals, he observed, but an increase in circulation at public libraries. Cheap reprints of earlier books moved onto the shelves and made it possible for many to buy and read the books they had missed when initially issued. "All in all, judging by the depression," he reflected, "by the time we all come to live on a four-day week our reading will amount to something."

According to Weeks, the "vigor and variety" of American literature was impressive. Sinclair Lewis's books, Stephen Vincent Benét's epic *John Brown's Body* (1928), Theodore Dreiser's novels, Charles A. Beard's histories – all were "books of quality, books quite all distinctive enough to keep people awake nights." He often reflected on writers and writing and wanted to help them get published and improve their work. He wrote, "Anyone who writes, anyone who tries to support himself on the perilous crutch of literature, will know that what American writers need most is encouragement, not prohibitions."

Thus in 1938 Sedgwick passed his title of *Atlantic Monthly* editor to a mature, savvy, well-known author and editor when he gave it to Weeks. Sedgwick's retirement was not really a surprise, the "secret" having been out a year before it happened. Weeks was clearly ready to take charge; his perception of magazines and editing led him to waste little time in moving in some different directions.

Weeks appreciated the tradition he had inherited from the nine editors who preceded him at the *Atlantic,* which had been founded in 1857. His predecessors were formidable ghosts – James Russell Lowell, James Thomas Fields, William Dean Howells, Thomas Baily Aldrich, Horace Elisha Scudder, Walter Hines Page, and Bliss Perry, before Sedgwick. But Weeks knew what all good editors know: "The *Atlantic* has survived because it has changed its editors more frequently than many of its larger competitors who are no longer in the land of the living. Whenever there was a serious sag in our circulation we brought in a new editor, a younger man who gave the magazine the lift it needed. It has survived because of our predilection for American writers, and because of our good fortune and good judgment in discovering them."

Weeks increased the amount of topical articles in relation to fiction. The format of the *Atlantic* was freshened, and the typeface modernized. The result was an all-time-high circulation of 117,000 by the end of 1943, putting the magazine ahead of *Harper's,* its leading competitor, and turning red ink to black on the balance sheet. By the end of 1947 circulation was more than 160,000. Each of forty thousand manuscripts received got a review from the nine-person staff, just as they had when Weeks started.

Weeks was as peripatetic an editor as one could find – he was both a lecturer and the host of a radio show on a regular basis, and he participated in selecting the winners of the Peabody Awards for broadcasting. In addition to those activities, Weeks found time to collaborate on several book projects and to help select the best examples from thousands of published articles for a volume celebrating the centennial of the *Atlantic.* He should also be remembered for his encouragement of authors, including Ralph McGill, Eudora Welty, Edwin O'Connor, *Last Hurrah* humorist Fred Allen, and scientist J. Robert Oppenheimer. The list is both long and impressive, representing writers and thinkers who will not fade immediately from the American consciousness.

Weeks retired from his editorship of the *Atlantic* in 1966, though he remained active as writer and reviewer and kept the title of editor emeritus of both the magazine and the Atlantic Monthly Press. In 1970 his first wife Frederica died. A year later he married Phoebe-Lou Adams, from the *Atlantic* staff.

Though his personal good humor and his love of fishing, reading, and the companionship of old friends did not change, Weeks grew more critical of American life and letters in his later years. Arguments between professional writers and professional academics had become too intense, he said – so much that the latter's criticism "breaks the skin." He also felt that contemporary fiction had become overwhelmingly violent and that its treatment of sex had grown "so stark that it has become objectionable." Writing in *Look,* Weeks found America's national self-confidence "demolished" in the wake of World War II. Cheap sex and banal television had added nothing worth remembering to American life. "America is more vulnerable than we think," he grumbled.

Despite his growing displeasure with American culture, Weeks was amiable and active to his last days. He had been working – though for Weeks reading and reviewing were as much pleasurable activities as they were work – in the *Atlantic* office only forty-eight hours before he died peacefully in his sleep at his weekend home in Thompson, Connecticut, at the age of ninety-one.

References:

John F. Baker, "Edward Weeks," *Publishers Weekly,* 221 (19 February 1982): 6–7;

Glenn Collins, "Edward A. Weeks, 91, an Editor of The Atlantic Monthly, Is Dead," *New York Times,* 24 March 1989, p. A16;

Edgar J. Driscoll, Jr., "Edward Weeks, longtime editor of the Atlantic Monthly; at 91," *Boston Globe,* 13 March 1989, p. 21;

"Edward A. Weeks, 1898–1989," *Atlantic Monthly,* 250 (May 1989): 104;

"Four Score and Ten," *Time,* 50 (3 November 1947): 52.

APPENDIX
Editorial Statements

Editorial Statements

"A Word of Thanks," From the Initial Issue of *Reader's Digest* (February 1922).

The Reader's Digest has been made possible by you, and by other charter subscribers who have responded during the past four months to a letter telling of our proposed plan.

In behalf, not only of ourselves, but of all those who have felt that the fulfillment of our plan would fill a very general need, we thank you. Without your advance support – and that of other charter subscribers – this magazine could not have materialized.

We believe you will find The Reader's Digest of even greater value and interest than you had anticipated: These features will no doubt appeal particularly:

1. Thirty-one articles each month – "one a day" – condensed from leading periodicals.

2. Each article of enduring value and interest – today, next month, or a year hence; such articles as one talks about and wishes to remember.

3. Compact form; easy to carry in the pocket and to keep for permanent reference.

4. A most convenient means of "keeping one's information account open" – of reading stimulating articles on a wide variety of subjects.

[signed] Lila 'Bell' Acheson.

From the Initial Issue of *American Mercury* (January 1924).

THE AIM of THE AMERICAN MERCURY is precisely that of every other monthly review the world has ever seen: to ascertain and tell the truth. So far, nothing new. But the Editors cherish the hope that it may be possible, after all, to introduce some element of novelty into the execution of an enterprise so old, and upon that hope they found the magazine. It comes into being with at least one advantage over all its predecessors in the field of public affairs: it is entirely devoid of messianic passion. The Editors have heard no Voice from the burning bush. They will not cry up and offer for sale any sovereign balm, whether political, economic or aesthetic, for all the sorrows of the world. The fact is, indeed, that they doubt that any such sovereign balm exists, or that it will ever exist hereafter. The world, as they see it, is down with at least a score of painful diseases, all of them chronic and incurable; nevertheless, they cling to the notion that human existence remains predominantly charming. Especially is it charming in this unparalleled Republic of the West, where men are earnest and women are intelligent, and all the historic virtues of Christendom are now concentrated. The Editors propose, before jurisprudence develops to the point of prohibiting skepticism altogether, to give a realistic consideration to certain of these virtues, and to try to save what is exhilarating in them, even when all that is divine must be abandoned. They engage to undertake the business in a polished and aseptic manner, without indignation on the one hand and without too much regard for tender feelings on the other. They have no set program, either destructive or constructive. Sufficient unto each day will be the performance thereof.

As has been hinted, the Editors are not fond enough to believe in their own varieties of truth too violently, or to assume that the truth is ascertainable in all cases, or even in most cases. If they are convinced of anything beyond peradventure, it is, indeed, that many of the great problems of man, and particularly of man as a member of society, are intrinsically insoluble – that insolubility is as much a part of their essence as it is of the essence of squaring the circle. But demonstrating this insolubility thus takes on something of the quality of establishing a truth, and even merely arguing it gathers a sort of austere virtue. For human progress is achieved, it must be manifest, not by wasting effort upon hopeless and exhausting enigmas, but by concentrating effort upon inquiries that are within the poor talents of man. In the field of politics, for example, utopianism is not only useless; it is also dangerous, for it centers attention upon what ought to be at the expense of what might be. Yet in the United States politics remains mainly utopian – an inheritance, no doubt, from the gabby, gaudy days of the Revolution. The ideal realm imagined by an A. Mitchell Palmer, a King Kleagle of the Ku Klux Klan or a Grand Inquisitor of the Anti-Saloon League, with all human curiosity and enterprise brought down to a simple passion for the goose-step, is as idiotically utopian as the ideal of an Alcott, a Marx or a Bryan. THE AMERICAN MERCURY will devote itself pleasantly to exposing the nonsensicality of all such hallucinations, particularly when they show a certain apparent plausibility. Its own pet hallucination will take the form of an hypothesis that the progress of knowledge is less a matter of accumulating facts than a matter of destroying "facts". It will assume constantly that the more ignorant a man is the more he knows, positively and indignantly. Among the great leeches and barber-surgeons who profess to medicate the body politic, it will give its suffrage to those who admit frankly that all the basic diseases are beyond cure, and who consecrate themselves to making the patient as comfortable as possible.

In some of the preliminary notices of THE AMERICAN MERCURY, kindly published in the newspapers, apprehension has been expressed that the Editors are what is called Radicals, *i.e.,* that they harbor designs upon the Republic, and are bound by a secret oath to put down 100% Americanism. The notion is herewith denounced. Neither is a Radical, or the son of a Radical, or, indeed, the friend of any known Radical. Both view the capitalistic system, if not exactly amorously, then at all events politely. The Radical proposals to destroy it at one blow seem to them to be as full of folly as the Liberal proposals to denaturize it by arousing its better nature. They believe that it is destined to endure in the United States, perhaps long after it has broken up everywhere else, if only because the illusion that any bright boy can make himself a part of it remains a cardinal article of the American national religion – and no sentient man will ever confess himself doomed to life imprisonment in the proletariat so long as the slightest hope remains, in fact or in fancy, of getting out of it. Thus class consciousness is not one of our national diseases; we suffer, indeed, from its opposite – the delusion that class barriers are not real. That delusion reveals itself in many forms, some of them as beautiful as a glass eye. One is the Liberal doctrine that a prairie demagogue promoted to the United States Senate will instantly show all the sagacity of a Metternich

H. L. Mencken, editor of the American Mercury *from 1924 to 1933 (Gale International Portrait Gallery)*

and all the high rectitude of a Pierre Bayard. Another is the doctrine that a moron run through a university and decorated with a Ph.D. will cease thereby to be a moron. Another is the doctrine that J. P. Morgan's press-agents and dish-washers make competent Cabinet Ministers and Ambassadors. Yet another, a step further, is the doctrine that the interests of capital and labor are identical – which is to say, that the interests of landlord and tenant, hangman and condemned, cat and rat are identical. Such notions, alas, seem to permeate all American thinking, the shallowness of which has been frequently remarked by foreign observers, particularly in the Motherland. It will be an agreeable duty to track down some of the worst nonsense prevailing and to do execution upon it – not indignantly, of course, but nevertheless with a sufficient play of malice to give the business a Christian and philanthropic air.

II

That air, of course, will be largely deceptive, as it always is. For the second time the nobility and gentry are cautioned that they are here in the presence of no band of passionate altruists, consecrated to Service as, in the late Mr. Harding's poignant phrase, "the supreme commitment". The Editors are committed to nothing save this: to keep to common sense as fast as they can, to belabor sham as agreeably as possible, to give a civilized entertainment. The reader they have in their eye, whose prejudices they share and whose woes they hope to soothe, is what William Graham Sumner called the Forgotten Man – that is, the normal, educated, well-disposed, unfrenzied, enlightened citizen of the middle minority. This man, as everyone knows, is fast losing all the rights that he once had, at least in theory, under American law. On the one hand he is beset by a vast mass of oppressive legislation issuing from the nether rabble of cowherds, lodge-joiners and Methodists, with prohibition as its typical masterpiece. And on the other hand he is beset by increasing invasions of his freedom of opinion, the product of craven nightmares among the usurers, exploiters and other rogues who own and try to run the Republic. If, desiring to entertain a guest in the manner universal among civilized men, he procures a bottle or two of harmless wine, he runs a risk of being dragged to jail by official blackmailers and fined and lectured by some political hack in the robes of a Federal judge. And if, disgusted by the sordid tyranny and dishonesty of the government he suffers under, he denounces it righteously and demands a return to the Bill of Rights, he runs a grave risk of being posted as a paid agent of the Bolsheviki.

This Forgotten Man, when he is recalled at all, is thus recalled only to be placarded as infamous. The normal agencies for relieving psychic distress all pass him over. The Liberals have no comfort for him because he refuses to believe in their endless series of infallible elixirs; most of these very elixirs, in fact, only help to multiply his difficulties. And the Tories who perform in the great daily newspapers and in the Rotary Club weeklies and in the reviews of high tone – these prophets of normalcy can see in his discontent nothing save subversion and worse. There is no middle ground of consolation for men who believe neither in the Socialist fol-de-rol nor in the principal enemies of the Socialist fol-de-rol – and yet it must be obvious that such men constitute the most intelligent and valuable body of citizens that the nation can boast. The leading men of science and learning are in it. The best artists, in all the arts, are in it. Such men of business as have got any imagination are in it. It will be the design of THE AMERICAN MERCURY to bring, if not alleviation of their lot, then at least some solace to these outcasts of democracy. That they will ever actually escape from the morass in which they now wander so disconsolately is probably too much to hope. But at all events there is some chance of entertaining them to their taste while they flounder.

III

In the field of the fine arts THE AMERICAN MERCURY will pursue the course that the Editors have followed for fifteen years past in another place. They are asking various other critics to share their work and they will thus be able to cover a wider area than heretofore, but they will not deviate from their old program – to welcome sound and honest work, whatever its form or lack of form, and to carry on steady artillery practise against every variety of artistic pedant and mountebank. They belong to no coterie and have no aesthetic theory to propagate. They do not believe that a work of art has any purpose beyond that of being charming and stimulating, and they do not believe that there is much difficulty, taking one day with another, about distinguishing clearly between the good and the not good. It is only when theories begin to enter into the matter that counsels are corrupted – and between the transcendental, gibberishy theory of a Greenwich Village aesthete and the harsh, moral, patriotic theory of a university pedagogue there is not much to choose. Good work is always done in the middle ground, between the theories. That middle ground now lies wide open: the young American artist is quite as free as he needs to be. The Editors do not believe that he is helped by nursing and coddling him. If the obscure, inner necessity which moves him is not powerful enough to make him function unassisted, then it is not powerful enough to make a genuine artist of him. All he deserves to have is aid against the obscurantists who occasionally beset him – men whose interest in the fine arts, by some occult Freudian means, seems to be grounded upon an implacable hatred of everything that is free, and honest, and beautiful. It will be a pleasure to pursue such obscurantists to their fastnesses, and to work the *lex talionis* upon them. The business is amusing and now and then it may achieve some by-product of good.

The probable general contents of the magazine are indicated by this first number, but there will be no rigid formula, and a number of changes and improvements, indeed, are already in contemplation. In the department of *belles lettres* an effort will be made to publish one or two short stories in each issue, such occasional short plays as will merit print, some verse (but not much), and maybe a few other things, lying outside the categories. The essays and articles, it is hoped, will cover a wide range; no subject likely to be of interest to the sort of reader before described will be avoided, nor will there be any limitation upon the free play of opinion, so long as it is neither doctrinaire nor sentimental. To the departments already set up others may be added later on, but this is a matter that will have to determine itself. The Editors will welcome communications from readers, and those that seem to be of general interest will be printed, perhaps with editorial glosses. No effort will be made in the book reviews to cover all the multitude of books that come from the publishers every month. The reviews will deal only with such books as happen to attract the staff of reviewers, either by their virtues or by their defects. The dramatic reviews will, however, cover the entire range of the New York theatre.

In general THE AMERICAN MERCURY will live up to the adjective in its name. It will lay chief stress at all times upon American ideas, American problems and American personalities because it assumes that nine-tenths of its readers will be Americans and that they will be more interested in their own country than in any other. A number of excellent magazines are already devoted to making known the notions of the major and minor seers of Europe; at least half a dozen specialize in the ideas emanating from England alone. This leaves the United States rather neglected. It is, as the judicious have frequently observed, an immense country, and full of people. These people entertain themselves with a vast number of ideas and enterprises, many of them of an unprecedented and astounding nature. There are more political theories on tap in the Republic than anywhere else on earth, and more doctrines in aesthetics, and more religions, and more other schemes for regimenting, harrowing and saving human beings. Our annual production of messiahs is greater than that of all Asia. A single session of Congress produces more utopian legislation than Europe has seen since the first meeting of the English Witenagemot. To explore this great complex of inspirations, to isolate the individual prophets from the herd and examine their proposals, to follow the ponderous revolutions of the mass mind – in brief, to attempt a realistic presentation of the whole gaudy, gorgeous American scene – this will be the principal enterprise of THE AMERICAN MERCURY.

"As I Was Saying," Joseph T. Shaw's Editorial Rationale in *Black Mask* (January 1927).

The following letter is typical of very many being received by *Black Mask* in almost every mail. Moreover, its inquiry forms such a happy introduction to our editorial purpose, that we cannot do better than reproduce it.

"The Editor,"
BLACK MASK:

"I hope you do not think that your readers are tired of Race Williams, Ed Jenkins and the like characters. We are not; for they are supreme in their line.

"Where is Hammett's 'Continental Crook'? Where is 'Mac,' that other sleuth, who was such a super-entertainer?

"You think it well, perhaps, to give us a change once in a while, but you must not let your old actors die, for they have won too firm a footing in the pages of *Black Mask.*

"I have become the bane of Los Angeles and 'Frisco booksellers, worrying them to get me all back numbers of *Black Mask* possible. My worldly troubles are many and varied but I forget them all when I take your excellent magazine in hand.

"E. W. J. . . . ."

And here is our answer:

Not long since we had a roundup with all the old, dependable contributors to *Black Mask* – the early builders of the magazine. We conveyed to them our purpose and inspiration – to make *Black Mask* bigger and better – the best of all. We invited them to sit in with us, take off their coats and accomplish this very thing. We looked around very carefully and asked a few more to join in – men worthy to take their places with this select group.

And their reply?

One and all, from the Atlantic to the Pacific, from the far North to the luring tropics, have sent in the message, in the inspiring words of Stanley Gardner: – "LETS GO!"

And it would seem that all at once the thing has started, with renewed life, with reawakened interest, with increased virility.

Carroll John Daly has commenced a brand new line for Race Williams, a great, ambitious work.

Erle Stanley Gardner has just sent us the first of a new Ed Jenkins series – a popular favorite in the most thrilling, gripping action we have seen in a long while.

J. Paul Suter, whose delightful style satisfies the most hard-boiled critic, is preparing some stiff problems for the Reverend McGregor Daunt to crack.

Dashiell Hammett has called back the Continental detective from his long retirement and is setting hm to work anew. Francis James is returning with a harder punch than ever. Tom Curry has injected new fire of life into the old reliable "Mac" and is broadening the scope of his activities. Raoul Fauconnier Whitfield is hitting on all eight cylinders in a new airplane series. Frederick L. Nebel is deep in startlingly realistic tales of the Underworld.

And this is but a mere suggestion of what the old favorites of *Black Mask* readers are at work upon.

Others, newcomers to our pages, are crowding forward and bringing no less enthusiasm than our old reliables who have taken the hunch.

There is much more that we could tell you, but now we will just say that neither E. W. J. nor any of our reader-friends need seek for past numbers of *Black Mask,* although – and here's more than a promise – you may soon find it advisable to place your orders in advance, with your newsdealer for the new ones.

For right now we can see the momentum of this new, concerted effort gathering force and volume.

Already we can add to Erle Stanley Gardner's rallying call, the assurance that – WE ARE ON THE WAY!

Statement From the Initial Issue of *Story* (April–May 1931).

The only purpose of Story is to present, regularly, from one place, a number of Short Stories of exceptional merit. It has no theories, and is part of no movement. It presents short narratives of significance by no matter whom and coming from no matter where.

It is not an anthology, but a sort of proof-book of hitherto unpublished manuscripts. Some of the stories will doubtless appear later in other, perhaps more permanent pages, and the rights remain vested in the authors, to whom communications may be addressed, or to the Editors of Story, 16 Poetzleinsdorferstrasse (xviii) Vienna. Thus the magazine is withheld by the editors from public sale in England and the United States, but may be obtained in Vienna, Paris, Nice, Budapest and Berlin.

Only Short Stories are considered, and if and when any articles are used, they will be as rare as Short Stories of creative importance are today in the article-ridden magazines of America.

Rationale From the Initial Issue of the *American Spectator* (November 1932).

The American Spectator has no policy in the common sense of that word. It advocates no panaceas; it has no axes to grind; it has no private list of taboos. It offers an opportunity for the untrammelled expression of individual opinion, ignoring what is accepted and may be taken for granted in favor of the unaccepted and misunderstood. Sincerity, authenticity, and passion are its editorial criterion. Its aim is to offer a medium for the truly valuable and adventurous in thought, and to invite contributions from every quarter where stimulating opinions may be expected. Clarity, vigor and humor are the three indispensable qualities which must inform the presentation of its ideas. Real knowledge and a decided point of view will replace the usual conventional comment on irrelevant or foregone conclusions.

The essential editorial problem of the better and more ambitious type of monthly magazine is that it is much too large. Any man who has ever served as an editor of such a magazine knows – and, if caught partly *inter pocula,* will sadly admit – that it is impossible to get enough good copy each month to fill the magazine. He is only too happy, indeed, if he can get even so many as two things that really please him. The rest of his magazine therefore represents a more or less unsatisfactory attempt to fill the established, arbitrary number of pages. For this reason, *The American Spectator* is limited to the size in which it here appears. That size will be increased only when and if the merit of sound copy on hand warrants it.

Another defect of the average magazine is that its editor often permits himself to remain in harness long after his imaginative oats have given out and the magazine thereafter continues simply as a matter of habit. The moment the editors feel that *The American Spectator* is becoming a routine job, is getting dull and is similarly continuing merely as a matter of habit, they will call it a day and will retire in a body to their estates.

The editors of *The American Spectator* have invited various distinguished writers in America, England, France, Germany, Austria and Italy to join them in contributing to its columns, and the almost unanimous response has been immensely gratifying. Each invited writer has been asked to write on what interests him most at the moment, and each writer will be his own editor. It will be the policy of *The American Spectator,* in short, to have no policy that will in any way interfere with or restrain any expression of opinion that any of its invited writers may desire to offer. And what applies to these writers will apply also to each of the editors.

We herewith, accordingly, present to you our first issue.

Prospectus From the Initial Issue of *Esquire* (Autumn 1933).

As for General Content ESQUIRE aims to become the common denominator of masculine interests – to be all things to all men. This is difficult to accomplish, all at a crack, and we would be foolish to expect to work out the formula down to the last little detail, in a first issue. One of the things that are needed, for the ultimate shaping of this magazine into what will be its final form, is a frank reaction from the readers. We won't know how to please you in future issues unless and until you tell us what you think of the way we started out. The one test that has been applied to every feature that is in this first issue has been simply and solely: "Is it interesting to men?" How often were we wrong? Come on, let's have it – we're leading with the chin.

As for Physical format In page layouts, typographic dress, and general makeup we have tried to allow this magazine to take on an easy natural masculine character to endow it, as it were, with a baritone voice. It would have been easier to be frank, to follow the much fancier handling that characterizes so many of the general magazines, that are calculated to captivate the woman reader, but we thought you'd welcome a change from that, so we have consciously tried to avoid all fuss and feathers, in dishing up this magazine's contents. Maybe in this matter, too, you can help us with suggestions. Is it easy to read? Do you like the page size? Enough pictures? Got any ideas?

As for the Color Pages Once we picked up an issue of one of the humor magazines containing a full page cartoon in color. We forget which one it was, or we'd be pleased to credit it, but anyway, turning to that colored cartoon was like coming upon the proverbial diamond in a coal heap. That accounts for the fact that so many of our color pages are devoted to cartoons. The use of color gives us a chance, also, to give the humorous drawings a variety of treatments that would not otherwise be possible. Some of them, we think, come very close to that ideal state of being classifiable, with equal applicability, under the heading of art as well as humor.

A Word to the Contributor We have known editorial staffs in which it seemed to be a matter of pride that a bevy of assistants inside such a formidable barrier that only a thin trickle of favored contributions ever penetrated to the inner editorial sanctum. We take an especial joy in applying reverse English to any such high hat policy and herewith solemnly promise that, at least as long as ESQUIRE: remains a quarterly, every contribution will get the attention of the editor and one of the publishers. This will also serve to explain why we may take an ungodly long time in returning scripts and drawings. All contributions should be addressed to the Chicago office, 919 North Michigan Avenue.

A Magazine for Men Only It is our belief, in offering ESQUIRE to the American male, that we are only getting around at last to a job that should have been done a long time ago – that of giving the masculine reader a break. The general magazines, in the mad scramble to increase the woman readership that seems to be so highly prized by national advertisers, have bent over backward in catering to the special interests and tastes of the feminine audience. This has reached a point, in some of the more extreme instances, where the male reader, in looking through what purports to be a general magazine, is made to feel like an intruder upon gynaecic mysteries. Occasionally, features are included for his special attention, but somewhat after the manner in which scraps are tossed to the patient dog beneath the table.

As for Selling The Old Man What we can't figure, for the life of us, is why woman-readership should be valued so highly as to make a step-child out of the interests of male readers. This is one magazine that is going to try to be general, but is determined to stay masculine. "Selling the wife" is an important job, but certainly not one that has ever suffered for the lack of help from us. We can think of a selling job, however, that has been sadly neglected, and that is the one of insurance against the destruction, all too frequent, of sales arguments that have been received by the little woman with a glow of approval, at the first skeptical grunt from the old man.

As for the Fashion Features ESQUIRE âims to be, among other things, a fashion guide for men.

But it never intends to become, by any possible stretch of the imagination, a primer for fops. We have been studying men, and men's clothes, for many years, and we have come to the conclusion that the average American male has too much inherent horse sense to be bothered very much by a lot of dress rules that nobody but a gigolo could find either time or inclination to observe. On the other hand, we feel that men have long since ceased to believe that there is anything effeminate or essentially unbusinesslike about devoting a little care and thought and study to the selection of clothes.

As for the Future Issues The launching of this magazine is an ambitious job, and already we have heard the wailing of countless Cassandras. "Why so many color pages – why so many features – how do you think you'll ever keep it up?" Well, a definite answer to the doubting Thomases is in preparation, in the shape of our second issue, which will be out December 1st. There we intend to show, not by promises but by performance, that the standard established by the first issue of ESQUIRE is meant to be a low mark rather than a high one, and that it will be not merely equaled but surpassed, in every issue from her out. For further details on this intriguing subject, and for a partial intimation of what is in store, see page 104.

"Within the Editorial Ken," Prospectus From the Initial Issue of *Ken* (7 April 1938).

This last page of Ken's first issue goes to press on one of the darkest days democracy has yet seen, the day of Hitler's entry into Vienna.

What makes the day so dark is the realization that as long as the Chamberlain government lasts, England cannot be counted in the ranks of the democracies. A democracy is not worthy of the name unless its government's actions reflect its people's wishes. The English people were overwhelmingly behind Eden. But Chamberlain sent Halifax to see Hitler, behind Eden's back, last November. Someday it will all come out. But meanwhile it is only too apparent that Hitler would no more have dared move on Austria, without the nod from Halifax, than Mussolini would have dared move on Ethiopia three years ago without the winks from Laval and Hoare.

France, since then, has tried desperately to live down Laval and the dirty diplomacy he stood for. But from Hoare to Halifax was a step deeper into the dirt of double dealing.

So long, then, as England is ruled by the present little gang of Tories, going directly counter to the desires for international decency expressed by the British public the last time they were given a chance to express themselves, we over here would be blithering idiots to take any more of that old eyewash about "the two great English-speaking democracies." For the moment there is only one great English-speaking democracy, and we are faced with a full-time job to keep it democratic.

And there, incidentally, is Ken's editorial policy. To show us the dangers that threaten this democracy. To remind us of the liberties we now enjoy, that we may be on the alert to safeguard them against attack from without or within.

Stop to think what it means to live in a democracy. Let's say you're a Republican. You could as well be a Democrat or a Socialist or a Communist or a Farmer-Laborite, but we'll say you're a Republican because that happens to be the biggest party out of power. Very well. You can read a Republican paper, openly, on the street car or bus, you can listen to Landon or Hoover or Hamilton on the radio, you can attend Republican club meetings or rallies or picnics if you feel like it. More important, you don't have to listen to F.D.R. on the radio if you don't want to. Nor do you have to attend Democratic rallies or picnics if you don't feel like it, which (remembering that you're a Republican) you naturally don't.

Does this bore you? Of course, the too-obvious is always boring, and besides you're not interested in "politics." All right, turn back to the sports pages, you don't have to be interested in politics – not yet. But if you aren't interested in politics now, then you will be, all of a sudden, when it's too late. And by no means will it bore you to discover that somebody on your block has a key to your house or apartment, that every fourth letter you get has been opened, that you have "subscribed" to numerous propaganda newspapers and magazines glorifying the new regime (that you will pay for promptly or wish you had), that you have "contributed" one-tenth of your income to the Party, that you have pledged yourself not to listen to certain stations on your radio, that you have "volunteered" to do physical culture exercises at fixed periods each week in company with everyone else on your block under the leadership of the fellow who has a key to all your dwellings, that you have "joined" a culture club that turns out to be under this same fellow's leadership, and that you and all the other members have "promised to attend" all mass-receptions that may be arranged for visiting Party officials.

And if, suddenly reminded of all these activities that sound so uncharacteristic of your rugged Republican individualism, you suggest that if it's even half true you ought to have your head examined, you will be obliged, and the examining instrument will be a rubber truncheon. It will probably work wonders for your memory, as well as for your interest in politics.

But should your memory still remain dull, the leader of your culture club will walk in some night with friends, to take you to a free memory clinic. There you will be asked to affirm or deny ownership of a pile of old magazines found in your basement. They will turn out to be copies of the now suppressed and notoriously Republican *Saturday Evening Post.* And you will be confronted by a waiter who distinctly remembers that you (or at any rate someone who looked very much like you) once sat at his table and remarked that you "couldn't imagine a crackpot like that ever running this country." From the context of the conversation it could readily be deduced, says the waiter, that you were referring to him who is now the Grand Factor of the Corporate State of the Americas.

They will let you write a postcard every two weeks thereafter, provided it says only what they dictate, and in time they may even let you out. But by then neither you nor this country will be recognizable.

At that, you will be better off than many a once-prosperous, once well-fed and well-established business or professional man who was for a while amused but soon bored by the rabble-rousing antics of an Austrian corporal who is today listening to the heady music of his followers' singing what was once an empty boast but is now half fulfilled: "Today all Germany is ours; tomorrow the whole world."

"The Saturday Evening Post reaffirms a policy," Ben Hibbs's Statement in *The Saturday Evening Post* (16 May 1942).

In our issue of March twenty-eighth appeared an article titled The Case Against the Jew, by Milton Mayer. It was the third of a series of three articles dealing with the place of the Jewish people in American life. The two others were written by Jerome Frank and Waldo Frank. All three of the authors are Jewish.

It was the hope of the former editor of the Post, who purchased the articles and placed them in the magazine several weeks before the change of editorship, that the three would be considered as a whole – that they would afford an intelligent basis for the discussion of a question which, through the malice and stupidity of Axis leaders, has caused untold grief in many parts of the world. The former editor of the Post believed that a frank airing of the whole question would serve to clear the atmosphere in this country and perhaps help prevent anti-Semitism from gaining a foothold here.

Unhappily, the third of the articles – Mr. Mayer's discussion – has been widely misunderstood. Mr. Mayer and the former editor of the Post looked upon it as a plea, directed at any Jewish people who may have strayed from the fold, to return to the faith of their fathers. That a good many Jews placed this interpretation on the article is amply demonstrated by approving letters which we have had from them. On the other hand, during the three weeks which have elapsed between the appearance of the Mayer article and the writing of this editorial, we have received several thousand letters from people – both Jews and Gentiles – who sincerely believe the article was intended as an attack on the Jewish people.

Naturally, we deeply regret this misunderstanding. The Post never has been, is not now and never will be anti-Semitic in belief or expression. It is not anti any group. We have always been as quick to publish material setting forth the noteworthy accomplishments of Jews as of Gentiles. We have done so because we have always believed that a good American is a good American regardless of race or creed. That this is still our policy will be demonstrated during the months to come by material some of which is already in the process of being written.

This editorial is being published not only to clear away a misunderstanding but because the new editor of the Post feels so deeply, so completely, that the only real cause in these anxious war days is the cause of America – the cause of freedom. We Americans are a cohesive people who get along with one another in peace and brotherhood. We are of many races; we came to these beloved shores from a hundred lands across the seas; and yet by some blessed alchemy we have all become Americans. For many years the Post has been, in a very real sense, the spokesman for the glories and the traditions of America – for the noble principles upon which this country was founded. It will continue to be just that – in these grim war years and afterward – for,

John H. Johnson, who founded Ebony *in 1945 (photograph by James L. Mitchell)*

to the new editor's way of thinking, there is nothing else in this stricken world even half so important as mankind's yearning for freedom and for brotherhood.

That one misunderstood article in the Post could have caused so much anxiety in the minds of its readers is a matter of very real sorrow to the new editor. He regrets, above all, that some hurt may have been done to America at a time when national unity is needed as it never was needed before. He asks all Post readers to believe that these words are written in the deepest sincerity.

[signed] Ben Hibbs

"Backstage," Statement From the Initial Issue of *Ebony* (November 1945).

WE'RE OFF! Like a thoroughbred stallion, we've been straining at the starting gate for months now waiting for the gun from the almighty, omnipotent, superduper War Production Board. We've brain-trusted and blueprinted, rehearsed and dummied over and over again anxiously keeping a weather eye pealed on Washington for the "go" signal. And sure enough, when the V-J whistle did blow, we were caught with our plans down.

Here's your paper and scram, the WPB boys suddenly said. And there we were with tons of slick, shiny stock, a sheaf of dummies but no magazine. But this story having a happing ending as do all good tales, we can confide that we pulled a reconversion act out of an ancient hat with slick style that would put magician Houdini to shame. And here we are.

As you can gather, we're rather jolly folks, we EBONY editors. We like to look at the zesty side of life. Sure, you can get all hot and bothered about the race question (and don't think we don't) but not enough is said about all the swell things we Negroes can do and will accomplish. EBONY will try to mirror the happier side of Negro life – the positive, everyday achievements from Harlem to Hollywood. But when we talk about race as the No. 1 problem of America, we'll talk turkey.

By now you should be hysterical with suspense wondering what all this has to do with the picture above of movie star Lena Horne with a shoe half off. No, it's not a pitchman's come-on. It's our way of taking you behind the scenes to get a peek at one of our coming attractions – a swell photo story by Dixon Gayer on the gent with his back so rudely to the camera.

He's sedate Phil Moore, who got his *Shoo, Shoo, Baby* inspiration from Lena on a Hollywood movie lot. His *I'm Gonna See My Baby* is now tops with the lads in khaki who are occupying Mr. Japrat. Next on his personal hit parade is a number called *I Want A Little Doggie,* which you should know by heart in a few months.

"Meet Mr. Moore" leads off our "Coming Attractions" and takes you behind the scenes for a recording session with Moore, Horne and Co. But Item 2 is also a hit opus – Earl Conrad's swell yarn "From Robbers To Cops." It's the picture tale of how a Washington flatfoot set the sergeant on his heels with a plan that turned D. C. Cow Town's little thieves into the corner cop's best friends.

"An Announcement to Our Readers," Gerard Piel's Statement in *Scientific American* (April 1948).

This page in the last four issues of this magazine has been devoted to the description of a new magazine of the sciences which is to be published under the century-old name of the SCIENTIFIC AMERICAN. Next month, May, will see the publication of the first issue of this new SCIENTIFIC AMERICAN.

In August 1845, when the first issue of the SCIENTIFIC AMERICAN was published, the meaning of science was the application of horse sense and mechanical ingenuity to improve the convenience of man's daily life. Nearly all of science was common knowledge. Under its great Editor, Orson Desaix Munn, the SCIENTIFIC AMERICAN became a fixture on the parlor table.

Now, a century later, our entire existence depends upon a science which is no longer common knowledge. The total of scientific information today exceeds the knowledge of any one man. It is the multiplied knowledge of science specialists in hundreds of separate fields.

During the past 50 years science has moved forward at a continually accelerating rate of progress; each new discovery has opened the way for many more. Whole new industries have now arisen at frontiers which were yesterday occupied by the advance forces of research science. Science has become a prime mover of modern history.

Demand For Scientific Information

This new role of science in human affairs has been recognized by a growing community of U.S. citizens. The members of this community have expressed an increasing demand for a source of authoritative and understandable information about science. Though they include experts in each field of science, they recognize that they are all, experts included, laymen before the sum total of scientific knowledge. They want to see science as a whole. They want to follow the major month-by-month advances of science no matter what field they occur in. They want to understand the new advances in the context of the history, the philosophy and the method of science which gives each discovery its meaning.

Their demand for scientific information is overlooked by the two kinds of magazine published today in the name of science. One is the technical journal in which the specialist reports his work to other specialists in the same field. The other is the "popular" magazine of science, published for mass audiences. To fill the gap between these extremes is the assignment of the new SCIENTIFIC AMERICAN.

The SCIENTIFIC AMERICAN, its name, goodwill and circulation have been purchased by a new publishing company. Under a new Board of Editors the SCIENTIFIC AMERICAN has become the vehicle for the creation of an entirely new magazine of the sciences.

Scientist and Journalist

The Board of Editors will collaborate directly with the men whose work they report in the production of every article that appears in the new SCIENTIFIC AMERICAN. Many articles will be written by scientists themselves. Others will be written by the Editors and the small fraternity of journalists who are qualified to write about science. In either case, all articles will represent the joint effort of the best talents of scientist and journalist working in close collaboration.

The articles in the new SCIENTIFIC AMERICAN will be written in plain English. Where words are inadequate, the new SCIENTIFIC AMERICAN will make use of the full range of the graphic arts for their power to convey the nature of the tools, the matter and the method of science.

The new SCIENTIFIC AMERICAN will find a unique place among U.S. magazines. It will serve as a universal medium for communication among men in the sciences, and between them and the public that is best equipped to understand their work and purpose. It will provide a much-needed "digest" of the technical press. More than a digest, it will organize and relate the basic documents on each subject, which are scattered among the many journals that make up the archives of science. Providing it achieves in performance the high editorial standards on which it has been designed, the new SCIENTIFIC AMERICAN will establish itself as indispensable to the community of U.S. citizens whose demand for scientific information has inspired its creation.

"*The Nation's* Future," Carey McWilliams's Editorial Policy in *Nation* (24 September 1955).

Down the years responsibility for the direction of *The Nation* has changed hands from time to time – in the 1930's it was sold twice within two years – but for long reaches of its history, ownership and management remained unaltered. Which is not to say that *The Nation* itself has been impervious to change. It changed radically when Oswald Garrison Villard became editor and no less radically when Freda Kirchwey succeeded him. Under Villard, *The Nation* ceased to be the largely literary journal it had become and dealt increasingly with social, economic, and political issues. With Freda Kirchwey's editorship, the rise of fascism and the sharp conflicts that came with the New Deal brought marked shifts in emphasis and direction. Despite all this, *The Nation* has managed to remain *The Nation.* Here is not, perhaps, so much another paradox of "permanence and change" as a reflection of the continuing influence of *The Nation's* tradition on succeeding editors. The 181 bound volumes of this magazine are more than a source of pride to the staff: they have a definite relevance to its future. They provide a touchstone, a guide, and, above all, a challenge to those who from time to time find themselves responsible for its management and direction. As a staff member for one decade and an occasional contributor for two before that, it should be fairly obvious that I honor the tradition of *The Nation* and intend to maintain it – come hell or high water.

Nevertheless, *The Nation* must change, as it has changed in the past, if only to encompass certain harsh realities of present-day American journalism. The constitutional guarantee of a free press finds justification in the obligation of the press to enlighten the people about their current affairs. But as Robert M. Hutchins has sourly observed, the great continuing debate which the framers of the First Amendment envisaged has in our time become a soliloquy. Within the last forty years, one-third of our daily newspapers and more than three thousand weeklies have ceased publication; at the moment ninety-four American cities are without competing papers. The same concentration of control appears elsewhere. In radio, one-fifth of the stations are interlocked with newspapers; four networks dominate national radio; less than two dozen advertisers account for 50 per cent of network income.

As the number of competing dailies and weeklies declines, the responsibility of the remaining independent publications increases. Today only a handful of national publications have been able to maintain complete freedom from business-office pressures in the face of steeply rising costs. Now more than ever before it becomes their special responsibility to report the significant happening that might otherwise go unreported, to air unpopular views and controversial issues, and, by careful selection and emphasis, to prevent the decisive considerations from being buried in an avalanche of irrelevant information. In these respects, *The Nation* is more urgently needed today than at any time in its history and, by the same token, its prospects were never brighter. For the same processes that have furthered and will continue to further monopoly control of the general press have created something very much like a monopoly for us. Never inclined to defy providence, we intend to exploit this opportunity to the fullest extent. In the future *The Nation* will devote even more space than it has in the past to unreported news of all kinds, local, national, and international. An independent national weekly is *not* the answer to the problem of a one-party press but it is part of the answer.

Even if *The Nation's* editors were inclined to evade the special responsibilities which new circumstances have imposed, its readers would not permit them to do so. These readers, as I can testify, are a special lot. One of the reasons why *The Nation,* with a small staff, has been able to provide a coverage of national affairs that publications with much larger staffs might envy is that its correspondents are about as numerous as its readers. *Nation* readers, moreover, are strategically well distributed, geographically and socially, vertically and horizontally. Despite an amazing range of differences of all sorts – racial, ethnic, religious, social, economic – they are alike in that they insist on doing their own thinking. No captive audience, this, but a live, responsive, critical, and exceptionally well-informed readership. With Brandies, our readers realize that "periodic, spasmodic indignation at wrong" is not enough; at the same time they would not want to see any wrong go unreported.

In the future as in the past *The Nation* will be consciously addressed to a special audience. It is an educated, intelligent audience, anxious to get the real facts, intensely interested in the free discussion of ideas on their merits, highly allergic to special pleading, propaganda, and double-talk. Readers of this kind are a permanent minority in any society. But they are more numerous in the America of today than they were thirty years ago, surface appearances to the contrary notwithstanding. Indeed, today's pressures for conformity are a measure of the respect reaction feels for their growing influence. Their ranks are swollen by those who are bored with most aspects of the mass media of communication. Here, too, is an opportunity which we intend to exploit. At the same time we hope to add recruits to the minority of independent liberals and give to American liberalism a new coherence and strength, thereby extending both their influence and our own. In neither case is influence a matter of numbers. By any reckoning the London *Economist* is one of the most influential journals in the world, yet its total circulation probably does not exceed 50,000. Editorial influence is a function not of mass but of quality. In much the same sense, the influence of an intellectual minority cannot be measured by counting noses; the thinking of this minority determines, in the caption of our editorial section, "the shape of things" to come.

The intellectual needs and interests, always varied, always changing, of this selective minority necessarily determine *The Nation's* content and coverage. For example, a publication addressed to such an audience does not need to "present both sides" of a question unless it is one on which the audience itself is sharply divided; its readers demand critical evaluations and the kind of reporting that winds up with a conclusion. Besides which, radio and television newscasts, as well as the availability of national news weeklies that provide excellently organized summaries of most major news items, have to some extent relieved publications like *The Nation* of a function which once was theirs, namely, of summarizing news developments. The mass media themselves, in turn, have become a major subject of critical attention. Science is another growing interest among the readers we hope to reach.

These new interests, reading habits, needs, and outlooks will determine the changes in content and coverage which readers of *The Nation* will note in the weeks to come. For a reason once suggested by Cyril Connolly I am reluctant to spell these changes out in detail. As I remember, Connolly once said that everyone has been victimized at one time or another by three persistent illusions: falling in love, starting a magazine, and the notion that one can make a living by keeping chickens. Projecting blueprints for magazines, to be and in being, is an occupational disease of editors; better that the changes should appear without announcement, fanfare, or forecast. But a few comments may not be indiscreet. In the last few years, for example, the "back-of-the-book" section has been severely curtailed. As rapidly as circumstances permit this section of the magazine will be enlarged, with more space given to books, music, art, theater, films, records, and also to radio and television. More space, too, will be found for letters and communications. Developments at the United Nations and in Washington will be followed more systematically than we have been able to do in recent years.

Now that Freda Kirchwey has been relieved of the publisher's burdens, she will be able to contribute more frequently to the editorial section than she has in the recent past. If ever an editor-publisher was entitled to surcease from the harassing responsibilities of management, Freda Kirchwey is that person. With courage, skill, and remarkable resourcefulness she has safely piloted *The Nation* through some of the stormiest years in its, and the nation's, history. During this period she has repeatedly had to withstand pressures that might well have broken the resistance of a battalion of stouthearted editors. Everyone admires Freda Kirchwey's moral courage and intellectual integrity but only those who have worked with her on a day-today basis can properly appreciate the patience, good humor, and imperturbable confidence with which she has faced, and surmounted, the crises that have arisen under her editorship. Her devotion to *The Nation,* her faith in it, and her unshakable determination that it should survive, have moved mountains and worked miracles.

For most of the period of her editorship Miss Kirchwey enjoyed the able assistance of Lillie Shultz as director of activities for the Nation Associates. Like Miss Kirchwey, Lillie Shultz has earned surcease from a heavy burden of care and responsibilities. Taking over as director in 1944, Miss Shultz made the Nation Associates a potent influence in American liberalism and a valuable aid to *The Nation.* Under her direction, the educational conferences of the Nation Associates were memorable affairs – "America's Opportunity to Create and Maintain Lasting Peace" (1944), "The Challenge of the

Atomic Bomb" (1945), "The Challenge of the Post-War World to the Liberal Movement" (Los Angeles, 1946), "The Palestine Problem and Its Relation to Peace" (1947), "The Atomic Era: Can It Produce Peace and Abundance?" (1950), "Freedom's Stake in the Middle East and North Africa" (1952), "Atoms for Peace" (1955). The immensely effective role that the Nation Associates played in the debate on Palestine before the United Nations and, in San Francisco in 1945, and later at the United Nations in New York, on the Spanish issue, was a reflection, also, of Miss Shultz's organizing drive and shrewd political judgment. Her services to *The Nation* cannot be adequately acknowledged in a brief note but they have been invaluable.

Changes in *The Nation's* editorship seem to have taken place, not too surprisingly, at key junctures in American life. Oswald Garrison Villard became editor during the last year of World War I – to face the fateful months of treaty-making, the revolutionary upheavals in Europe, the years of post-war corruption and reckless expansion, the predestined plunge into economic depression. Freda Kirchwey became editor in the middle of the depression decade – with the shadow of European fascism extending across the Atlantic, with Roosevelt battling for the New Deal reforms and collective security, with war in Spain and a new world war just over the horizon. This year, too, marks a watershed of a sort – the cold war shows signs of abating, the witch hunt is less frenzied, the atomic era was formally inaugurated at Geneva, domestic, social, and economic issues have taken on new dimensions, a "revolution of rising expectations" has everywhere inspired in people a new confidence in their ability to manage their affairs, while the achievements of science have given substance to the belief. The century of ideologies is about over. As David Thomson pointed out in our issue of September 10, the key to the politics of the future is to be found in "a more rational and effective democracy, linked to the actualist methods and spirit of science." American liberalism is emerging from a partial eclipse and should be the stronger for the experience of the last decade. Thus the general omens are good. With George G. Kirstein, I feel that the opportunity to achieve the long-sought goal of rescuing *The Nation* from the class of so-called "deficit publications" was never better and I share his feeling, too, that only by making the publication self-supporting – although it will not be that for some time – can we safeguard its future.

Not only are the political weather signs favorable, but we start with a clean slate. As readers will note from page 272 of this issue, a stipulation has been signed for the dismissal of the libel action which Nation Associates, Inc., brought against the *New Leader* in 1951. Negotiations to this end were initiated some months before the present reorganization of *The Nation* was even contemplated; the new management is glad the action has been dismissed by agreement of both parties.

It has been said that the only way American liberals can live in the present without repudiating the past is to believe in the future. *The Nation* is proud of its past and confident of the future. One of its best friends, the late Henry W. Nevinson, adopted for his motto words which *Nation* editors have appropriated on an occasion similar to this in the past and which is still a good motto for us in the years ahead: "The older, the bolder."

Publisher's Statement From the Initial Issue of *National Review* (19 November 1955).

There is, we like to think, solid reason for rejoicing. Prodigious efforts, by many people, are responsible for NATIONAL REVIEW. But since it will be the policy of this magazine to reject the hypodermic approach to world affairs, we may as well start out at once, and admit that the joy is not unconfined.

Let's face it: Unlike Vienna, it seems altogether possible that did NATIONAL REVIEW not exist, no one would have invented it. The launching of a conservative weekly journal of opinion in a country widely assumed to be a bastion of conservatism at first glance looks like a work of supererogation, rather like publishing a royalist weekly within the walls of Buckingham Palace. It is not that, of course; if NATIONAL REVIEW is superfluous, it is so for very different reasons: It stands athwart history, yelling Stop, at a time when no one is inclined to do so, or to have much patience with those who so urge it.

NATIONAL REVIEW is out of place, in the sense that the United Nations and the League of Women Voters and the *New York Times* and Henry Steele Commager are *in* place. It is out of place because, in its maturity, literate America rejected conservatism in favor of radical social experimentation. Instead of covetously consolidating its premises, the Untied States seems tormented by its tradition of fixed postulates having to do with the meaning of existence, with the relationship of the state to the individual, of the individual to his neighbor, so clearly enunciated in the enabling documents of our Republic.

"I happen to prefer champagne to ditchwater," said the benign old wrecker of the ordered society, Oliver Wendell Holmes, "but there is no reason to suppose that the cosmos does." We have come around to Mr. Holmes' view, so much so that we feel gentlemanly doubts when asserting the superiority of capitalism to socialism, of republicanism to centralism, of champagne to ditchwater – of anything to anything. (How curious that one of the doubts one is *not* permitted is whether, at the margin, Mr. Holmes was a useful citizen!) The inroads that relativism has made on the American soul are not so easily evident. One must recently have lived on or close to a college campus to have a vivid intimation of what has happened. It is there that we see how a number of energetic social innovators, plugging their grand designs, succeeded over the years in capturing the liberal intellectual imagination. And since ideas rule the world, the ideologues, having won over the intellectual class, simply walked in and started to run things.

Run just about *everything*. There never was an age of conformity quite like this one, or a camaraderie quite like the Liberals'. Drop a little itching powder in Jimmy Wechsler's bath and before he has scratched himself for the third time, Arthur Schlesinger will have denounced you in a dozen books and speeches, Archibald MacLeish will have written ten heroic cantos about our age of terror, *Harper's* will have published them, and everyone in sight will have been nominated for a Freedom Award. Conservatives in this country – at least those who have not made their peace with the New Deal, and there is serious question whether there are others – are nonlicensed nonconformists; and this is dangerous business in a Liberal world, as every editor of this magazine can readily show by pointing to his scars. Radical conservatives in this country have an interesting time of it, for when they are not being suppressed or mutilated by the Liberals, they are being ignored or humiliated by a great many of those of the well-fed Right, whose ignorance and amorality have never been exaggerated for the same reason that one cannot exaggerate infinity.

There are, thank Heaven, the exceptions. There are those of generous impulse and a sincere desire to encourage a responsible dissent from the Liberal orthodoxy. And there are those who recognize that when all is said and done, the market place depends for a license to operate freely on the men who issue licenses – on the politicians. They recognize, therefore, that efficient getting and spending is itself impossible except in an atmosphere that encourages efficient getting and spending. And back of all political institutions there are moral and philosophical concepts, implicit or defined. Our political economy and our high-energy industry run on large, general principles, on ideas – not by day-to-day guess work, expedients and improvisations. Ideas have to go into exchange to become or remain operative; and the medium of such exchange is the printed word. A vigorous and incorruptible journal of conservative opinion is – dare we say it? – as necessary to better living as Chemistry.

We begin publishing, then, with a considerable stock of experience with the irresponsible Right, and a despair of the intransigence of the Liberals, who run this country; and all this in a world dominated by the jubilant single-mindedness of the practicing Communist, with his inside track to History. All this would not appear to augur well for NATIONAL REVIEW. Yet we start with a considerable – and considered – optimism.

After all, we crashed through. More than one hundred and twenty investors made this magazine possible, and over fifty men and women of small means, invested less than one thousand dollars apiece in it. Two men and one woman, all three with overwhelming personal and public commitments, worked round the clock to make publication possible. A score of professional writers pledged their devoted attention to its needs, and hundreds of thoughtful men and women gave evidence that the appearance of such a journal as we have in mind would profoundly affect their lives.

Our own views, as expressed in a memorandum drafted a year ago, and directed to our investors, are set forth in an adjacent column. We have nothing to offer but the best that is in us. That, a thousand Liberals who read this sentiment will say with relief, is clearly not enough! It isn't enough. But it is at this point that we steal the march. For we offer, besides ourselves, a position that has not grown old under the weight of a gigantic, parasitic bureaucracy, a position untempered by the doctoral dissertations of a generation of Ph.D's in social architecture, unattenuated by a thousand vulgar promises to a thousand different pressure groups, uncorroded by a cynical contempt for human freedom. And that, ladies and gentlemen, leaves us just about the hottest thing in town.

[signed] WM. F. BUCKLEY, JR.

Checklist of Further Readings

Aaron, Daniel. *Writers on the Left: Episodes in American Literary Communism.* New York: Harcourt, Brace & World, 1961.

Allen, Charles. "The Advance Guard," *Sewanee Review,* 51 (1943): 410–429.

Allen. "Regionalism and the Little Magazines," *College English,* 7 (October 1945): 10–16.

Allen, Frederick Lewis. "American Magazines, 1741–1941," *Bulletin of the New York Public Library,* 45 (June 1941): 439–445.

Anderson, Elliott, and Mary Kinzie, eds. *The Little Magazine in America: A Modern Documentary History.* Yonkers, N.Y.: Pushcart Press, 1978.

Arndt, Karl J. R., and May E. Olson. *German-American Newspapers and Periodicals, 1732–1955.* Heidelberg: Quelle & Meyer, 1961.

Atherton, Gertrude. "Literary Merchandise," *New Republic,* 3 (July 1915): 223–224.

Bakeless, John E. "Aristocrats of Publishing," *Vanity Fair,* 40 (August 1933): 42–44, 52.

Bakeless. *Magazine Making.* New York: Viking, 1931.

Baker, Harry T. "Periodicals and Permanent Literature," *North American Review,* 212 (December 1920): 777–787.

Baughman, James L. *Henry R. Luce and the Rise of the American News Media.* Boston: Twayne, 1987.

Berelson, Bernard, and Patricia J. Salter. "Majority and Minority Americans: An Analysis of Magazine Fiction," *Public Opinion Quarterly,* 10 (Summer 1946): 168–190.

Bixler, Paul. "Little Magazine, What Now?," *Antioch Review,* 8 (March 1948): 63–77.

Brainerd, Marion. "Historical Sketch of American Legal Periodicals," *Law Library Journal,* 14 (October 1921): 63–69.

Brown, Dorothy M. "The Quality Magazines in the Progressive Era," *Mid-America,* 53 (July 1971): 139–159.

Burgess, Gelett. *Bayside Bohemia: Fin de Siècle San Francisco & Its Little Magazines.* San Francisco: Book Club of California, 1954.

Canby, Henry Seidel. "Free Fiction," *Atlantic Monthly,* 116 (July 1915): 60–68.

Chenery, William L. "American Magazines, 1741–1941," *Bulletin of the New York Public Library,* 45 (June 1941): 445–448.

Chielens, Edward E., ed. *The Literary Journal in America, 1900–1950.* Detroit: Gale Research Company, 1977.

Colvert, James B. "The Function of the Academic Critical Quarterly," *Mississippi Quarterly,* 23 (1969–1970): 95–101.

Compaine, Benjamin M. *The Business of Consumer Magazines.* White Plains, N.Y.: Knowledge Industry Publications, 1982.

Compaine. "The Magazine Industry: Developing the Special Interest Audience," *Journal of Communication,* 30 (Spring 1980): 98–103.

Cook, Michael L. *Mystery, Detective, and Espionage Magazines.* Westport, Conn.: Greenwood Press, 1983.

Cort, David. *The Sin of Henry Luce: An Anatomy of Journalism.* Secaucus, N.J.: Stuart, 1974.

Daniel, Walter C. *Black Journals of the United States.* Westport, Conn.: Greenwood Press, 1982.

Davenport, Walter, and James C. Derieux. *Ladies, Gentlemen, and Editors.* Garden City, N.Y.: Doubleday, 1960.

Deats, Ruth Z. "Poetry for the Populace: Trends in Poetic Thought in American Popular Magazines," *Sewanee Review,* 50 (July–September 1942): 374–388.

Ditzion, Sidney. "The History of Periodical Literature in the United States: A Bibliography," *Bulletin of Bibliography,* 15 (January/April 1935): 110; (May/August 1935): 129–133.

Drewry, John Eldridge. "American Magazines To-Day," *Sewanee Review,* 36 (July 1928): 342–356.

Drewry. *Some Magazines and Magazine Makers.* Boston: Stratford, 1924.

Elson, Robert T. *Time, Inc.: The Intimate History of a Publishing Enterprise, 1923–1941,* edited by Duncan Norton-Taylor. New York: Atheneum, 1968.

Elson. *The World of Time, Inc.: The Intimate History of a Publishing Enterprise, 1941–1960,* edited by Norton-Taylor. New York: Atheneum, 1973.

Emmart, A. D. (Richel North). "The Limitations of American Magazines," *Modern Quarterly,* 1 (March 1923): 2–12; (July 1923): 18–30; (December 1923): 17–26.

Faxon, Frederick W. "Magazine Deterioration," *Bulletin of Bibliography,* 9 (April 1916): 34–35.

Felker, Clay S. "Life Cycles in the Age of Magazines," *Antioch Review,* 29 (Spring 1969): 7–13.

Ferguson, Marjorie. *Forever Feminine: Women's Magazines and the Cult of Femininity.* London & Exeter, N.H.: Heinemann, 1983.

Fletcher, Alan D. "City Magazines Find a Niche in the Media Marketplace," *Journalism Quarterly,* 54 (Winter 1977): 740–743.

Fletcher, D., and Bruce G. VandenBergh. "Numbers Grow, Problems Remain for City Magazines," *Journalism Quarterly,* 59 (Summer 1982): 313–317.

Ford, James L. C. *Magazines for Millions: The Story of Specialized Publications.* Carbondale: Southern Illinois University Press, 1969.

Geiger, Louis G. "Muckrakers – Then and Now," *Journalism Quarterly,* 43 (Autumn 1966): 469–476.

Gillespie, Harris. "Magazine Mortality," *Magazine World,* 1 (October 1945): 27–30.

Goldwater, Walter. *Radical Periodicals in America, 1890–1950; A Bibliography with Brief Notes: With a Genealogical Chart and a Concise Lexicon of the Parties and Groups Which Issued Them.* New Haven: Yale University Library, 1964.

Goodstone, Tony, ed. *The Pulps: Fifty Years of American Pop Culture.* New York: Chelsea House, 1970.

Goulart, Ron. *Cheap Thrills: An Informal History of the Pulp Magazines.* New Rochelle, N.Y.: Arlington House, 1972.

Greene, Theodore P. *America's Heroes: The Changing Models of Success in American Magazines.* New York: Oxford University Press, 1970.

Griffin, Max L. "A Bibliography of New Orleans Magazines," *Louisiana Historical Quarterly,* 18 (July 1935): 491–556.

Guenther, Paul, and Nicholas Joost. "Little Magazines and the Cosmopolitan Tradition," *Papers on Language and Literature,* 6 (Winter 1970): 100–110.

Hamblin, Dora Jane. *That Was the Life.* New York: Norton, 1977.

Hamilton, Ian. *The Little Magazines: A Study of Six Editors.* London: Weidenfeld & Nicolson, 1976.

Hamilton, William B. "Fifty Years of Liberalism and Learning," *South Atlantic Quarterly,* 51 (January 1952): 7–32.

Hamilton, ed. *Fifty Years of the South Atlantic Quarterly.* Durham, N.C.: Duke University Press, 1952.

Handbook of Magazine Publishing. New Canaan, Conn.: Folio Magazine, 1978.

Hausdorff, Don. "Magazine Humor and Popular Morality, 1929–34," *Journalism Quarterly,* 41 (Autumn 1964): 509–516.

Hausdorff. "Magazine Humor and the Depression Years," *New York Folklore Quarterly,* 20 (1964): 199–214.

Hirsch, Paul M. "An Analysis of *Ebony*: The Magazine and Its Readers," *Journalism Quarterly,* 45 (Summer 1968): 261–270.

Hoffman, Frederick J. "Little Magazines and the Avant-Garde," *Art in Society,* 1 (Fall 1960): 32–37.

Hoffman. "The Little Magazines: Portrait of an Age," *Saturday Review of Literature,* 26 (25 December 1943): 3–5.

Hynds, Ernest C. "City Magazines, Newspapers Serve in Different Ways," *Journalism Quarterly,* 56 (Autumn 1979): 619–622.

Ingraham, Charles A. "American Magazines, Past and Present," *Americana,* 15 (October 1921): 325–333.

Janssens, Gerardus Antonius Mario. *The American Literary Review: A Critical History 1920–1950.* The Hague & Paris: Mouton, 1968.

Jillson, Willard Rouse. *The Newspapers and Periodicals of Frankfort, Kentucky, 1795–1945.* Frankfort: Kentucky State Historical Society, 1945.

Johns-Heine, Patricke, and Hans H. Gerth. "Values in Mass Periodical Fiction, 1921–1940," *Public Opinion Quarterly,* 13 (Spring 1949): 105–113.

Johnson, Charles S. "The Rise of the Negro Magazine," *Journal of Negro History,* 13 (January 1928): 7–21.

Joost, Nicholas. *Ernest Hemingway and the Little Magazines: The Paris Years.* Barre, Mass.: Barre Publishers, 1968.

Kahan, Robert S. "Magazine Photography Begins: An Editorial Negative," *Journalism Quarterly,* 42 (Winter 1965): 53–59.

Kelly, R. Gordon, ed. *Children's Periodicals of the United States.* Westport, Conn.: Greenwood Press, 1984.

King, Alexander. "The Sad Case of the Humorous Magazines," *Vanity Fair,* 41 (December 1933): 26–27, 68, 71.

Klingberg, Frank J. "The Value of Regional Literature," *Historical Magazine of the Protestant Episcopal Church,* 10 (December 1941): 399–401.

Kosinski, Jerzy. "Packaged Passion," *American Scholar,* 42 (Spring 1973): 193–204.

Lazarsfeld, Paul F., and Rowena Wyant. "Magazines in 90 Cities – Who Reads What?," *Public Opinion Quarterly,* 1 (October 1937): 29–41.

Libbey, James K. "Liberal Journals and the Moscow Trials of 1936–38," *Journalism Quarterly,* 52 (Spring 1975): 85–92, 137.

Littlefield, Daniel F., Jr., and James W. Parins. *American Indian and Alaskan Native Newspapers and Periodicals, 1826–1985,* 3 volumes. Westport, Conn.: Greenwood Press, 1984–1986.

MacMullen, Margaret. "Pulps and Confessions," *Harper's,* 175 (June 1937): 94–102.

Makosky, Donald Robin. "The Portrayal of Women in Wide-Circulation Magazine Short Stories, 1905–1955," Ph.D. dissertation, University of Pennsylvania, 1966.

Manchester, Harland. "The Farm Magazines." *Scribner's Magazine* (October 1938): 25–29, 58–59.

Matthews, Brander. "American Magazines," *Bookman,* 49 (July 1919): 533–541.

Meyer, Susan E. *America's Great Illustrators.* New York: Abrams, 1978.

Mondello, Salvatore. "The Magazine *Charities* and the Italian Immigrants, 1903–14," *Journalism Quarterly,* 44 (Spring 1967): 91–98.

Moon, Ben L. "City Magazines Past and Present," *Journalism Quarterly,* 47 (Winter 1970): 711–718.

Mott, Frank Luther. "College Literary Magazines," *Palimpsest,* 44 (1963): 303–310.

Mott. *A History of American Magazines,* 5 volumes. Cambridge, Mass.: Harvard University Press, 1938–1968.

Mugleston, William F. "The Perils of Southern Publishing: A History of *Uncle Remus's Magazine,*" *Journalism Quarterly,* 52 (Autumn 1975): 515–521, 608.

O'Brien, Edward J. "The Little Magazines," *Vanity Fair,* 41 (October 1933): 20–21, 58.

Oursler, Fulton. "American Magazines, 1741–1941," *Bulletin of the New York Public Library,* 45 (June 1941): 448–456.

Peterson, Martin Severin. "Regional Magazines," *Prairie Schooner,* 3 (Fall 1929): 292–295.

Peterson, Theodore. *Magazines in the Twentieth Century.* Urbana: University of Illinois Press, 1964.

Peterson. "The Role of the Minority Magazine," *Antioch Review,* 23 (Spring 1963): 57–72.

Porter, William. "The Quality Magazines and the New American Reader," *Gazette,* 6 (1960): 305–310.

Pound, Ezra. "Small Magazines," *English Journal,* 19 (1930): 689–704.

Regier, C. C. *The Era of the Muckrakers.* Chapel Hill: University of North Carolina Press, 1932; Gloucester, Mass.: Smith, 1957.

Repplier, Agnes. "American Magazines," *Yale Review,* 16 (January 1927): 261–274.

Reuss, Carol. "*The Ladies' Home Journal* and Hoover's Food Program," *Journalism Quarterly,* 49 (Winter 1972): 740–742.

Rice, Philip Blair. "The Intellectual Quarterly in a Non-Intellectual Society," *Kenyon Review,* 16 (Summer 1954): 420–439.

Riley, Sam G. *Index to Southern Periodicals.* Westport, Conn.: Greenwood Press, 1986.

Riley. *Magazines of the American South.* Westport, Conn.: Greenwood Press, 1986.

Riley. "The New Money and the New Magazines," *Journal of Regional Cultures* (Fall/Winter 1982): 107–115.

Riley. "Specialized Magazines of the South," *Journalism Quarterly,* 59 (Autumn 1982): 447–450, 455.

Riley and Gary W. Selnow, eds. *Index to City and Regional Magazines of the United States.* Westport, Conn.: Greenwood Press, 1989.

Rollins, Hyder E. "O. Henry's Texas Days," *Bookman,* 40 (October 1914): 154–165.

Root, Robert, and Christine V. Root. "Magazines in the United States: Dying or Thriving?," *Journalism Quarterly,* 41 (Winter 1964): 15–22.

Ryant, Carl G. "From Isolation to Intervention: *The Saturday Evening Post,* 1939–1942," *Journalism Quarterly,* 48 (Winter 1971): 679–687.

Sampson, Robert. *Yesterday's Faces: A Study of Series Characters in the Early Pulp Magazines.* Bowling Green, Ohio: Bowling Green University Popular Press, 1983.

Schacht, J. H. *A Bibliography for the Study of Magazines,* fourth edition. Urbana, Ill.: College of Communications, 1979.

Schoenfeld, A. Clay. "The Environmental Movement as Reflected in the American Magazine," *Journalism Quarterly,* 60 (Autumn 1983): 470–475.

Severance, Frank Hayward. "The Periodical Press of Buffalo, 1811–1915," Buffalo Historical Society, *Publications,* 19 (1915): 177–280.

Singerman, Robert. *Jewish Serials of the World: A Research Bibliography of Secondary Sources.* Westport, Conn.: Greenwood Press, 1986.

Sloane, David E., ed. *American Humor Magazines and Comic Periodicals.* Westport, Conn.: Greenwood Press, 1987.

Smith, C. Zoe. "Black Star Picture Agency: *Life*'s European Connection," *Journalism History,* 13 (Spring 1986): 19–25.

Smith. "Germany's Kurt Korff: An Emigré's Influence on Early *Life,*" *Journalism Quarterly,* 65 (Summer 1988): 412–419, 424.

Smith, James Steel. "American Magazine Missionaries of Culture," *Journalism Quarterly,* 43 (Autumn 1966): 449–458.

Stephens, Ethel. "American Popular Magazines, A Bibliography," *Bulletin of Bibliography Pamphlets,* no. 23, 1916.

Stinson, Robert. "McClure's Road to *McClure's:* How Revolutionary Were 1890s Magazines?," *Journalism Quarterly,* 47 (Summer 1970): 256–262.

Stuntz, Stephen Conrad. *List of Agricultural Periodicals of the United States and Canada Published during the Century July 1810 to July 1910.* U.S. Department of Agriculture, "Miscellaneous Publication," no. 398. Washington, D.C.: Government Printing Office, 1941.

Swallow, Alan. "The Little Magazines," *Prairie Schooner,* 16 (December 1942): 238–243.

Swanberg, W. A. *Luce and His Empire.* New York: Scribners, 1972.

Tassin, Algernon de Vivier. *The Magazine in America.* New York: Dodd, Mead, 1916.

Tate, Allen. "The Function of the Critical Quarterly," *Southern Review,* 1 (1936): 551–559.

Tebbel, John. *The American Magazine: A Compact History.* New York: Hawthorn Books, 1969.

Terwilliger, W. Bird. "A History of Literary Periodicals in Baltimore," Ph.D. dissertation, University of Maryland, 1941.

Thomas, Dana L. *The Media Moguls.* New York: Putnam, 1981.

Torrence, Clayton. "The Semi-Centennial of the *Virginia Magazine of History and Biography,*" *Virginia Magazine of History and Biography,* 51 (July 1943): 217–225.

Towne, Charles Hanson. *Adventures in Editing.* New York & London: Appleton, 1926.

Towne. "The One-Man Magazines," *American Mercury,* 63 (July 1946): 104–108.

Wainwright, Loudon. *The Great American Magazine: An Insider History of* Life. New York: Knopf, 1986.

White, Helen, and Redding S. Sugg, Jr., eds. *From the Mountain.* Memphis: Memphis State University Press, 1972.

Whittemore, Reed. *Little Magazines.* Minneapolis: University of Minnesota Press, 1963.

Wolseley, Roland E. *The Changing Magazine: Trends in Readership and Management.* New York: Hastings House, 1973.

Wolseley. *Understanding Magazines,* revised edition. Ames: Iowa State University Press, 1966.

Wood, James Playsted. *Magazines in the United States, Their Social and Economic Influence.* New York: The Ronald Press, 1971.

Zuilen, A. J. van. *The Life Cycle of Magazines.* Uithoorn, The Netherlands: Graduate Press, 1977.

Contributors

Edd Applegate .... *Middle Tennessee State University*
Michael D. Applegate .... *University of Northern Colorado*
Donald R. Avery .... *Eastern Connecticut State University*
Nora Baker .... *Southern Illinois University at Edwardsville*
Donald Allport Bird .... *Long Island University, Brooklyn*
Peyton Brien .... *University of Toronto*
Sam Bruce .... *Columbia, South Carolina*
Jack Colldeweih .... *Fairleigh Dickinson University*
Wallace B. Eberhard .... *University of Georgia*
Ralph Engelman .... *Long Island University*
James S. Featherston .... *Louisiana State University*
Vincent Fitzpatrick .... *Enoch Pratt Free Library, Baltimore*
James W. Hipp .... *Columbia, South Carolina*
W. J. Hug .... *Jacksonville State University*
Terry Hynes .... *California State University, Fullerton*
A. J. Kaul .... *University of Southern Mississippi*
Daniel Morris .... *Harvard University*
Shirley M. Mundt .... *Louisiana State University*
Whitney R. Mundt .... *Louisiana State University*
Sharon M. Murphy .... *Marquette University*
Michael D. Murray .... *University of Missouri at Saint Louis*
Jack A. Nelson .... *Brigham Young University*
Kathryn News .... *Temple University*
Janet M. Novey .... *Brooklyn, New York*
Alf Pratte .... *Brigham Young University*
Howard Price .... *Eastern Illinois University*
Sam G. Riley .... *Virginia Polytechnic Institute & State University*
Kenneth A. Robb .... *Bowling Green State University*
Patt Foster Roberson .... *Southern University, Baton Rouge*
Garyn G. Roberts .... *Michigan State University*
Norman Sims .... *University of Massachusetts – Amherst*
Eileen Stewart .... *Marquette University*
James T. F. Tanner .... *University of North Texas*
J. Douglas Tarpley .... *CBN University*

Cumulative Index

Dictionary of Literary Biography, Volumes 1-137
Dictionary of Literary Biography Yearbook, 1980-1992
Dictionary of Literary Biography Documentary Series, Volumes 1-11

Cumulative Index

DLB before number: *Dictionary of Literary Biography,* Volumes 1-137
Y before number: *Dictionary of Literary Biography Yearbook,* 1980-1992
DS before number: *Dictionary of Literary Biography Documentary Series,* Volumes 1-11

A

B

C

D

E

F

G

H

I

K

L

M

N

O

P

Q

S

W

Y

Z

ISBN 0-8103-5396-2

90000

9 780810 353961

(Continued from front endsheets)

116 *British Romantic Novelists, 1789-1832,* edited by Bradford K. Mudge (1992)

117 *Twentieth-Century Caribbean and Black African Writers,* First Series, edited by Bernth Lindfors and Reinhard Sander (1992)

118 *Twentieth-Century German Dramatists, 1889-1918,* edited by Wolfgang D. Elfe and James Hardin (1992)

119 *Nineteenth-Century French Fiction Writers: Romanticism and Realism, 1800-1860,* edited by Catharine Savage Brosman (1992)

120 *American Poets Since World War II,* Third Series, edited by R. S. Gwynn (1992)

121 *Seventeenth-Century British Nondramatic Poets,* First Series, edited by M. Thomas Hester (1992)

122 *Chicano Writers,* Second Series, edited by Francisco A. Lomelí and Carl R. Shirley (1992)

123 *Nineteenth-Century French Fiction Writers: Naturalism and Beyond, 1860-1900,* edited by Catharine Savage Brosman (1992)

124 *Twentieth-Century German Dramatists, 1919-1992,* edited by Wolfgang D. Elfe and James Hardin (1992)

125 *Twentieth-Century Caribbean and Black African Writers,* Second Series, edited by Bernth Lindfors and Reinhard Sander (1993)

126 *Seventeenth-Century British Nondramatic Poets,* Second Series, edited by M. Thomas Hester (1993)

127 *American Newspaper Publishers, 1950-1990,* edited by Perry J. Ashley (1993)

128 *Twentieth-Century Italian Poets,* Second Series, edited by Giovanna Wedel De Stasio, Glauco Cambon, and Antonio Illiano (1993)

129 *Nineteenth-Century German Writers, 1841-1900,* edited by James Hardin and Siegfried Mews (1993)

130 *American Short-Story Writers Since World War II,* edited by Patrick Meanor (1993)

131 *Seventeenth-Century British Nondramatic Poets,* Third Series, edited by M. Thomas Hester (1993)

132 *Sixteenth-Century British Nondramatic Writers,* First Series, edited by David A. Richardson (1993)

133 *Nineteenth-Century German Writers to 1840,* edited by James Hardin and Siegfried Mews (1993)

134 *Twentieth-Century Spanish Poets,* Second Series, edited by Jerry Phillips Winfield (1994)

135 *British Short-Fiction Writers, 1880–1914: The Realist Tradition,* edited by William B. Thesing (1994)

136 *Sixteenth-Century British Nondramatic Writers,* Second Series, edited by David A. Richardson (1994)

137 *American Magazine Journalists, 1900–1960,* Second Series, edited by Sam G. Riley (1994)

Documentary Series

1 *Sherwood Anderson, Willa Cather, John Dos Passos, Theodore Dreiser, F. Scott Fitzgerald, Ernest Hemingway, Sinclair Lewis,* edited by Margaret A. Van Antwerp (1982)

2 *James Gould Cozzens, James T. Farrell, William Faulkner, John O'Hara, John Steinbeck, Thomas Wolfe, Richard Wright,* edited by Margaret A. Van Antwerp (1982)

3 *Saul Bellow, Jack Kerouac, Norman Mailer, Vladimir Nabokov, John Updike, Kurt Vonnegut,* edited by Mary Bruccoli (1983)

4 *Tennessee Williams,* edited by Margaret A. Van Antwerp and Sally Johns (1984)

5 *American Transcendentalists,* edited by Joel Myerson (1988)

6 *Hardboiled Mystery Writers: Raymond Chandler, Dashiell Hammett, Ross Macdonald,* edited by Matthew J. Bruccoli and Richard Layman (1989)

7 *Modern American Poets: James Dickey, Robert Frost, Marianne Moore,* edited by Karen L. Rood (1989)

8 *The Black Aesthetic Movement,* edited by Jeffrey Louis Decker (1991)

9 *American Writers of the Vietnam War: W. D. Ehrhart, Larry Heinemann, Tim O'Brien, Walter McDonald, John M. Del Vecchio,* edited by Ronald Baughman (1991)

10 *The Bloomsbury Group,* edited by Edward L. Bishop (1992)

11 *American Proletarian Culture: The Twenties and The Thirties,* edited by Jon Christian Suggs (1993)

Yearbooks

1980 edited by Karen L. Rood, Jean W. Ross, and Richard Ziegfeld (1981)

1981 edited by Karen L. Rood, Jean W. Ross, and Richard Ziegfeld (1982)

1982 edited by Richard Ziegfeld; associate editors: Jean W. Ross and Lynne C. Zeigler (1983)

1983 edited by Mary Bruccoli and Jean W. Ross; associate editor: Richard Ziegfeld (1984)

1984 edited by Jean W. Ross (1985)

1985 edited by Jean W. Ross (1986)

1986 edited by J. M. Brook (1987)

1987 edited by J. M. Brook (1988)

1988 edited by J. M. Brook (1989)

1989 edited by J. M. Brook (1990)

1990 edited by James W. Hipp (1991)

1991 edited by James W. Hipp (1992)

1992 edited by James W. Hipp (1993)